New Perspectives on

MACROMEDIA®
DREAMWEAVER® MX

Comprehensive

KELLY HART AND MITCH GELLER
Nu-Design.com

THOMSON
™
COURSE TECHNOLOGY

Australia • Canada • Mexico • Singapore • Spain • United Kingdom • United States • Japan

THOMSON

COURSE TECHNOLOGY

New Perspectives on Macromedia® Dreamweaver® MX—Comprehensive
is published by Course Technology.

Managing Editor:
Rachel Crapser

Senior Product Manager:
Kathy Finnegan

Technology Product Manager:
Amanda Young Shelton

Product Manager:
Karen Stevens

Associate Product Manager:
Brianna Germain

Editorial Assistant
Emilie Perreault

Marketing Manager:
Rachel Valente

Developmental Editor:
Robin M. Romer,
Katherine T. Pinard

Production Editor:
Anne Valsangiacomo

Composition:
GEX Publishing Services

Text Designer:
Meral Dabcovich

Cover Designer:
Efrat Reis

Disclaimer
Course Technology reserves the right to revise this publication and make changes from time to time in its content without notice.

TRADEMARKS
Macromedia, the Macromedia and Macromedia Education logos, Authorware, ColdFusion, Director, Dreamweaver, Fireworks, FreeHand, JRun, Macromedia Flash and Shockwave are trademarks or registered trademarks of Macromedia, Inc. in the United States and/or other countries. Third party products, services, company names, logos, design, titles, words, or phrases within these materials may be trademarks of their respective owners.

"Avon," an essay from a collection of writings entitled *Punch* appears in Case Problem 3 in all tutorials courtesy of Kelly Hart. *Avon* and *Punch* are © Copyright Kelly Hart, 2002. All rights reserved.

The following images, which appear on the Data Disk and are used in Case Problem 2 in all tutorials, are provided courtesy of the Sid Richardson Museum of Western Art (www.sidrmuseum.org), Fort Worth, Texas:
"A Quiet Day in Utica" by Charles M. Russell, 1907, Oil on canvas.

"Cow Punching Sometimes Spells Trouble" by Charles M. Russell, 1889, Oil on canvas.
"Indians Hunting Buffalo" by Charles M. Russell, 1894, Oil on canvas.
"The Bucker" by Charles M. Russell, 1904, Pencil, watercolor, and gouache on paper.
"Deer in Forest" by Charles M. Russell, 1917, Oil on canvas.
"Buffalo Runners—Big Horn Basin" by Frederic Remington, 1909, Oil on canvas.
"A Figure of the Night" by Frederic Remington, 1908, Oil on canvas.
"The Cow Puncher" by Frederic Remington, 1901, Oil (black and white) on canvas.
"The Love Call" by Frederic Remington, 1909, Oil on canvas.
"Among the Led Horses" by Frederic Remington, 1909, Oil on canvas.
"The Luckless Hunter" by Frederic Remington, 1909, Oil on canvas.
"The Riderless Horse" by Frederic Remington, 1886, Pencil, pen and ink, and watercolor on paper.

All media elements used in Case Problem 1 are provided courtesy of Dr. Jerold A Edmondson and are © Copyright Dr. Jerold A Edmonson, 2003. All rights reserved.

ISBN 0-619-02077-6

Preface

Course Technology is the world leader in information technology education. The New Perspectives Series is an integral part of Course Technology's success. Visit our Web site to see a whole new perspective on teaching and learning solutions.

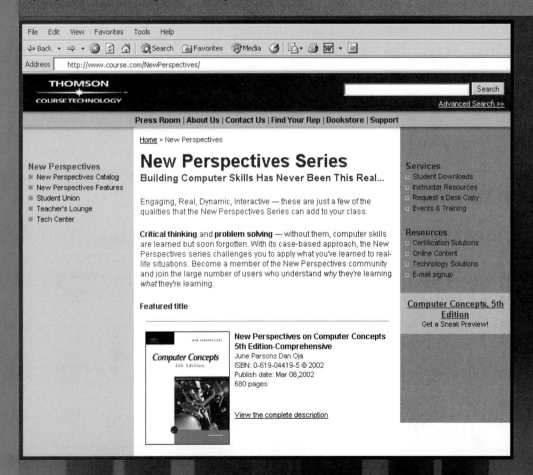

New Perspectives—Building Computer Skills Has Never Been This Real

Why New Perspectives will work for you.

Critical thinking and **problem solving**—without them, computer skills are learned but soon forgotten. With its **case-based** approach, the New Perspectives Series challenges students to apply what they've learned to real-life situations. Become a member of the New Perspectives community and watch your students not only **master** computer skills, but also **retain** and carry this **knowledge** into the world.

New Perspectives catalog
Our online catalog is never out of date! Go to the Catalog link on our Web site to check out our available titles, request a desk copy, download a book preview, or locate online files.

Complete system of offerings
Whether you're looking for a Brief book, an Advanced book, or something in between, we've got you covered. Go to the Catalog link on our Web site to find the level of coverage that's right for you.

Instructor materials
We have all the tools you need—data files, solution files, figure files, a sample syllabus, and ExamView, our powerful testing software package.

How well do your students know Microsoft Office?
Experience the power, ease, and flexibility of SAM XP and TOM. These innovative software tools provide the first truly integrated technology-based training and assessment solution for your applications course. Click the Tech Center link to learn more.

Get certified
If you want to get certified, we have the titles for you. Find out more by clicking the Teacher's Lounge link.

Interested in online learning?
Enhance your course with rich online content for use through MyCourse 2.0, WebCT, and Blackboard. Go to the Teacher's Lounge to find the platform that's right for you.

Your link to the future is at
www.course.com/NewPerspectives

What you need to know about this book.

- Student Online Companion takes students to the Web for additional work.

- ExamView testing software gives you the option of generating a printed test, LAN-based test, or test over the Internet.

- Students will appreciate the detailed, real-world scenarios that provide the context of the case problems in each tutorial.

- For Macintosh users, a Macintosh Users Guide to New Perspectives on Macromedia Dreamweaver MX is available for downloading in the Student Downloads and Instructor Resources sections of course.com.

- Students will gain confidence as they learn how to use Dreamwever to create and manage complex Web sites.

- In addition to teaching how to use Dreamweaver, this book provides extensive information about planning and designing a Web site, including information architecture. Also included is extensive coverage of marketing research, researching the target audience, and end-user analysis and profiling.

- The various methods of accomplishing different tasks in Dreamweaver are presented along with a discussion of the pros and cons of each method.

- Each chapter includes a section in which the students examine the HTML code behind the page they just built.

CASE	TROUBLE?	SESSION 1.1	QUICK CHECK	RW
Tutorial Case Each tutorial begins with a problem presented in a case that is meaningful to students. The case sets the scene to help students understand what they will do in the tutorial.	**TROUBLE? Paragraphs** These paragraphs anticipate the mistakes or problems that students may have and help them continue with the tutorial.	**Sessions** Each tutorial is divided into sessions designed to be completed in about 45 minutes each. Students should take as much time as they need and take a break between sessions.	**Quick Check Questions** Each session concludes with conceptual Quick Check questions that test students' understanding of what they learned in the session.	**Reference Windows** Reference Windows are succinct summaries of the most important tasks covered in a tutorial. They preview actions students will perform in the steps to follow.

BRIEF CONTENTS

TABLE OF CONTENTS

Tutorial 4   DRM 4.01

Working with Graphics, Mouseovers, and Tables

Organizing Content and Layout in the Catalyst Web Site

Acknowledgments

The authors wish to thank:

Robin Romer, our editor extraordinaire, for skillfully guiding us to shape our ramblings into a "real book" and Kitty Pinard for jumping right into the fray when Robin left to work on "the Jake project" and for having such patience with us. Thank you both for all your hard work and dedication.

Charlie Lindahl (aka CyberChuck) for introducing us to an amazing new thing called the Web on his new Mosaic Version 0.2A browser (1993), for helping us to keep up with the latest developments ever since, and for his never-ending encouragement and enthusiasm.

Richard Strittmatter and Meshnet.com for building our server, for continuing to come up with definitive answers for the complex and often misunderstood technologies of the Internet, and for graciously providing hosting and support for our test cases.

The staff of the Sid Richardson Museum and Store (www.sidrmuseum.org/store) for their support and generosity in allowing us to use images from the Sid Richardson Collection of Western Art.

Dr. Jerold A Edmondson, for providing the inspiration and media for Case Problem 1. His research is available at *http://ling.uta.edu/~jerry/research/*.

Our wonderful reviewers: Eric Infanti of The Language of Technology Consulting Group; Nancy Peaslee; Art Schneider of Portland Community College—Sylvania Campus; and Rebekah Tidwell of Carson Newman College; and Rachel Crapser, Donna Gridley, and Anne Valsangiacomo from Course Technology for their help and support.

Mitch would like to thank Edyie and Joe Geller and the rest of the family for their love and support...you guys are the greatest!

Kelly would like to thank Mary O'Brien for her culinary, caffeination, and grammatical assistance, along with the rest of the Nu-Design.com team and Brian and Matt for their support.

New Perspectives on

MACROMEDIA
DREAMWEAVER MX

Read This Before You Begin

To the Student

Data Disks

To complete the tutorials, Review Assignments, and Case Problems, you need **two** Data Disks. Your instructor will either provide you with these Data Disks or ask you to make your own.

If you are making your own Data Disks, you will need **two** blank, formatted high-density disks. You will need to copy a set of files and/or folders from a file server, standalone computer, or the Web onto your disks. Your instructor will tell you which computer, drive letter, and folders contain the files you need. You could also download the files by going to www.course.com and following the instructions on the screen. You will copy the Tutorial.01, Tutorial.02, Tutorial.03, and Tutorial.04 folders onto one blank formatted high-density disk and label it **Data Disk 1: Tutorials 1-4**; and you will copy the Tutorial.05 and Tutorial.06 folders onto a second blank formatted high-density disk and label it **Data Disk 2: Tutorials 5-6**.

Before creating your Data Disks, check with your instructor to find out where you will be storing your Web sites. It is assumed that you are working from the hard drive of your computer; if you are working from a removable disk then you'll need to substitute the appropriate drive letter when instructed to navigate to a location.

When you begin each tutorial, Review Assignment, or Case Problem, be sure you are using the correct Data Disk. Refer to the "File Finder" chart at the back of this text for more detailed information on which files are used in which tutorials.

See the inside back cover of this book for more information on Data Disk files, or ask your instructor or technical support person for assistance.

Installation Information

We assume a default installation of Macromedia Dreamweaver MX. The screenshots in this book were taken using a machine running Windows XP Professional and, when showing a browser, Internet Explorer 6. If you are using a different operating system or a different browser, your screen might differ from the figures in these tutorials.

Using Your Own Computer

If you are going to work through this book using your own computer, you need:

- **Computer System** A text editor and a Web browser (preferably Internet Explorer or Netscape Navigator, versions 4.0 or higher) must be installed on your computer. If you are using a non-standard browser, it must support frames and HTML 4.0 or higher.

- **Data Disks** You will not be able to complete the tutorials or exercises in this book using your own computer until you have your Data Disks.

Visit Our World Wide Web Site

Additional materials designed especially for you are available on the World Wide Web. Go to www.course.com/NewPerspectives.

To the Instructor

The Data Disk files are available on the Instructor's Resource Kit for this title. Follow the instructions in the Help file on the CD-ROM to install the programs to your network or standalone computer. For information on creating Data Disks, see the "To the Student" section above.

You are granted a license to copy the Data Disk files to any computer or computer network used by students who have purchased this book.

INTRODUCING
DREAMWEAVER MX
Exploring the Catalyst Web Site

Catalyst

Catalyst is an independent record label in Denton, Texas, just north of Dallas, that was started by Sara Lynn in 2000. Most of the groups affiliated with the label originated as part of the underground Denton music scene, which centers around the University of North Texas. A year ago, Catalyst created a Web site to promote its bands. Since that time, some of the bands have developed a national following. Sara believes that this success is due, in part, to the exposure from the Catalyst Web site. She also believes that further development of the Web site will generate more national publicity as well as increase CD sales. Therefore, she wants to redesign and expand the Web site.

Brian Lee, who is responsible for public relations and marketing at Catalyst, has a background in multimedia development and will head the Web development team. The new Catalyst Web site will be developed using Macromedia Dreamweaver MX. Brian's team will research the current market trends as well as design and create a new Web site for Catalyst. You will work with Brian and his team to develop this site.

You'll start by reviewing the history and structure of the Internet and the World Wide Web. Then you'll explore the components of a basic Web page. Finally, you'll examine the Dreamweaver tool set and learn how to use the Dreamweaver Help features.

SESSION 1.1

In this session, you will learn about the Internet and the World Wide Web. You will explore the relationship between Web servers and Web clients. Finally, you will open and review a Web site in a browser and examine the components of a basic Web page.

Dreamweaver and the Internet

Dreamweaver is a Web site creation and management tool. To better understand what this means, you'll need to review some basic terms and concepts associated with Web sites.

The Internet and the World Wide Web

A **network** is a series of computers that are connected together to share information and resources. Within each network, one (or more) machine is designated as the **server**, which is the computer that stores and distributes information to the other computers in the network. The **Internet** is a huge, global network made up of millions of smaller computer networks that are all connected together. The Internet provides a way for people to communicate and exchange information via computer, whether they are across the street or across the globe. All of the computers connected to the Internet can communicate and exchange information. Figure 1-1 illustrates the Internet as a series of interconnected roadways. Each roadway represents a computer network.

Figure 1-1   ILLUSTRATION OF THE INTERNET

As the Internet evolved, different protocols were developed to allow information to be shared in different ways. A **protocol** is a set of technical specifications that define a format for sharing information. Creating an agreed-upon protocol enables a programmer to create software that can interact with all the other software that uses the same protocol. For example, **Simple Mail**

Transfer Protocol (SMTP) is an agreed-upon format used by some e-mail software. Without this standard protocol, there would be many incompatible e-mail formats, and you would be able to exchange e-mail only with people who were using the same e-mail software. Another common Internet protocol is **File Transfer Protocol (FTP)**, which is used to copy files from one computer to another over the Internet.

In 1989, Timothy Berners-Lee and his team of scientists at CERN (the European Organization for Nuclear Research) created what we call the World Wide Web as a means for scientists to more easily locate and share data. The **World Wide Web (WWW** or **Web)** is a subset of the Internet with its own protocol, **HTTP (Hypertext Transfer Protocol)**, and its own document structure, called **HTML (Hypertext Markup Language)**. HTTP controls the transfer of Web pages over the Internet, whereas HTML provides instructions for how to format Web pages for display. **Web pages** are the electronic documents of information on the Web; a group of related and interconnected Web pages is referred to as a **Web site**. Figure 1-2 shows how the Web page vehicles must follow the HTTP rules of the road to travel the Internet.

Figure 1-2   **ILLUSTRATION OF THE WORLD WIDE WEB**

Web page

Web protocol

In addition to standards for transfer and display of information, the Web introduced the technology for hyperlinks to the Internet. **Hyperlinks** (or **links**) are nodes that provide the ability to cross reference information within a document or a Web page and enable the user to move from one document or Web page to another.

Web Servers and Clients

You must have access to the Internet to view a Web site. Most people connect to the Internet through an Internet service provider. An **Internet service provider (ISP)** is a company that has direct access to the Internet and sells access to other smaller entities. Some large institutions, such as universities, have direct links to the Internet and are, in essence, their own ISPs.

There are two general categories for the computers involved in accessing Web pages: Web servers and Web clients. When you create a Web page or a Web site, you must post a copy of your work to a Web server to share the page with the world. A **Web server** (or server) is a specialized server that stores and distributes information to computers that are connected to the Internet.

A **Web client** (or client) is the computer an individual uses to access information, via the Internet, that is stored on Web servers throughout the world. A home computer with Internet access is considered a Web client. In addition to being connected to the Internet to view a Web site, you must have a Web browser installed on your client computer that can interpret and display Web pages. A **Web browser** is the piece of software installed on a client computer that allows users to view Web pages. Two of the most common Web browsers are Microsoft Internet Explorer and Netscape Navigator.

Web Pages and Web Sites

Now that you understand what a Web page is and how your computer accesses a Web page on the Internet, you'll examine some elements that are common to all Web pages: Web address, hyperlinks, and content.

Web Address

Every Web page that is posted to the Internet has a Web address. Just like your residence has a unique street address that people use to locate where you live, and a file on your computer has a unique path used to locate where it is stored, every Web page has a unique address, called a **Uniform Resource Locator (URL)**, that Web browsers use to locate where that page is stored. A URL includes the information identified in Figure 1-3.

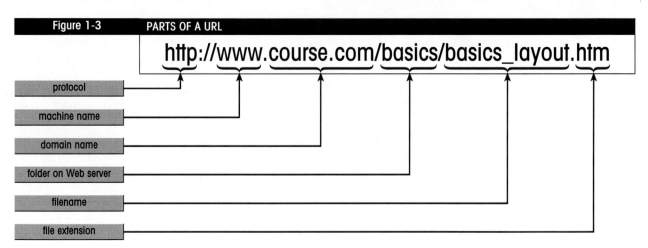

Figure 1-3   PARTS OF A URL

http://www.course.com/basics/basics_layout.htm

- protocol
- machine name
- domain name
- folder on Web server
- filename
- file extension

The first portion of the URL indicates the protocol, which is usually HTTP but can be **HTTPS (Hypertext Transfer Protocol Secure)**. HTTPS means that the site is secure because it encrypts data transferred between your browser and the server. **Encryption** is the process of coding data so that only the sender and/or receiver can read it, preventing others from being able to understand it. This is important when you plan to submit confidential or credit card information over the Web.

The protocol is immediately followed by "://" which originated from UNIX (a server operating system) and essentially says "what follows should be interpreted according to the indicated protocol." When typing a URL into a browser, if you omit the protocol, the browser assumes you mean *http://*.

The next part of the URL is the **machine name**, which is a series of characters that the server administrator assigns to the Web server. Often, the machine name is *www*, but it can be any word, phrase, or acronym, or it can be omitted entirely. For example, the URL *home.netscape.com* for Netscape uses *home* as the machine name, and the URL *CNN.com* for CNN omits the machine name entirely. Many servers are configured to route the URL both with and without a *www* to the same location. For example, *www.course.com* and *course.com* both go to the same place. Because so many sites use *www* as the machine name, it is good to include it if you are not sure of the exact URL for a site.

The machine name is followed by the domain name. The **domain name** is a unique name for a Web site chosen by the site owner combined with a top-level domain. A **top-level domain** is the highest category in the Internet naming system. The top-level domain may indicate the Web site's type of entity or country of origin. Common top-level domains are commercial (.com), organization (.org), network (.net), U.S. educational (.edu), and U.S. government (.gov). Although .com and .org are generally available to anyone, .edu must be some type of educational entity in the United States and .gov is reserved for the United States government. Some top-level domains for countries are United States (.us), Canada (.ca), United Kingdom (.uk), and Japan (.jp). Domain names are often a word or phrase related to an organization or individual. For example, *course.com* is the domain name for Course Technology, the publisher of this book. Domain names must be registered for a fee with a domain registrar and are regulated by ICANN (Internet Corporation for Assigned Names and Numbers). Domain names can be purchased for a period of 1 to 10 years, and the owner has the opportunity to renew before anyone else can buy the name. Once you own a domain name, no one else can use it. As of 2001, there were more than 20 million domain names. Each domain name can have one or more machine names.

The top-level domain might be followed by nested directories (or folders), which indicate the location of the file on the Web server. The last name in the series is usually the filename, as indicated by the .html or .htm extension. The folders and filenames are separated by slashes (/).

By knowing the parts of a URL and what they indicate, you can gather some information about the site you are visiting. You can also make an educated guess when trying to determine the correct URL for a site you want to visit.

REFERENCE WINDOW   **RW**

Opening a Remote Web Page in a Browser
- Double-click the Internet Explorer icon on the desktop.
- Type the URL of the Web page you want to open in the Address text box at the top of the browser window, then press the Enter key.

You'll use a URL to open the Course Technology Web site.

To open a remote Web page in a browser:

1. Verify that your computer is on and that the Windows desktop is running. See Figure 1-4.

   TROUBLE? If you are using a Macintosh, go to www.course.com, navigate to the Student Downloads page, and then download the *Macintosh User's Guide to New Perspectives on Macromedia Dreamweaver MX*.

Figure 1-4   WINDOWS XP DESKTOP

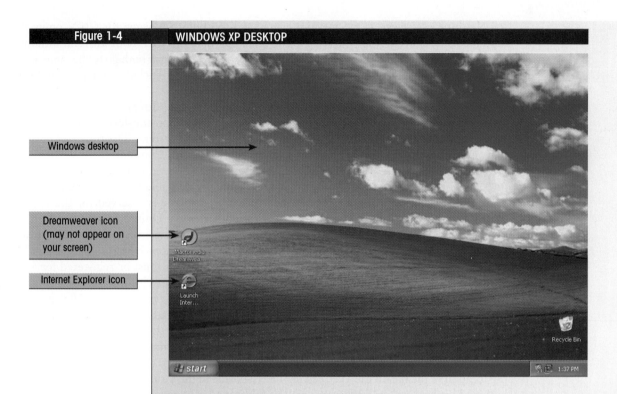

Windows desktop

Dreamweaver icon
(may not appear on
your screen)

Internet Explorer icon

TROUBLE? If the icons or the background on your desktop differ from those in Figure 1-4, don't be concerned.

2. Double-click the **Internet Explorer** icon on the desktop. The Web browser opens and displays the default page. You'll open the Course Technology Web site by entering its URL.

    TROUBLE? If you don't see on the desktop, then click the Launch Internet Explorer Browser icon on the Quick Launch toolbar. If you don't see the icon, click the Start button, point to All Programs, and then click Internet Explorer. If you are using Netscape Navigator or a different Web browser, use the desktop icon or Start menu to open that browser.

3. Click in the **Address** text box at the top of the window to select its contents.

4. Type **www.course.com** in the Address text box, and then press the **Enter** key. The main page for the Course Technology Web site opens.

    TROUBLE? If you do not have Internet access, you will not be able to view the Course Technology Web site. Continue with Step 5.

    TROUBLE? If you are using Netscape Navigator, type the URL into the Location text box, and then press the Enter key.

5. If necessary, click the **Maximize** button on the Internet Explorer title bar to maximize the window. See Figure 1-5.

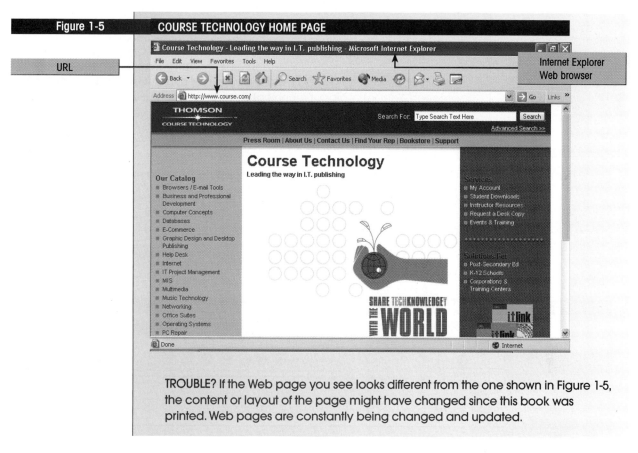

Figure 1-5 | **COURSE TECHNOLOGY HOME PAGE**

URL

Internet Explorer
Web browser

TROUBLE? If the Web page you see looks different from the one shown in Figure 1-5, the content or layout of the page might have changed since this book was printed. Web pages are constantly being changed and updated.

Sometimes you'll need to view a Web page that is not posted to the Web. For example, a client may hand you files on a disk or a coworker may ask you to view a Web page from a local source such as a disk, computer hard drive, or local network server before the Web page is posted to the Web. You can view a local copy of a Web page in your browser by typing the file path instead of the URL.

REFERENCE WINDOW **RW**

Opening a Local Web Page in a Browser
- Click File on the menu bar, and then click Open.
- Click the Browse button, click the Look in list arrow, and then navigate to the location where the Web page is stored.
- Click the Web page filename to select it, and then click the Open button.
- Click the OK button in the Open dialog box.

Brian asks you to view a copy of the existing Catalyst Web site, (located on your Data Disk). You'll start by opening the site's **home page**, which is the main page of a Web site. You can type the file path in the Address text box or browse to locate the file.

To open a local Web page in a browser:

1. Insert your Data Disk into the appropriate disk drive.

   TROUBLE? If you don't have a Data Disk, you need to get one before you can proceed. Your instructor or technical support person will either give you one or ask you to make your own by following the instructions on the "Read This Before You Begin" page preceding Tutorial 1. See your instructor or technical support person for more information.

2. Click **File** on the menu bar, and then click **Open**. The Open dialog box appears.

3. Click the **Browse** button, click the **Look in** list arrow, navigate to the **Catalyst** folder within the **Tutorial** folder within the **Tutorial.01** folder, click **index.htm**, and then click the **Open** button.

4. Click the **OK** button in the Open dialog box. The home page for the Catalyst Web site opens. See Figure 1-6.

Figure 1-6	CATALYST HOME PAGE

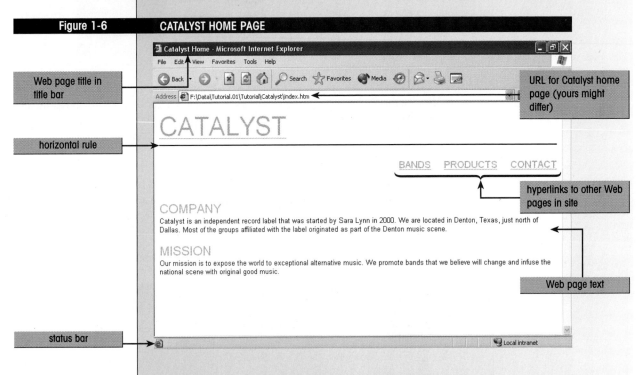

TROUBLE? If the Catalyst Web site does not open, make sure your Data Disk is in the appropriate disk drive and try again. If your instructor has provided you with different steps to access the Catalyst Web site, use that method.

TROUBLE? If a Dial-up Connection dialog box opens, the browser is trying to connect to the Internet. Click the Work Offline or Cancel button to close the dialog box. It is not necessary to connect to the Internet to complete these steps.

Web sites are **nonlinear**, which means that information branches out from the home page in many directions much like railroad tracks branch out from a train station. You can think of the home page as the hub or "train station" of a Web site. Just as people go to a train station to begin a train trip, the home page is where most people start when they want to explore a Web site. The major categories of information contained in the Web site branch out from the home page. Just as different sets of train tracks overlap, the branches of a Web site interconnect (through links), and just as one train station is connected to other train stations, your Web site can be linked to other Web sites.

Hyperlinks

Hyperlinks can be graphics, text, or buttons with **hot spots** (active areas) that, when clicked with a mouse, take you to another related section. The related section can be on the same Web page, another Web page on the same site, or on another Web site altogether. This interlinking of information from various places gives the Web its nonlinear nature and even its name. There are several ways that links are indicated on a Web page. When positioned over a link, the mouse pointer will change from an arrow to a hand with a pointing finger.

Text links are often underlined and appear in a different color to distinguish them from other text. A **graphic** is a visual representation, such as a drawing, painting, or photograph. Images, like the CD covers on the Products page, are a type of graphic. Graphic links are not usually visually distinguishable from graphics that are not links, but the mouse pointer changes to the pointing finger when it is positioned over a graphic link.

The Catalyst company logo, located at the upper-left corner of the Web page, is also a link. A **logo** is usually a graphic used by a company for the purposes of brand identification. In this case, the company logo is actually formatted text. A company logo is often used as a link to the Web site home page.

You need to become familiar with the artists that Catalyst represents and the CDs that they sell, so Brian asks you to review the Bands and Products pages of the Web site. You'll use links to move between the pages.

To use a link:

1. Point to the **BANDS** hyperlink, but do not click it. The pointer changes to 🖑 to indicate that you are pointing to a hyperlink. The URL for the new page appears on the left side of the **status bar**, a banner of details about the window's contents that appears at the bottom of the browser window.

2. Click the **BANDS** hyperlink. The Bands page replaces the home page in the browser window. See Figure 1-7.

Figure 1-7   BANDS PAGE

3. Click the **PRODUCTS** hyperlink. The Products page replaces the Bands page in the browser window. See Figure 1-8.

Figure 1-8   PRODUCTS PAGE

4. Point to the **Catalyst logo** on the Products page but do not click. The pointer changes shape and the home page URL appears in the status bar.

5. Click the **Catalyst logo**. The home page reappears in your browser.

After you view two or more Web pages, you can quickly move between the pages you have opened by using buttons on the browser toolbar. Rather than reloading the home page, you can use the Back button to return to the previous page. Once you return to a previously opened page, the Forward button becomes active so you can redisplay a later page.

To go back or forward to a previously viewed page:

1. Click the **Back** button ⬅ on the browser toolbar. The Products page reappears in the browser window.

2. Click the **Forward** button ➡ on the browser toolbar. The Catalyst home page reappears in the browser window.

You have used links to move through the Catalyst Web site.

Content

The main purpose of most Web sites is to provide information, which is conveyed through the content. **Content** is the information presented on a Web page. A Web page usually contains a combination of text, graphics, and possibly multimedia elements such as video, animation, or interactive content. The blend of these elements is determined by deciding what will most effectively convey the intended message or information. Ignoring the content of a Web site is a common mistake made by inexperienced designers.

Brian asks you to review the content of the Catalyst Web site, looking for content and design elements that you think should be added or changed when you start to redesign the site.

To review site content:

1. Read the content on the home page of the Catalyst Web site, considering what information might be appropriate to add and what design changes you'd like to see.

2. Click the **BANDS** hyperlink.

3. Review the content of the Bands page, considering what information might be appropriate to add and what design changes you'd like to see.

4. Click the **PRODUCTS** hyperlink.

5. Review the content of the Products page, considering what information might be appropriate to add and what design changes you'd like to see.

6. Click the **CONTACT** hyperlink.

7. Review the content on the Contact page, considering what information might be appropriate to add and what design changes you'd like to see.

From your review of the site content, you might have a list of changes you would suggest to Brian. For example, readers might want more information in the descriptions on the Bands page. The Products page might also include song titles for each CD. You're done looking at the Catalyst site from the browser, so you'll close the site and the browser for now.

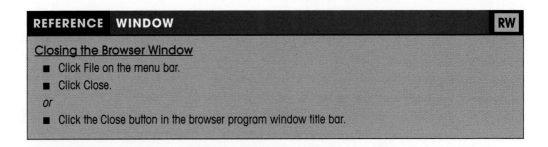

To close the browser window:

1. Click **File** on the menu bar, and then click **Close**. The browser window closes. You can also click the Close button ☒ in the program window title bar to exit your browser.

So far you have learned about the Internet, the Web, Web servers, and clients. You have explored the different components of a Web page, and you have opened the existing Catalyst Web site in a browser. In the next session, you will view the existing Catalyst Web site from within Dreamweaver.

Session 1.1 QUICK CHECK

1. What is the Internet?

2. What is the World Wide Web?

3. Explain the difference between a Web server and a Web client.

4. What is a Web browser?

5. What is a URL?

6. In the following URL, what is the domain name: http://www.course.com/index.html?

7. Define hyperlinks.

8. Explain the purpose of content on a Web site.

SESSION 1.2

In this session, you will review the history of Web design tools. You will start Dreamweaver, arrange its windows and toolbars, and create a site definition. Finally, you will explore the Dreamweaver tool set.

Evolving Web Design Tools

In the early days of Web design, most Web pages contained only text and were created by typing HTML into documents using a simple text editor (such as Notepad or Simple Text). To create a Web page, you had to know how to write HTML from scratch. As the Web evolved, Web authors began to create more complex graphical interfaces. This made creating Web pages from scratch very cumbersome. HTML was designed by scientists as a means of sharing information. Using HTML for graphically complex interfaces involves complex HTML structures that are not practical (for most people) to type. Furthermore, artists, graphic designers, business people, and nonprogrammers who wanted to create Web pages did not necessarily want to learn all of the intricacies of HTML. This led to the development of software packages that allowed the user to design Web pages by typing, placing, and manipulating content in an environment that more closely approximated the look of the Web page the designer wanted to create. The software actually wrote the HTML for them. These software packages were originally referred to as **WYSIWYG** (What You See Is What You Get) programs, because the Web page is displayed in the program window as it will appear to the end user and the code is hidden from sight. Today, the acronym WYSIWYG is not often used because almost all software is designed to show you what you will get as you work. Also, this has been critiqued as a bit of a misnomer with Web software because what you get really depends on the specific browser and version used to view the page.

With these Web software packages, people who were not programmers were able to design Web pages, and designers gained even more control over the look of their sites across the various browsers. Dreamweaver grew out of this need for easy-to-use, visual tools that allow Web authors to rapidly develop reliable and well-coded Web pages. Dreamweaver has become one of the most widely used site development and management tools because of its ease of use, accurate HTML output, and powerful tool set. With Dreamweaver, you can create a successful Web site without knowing any HTML. However, some familiarity with HTML enables you to make the site work better, fix problems that arise, and create elements that are complex or impossible to create in Dreamweaver.

Comparing Page-Centric and Site-Centric Design Tools

There are two popular ways that Web development programs approach Web site design—page-centric design and site-centric design. Many software packages use a **page-centric design** approach, which concentrates on designing and creating the Web pages individually and then linking them together, rather than concentrating on the Web site as a whole. Designers create one page, then they create a second page and attach it to the first page, then they create a third page to attach to the first two, and the site grows from there.

Dreamweaver takes the opposite approach—site-centric design. A **site-centric design** approach focuses on planning the Web site structure and design before creating any pages. Designers associate the parameters with the site, and the parameters are then used by all the pages of the site. One of the benefits of site-centric design is that if the designer wants to change some aspect of the site, such as a heading color or page background color, the change is made once and all the pages associated with the site reflect the change. Professional Web designers tend to prefer site-centric design tools, like Dreamweaver, which are more comprehensive than page-centric design tools.

Starting Dreamweaver and Selecting a Workspace Layout Configuration

To get started you will need to open Dreamweaver and set the workspace layout configuration. The Dreamweaver program window consists of several smaller windows, toolbars, and panels. There are three preset workspace layout configurations to choose from. In addition, the user can move windows and adjust the workspace to suit his or her work style. Dreamweaver opens in the same state it was in when it was last closed, so—depending on the working method of the person who last used the computer that you are working on—Dreamweaver could open in any number of configurations. The three preset workspace layout configurations are:

- **Dreamweaver MX Workspace**. The Dreamweaver MX workspace layout configuration is the default layout and is the configuration that is recommended for most users. It is the configuration that you will be using in these tutorials. It is an integrated workspace that uses multiple document interface. **Multiple document interface (MDI)** enables all of the document windows and panels to be integrated in one large application window. In the default setting, the panels are docked on the right side of the window.

- **HomeSite/Coder-Style**. The HomeSite/Coder-Style workspace layout uses the same integrated workspace as the Dreamweaver MX workspace layout, but the panels are arranged to be similar to two other Macromedia software products, HomeSite and ColdFusion Studio. In this configuration, the document window also shows the Code view by default. This configuration is used primarily by people who are familiar with HomeSite and ColdFusion.

- **Dreamweaver 4**. This workspace layout is similar to the layout used in Dreamweaver 4 (the previous version of Dreamweaver). In this configuration, each window and panel group is a separate floating entity and there is no larger application window to integrate the various features.

You will use the Dreamweaver MX workspace layout configuration for these tutorials. If someone else has used your computer and changed the Dreamweaver layout configuration, you can reset Dreamweaver to its default Dreamweaver MX workspace layout.

REFERENCE WINDOW	RW

Selecting the Default Dreamweaver MX Workspace
- Click Edit on the main menu bar, and then click Preferences.
- Make sure General is selected in the Category list, and then click the Change Workspace button.
- Click the Dreamweaver 4 workspace option button, click OK, and then click OK.
- Click the Change Workspace button again, click the Dreamweaver MX workspace option button, click OK, and then click OK.
- Click the OK button in the Preferences dialog box, click File on the main menu bar, and then Exit to exit Dreamweaver.
- Start Dreamweaver again.

In this tutorial, you'll set up Dreamweaver in the default Dreamweaver MX workspace layout. The figures in this book show Dreamweaver in this default layout. As you become more proficient with Dreamweaver, you may find that you prefer a different setup.

MACINTOSH USERS If you are working on a Macintosh, go to www.course.com, navigate to the Student Downloads page, and then download the *Macintosh User's Guide to New Perspectives on Macromedia Dreamweaver MX*. The steps in this book were written for Dreamweaver MX for Windows, and the figures show Dreamweaver MX running on a Windows XP system. In the *Macintosh User's Guide*, you will find instructions for arranging the Dreamweaver windows on your screen so that they more closely match the screens shown in the figures in this book, and, when necessary, alternate steps for performing actions on the Macintosh to obtain the results indicated in the steps.

To start Dreamweaver and select the Dreamweaver MX workspace layout:

1. Click the **Start** button on the taskbar, point to **All Programs**, point to **Macromedia**, and then click **Macromedia Dreamweaver MX**. Dreamweaver starts with various windows and toolbars displayed.

   TROUBLE? If you do not see the Macromedia folder, click Macromedia Dreamweaver MX on the Programs menu. If you can't find Macromedia Dreamweaver MX on the Programs menu, press the Esc key to close the Start menu, and then double-click the Dreamweaver program icon on your desktop.

   TROUBLE? If this is the first time Dreamweaver has been started on this computer, the Workspace Setup dialog box opens. Make sure the Dreamweaver MX Workspace option button is selected, then click OK.

   TROUBLE? If the Welcome screen appears, click the Close button ☒ in the window.

2. Click **Edit** on the main menu bar, and then click **Preferences** to open the Preferences dialog box.

3. Click **General** in the Category list, if necessary, and then click the **Change Workspace** button to open the Workspace Setup dialog box.

4. Click the **Dreamweaver 4 Workspace** option button, and then click **OK**.

5. Click **OK** in the dialog box that appears warning you that the change will take effect the next time you start Dreamweaver.

6. Click the **Change Workspace** button again, click the **Dreamweaver MX Workspace** option button, click **OK**, and then click **OK** in the warning dialog box.

   This clears any configuration changes that might have been made by another user from memory, and returns the layout to the default position.

7. Click the **OK** button to close the Preferences window, click **File** on the menu bar, and then click **Exit** to exit Dreamweaver.

8. Repeat Step 1 to start Dreamweaver again. The Dreamweaver workspace will not change configurations until the program has been closed and reopened.

9. Click the **Maximize** button ☐ in the program window title bar if necessary. See Figure 1-9.

Figure 1-9	DEFAULT DREAMWEAVER WORKSPACE LAYOUT

The elements of the Dreamweaver MX workspace layout are labeled in Figure 1-9. For example, the **main menu bar**, located at the top of the work area, is a categorized series of menus that provide access to all the tools and features available in Dreamweaver. The Site menu, for example, has commands for creating, defining, and viewing sites.

Each of the **panel groups** on the right side of the screen contains related panels. **Panels** contain related commands, controls, and information about different aspects of working with Dreamweaver. You will learn about the other elements in the Dreamweaver window as you use them.

Now that Dreamweaver is open and in the default layout, you'll open the Catalyst Web site in Dreamweaver. But first you must create a Local Site Definition for the Catalyst Web site.

Creating a Site Definition

Working on a Web site is a lot like working on a report. Usually you keep the original report locally on your computer and distribute a copy of the report to others to review. In the case of a Web site, you work on the original site on your computer and then have Dreamweaver post a copy to a publicly viewable space, such as a Web server. The original site stored on your computer is the local version, and the copy Dreamweaver posts is the remote version. You make all changes and revisions to the local site and then have Dreamweaver update the remote site. A **site definition** is the information that tells Dreamweaver where to find the local and remote files for the Web site, along with other parameters that affect how the site is set up within Dreamweaver. Dreamweaver stores a local Web site in the same format as it will be posted on the Web. The program stores the local version of the site on which you work in a local root folder. You can use files stored anywhere on your hard drive or network to create your site; Dreamweaver prompts you to copy these files into the local root folder so that everything you need will be located in one convenient location.

Note that the site definition is not kept as part of the site; instead it is stored in the Windows registry. If you move to another computer to work, you must re-create the site definition on that computer.

There are two main categories in a site definition—local information and remote information. You should create the local information for the site definition (referred to as the Local Site Definition) before you begin working on a Web site. It is acceptable to wait to create the remote information for the site definition (referred to as the Remote Site Definition) until you are ready to post a copy of the site to a Web server.

Creating a Local Site Definition

A **Local Site Definition** is the information stored on the computer that you are using that tells Dreamweaver where the local root folder is located. The **local root folder** is the location where you store all the files used by the local version of the Web site. If you use a different computer for a later work session, you'll need to re-create the Local Site Definition on that computer.

You can place the local root folder on a hard drive or on a removable disk. Be aware, however, that working on a site stored on a removable disk can be slower than working on a site stored on a hard drive. Also, when you create the Local Site Definition, you need to be sure to use the most recent version of the site.

There are two ways to create a Local Site Definition. You can click the Basic tab in the Site Definition dialog box and use the Site Definition Wizard to walk you through the process of setting up a site; however, using the Site Definition Wizard prompts you to set your Remote Site Definition as well. The second method is to click the Advanced tab in the Site Definition dialog box and input the information yourself. For these exercises you will input the information yourself so that you can gain a better understanding of the process of creating a Local Site Definition.

REFERENCE WINDOW   **RW**

Creating a Local Site Definition

- Click Site on the main menu bar or on the Site panel menu bar, and then click New Site.
- Click the Advanced tab.
- Click Local Info in the Category list.
- Type a name in the Site Name text box.
- Type a path in the Local Root Folder text box (*or* click the Browse button, navigate to the Web site's folder, and then click the Select button).
- Click the Refresh Local File List Automatically checkbox to check it.
- Click the Enable Cache checkbox to check it.
- Click the OK button.

You'll need to enter several pieces of information and select a few options to set up a Local Site Definition. Refer to the following list for an explanation of the parts of a Local Site Definition:

- **Site Name.** An internal name you give the Web site for your reference. This name appears on the Site menu in the Document window and in the Site panel.

- **Local Root Folder.** The location where you want to store all the files used by the local version of the Web site. You choose where to place the local root folder on your computer, network, or removable disk.

  When creating the local root folder, use a logical folder structure and a descriptive naming system. A logical folder structure helps keep the Web site files organized. For example, it is a good idea to store each project in its own folder and to create a Dreamweaver subfolder within each project folder so that the Dreamweaver files remain separate from any original, uncompressed artwork and working files that you have not yet added to the Web site. You might, for instance, create a Catalyst project folder that contains a Dreamweaver subfolder. Any text files or graphics that you have not yet added to the Web site would be stored in the Catalyst folder. The Dreamweaver subfolder would be the local root folder for the new Catalyst Web site project. Remember that folder names can include any series of letters, numbers, hyphens, and underscores. They should not include spaces, symbols, or special characters, which can cause problems on some servers. Symbols and special characters also can have different meanings on different platforms.

- **Refresh Local File List Automatically.** An option that enables Dreamweaver to update the list of local files any time you add, delete, move, or rename a file used in the Web site. You'll usually leave this option checked.

- **HTTP Address.** The URL of your Web site, which Dreamweaver uses to automatically verify links. You will enter this URL in a later tutorial when you publish the Catalyst Web site.

- **Cache: Enable Cache.** An option that enables Dreamweaver to use a **cache**, a temporary local storage space, to speed up the processing time needed to update links when you move, rename, or delete a file. You'll usually leave this option checked.

You must create a Local Site Definition before you can view the Catalyst Web site from within Dreamweaver on your computer.

To create the Local Site Definition:

1. Click **Site** on the main menu bar, and then click **New Site**. The Site Definition for Unnamed Site 1 dialog box opens.

2. Click the **Advanced** tab, and then click **Local Info** in the Category list, if necessary. See Figure 1-10.

Figure 1-10   ADVANCED TAB IN THE SITE DEFINITION FOR UNNAMED SITE 1 DIALOG BOX

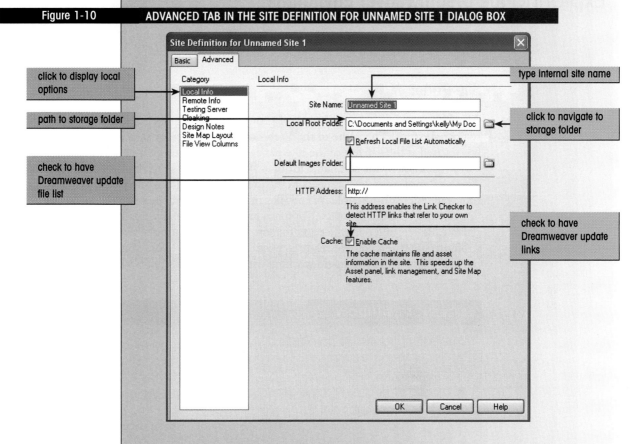

3. If necessary, drag to select the text in the Site Name text box, and then type **Catalyst**. Catalyst is the name you will use to reference the site; this name will not be used outside the Dreamweaver environment.

4. Click the **Local Root Folder Browse** button to open the Choose Local Root Folder for Site Catalyst dialog box, navigate to the **Catalyst** folder within the **Tutorial** folder within the **Tutorial.01** folder on your Data Disk (the location where the Catalyst Web site is stored), and then click the **Select** button to open the folder.

5. Click the **Refresh Local File List Automatically** checkbox to check it, if necessary. Dreamweaver will update your file list whenever you add, move, delete, or rename a file in your Web site.

6. In the Cache section, click the **Enable Cache** checkbox to check it, if necessary. Dreamweaver will quickly update links whenever you move, rename, or delete a file.

7. Click the **OK** button to close the Site Definition dialog box. Dreamweaver scans the existing files and creates the file list for the site.

TROUBLE? If a dialog box opens with the message that the initial site cache will now be created, click the OK button.

Next, you will explore the Catalyst Web site from within Dreamweaver.

Exploring the Dreamweaver Environment

Brian wants you to explore the Catalyst Web site from within Dreamweaver. As you are reviewing the site, you will also explore the basic Dreamweaver windows and toolbars.

Site Panel

The **Site panel** is in the Files panel group and is the panel you use to manage local and remote site files. The name of the Web site that is currently selected appears in the Site list box located at the top left of the Site panel. Once you create a Local Site Definition on your current computer, the site name for that Web site is added to the list (in this case, Catalyst). The local root site folder appears in the lower portion of the Site panel. When you open the root folder, a list of the folders and files in the local site appears in the lower portion of the Site panel. From the Site panel, you can create new Web pages as well as view, move, copy, rename, delete, and open files and folders. You can also use the Site panel to transfer files to a remote site when you are ready to post the site to the Web. You will use these features of the Site panel when you begin working with the remote site.

REFERENCE WINDOW   **RW**

Viewing the File List and Site Map in the Site Panel
- Click the View list arrow on the Site panel toolbar (the list arrow on the right), and then click Local View to view the file list.
- Click the Site list arrow on the Site panel toolbar, and then click the Web site name.
- Click the Expand button next to the Web site folder in the list.
- Click the Collapse arrow in the Answers panel to contract it, if necessary.
- Click the View list arrow on the Site panel toolbar, and then click Map View to view the site map.
- Click the Expand/Collapse button on the Site panel toolbar to view the file list and the site map simultaneously.
- Click the Expand/Collapse button on the Site panel toolbar again to collapse the view.

The Site panel consists of a menu bar, a toolbar, the list of files in the local root folder, and an integrated file browser. The **integrated file browser**, located below the local root folder file list, enables you to browse files that are outside of your site. Once you set up a remote site, you can select Remote View from the View drop-down list, and a list of the files and folders in the remote site will appear in the lower portion of the Site panel. You can expand the Site panel to fill the work area. When the Site panel is expanded, the lower portion of the panel is divided into two panes so you can display both the local and remote views of your site simultaneously.

To view the file list of a local Web site in the Site panel:

1. Click the **list arrow** on the right side of the Site panel toolbar, and then click **Local View**, if necessary. The list arrow on the right side of the toolbar is the View list arrow.

2. Click the **list arrow** on the left side of the Site panel toolbar, and then click **Catalyst**, if necessary. The list arrow on the left side of the toolbar is the Site list arrow. The Catalyst Web site appears in the list below the toolbar.

3. Click the plus (+) button ⊞ next to the Site - Catalyst folder, if necessary, and then click the **Collapse** button ▼ at the top of the Answers panel to contract the Answers panel. The graphics folder and the Catalyst Web page files appear in the list. See Figure 1-11.

Figure 1-11	SITE PANEL WITH SITE FILE LIST

When a Web site is selected, the folders and pages in the local root directory of that site are displayed. Currently, the folders and pages in the local root folder of the Catalyst Web site are visible. A folder icon precedes the folder name, whereas a Dreamweaver Web page icon precedes the Web page filenames. Each filename is followed by a **file extension**, which is used by Windows to determine the file type. The file extension for Web pages can be either .htm or .html. Depending on how your Web server is set up, you might be required to use one or the other for the entire site or for only the default page.

Another way to view the files and folders in a Web site is with the site map. A **site map** is a visual representation of how the pages in a Web site are interrelated. You can display the site map in the Site panel by selecting Map View from the View drop-down list. You might need to resize the Site panel to view the entire site map.

You'll view the site map for the Catalyst Web site.

To view the site map and to view the site map and the local file list simultaneously:

1. Click the **View** list arrow on the Site panel toolbar, and then click **Map View**. The site map appears in the Site panel. See Figure 1-12.

Figure 1-12   SITE PANEL WITH SITE MAP

2. Click the **Expand/Collapse** button ⬚ on the Site panel toolbar to expand the Site panel and display both the Map View and the Local View simultaneously. See Figure 1-13.

Figure 1-13   SITE PANEL WITH FILE LIST AND SITE MAP

3. Click ⬚ to return the panel to its original size

4. Click the **View** list arrow, and then click **Local View** to return to Local view.

You can open any page in the Web site by double-clicking its filename in the file list or the site map. Each page opens in a separate Document window. You can open multiple pages at one time. Although there are other methods for opening Web pages in Dreamweaver, this method ensures that you always open the file from the root folder (rather than from a backup copy or another location). You can move between the open pages by clicking the Document window title bar of the page you want to make active. The active page appears in the foreground and has a blue title bar.

You'll use the Site panel to open the Bands and Products pages in their own Document windows.

To open Web pages from the Site panel:

1. Double-click **bands.htm** in the Site panel. The Catalyst-bands page opens in its own Document window to the left of the Site panel.

2. Double-click **products.htm** in the Site panel. The Catalyst-products page opens in its own Document window, and now is the active page. See Figure 1-14.

Figure 1-14	WEB PAGES OPENED FROM SITE PANEL

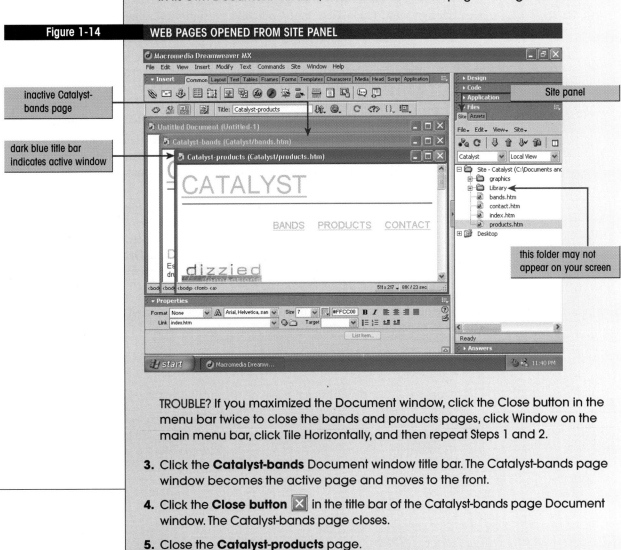

inactive Catalyst-bands page

dark blue title bar indicates active window

this folder may not appear on your screen

TROUBLE? If you maximized the Document window, click the Close button in the menu bar twice to close the bands and products pages, click Window on the main menu bar, click Tile Horizontally, and then repeat Steps 1 and 2.

3. Click the **Catalyst-bands** Document window title bar. The Catalyst-bands page window becomes the active page and moves to the front.

4. Click the **Close button** X in the title bar of the Catalyst-bands page Document window. The Catalyst-bands page closes.

5. Close the **Catalyst-products** page.

6. Close the **Untitled Document** page.

Document Window

The **Document window** is the main work area where you create and edit a Web page. You use tools from the various panels, toolbars, and inspectors to manipulate the page that is open in the Document window.

The **Document toolbar**, located below the Insert bar at the top of the main work area, includes buttons for the most commonly used commands related to the Document window. At the top of the Document window is the **title bar**, which displays the page title and the filename of the Web page. The **page title** is the name you give a Web page; it will appear in the title bar of the browser. The **filename**, the name under which a Web page is saved, appears in parentheses to the right of the page title in the title bar. If an asterisk (*) appears after the filename, it means that the page has been modified without being resaved. Usually, the page that opens by default when you visit a Web site has the filename index.htm or default.htm. A Web server will display the index.htm or default.htm page if the viewer has not requested a specific file in the URL.

The middle of the Document window is the document work area where you create and edit Web pages. There are three ways to display the information in the document work area: Design view, Code view, and Code and Design view. The buttons that control the views are located on the Document toolbar.

- **Design view**. Displays the page as it will appear in a browser. Design view is the primary view used when you are designing and creating a Web page. In Design view, all of the HTML code is hidden so you can focus on how the finished product will look. When you view the home page of the Catalyst Web site in Design view, it will look the same as it does in a browser.

- **Code view**. Displays the underlying HTML code that Dreamweaver automatically generates as you create and edit a page. You can also enter or edit HTML code in this window. This view is used primarily when you want to work directly with the HTML code.

- **Code and Design view**. Splits the Document window into two panes: the upper pane showing the underlying code and the lower pane showing the page as it will appear in the browser. You can easily move between the panes to either edit the HTML code or change the design using the Dreamweaver tools. This view is used primarily when you want to debug or troubleshoot a page.

You'll look at the Catalyst Home page in the different views. The filename of the home page is index.htm, because it is the page that displays by default when the viewer has not requested a specific file in the URL.

> **To display a Web page in different views:**
>
> **1.** Double-click **index.htm** in the Site panel. This opens the Catalyst home page.
>
> **2.** Click the **Show Design View** button ▦ on the Document window toolbar, if necessary. The home page Document window appears in Design view. See Figure 1-15.

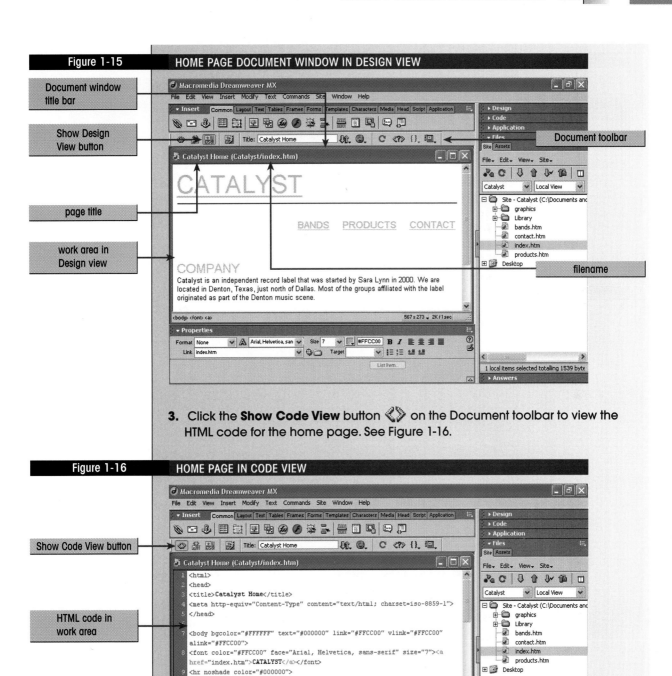

| Figure 1-15 | HOME PAGE DOCUMENT WINDOW IN DESIGN VIEW |

Document window title bar

Show Design View button

page title

work area in Design view

Document toolbar

filename

3. Click the **Show Code View** button on the Document toolbar to view the HTML code for the home page. See Figure 1-16.

| Figure 1-16 | HOME PAGE IN CODE VIEW |

Show Code View button

HTML code in work area

4. Click the **Show Code and Design Views** button on the Document toolbar to view both the code and the design of the home page. See Figure 1-17.

Figure 1-17   HOME PAGE IN CODE AND DESIGN VIEWS

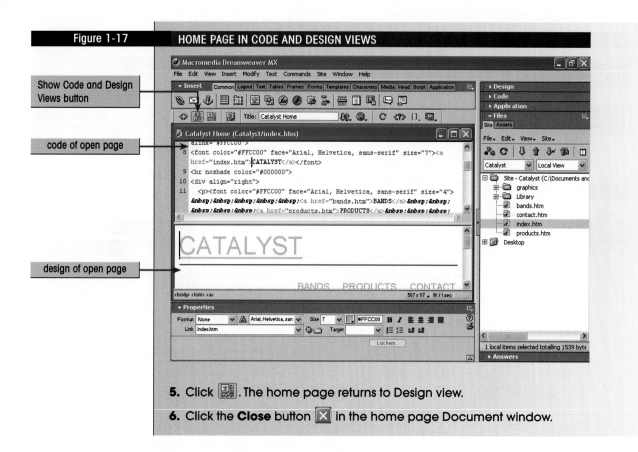

Show Code and Design Views button

code of open page

design of open page

5. Click ▦ . The home page returns to Design view.

6. Click the **Close** button ☒ in the home page Document window.

The **status bar** is located at the bottom of the Document window. Three things always appear in the status bar: the tag selector, the Window Size menu, and the Document Size/Estimated Download Time.

- **Tag selector**. Displays all the HTML tags surrounding the current selection in the work area.

- **Window Size menu**. Displays the Document window's current dimensions in pixels. A **pixel**, which stands for picture element, is the smallest adjustable unit on a display screen. The numbers change when you resize the Document window. You can set the window dimensions by manually resizing the window or by selecting one of the common monitor sizes from the menu.

- **Document Size/Estimated Download Time**. Displays the size of the current page in kilobytes (K) and the approximate amount of time in seconds it would take to download the page over a 28Kbps modem.

You'll review the status bar items as you explore and modify the Bands page.

To explore the status bar:

1. Open the **Catalyst-bands** page.

2. Drag to select the **Catalyst logo** at the top of the Catalyst-bands page. The status bar tag selector shows the HTML tags associated with the selected text. See Figure 1-18.

Figure 1-18   **STATUS BAR ITEMS**

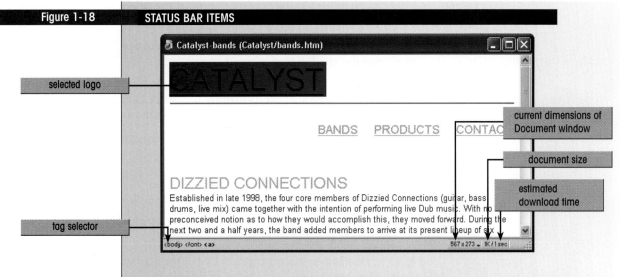

selected logo

tag selector

current dimensions of Document window

document size

estimated download time

TROUBLE? If you don't see the <font> and <a> tags in your status bar, don't worry. That means that the tags aren't selected in the underlying code.

3. Drag to select some of the text below the Dizzied Connections heading. Notice the HTML tags that now appear in the Tag selector: <body>, <div>, <p>, and <font>.

4. Click the **Window Size** menu on the status bar to display a list of common monitor sizes, and then click **536 x 196**. The Document window reduces to approximately half its current size.

5. Click the **Window Size** menu on the status bar, and then click **955 · 600**. The Document window expands to fill most of the screen.

   TROUBLE? If a dialog box opens with the message that the chosen size won't fit your current screen and that the screen size will be used, then your monitor size is smaller than 955 × 600. Click the OK button to resize the window to your screen size.

6. Manually resize the Document window to its previous dimensions.

   TROUBLE? If you can't see the resize button in the lower right corner of the Document window, click Window on the main menu bar, then click Tile Horizontally to have the Document window automatically fill the work area.

7. Review the **Document Size/Estimated Download Time** for the Catalyst-bands page.

8. Close the **Catalyst-bands** page.

Next, you'll explore the Property inspector.

Property Inspector

The most frequently used tool is the **Property inspector**, a toolbar with buttons for examining or editing the attributes of any element that is currently selected on the page displayed in the Document window. A **page element** is either an object or text. The Property inspector buttons and options change to reflect the attributes of the selected element. When text is selected, the Property inspector has two modes:

- **HTML mode.** The HTML mode enables you to apply HTML formatting to change the attributes of selected text.
- **CSS mode.** The CSS mode, or **Cascading Style Sheet mode**, enables you to apply Cascading Style Sheet formatting to change the attributes of selected text. (Cascading Style Sheets will be explained in more detail in later tutorials.)

You'll set the Property inspector to HTML mode and explore the attributes of different objects on the Catalyst site.

To explore object attributes using the Property inspector:

1. Open the **Catalyst Home** page in the Document window. (Remember, the filename of the home page is index.htm.)

2. Drag to select the text in the paragraph below the Company heading in the Document window.

3. Click the **Options menu** button 📇 on the right side of the Property inspector title bar, then click **HTML Mode.** The Property inspector attributes reflect the selected text. The attributes associated with text are similar to those in a word processing program, such as text size, color, styles (bold and italics), alignment, and indents. See Figure 1-19.

Figure 1-19	PROPERTY INSPECTOR SHOWING ATTRIBUTES FOR SELECTED TEXT

4. Drag to select the **BANDS** link at the top of the page in the Document window. The Property inspector attributes change to reflect the selected text and includes the link information. See Figure 1-20.

Figure 1-20	PROPERTY INSPECTOR SHOWING ATTRIBUTES FOR SELECTED LINK TEXT

selected link text

link information for selected text

5. Close the **Catalyst Home** page.

6. Open the **Catalyst-products** page.

7. Click the **Dizzied Connections CD cover image** in the Document window to select it, and then observe the attribute changes in the Property inspector. Notice the attributes related to images, such as height and width dimensions, borders, and so forth. See Figure 1-21.

Figure 1-21	PROPERTY INSPECTOR SHOWING ATTRIBUTES FOR SELECTED IMAGE

selected image

click to expand or shrink Property inspector

TROUBLE? If the Property inspector did not expand to show a second row of attributes, click the down arrow ▽ in the lower right corner of the Property inspector.

8. Close the **Catalyst-products** page.

Next you'll explore the Insert bar.

Insert Bar

In Dreamweaver, anything that you create or insert into a page is called an **object**. For example, tables, images, and links are objects. Whenever you want to create a new object, you use the **Insert bar**. The Insert bar contains tabs which reflect categories of objects. Each tab contains buttons for working with that category of objects. The tasks you can perform on each of the tabs on the Insert bar are described in Figure 1-22.

Figure 1-22	INSERT BAR CATEGORIES

CATEGORY (TAB)	DESCRIPTION OF TASKS
Common	Create and insert the most frequently used objects, such as images, layers, and tables.
Layout	Draw and insert tables and layers as well as buttons to switch between Standard view and Layout view.
Text	Insert text and list formatting tags such as bold (b), emphasis (em), and paragraph (p).
Tables	Insert tables and specific table tags.
Frames	Insert common, prefabricated frameset layouts.
Forms	Create and insert form elements in pages that include interactive forms.
Templates	Create page templates, including inserting editable, optional, and repeating regions into template files.
Characters	Insert special characters, such as the copyright symbol, line break character, and non-breaking space character.
Media	Insert animated and interactive media elements such as Flash, Shockwave, and Java applets.
Head	Insert elements that are found in the head section of the page, such as meta tags, keywords, and base tags.
Script	Insert a script, a noscript section, or a server-side include.
Application	Insert dynamic elements, such as recordsets, repeated regions, and dynamic tables and text.

The Insert bar displays the Common category tab by default. You'll explore some of the category tabs in the Insert bar.

To explore the category tabs in the Insert bar:

1. Open the **Catalyst-products** page.

2. Click the **Common** tab on the Insert bar, if necessary. A toolbar containing buttons in the Common category appears. See Figure 1-23. You can add objects to the Insert bar, so your Insert bar might include additional items.

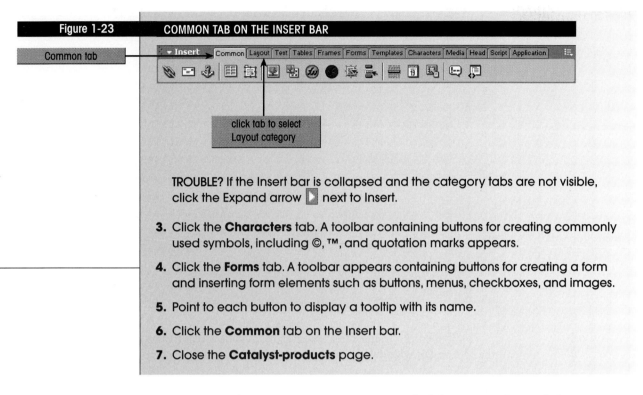

Figure 1-23   **COMMON TAB ON THE INSERT BAR**

Common tab

click tab to select
Layout category

TROUBLE? If the Insert bar is collapsed and the category tabs are not visible, click the Expand arrow ▶ next to Insert.

3. Click the **Characters** tab. A toolbar containing buttons for creating commonly used symbols, including ©, ™, and quotation marks appears.

4. Click the **Forms** tab. A toolbar appears containing buttons for creating a form and inserting form elements such as buttons, menus, checkboxes, and images.

5. Point to each button to display a tooltip with its name.

6. Click the **Common** tab on the Insert bar.

7. Close the **Catalyst-products** page.

As you are working in Dreamweaver, you may find that you need some help.

Getting Help in Dreamweaver

As you develop a Web site, you might run into a question about the purpose of a certain feature or want to review the steps for completing a specific task. Dreamweaver has a comprehensive Help system that provides a variety of ways to get the information you need.

Dreamweaver includes a Help command called **Using Dreamweaver**, which includes information about all of the Dreamweaver features. To open this Help window, you click Help on the main menu bar, and then click Using Dreamweaver to open the Using Dreamweaver MX window. Once open, there are three tabs that give you access to the Help topics: Contents, Index, and Search. **Contents** arranges the information by subject categories, similar to the table of contents in a printed book. **Index** arranges the information alphabetically by topic. **Search** allows you to look up information by typing a keyword or phrases. The relevant Help topic appears in the right pane of the browser window and can include explanations, descriptions, figures, and links to related topics.

REFERENCE WINDOW   RW

<u>Getting Help in Dreamweaver</u>

- Click Help on the main menu bar, and then click Using Dreamweaver.
- Click the Contents tab, and then click a topic or subtopic in the Contents list to display that Help topic.
- Click the Index tab, type a letter or word into the text box, and then double-click a topic or subtopic in the Index list (*or* click a topic or subtopic, and then click the Display button).
- Click the Search tab, type keywords into the text box, click the List Topics button, click a topic in the Select topic to display list, and then double-click a topic and/or subtopic in the Topic list (or click a topic or subtopic, and then click the Display button).
- Click the Close button in the Help window title bar and, if necessary, click the Close button in the Search window.

or

- Click the Help button in any window or toolbar, or right-click any panel tab and then click Help on the context menu to open the Using Dreamweaver MX window to a context-sensitive Help topic.
- Click the Close button in the Help window title bar.

You'll open the Using Dreamweaver MX window features to look up information about the Document window, the Insert bar, and the Property inspector.

To look up information in Using Dreamweaver MX:

1. Open the **Catalyst Home** page in the Document window.

2. Click **Help** on the main menu bar, and then click **Using Dreamweaver**. The Using Dreamweaver MX window opens.

3. Click the **Contents** tab, click **Dreamweaver Basics** in the Contents list, click **Exploring the Workspace**, click **Using windows and panels in Dreamweaver**, and then click **About the Document window**. The Document window Help topic appears in the right pane of the Using Dreamweaver MX window.

4. Click the **Maximize** button in the Using Dreamweaver MX window, if necessary. Notice the links to a related topic. See Figure 1-24.

Figure 1-24   CONTENTS TAB IN USING DREAMWEAVER MX WINDOW

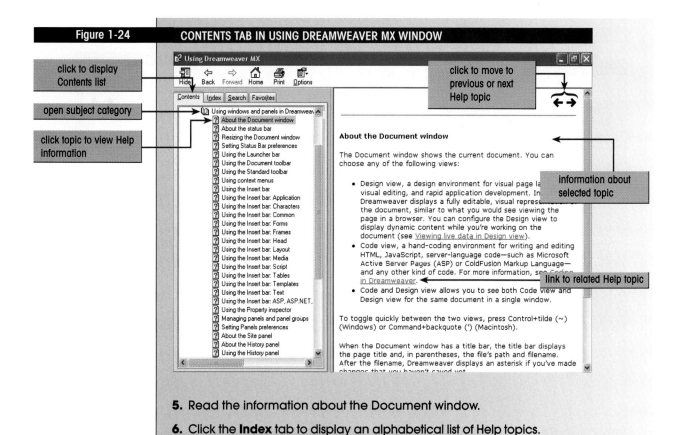

5. Read the information about the Document window.

6. Click the **Index** tab to display an alphabetical list of Help topics.

7. Type **insert** in the keyword text box to display a list of Help topics that begin with "insert," and then double-click **categories** under the Insert bar heading in the list. The Using the Insert bar Help topic appears in the right pane. See Figure 1-25.

Figure 1-25   INDEX TAB IN USING DREAMWEAVER MX WINDOW

click to display Index list

type letter or word to
scroll alphabetical list
of topics

double-click a topic
to view

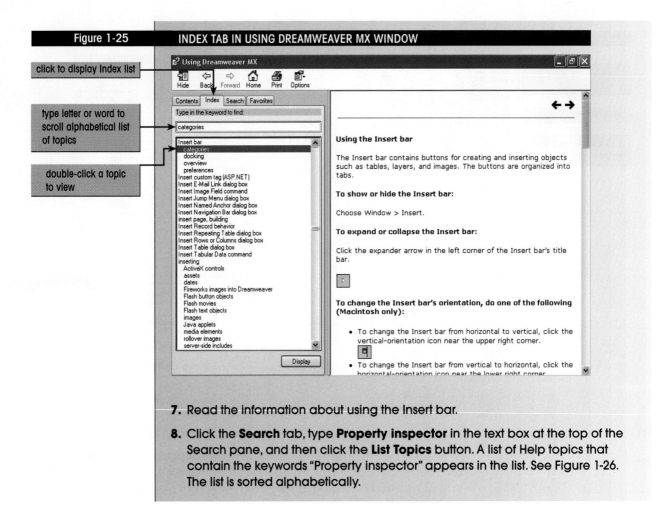

7. Read the information about using the Insert bar.

8. Click the **Search** tab, type **Property inspector** in the text box at the top of the
Search pane, and then click the **List Topics** button. A list of Help topics that
contain the keywords "Property inspector" appears in the list. See Figure 1-26.
The list is sorted alphabetically.

Figure 1-26	SEARCH TAB IN USING DREAMWEAVER MX WINDOW

type keywords here

click to display
documents containing
keywords

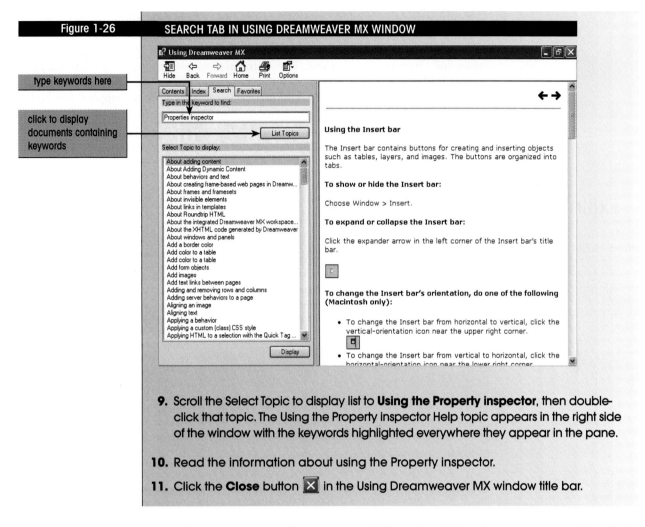

9. Scroll the Select Topic to display list to **Using the Property inspector**, then double-click that topic. The Using the Property inspector Help topic appears in the right side of the window with the keywords highlighted everywhere they appear in the pane.

10. Read the information about using the Property inspector.

11. Click the **Close** button ☒ in the Using Dreamweaver MX window title bar.

Another way to access Dreamweaver Help topics is by using **context-sensitive help**, which opens the Help topic related to the feature you are using. You access context-sensitive Help by clicking the Help button in any dialog box or toolbar about which you have a question, or by right-clicking any panel tab and then clicking Help.

You'll use context-sensitive Help to learn more about the text formatting features of the Property inspector.

To use context-sensitive Help:

1. Select the block of body text below the Company heading on the home page.

2. Click the **Help** button ⑦ in the upper-right corner of the Property inspector. The Using Dreamweaver MX window opens.

3. Read the Help information about setting text property options.

4. Close the Help window.

Dreamweaver also provides you with additional information about the program with a Welcome tour and Tutorials. These features are accessed from the Help menu. The **Welcome tour** contains animations that provide overviews of the Web development process and Dreamweaver features. The **Tutorials** provide hands-on experience in creating a sample Web site in Dreamweaver.

Finally, Macromedia provides additional Dreamweaver product support and Help features on its Web site (*www.macromedia.com*). The Web site provides you with the latest information on Dreamweaver, advice from experienced users, and advanced Help topics, as well as examples, tips, and updates. You can also join a discussion group to converse with other Dreamweaver users.

Exiting **Dreamweaver**

When you are finished working, you need to close the Web site and exit the Dreamweaver program. The Exit command on the File menu exits Dreamweaver and closes all open windows. You can also use the Close command or the Close button on the window title bars to close each open window until the program exits. Dreamweaver will prompt you to save any Web pages that you haven't yet saved.

REFERENCE   WINDOW   **RW**

Exiting Dreaweaver
- Click File on the menu bar, and then click Exit.

or

- Click the Close button in the Dreamweaver program window title bar.

Because you haven't made any changes to the Catalyst site, you can close any open pages without saving, and then exit the site.

To exit Dreamweaver:

1. Close the **Catalyst Home** page.

2. Click **File** on the menu bar, and then click **Exit**. Dreamweaver exits. You can also click the Close button ☒ in the program window title bar to exit Dreamweaver.

You've reviewed the existing Catalyst site and are ready to begin planning the new Web site.

Session 1.2 QUICK CHECK

1. Do you need to know HTML to create a successful Web site in Dreamweaver? Why or why not?

2. Explain the difference between a page-centric design approach and a site-centric design approach.

3. What is the difference between the local site and the remote site in Dreamweaver?

4. What is a site definition, and where is it stored?

5. What is the local root folder?

6. Which window or panel do you use to manage local and remote site files?

7. Which view in the Document window displays the underlying HTML code that Dreamweaver automatically generates as you create and edit a Web page?

8. Where would you turn for information about all of the Dreamweaver features?

REVIEW ASSIGNMENTS

Brian Lee is getting ready to have his team begin to plan the new Catalyst Web site. In preparation for this, he wants you to review the Web sites of bands that you like. While looking, keep your eyes open for possible improvements that could be incorporated into the new Catalyst site.

1. Start your Web browser.

Explore　　2. Type the URL for the Web site of a favorite band in the Address text box, and then press the Enter key. (*Hint:* If you don't know the URL for the band's Web site, try typing "*www.thenameoftheband.com*" in the Address text box, using the actual band name.)

3. Review the home page of the band's Web site to see what information is included and how the information is arranged.

4. Use hyperlinks to explore the site. Look at how information is presented and whether you can move easily between sections.

5. Click the band's logo, if there is one. Notice whether the logo is a hot spot, and, if it is, where it takes you.

Explore　　6. Use a search engine to find the Web site for another of your favorite bands. Type the URL for a search engine into the Address text box, and press the Enter key to open the search engine. (Two popular search engines are *www.google.com* and *www.dogpile.com*.) Search for the band's Web site by typing the name of the band into the Search text box, and then clicking the Search button. The search engine displays a list of pages that contain the words in your search. (*Hint:* If too many unrelated choices appear, narrow the search by typing quotation marks around the band's name and clicking the Search button again. If no matches appear, check the spelling and try again. If there are still no matches, try searching for a different band.)

7. Click the link for the band's Web site to open the home page.

8. Repeat Steps 3 through 5 to explore the Web site and review the information it contains.

Explore

9. Compare the two sites that you explored. Write down your responses to the following questions:

   a. What are the similarities and the differences between the sites?
   b. Which features do you prefer? Why?
   c. Can any of the features from these sites be incorporated into the Catalyst Web site?
   d. How would the changes improve the site?

10. Exit your browser.

11. Start Dreamweaver.

12. Open the Contents tab in the Using Dreamweaver MX window.

13. Click Getting Started in the Contents list, then click Introduction.

Explore

14. Read the information in the Introduction pane, and then click the Next arrow link (the right arrow) at the end of the overview to move to the next topic. (*Hint:* The left and right arrows are links that move you consecutively through the Help topics.)

15. Read the next three Help topics, using the Next arrow link to move to the consecutive pages.

16. Close the Using Dreamweaver MX window.

Explore

17. View the Welcome tour. Click Help on the menu bar, click Welcome to open the Welcome window, and then click the Design button.

Explore

18. Read the information on each page, clicking the camera icon when available to view the screen shots, and then click the Play button (the right arrow at the bottom of the window) to move to the next page.

19. When the movie ends (the Play button is grayed out and unavailable), click the Close button in the Welcome window title bar to close the tour.

20. Exit Dreamweaver.

CASE PROBLEMS

Case 1. Hroch University Anthropology Department   Dr. Matt Hart is a social anthropologist at Hroch University, which has an internationally acclaimed anthropology department renowned for its research. Matt has lived in Asia for the last two years collecting data on small rural communities in northern Vietnam. He wants to create a Web site to present his research findings and accompanying graphics. He asks you to review existing Web sites that deal with social anthropology and northern Vietnam in preparation for designing his Web site. He also asks you to find out what image file formats are compatible with Dreamweaver.

1. Start your Web browser.

Explore

2. Use a search engine to find Web sites related to social anthropology. Type the URL for a search engine into the Address text box, and press the Enter key to open the search engine. (Two popular search engines are *www.google.com* and *www.dogpile.com*.)

Explore

3. Search for relevant Web sites by typing the term "social anthropology" into the search text box and then clicking the Search button. The search engine displays a list of pages that contain the words in your search. (*Hint:* If too many unrelated choices appear, narrow the search by typing quotation marks around the keywords and clicking the Search button. If no matches appear, check your spelling and try again.)

4. Click the link for an appropriate page to open the Web site, and then explore the Web site, making notes about what information is included, how the material is organized, and what images are included.

5. Click the Back button on the browser toolbar until you return to the search engine. Then investigate a second Web site, taking notes about its content and organization.

Explore 6. Return to the search engine and search for Web sites related to "northern Vietnam." Explore at least one Web site, taking notes about its content and organization.

7. Write a memo to Matt giving a brief description of the sites' similarities and differences, and list features you would like to incorporate into the new Web site. Include the URL for each site analyzed.

8. Close the browser.

9. Start Dreamweaver, and then select the Dreamweaver MX workspace layout.

10. Open Using Dreamweaver MX Help.

11. Use the Contents tab to display Inserting Images from the Adding Content category.

12. Read the About images topic to learn about the image file formats that Dreamweaver uses.

13. Add to your memo a brief explanation of which image file formats are compatible with Dreamweaver.

14. Exit Dreamweaver.

Case 2. Museum of Western Art The Fort Worth Museum of Western Art has been a premier gallery for many years. As part of the museum's plan to further community education about western art, Tika Hagge, the museum manager and curator, wants to expand the museum Web site. She has contracted C. J. Strittmatter to design and maintain the new site. You'll work with C. J. on the site. To start, you'll review the museum's current Web site.

1. Start Dreamweaver, and then select the Dreamweaver MX workspace layout.

2. Create a Local Site Definition for the museum's Web site. Use "Museum of Western Art" as the site name, set the path Tutorial.01\Cases\Museum\Dreamweaver on your Data Disk as the local root folder, check the Refresh Local File List Automatically checkbox, and check the Enable Cache checkbox.

3. Select Museum of Western Art in the Site list in the Site panel in Local view.

4. Expand the folder list if necessary. How many pages are in the site?

5. Display the site map in the Site panel. How are the pages connected?

Explore 6. Click the plus (+) button next to the contact.htm page. Notice the globe icon, which indicates a file on another site or a special link (such as an e-mail link).

Explore 7. Display the page titles in the site map by clicking View on the Site panel menu bar, and then clicking Show Page Titles.

Explore 8. Display the filenames by turning off the Show Page Titles command.

Explore 9. Right-click the Files panel group name, and then click Help on the context menu to open context-sensitive Help.

10. Read the Using the Site panel Help topic, and then close the Help window.

11. Display the site map and the files list in the Site panel. (*Hint*: Click the Expand/Collapse button to display both the map and the file list.)

12. Collapse the Site panel, and then display only the local files list.

13. Open the site's home page (index.htm) from the Site panel, and then read the page's content.

14. Open the site's contact page (contact.htm) from the Site panel, and then read the contents of the page.

15. Make the home page the active page.

16. Change the view to Code and Design view.

17. Close all open pages.

18. Exit Dreamweaver.

Case 3. NORM NORM is an independent publishing company in California that concentrates on cultivating fringe writings of all sorts. Norman Blinkered started the company in 1988, using his kitchen as an office. Since then, NORM has grown and prospered. Norman recently hired Mark Chapman to design and maintain a Web site for the company in hopes of expanding NORM's market through Internet exposure. Mark asks you to research the Web sites of other independent publishing companies. Norman has provided a list of some competitors: Seven Stories Press, Akashic Books, Soft Skull Press, and Verso. You'll use a search engine to find the Web sites of NORM's competitors. Then you'll investigate the sites you find.

1. Start your Web browser.

Explore   2. Use a search engine to find the Web sites for NORM's competitors. Type the URL for a search engine into the Address text box, and press the Enter key to open the search engine. (Two popular search engines are *www.google.com* and *www.dogpile.com*.)

Explore   3. Search for a competitor's Web site by typing the company's name in the search text box and then clicking the Search button. The search engine displays a list of pages that contain the words in your search.

4. Click the link for an appropriate page to open the Web site. Then explore the Web site, making notes about the site's design, what information is included, how the material is organized, and to whom the site would appeal.

5. Click the Back button on the browser toolbar until you return to the search engine.

6. Repeat Steps 3 through 5 for each of NORM's competitors.

Explore   7. Return to the search engine and search for Web sites for independent publishing companies. Explore at least one Web site, taking notes about its content and organization.

8. Write a brief description of the sites' similarities and differences, listing both content and design features you would like to incorporate into the new Web site. Include the URL for each site.

9. Close the browser.

Case 4. Sushi Ya-Ya Sushi Ya-Ya is a small sushi restaurant that will be opening soon in the French Quarter of New Orleans. Charlie Lindahl, the store's owner, has decided that a Web site with online ordering features would help create publicity for the new restaurant and garner lunch sales by encouraging carry-out orders by local businesses. Charlie hired Mary O'Brien to create and design the site. You will assist Mary in building the site. Mary asks you to research what other sushi restaurants have done with their Web sites. Then she asks you to use Dreamweaver to find information about basic HTML.

1. Start your Web browser.

Explore

2. Use a search engine to find the Web sites for sushi restaurants. Type the URL for a search engine into the Address text box, and press the Enter key to open the search engine. (Two popular search engines are *www.google.com* and *www.dogpile.com*.)

Explore

3. Search for sushi restaurant Web sites by typing the appropriate keywords in the search text box and then clicking the Search button. The search engine displays a list of pages that contain the words in your search.

4. Explore at least three sushi restaurant sites. For each site, write down the site's URL and any useful information about the site's content, organization, and design. (*Hint:* Use the Back button on the browser toolbar to return to the search results and link to a different restaurant.)

5. Write a brief description of the sites' similarities and differences, listing both content and design features you would like to incorporate into the new Sushi Ya-Ya Web site. Include the URL for each site.

6. Close your browser.

7. Start Dreamweaver, and then select the Dreamweaver MX workspace layout.

8. Open Using Dreamweaver MX Help.

9. Select Search and type "HTML styles" into the Type in the keyword to find text box, and then click the List Topics button.

10. Open the Setting Up a Document topic, and read it.

11. Open the Using HTML styles to format text topic and read it.

12. Close the Help window.

13. Exit Dreamweaver.

QUICK | CHECK ANSWERS

Session 1.1

1. the world's largest computer network used for communicating and exchanging information via computer

2. a subset of the Internet with its own protocol (HTTP) and document structure (HTML)

3. A Web server is a specialized server that stores and distributes information to computers that are connected to the Internet. A Web client is a computer that an individual uses to access Internet information via a Web server.

4. the software installed on a client computer that allows users to view Web pages

5. a unique address that Web browsers use to locate where a specific Web page is stored

6. course.com

7. Hyperlinks are graphics, text, or buttons with hot spots that when clicked with a mouse take you to another related section on the same Web page, another Web page on the same site, or another Web site entirely.

8. to effectively convey the Web site's intended message or information—usually with a combination of text, graphics, and possibly multimedia elements such as video, animation, or interactive content

Session 1.2

1. No. However, some familiarity with HTML enables you to make the site work better, fix problems that arise, and create elements that are complex or impossible to create in Dreamweaver.

2. Page-centric design concentrates on designing and creating Web pages individually and then linking them. Site-centric design focuses on planning the Web site structure and design before creating any pages.

3. The local site is stored on your computer and is the version you work on; the remote site is a copy of the local site that Dreamweaver posts to a publicly viewable space, such as a Web server.

4. A site definition is the information that tells Dreamweaver where to find the local and remote files for the Web site. It also defines other parameters that affect how the site is set up within Dreamweaver. It is stored in the Windows registry. If you move to another computer to work, you must re-create the site definition on that computer.

5. the location where you want to store all the files used by the local version of the Web site

6. Site panel

7. Code view

8. Using Dreamweaver Help

In this tutorial you will:

- Determine the site goals

- Identify the target audience

- Conduct market research

- Create end-user scenarios

- Design the information architecture

- Create a flow chart and site structure

- Create a site concept and metaphor

- Design the site navigation structure

- Develop the aesthetic concept for the site

- Create a new site

PLANNING AND DESIGNING A SUCCESSFUL WEB SITE

Developing a Web Site Plan and Design for Catalyst

Catalyst

Before you can create a Web site in Dreamweaver, a considerable amount of planning must take place. Remember, Dreamweaver uses a site-centric approach for designing Web sites. While planning may seem like a lot of work, it will help you avoid reworking site elements; in the end, it will save you time and frustration. Also, it is almost impossible to create an effective Web site without having a clear idea of what the goals for the site are. Planning enables you to determine what you need from your Web site and how the site will meet those needs.

Brian Lee, the public relations and marketing director at Catalyst, has asked you to work with him to plan the new Web site for Catalyst. First, you will determine site goals and identify your target audience. To do this, you will conduct market research and create end-user scenarios. Then, you will design the information architecture, create a flow chart and site structure, design the site navigation structure, and develop the aesthetic concept for the site. Finally, you will create the new site.

SESSION 2.1

In this session, you will plan the structure of the new Catalyst Web site. You'll determine the site's goals. You will define a target audience and create an end-user profile. You will research the intended market. You will create end-user scenarios. Finally, you will use this information to make preliminary decisions about the new Catalyst Web site.

Creating a Plan for a New Web Site

Whether you are part of an in-house Web team or an independent designer hired to create a Web site, the first order of business for designing a professional Web site is to determine the goals, the target audience, and the expectations for the site. You obtain this information from the client, the person or persons for whom you are creating the site. This process can be accomplished in a single meeting, but more often it requires a series of meetings and considerable time.

This is a crucial part of the planning process, because it is impossible to design a Web site that will effectively meet the client's needs until you determine exactly what those needs are. You should explain clearly to clients what information you will need from them and what value their contribution will make to the final Web site. By making the client aware of what to expect and by communicating effectively with the client throughout the process, you help to insure a successful project and a satisfied client.

It is important to understand that there are many possible paths in any creative process. However, as you gain experience in planning, designing, and creating Web sites, you'll find that some things work better than others. You will come up with your own ideas about the site's goals, the target audience, and so forth, and then compare them to those approved by Brian. You will then compare how your plan is similar to and different from the final Catalyst Web site plan, and consider the benefits of doing it another way.

Determining Site Goals

The first question you should ask when you begin to plan a site is: What are the primary goals of the Web site? A Web site can have one goal or many goals. It is a good idea to brainstorm with the client, in this case Brian, and create a list of all the goals you can think of for the site. For example, the goals of a commercial Web site might be to:

- Provide information about a product
- Sell a product
- Increase brand recognition
- Provide help or operational instructions

This list, which could go on and on, is very general. The goal list for an actual site would be much more specific. For example, it would state what the product or products would be.

There are a few guidelines to keep in mind as you develop the list of site goals. First, write site goals in an active voice rather than passive. Second, use action verbs to help you select achievable goals rather than concepts. For example, brand recognition is a concept, not a goal; *increasing* brand recognition is a goal. Action verbs include words such as achieve, increase, and provide. Third, think about the different aspects of the site. For example, in addition to selling products, you may want to provide reliable support. Finally, make a comprehensive list. You should have at least 10 goals in your original list.

Once you have a list of possible site goals, review the list and place the goals in order of importance. For example:

- Sell a product
- Increase brand recognition

■ Provide information about a product

■ Provide help or operational instructions

Review your list and, if possible, combine goals; then reprioritize if necessary. Some of the lower-priority goals might actually be part of higher-priority goals. For example, in some cases, providing help or operational instructions may be incorporated into the general goal of providing information about the product. There is a limit to the number of goals that a Web site can effectively achieve; therefore, the first four or five goals are probably the ones you will want to focus on. Remember, site goals are most effective if they are the result of collaboration with the client.

Brian asks you to develop a list of goals for the new Catalyst site. As you gain experience in designing Web sites, your ability to identify and articulate goals will continue to improve.

To create a list of goals for the new Catalyst site:

1. Write down at least 20 possible site goals.

2. Review the list to be sure that all statements are in the active voice and use action verbs.

3. Prioritize the goals in order of importance.

4. Review your list, combining goals if possible, and reprioritizing them if necessary.

5. Review the top five goals. Think about what you want to accomplish with the site and make sure that your list of goals will help achieve a successful site.

Brian created a list of goals for the new Catalyst Web site, and then prioritized and combined them.

6. Compare your list to Brian's goal list shown in Figure 2-1.

Figure 2-1	CATALYST WEB SITE GOALS

1. Enhance label identity.
2. Increase band recognition.
3. Promote band image.
4. Boost sales of CDs and promotional products.
5. Provide tour date information.
6. Provide information about individual band members.
7. Provide press information.
8. Create cross interest between bands with similar sounds.
9. Link to fan sites.
10. Produce a sound library (long-term, not immediate).
11. Construct and link to individual band sites (long-term, not immediate).
12. Create a photo library for each band (long-term, not immediate).
13. Create other materials (such as Flash animations) to increase interest (long-term, not immediate).

You will use the site goals to make decisions about the site organization and structure. The site's primary goal is to enhance label identity—in other words, to make people aware of Catalyst and to associate the label with certain types of bands. The site will be organized to emphasize the Catalyst name and logo. The home page will include information about the label, followed by band information. The label logo will appear at the top of every page, and the site navigation will be organized so that a "label information" category is included on the top level of the site.

The priority of the goals helps to determine the site's layout. If the first two goals were switched and increased band recognition was the primary goal, the site structure might be organized differently. The band information could appear above the label information. The band logos could appear at the top of all of the pages instead of the label logo. The individual bands could be placed in their own category in the top level of navigation. This is just one set of many possible changes.

When you start to examine the way that site goals can affect the structure of the final site, you can see just how important it is to carefully consider what you want to accomplish. Taking the time to establish goals and expectations from the very beginning will make a world of difference in the final site.

Identifying the Target Audience

The **target audience** for a Web site is the group of users that you would *most* like to visit the site. You identify the target audience by creating a user profile. The **user profile** is the information that you gather from a list of questions, as shown in Figure 2-2. The user profile is a tool designed to help you determine the characteristics of the group of people you are trying to reach—the target audience. (In this case, the word "user" refers to the target user group, not an individual user.)

Figure 2-2	GENERAL USER PROFILE QUESTIONS

User Profile Questions:

1. **What is the age range of the user?** (Sites can appeal to a range of ages. The age range will depend on the site goals. Generally, the group members are linked because they share a commonality, such as a habit, a characteristic, or a developmental stage.)

2. **What is the gender of the user?** (Sites can be targeted to males only, females only, or males and females. Not all sites are targeted to a specific gender.)

3. **What is the education level of the user?** (Education level will be a range. Designate education level either by the current year in school, e.g., senior in high school, or the degree earned if out of school, e.g., associates degree.)

4. **What is the economic situation of the user?** (Economic situation refers to the annual income level of the user as well as other extenuating economic factors like parental support or student loans. For example, the user may be a student who has only a part time job. As a student, the user may have a lower income bracket, earning only $20,000 a year, but extenuating economic factors like parental support and student loans may affect the user's buying power. All of this information should factor into the user's economic situation.)

5. **What is the geographic location of the user?** (Is the site targeted at users in a specific city, a specific region, or a specific country?)

6. **What is the primary language of the user?**

7. **What is the ethnic background of the user?** (Most sites are targeted at a user group with diverse cross-sections of ethnic backgrounds; however, sometimes ethnicity is a factor in your target audience. For example, *Jet Magazine* is targeted at African-American users.)

8. **Are there other unifying characteristics that are relevant to the user?** (If you know that the target group has a common characteristic that may be of use in designing the Web site, list it here. Unifying characteristics are useful if they are related to the topic of the Web site or if they could affect the goals of the site. For example, unifying characteristics might include things such as: target users have diabetes [for a diabetes disease-management site], target users ride dirt bikes [for a BMX motor cross site], target users listen to club music [for an alternative music site], and so forth.)

You can also use other resources to help you create a user profile. If the client has an existing Web site, you may be able to obtain specific data about current users from usage logs and user registration data. Usage logs are exact records of every visit to the site; they include information such as the time and date of the visit, the visitor's ISP, the visitor's pathway through the site, the visitor's browser and operating system, and so forth. Some sites require users to register before being allowed access by creating a user ID and providing personal information. You can analyze this registration information when it's available to further define the target audience.

Brian asks you to create a user profile that identifies the target audience of the Catalyst Web site.

To identify the target audience for the new Catalyst Web site:

1. Answer the User Profile Questions listed in Figure 2-2.

2. Review your answers to ensure that the target audience you identified reinforces the final site goals listed in Figure 2-1.

3. Compare your answers to the User Profile Questions to those compiled by Brian, shown in Figure 2-3.

Figure 2-3	USER PROFILE FOR CATALYST SITE

1. Age: 18 to 29
2. Gender: male and female
3. Education level: late high school to college
4. Economic situation: students with expendable income from parental support/financial aid; recent college graduates entering the workplace
5. Geographic location: United States and Canada; the label has concentrated on signing bands from the Denton, Texas area but wants to target a larger area with its Web site
6. Primary language: target user will speak/read English
7. Ethnic background: the Catalyst Web site will not target a specific ethnic background
8. Other unifying characteristics: participation in the "indie" (independent) college music scene

Sometimes clients and designers are hesitant to identify the target audience because they think it will limit the reach of the Web site. However, a very broad target audience can be even more restrictive than having a very narrow target audience. A site that must appeal to many different groups of people must be more generic in some ways. For example, if the new Catalyst Web site is intended to appeal to an older audience (50 to 60 years of age) as well as to a college age audience (18 to 29 years of age), you can include only elements that will be attractive and communicate effectively with both age groups. You can see how this might limit some stylistic options (such as graphic choice, word choice, and color choice) that would be available to a Web site with a target audience that included only a college-aged group.

Some sites are intended to appeal to a broad target audience. Consider the Internal Revenue Service (IRS). The IRS Web site (*www.irs.gov*) is designed to be an informational site available to a diverse group of people. The site contains a huge amount of information about U.S. tax laws and tax preparation. Knowing that the target audience for the IRS site is broad and that the goal of the site is to dispense information, designers chose to create a text-based site with very few graphic elements that will be accessible to the broadest possible group of users. The IRS site is very effective at achieving its goals. However, this primarily text-based design would not be effective if the main goal was entertainment because—although informationally rich—the site is not very entertaining.

Once you have identified a target audience, you can use the general information from the user profile as a basis to research and make more advanced decisions about user wants, needs, technical proficiencies, and so forth. When used appropriately, the target audience information is a great tool for focusing a Web site to achieve the site goals. However, be careful not to get lost in stereotypes. It is easy to draw general conclusions about the target audience without backing up those assumptions with research. This can lead to a Web site that seems targeted to your intended audience, but, in fact, does not actually appeal to them. For example, we have all been sitting in front of the television when a commercial that is supposed to appeal to our gender and/or age group comes on the screen. Think about your reaction to a commercial that has the right look but underestimates your intelligence or misinterprets your styles, habits, and so forth. Use the target audience information as a starting point for your research.

Conducting Market Research

Market research is the careful investigation and study of data about the target audience's preferences for a product or service. It also includes evaluating the products or services of competitors. The user profile provides information about your target audience. Once you've created the user profile, you need to investigate the habits, interests, likes, and dislikes of that group of people, as well as what Catalyst's competitors are doing to attract them.

Advertising and design agencies spend a substantial amount of money subscribing to services that provide in-depth market analysis of products or services and their target audiences (like *www.ipsos-asi.com* or *www.imarketinc.com*), but the average designer has to rely on his or her own research. You will look for information that will help you to build a Web site tailored to the target audience Catalyst wants to attract. Technical information—such as the screen size and the speed of the computer and Internet connection that the target audience uses—tells you the technical limitations of an effective site. Information on the spending habits of the target audience tells you the potential profitability of the Web site. Information on the interests of the target audience tells you what will appeal to the target audience and what elements you might include in the site to draw them in. Information about the culture and the customs of the target audience tells you what colors, symbols, fashions, styles, and so forth will be effective in communicating with the target audience. Finally, information about competing Web sites tells you what the competition believes is effective in attracting and communicating with the target audience.

The fastest way to obtain information about the habits, interests, and likes of a target audience is to use a search engine such as *www.altavista.com* or *www.google.com* to locate Web sites with statistics and other data about the target audience's lifestyle and preferences. A **search engine** is a Web site whose primary function is to gather and report what information is available on the Web about specified keywords or phrases. Brian spent some time online and compiled the information shown in Figure 2-4.

Figure 2-4	CATALYST TARGET AUDIENCE INFORMATION

- 78% of college students own computers.
- Student shoppers tend to go off-campus or online to find the most competitive pricing.
- 72% of students use online services on a daily basis. 52% use search engines to locate stores online. (Yahoo, AltaVista, and Google are among the most frequently used.)
- College students spend an average of $480 online annually. Among the most commonly purchased items are music (46% of students buy their music online), books (37%), tickets for air travel (32%), concert and other event tickets (22%), and computer software (14%).
- 58% of college students downloaded music from the Internet in the last year.
- 65% of college students have and use credit cards.

You'll look for additional information about the target audience for the Catalyst Web site. Make sure that you note the source of the information and the URL of the Web page in case you need to refer to that source in the future.

To gather information on your target audience:

1. Start your browser, type **www.dogpile.com** in the Address text box, and then press the **Enter** key. The Dogpile home page opens.

   TROUBLE? If the Dogpile search engine is unavailable (sometimes sites go down), you can try another search engine. Type www.google.com (or the URL for your favorite search engine) in the Address text box, and then press the **Enter** key.

2. Type **market research student spending** into the text box at the top of the page and start the search.

3. Review the list of Web sites, click the link for a Web site that looks promising, and then explore that Web site.

4. Write down any pertinent information. Make sure to note the source of the information and the URL of the Web page in case you need to refer to that source in the future.

5. Click the **Back** button ⬅ on the toolbar to return to the search results, and then repeat Steps 3 and 4.

By now you should have an understanding of the target audience's habits and likes. Now, it is time to switch your focus from the habits of the target audience to what you can do with the Web site to attract the target audience. Next, you'll investigate Web sites that the target audience frequents, as well as the Web sites of Catalyst competitors. You will have to make assumptions about which sites are popular with the target audience based on the information that you gathered about its habits and preferences. By exploring sites that are popular with the target audience and the sites of competitors, you can familiarize yourself with graphic styles that the target audience is accustomed to, as well as the colors, symbols, fashions, styles, and slang terms that have been effective in communicating with the target audience.

While you are exploring Web sites, pay close attention to their design. What colors do the sites use? How is the information laid out? What are the navigation systems like? Is there anything unique about the sites? What aspects of the sites might appeal to the target audience? How is the space used? Can you ascertain what the sites' goals might be? Is the content presented in straightforward language or in slang specific to the target audience? Is there a lot of text on each page or is the text broken into smaller segments?

Brian asks you to explore some music-related Web sites.

To explore other music Web sites:

1. Type **www.mtv.com** in the Address text box, and then press the **Enter** key. The MTV home page opens.

2. Navigate through the Web site, evaluating the colors, information layout, navigation system, use of space, content, language style (formal, conversational, slang, etc.), and so forth.

3. Record your findings and make notes about anything you feel is important about the site.

4. Repeat Steps 1 through 3 for **www.click2music.com**, a BMG Music Web site.

5. Search for and explore other sites that the target audience might frequent.

6. Look at two other music labels' sites. What information do they include? Does the information change when the label is trying to target a different audience? Think about what you like and dislike about the sites.

By this point, you should have a clear idea of the target audience, including the user's habits, interests, and so forth. You should also have an understanding of what you can do with the Web site to attract the target audience. You will use this information to develop end-user scenarios.

Creating End-User Scenarios

End-user scenarios are imagined situations in which the target audience might access a Web site. End-user scenarios are used to envision actual conditions that an end user will be in while experiencing the Web site. Scenarios enable you to visualize an abstract target audience as real people. By placing characters in realistic situations, you can get a better sense of what factors might affect the users' experience with the Web site. Then, you can anticipate the end users' needs and build a Web site that incorporates these factors into its design.

Brian created two scenarios for the Catalyst Web site, as shown in Figure 2-5. The scenarios provide insights that go beyond statistics and facts. For example, from Scenario 1, you learn that there is a good chance that the target audience will not have access to audio on the Web site; therefore, you can conclude that the audio should not be a primary component.

Figure 2-5	END-USER SCENARIOS FOR CATALYST SITE

Scenario 1

Tim Roth is a junior at the University of North Texas in Denton, Texas. He is 21 and lives on campus in one of the older dorms. Tim has a computer, but the dorms are not equipped with high-speed Internet connections; therefore, when Tim wants to surf from his room, he must do it via a 56k modem. He does most of his surfing late at night in the computer science lab that has 24-hour access. Because the lab computers have no speakers, Tim can listen to sound only if he brings his headphones.

Tim is a fan of Surface Suction and attends the band's shows regularly. He visits the Catalyst site frequently to check out new bands. The feature that he would most like to see added to the Catalyst site is a regularly updated list of live shows. Tim's other favorite sites are the Rubber Gloves Rehearsal Studio Web site and The Good Records Web site.

Scenario 2

Sita Owanee, 26, is a recent graduate of Syracuse University's art media studies MFA program. She is now living in New York City and is working as a graphic designer. Because Sita has just started her career and has little expendable income, she has access to the Web via only a 56k modem and a moderately equipped computer.

Sita has a passion for dub music. Dizzied Connections is one of her favorite bands. She discovered the Catalyst Web site when Dizzied Connections moved to the label and has since become a regular visitor. She visits the site to keep up with Dizzied Connections and to see if Catalyst has signed other bands with the same sound. Sita would most like to see an expanded section featuring her favorite band. Regularly updated news about the band would keep her interested in the site. Sita's other favorite sites include the Knitting Factory Web site and the Village Voice Web site.

Brian asks you to create a third scenario for the Catalyst site.

To create an end-user scenario:

1. Review the Catalyst site goals, user profile, and market research.

2. Create a character who might visit the Catalyst Web site. Give the character a name and attributes, such as age, gender, location, and so forth.

3. Place the character in a situation where he or she is accessing the Web site. Describe the user's surroundings and the user's experience with the site.

Planning might seem time-consuming and difficult, but a few hours of advanced preparation will save you many hours of redesign work later. In the next session, you will work on the Catalyst site's informational structure and aesthetic design.

Session 2.1 QUICK CHECK

1. True or False? There is only one plan and design for a Web site.

2. What is the purpose of listing site goals?

3. How many goals can a Web site achieve effectively?

4. What is a target audience for a Web site?

5. Why would you create a user profile?

6. What happens if you draw general conclusions about the target audience without backing up those conclusions with research?

7. Why would you conduct market research?

8. What are end-user scenarios?

SESSION 2.2

In this session, you will create the information architecture for the Catalyst Web site, which includes creating a flow chart and organizing information categories. Then you will design the site. To do this, you will develop a site metaphor. You will also establish a color palette, a font set, a graphic style, and a layout design for the site.

Information Architecture

Information architecture is the process of determining what you need a site to do, and then creating a framework that will allow you to accomplish those goals. It applies the principles of architectural design and library science to Web site design by providing a blueprint for Web page arrangement, Web site navigation, and page content organization. The basic process for creating the information architecture for a site is to construct information categories, draw a flow chart, and organize the available information into pages. You'll work on the information architecture for the new Catalyst site.

Creating Categories for Information

Categories provide structure for the information in a Web site and are used to create the main navigation system. The main **navigation system** is the interface that visitors use to move through a Web site. This interface appears on every page in the site. The main categories of a Web site are like the subject sections of a library or bookstore (fiction, poetry, reference material, etc.); they show the user what types of information are included in the Web site. The categories should be based on the site goals and the information gathered during the preliminary planning stages. When you create the Catalyst categories, think about how the information should be organized to achieve the site goals, then use what you learned from visiting other sites to create logical groupings of information. You should include no more than five main categories on a Web site, because more than five main categories make the pages seem cluttered.

Categories can be divided into subcategories, just like the fiction section in a library or bookstore might be divided into history novels, mysteries, literature, science fiction, and so forth. Subcategories should be arranged in hierarchical order, placing the most important subcategories first. Once you know the major categories for the Catalyst site, you can list all the subcategories that will fall under each category in a hierarchical order. You should include no more that five subcategories for each main category, because fragmenting information into too many subcategories makes the Web site more difficult to navigate.

For more complex sites, individual subcategories can be divided into third-level subcategories. Before creating third-level subcategories, make sure that there is enough information to warrant the breakdown. Visitors dislike having to link too far down into a site to find relevant information. Third-level subcategories are appropriate only when a Web site is incredibly information intensive, like a research site, and there is no other means to effectively convey the information.

The best way to present the major categories and the subcategories for a Web site is in a standard outline format. Brian created the outline shown in Figure 2-6 to show how the Catalyst site content can be structured.

Figure 2-6	CATALYST WEB SITE CATEGORIES

Catalyst Web Site Category Outline

I. Home Page
   a. Label
      i. News
      ii. Mission statement
      iii. Company history
      iv. Employee biographies
   b. Bands
      i. Dizzied Connections
      ii. Sloth Child
      iii. Life in Minor Chords
   c. Catalogue
      i. CDs
      ii. Vinyl
   d. Tour Dates
      i. Tour schedules
      ii. Venues and ticket information
   e. Contact
      i. Company contact information
      ii. Directions
      iii. E-mail form

Brian asks you to create an alternate outline with another possible version of the categories and subcategories for the Catalyst Web site.

To create an information category outline:

1. Review the site goals and your research, and then use that information to create a list of five categories of information for the Catalyst Web site.

2. Start an outline using the categories you listed in Step 1 as section headings.

3. List all the subcategories that will be included in the first section of your outline, and then arrange them in hierarchical order.

4. Break the subcategories into their respective subcategories, where applicable, and arrange them in hierarchical order.

5. Repeat Steps 3 and 4 for each section of your outline.

6. Compare your outline to Brian's outline shown in Figure 2-6.

Next you'll work on the flow chart for the Catalyst site.

Creating a Flow Chart

A **flow chart** is a diagram of geometric shapes connected by lines that shows steps in sequence. The shapes represent steps, decision points, and dead ends. The lines represent the connection of steps. If steps must be followed in a particular order or direction, then arrows are attached to the lines. In Web design, a flow chart provides a visual representation of the hierarchical structure of the pages within the site. The shapes represent pages and the lines represent their connection.

You create a flow chart from the information category outline. The main categories become the major branches of the flow chart and the subcategories become the subbranches. Most of the time, visitors can move between pages of a Web site in any direction, so arrows are usually not included. You can use shapes to designate different types of pages in the Web site. For example, all form pages can be hexagons while regular pages can be squares. There is no widely recognized standard for the shapes used to designate different Web pages; therefore, a key or legend for deciphering what the shapes represent is often included in the chart. Figure 2-7 shows the flow chart that Brian created for the new site.

Figure 2-7   CATALYST WEB SITE FLOW CHART

Brian asks you to create a flow chart using the outline that you created. You can create a flow chart using flow-charting software or sketch a flow chart using pen and paper.

To create a flow chart:

1. Draw a square at the top of the page and label it **Home Page**.

2. Draw five squares in a horizontal row below the Home Page square for each of the main categories of your outline, and label each square with one category.

3. Draw a line from each main category page to the home page to connect them.

4. Repeat Steps 2 and 3 to add the subcategory pages below the category pages. Continue until all of the information from your outline is represented in the flow chart.

5. Create a key for your flow chart by drawing and labeling the shapes you used.

6. Compare your flow chart to the flow chart Brian created, shown in Figure 2-7.

Next, you'll work on the page content for the Catalyst site.

Gathering and Organizing Information

The next step in the process of creating the information architecture is to gather and organize all possible sources of information. The materials that you collect will be used to create the content for the site. It is best to err on the side of excess at this stage, because the more raw materials you have to work with, the better job you can do once you actually start to create content.

Gathering information is often like detective work; you'll need to use your instincts, follow leads, do research, and talk to others to gather everything you can. Based on the site goals, the market research, the information outline, and the flow chart, you and Brian will need information about:

- the company and the management team
- the bands and the band members
- the products (CDs)

You will find this information in a variety of places. Much of the information you need can be found in promotional materials such as brochures, flyers, press releases, reviews, and articles. Gather all of the available graphic materials and any pertinent company documents (such as the company's mission statement and employee biographies.) Outside resources can also provide some information. Outside resources include reviews, articles, and other Web sites that reference the product or service. You'll want a paper copy of all the information for ease of organization. Once all the information is compiled and printed, you are ready to start organizing it.

Organizing the data lets you see exactly what you have gathered about each relevant topic. You need to sort the collected materials, piece-by-piece, into the categories and subcategories you established earlier. You may need to split some items, such as a brochure, into more than one category. Information that fits more than one category should be placed in the category that seems most appropriate. Review any information that is relevant but doesn't fit the planned pages. Try to find a place in the existing structure where the information might fit. You might also consider whether it warrants creating a separate section or a new page. After you have designed the aesthetic structure of the site, you will create page content out of the materials that you have assembled and organized.

Designing a Web Site

The phrase "look and feel" is used to describe the overall external characteristics of a Web site. It refers to how all the elements of the site design interact to create an experience for the user. The look and feel is achieved from a mixture of many smaller choices, including which colors, fonts, graphic style, and layout are selected for the design. To combine all these elements effectively, you start by creating a concept and metaphor for the site.

Creating a Site Concept and Metaphor

A good concept is the basis for developing an aesthetically cohesive Web site. A **site concept** is a general underlying theme that unifies the various elements of a site and contributes to the site's look and feel. To develop a site concept, review some of the artwork and Web sites that appeal to your target audience and look for common underlying themes. Next, make a list of words that describe what you would like the site to convey. Try to think of words that will reinforce the site goals and words that will communicate something to your target audience. Finally, write the concept out on a piece of paper.

Once you have developed a site concept, you create a metaphor for the site. A **metaphor** is a comparison in which one object, concept, or idea is represented as another. For example, the expression "at that moment, time was molasses" and Shakespeare's famous observation that "all the world's a stage" are metaphors. The site metaphor should be a visual extension of the site concept, thereby reinforcing the site message and the site goals. The metaphor helps to create a unified site design. It does not have to be concretely represented in the site. For example, if the site concept is fluidity, the metaphor might be a river. In this case, the site might not be designed to look like a river, but instead would integrate elements that are commonly identified with rivers: a series of small, partially transparent, wavy lines in the page background; a flowing theme in the graphic design; and colors that are cool, like muted blues and silvers. The river metaphor is an instrument to focus the aesthetic choices.

For the new Catalyst Web site, Brian came up with a list of words to describe the site: *hip, retro, logical, underground, alternative, minimalist,* and *intuitive.* Some words apply to a look that is popular with the target audience (hip, retro); other words apply to the flow of information (logical, intuitive). Next, he reviewed the CD cover art on the current Catalyst Web site as well as the CD cover art of other bands in the same genre of music to get a feel for the artwork styles that are popular with the Catalyst target audience. Finally, he decided on the site concept—appropriation of items from the past to create a new look—and the metaphor—recycling. In later sections, you will see how the recycling metaphor helps to shape the site design by providing a foundation for color choice, font choice, graphics choice, and layout.

Brian asks you to develop another concept and metaphor for the new Catalyst Web site.

To develop a site concept and metaphor:

1. List at least five words that describe the site.

2. In your browser window, click **File** on the menu bar, click **Open**, click the **Browse** button, click the **Look in** list arrow, navigate to the **Catalyst** folder within the **Tutorial** folder within the **Tutorial.02** folder on your Data Disk, click **index.htm**, click the **Open** button, and then click the **OK** button. The current Catalyst Web site opens in your Web browser.

3. Click the **PRODUCTS** link, review the CD cover art on the Products page, and then close the Catalyst Web site.

4. Review other artwork that appeals to the target audience.

5. Choose a site concept.

6. Choose a site metaphor.

7. Write a paragraph that explains how you could integrate the concept and the metaphor into the site.

In the next session you will learn how to make your site accessible to people with disabilities.

Considering Accessibility Issues

The Web is a public venue used by a variety of people, including people with disabilities. With regard to Web design, **accessibility** refers to the quality and ease of use of a Web site by people who use assistive devices or people with disabilities. (**Assistive devices** are apparatus that provide a disabled person with alternate means to experience electronic and information technologies.) Some ways you might enhance the accessibility of a Web site include providing alternate text descriptions that can be read by audio assistive devices for any graphics on the site, and establishing basic text links in addition to graphical navigation structures

Effective June 21, 2001, Section 508 of the federal Rehabilitation Act requires all United States federal government agencies, as well as public colleges and universities, to make their electronic and information technology accessible to people with disabilities. Although private companies are under no legal obligation to make their sites accessible, many try to ensure that their sites are at least partially in line with current federal guidelines. Because technologies change rapidly, the Web is the best source for current accessibility guidelines and accessibility-checking tools.

Macromedia offers a number of tools to help you develop accessible Web sites, including templates and checking utilities. Search the Macromedia Web site (*www.macromedia.com*) using the keyword "accessibility" for information. You can also activate Accessibility dialog boxes within Dreamweaver. When the Accessibility dialog boxes are activated, every time you insert an object into your Web page, Dreamweaver will prompt you for the information you need to add accessibility.

The World Wide Web Consortium (W3C) also provides information about accessibility technology, guidelines, tools, education and outreach, and research and development. It has created a Web Accessibility Initiative (WAI) whose mission is to promote usability of the Web for people with disabilities. (For more information on this, go to their Web site at *www.w3.org/WAI*.)

Another place to find help in adding accessibility to your Web site is the Center for Applied Special Technology (CAST). CAST is a nonprofit organization whose mission is to expand opportunities for people with disabilities through innovative uses of computer technology. CAST developed Bobby, a tool that checks Web pages for accessibility issues and returns a detailed report with suggestions for improvement. Bobby is now owned by Watchfire. (Go to *bobby.watchfire.com* for more information about Bobby.)

For now, Brian wants to adjust the new Web site design for accessibility without changing the site's look and feel. This will make the site available to as wide an audience as possible while maintaining a look and feel that appeals to the target audience. Brian decides to implement basic accessibility modifications into the design for the new site, and then create a parallel site next year that will meet all of the current accessibility guidelines.

Based on a review of the current guidelines, Brian has decided to include alternate text descriptions for graphics and graphic links. This alternate text can be "read" by audio assistive devices. Depending on the browser, this information will appear in place of a graphic or when the user points to an image or link. Brian wants to make the alternate text as descriptive as possible so that anyone can appreciate the site content even without seeing it. He also wants to run the completed site through Bobby. Based on the suggestions made in that report, Brian will begin to plan the parallel site that Catalyst will build next year.

Selecting Colors

Color is an interesting component of design because it affects the emotional response that a user has to the site. The colors you choose will set the tone of the site. Before selecting colors for a Web site, you'll need a basic understanding of how color applies to Web design.

There are two major systems of color. The traditional **subtractive color system** uses cyan, magenta, and yellow as its primary colors; all other colors are created by mixing these primary colors. It is called the subtractive color system because new colors are created by adding pigment such as ink and paint and removing light. If the primary colors of the subtractive color system were combined in equal amounts, they would make black, the absence of light. The **additive color system** uses red, green, and blue as its primary colors. This system is also called the **RGB system** (for red, green, and blue). As with the subtractive color system, all other colors are created by combining these primary colors. It is called the additive color system because it works like a prism—new colors are created by adding varying amounts of light. If all of the primary colors of the additive system are combined in equal amounts, they create pure white light. Figure 2-8 shows how the primary colors (red, green, and blue) can be mixed in various combinations to create secondary colors (cyan, magenta, and yellow), and how the primary colors can be combined equally to create white.

Figure 2-8 **RGB COLOR SYSTEM**

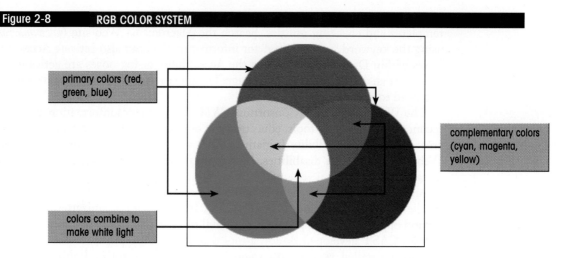

Web sites are a digital media designed to be viewed on monitors. A monitor combines hundreds of thousands of **pixels** (tiny dots of light that glow in different color intensities) to create images. Because monitors work with light, they use the additive RGB color system. When creating or saving graphics for the Web, you should use RGB color.

Color is a good tool for emphasizing information, such as headlines from body text, or for drawing the eye to a specific area of the page. Color also can distinguish segments of the Web site (when you use a different color for each major category, for example).

Choosing a color palette can be difficult. There is no precise scientific method to ensure that you choose the perfect colors. This is why most design teams include a graphic artist who is trained in color theory. However, even without extensive color training, you can select attractive and effective colors for a Web site. Keep in mind the following basic color concepts and strategies:

- **Keep it simple.** With color choice, more is definitely not better. Everyone has seen a Web site that looks as if it erupted from a rainbow. Too many competing colors cause the eye to race around the page, leaving the user dazed and confused.

- **Include three to six colors per site.** You'll use these same colors for all of the site's elements, including the text, background, links, logo, buttons, navigation bar, and graphics. Black and white count as colors when selecting a palette. (This rule does not apply to the use of photographic images, which have many colors and can enhance your site.)

- **Consider the mood you want to create.** Colors create a mood. Studies have shown that colors have a psychological effect on people. For example, blue is calming, whereas red is hot or intense. Think about what things your target audience might associate with a color when choosing a palette for a Web site.

- **Keep in mind the target audience.** Different cultures do not always have the same psychological associations with specific colors. For example, the United States associates white with purity and red with danger, whereas some countries associate white with death and red with marriage. If a Web site has a global or foreign target audience, you might need to research the customs and symbols of the target culture.

One way to develop a color palette is to look to other works of art for inspiration. Think of what emotions and feelings you want to evoke with the Web site, and then find a painting, photograph, or other work of art that stirs those feelings in you. Evaluate the colors the artist used. Consider how the colors interact. Try to pinpoint colors that are causing the emotion. Consider how the color palette works with your metaphor. Think about how you might use that color palette in the Web site.

Brian chose the colors shown in Figure 2-9 for the new Catalyst Web site. This color palette retains the two colors used in the current Catalyst site, and adds a third color so that the designer can combine the colors in different ways, providing additional flexibility. Black and white will be the other colors used in the site. Because the number one site goal is to increase label identity, Brian didn't want to discard the palette that is currently identified with Catalyst; instead, he decided to retain the original palette and add an additional color. The first two colors are already associated with the Catalyst label. They are used in the logo as well as other print materials. The color palette also fits nicely into the recycling design metaphor because the varying shades of yellow and orange are reminiscent of colors popular in the early 1970s. In the site, all three colors will be used in the logo, Yellow-Yellow-Orange will be used in a strip across the top of the site, and Dark-Hard-Orange will be used in a smaller strip below the top strip. Font colors will be discussed in the next section.

Figure 2-9	COLOR PALETTE FOR THE NEW CATALYST WEB SITE

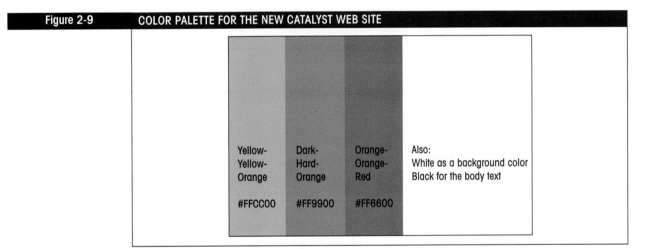

In the figure the colors are referred to by their color names as well as their hexadecimal color codes. While color names are easy to remember and may have more meaning to the average person, they can be unreliable when trying to communicate specific color values. One person may use the word red to refer to the generic red family of colors, another person may be referring to the specific color designated as red in the Web Safe Color Palette, while still another person may be referring to a red in another color palette. The names used in these tutorials are the Web Safe Color Palette names. The **Web Safe Color Palette** consists of 216 colors and was created so that Web designers would have a reliable color palate to work with. The Web Safe Color Palette was created when many computers could display only 256 colors at a time. Since current computers can display 16+ million colors and many designers have disregarded the Web Safe Color Palette, many of the colors currently in use in Web sites do not have reliable color names. All colors, however, have hexadecimal color codes; so, to insure that the color you specify is understood by the browser and displayed properly, well-coded HTML uses hexadecimal color codes instead of color names. **Hexadecimal** is a number system that uses the digits 0-9 to represent the decimal values 0-9, plus the letters A-F to represent the decimal values 10 to 15. These color codes are six-digit numbers in the form of #RRGGBB where RR is replaced by the hexadecimal color value for red, GG is replaced with the green value, and BB is replaced with the blue value. The specified amounts of each of these colors are mixed together by the system to create the color you specify. You do not need to know the hexadecimal color codes when you are using

Dreamweaver. When you are choosing colors, you click the color you want to use and Dreamweaver will display the hexadecimal code for that color.

Brian asks you to select a color palette that will work with the site metaphor you developed. You can use a graphic program (such as Adobe Photoshop, Macromedia Fireworks, or Adobe Illustrator), crayons, markers, or colored paper to create your color palette.

To choose a color palette:

1. Envision a set of colors that will work with your site concept and metaphor.

2. Look at works of art for inspiration.

3. Think about the psychological associations of the colors. Are these in line with your site goals?

4. Draw a series of rectangles (one for each color in your palette) side by side, and then fill each with one color.

5. Write a brief explanation of your color choice and how it reinforces the site concept and metaphor. Describe where and how you intend to use the colors in the site.

Next, you'll work on font choice.

Selecting Fonts

Font refers to a set of letters, numbers, and symbols in a unified typeface. Font choice is important in creating an effective Web site because a font conveys a wealth of subtle information and often creates an impression about the content before it is even read. Think about the different fonts that might be used on Web sites that present current news and events, Far East travel, and science fiction movies.

There are three categories of typefaces, serif, sans-serif, and mono. These categories are also referred to as **generic font families**. In **serif typefaces** there is a delicate, horizontal line which finishes off the main strokes of each character; an example would be the horizontal bars at the top and bottom of an uppercase M. The most common serif typeface is Times New Roman. **Sans-serif typefaces** are typefaces in which these lines, or serifs, are absent. (*Sans* means without, so *sans serif* means *without serif*.) The most common sans-serif typeface is Helvetica. A third category, mono, is sometimes used. *Mono* is short for *monospaced*. A **monospaced font** is one in which each letter takes exactly the same width in the line; for example, the letter *i* (a thin letter) would take the same amount of space as the letter *m*. Monospaced fonts are serif fonts, but they are considered a separate generic font family in Dreamweaver. (Fonts that are not monospaced are **proportional fonts**, because each letter takes up a different width on the line proportional to the width of the letter—for example, the letter *i* takes less space than the letter *m*).

A font must be installed on the end-user's machine for the page to be displayed using that font. If a font is not found on the client machine, the page will be displayed in the default font the end user has chosen for his or her browser. Dreamweaver arranges fonts into groups, which provide designers with the best chance for achieving the desired look for the page. Figure 2-10 lists the default Dreamweaver font groupings. Each group contains the most common names for the selected font; these common names include at least the most common PC name, the most common Mac name (when different), and the generic font family name. When you apply a font grouping to text, Dreamweaver places an HTML font tag that contains all three choices around the specified text, thus ensuring maximum potential for aesthetic continuity across all platforms and all machines.

Figure 2-10	DEFAULT FONT GROUPS IN DREAMWEAVER

Arial, Helvetica, sans-serif
Times New Roman, Times, serif
Courier New, Courier, mono
Georgia, Times New Roman, Times, serif
Verdana, Arial, Helvetica, sans-serif
Geneva, Arial, Helvetica, sans-serif

Selecting a font also involves choosing a font color and font size, and sometimes a font style. **Font color** refers to the color that is applied to the font. The font color should be chosen from the colors you selected for the site's color palette. **Font size** refers to the size of the font. In HTML there is no fixed font size. Instead, all font sizes are relative to the default font size that the end user has set for his or her browser. Font sizes range from 1 to 7, where 1 and 2 are smaller than the browser's default font size, 3 is equal to the browser's default font size, and 4 through 7 appear larger than the browser's default font size. **Font style** refers to the stylistic attributes that are applied to the font. Stylistic attributes include bold, italic, and underline.

As you select fonts for a Web site, keep in mind the following strategies:

- **Less is more.** In general, you should use no more than two fonts in a Web site so that the site will have a consistent look. You should use one font, one font size, and one font color for the general body text (although text links in the body text will be distinguished by a different color). You can use a second font, size, and color for headings.

- **Convert headings to images.** Sometimes headings and logos are actually text that has been converted to an image in a graphics program. By converting text into an image, the designer has greater control over the look of the final site, because the designer can choose a font that is not in the Dreamweaver font list and may not be found on every computer.

- **Consider what you are trying to convey.** Fonts create an impression about the content of the site. Different fonts are associated with specific types of content. For example, the titles of old horror movies always appeared in a gothic font; therefore, that font is usually associated with horror movies. Choose fonts that will support the concept and metaphor for the site.

- **Consider accessibility.** Visually impaired users of the Web site may have a hard time reading certain fonts or smaller sizes. Review accessibility Web sites to find guidelines about fonts and font size.

Brian decided to use black; size 3; Arial, Helvetica, sans-serif as the general body text on the Catalyst Web site. Brian selected the Arial, Helvetica, sans-serif grouping because of its simplicity, which will help give the site a minimalist look. He used black text and the default font size because it is easy to read. The logo, headings, and site navigation categories will be graphics made from text using the Bauhaus Lt Bt font and a combination of the Web site palette colors. Brian selected the Bauhaus font, which was used prevalently on T-shirts and in advertising in the early 1970s, because it supports the site metaphor. Although it is not necessary, designers often choose to have links formatted in different colors depending on their state. For example, in the NewCatalyst site, a **text link**, which is a hyperlink that has not yet been clicked, will be the color Yellow-Yellow-Orange; an **active link**, which is a text hyperlink that is in the process of being clicked, will be the color Dark-Hard-Orange; and a **visited link**, which is a text hyperlink that has been clicked, will be the color Orange-Orange-Red. See Figure 2-11.

Figure 2-11 FONT CHOICES FOR NEW CATALYST SITE

In the NewCatalyst Web site:

Page Headings will be:
font: Arial, Helvetica, sans-serif; size: +4; color: Dark-Hard-Orange

Sub-headings will be:
font: Arial, Helvetica, sans-serif; size: +2; color: Dark-Hard-Orange

linked text will be:
font: Arial, Helvetica, sans-serif; color: Yellow-Yellow-Orange

active links will be:
font: Arial, Helvetica, sans-serif; color: Dark-Hard-Orange

visited links will be:
font: Arial, Helvetica, sans-serif; color: Orange-Orange-Red

body text will be:
font: Arial, Helvetica, sans-serif; size: None(3); color: Black

Brian asks you to select a set of fonts that will go with the concept and metaphor you developed for the Catalyst site.

To choose fonts:

1. Review accessibility Web sites for information about font choice, and then exit your browser.

2. Envision a font for the general body text that will work with the site concept and metaphor. Review the list in Figure 2-10 for a list of font grouping options.

3. Choose a font color from your site color palette for the body text.

4. Choose a color from your color palette for any text hyperlinks that will appear in the body text. Choose a different color for visited links.

5. Choose a font size for the body text.

6. Choose a font, color, and size for the headings.

7. Write a brief explanation of your font choices.

Next, you'll select a graphic style.

Choosing a Graphic Style and Graphics

The graphics in a Web site provide the personality of the site. Recall that graphics can include images, photographs, buttons, logos, and so forth. **Graphic style** refers to the look of the graphic elements of the site. Designing a consistent look for all the graphics in a Web site is one of the keys to developing a cohesive, well-made Web site.

When selecting a graphic style, keep in mind the following strategies:

- **Be consistent.** If you use a cartoonish drawing for one button, then use cartoonish drawings for all the buttons. If you add a photographic image to the upper right corner of one page, then consider adding photographic images to the upper right corners of all the pages. Consistency in choosing graphics gives your site a cohesive look.

- **Design with purpose.** When you add a graphic to a page, ask yourself what the graphic adds to the page. Make sure that you have a reason for adding each graphic to the site.

- **Consider size.** Reduce all of the graphics to the smallest possible file size that you can get without sacrificing the quality of the image. The file size of each graphic contributes to the file size of your Web pages; and the smaller you can keep the file size of your Web pages, the faster they will load in the user's browser. You will have to use a graphics program like Photoshop or Fireworks to do this.

- **Consider the target audience.** Review the user profile and consider the technical capabilities of the target audience. Choose graphics that will not keep users from enjoying the site by making the pages load too slowly.

- **Support your concept and metaphor.** Choose graphics that reinforce the concept and metaphor of the site. Visual symbols are very powerful tools for conveying information. Make sure you consider what each graphic adds to the site, and make sure that each graphic reinforces the site metaphor.

Based on the Catalyst site goals, the CD cover art for the bands represented by the Catalyst label, the color palette, font choices, and site metaphor, Brian selected a graphic style that mimics the flat, traditional, two-dimensional style prevalent in magazine advertisements during the 1950s and 1960s. Any graphics used on the site will be combined with processed industrial photographs to create a "hip" recycled look. By juxtaposing design styles and images from an earlier time with modern music and content, the site will deconstruct both the old and the new, creating a style and depth that should appeal to the target audience. Figure 2-12 shows the new Catalyst logo as a sample of the graphic style that was chosen.

Figure 2-12	SAMPLE OF GRAPHIC STYLE FOR NEW CATALYST SITE

You should make a list of the graphics that you want to include in the site. Include logos, buttons, illustrations, and so forth.

Brian asks you to choose a graphic style for the site concept that you have chosen.

To choose a graphic style and graphics:

1. Review the concept and metaphor for the site, the user profile, and the research that you gathered about sites that appeal to the target audience.

2. Make a list of the graphics that you want to include in the site (logos, buttons, illustrations, etc.).

3. Write a paragraph that describes the graphic style for your site. Explain how this graphic style supports your metaphor.

With the colors, fonts, and graphic style in place, you'll next determine the site's layout.

Sketching the Layout

The term *layout* comes from traditional print design. **Layout** is the position of elements, in this case, on the screen. When creating the layout, you decide where on the Web pages to place the navigation system, text, logo, artwork, and so forth. The layout should support the site goals and metaphor. It should be easy for a user to follow, and it should appeal to the target audience. Often, two or three effective layouts are possible. Initially, designers create rough sketches of possible layout designs. The client and design team then choose the sketch that they like best, and then create **comps** (comprehensive drawings) from the sketch. The comps are fully developed, detailed drawings that provide a complete preview of what the final design will look like.

Brian developed rough sketches of two possible layouts for the new Catalyst Web site, as shown in Figure 2-13. The first sketch places the site navigation system at the top of the page, whereas the second sketch places the site navigation system along the left side of the page. Although both layouts are effective, Brian decided to go with Layout 1. The top navigation system makes better use of the available space and appears to flow better with the selected graphic style.

Figure 2-13	LAYOUT SKETCHES FOR NEW CATALYST SITE

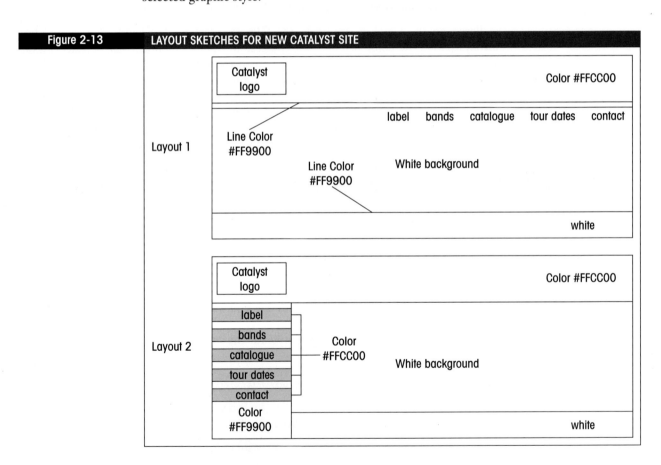

Brian asks you to draw a rough sketch of a layout that will support the site metaphor you have chosen.

To create a rough sketch of the site layout:

1. Draw a rough sketch of your site layout.

2. Add objects to represent items that you cannot draw, and label them. For example, draw a square the size of a photograph you plan to include and write a brief description of the photograph inside the square.

3. Add labels to identify the colors of each section and the lines (for example, write "white background" across the background).

4. Write a paragraph that explains why you selected this layout. Describe how the layout reinforces the site concept and metaphor and helps to achieve the site goals.

Before the design is considered complete, you need to review its logic.

Checking the Design for Logic

The final step of designing a site is to check the design for logic. It is important that the end user is able to navigate easily through the site. A Web site that is attractive to view but confusing to navigate is not well designed. When you check a design for logic, look at all of the elements of the site plan as though you were seeing them for the first time and answer the following questions:

- Is the navigation system easy to follow?
- Does the graphic style support the site metaphor?
- Do the individual elements flow together to create a consistent look for the site?

If you find problems or inconsistencies in any area, you'll need to work through the steps that pertain to the trouble area again, addressing the problems as you go. Brian has checked the new Catalyst Web site design and is satisfied that it is logical and consistent.

With the planning and design complete, you're ready to start building the site. You'll do this in Session 2.3.

Session 2.2 QUICK | CHECK

1. What is information architecture?

2. What is the purpose of categories?

3. How is a flow chart used in Web design?

4. Why is gathering information similar to detective work?

5. What is a site concept?

6. Why would you want to consider accessibility issues when creating a Web site?

7. What are four color concepts and strategies?

8. True or False: Designing a consistent look for all the graphics in a Web site is one of the keys to developing a cohesive, well-made Web site.

9. What does the term *layout* mean?

SESSION 2.3

In this session, you will create a new site. First, you'll set up the site definition for both the local and remote information. Then, you'll add pages to the site and set their page properties. Next, you'll preview the site in a browser and on the Web. Finally, you'll review the HTML tags that Dreamweaver compiled for the site.

Creating a New Site

With the planning and design for the new Catalyst Web site complete, you're ready to create the site. You create a new site in Dreamweaver by setting up the site definition for the site. Remember that a site definition has two main parts—the local info and the remote info.

Creating a Local Site Definition

The process for creating the Local Site Definition for a new site is the same as the process for creating one for an existing site. You need a site name and a local root folder to create the Local Site Definition.

You'll use "NewCatalyst" as the site name to reference the site within Dreamweaver. Spaces are not used in site names or filenames because they can cause problems with some operating systems. You can capitalize the first letter of each word to make each site or filename more readable. The local root folder for the site will be Dreamweaver, which will be stored in a project folder named Catalyst on the drive you select. This folder structure keeps the Dreamweaver files separate from original, uncompressed artwork and working project files that you have not yet added to the Web site.

To create the Local Site Definition:

1. Start **Dreamweaver**, close any pages that are open, then set your workspace layout preference to **Dreamweaver MX**, if it is not already set.

2. Click **Site** on the main menu bar, and then click **New Site**. The Site Definition for Unnamed Site 1 dialog box opens.

3. Click the **Advanced** tab, and then click **Local Info** in the Category list, if necessary.

4. Drag to select the text in the Site Name text box, if necessary, and then type **NewCatalyst** (do not type a space between the words). NewCatalyst is the name you will use to reference the site.

5. Click the **Browse** button ▭ next to the Local Root Folder text box to open the Choose Local Root Folder for Site NewCatalyst dialog box.

6. Navigate to the location where you will be storing your Web site files, if necessary, click the **Create New Folder** button ▭ in the Choose Local Root Folder for Site NewCatalyst dialog box, type **Catalyst**, press the **Enter** key, double-click the **Catalyst** folder, click ▭, type **Dreamweaver**, press the **Enter** key, double-click the **Dreamweaver** folder.

7. Click the **Select** button to open the folder. You can also type the path to the local root folder in the Local Root Folder text box.

TROUBLE? If you are storing your Data Files on a different drive or in a different folder, your instructor might provide you with another location than the one created in Step 6. Ask your instructor or technical support person for help if you are unsure of the location in which to store the Catalyst Web site.

8. Click the **Refresh Local File List Automatically** checkbox to check it, if necessary.

9. Click the **Enable Cache** checkbox to check it, if necessary. See Figure 2-14.

Figure 2-14 | LOCAL SITE DEFINITION FOR NEWCATALYST SITE

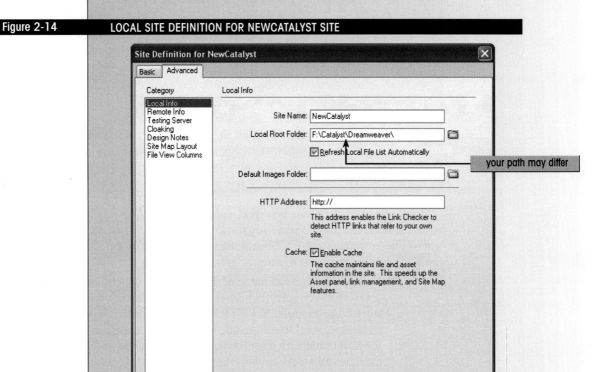

Sometimes, Dreamweaver creates a folder in the local root folder named "_notes." Do not delete this folder, as it is necessary for Dreamweaver to display the site properly; however, you can ignore it.

Before you close the Site Definition dialog box, you'll create the Remote Site Definition.

Creating a Remote Site Definition

A **Remote Site Definition** is the information stored on the computer that you are using that tells Dreamweaver where the remote server is located and how to connect to it. Creating a Remote Site Definition enables you to put the Web site on a Web server so that it can be seen on the Web. Viewing a site in a browser on the Web enables you to verify that the features of your Web site work in the browser and when viewed by others over the Web. You set the Remote Site Definition in much the same way as you do the Local Site Definition.

REFERENCE   **WINDOW**   **RW**

Creating a Remote Site Definition for FTP Access

- Click Site on the main menu bar or on the Site panel menu bar, and then click Edit Site.
- Click the site name in the list in the Edit Sites dialog box.
- Click the Edit button.
- Click Remote Info in the Category list.
- Click the Access list arrow, and then click FTP.
- Type the FTP host address where the public version of your Web site will be hosted in the FTP Host text box.
- Type the host directory name in the Host Directory text box.
- Type your login name in the Login text box.
- Type your password in the Password text box, and then check the Save checkbox if you want Dreamweaver to remember your password.
- Click the Use Passive FTP checkbox to check it.
- Verify that the Enable File Check In and Check Out checkbox is not checked.
- Click the OK button.
- Click the Done button in the Edit Sites dialog box.

First, you need to choose how you will access your Web server. Remote access is usually via FTP, although some larger organizations provide remote access through a local network. These tutorials use FTP in the Remote Site Definition. The following list describes the FTP options you need to set:

- **FTP Host.** The full name of the FTP host, which is what you will use to access the Web server where the public version of your Web site will be stored. For example, the FTP host might be *www.domain.com* or *ftp.domain.com*. Do *not* include a protocol. (A common mistake is to precede the host name with a protocol, such as FTP:// or HTTP://.) The FTP host name is available from your hosting provider.

- **Host Directory.** The location where your Web site files are located on the Web server. For example, the host directory might be *public_html*. You often see more folders and files if you log on the host directory through FTP rather than with a Web browser; the Web folder is usually but not always a subfolder of your default FTP folder. The Host Directory is available from your hosting provider.

- **Login.** Your assigned login name. Be careful when typing your login name as it may be case-sensitive.

- **Password.** Your assigned password. Be careful when typing your password as it may be case-sensitive.

  Dreamweaver has the ability to save your password. During your work session, you should leave the Save checkbox checked. If you leave the Save checkbox unchecked, then you may have to reenter your password periodically throughout your work session. If you are working on a public system, however, before ending your work session, open the Remote Info category of the Site Definition and uncheck the Save checkbox. This ensures that the next person to use the computer cannot load your site definition and log into your account. *If you do not uncheck the Save checkbox, then your password remains on the computer.*

- **Use Passive FTP.** A server parameter. This information is available from your hosting provider. If you cannot obtain this information, leave the checkbox checked. If you have difficulties when you preview the site on the Web, reopen the Site Definition dialog box and uncheck the Use Passive FTP checkbox.

■ **Use Firewall.** This option is relevant only if your computer includes a firewall that prevents outbound connections. (This is a rare occurrence, especially in schools, because most firewalls restrict only inbound traffic.) A **firewall** is a hardware or software device that restricts access between the computer network and the Internet, thereby protecting the computer behind the firewall.

■ **Check In/Out.** An option that enables multiple users to access files on the Web site. This will be discussed in a later tutorial.

You'll create a Remote Site Definition so you'll be able to preview the Catalyst Web site on the Web. If you do not have access to FTP, then you will not be able to create and preview the remote Web site.

To create the Remote Site Definition:

1. Click **Remote Info** in the Category list.

TROUBLE? If you do not have access to an FTP host on a Web server, you cannot create a Remote Site Definition using these steps. Your instructor may provide you with directions for creating a Remote Site Definition using a local network. If you do not have access to an FTP host on a Web server, continue with Steps 11 and 12 to save the Local Site Definition.

2. Click the **Access** list arrow, and then click **FTP**. Additional options appear in the dialog box. See Figure 2-15.

| Figure 2-15 | SITE DEFINITION FOR NEWCATALYST DIALOG BOX |

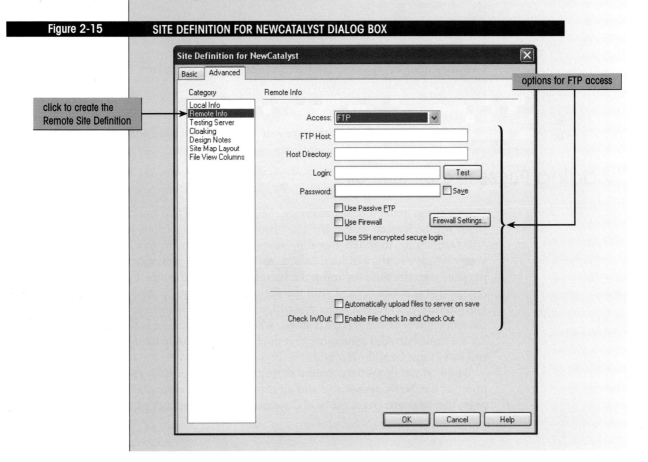

3. Click in the **FTP Host** text box and then type the address to the FTP Host, which enables you to connect to the server where the public version of your Web site will be hosted.

4. Press the **Tab** key to move the insertion point to the Host Directory text box, and then type the host directory name.

5. Press the **Tab** key to move the insertion point to the Login text box, and then type your login name. Remember that on many systems, the login ID is case-sensitive.

6. Press the **Tab** key to move the insertion point to the Password text box, and then type your password. Remember that on many systems, the password is case-sensitive.

7. Click the **Save** checkbox to check it, if necessary. Dreamweaver will remember your password. If you are working on a public computer, you'll need to uncheck the Save checkbox before you end your work session.

8. Click the **Use Passive FTP** checkbox to check it.

9. If your computer uses a firewall that restricts outbound connections, click the **Use Firewall** checkbox to check it.

10. Verify that the **Enable File Check In and Check Out** checkbox is unchecked.

11. Click the **OK** button. The Site Definition dialog box closes and the site definition is saved.

    A dialog box might open with the message that the initial site cache will be created.

12. If necessary, click the **OK** button to close the dialog box. The site definition for your Web site is complete.

You will now create pages that are automatically associated with the site.

Adding Pages to a Defined Site

Once a site is defined, you can create the pages that will be associated with the site. These pages will be located within the local root folder you specified when setting up the Local Site Definition. Although there are several ways to create new pages, including creating your first page in the Untitled Document window, the only way to automatically associate the page with the site is by using the New File command on the File menu in the Site panel. A page that is not associated with the site can cause erratic behavior in Dreamweaver in the future. After you create a page, you will give the page a filename. Recall that the filename is the name under which a page is saved, whereas the page title is the text that appears in the browser title bar. Also remember that the home page should have the filename of index.htm and *index* must be all lowercase.

Based on the flow chart created during the planning, Brian asks you to create the home page for the NewCatalyst site and all the first-level Web pages: the label page, the bands page, the catalogue page, the tour dates page, and the contact page.

To add a new page to a site:

1. Click **File** on the Site panel menu bar, and then click **New File**. The new page is added to the local folder in the Site panel and its filename—untitled.htm—is highlighted, ready for you to replace it with a more descriptive filename. See Figure 2-16.

Figure 2-16 | NEW PAGE IN SITE PANEL

2. Type **index.htm**, and then press the **Enter** key. Notice that the new file in the Site panel now has the appropriate filename for the home page.

3. Repeat Steps 1-2 for the remaining pages, using the following filenames: **label.htm**; **bands.htm**; **catalogue.htm**; **tourdates.htm**; and **contact.htm**.

4. Click the **Refresh** button **C** on the Site panel toolbar to refresh the display. All of the pages you added now appear in alphabetical order in the local folder in the Site panel.

Note that you used lowercase letters for all of the filenames. It is important to keep the case of the filenames consistent because, although some operating systems are not case sensitive, some are.

Saving Pages

It is important to save frequently—at least every ten minutes—and whenever you have finished modifying a page. You should also make sure all pages in the site are saved before you preview the site. Anyone who has worked on a computer for any length of time can confirm that programs crash at the least opportune moment. Saving your work frequently prevents large losses.

There are a few measures built into Dreamweaver to help you keep your work safe. If you have not saved a page after you have edited it and you try to close the page or exit the program, Dreamweaver will ask if you want to save the changes you made to that page. If you use an element, such as a graphic, in a page, and that element is not yet part of the site, Dreamweaver will ask if you want to save a copy of the element in the local root folder. By including copies of all of the files associated with a site within its local root folder, you prevent a myriad of complications from occurring.

To keep your local root folder organized, it's a good idea to set up additional folders before you begin working on a site, and then to save all the site files to the folders you designated for them as you go. You created your local root folder named Dreamweaver when you created your Local Site Definition; now you will create a Graphics folder within the local root folder so that you will have a designated place within the root folder to keep the copies of the graphics that you use in your site. Brian asks you to create a Graphics folder for the site, then open each page that you have created, give the page a page title, and save the page.

To save a page:

1. Click **File** on the Site panel menu bar, and then click **New Folder**. A new folder named *untitled* appears below the page filenames in the local file list in the Site panel.

2. Type **Graphics**, then press the **Enter** key.

3. Double-click **index.htm** in the Site panel to open the home page in the Document window.

4. Drag to select **Untitled Document** in the Title text box on the Document toolbar, and then type **Catalyst - Home**. See Figure 2-17.

| Figure 2-17 | PAGE TITLE IN THE DOCUMENT WINDOW |

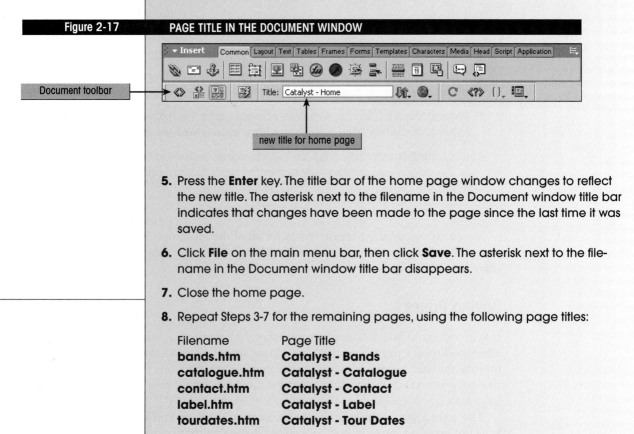

Document toolbar

new title for home page

5. Press the **Enter** key. The title bar of the home page window changes to reflect the new title. The asterisk next to the filename in the Document window title bar indicates that changes have been made to the page since the last time it was saved.

6. Click **File** on the main menu bar, then click **Save**. The asterisk next to the filename in the Document window title bar disappears.

7. Close the home page.

8. Repeat Steps 3-7 for the remaining pages, using the following page titles:

Filename	Page Title
bands.htm	**Catalyst - Bands**
catalogue.htm	**Catalyst - Catalogue**
contact.htm	**Catalyst - Contact**
label.htm	**Catalyst - Label**
tourdates.htm	**Catalyst - Tour Dates**

Setting **Page Properties**

Once you have created a page, the next step is setting the page properties, which are attributes that apply to an entire page rather than to only an element on the page. Page properties include:

- **Page Title.** The name that will appear in the browser title bar (can also be set in the Document toolbar, as you just did).

- **Background.** A Web page background can be an image, a color, or both. If both are used, the color will appear while the image is downloading, and then the image will cover up the color. If the image contains transparent pixels, then the background color will show through. The default background is no color, and most browsers display an absence of color as white. You'll use white, which has the hexadecimal code #FFFFFF for the background color of the new Catalyst site. You will also use a background image for the new Catalyst site. The filename for the background image will be background.gif.

- **Colors.** You can set a default color for text and hyperlinks on the page. The default text color is black, and the hexadecimal code for black is #000000. If you do not specify a color for visited or active links, the browser's default colors will be used. The new Catalyst Web site will use Yellow-Yellow-Orange for the links, Orange-Orange-Red for the visited links, and Dark-Hard-Orange for the active links. When you want to select a color and do not know the hexadecimal code, you can select the color from a visual display in Dreamweaver, and Dreamweaver will display the hexadecimal code. You do this by clicking the color box to the left of the text box where you would type the hexadecimal code to open the color picker, and then clicking the color swatch you want. It is always best to use the hexadecimal number, if you know it, so that you are selecting the exact same color each time you insert the color. Figure 2-18 shows the color picker in the Page Properties dialog box.

Figure 2-18	PAGE PROPERTIES DIALOG BOX WITH COLOR PICKER OPEN

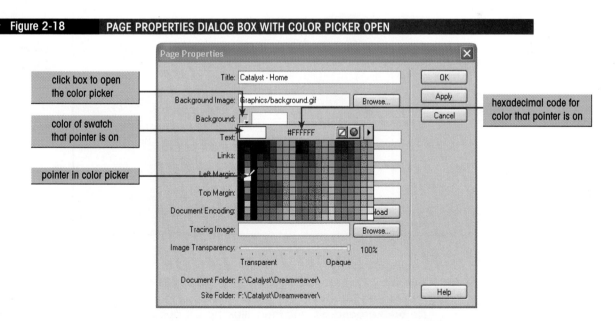

- **Margins.** Margins are measurements that specify where page content is placed on the page. There are two sets of margin controls in the Page Properties dialog box because Netscape uses Margin Width and Margin Height attributes of the body tags, while Internet Explorer uses Left Margin and Top Margin attributes of the body tags. You should always set both to maintain consistency when the page is viewed in different browsers. The new Catalyst site will have a Left Margin/Margin Width of 5 and a Top Margin/Margin Height of 0.

■ **Document Encoding.** Document encoding specifies how the digital codes will display the characters in the Web page. The default Western [Latin1] setting is the setting for English and other Western European languages.

■ **Tracing Image.** The Tracing Image setting is used to select an image as a guide for re-creating a design or mock-up that was originally created in a graphics program. For example, if you created a mock-up of your site in Photoshop, you could import a copy of that mock-up into Dreamweaver as a Tracing Image. Then you could use that image as a reference while you were re-creating the individual elements in Dreamweaver. The Tracing Image is visible only in the Dreamweaver environment.

You must resave the open page after changing the page properties to associate the new properties with that page.

You'll set the page properties for the Catalyst - Home page.

To set page properties:

1. Double-click the **index.htm** page in the Site panel to open the Catalyst - Home page of the NewCatalyst site.

2. Click **Modify** on the main menu bar, and then click **Page Properties**. The Page Properties dialog box opens. See Figure 2-19.

Figure 2-19   **PAGE PROPERTIES DIALOG BOX**

3. Press the **Tab** key to move the insertion point to the **Background Image** text box, click the **Browse** button to open the Select Image Source dialog box, navigate to the **Tutorial** folder in the **Tutorial.02** folder on your Data Disk, click the file **background.gif**, and then click the **OK** button. A dialog box opens asking you if you want to copy the file to the root folder.

4. Click **Yes** to open the Copy File As dialog box, double-click the **Graphics** folder in the Dreamweaver root folder, and then click the **Save** button. Once you have added a copy of the graphic to the site, you can browse to this copy of the graphic when you want to use the graphic again anywhere in the site.

5. Click the **Background color box/swatch** ⬜, and then point to the **white swatch** in the pop-up color picker. Notice that the hexadecimal color code at the top of the color picker changes as you move the pointer over the color swatches.

6. Click the **white swatch** in the color picker to select white as the Background color. #FFFFFF appears in the Background text box.

7. Click in the **Text** text box, type **#000000**, which is the hexadecimal color code for black, and then press the **Tab** key. The color box next to the Text text box changes to black to match the color code you just typed.

8. Press the **Tab** key to move the insertion point to the Visited Links text box, and then type **#FF6600**, which is the hexadecimal color code for Orange-Orange-Red.

9. Press the **Tab** key twice to move the insertion point to the Links text box, and then type **#FFCC00**, which is the hexadecimal color code for Yellow-Yellow-Orange.

10. Press the **Tab** key twice to move the insertion point to the Active Links text box, and then type **#FF9900**, which is the hexadecimal color code for Dark-Hard-Orange.

11. Press the **Tab** key to move the insertion point to the Left Margin text box, and then type **5**.

12. Press the **Tab** key to move the insertion point to the Margin Width text box, and then type **5**.

13. Press the **Tab** key to move the insertion point to the Top Margin text box, and then type **0**.

14. Press the **Tab** key to move the insertion point to the Margin Height text box, and then type **0**.

The Document Encoding is set to Western (Latin 1) by default and there is no Tracing Image on this page, so you are finished setting the page properties.

15. Click the **OK** button. The Page Properties dialog box closes, applying the property settings to the page. See Figure 2-20.

Figure 2-20   **CATALYST - HOME PAGE AFTER NEW PAGE PROPERTIES ARE APPLIED**

asterisk indicates
changes have
not been saved

16. Click **File** on the Document window menu bar, and then click **Save**. The page properties are saved with the page.

17. Close the **Catalyst - Home page** Document window.

Now that the page properties are set, you'll examine the HTML tags.

Reviewing the HTML Tags

The most common language of the Web is **Hypertext Markup Language (HTML)**, which provides instructions for how to format Web pages for display. Because many types of computers are connected to the Web and people use different operating systems and software on their computers, Web pages are not tied to any specific software package; rather they are created in a common markup language that is viewable by a variety of software packages (including Web browsers). HTML uses a series of tags to tell a browser what to do with the information on a Web page and how to display it.

Even though Dreamweaver provides a graphical interface for creating a Web site in HTML, it is important to have a basic understanding of HTML in order to gain a true sense of what is going on. Web pages are text documents that include specific markup tags that tell a Web browser how to display the elements. Tags almost always appear in sets, and each tag is included within angle brackets, < and >. The opening tag tells a browser that a certain type of information will be following. The opening tag also contains any parameters or attributes that are to be applied to that information. The closing tag always starts with a forward slash, /, which tells the browser that the type of information that had been started is now finished.

Some tags are required for every Web page. These tags—HTML, head, title, and body—are described in Figure 2-21.

Figure 2-21	BASIC HTML TAGS		
NAME	**OPENING TAG**	**CLOSING TAG**	**DESCRIPTION**
HTML	<html>	</html>	Signify where the HTML coding begins and ends; usually appear at the beginning and ending of a Web page. Everything inside the <html> and </html> tags is HTML unless specifically denoted as something else by another type of tag.
head section	<head>	</head>	Contains the page title, the descriptive information for the page which is not seen in the browser, and programming scripts.
title	<title>	</title>	Surround the page title, which appears in the title bar of the browser window when a viewer opens that page.
body	<body>	</body>	Surround all the content or visible elements on the page. Includes other tags to format the content. Also contains some scripts.

Many other tags appear within the body of a document to format the content. You'll see these additional tags as you continue to build the pages for the new Catalyst Web site.

You want to review the HTML tags that Dreamweaver generated when you created the Web pages and set their properties.

To review the HTML tags of Web pages:

1. Double-click **index.htm** in the Site panel. The Catalyst - Home page opens in a Document window.

2. Click the **Show Code View** button ◇ on the Document toolbar. The Document window shows the underlying HTML coding of the home page. See Figure 2-22. Note that the line numbers are for the user's reference only; the line numbers shown in the figure may not match the ones on your screen. Also, the lines of code on your screen may wrap differently than those in the figure.

   TROUBLE? If you cannot see all of the code, make sure that the horizontal scroll box is all the way on the left edge of the horizontal scroll bar.

Figure 2-22	HTML CODE FOR CATALYST - HOME PAGE

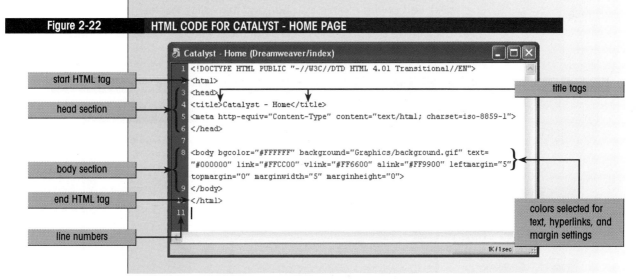

You want to copy the Page Properties from the Catalyst - Home page to the other pages in the site. Instead of reopening the Page Properties dialog box, you'll use Code and Design views to make this change.

To copy the Page Properties in Code and Design view:

1. Click the **Show Code and Design Views** button ⚏ on the Document window toolbar. The home page appears in a graphical format and as HTML coding.

2. Drag to select the entire body section in the Code pane, including the opening and closing body tags. See Figure 2-23.

   TROUBLE? You may need to scroll down to see the body tags.

| Figure 2-23 | CATALYST - HOME PAGE IN CODE AND DESIGN VIEWS WITH THE BODY SECTION SELECTED |

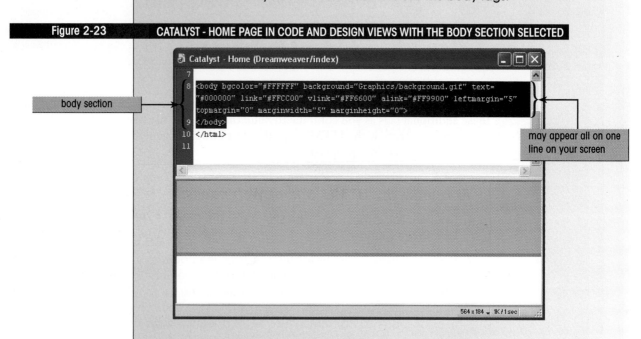

body section

may appear all on one
line on your screen

3. Click **Edit** on the main menu bar, and then click **Copy**.

4. Open the **Catalyst - Bands** page, drag to select the body tags in the code, click **Edit** on the main menu bar, and then click **Paste**.

5. Click in the Design pane in the Document window to see the changes in the bands page. See Figure 2-24.

| Figure 2-24 | CATALYST - BANDS PAGE IN CODE AND DESIGN VIEW WITH THE NEW BODY SECTION |

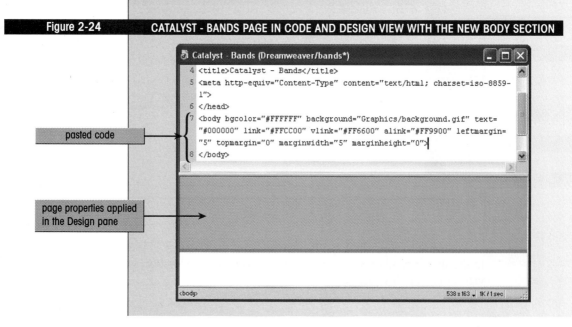

pasted code

page properties applied
in the Design pane

6. Click **File** on the main menu bar, and then click **Save**. The changes you made to the Bands page are saved.

7. Click the **Close** button ☒ on the Catalyst - Bands Document window title bar to close the page.

8. For each of the other pages in the Web site—**catalogue.htm**, **contact.htm**, **label.htm**, and **tourdates.htm**—repeat Steps 4 through 7 to paste the body tags you copied from the Catalyst - Home page. Save your changes on each page.

9. Click ☒ on the Catalyst - Home Document window title bar to close the page.

You have finished creating the pages for the new Catalyst Web site and setting the page properties. Now you will preview the site.

Previewing a Site in a Browser

There are often differences in the way that different browsers display Web pages; there are even differences in the way that different versions of the same browser will display Web pages. That is why, once you have started building a Web site, you should preview it in the various browsers that you are planning to support. Catalyst plans to support both Internet Explorer and Netscape Navigator, the two most commonly used browsers.

You can preview your site in any browser that is in the Dreamweaver Preview list. You may need to add the browser in which you want to preview your Web pages to the Preview list. The two browsers you consider most important can be designated as the primary and secondary browsers. Dreamweaver will default to the primary browser when you are previewing your work, and both the primary and secondary browsers have keyboard shortcuts.

To make a browser your primary browser, you check the Primary Browser checkbox when adding the browser to your list. To make a browser the secondary browser you check the box next to Secondary Browser. If you do not check either the Primary or Secondary checkbox, the browser will be added to the Preview in Browser list on the File menu but it will not have a keyboard shortcut. These tutorials use Internet Explorer version 6 as the primary browser.

To add a browser to the Preview list:

1. Click **File** on the Site panel menu bar, point to **Preview in Browser**, and then click **Edit Browser List**. The Preferences dialog box opens with Preview in Browser selected in the Category list. See Figure 2-25.

Figure 2-25 PREFERENCES DIALOG BOX

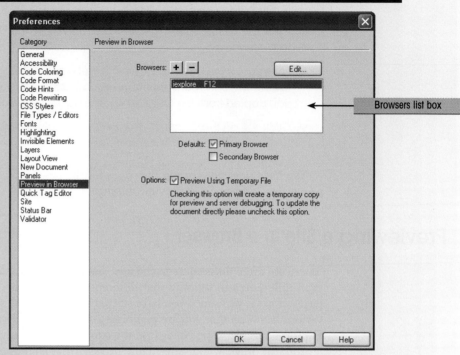

2. Look for the browser that you use in the Browsers list box. If the browser is listed, click it to select it, and then skip to Step 8. If the browser is not listed, continue with Step 3.

3. If you need to add a browser, click the Browsers **Plus (+)** button ⊞. The Add Browser dialog box opens. See Figure 2-26.

Figure 2-26 ADD BROWSER DIALOG BOX

4. Type the name of the browser you are adding in the Name text box.

5. Click the **Browse** button to open the Select Browser dialog box, navigate to the folder containing the browser that you want to add, click the browser program icon, and then click the **Open** button. The path to the file that you selected appears in the Application text box.

TROUBLE? If you cannot find the browser program icon on the computer that you are using, ask your instructor or technical support person for help.

6. Click the **Primary Browser** checkbox to check it if you want Dreamweaver to default to this browser when you preview your work. Check the **Secondary Browser** checkbox to check it if you want this to be the secondary browser choice that you can access when previewing your work. If you do not check either the Primary or Secondary checkbox, the browser will be added to the Preview in Browser list on the File menu, but it will not have a keyboard shortcut.

7. Click the **OK** button in the Add Browser dialog box.

8. Click the **OK** button in the Preferences dialog box.

Once a browser has been added to Dreamweaver, you can preview the pages you created for the new Catalyst site. You'll start by previewing the home page.

To preview a page in a browser:

1. Click **index.htm** in the Site panel. This selects the Catalyst - Home page.

2. Click **File** on the Site panel menu bar, point to **Preview in Browser**, and then click **iexplore** or the name of your browser. The browser opens with the home page. See Figure 2-27.

| Figure 2-27 | CATALYST - HOME PAGE OPEN IN INTERNET EXPLORER |

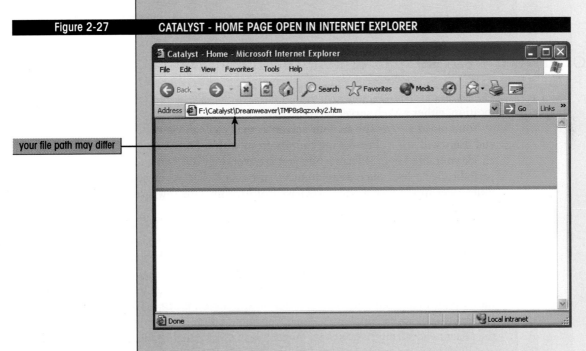

your file path may differ

TROUBLE? Some versions of Internet Explorer do not work correctly in preview mode. If your Web page does not look like the one shown in Figure 2-27 ask your instructor for help.

3. Review the page, looking at its background. The background image should be displayed. Look at the page title in the title bar.

4. Click the **Close** button ⊠ on the browser window title bar to close the page and the browser.

5. Repeat Steps 1 through 4 to preview the **bands.htm**, **catalogue.htm**, **contact.htm**, **label.htm**, and **tourdates.htm** pages.

When Dreamweaver previews a page, it creates a temporary file with a filename that consists of random symbols, letters, and numbers. Most of the time Dreamweaver deletes these temporary files after you close the browser. However, sometimes it leaves these files in the file list in the root folder. After previewing a page, you should confirm that the temporary file is deleted so that your root folder does not become cluttered and you do not become confused. If you find these files in your Web site directory, you should delete them.

To delete a temporary file from the root folder:

1. Click the **Refresh** button 🗘 on the Site panel toolbar to refresh the local file list.

2. Select the temporary filename from the local file list in the Site panel, if necessary.

3. Click **File** on the Site panel menu bar, click **Delete**, and then click the **OK** button.

Now you will preview your site from the Web.

Uploading a Web Site to a Remote Location

Once you have created pages in your Web site, you should upload the site to your remote location, either a Web server or your network server.

You upload a Web site to your server so that you can view the site over the Web as the end users will see it. Previewing the site from within Dreamweaver is a convenient way to check your site for problems while you are working, but you should also upload your site periodically (at least once a day) to make sure that it displays correctly. Sometimes there are differences in the way a page previews from within Dreamweaver and the way it actually looks when it is viewed on the Web.

You set the parameters when you created the Remote Site Definition, so the rest is easy. You upload Web sites from the Site panel. First, you connect to the remote server where your site will be located, using the Connects to remote host button on the Site panel toolbar. Then, you select the files in the local root folder that you want to upload, pressing the Ctrl key as you select nonadjacent files or pressing the Shift key to select a block of adjacent files. Finally, you "put" the selected files on the server, using the Put File(s) button on the Site panel toolbar. When you are done, you should disconnect from the remote server using the Disconnects from remote host button on the Site panel toolbar.

All of the files that the remote version of a Web site will use must be located on the Web server. The first time you upload a site, you must include all the files and folders for the site, including the graphics located in the Graphics folder. From then on, you update the remote site by uploading only files that you have changed. When you upload a Web page or group of pages, Dreamweaver will ask you if you would like to upload the dependent files. **Dependent files** are files like the graphics files that are used in the Web page. If you have had to include a copy of the element in the local root folder, then it is a dependent file because the file will be needed for that element to be viewed on the page. If you have not yet uploaded these files, or if you have modified them, you will need to upload these dependent files. However, if you have already uploaded them and you have not modified them, it is not necessary to upload them again.

When you upload the pages to the remote server, be careful to use the Put File(s) button on the Site panel toolbar, not the Get File(s) button. The Get File(s) button downloads the files from the remote server to your local folder, and you might overwrite the more current files in your local folder.

You will upload the NewCatalyst site to the remote server so you can preview it on the Web.

To upload a site to the remote server:

1. Click the **Connects to remote host** button on the Site panel toolbar. When Dreamweaver is connected to the remote host, you see a green light on the Connects to remote host button. Dreamweaver connects to the remote host, and the Site panel changes to Remote view.

   TROUBLE? If you do not have access to a remote host, you cannot upload your site. Check with your instructor to see if he or she has alternate instructions. If not, skip to Step 9.

2. Click the **View** list arrow on the Site panel toolbar, and then click **Local View**.

3. Click the **Graphics** folder, press and hold the **Shift** key, and then click **tour-dates.htm** to select all of the files in the local file list. These are the files you want to upload to the server.

4. Click the **Put File(s)** button on the Site panel toolbar. A dialog box opens, asking if you want to include dependent files. You have already selected all of the dependent files for the site—the Graphics folder—in addition to the pages.

5. Click the **No** button.

6. Click the **View** list arrow, and then click **Remote View**. The Site panel switches to Remote view and you see the list of files you uploaded to the remote server.

7. Click the **Expand/Collapse** button on the Site panel toolbar. The Site panel expands to display both the Remote and Local views. See Figure 2-28.

| Figure 2-28 | SITE PANEL WITH REMOTE AND LOCAL VIEWS DISPLAYED |

8. Click the **Disconnects from remote host** button 🔌 on the Site panel toolbar, click the **Expand/Collapse** button ⬚ on the Site panel toolbar to collapse the Site panel, click the **View** list arrow, and then click **Local View** to return to Local view.

   If you are working on a public computer, continue with Step 9; otherwise skip to Step 11.

9. If you are working on a public computer, click **Site** on the Site panel menu bar, click **Edit Sites** to open the Edit Sites dialog box, make sure **NewCatalyst** is selected in the list, then click the **Edit** button. The Site Definition for NewCatalyst dialog box opens.

10. Click **Remote Info** in the Category list, click the **Save** checkbox to uncheck it, click the **OK** button, then click the **Done** button in the Edit Sites dialog box. Now, the next person who uses the computer cannot load your site definition and log into your account.

11. Exit Dreamweaver.

Next, you'll preview your Web site on the remote server.

Previewing on the Web

Once the files are uploaded to the remote site, you and others can view them in a browser. You'll explore the remote site using a browser to check if the page looks the same on the Web as it does in Dreamweaver. If you find differences, like extra spaces or different fonts, write them down and discuss them with your instructor. At this point, the only difference that you should see is in the site address. When you preview over the Web, the site will have an actual Web address instead of a file path.

To view a site from a remote location:

1. Start your browser, type the URL of your remote site into the Address text box on the browser toolbar, and then press the **Enter** key. The index.htm page of the NewCatalyst site from the remote server loads in the browser window. See Figure 2-29.

Figure 2-29   CATALYST - HOME PAGE IN INTERNET EXPLORER, VIEWED OVER THE WEB

TROUBLE? If the browser window displays the list of files stored on the remote site, double-click the index.htm file to open the home page.

TROUBLE? If the browser displays a warning which says that the listing was denied, type the base URL of the remote site, then / (a forward slash), and then "index.htm" into the Address box in your browser's toolbar.

TROUBLE? If any pages or items are missing or do not display correctly, the files might have been corrupted during the upload process or you might not have uploaded all the dependent files. Repeat the previous set of steps to upload all of the files to the remote location. If you still have problems with your remote site, you might need to edit the Remote Site Definition and click the Use Passive FTP check box to uncheck it. Ask your instructor or technical support person for help.

2. Go to each page of the site by typing the URL of the remote site, then / (a forward slash), and then the page's filename into the Address box in your browser's toolbar. Review each page to make sure that everything was successfully uploaded. (At this point you will see only a background and a page title for each page.)

3. Click the **Close** button ☒ on the browser title bar to close your browser.

You have finished creating the pages for the new Catalyst Web site, setting the page properties, and previewing the pages. In the next tutorial, you'll add and format the text on each page.

Session 2.3 QUICK CHECK

1. What are the two main parts of the site definition?

2. What is the purpose of creating a Remote Site Definition?

3. What happens when you click the New File command on the File menu in the panel?

4. Explain what page properties are.

5. When should you save your work?

6. What are two ways to preview a site you are creating?

7. True or False? Web pages are created in a markup language that is viewable by only specific software packages.

REVIEW ASSIGNMENTS

Web design teams often develop two or three Web site layouts and designs for a client, who then chooses one concept for development. The alternate design can have a different metaphor, be based on reordered site goals, or geared for another target audience. Sara is considering expanding the Catalyst label to include Texas Blues bands. Brian asks you to plan and design an alternate Catalyst site for a band lineup devoted to Texas Blues bands.

1. Define a list of site goals for the alternate Catalyst site.

2. Do research and identify the target audience for the alternate Catalyst site.

3. Create a user profile for the alternate Catalyst site.

4. Conduct market research to gather information about Texas Blues music Web sites and other Web sites that cater to your target audience.

5. Develop two end-user scenarios for the alternate Catalyst site.

6. Create an information category outline arranged in hierarchical order for the alternate Catalyst site.

7. Create a flow chart for the alternate Catalyst site.

8. Develop a site concept and a metaphor for the alternate Catalyst site.

9. Go to *www.w3.org/WAI*, the Web site of the Web Accessibility Initiative (WAI) developed by the World Wide Web Consortium (W3C), and research accessibility guidelines.

10. Choose a color palette, fonts, and a graphic style for the alternate Catalyst site.

11. Create a rough sketch of the layout for the alternate Catalyst Web site.

Explore 12. Check the design for logic by reviewing the decisions that you have made. Make sure that your design reinforces the site goals and supports the site metaphor.

13. Create a Local Site Definition using "CatalystBlues" as the site name and use the Browse button to identify the local root folder as a Dreamweaver folder that you create within a folder named CatalystBlues in the location where you are storing your Web site files. Refresh the local file list automatically, and enable cache.

14. Create a Remote Site Definition using FTP access for the CatalystBlues site. (*Hint*: If you already closed the Site Definition dialog box, click Edit on the main menu bar, click Edit Sites, click CatalystBlues in the list, and then click the Edit button.)

Explore ▶ 15. In the Site panel, add the home page and first-level pages to the CatalystBlues site, based on your site plan, and then rename them with descriptive filenames.

Explore ▶ 16. Open each page in a Document window, set the appropriate page title, background, and colors in the Page Properties dialog box, and then save and close each page. (*Hint*: Remember that you can copy the body tags.)

17. Review the HTML tags for the home page in Code view.

Explore ▶ 18. Switch to Code and Design view, and then change the background color of the home page to another color in the CatalystBlues color palette.

19. Preview the pages in your browser, looking for consistency in display. Each page should have the same background, and each page should have the page title that you assigned to it displayed in the browser title bar.

20. Preview the pages on the Web, looking for consistency in display. Again, each page should have the same background and each page should have the page title that you assigned to it displayed in the browser title bar.

21. Save and close the home page.

22. Exit Dreamweaver.

CASE PROBLEMS

Case 1. Hroch University Anthropology Department You are working with Dr. Matt Hart, a social anthropologist at Hroch University, to create a Web site to present his research findings and accompanying graphics about the small rural communities of northern Vietnam. To initiate the planning and design, you asked Dr. Hart to provide you with a list of site goals, ideas on a target audience, and the material that he wants to include on the site. Dr. Hart has responded with a memo that outlines the decisions he made. You'll use the information from the memo to plan the Web site. Dr. Hart, however, did not provide all the information that you requested (a common occurrence when working with clients). You'll use the information Dr. Hart provided as a starting point. It will be necessary for you to research and make some decisions on your own.

1. Start Word (or another word processing program), open the HartMemo.doc document file located in the Cases folder within the Tutorial.02 folder on your Data Disk, and then read the memo.

2. Review the goals that Dr. Hart listed, and then create a list of site goals for the Web site. Consider the order of importance and wording.

3. Define a target audience and a user profile for the site. (*Hint:* Search online sources to learn more about the groups of people listed in the memo.)

4. Conduct market research. Find and review at least four Web sites that deal with the lesser-known areas of northern Vietnam, provide information on social anthropology, or are targeted at presenting research online.

Explore ▶ 5. Write a paragraph documenting the findings from your market research. Include the URLs of the Web sites that you visited, as well as information about categories of information, graphic style, layout, and site metaphor.

6. Create three end-user scenarios for the site.

7. Develop an information category outline. Base the categories and hierarchy on the memo and your market research.

8. Create a flow chart for the site.

9. Develop a site concept and metaphor for the site. (Even sites that have minimal design can benefit from a site metaphor.)

Explore 10. Investigate usability guidelines that deal with text. Research these guidelines at *www.w3.org/WAI*. Write down your findings and use them when making font choices.

11. Design a color palette for the site. Write a paragraph explaining your choice.

12. Choose the fonts for the site. Write a paragraph explaining your choice.

13. Plan the graphic style of the site. Write a paragraph explaining your choice.

14. Create a rough sketch of the layout of the site. Write a paragraph explaining your choice.

Explore 15. Check the design for logic by reviewing the decisions that you have made. Make sure that your design reinforces the site goals and supports the site metaphor.

16. Create a Local Site Definition, using "Hart" as the site name, and "Hart\Dreamweaver" in the folder and location where you are storing your Web site for the local root folder. Refresh the local file list automatically, and enable cache.

17. Create a Remote Site Definition using FTP access for the Hart site.

18. Create a Graphics folder in the root folder in the Local view of the Site panel.

Explore 19. In the Site panel, add pages with the following filenames: index.htm, Contact.htm, CulturalCrossPollination.htm, LinguisticDifferences.htm, ProfHart.htm, and RitualsAndPractices.htm.

Explore 20. Open each page in a Document window. Then open the Page Properties window and set the background image to the HartBackground.gif file located in the Cases folder within the Tutorial.02 folder on your Data Disk (remember, once you add a copy of the graphic to your Graphics folder, you can select it from the Graphics folder), set the background color to white and the text color to black, and then save and close each page. Set the page title from the following list:

Filename	Page Title
index.htm	Hroch University Anthropology Dept. - Prof. Hart - Home
Contact.htm	Hroch University Anthropology Dept. - Prof. Hart - Contact
CulturalCrossPollination.htm	Hroch University Anthropology Dept. - Prof. Hart - Cultural Cross-pollination
LinguisticDifferences.htm	Hroch University Anthropology Dept. - Prof. Hart - Linguistic Differences
ProfHart.htm	Hroch University Anthropology Dept. - Prof. Hart
RitualsAndPractices.htm	Hroch University Anthropology Dept. - Prof. Hart - Rituals and Practices

21. Preview the pages in your browser, looking for consistency in display. Each page should have the same background, and each page should have the page title that you assigned to it displayed in the browser title bar.

22. Preview the pages on the Web, looking for consistency in display. Again, each page should have the same background and each page should have the page title that you assigned to it displayed in the browser title bar.

23. Review the HTML tags for the home page in Code view.

24. Close the Hart site.

Case 2. Museum of Western Art C. J. Strittmatter, who has been hired to design the Web site for the Fort Worth Museum of Western Art, asks you to work on the plan and design of the new Web site. To develop a feasible plan, you'll need to conduct marketing research on other western art museum sites. In addition, C. J. asks you to research the current accessibility guidelines for using alternate text descriptions on graphics. You'll then create the new site, add the home page and top-level pages to the site, and then set the page properties.

1. Define the goals for the site.

2. Define a target audience and a user profile for the site.

3. Conduct market research. Find and review at least four Web sites that deal with western art. (*Hint:* Use a search engine to search the keywords "western art," "cowboy art," and "Texas museums.")

Explore 4. Write a paragraph documenting the findings from your market research. Include the URLs of the Web sites that you visited, as well as information about categories of information, graphic style, layout, and site metaphor.

5. Create two end-user scenarios for the site.

6. Develop an information category outline for the site.

7. Create a flow chart for the site.

8. Develop a site concept and metaphor for the site. Write a paragraph explaining your choices.

Explore 9. Investigate usability guidelines that deal with Alt messages. Alt messages are text messages that can be read by assistive devices. They are used with graphic buttons and so forth to make the site more accessible. Research these guidelines at *www.w3.org/WAI*. Write down your findings to use when working on the site's graphics.

10. Design a color palette, choose the fonts, and select a graphic style for the site. Write a paragraph explaining your choices.

11. Create rough sketches of two layouts for the site. Write a paragraph explaining which layout you prefer and why.

Explore 12. Check the logical layout of the design you prefer by reviewing the decisions that you have made. Make sure that your design reinforces the site goals and supports the site metaphor.

13. Create a Local Site Definition, using "Museum" as the site name and "Museum\Dreamweaver" as the folder and location where you are storing your Web sites as the local root folder. Refresh the local file list automatically, and enable cache.

14. Create a Remote Site Definition using FTP access for the Museum site.

15. Create a Graphics folder in the root folder in the Local view of the Site panel.

Explore 16. In the Site panel, add pages to the Museum site and name them index.htm, Art.htm, Artists.htm, Location.htm, and Museum.htm.

17. Open each page in a Document window and set the page title using the list below, and then save and close each page.

Filename	Page Title
Index.htm	Museum of Western Art - Home
Art. htm	Museum of Western Art - Art
Artists.htm	Museum of Western Art - Artists
Location.htm	Museum of Western Art - Location
Museum.htm	Museum of Western Art - Museum

18. Open the home page; set the background color to #CC6600; set the text, links, visited links, and active links color to #ECB888 in the Page Properties window; and then save the page.

Explore
19. Switch to Code and Design view and review the HTML tags for the home page in Code view. Copy all of the body tag information from the home page, open the other pages of your site, and then paste the body tags into them.

20. Save and close each page.

21. Preview the pages in your browser, looking for consistency in display. Each page should have the same background, and each page should have the page title that you assigned to it displayed in the browser title bar.

22. Preview the pages on the Web, looking for consistency in display. Again, each page should have the same background and each page should have the page title that you assigned to it displayed in the browser title bar.

23. Close the Museum site.

Case 3. NORM You are working on the new Web site for NORM, an independent publishing company in California that concentrates on cultivating fringe writings of all sorts. The Web design team is in the initial planning phase of designing the new NORM Web site. Using your research on NORM competitors, you'll develop a plan for the new NORM site. Then you create the new site, add the home page and top-level pages to the site, and set the page properties.

1. Define a list of goals for the site.

2. Define a target audience and a user profile for the site.

3. Conduct market research as needed by visiting competitors' sites.

4. Compose two end-user scenarios for the site.

5. Develop an information category outline for the site.

6. Create a flow chart for the site.

7. Develop a site concept and metaphor for the site. Write a paragraph explaining your choices.

8. Design a color palette, choose the fonts, and select a graphic style for the site. Write a paragraph explaining your choices.

9. Create a rough sketch of the layout of the site. Write a paragraph explaining your choice.

Explore
10. Check the layout of the design for logic by reviewing the decisions that you have made. Make sure that your design reinforces the site goals and supports the site metaphor.

11. Create a Local Site Definition, using "NORM" as the site name and "NORM\Dreamweaver" in the folder and location where you are storing your Web sites as the local root folder. Refresh the local file list automatically, and enable cache.

12. Create a Remote Site Definition using FTP access for the NORM site.

13. Create a Graphics folder in the root folder in the Local view of the Site panel.

14. Create new pages in the Site panel and name the pages: index.htm, books.htm, company.htm, contact.htm, and links.htm.

Explore ▶ 15. Open each page in a Document window and set a page title based on the filename. Set the background image to the NORMBackground.gif document file located in the Cases folder within the Tutorial.02 folder on your Data Disk (remember, once you add a copy of the graphic to your Graphics folder you can select it from the Graphics folder). Set the background color to #003366; the text color to #FFFFFF; and the links, visited links, and active links color to #CCCFE6.

16. Save and close each page.

17. Preview the pages in your browser, looking for consistency in display. Each page should have the same background, and each page should have the page title that you assigned to it displayed in the browser title bar.

Explore ▶ 18. Review the HTML tags for the home page in Code view.

Explore ▶ 19. Switch to Design and Code view, and then change the background color of the home page to another color that would complement the colors you set in Step 15 in the color palette.

20. Save and close the home page.

21. Preview the pages on the Web, looking for consistency in display. Each page should have the same background except for the home page, and each page should have the page title that you assigned to it displayed in the browser title bar.

22. Close the NORM site.

Case 4. **Sushi Ya-Ya**   You are working with Mary O'Brien to create and design a Web site for Sushi Ya-Ya, a small sushi restaurant that will be opening soon in the French Quarter of New Orleans. Mary asks you to develop a Web site plan and design to present to Charlie Lindahl, the restaurant's owner, for review at the next scheduled meeting. Because Sushi Ya-Ya is not yet open, there is no established customer base. You know that the client wants to attract the employees of local businesses for its lunch clientele. You will have to do further research to define the target audience as well as to develop content for the site, as the business has not yet generated any informational materials.

1. Research restaurant Web sites (sushi restaurants in particular) and the French Quarter in New Orleans. Make notes about your findings.

2. Construct a list of goals for the site.

3. Define a target audience and a user profile for the site.

4. Complete your market research. Review at least eight Web sites, including restaurant sites, sites geared at your target audience, sites about New Orleans and the French Quarter, and sites about sushi.

5. Write a paragraph documenting the findings from your market research. Include the URLs of the Web sites that you visited.

6. Compose two end-user scenarios for the site.

7. Develop an information category outline for the site.

8. Create a flow chart for the site.

9. Develop a concept and metaphor for the site. Be creative, but make sure that your metaphor will support the site goals.

10. Design a color palette, choose the fonts, and select a graphic style for the site. Write a paragraph explaining your choices.

11. Create rough sketches of two layouts of the site. Write a paragraph explaining which layout you prefer and why.

Explore 12. Check the layout of the design you prefer for logic by reviewing the decisions that you have made. Make sure that your design reinforces the site goals and supports the site metaphor.

13. Create a Local Site Definition, using "SushiYaYa" as the site name and "SushiYaYa\Dreamweaver" in the folder and location where you are storing your Web sites as the local root folder. Refresh the local file list automatically, and enable cache.

14. Create a Remote Site Definition using FTP access for the SushiYaYa site.

15. Create a Graphics folder in the root folder in the Local view of the Site panel.

Explore 16. In the Site panel, add the first-level pages to the SushiYaYa site based on your site plan and flow chart, and then rename them with descriptive filenames.

Explore 17. Open each page in a Document window, set the appropriate page title, background, and colors in the Page Properties dialog box, and then save and close each page.

18. Preview the pages in your browser, looking for consistency in display. Each page should have the same background, and each page should have the page title that you assigned to it displayed in the browser title bar.

19. Review the HTML tags for the home page in Code view.

Explore 20. Switch to Code and Design views, and then change the background color of the home page to another color in the color palette.

21. Save and close the home page.

22. Preview the pages on the Web, looking for consistency in display. Again, each page should have the same background and each page should have the page title that you assigned to it displayed in the browser title bar.

23. Close the SushiYaYa site.

QUICK | CHECK ANSWERS

Session 2.1

1. False; there are many possible paths in any creative process.
2. to make decisions about the site's organization and structure
3. four or five
4. the group of users that you would most like to visit the site
5. to help identify the target audience by determining the characteristics of the group of people you are trying to reach
6. You may create a Web site that seems targeted to the intended audience but that does not actually appeal to them.

7. to find out the target audience's preferences for a product or service; investigate the target audience's likes, dislikes, and interests; and evaluate competitors' products or services

8. imagined situations in which members of the target audience might access a Web site

Session 2.2

1. the process of determining what you want a site to do and then creating a framework that will allow you to accomplish those goals

2. Categories provide structure for the information in a Web site and are used to create the main navigation system.

3. A flow chart provides a visual representation of the hierarchical structure of the pages within the site.

4. because you need to use your instincts, follow leads, do research, and talk to others to gather everything you can

5. a general underlying theme that runs through the site and is used as a unifying mechanism for various elements that contribute to the site's look and feel

6. because the Web is a publishing venue used by a variety of people, including people with disabilities

7. keep it simple; include three to six colors per site; consider the mood you want to create; and keep in mind the target audience

8. True.

9. the position of elements (navigation system, text, logo, artwork, etc.) on a Web page

Session 2.3

1. local info and remote info

2. to put a Web site on a Web server so it can be seen on the Web, enabling you to verify that the Web site's features work in the browser and over the Web

3. a new page is created that is automatically associated with the defined site

4. attributes that apply to an entire page rather than to an element on the page, such as a page title, background, text and link colors, and margins

5. at least every ten minutes and whenever you have finished modifying a page

6. in a browser; on the Web

7. False; HTML is a common markup language that is viewable by a variety of software packages, including Web browsers.

In this tutorial you will:

- Add text to a page

- Format text using font tags

- Create and format text links

- Learn about the underlying HTML involved with text

- Create HTML styles

- Create Cascading Style Sheets

- Export CSS styles to an external style sheet

- Edit CSS styles

- Examine a style sheet in Code view

- Upload a site to the Web server

ADDING
AND FORMATTING TEXT

Working with Text on the Catalyst Web Site

CASE

Catalyst

Each page of the Catalyst site will contain at least three text elements: the page heading, sub-headings, and body text. Formatting provides a way for you to distinguish between these different types of text. Based on the design plan that was finalized and approved, the page heading will be formatted as Arial, Helvetica, sans-serif font grouping; a +4 font size; and the Dark-Hard-Orange color. Sub-headings will be formatted as Arial, Helvetica, sans-serif font grouping; a +2 font size; and the Dark-Hard-Orange color. The body text will be formatted with the Arial, Helvetica, sans-serif font grouping. Because black was already selected as the default text color in the Page Properties, and the body text will be in the default base size for the page, you will not need to change the color or size format of the body text.

Sara Lynn, the president of Catalyst, and Brian Lee, the public relations and marketing director, have approved the design plan for the new Catalyst Web site. The next step is to add text to the site's pages and to format the text based on the design plan. To do this, you will type some of the text directly onto the page, and import some of the text from text files. You will apply some formatting directly, and you will create and apply styles to make the formatting consistent from one page to another.

Understanding Text Basics

The way that HTML displays and formats text has evolved over time. Each evolutionary step has provided better control over the way text is formatted and displayed.

The World Wide Web Consortium (W3C) publishes recommendations for HTML standards. As new versions of HTML are developed and then accepted, the W3C assigns version numbers to these standards (a lower number = an older standard). New HTML versions contain new elements, tags, and updated methods of doing things. Tags that have been replaced in new versions of HTML are kept around for compatibility with older browsers. These older tags that are in the process of becoming obsolete are called **deprecated**. Because many people use older browsers that rely on the earlier versions of HTML, deprecated tags are phased out slowly.

In the earliest days of the Web, designers had limited control over the way text was displayed in a browser. Text was displayed in the default font and size set by the user's browser. The way it looked was also affected by the user's operating system. Designers had no font control within a Web page except for the six predefined heading tags that could be used to denote importance of text by changing the relative size of the headings. In HTML 2, bold, italic, and underline attributes were added. In HTML 3.2, another milestone in controlling the display of text was added—the HTML font tag (or just font tag). The **font tag** allowed designers to designate which font and which relative font size the Web page should be displayed in (as long as the designated font was installed on the user's computer). The techniques for adding and formatting basic text that you will explore in this session use the font tag and its attributes to control the way text is displayed. In HTML 4.01, font tags were deprecated and their functions replaced and expanded upon by Cascading Style Sheets (which you will work with in Session 3.2). Even though font tags were deprecated, there are several important reasons to learn to format text with font tags:

1. You may need to update older HTML pages. Familiarity with the version of HTML in which the older pages were created makes the task much easier and more efficient.

2. Your target audience may include users of older browsers or technology. It is impossible for these people to reliably view HTML pages that use the latest specifications. (We all know someone who has a 5-year-old computer that they use but never update.)

3. Some new portable devices, specialized Web access tools, Web appliances and devices, and other programs are not compliant with the latest specifications and still rely on HTML 3.2 or earlier.

4. Some Web content management systems (for example, systems that dynamically create educational pages for online courses) do not support current formats.

Because specifications and standards change rapidly, there is no easy way to predict exact adoption rates for newer standards and technologies. The W3C Web site (*www.w3.org*) is a good reference to keep up with current trends and changes.

Adding **Text to a Web Page**

Almost every Web page includes text elements. In fact, text is the basis of most Web sites. To ensure maximum readability, you'll want to be sure that the text you add to a Web page is clearly written and free from spelling, punctuation, and grammatical errors. Well-written Web content is concise, effective in communicating your point, and written with the end-user in mind. By the time you are ready to add the content to your Web site, you will already have the information architecture, which will tell you what you need to include on each page, and you will have all of the raw materials, including the text and the graphics, so that you are not composing on the fly.

There are two ways to add text to a page in Dreamweaver. You can simply type in the work area of the Document window to add text to the page. This is a good method for adding small amounts of text or text that will be heavily formatted. You can also copy existing text from another file (whether a text document or a Web page) and paste it into the work area of the Document window in Design view. This is a good method for adding text to your site if there is a great deal of text to contend with; most word processing programs have better spell checking and grammar checking features, as well as well as a built-in thesaurus. However, sometimes there are errors—such as extra spaces, oddly positioned text, or misinterpreted symbols—that appear on the Web page when text is imported from another program. Whenever you copy text from another source, it is important to read over the text and correct any errors that have been introduced. Note that, when you copy text from a text file, any formatting from the original file is lost when you paste the text into Dreamweaver. Line breaks, however, are maintained.

Brian asks you to add text to the bands page of the NewCatalyst site. He has already typed the text into a Word document.

To add text to a Web page:

1. Start **Dreamweaver**, open the **NewCatalyst** site you modified in Session 2.3, and then close the Untitled Document in the Document window.

   TROUBLE? If you are working on a different computer than you did in Session 2.3, you will need to re-create the site definition on this computer (both the local info and the remote info).

2. Double-click the **bands.htm** page in the Site panel to open it in a Document window, and then click the **Show Design View** button 🖾 on the Document toolbar, if necessary, to switch to Design view.

3. Press the **Enter** key five times to move the insertion point a few lines below the colored portion of the page background, and then type **CATALYST BANDS**. The text you typed appears in the Document window. See Figure 3-1.

Figure 3-1   TEXT TYPED ON BANDS PAGE

typed text

Catalyst - Bands (Dreamweaver/bands*)

CATALYST BANDS

<body> <p>   564 x 314   1K / 1 sec

4. Start **Word** or another word processing program, and then open the **Tutorial.03/Tutorial/Bands.doc** file located on the Data Disk. This document contains the rest of the text you want to add to the bands page. Notice that the paragraph headings are bold.

5. Press the **Ctrl+A** keys to select all the text in the document, press the **Ctrl+C** keys to copy the text to the Windows Clipboard, and then click the **Close** button ☒ on the title bar of the word processing program to close the document and exit the word processing program.

6. Click to place the insertion point after the text you typed in the Catalyst - Bands Document window, if necessary, and then press the **Enter** key to move the insertion point down a line.

7. Click **Edit** on the main menu bar, and then click **Paste**. The text you copied from the Bands.doc document is pasted into the Catalyst - Bands page.

8. Scroll to the top of the page. See Figure 3-2.

Figure 3-2   TEXT COPIED FROM WORD DOCUMENT

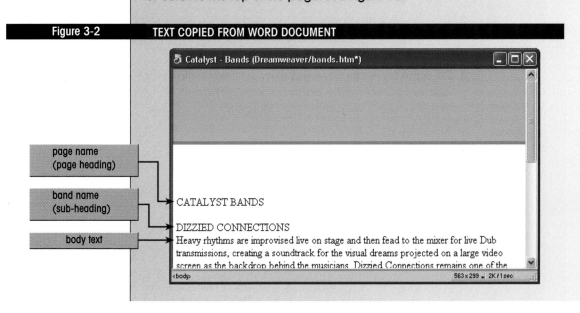

page name
(page heading)

band name
(sub-heading)

body text

Catalyst - Bands (Dreamweaver/bands.htm*)

CATALYST BANDS

DIZZIED CONNECTIONS
Heavy rhythms are improvised live on stage and then fead to the mixer for live Dub transmissions, creating a soundtrack for the visual dreams projected on a large video screen as the backdrop behind the musicians. Dizzied Connections remains one of the

<body>   563 x 299   2K / 1 sec

9. Scroll as needed and read the bands page text. Notice that the paragraph headings are not bold as they were in the text document. Before you continue, you'll save the page with the text.

10. Click **File** on the main menu bar, and then click **Save**.

Before you format the text on the Catalyst - Bands page, you want to check the spelling.

Checking the Spelling on Web Pages

It is important to proofread all of the text that you add to your Web pages, whether you typed it directly onto the Web page or you copied it from another file. You can't assume that text you receive from someone else has been proofed and corrected. You should also use Dreamweaver's built-in spell checker to double-check for errors. Errors in spelling and grammar can detract from the overall impression of the site. They can make the company, product, or service seem unprofessional.

Brian asks you to proofread the bands page and then to use the spell-checker tool to double-check for spelling errors. The spell checker is not foolproof, so when you proof-read the page, it is a good idea to look for errors that a spell checker won't catch, such as incorrectly used homonyms (for example, *there*, *their*, and *they're*), a correctly spelled word that is wrong in context (such as *from* versus *form*), or missing words.

To check a page for spelling errors:

1. Scroll to the top of the bands page, click to place the cursor above the text, click **Text** on the main menu bar, and then click **Check Spelling**. The Check Spelling dialog box opens, displaying the first word that it finds that does not match any words in the built-in dictionary, in this case the word "fead."

2. Drag the Check Spelling window by its title bar so that you can see the sentence with the highlighted word in the Document window. The word should be "fed."

3. Click **fed** in the Suggestions list. See Figure 3-3.

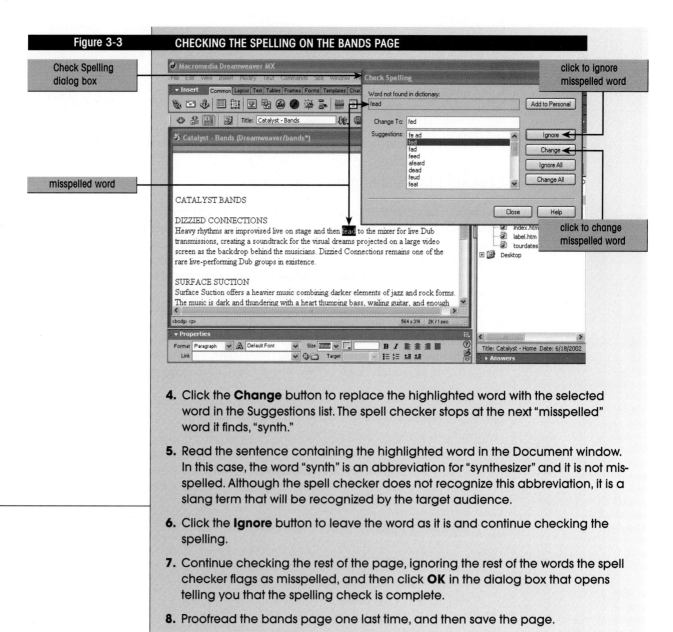

Figure 3-3 CHECKING THE SPELLING ON THE BANDS PAGE

4. Click the **Change** button to replace the highlighted word with the selected word in the Suggestions list. The spell checker stops at the next "misspelled" word it finds, "synth."

5. Read the sentence containing the highlighted word in the Document window. In this case, the word "synth" is an abbreviation for "synthesizer" and it is not misspelled. Although the spell checker does not recognize this abbreviation, it is a slang term that will be recognized by the target audience.

6. Click the **Ignore** button to leave the word as it is and continue checking the spelling.

7. Continue checking the rest of the page, ignoring the rest of the words the spell checker flags as misspelled, and then click **OK** in the dialog box that opens telling you that the spelling check is complete.

8. Proofread the bands page one last time, and then save the page.

Formatting **Text Using Font Tags**

The simplest way to format text in Dreamweaver is to select the text in the Document window and set the attributes for the text in the Property inspector. You can set the attributes for a single letter, a word, a line of text, or an entire block of text. The attributes for text formatting are similar to those you will find in a word processing program; however, when text is formatted in Dreamweaver, HTML tags are added in the background. Text formatting attributes include format, font, font size, font color, emphasis, alignment, lists, and indents.

The **format** attributes are a list of standardized HTML tags used for text formatting. These include the paragraph tag and a variety of heading tags.

The **font** attributes are a list of the fonts available for use. The Default Font option displays the text in the default font of the end-user's browser. To maintain greater control of the aesthetic look of a page, you can choose a font group from the list. When a font group is selected, Dreamweaver places a font tag containing all of the choices in the font group around the specified text. You can also add fonts to the list, but it is recommended that you use caution when doing this because a font must be installed on the end-user's machine to display the text in that font. If the font is not installed on the end-user's machine, the text will be displayed in the browser's default font.

The **font size** attributes are a list of available font sizes. Unlike word processing programs, HTML has no fixed font size. Instead, when you choose a font size from the list, you are choosing from a scalar range of sizes relative to a **base font size**. The default base font size is 3; however, you can set the base font size for the Web page to a different value by inserting a basefont tag designating a different base font size into the head portion of your Web page. (You will learn about the basefont tag later in this session.) If you do not choose a value from the font size list, your text will be displayed at the base font size that you have selected for that page. If you have not added a base font tag, the text will be a 3. If you have added a base font tag, the text will be displayed at the designated size.

When you choose a value from the font size list, Dreamweaver inserts a fontsize tag into the HTML of your page. The first seven choices in the font size list are absolute font sizes (1 to 7). **Absolute font sizes** are based on the standard default base size of 3. Sizes 1 and 2 are smaller than 3, while sizes 4 through 7 appear progressively larger than 3. If you choose an absolute font size, the fontsize tag will override the basefont tag and the text you select will be displayed at the designated size regardless of the base font size. The remaining choices in the font size list are relative font sizes (-7 to +7). **Relative font sizes** add or subtract from the base font size. For example, a +2 value increases the base font size by two sizes, and a -2 value reduces the base font size by two sizes. Relative font sizes are the best choice because they ensure that text will be proportionately scaled in the browser window. For example, if you change the base font size for the page to the absolute size 4, a +2 value adds 2 sizes to size 4; if you later change the base font size for the page to the absolute size 3, the +2 value adds 2 sizes to size 3.

In addition to the font sizes that you create for a Web page, users can change the overall size of text that appears in their browser—essentially scaling the size that text appears in their browser. The default size for text in a browser is Medium, and that is the size that you should use when you preview your Web pages. A visually impaired user might set the browser text to Larger to increase the readability of text on Web pages.

The **font color** attributes enable you to change the color of selected text. The default font color for a page is the color you selected in the Page Properties dialog box. To change the color of a selected block of text, you can type the hexadecimal color code into the color text box or select a color with the color picker.

The buttons in the Property inspector enable you to change the emphasis of selected text with boldface and italics; apply a left, center, or right alignment to a paragraph; turn paragraphs into items in an unordered (bulleted) or ordered (numbered) list; and apply or remove indents from paragraphs.

REFERENCE   WINDOW   **RW**

Formatting Text Using the Property Inspector

- Click the Options menu button in the Property inspector, and then click HTML mode.
- Select the text in the Document window that you want to format.
- To change the font, click the Font list arrow in the Property inspector, and then click the font grouping you want.
- To change the font size, click the Size list arrow in the Property inspector, and then click the size you want.
- To change the color, click in the Text Color text box in the Property inspector and type the hexadecimal code of the color you want, or click the Text Color color box in the Property inspector and click the color swatch you want using the color picker.
- To change the style, click the Bold or Italic button in the Property inspector.
- To change the alignment, click one of the alignment buttons in the Property inspector.
- To create a text hyperlink, select the text, click the Browse for File button in the Property inspector, and then browse to the file to which you want to link, or click the Point to File icon in the Property inspector and then drag to the file to which you want to link, or type the external URL in the Link text box.

Next, you'll format the text on the Catalyst - Bands page. The page heading—CATALYST BANDS—will be formatted with the Arial, Helvetica, sans-serif font grouping, a +4 font size, and the Dark-Hard-Orange (#FF9900) color. You can make all these changes in the Property inspector.

To format the page heading with the Property inspector:

1. Select **CATALYST BANDS** in the Document window, click the **Options menu** button in the Property inspector, and then click **HTML Mode**. The Property inspector shows the HTML formatting mode and that there is no formatting to the selected text. See Figure 3-4.

Figure 3-4	PROPERTY INSPECTOR FOR UNFORMATTED PAGE HEADING TEXT

Font list arrow

Font Size list arrow

Font Color text box

Options menu button

2. Click the **Font** list arrow, and then click **Arial, Helvetica, sans-serif**. The font of the selected text changes to the Arial, Helvetica, sans-serif font group.

3. Click the **Size** list arrow, and then click **+4**. The font size of the selected text changes to +4, four sizes larger than the default font size.

4. Click in the **Font Color** text box, type **#FF9900**, and then press the **Enter** key. The color of the selected text changes to #FF9900 (Dark-Hard-Orange).

5. Click in the selected line of text in the Document window to deselect the page heading and leave the insertion point in the text. See Figure 3-5.

Figure 3-5 **FORMATTED PAGE HEADING**

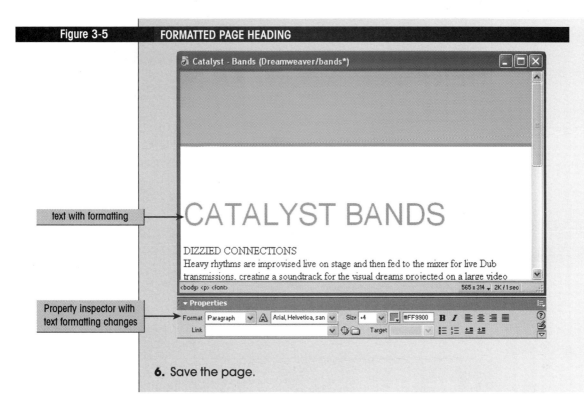

text with formatting

Property inspector with text formatting changes

6. Save the page.

Next, you'll format the band names in the paragraph headings—Dizzied Connections, Surface Suction, Sloth Child, and Life in Minor Chords—as sub-headings using the Property inspector. These sub-headings will be similar to the page heading, but smaller. You'll format them with the Arial, Helvetica, sans-serif font grouping, a +2 font size, and the Dark-Hard-Orange (#FF9900) color.

To format the band names with the Property inspector:

1. Scroll down in the Document window, if necessary, and then select **DIZZIED CONNECTIONS**.

2. Change the font to **Arial, Helvetica, sans-serif**, the size to **+2**, and the color to **#FF9900** in the Property inspector.

3. Click in the selected line of text in the Document window to deselect the text and leave the insertion point in the formatted line. See Figure 3-6.

Figure 3-6   **FORMATTED SUB-HEADING**

formatted band name →

relative font size
for band names

4. Repeat Steps 1–3 for the three other paragraph sub-headings on the page: **SURFACE SUCTION**, **SLOTH CHILD**, and **LIFE IN MINOR CHORDS**.

5. Save the page.

Next, you'll format the body text below each band name with the Arial, Helvetica, sans-serif font group. You'll set the font size to None so the font size will default to the base font size, which is 3 because you have not added a basefont tag. You will not enter a hexadecimal number in the Color text box, so the body text color will appear black (the default color you set in the Page Properties dialog box).

To format the band text with the Property inspector:

1. Select all of the paragraph text below the DIZZIED CONNECTIONS heading in the Document window.

2. Change the font to **Arial, Helvetica, sans-serif**, make sure that the font size is set to **None**, and then click in the selected text in the Document window. See Figure 3-7.

Figure 3-7 **FORMATTED CATALYST - BANDS PAGE**

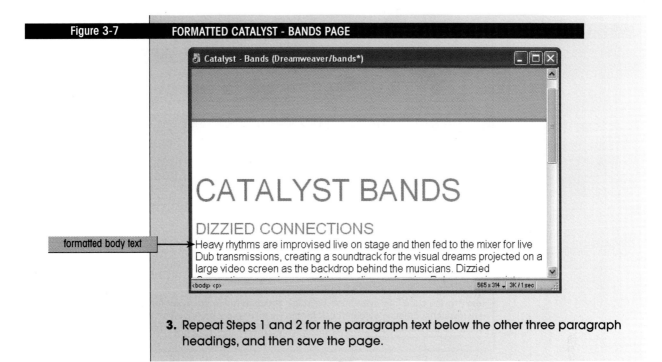

3. Repeat Steps 1 and 2 for the paragraph text below the other three paragraph headings, and then save the page.

Finally, you'll preview the page in a browser and change the browser settings for text size to see how they affect the way the page looks.

To change the text size in a browser:

1. Click **bands.htm** in the Site panel to select it, click **File** on the Site panel menu bar, point to **Preview in Browser**, and then click **iexplore** or the name of your browser to preview the bands page in your browser.

2. Click **View** on the menu bar in the browser window, point to **Text Size**, and then click **Larger**. See Figure 3-8.

Figure 3-8   BANDS PAGE IN BROWSER WITH LARGER TEXT SELECTED

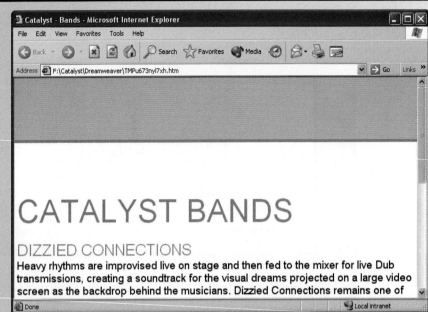

TROUBLE? If you are not using Internet Explorer, ask your instructor to help you locate the text sizing command for your browser.

3. Click **View** on the menu bar in the browser window, point to **Text Size**, and then click **Largest**. See Figure 3-9.

Figure 3-9   BANDS PAGE IN BROWSER WITH LARGEST TEXT SELECTED

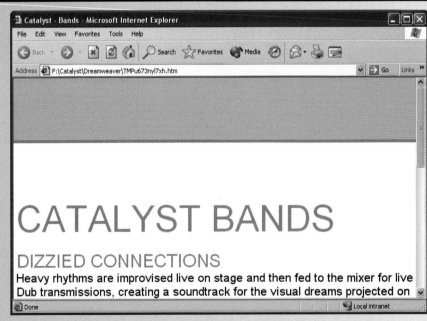

4. Click **View** on the menu bar in the browser window, point to **Text Size**, and then click **Medium**.

5. Close the browser.

The Catalyst Web site plan calls for text hyperlinks at the top of each page. You'll add these next.

Creating **Text Hyperlinks**

Hyperlinks enable users to move between pages in a Web site and to connect to pages on other Web sites. For the Catalyst Web site, you will create text hyperlinks for the main navigation system as called for in the site plan. First, you'll add the link text to one of the pages in the site and format it. Then, you'll create the hyperlinks. Finally, you will copy the links to the rest of the pages in the site.

Adding and Formatting Hyperlink Text

You'll insert the text for the hyperlinks—label, bands, catalogue, tour dates, and contact—on a blank line just below the colored part of the page background. You want to separate each word with two **non-breaking spaces**, which are special, invisible characters used to create more than one space between text and other elements. In HTML, only one regular space will display between items no matter how many spaces you type using the Spacebar. Using the non-breaking space allows you to separate items with more than one space between them.

After you insert the link text, you'll format it by setting the font, size, and alignment. You won't set any colors for the link text because you specified them when you set the page properties.

To add and format text for hyperlinks on a Web page:

1. Click to position the insertion point just below the colored portion of the background.

2. Type **label**, click the **Characters** tab on the Insert bar, and then click the **Non-Breaking Space** button ⬇ twice. Two non-breaking spaces are inserted after the text. (A breaking space and a non-breaking space look the same in Design view.)

You can also insert non-breaking spaces using the keyboard.

3. Type **bands**, press the **Ctrl+Shift+Spacebar** keys twice to insert two non-breaking spaces.

4. Type **catalogue**, insert two non-breaking spaces, type **tour dates**, insert two non-breaking spaces, type **contact**, and insert two non-breaking spaces. The text for each link is followed by two non-breaking spaces. See Figure 3-10.

Figure 3-10   UNFORMATTED LINK TEXT

unformatted link text →

Catalyst - Bands (Dreamweaver/bands*)

label bands catalogue tour dates contact

CATALYST BANDS

DIZZIED CONNECTIONS
Heavy rhythms are improvised live on stage and then fed to the mixer for live
Dub transmissions, creating a soundtrack for the visual dreams projected on a
large video screen as the backdrop behind the musicians. Dizzied

\<body\> \<p\>   565 x 314   3K / 1 sec

5. Select all of the link text and non-breaking spaces in the Document window, and then use the Property inspector to change the font to **Arial, Helvetica, sans-serif** and the size to **+1**.

6. Click the **Align Right** button ≣ in the Property inspector, and then click in the selected line of text. The formatted text for the links aligns to the right of the page. See Figure 3-11.

Figure 3-11   FORMATTED AND ALIGNED LINK TEXT

Catalyst - Bands (Dreamweaver/bands*)

label bands catalogue tour dates contact

CATALYST BANDS

DIZZIED CONNECTIONS
Heavy rhythms are improvised live on stage and then fed to the mixer for live
Dub transmissions, creating a soundtrack for the visual dreams projected on a
large video screen as the backdrop behind the musicians. Dizzied

\<body\> \<p\> \<font\>   565 x 314   3K / 1 sec

7. Save the page.

You'll convert the formatted text to hyperlinks.

Creating Links from Text

You can create text hyperlinks using the Property inspector to associate the text with a specific file or Web page. The first time you link to a file, you select the link text, then you use the Browse for File button or the Point to File icon next to the Link text box in the Property inspector to select the appropriate file. Dreamweaver will then create the link for you. (You can also type the URL into the Link text box in the Property inspector, but if you mistype the URL or path, the link will not work.) If the page you link to is outside the local root folder, Dreamweaver prompts you to include a copy of the page in the site (that is, in the local root folder). Remember to keep all of the elements that you will use in your site within the site's local root folder. In this way, the elements will be accessible when you publish the site and Dreamweaver can manage the site and its elements for you.

Once you link to a file, it will appear in the Link list when you click the Link list arrow in the Property inspector. If you need to add another link to that file, first select the new link text, and then click the Link list arrow and select the file from the list.

There are two types of links, relative links and absolute links. Relative links can be relative to the document or to the site's root folder. **Document relative links** don't specify the entire URL of the Web page you are linking to; instead, they specify a path from the current page. You use document relative links when you are linking to pages within your site, because you can move the site to a different server location or different domain, and the links will still work. In addition to standard document relative links, Dreamweaver includes an option to create site root relative links. **Site root relative links** specify a path from the site root folder to the linked document. You can use site root relative links when you work on large sites with complex folder structures that change frequently. When you link to a page anywhere within your local root folder, Dreamweaver creates a relative link. In these tutorials you will use document relative links.

When you link to a page in another site, you use an absolute link. An **absolute link** contains the complete URL of the page you are linking to, which includes *http://www.domainname.com/* plus the filename of the page to which you are linking. You use an absolute link when you want to link to Web pages outside of your site.

Next, you'll create hyperlinks from the link text you just added and formatted. Each link will be associated with the appropriate existing Web page. You will also create a link from the link text for the current page to itself (for example, on the Catalyst - Contact page, you will link the link text "contact" to the Catalyst - Contact page). Although the link will not go anywhere, formatting it as a link will maintain consistency in the look of the text in the navigation system, and, when you copy the navigation system to other pages of the site, you will not have to create additional links. Remember, when you set the page properties, you designated various colors for the three types of links (text links, active links, and visited links).

To create hyperlinks from text:

1. Select **label** in the Catalyst - Bands Document window.

2. Click the **Browse for File** button ▢ in the Property inspector. The Select File dialog box opens. The Look in list box lists the folder in which the dialog box was last closed.

3. Navigate to the **Dreamweaver** folder (which is the local root folder) for the Catalyst site in the location where you are storing your site files.

4. Click **label.htm** in the file list. See Figure 3-12.

Figure 3-12　　**SELECT FILE DIALOG BOX**

file list

relative URL created automatically

type of relative link

5. Click the **OK** button, and then click the selected text in the Document window to deselect the text and leave the cursor in the new link text. The word "label" is now a hyperlink to the label page of the NewCatalyst Web site. See Figure 3-13.

Figure 3-13　　**LABEL TEXT CONVERTED TO A HYPERLINK**

text hyperlink

link path and filename

6. Select **bands** in the Document window, click the **Point to File** icon ✿ in the Property inspector (do not release the mouse button), and then drag the pointer to the **bands.htm** file in the Site panel, as shown in Figure 3-14.

| Figure 3-14 | CREATING A HYPERLINK USING THE POINT TO FILE ICON |

arrow indicates to which file the link will be created

Point to File icon

7. Release the mouse button. The link text "bands" is now linked to the bands page.

8. Repeat Steps 6 and 7 to create hyperlinks for **catalogue**, **tour dates**, and **contact**, associating each with its corresponding file. (For the tour dates link, make sure you select both words before you create the link.)

9. Save the **bands** page, click **bands.htm** in the Site panel to select it, and then preview it in your browser. See Figure 3-15.

| Figure 3-15 | CATALYST - BANDS PAGE PREVIEWED IN BROWSER |

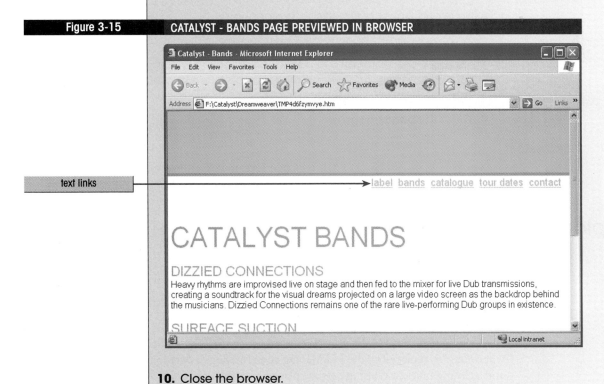

text links

10. Close the browser.

You want to add these same hyperlinks to the rest of the Web pages in the Catalyst site. Although you could open each page, type and format the link text, and then link the text to the appropriate page, it's faster to copy the links you created on the Catalyst - Bands page to the other pages in the site.

To copy and paste hyperlinks between Web pages:

1. Click to position the insertion point at the top of the colored area at the top of the Design window, press and hold the **Shift** key, and then press the **down arrow** key five times to select the blank lines above the hyperlinks you created, the hyperlinks, and the blank line below the hyperlinks.

   TROUBLE? If the page heading "CATALYST BANDS" is selected, press and hold the Shift key, and then press the up arrow key once.

2. Click **Edit** on the main menu bar, and then click **Copy HTML**. You need to use the Copy HTML command instead of the Copy command so that Dreamweaver will copy the underlying HTML code as well as the text.

3. Open the **catalogue.htm** page in a Document window.

4. Click **Edit** on the main menu bar, and then click **Paste HTML**. The blank lines and hyperlinks are copied into the Catalyst - Catalogue page.

   TROUBLE? If you cannot see the links in the new page, place the insertion point at the top of the new page and then press the Enter key to add blank lines. (The links are the same color as the background, and they will be invisible if they are pasted too high on the page.)

5. Select the hyperlinks, and verify that their formatting is **Arial, Helvetica, sans-serif** font, **+1** font size, and **right aligned**.

6. Save and close the Catalyst - Catalogue page.

   You'll repeat this process to add the hyperlinks to the remaining pages of the site.

7. Repeat Steps 3 through 6 to paste the navigation system into each of the remaining pages in the NewCatalyst Web site: **contact.htm**; **index.htm**; **label.htm**; and **tourdates.htm**.

8. Close the **bands** page.

Next, you'll look at the HTML tags that Dreamweaver inserted when you formatted text and created hyperlinks.

Exploring **HTML Tags for Text and Hyperlinks**

HTML tags, whether they apply to text, hyperlinks, or other elements, follow a specific format. As you have already seen, most HTML tags come in pairs with an opening and closing tag that surrounds the text to which the tag is applied, as in the following example:

```
<tag>Some Text</tag>
```

Opening tags are placed before the text to which they are applied, and take the form <tag>, where "tag" is replaced by the HTML tag you are using. There is an opening bracket, the tag, and a closing bracket. Closing tags are placed after the text to which they are applied, and take the form </tag>. Again, there are opening and closing brackets, but in a closing tag, there is a forward slash before the tag itself.

Tags can also be used together, or nested. **Nesting** means placing one set of tags around another set of tags so that both sets apply to the text they surround, such as:

`<tag2><tag>Some Text</tag></tag2>`

When working with nested tags, you must keep the opening and closing tags correctly paired. For example, it would be incorrect to write:

`<tag><tag2>Some Text</tag></tag2>`

Remembering the phrase "first tag on, last tag off" can help you to remember that the outside opening and closing tags belong together and so forth.

REFERENCE WINDOW   RW

Examining HTML Tags
- Click the Show Code View button or the Show Code and Design Views button.
- If the lines of code do not wrap in the Document window, click View on the menu bar, point to Code View Options, and then click Word Wrap.
- Select the tag you want to examine in the Code pane, and then click the Reference button on the Document toolbar to open the Reference panel.

Some tags also contain attributes, such as size, color, and alignment. These attributes are placed within the opening tag. Tag attributes are separated by a blank space and the value of each attribute is usually placed in quotation marks, such as:

`<tag color="x" size="x">Some Text</tag>`

The specific tags that are used depend on the applied formatting and the type of element, such as text or a hyperlink. Some helpful reference sites for HTML tags include *www.webmonkey.com* (try the HTML cheatsheet) and *www.w3.org*.

You will learn about some of the HTML tags that apply to text by examining the tags that Dreamweaver applied when you formatted the text on the bands page.

Exploring HTML Tags that Apply to Text

When you format text in Design view, Dreamweaver places the appropriate HTML tags around the text for you. To see the HTML tags, you need to make the code visible by switching to either Code view or Code and Design views. Many HTML tags can be used to manipulate text. Some of the more common text tags are described in Figure 3-16.

Figure 3-16	COMMON HTML TAGS FOR TEXT		
TAG NAME	**TAG DESCRIPTION**	**TAG SAMPLE**	**BROWSER DISPLAY**
Font	Contains the font face grouping, font size, and font color attributes. When you format text using the HTML mode in the Properties Inspector, Dreamweaver uses font tags to format the text.	`<color="#000000", size="3", font face="Arial, Helvetica, sans-serif">` `Some text</font>`	Some text
Italic	Adds italic style to text. Accessibility guidelines recommend that you use the Emphasis tag instead of the Italic tag because the Italic tag is used to create a visual presentation effect while the Emphasis tag is used to indicate structural emphasis.	`<i>Some text</i>`	*Some text*

Figure 3-16   **COMMON HTML TAGS FOR TEXT (CONTINUED)**

TAG NAME	TAG DESCRIPTION	TAG SAMPLE	BROWSER DISPLAY
Emphasis	Adds structural meaning to text and is to be rendered differently from other body text to designate emphasis. When you use the Italicize button, Dreamweaver places Emphasis tags around the selected text because accessibility guidelines recommend using the Emphasis tag in place of the Italics tag. Both Internet Explorer and Netscape italicize text that is surrounded by the Emphasis tag.	`<em>Some text</em>`	*Some text*
Bold	Adds bold style to text. Accessibility guidelines recommend that you use the Strong tag instead of the Bold tag because the Bold tag is used to create a visual presentation effect while the Strong tag is used to indicate structural emphasis.	`<b>Some text</b>`	**Some text**
Strong	Adds structural meaning to text and is to be rendered differently from other body text to designate a stronger emphasis than the Emphasis tag. When you use the Bold button, Dreamweaver places Strong tags around the selected text because accessibility guidelines recommend using the Strong tag in place of the Bold tag. Both Internet Explorer and Netscape bold text that is surrounded by the Strong tag.	`<strong>Some text </strong>`	**Some text**

Unordered List	Creates a list of bulleted items.	`<ul>`
		`<li>Item1</li>`
		`<li>Item2</li>`
		`</ul>`
			■ Item1
			■ Item2

Ordered List	Creates a list of numbered items.	`<ol>`
		`<li>Item1</li>`
		`<li>Item2</li>`
		`</ol>`
			1. Item1
			2. Item2

Paragraph	Designates a block of text that starts and ends with a break (a skipped line) and by default is left aligned with a ragged right edge. Dreamweaver places paragraph tags around blocks of text when you press the Enter key.	`<p>Some text`
		`in a paragraph.`
		`</p>`
		`<p>Another`
		`paragraph.</p>`
			Some text in a paragraph.
			
			Another paragraph.

Blockquote	Usually indents text from both the left and right margins, and can be nested for deeper indents. Added in Dreamweaver with the Text Indent button (ScreenTip is "indent"); the Outdent button removes a blockquote tag.	`<p>Introductory text`
		`</p>`
		`<blockquote><p>Some`
		`text</p></blockquote>`
		`<p>Closing text</p>`
			Introductory text
			
			Some text
			
			Closing text

Div	Divides a page into a series of blocks; for example, applying the Align attribute in the Property Inspector sometimes creates a div tag with a value of left, center, or right to align the text.	`<div align="right">`
		`Some text, a`
		`paragraph, or other`
		`element</div>`
			Some text, a paragraph, or other element

Pre	Preserves the exact formatting of a block of text when it is displayed in a Web page by rendering text in a fixed pitch font, and by preserving the associated spacing with whitespace characters. For example a poem with Pre tags around it would maintain indentions, multiple spaces between words, and new lines that would otherwise be discarded when it was rendered in a browser.	`<pre>    Some`
		`preformatted    text`
		`might`
		`    look        like`
		`this. </pre>`
			` Some`
			`preformatted   text`
			`might`
			`  look    like`
			`this.`

Figure 3-16		COMMON HTML TAGS FOR TEXT (CONTINUED)	
TAG NAME	**TAG DESCRIPTION**	**TAG SAMPLE**	**BROWSER DISPLAY**
Break	Forces a line break on a page. Used singly without a closing tag because it does not surround text and add attributes. Add by pressing the Shift+Enter keys or clicking the Break object from the Characters tab of the Insert panel.	`Some text`	Some text
Non-breaking space	Inserts a space that will be displayed by the browser. (Browsers will only display one regular space between items in a Web page, regardless of how many regular spaces are entered) Use non-breaking spaces when you want to add more than one visible space between items. The non-breaking space is a special character (not a tag) that is often used like a tag to format text. Insert by pressing the Ctrl+Shift+Spacebar keys or by clicking the Non-Breaking Space button on the Characters tab on the Insert bar.	`Some  ` ` text`	Some text
Basefont	Changes the attributes of the default font on which all of the text contained in the Web page is based and overrides the default font settings in the users browser. The basefont tag is placed in the head or body of the page and is used with the size attribute to change the size of the base font for the page. (When an absolute font size is used as the size value in the font tag it overrides the basefont tag. When a relative font size is used as the size value in the font tag it adds or subtracts from the size value you designate in the basefont tag.)	`<basefont size="6">` `Text at basefont size`	Text at basefont size

When viewing the tags in Code view, you might not recall the purpose of a specific tag. To see a description of a tag, you can click the Reference button on the Document toolbar to display information about the tag. In Code view, most HTML code is blue; however, the code for hyperlinks is green. Regular text is black in Code view .

You'll review the HTML tags that Dreamweaver added when you formatted the text on the Catalyst - Bands page.

To examine HTML tags for text:

1. Open the **bands.htm** page of the NewCatalyst Web site in a Document window.

2. Click the **Show Code and Design Views** button on the Document window toolbar. The Document window splits into two panes.

   If the Word Wrap option is not turned on, the code extends beyond the right margin of the Document window and you cannot see all the text and tags. You'll turn on the Word Wrap option so that all the text and tags appear within the viewing area. This option affects the code only in Dreamweaver.

3. Click **View** on the main menu bar, and then point to **Code View Options**.

4. If **Word Wrap** does not have a check mark next to it, click **Word Wrap**; if **Word Wrap** has a check mark next to it, click anywhere in the Document window to close the menu. The code rewraps so that all the text and tags are visible within the Document window.

5. Select **CATALYST BANDS** in the Design pane at the bottom of the Document window. The corresponding text is also selected in the Code pane. Notice that the paragraph and font tags surround the page heading. See Figure 3-17.

Figure 3-17 | CATALYST - BANDS PAGE IN CODE AND DESIGN VIEWS

opening font tag

opening paragraph tag

selected text

drag to resize panes

TROUBLE? If the Code and Design panes in the Document window are unequal sizes, you can resize the panes. Drag the border between the two panes up or down to adjust the panes until the window is more evenly divided between the panes.

6. Select the entire opening font tag for the page heading, and then click the **Reference** button ⟨?⟩ on the Document toolbar. The Reference panel opens in the Code panel group with information about the selected HTML element. See Figure 3-18.

Figure 3-18 | REFERENCE PANEL OPEN FOR SELECTED HTML TAG

selected opening font tag

click to hide panel group pane

drag to expand the width of the panel groups

Reference panel

Select Tag list arrow

Select Attribute list arrow

7. Position the pointer over the left edge of the panel group pane so that it changes to ⟷, drag the edge to the left to open the panel wider, and then read the text in the Reference panel.

   TROUBLE? If the pane containing the panel groups disappeared, you accidentally clicked the arrow that collapses the panel group pane. Position the pointer over the small triangle on the right edge of the screen so that the rectangle around it turns blue, and then click. You can also click Window on the main menu bar, and then click Site to re-expand the panel group pane.

8. Click the **Select Attribute** list arrow in the Reference panel, click **color**, and then read the text in the Reference panel describing the color attribute of the font tag.

9. Click the **Select Attribute** list arrow in the Reference panel, click **size**, and then read the description about the size attribute of the font tag.

10. Click the **Select Tag** list arrow in the Reference panel, scroll down and click **P** (the paragraph tag), and then read the description of the paragraph tag.

11. Click the **Select Tag** list arrow in the Reference panel, scroll up and click **B** (the bold tag), and then read the description of the bold tag.

12. Select and read the descriptions of the **STRONG** (strong) and **BR** (break) tags.

13. Drag the left edge of the panel group pane to the right to restore it to its original width.

Next, you'll look at the HTML tags for hyperlinks.

Exploring HTML Tags that Apply to Hyperlinks

Hyperlinks are created in HTML with the **anchor tag**, which has the general format:

```
<a href="absolute or relative path">Link Text</a>
```

where "href" is short for hypertext reference, "absolute or relative path"—the URL or page for the link—is the value for href, and "Link Text" indicates the text on the Web page that users click to use the link. Absolute, document relative, and site root relative links have different path information in the href attribute. Figure 3-19 shows the anchor tag with the three types of links.

Figure 3-19	ANCHOR TAGS FOR ABSOLUTE AND RELATIVE LINKS	
LINK	**ANCHOR TAG**	**DESCRIPTION**
Absolute	`<a href="http://www.websitename.com">Text link to a Web page outside current site</a>`	Specifies the absolute or complete path to the linked page.
Document Relative	`<a href="anotherpage.htm">Text link to another page within current site</a>`	Specifies the location of the linked page relative to the current page. Commonly used.
Site Root Relative	`<a href="/subfolder/anotherpage.htm">Text link to another page within current site</a>`	Specifies the location of the linked page relative to the root folder. Used sometimes when sites have a lot of subfolders that change frequently within the root folder.

One of the attributes you can specify with an anchor link is the target attribute. The **Target** attribute specifies where the link opens—in the current browser window or a new browser window. The default is for the new page to be opened in the current browser window, replacing the page from which you linked. If you want the new page to replace the current page, you do not need to include a target attribute. If you specify "_blank" as the target attribute, the linked page opens in a new browser window. The complete anchor tag for opening a page in a new browser window takes the format:

`<a href="absolute or relative path" target="_blank">Link Text</a>`

Another anchor tag attribute is the name attribute. The **Name** attribute associates a name with a specific named location within a Web page. With the name attribute, you can link to the named location on the current page or another page, much like a bookmark. You use the anchor tag with the name attribute in the format:

`<a name="anchor_name">Some Text</a>`

where "anchor_name" is the name you give the anchor, and "Some Text" is the text that is being named as the anchor. Anchor names are case-sensitive. When you create a named anchor, Dreamweaver inserts an anchor icon into the Document window beside the text. The anchor icon is not visible in a browser.

Once a location on a page has a named anchor, you can create links to it from other locations on the same page or from other pages. For example, you can select the page heading and create an anchor to the text named "top," then type "back to the top" at the bottom of the page and create a link from that text to the "top" anchor. This enables the user to jump from the bottom to the top of the Web page by clicking the "back to the top" link. The format for an anchor tag that links to a named anchor on the same page is:

`<a href="#anchor_name">Link Text</a>`

If you are linking to a named anchor on a different page, you need to include the path and filename to the page containing the named anchor in the following general format:

`<a href="absolute or relative path#anchor_name">Link Text</a>`

The # symbol always precedes the anchor name when it is used in a link.

You'll look at the HTML for the hyperlinks you created on the Catalyst - Bands page.

To examine HTML tags for hyperlinks:

1. Select the **contact** link on the Catalyst - Bands page in the Design pane of the Document window.

2. Examine the anchor tag that surrounds the selected text in the Code pane of the Document window. See Figure 3-20.

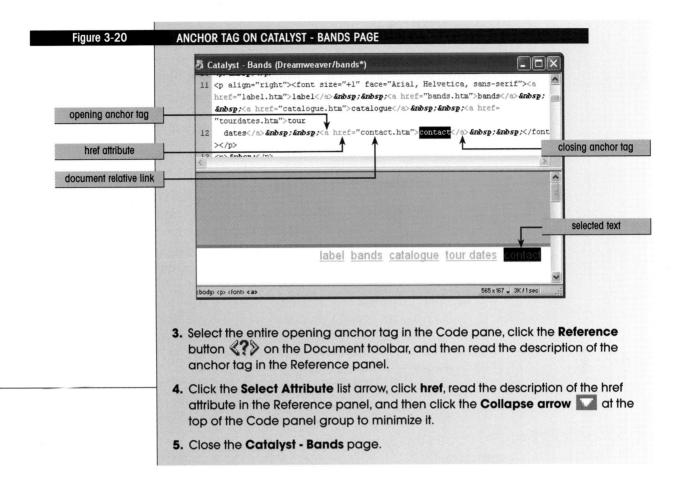

| Figure 3-20 | ANCHOR TAG ON CATALYST - BANDS PAGE |

3. Select the entire opening anchor tag in the Code pane, click the **Reference** button 〈?〉 on the Document toolbar, and then read the description of the anchor tag in the Reference panel.

4. Click the **Select Attribute** list arrow, click **href**, read the description of the href attribute in the Reference panel, and then click the **Collapse arrow** ▼ at the top of the Code panel group to minimize it.

5. Close the **Catalyst - Bands** page.

Creating and Applying HTML Styles

Formatting text can be tedious and time consuming, especially if you are applying the same formatting repeatedly throughout a Web site. Instead of applying each attribute separately, you can create an **HTML style**, which is a group of text attributes that you save with a name and reuse within the same Web site. HTML styles are a time-saving feature in Dreamweaver rather than a part of HTML. When you apply an HTML style to either selected text or a paragraph, Dreamweaver inserts all of the same HTML tags around the text that it would if you applied each attribute separately. The difference is that you save time by applying the entire group of attributes at one time. Using HTML styles saves you time and ensures that each element within the site has consistent formatting. HTML styles are supported by all of the browsers that support the individual attributes that you select for the style, because no extra tags are added to the Web page.

The drawback to using HTML styles is that there is no automatic update capability associated with them. This means that if you want to change some aspect of an element's formatting, such as the font color for the band names, simply revising the HTML style will not reformat all of the text to which the style was previously applied. You can either edit the style and reapply it to each occurrence, or you can manually change the formatting for each occurrence. HTML styles simply prevent you from having to apply each formatting attribute to text separately, nothing more.

Creating HTML Styles

You create and edit HTML styles in the HTML Styles panel. When you create a new HTML style, you have a variety of attribute choices. The attributes associated with HTML styles include:

- **Name.** A descriptive and unique name you give the HTML style. For example, you might use "Main Headings" as the name for the HTML style for the main headings in the Web site.
- **Apply To.** The option to apply the HTML style to the paragraph level or selection level. Selection level styles affect only the selected text; paragraph level styles affect the entire paragraph whether you select any or all of the paragraph text or just position the insertion point within the paragraph. Paragraph level styles have additional attribute options available.
- **When Applying.** The option to add the formatting attributes to any existing formatting or to replace all the existing formatting with the formatting attributes of the HTML style.
- **Font Attributes.** Text formatting attributes that you can select for the HTML style, including font, size, color, and style such as bold or italics. Font attributes apply to both paragraph level and selection level styles. You can quickly set text formatting attributes for an HTML style by selecting text with the appropriate attributes prior to defining a new HTML style; the attributes of the selected text will appear and you can change them as necessary.
- **Paragraph Attributes.** Paragraph formatting attributes that you can select for paragraph level styles, including format and alignment.

REFERENCE WINDOW | **RW**

Creating a New HTML Style

- Click the Expand arrow in the Design panel group, if necessary, and then click the HTML Styles tab.
- If you are creating a new style based on previously formatted text, select the formatted text.
- Click the New Style button in the HTML Styles panel to open the Define HTML Style dialog box.
- Type a name for the new style.
- Click the desired Apply To option button.
- Click the desired option button next to When Applying.
- Select the desired options in the Font or Paragraph Attributes section.
- Click the OK button.

Brian asks you create HTML styles to format the contact page of the NewCatalyst site.

To add the text to the Contact page:

1. Start **Word** or another word processing program, and then open the **Tutorial.03/Tutorial/Contact.doc** file located on your Data Disk.

2. Press the **Ctrl+A** keys to select all the text, press the **Ctrl+C** keys to copy the selected text to the Windows clipboard, and then exit the word processor.

3. Open the **contact.htm** page of the NewCatalyst site in a Document window, and then click the **Show Design View** button 📟 on the Document toolbar.

4. Position the insertion point at the end of the line that contains the links to the other pages on the site (after the two non-breaking spaces after the contact link), press the **Enter** key to move the insertion point to a new line, and then click the **Align Left** button ☰ in the Property inspector to move the insertion point to the left margin.

5. Click **Edit** on the main menu bar, and then click **Paste**. The unformatted text for the page appears below the links.

6. Scroll up so that you can see all of the contact information. See Figure 3-21.

Figure 3-21   **UNFORMATTED CONTACT PAGE**

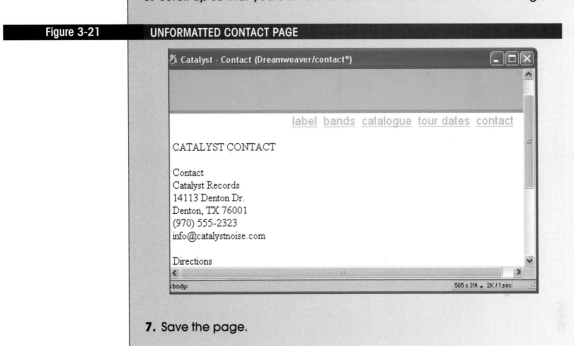

7. Save the page.

You'll start by creating the style for the main heading on the page. The main heading should match the formatting you applied to the Catalyst Bands heading on the Catalyst - Bands page.

To create a new HTML style:

1. Click the **Expand** arrow ▶ next to Design to open the Design panel group, and then click the **HTML Styles** tab. The HTML Styles panel opens. See Figure 3-22.

Figure 3-22   **HTML STYLES PANEL**

2. Click the **New Style** button in the lower right corner of the HTML Styles panel. The Define HTML Style dialog box opens.

You'll enter the formatting attributes for the style.

3. Type **page heading** in the Name text box.

4. Click the **Paragraph** option button in the Apply To section.

5. Click the **Clear Existing Style** option button in the When Applying section, if necessary.

6. In the Font attributes section, select **Arial, Helvetica, sans-serif** from the Font list, type **#FF9900** in the Color text box, and then select **+4** from the Size list. See Figure 3-23.

Figure 3-23	COMPLETED DEFINE HTML STYLE DIALOG BOX

7. Click the **OK** button. The Define HTML Style dialog box closes and the new page heading style appears in the HTML Styles panel. You will apply this style to the page heading in the next section.

Dreamweaver sometimes creates a folder named "Library" in the local root folder in which it saves the information it will need when you apply HTML styles. This information is for Dreamweaver's use only; you do not need to worry about it.

Next, you'll create the style for the secondary heading. You'll use the same format as you did for the band names on the Catalyst - Bands page. To ensure that the attributes you use in the style match the formatting you already applied to those headings, you will first select the formatted text. The formatting attributes will then be selected in the Define New Style dialog box when it opens.

To create a new HTML style based on sample text:

1. Open the **bands** page of the NewCatalyst site in a Document window.

2. Scroll down and select **DIZZIED CONNECTIONS** in the Document window.

3. Click the **New Style** button ⊞ in the HTML Styles panel. The Define HTML Style dialog box opens with the font attributes of the selected text displayed.

4. Type **sub-heading** in the Name text box, and then click the **OK** button.

5. Select the text in the paragraph below DIZZIED CONNECTIONS, and then create a new style with the name **body text**. The new styles appear in the HTML Styles panel. See Figure 3-24.

| Figure 3-24 | HTML STYLES PANEL WITH NEW STYLES |

6. Close the **bands** page.

You can edit existing styles as needed to change any of the formatting attributes. Before you open the Define HTML Style dialog box to make your changes, make sure no text is selected in the Document window. Also, make sure that the Auto Apply checkbox does not contain a check mark (or the existing style will be applied when you select it). Then right-click the style you want to edit, click Edit on the context menu to open the Define HTML Style dialog box, and make whatever changes are needed. Remember that Dreamweaver does not update any text that was already formatted using that HTML style.

Now that you've created the styles you need, you can use them to format the Contact page.

Applying HTML Styles

Once you've created HTML styles, you can use them to quickly format text on other pages in a Web site. The HTML styles give you the assurance that the same elements will include the exact same formatting attributes. If the Auto Apply checkbox in the HTML Styles panel is checked, the style is applied when you click its name. If the Auto Apply checkbox is not checked, you must click the style name and then click the Apply button.

Applying an HTML Style

- Select the text or paragraph to which you want to apply the style.
- Click the Auto Apply checkbox in the HTML Styles panel to check it.
- Click the style name that you want to apply in the HTML Styles panel.

or

- Click the style name that you want to apply in the HTML Styles panel.
- Click the Apply button in the HTML Styles panel.

If you want to remove formatting previously applied to text, you can use the Clear Selection Style and the Clear Paragraph Style built-in styles in the HTML Styles panel. These built-in styles remove any formatting already applied with the HTML Styles panel or the Property inspector.

You'll use the HTML styles that you just created to format the Contact page.

To apply HTML styles:

1. Make sure the **contact** page is still open, and then, if necessary, click the **Auto Apply** checkbox in the HTML Styles panel to check it.

2. Select **CATALYST CONTACT** in the Document window.

3. Click the **page heading** style in the HTML Styles panel to apply the style to the selected heading.

4. Select **Contact** directly below the page heading in the Document window (do not select the contact link), and then click the **sub-heading** style in the HTML Styles panel. The style is applied to the text.

5. Select **Directions** in the Document window, and then apply the **sub-heading** style to the text.

6. Apply the **body text** style to all the text below the sub-headings. See Figure 3-25.

Figure 3-25   FORMATTED CONTACT PAGE

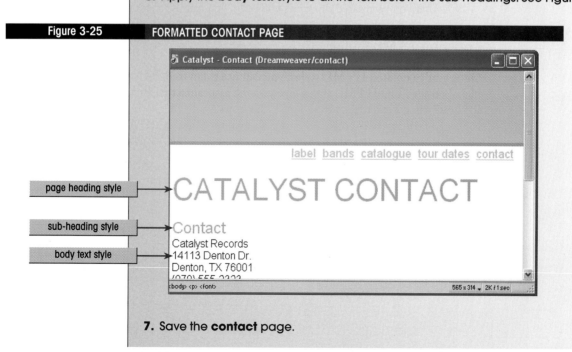

7. Save the **contact** page.

You could continue to apply these styles to the rest of the Catalyst Web site.

Deleting HTML Styles

As you develop a Web site, the list of HTML styles that you create can become quite long. As you work, you might find that you no longer are using a certain style. To keep the HTML Styles panel current and accurate, you can delete unneeded styles.

You'll delete the body text style. Deleting the body text style will not delete it from the text to which it was already applied.

REFERENCE WINDOW   **RW**

Deleting HTML Styles
- Click the Auto Apply checkbox in the HTML Styles panel to uncheck it, if necessary.
- Click the style in the HTML Styles panel that you want to delete.
- Click the Delete Style button in the HTML Styles panel.
- Click the OK button in the warning dialog box.

To delete HTML styles:

1. Click the **Auto Apply** checkbox in the HTML Styles panel to uncheck it.

2. Click the **body text** style in the HTML Styles panel to select it.

3. Click the **Delete Style** button 🗑 in the lower-right corner of the HTML Styles panel.

   A dialog box opens, indicating that you cannot undo deleting a style.

4. Click the **OK** button. The body text style is removed from the HTML Styles panel.

TROUBLE? If a dialog box did not open and the body text style was deleted, then this message was disabled in your Dreamweaver setup. Continue with Step 5.

5. Minimize the Design panel group by clicking the **Collapse arrow** at the top of the Design panel group.

6. Close the **contact** page.

So far, you have formatted text using HTML tags, you have learned about the HTML tags used for formatting and hyperlinking text, and you have created HTML styles. In the next session, you will format text using Cascading Style Sheets.

Session 3.1 QUICK CHECK

1. Older HTML tags that are in the process of becoming obsolete are called _____.

2. Why do you need to learn to format text with font tags?

3. There are two ways to add text to a page in Dreamweaver. You can _____ in the work area of the Document window to add text to the page, or you can _____ text from another document and _____ it into the page.

4. _____ font sizes add or subtract from the base font size.

5. _____ enable users to move between pages in a Web site and to connect to pages on other Web sites.

6. When you link to a page in your local root folder, what type of link is created by default?

7. The general format for the HTML code for the bold tag is _____.

8. The _____ tag is used to create hyperlinks.

SESSION 3.2

In this session, you will create Cascading Style Sheets. You will use CSS styles to modify an existing HTML tag, and you will create a custom style class. Finally, you will customize the appearance of text links.

Understanding Cascading Style Sheets

Cascading Style Sheets were created as the answer to the limitations of HTML styles. A **Cascading Style Sheet (CSS)** is a collection of styles that is either inserted in the head of the HTML of a Web page and used throughout that page, or is attached as an external document and used throughout the entire Web site. A **CSS style** is a rule that defines the appearance of an element in a Web page either by redefining an existing HTML tag or by creating a custom style (also called a class style or a custom style class). CSS styles primarily define text appearance and layout and allow you to specify more parameters of the design than earlier HTML specifications; for example, you can create custom list bullets.

A custom style sheet provides a convenient way to create styles that can be defined in one location and then applied to content residing in many different locations. This ability to separate the look of the site from the content of the site enables the designer to more easily update the Web site's appearance. In addition, unlike with HTML styles, designers can redefine a CSS style after it has been applied, and any content to which the style has been applied is updated as well. So, changing the font for all headings on a site or changing the color of body text on all the pages becomes a simple task.

Some limitations exist with CSS styles. CSSs were adopted as part of HTML 4 and are not fully compatible with older browsers. If you are working on a Web site that supports browser versions 3.0 and older, you will need to use the pre-CSS formatting alternatives that you learned in the last session. Even current browsers do not display all of the features of CSS styles properly; but as new versions of browsers are released, this is changing rapidly. Eventually, all of the CSS style elements will be fully supported. Previewing the Web site in all the browsers and browser versions you are planning to support before making the site public is the best way to verify that all aspects of the site work and display as you expect.

When you create a CSS style, you will first need to choose the the type of style; then you choose the name, tag, or selector of the style; and finally, you choose the location of the style. These options are described below:

- **Type.** The type of CSS style you will create. There are three types of CSS styles available in Dreamweaver. A **redefined HTML tag** is an existing tag you modify; this is probably the most common type of CSS style. When you redefine an HTML tag, the CSS style is used in every instance of that tag. A **custom style** (also called a **custom style class**) is a style you create from scratch and apply to the element you have selected on the page. A **CSS selector** is used in a style you create to redefine formatting for particular combinations of tags; this style is most commonly used to customize the appearance of text links.

- **Name/Tag/Selector.** The name you specify for the custom style, the redefined HTML tag, or the redefined selector, depending on the type of CSS style you select.

- **Define in.** The option to save the style you are creating in a new style sheet file, in an existing external style sheet file, or within only the current document. An **external style sheet** is a separate file that contains all of the CSS styles connected with a Web site. When you save the file in the current document, Dreamweaver creates an **internal style sheet** that embeds (or inserts) the styles in the head of the current Web page and applies them only throughout that document.

Once you select the name, type, and location of the style, you can choose the various attributes for that style. There are eight categories of attributes that can be applied to create a style:

- **Type.** Text attributes similar to those available for the font tag (such as font, font size, font color, and so on), as well as additional attributes such as line height and decoration. You will use the Type attributes most frequently.

- **Background.** A color or an image, fixed or scrolling, that appears behind a page element, like a block of text. CSS background attributes overlay the Web page background designated with the page properties.

- **Block.** The spacing between words, letters, and lines of text, the horizontal and vertical alignment of text, and the indent applied to the text. This attribute is usually applied to blocks of text.

- **Box.** Attributes that control the placement of elements on the page. When you select a letter, a word, or a group of words, you can see the selection box that surrounds all text elements. Box attributes control the characteristics of the selection box.

■ **Border.** The dimensions, color, and line styles of the borders of the selection box that surrounds the text elements.

■ **List.** The number format or the bullet shape or image and its position used with ordered and unordered lists.

■ **Positioning.** The placement of text on the screen. Currently, positioning is only available as a custom style class.

■ **Extensions.** Attributes that control page breaks during printing, the appearance of the pointer when positioned over objects on the page, and special effects to objects. Many browsers do not support extensions attributes.

Some attributes used in CSS styles are not visible within the Dreamweaver environment. You must preview the page in a browser to view the page with all attributes of the styles applied.

Modifying Existing HTML Tags

The simplest way to create a CSS style is to redefine an existing HTML tag. When you create a CSS style to modify an HTML tag, Dreamweaver provides you with an extensive list of tags from which to choose from. You can change and remove existing attributes or add new attributes to any tag. When you modify the attributes associated with a tag, the changes you make will apply to every instance of that tag.

REFERENCE WINDOW	RW

Modifying an Existing HTML Tag
- Open the CSS Styles panel in the Design panel group.
- Click the New CSS Style button in the CSS Styles panel to open the New CSS Style dialog box.
- Click the Redefine HTML Tag option button.
- Click the Tag list arrow, then click the tag that you want to modify.
- Click the appropriate Define In option button.
- Click the OK button to open the CSS Style definition dialog box.
- Click a category in the Category list, and then set the options you want.
- Click the OK button.

Sometimes modifying an existing HTML tag can make it more useful. For example, consider the Heading 1 tag, <h1>, which is the largest heading. Its format changes based on how users' browsers interpret the tag, making its layout and appearance inconsistent. To maintain more control over the appearance of your Web page, you can create a CSS style that redefines the <h1> tag to include all the attributes that you want your Web page headings to include. This gives you a consistency that the <h1> tag would otherwise lack and makes the <h1> tag more useful. Many designers prefer to redefine HTML tags when creating CSS styles because tags, like the paragraph tag and the body tag, often are automatically inserted for them, and older browsers that don't support CSS styles will apply the standard formatting of the HTML tags.

Brian asks you to modify the text on the Catalyst - Bands page using CSS styles to modify the existing tags. You'll start by redefining the existing <h1> HTML tag.

To modify an existing HTML tag:

1. If you took a break after the last session, make sure **Dreamweaver** is running and the **NewCatalyst** site is open.

2. Open the **bands.htm** page in a Document window.

3. Click the **Expand** arrow ▷ on the Design panel group to open the Design panel group, and then click the **CSS Styles** tab. See Figure 3-26.

Figure 3-26	CSS STYLES PANEL

click to apply styles

click to edit styles

click to create a
new CSS style

4. Click the **New CSS Style** button in the lower right corner of the CSS Styles panel. The New CSS Style dialog box opens. See Figure 3-27.

Figure 3-27	NEW CSS STYLE DIALOG BOX

click to change Name
text box to Tag text box

5. Click the **Redefine HTML Tag** option button in the Type section. A list of tags is now available in the Tag list at the top of the dialog box.

6. Click the **Tag** list arrow, scroll down, and then click **h1**. This specifies that you'll modify the <h1> tag.

7. Click the **This Document Only** option button, if necessary. This creates an internal style sheet.

8. Click the **OK** button. The CSS Style definition for h1 dialog box opens.

9. Click **Type** in the Category list box, if necessary.

10. Click the **Font** list arrow, and then click **Arial, Helvetica, sans-serif**.

11. Click in the Size text box, type **50**, and then, if necessary, click the right **Size** list arrow, and then click **pixels**.

12. Click the **Weight** list arrow, and then click **normal**.

13. Click the **Case** list arrow, and then click **uppercase**.

14. Click in the **Color** text box, type **#FF9900**, and then press the **Tab** key. See Figure 3-28.

Figure 3-28   **COMPLETED CSS STYLE DEFINITION FOR H1 DIALOG BOX**

15. Click the **OK** button.

You don't see any changes to the look of the existing bands page because there are no styles applied to the content.

Modified HTML tags are not listed in the CSS panel list because there is no need for a special list. For example, Dreamweaver applies the paragraph tag whenever you press the Enter key. If you modify the paragraph tag, Dreamweaver will automatically insert the new formatting anywhere a paragraph tag is found in the Web page. The redefined HTML tag is applied in the same way that the tag would normally be applied.

If you do not remove any previously applied formatting, including font tags and so forth, before applying a CSS style, the content might display incorrectly in the user's browser. For example, the older formatting might override the CSS style you applied or, in some cases, it might combine with the CSS style, causing the text to display differently than you had intended.

To remove formatting and apply a modified HTML tag:

1. Select all of the text on the bands page.

2. Click the **HTML Styles** tab in the Design panel group, and then click the **Auto Apply** checkbox to check it, if necessary.

3. Click **Clear Selection Style** in the HTML Styles panel, and then click **Clear Paragraph Style** in the HTML Styles panel to clear all of the HTML Styles from the text.

    Now you need to make the link text right-aligned again.

4. Select the link text in the Document window, and then click the **Align Right** button ≡ in the Property inspector.

5. Select **CATALYST BANDS** in the Document window.

6. Click the **Format** list arrow, and then click **Heading 1**. The h1 tag that you modified in the New CSS Style dialog box is applied to the selected text. The list of tags in the Format list is also available in CSS mode in the Property inspector. This is because designers frequently start designing by redefining the HTML tags that are most commonly used, and then they use CSS for the rest of the styles. They use these HTML tags in conjunction with the custom style classes that they create.

7. Save the page.

8. Preview the page in a browser. See Figure 3-29.

Figure 3-29	CATALYST - BANDS PAGE IN BROWSER

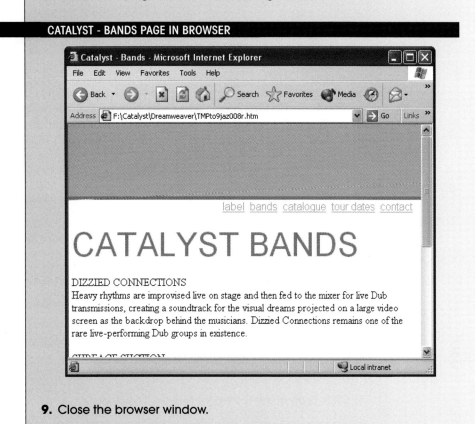

9. Close the browser window.

Creating and Applying Custom Style Classes

Modifying text attributes is not limited to the redefinition of existing HTML tags. You can also create custom style classes, which are styles you build from scratch and give a unique name. The process for creating a custom style class is similar to redefining an HTML tag, except that you name the style and specify all the attributes you want the style to include. Some designers prefer to create custom style classes instead of redefining existing tags (like the heading tags) so they can use a descriptive and meaningful name for each style. This is especially helpful for sites that have many heading styles. Custom style classes appear in the CSS Styles panel and in the Property inspector when it is in CSS mode, and they can be applied to any selected text.

Creating a Custom Style Class
- Click the CSS Styles tab in the Design panel group.
- Click the New CSS Style button in the CSS Styles panel to open the New CSS Style dialog box.
- Click the Make Custom Style (class) option button.
- Select all of the text in the Name list box, and then type the name of the new custom style class.
- Click the appropriate Define In option button.
- Click the OK button to open the CSS Style definition dialog box.
- Click a category in the Category list, and then set the options you want.
- Click the OK button.

You'll create a custom style class for the subheadings on the Catalyst - Bands page. You'll name the style .CatalystSubHeadings. By convention, the name of a custom style class always begins with a period, has no spaces, and cannot contain any special characters. (If you forget to add the period, Dreamwaever will add it for you.) In addition to a font, size, and color, you'll include a background color.

To create a custom style class:

1. Click the **CSS Styles** tab in the Design panel group, and then click the **New CSS Style** button in the CSS Styles panel. The New CSS Style dialog box opens.

2. Click the **Make Custom Style (class)** option button in the Type category.

3. Select all of the text in the Name text box, and then type **.CatalystSubHeadings** (including the period before the name).

4. Click the **This Document Only** option button in the Define In section, if necessary, and then click the **OK** button. The CSS Style definition for .CatalystSubHeadings dialog box opens.

5. Click **Type** in the Category list box, if necessary.

6. Change the font to **Arial, Helvetica, sans-serif**, change the size to **24 pixels**, change the case to **uppercase**, and then type **#FF9900** in the Color text box. You need to change the category so you can add the background color.

7. Click **Background** in the Category list box.

8. Click in the **Background Color** text box, type **#FFCC00**, and then click the **OK** button. The name of the new style appears in the CSS Styles panel.

Once you create a custom style class, you need to apply it to the text you want to format. You apply a custom style class to selected text from the CSS Style panel or from the Property inspector when it is in CSS mode. You'll apply the .CatalystSubHeadings style to all the band names on the bands page.

To apply a custom style class:

1. Select **DIZZIED CONNECTIONS** in the bands page Document window.

2. Click **CatalystSubHeadings** in the CSS Styles panel. The style is applied to the selected band name.

   You want to apply the custom style to the rest of the band names on the page.

3. Apply the style to the other band names on the page: **SURFACE SUCTION**, **SLOTH CHILD**, and **LIFE IN MINOR CHORDS**.

4. Scroll back up to the top of the page. See Figure 3-30.

Figure 3-30	CUSTOM STYLE CLASS APPLIED TO BAND NAMES

formatted band names

5. Save the page, and then preview the page in a browser.

6. Close the browser.

You can also create CSS styles to format the text links for the site.

Using the CSS Selector

Using CSS styles to customize the appearance of text links provides you with greater control over the way text links will look. Think about a Web site where the text links were not underlined text, but instead were distinguished by specific colors and fonts, and when you positioned the pointer over a link, the link changed color. You cannot achieve this look using HTML styles, modified HTML tags, or custom style classes; instead you need to use the CSS Selector. When you use the CSS Selector, you redefine the formatting for a group of tags or for tags containing a specific id attribute. To do this, you create a CSS style for each part of a tag. For example, the anchor tag <a> is broken into four parts: a:link, a:hover, a:active, and a:visited. Each of these controls a portion of the hyperlink functionality of the anchor tag. The a:link portion of the tag controls the way the link text looks before the link has been visited. The a:hover portion of the tag controls the way the link text looks while the pointer is over the text. (The a:hover portion of the tag is not supported by Netscape version 4.) The a:active portion of the tag controls the way the link text looks while it is being clicked. (The a:active portion of the tag is buggy in Internet Explorer on Windows.

Sometimes it will stay active until you click another link.) The a:visited portion of the tag controls the way the linked text looks after the link has been visited. You can use the CSS Selector to modify each part of the anchor tag in the same way you would use Modify HTML tag to modify a regular tag.

REFERENCE   WINDOW   **RW**

<u>Customizing the Appearance of Hyperlinks Using the CSS Selector</u>
- Click the CSS Styles panel in the Design panel group.
- Click the Edit Styles option button in the CSS Styles panel, and then click the New CSS Style button in the CSS Styles panel to open the New CSS Style dialog box.
- Click the Use CSS Selector option button.
- Click the Selector list arrow, then click the selector you want to modify.
- Click the appropriate Define In option button.
- Click the OK button to open the CSS Style definition dialog box.
- Click a category in the Category list, and then set the options you want.
- Click the OK button.

When you define the parts of the anchor tag, you must define them in the order in which they appear in the CSS Selector drop-down list. You must place a:hover after the a:link and a:visited styles, or they will hide the color property of the a:hover style. Similarly, you must place the a:active style after the a:hover style or the a:active color property will apply when the user both activates and hovers over the linked text. You can view the styles in the order that you apply them by selecting Edit Styles view in the CSS Styles panel.

You'll customize the appearance of the text links in the bands page of the NewCatalyst site using the CSS Selector to create a style for the a:link, a:hover, and a:visited parts of the anchor tag.

To customize the appearance of hyperlinks using the CSS Selector:

1. Click the **Edit Styles** option button in the CSS Styles panel, and then click the **New CSS Style** button ⊞ in the CSS Styles panel. The New CSS Style dialog box opens.

2. Click the **Use CSS Selector** option button in the Type section, click the **Selector** list arrow, click **a:link**, click the **This Document Only** option button in the Define In category, if necessary, and then click the **OK** button. The CSS Style definition for a:link dialog box opens.

3. Click **Type** in the Category list box, if necessary, and then select **Arial, Helvetica, sans-serif** from the Font list, type **#FF9900** in the Color text box, click the **none** checkbox in the Decoration section to check it, and then click the **OK** button. The a:link is customized for the Catalyst site, and is added to the CSS Styles list in Edit view in the CSS Styles panel. See Figure 3-31.

Figure 3-31   **CSS STYLES PANEL IN EDIT STYLES VIEW**

You'll repeat this process for a:visited and a:hover.

4. Click ⬆ in the CSS Styles panel to open the New CSS Style dialog box.

5. Make sure the **Use CSS Selector** option button is selected, select **a:visited** from the Selector list, make sure the **This Document Only** option button is selected, and then click the **OK** button. The CSS Style definition for a:visited dialog box opens.

6. Click **Type** in the Category list box, if necessary, select **Arial, Helvetica, sans-serif** from the Font list, type **#FF9900** in the Color text box, click the **none** checkbox in the Decoration section to check it, and then click the **OK** button. The a:visited portion of the tag is customized.

Next, you'll customize the a:hover portion of the tag.

7. Click ⬆ in the CSS Styles panel.

8. Make sure the **Use CSS Selector** option button is selected, select **a:hover** from the Selector list, make sure the **This Document Only** option button is selected, and then click the **OK** button.

9. Click **Type** from the Category list box, if necessary, select **Arial, Helvetica, sans-serif** in the Font list, type **#FF6600** in the Color text box, click the **underline** checkbox in the Decoration section to check it, and then click the **OK** button.

10. Save the page.

You'll preview the bands page in a browser so you can try the links. The links on the other pages in the Catalyst site will not be modified, because you have changed the links only for the Bands page.

To preview the customized text links in a browser:

1. Preview the **bands** page in a browser. The custom a:link style is visible.

2. Point to the **catalogue** link. The hover style is visible. See Figure 3-32.

Figure 3-32   **CUSTOMIZED HYPERLINKS IN BROWSER**

custom hover style

custom link style

3. Click the **catalogue** link. The Catalyst - Catalogue page opens in the browser.

4. Click the **bands** link on the Catalogue page. The Catalyst - Bands page reloads.

5. Close the browser, and then close the **bands** page.

So far, you have created CSS styles in the bands page using the modify HTML tag, custom style, and CSS Selector methods. In the next session, you will create CSS styles in an external style sheet and learn to attach the external style sheet to the pages of your site.

Session 3.2 QUICK CHECK

1. A rule that defines the appearance of an element in a Web page by redefining an existing HTML tag or by creating a custom style is a _____.

2. When you redefine a CSS style after it has been applied, does the content to which the style has been applied update as well?

3. A CSS style that you create from scratch is called a _____.

4. Can you save CSS styles in a style sheet that can be applied to all of the pages in a site?

5. How does modifying an HTML tag make it more useful?

6. Why do some designers prefer to create custom style classes instead of redefining existing HTML tags?

7. What do custom style class names start with?

<table>
<tr><td>**SESSION
3.3**</td><td>In this session, you will create a CSS style in an external style sheet. You will export a style that was created within a Web page to an external style sheet and attach an external style sheet to Web pages. Finally, you will edit an existing style, examine CSS styles in Code and Design views, and upload your modified site to the Web server.</td></tr>
</table>

Using External Style Sheets

Having all the styles for a Web site located in one place is one of the greatest advantages of using CSS. Using an external style sheet enables you to separate the style of your Web site from the content of your Web site, thus enabling you to make site-wide stylistic changes by updating a single file. So far, you have created and used styles within one document, or page, of the Catalyst site. To use the styles you created throughout a site, they must be located in an **external style sheet**, a file that contains the CSS styles defined for a Web site. This file has the file extension .css. You can have as many external style sheets as you would like for your site, but it is usually easier to incorporate all of your styles in one external style sheet. You can either create a style in an external style sheet or you can export the styles you created within a Web page to an external style sheet.

Exporting Styles to an External Style Sheet

If you've already created styles in a specific document, you can export those styles to an external style sheet rather than re-create them. This enables you to use those styles throughout the Web site. To keep the files in a Web site organized, you will create a folder named "Stylesheets" in the local root directory of the Web site, and then save the external style sheet file with a descriptive name, such as "CatalystStyles," within the Stylesheets folder. In order to export CSS styles to an external style sheet, the Web page where the styles are currently located must be open.

REFERENCE WINDOW   **RW**

Exporting Styles to an External Style Sheet
- Open the Web page whose styles you want to export.
- Click File on the main menu bar, point to Export, and then click CSS styles to open the Export Styles As CSS File dialog box.
- Navigate to the folder in which you are saving your style sheets in the local root folder.
- Type a name for the style sheet in the File name text box.
- Click the Save button.

Because you want to use the styles you created for the bands page on all the other pages in the Web site, you'll export those styles to an external style sheet. In this case, you will create the style sheet when you export the files from the bands page.

To export styles to an external style sheet:

1. If you took a break after the last session, make sure **Dreamweaver** is running and the **NewCatalyst** site is open.

2. Open the **bands.htm** page in the Document window.

3. Make sure **bands.htm** is selected in the Site panel, click **File** on the main menu bar, point to **Export**, and then click **CSS Styles**. The Export Styles As CSS File dialog box opens.

You need to create a new folder in which to store the external style sheet.

4. Verify that the Save in box is open to the local root folder of your NewCatalyst Web site (the Dreamweaver folder).

5. Click the **Create New Folder** button 📝 on the dialog box toolbar, type **Stylesheets**, and then press the **Enter** key. The Stylesheets folder is created within the local root of the NewCatalyst Web site.

6. Double-click the **Stylesheets** folder. You want to save the external style sheet in this folder.

Next, you'll name the external style sheet with a descriptive name.

7. Click in the **File name** text box and then type **CatalystStyles**. See Figure 3-33.

Figure 3-33	EXPORT STYLES AS CSS FILE DIALOG BOX

current folder

enter style sheet name

style sheet files have the .css file extension

8. Click the **Save** button. The external style sheet file is saved within the folder you created.

9. Click the **Refresh** button ↻ on the Site panel toolbar to refresh the file list, and then click the **Plus (+)** button beside the Stylesheets folder to view the CatalystStyles.css file in the file list. See Figure 3-34.

Figure 3-34	STYLE SHEET IN LOCAL FILE LIST

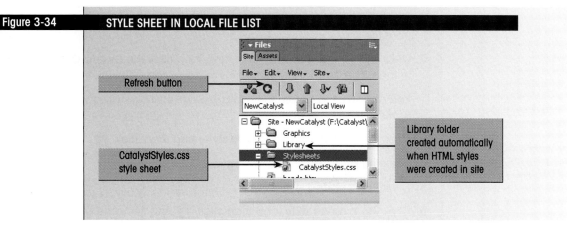

Once you have exported styles, you should remove them from the document.

Deleting Styles from a Style Sheet

You must delete styles that you have created within a document after you export those styles to an external style sheet. Otherwise, you will end up with multiple sets of styles with the same names, which can cause confusion. Further, if you use both sets of styles, this can negate some of the benefits of using style sheets because it prevents you from having one centralized set of styles that is easily updated and used throughout the site. When you delete the styles from your page, the text will return to its original formatting. You can also delete a style if you are not going to use it in the site. Deleting styles that you are not using in a site helps to keep the site's files organized and lean. External style sheets are uploaded to the Web server along with the Web pages, graphics, and other files associated with the site. By deleting unused styles, you are eliminating unnecessary materials from the site, reducing the size of the files and eliminating clutter.

Because you exported the styles from the bands page to the external style sheet, you can delete the styles located within the bands page.

To delete a style from within a document:

1. Click the **Edit Styles** option button at the top of the CSS Styles panel, if necessary. The CSS Styles panel displays a list of the styles created within the bands page. (You will not see the external style sheet in this panel until you attach the external style sheet to the page.) See Figure 3-35.

Figure 3-35	CSS STYLES ON BANDS PAGE

You want to delete the h1 style, which you copied to the external style sheet, from the list.

2. Click **h1** in the CSS Styles panel, and then click the **Delete CSS Style** button 🗑 in the CSS Styles panel. The style is removed from the list.

You also want to delete the .CatalystSubHeading style and the three anchor styles you created earlier.

3. Click the **.CatalystSubHeading** style, and then click 🗑.

4. Click the **a:link** style, and then click 🗑.

5. Click the **a:visited** style, and then click 🗑.

6. Click the **a:hover** style, and then click 🗑. The filename of the open page, bands.htm, followed by the words "(no styles defined)" appear in the CSS Styles panel, and the formatting of the text in the bands page is removed.

7. Save the **bands** page.

Next, you'll attach the external style sheet to the bands page.

Attaching a Style Sheet to Pages

When the styles for formatting a Web site are located in an external style sheet, you must attach each Web page that you want to format with those styles to the style sheet. You can attach the style sheet to each Web page when you create your pages (if the style sheet has already been created), or you can attach the style sheet to each page when you need the styles to format text. If the styles in the external style sheet were exported from a page in your Web site, the styles will be automatically applied to that page when the external style sheet is attached to the page.

The process for applying a CSS style saved in an external style sheet to the rest of the pages in your site is the same as the process for applying CSS styles created within a document. If the style is a custom style, you select the text to which you want to apply the style, and then click the style in the CSS Styles panel. If the style is a modified HTML tag or a CSS Selector, you apply the tag in the regular way and the modified attributes of the tag will be included. To attach an external style sheet to a Web page, you must open the page in a Document window, click the Attach Style Sheet button in the CSS Styles panel, and then choose the desired style sheet. Before you attach the style sheet, you need to remove the current formatting; otherwise, the older formatting might override the CSS style you apply or it might combine with the CSS style, causing the text to display differently than you had intended.

REFERENCE WINDOW	RW

Attaching an External Style Sheet to a Web Page
- Open the CSS Styles panel in the Design panel group.
- Click the Apply Styles option button.
- Click the Attach Style Sheet button to open the Link External Style Sheet dialog box.
- Click the Browse button, navigate to the folder within the local root folder that contains the style sheets, click the name of the style sheet you want to attach to the Web page, and then click the OK button.
- Click the Link option button.
- Click the OK button.

You'll attach the CatalystStyles style sheet to all of the pages in the NewCatalyst Web site, starting with the bands page.

To attach an external style sheet to a Web page:

1. Click the **Apply Styles** option button in the CSS Styles panel, and then click the **Attach Style Sheet** button at the bottom of the CSS Styles panel. The Link External Style Sheet dialog box opens.

2. Click the **Browse** button, double-click the **Stylesheets** folder in the local root folder of your NewCatalyst site, click **CatalystStyles.css**, and then click the **OK** button to select the external style sheet you want to attach to the page.

3. Click the **Link** option button, if necessary, and then click the **OK** button. When a custom style is located in an external style sheet, appears before it in the CSS Styles panel in the Apply Styles view. See Figure 3-36.

| Figure 3-36 | CSS STYLES PANEL AFTER ATTACHING CATALYSTSTYLES.CSS |

The external style sheet is attached, and the styles in the external style sheet are applied to the content on the bands page.

4. Save and close the page.

You will remove the old formatting from the text in the other pages of the site, and then attach the CatalystStyles external style sheet to the rest of the pages in the Catalyst Web site.

To attach the rest of the Web pages to the external style sheet:

1. Open the **catalogue.htm** page in a Document window, click **Edit** on the main menu bar, click **Select All**, and then click the **Toggle CSS/HTML Mode** button in the Property inspector to toggle to HTML mode, if necessary.

2. Click the **Size** list arrow in the Property inspector, click **None**, click the **Font** list arrow, and then click **Default Font** to remove the previous formatting from the text.

3. Click the **Attach Style Sheet** button in the CSS Styles panel. The Link External Style Sheet dialog box opens.

4. Click the **Browse** button, make sure the **Stylesheets** folder in the local root folder of the NewCatalyst site is the current folder, click **CatalystStyles.css**, click the **OK** button, make sure the **Link** option button is selected, and then click the **OK** button in the Link External Style Sheet dialog box. The modified selectors are applied to the hyperlinked text on the page.

5. Save the page, and then preview the page in a browser to view the hyperlink styles.

6. Close the browser, and then close the page.

7. Repeat Steps 1 through 6 for the **index.htm** page, the **label.htm** page, and the **tourdates.htm** page.

   On the contact.htm page, you need to remove the current formatting from all of the text on the page before attaching the external style sheet.

8. Open the **contact.htm** page, drag to select all of the text on the page, including the link text, click the **HTML Styles** panel, make sure the **Apply** checkbox is checked, click **Clear Selection Style**, and then click **Clear Paragraph Style**.

9. Select the link text, and then click the **Align Right** button ≣ in the Property inspector.

10. Click the **CSS Styles** panel, and then attach the **CatalystStyles.css** style sheet, stored in the **Stylesheets** folder in the local root folder, to the contact page.

11. Select the page heading, **CATALYST CONTACT**, in the Document window, click the **Format** list arrow in the Property inspector, and then click **Heading 1** to apply the modified h1 tag.

12. Select **Contact** in the Document window (not the contact link), click the **Toggle CSS/HTML Mode** button 🅰 in the Property inspector, click the **CSS Styles** list arrow (the list box currently says No CSS Style), and then click **CatalystSubHeadings**.

13. Select **Directions** in the Document window, click the **CSS Styles** list arrow in the Property inspector, click **CatalystSubHeadings**, and then click in the selected line of text. See Figure 3-37.

| Figure 3-37 | CONTACT PAGE WITH EXTERNAL STYLE SHEET ATTACHED |

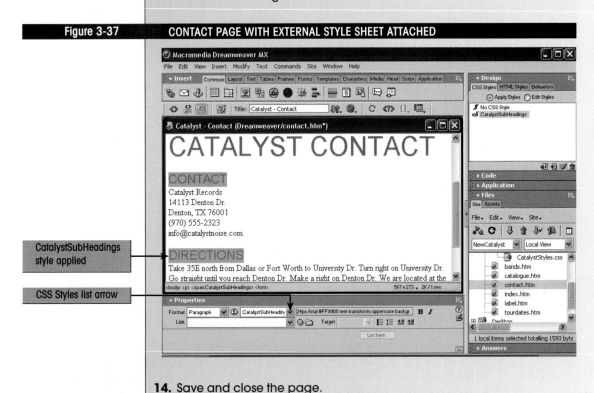

14. Save and close the page.

The same external style sheet is now attached to all the pages in the Web site, and the existing text has been formatted.

Creating a Style in an External Style Sheet

Once an external style sheet is created, you can add new styles to it at any time. Just choose the style sheet by name when you create the new style.

REFERENCE WINDOW   **RW**

Defining a Style in an External Style Sheet
- Open the CSS Styles panel in the Design panel group.
- Click the New CSS Style button in the CSS Styles panel to open the New CSS Style dialog box.
- Click the Make Custom Style (class) option button.
- Click the Name list arrow, and then type a name for the new style in the Name list box.
- Click the appropriate Define In option button.
- Click the OK button to open the CSS Style definition dialog box.
- Click a category in the Category list, and then set the options you want.
- Click the OK button.

You need to create a style for the copyright information that will appear at the bottom of each page. Because this style will be used on each page in the NewCatalyst Web site, you'll define the new style in the CatalystStyles.css external style sheet.

To define a style in an external style sheet:

1. Open the **bands** page in a Document window.

2. Click the **New CSS Style** button ⊞ in the CSS Style panel.

3. Click the **Make Custom Style (class)** option button, if necessary, select any text in the **Name** text box, and then type **.CatalystFooter**.

4. Click the top **Define In** option button, make sure **CatalystStyles.css** is listed in the Define In list box, and then click the **OK** button to open the CSS Style Definition for .CatalystFooter in CatalystStyles.css dialog box.

5. Click **Type** in the Category list, if necessary, set the font to **Arial, Helvetica, sans-serif**, set the size to **10 pixels**, and then type **#000000** in the Color text box.

6. Click **Block** in the Category list.

7. Click the **Text Align** list arrow, and then click **center**.

8. Click the **OK** button. The CatalystFooter style appears in the CSS Styles panel. See Figure 3-38.

Figure 3-38   **CSS STYLES PANEL WITH NEW STYLE ADDED**

new CSS style
in style list

You'll add copyright text to the bands page, and then apply the CatalystFooter style to it.

To add text and apply an external style:

1. Press the **Ctrl+End** keys to move the insertion point to the end of the text on the bands page, and then press the **Enter** key twice. This is the location where you'll type the copyright information.

2. Click the **Characters** tab on the Insert bar, and then click the **Copyright** button ⓒ. The copyright symbol © is inserted at the beginning of the line.

3. Press the **Right Arrow** key to deselect the copyright symbol, press the **Spacebar**, and then type **copyright Catalyst, Inc. 2004**.

   Next, you'll apply the CatalystFooter style to the copyright line.

4. Select the copyright symbol and text, click **CatalystFooter** in the CSS Styles panel, and then click anywhere in the Document window to deselect the text. The style is applied to the text. See Figure 3-39.

Figure 3-39   **CATALYSTFOOTER CSS STYLE APPLIED**

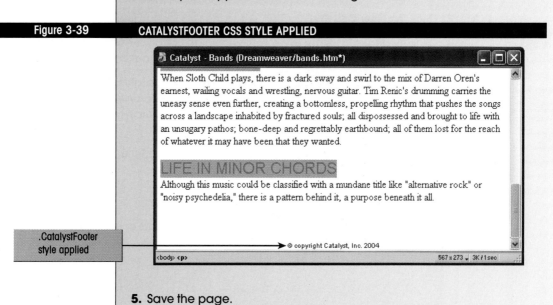

.CatalystFooter
style applied

5. Save the page.

Next, you will redefine an existing HTML tag—the paragraph tag—and add that style to the CatalystStyle style sheet. You can use this modified tag to customize the attributes of the body text for your Web pages. Dreamweaver will automatically add the customized attributes to all the text in the site that is surrounded by paragraph tags.

Brian asks you to modify the paragraph tag to include a font attribute.

To create a CSS style in an existing external style sheet:

1. Click the **New CSS Style** button in the CSS Style panel.

2. Click the **Redefine HTML Tag** option button, click the **Tag** list arrow, click **p**, make sure the top **Define In** option button is selected and **CatalystStyles.css** is listed in the Define In list box, and then click the **OK** button to open the CSS Style Definition for p in CatalystStyles.css dialog box.

3. Click **Type** in the Category list, if necessary, change the font to **Arial, Helvetica, sans-serif**, and then click the **OK** button. The body text in the bands page changes to Arial, Helvetica, sans-serif. See Figure 3-40.

Figure 3-40	BANDS PAGE WITH MODIFIED PARAGRAPH TAG APPLIED

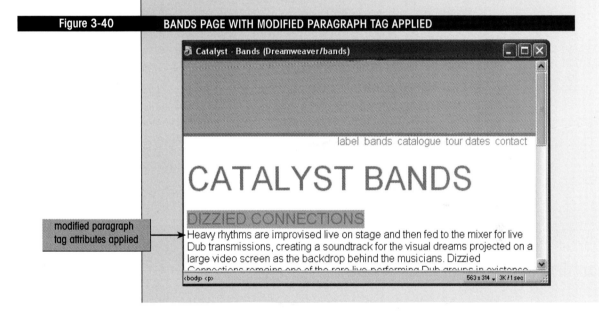

modified paragraph tag attributes applied

Editing CSS Styles

One of the most powerful aspects of Cascading Style Sheets is the ability to edit styles. You edit a style by adding or removing formatting from an existing style. When you edit a style, any element to which the style is applied is updated automatically to reflect the changes you made. This helps you to maintain a consistent look throughout a Web site, whether it includes a few pages or many. It also enables you to control the look of an entire Web site from one centralized set of specifications.

REFERENCE WINDOW   **RW**

Editing a Style
- Open the CSS Styles panel in the Design panel group.
- Click the Edit Styles option button in the CSS Styles panel.
- Double-click the name of the style you want to modify to open the CSS Style Definition dialog box.
- Make the desired changes.
- Click the OK button.

After reviewing the site, Brian asks you to edit the CatalystSubHeadings style to remove the background color.

To edit a style:

1. Click the **Edit Styles** option button in the CSS Styles panel. The list of styles appears in the CSS Styles panel.

2. Double-click the **.CatalystSubHeadings** style to open the CSS Style Definition for .CatalystSubHeadings in CatalystStyles.css dialog box. (You can also right-click the style name, and then click Edit on the context menu.)

3. Click **Background** in the Category list, select the text in the **Background Color** text box, press the **Delete** key, and then click the **OK** button. The background color is removed from every subheading to which the style was applied.

4. Preview the page in a browser.

5. Close the browser.

6. Click the **Collapse arrow** [icon] in the Design panel group, and then close the page.

Examining Code for CSS Styles

As you created and applied CSS styles to format the text on the pages of the NewCatalyst Web site, Dreamweaver added the appropriate HTML code within the head of each page. The **head** of a Web page is the portion of the HTML between the head tags. The actual code included within the head differs based on whether you created an internal style sheet or an external style sheet.

When you create styles that apply only to the document in which you are working, the code for those styles is placed in the head of that page. If you attach a Web page to an external style sheet, a link tag to the style sheet is placed in the head portion of the HTML code for that page. The link tag allows the Web page to access the content of the external style sheet. You will examine the HTML code in the head of the bands page, as well as the additional tags that appear throughout the Web page.

Viewing Code for Internal Style Sheets

When styles are defined in the current document only, the code is in an internal style sheet, which is also called an **embedded style sheet** because the styles are embedded (or placed) in the head of the Web page. The embedded styles can be used throughout the current Web page, but not on any other page. The code usually takes the format:

```
<style type="text/css">

<!--

name {attribute-name: attribute value; attribute2-name:
attribute2 value}

-->

</style>
```

where **name** is the style name, the HTML tag name, or the tag and selector name.

The style definitions all appear inside the style tags, which are in the format:

```
<style type="text/css">style definitions</style>
```

where type="text/css" indicates the format of the style that will follow. Currently "text/css" is the only style type; however, the current HTML guidelines recommend that you include the style type to prevent problems if other style types are introduced in the future.

Nested within the style tag is the **comment tag**, which is in the format:

```
<!-- style definitions -->
```

Comment tags hide the style definitions from older browsers that do not support CSS. Browsers tend to ignore tags that they do not understand. Browsers that do not understand CSS style tags will ignore the tags, but the content of the style tag (the style definitions) will be displayed in the Web page as text. To avoid this problem, comment tags are placed around the style definitions to prevent older browsers from displaying them in the Web page.

The format for the style definition is:

```
style name {attribute-name: attribute value; attribute2-name:
                  attribute2 value}
```

You can tell by the style name whether the style is a custom style, a redefined tag, or a tag created using the CSS selector. When a custom style class is created, a period precedes the name of the new style (for example, .CatalystFooter). If an existing tag is redefined, the tag name appears at the beginning of the style (for example, h1). If you use the CSS Selector, the tag name is followed by a colon and the customized tag (for example, a:active) appears at the beginning of the style definition. The style definition is a series of attributes: values separated by semicolons and surrounded by brackets. Styles follow this same format whether they are embedded within a page or located within an external style sheet.

You can view the embedded style sheet for a page by opening the page in a Document window and switching to Code view. Figure 3-41 shows the code for the styles that were embedded in the bands page of the NewCatalyst Web site before they were exported to an external style sheet and deleted from the page.

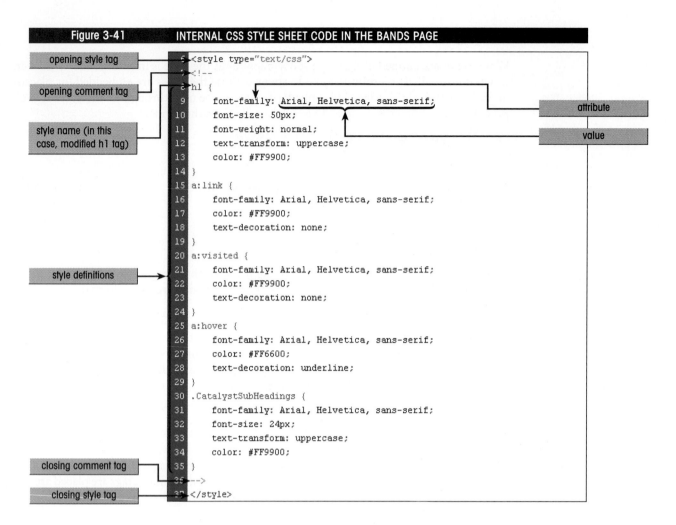

Figure 3-41   INTERNAL CSS STYLE SHEET CODE IN THE BANDS PAGE

opening style tag

opening comment tag

style name (in this case, modified h1 tag)

attribute

value

style definitions

closing comment tag

closing style tag

```
 5  <style type="text/css">
 7  <!--
 8  h1 {
 9      font-family: Arial, Helvetica, sans-serif;
10      font-size: 50px;
11      font-weight: normal;
12      text-transform: uppercase;
13      color: #FF9900;
14  }
15  a:link {
16      font-family: Arial, Helvetica, sans-serif;
17      color: #FF9900;
18      text-decoration: none;
19  }
20  a:visited {
21      font-family: Arial, Helvetica, sans-serif;
22      color: #FF9900;
23      text-decoration: none;
24  }
25  a:hover {
26      font-family: Arial, Helvetica, sans-serif;
27      color: #FF6600;
28      text-decoration: underline;
29  }
30  .CatalystSubHeadings {
31      font-family: Arial, Helvetica, sans-serif;
32      font-size: 24px;
33      text-transform: uppercase;
34      color: #FF9900;
35  }
36  -->
37  </style>
```

Viewing Code for External Style Sheets

An external style sheet can be used in any Web page that contains a link to the style sheet in its head. External style sheets are also called linked style sheets. When an external style sheet is attached to a page, a link tag appears within the head of the Web page. These link tags do not include a closing tag or any style content information; they only convey relationship information about the linked document. Link tags can appear only within the head of a Web page.

Link tags appear in the following general format:

```
<link rel="stylesheet" href="stylesheeturl.css" type="text/css">
```

The first part of the tag, link, identifies the type of tag. The second part of the tag, rel=, indicates the relationship between the linked document and the Web page. The relationship itself appears within quotation marks; in this case, the relationship is "stylesheet," meaning that the linked document contains the style information used to format the text in the original document. Next, href="stylesheeturl.css" is the URL of the linked document. The URL appears within quotation marks. Finally, type= indicates that will follow. MIME type is the standard for indentifying content type on the Internet. The type also appears within quotation marks.

You'll look at the link to the external style sheet on the bands page.

To view the code in the bands page:

1. Open the **bands** page in a Document window.

2. Click the **Show Code View** button on the Document toolbar, and then scroll to the top of the bands page in the Document window.

3. Locate the link tag in the head of the bands page. See Figure 3-42.

Figure 3-42 **BANDS PAGE WITH EXTERNAL STYLE SHEET ATTACHED**

link tag to the external style sheet CatalystStyles

Next, you will view style tags.

Viewing Style Tags

When you use CSS styles to modify or customize HTML tags, you will not see any additional code in the body of your Web pages. The existing tags simply reference the new definitions, which are located either in the head portion of the Web page or in an external style sheet.

When you select text and apply a custom style class, Dreamweaver adds the attributes of that custom style class to the text by inserting additional code within the Web page in one of three ways:

■ **Adding attributes to an existing tag.** When you apply a custom style class to text that is already surrounded by a tag, Dreamweaver adds the additional attributes of the custom style class to the existing tag. For example, if you apply a custom style class named "ClassName" to a block of text that is already surrounded by a paragraph tag, Dreamweaver adds the attributes of the custom style to that paragraph tag in the following manner:

```
<p class="ClassName">Content of text block</p>
```

where class="ClassName" tells the browser to format the text according to the definition in the custom style class named "ClassName." (The custom style class definition will be located either in the head of the Web page or in an external style sheet.)

■ **Applying a custom style class to a block of text.** When you apply a custom style class to a block of text that is not already encompassed by a tag, Dreamweaver surrounds the entire block of text with the div tag that inserts the custom style attributes. The div tag appears in the general format

`<div class="ClassName">Content of text block</div>`

■ **Applying a custom style class to a text selection.** When you apply a custom style class to a selection smaller than a text block (such as a word, a phrase, or a portion of a text block), Dreamweaver surrounds the selection with a span tag that inserts the custom style attributes. The span tag appears in the following general format:

`<span class="ClassName">Content of text selection</span>`

You will view the subheadings and footer on the bands page in Code and Design views to examine the code that Dreamweaver inserted into the page.

To examine the bands page in Code and Design views:

1. Click the **Show Code and Design Views** button ⌖ on the Document toolbar, and then select **DIZZIED CONNECTIONS** in the Design pane.

2. Examine the code in the Code pane. The custom style class information was inserted with a span tag. See Figure 3-43.

Figure 3-43	BANDS PAGE WITH A SUBHEADING SELECTED AND CODE REVEALED

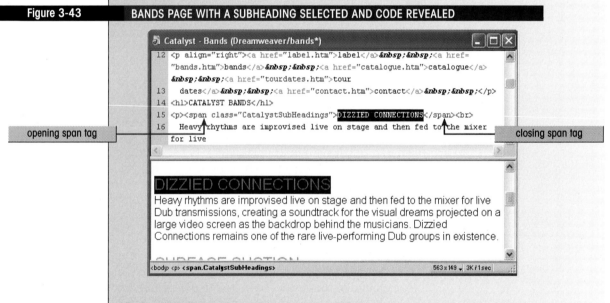

3. Scroll to the bottom of the page in the Design pane, select the footer text, and then examine the code in the Code pane. The custom style class information is inserted into the paragraph tag. See Figure 3-44.

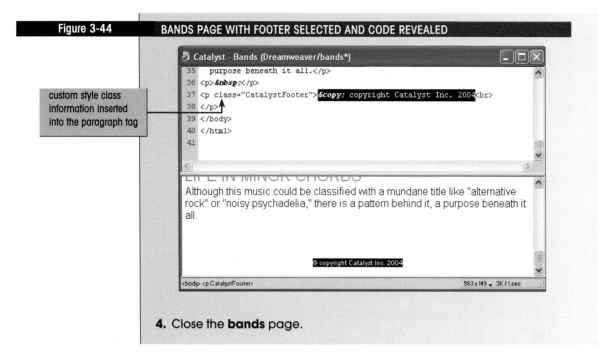

Figure 3-44 **BANDS PAGE WITH FOOTER SELECTED AND CODE REVEALED**

custom style class
information inserted
into the paragraph tag

4. Close the **bands** page.

As a final step, you'll post the updated files for the Catalyst Web site to your remote location.

Updating a Web Site on a Remote Server

As a final review of the text you added to the NewCatalyst Web site, you'll update the files on the remote server. Because you have uploaded the entire site, you need only to upload the files that you have changed to update the remote site. This includes the bands.htm page, the catalogue.htm page, the contact.htm page, the index.htm page, the label.htm page, the tourdates.htm page, and the external style sheet located in the Stylesheets folder. You will upload the modified pages and new dependent files in the NewCatalyst site to the remote server. Then you'll preview the site on the Web.

REFERENCE WINDOW **RW**

Uploading a Site to the Remote Server
- Click the Connects to remote host button on the Site panel toolbar.
- Click the View list arrow on the Site panel toolbar, and then click Local View.
- Press and hold the Ctrl key, and then click all of the files and folders on the local site that have been modified or added.
- Click the Put File(s) button on the Site panel toolbar.
- Click the No button in the dialog box that opens asking if you want to include dependent files.
- Click the View list arrow on the Site panel toolbar, and then click Remote View.
- Click the Disconnects from remote host button on the Site panel toolbar.

To upload a site to the remote server:

1. Click the **Connects to remote host** button on the Site panel toolbar. Dreamweaver connects to the remote host.

2. Click the **View** list arrow on the Site panel toolbar, and then click **Local View**.

3. Click the **Stylesheets** folder in the Site panel, press and hold the **Shift** key, click **tourdates.htm**, and then click the **Put File(s)** button on the Site panel toolbar.

4. Click the **No** button when asked if you want to include dependent files. You already selected the new dependent file for the site when you selected the Stylesheets folder.

5. Click the **View** list arrow in the Site panel toolbar, and then click **Remote View**. A copy of the Stylesheets folder and the updated files appear in the remote file list in the Site panel.

6. Click the **Disconnects from remote host** button on the Site panel toolbar.

7. Exit **Dreamweaver**.

Next, you'll preview the updated site in a browser. The site will include all of the new styles and text that you added to your local version.

To preview the updated site in a browser:

1. Start your browser, type the URL of your remote site into the Address text box on the browser toolbar, and then press the **Enter** key.

2. Explore the remote site within the browser, clicking each of the links to make sure that the pages were successfully uploaded, and read the text on each of the pages.

3. Exit the browser.

Session 3.3 QUICK CHECK

1. What is the file extension for an external style sheet?

2. Can you apply CSS styles that you create in one Web page to text on another Web page in your site?

3. Why is it a good idea to delete unneeded styles from a style sheet?

4. Why do you need to remove the current formatting from text on a Web page before attaching an external style sheet?

5. Can you add new styles to an external style sheet?

6. What happens when you edit a CSS style?

7. Why is an internal style sheet also called an embedded style sheet?

8. Does a link tag have a closing tag?

REVIEW ASSIGNMENTS

Brian wants you to continue adding and formatting the text on the NewCatalyst Web site. First, you'll add text on the catalogue page and the label page. You'll use existing CSS styles and create new styles to format the text you added, including a third-tier subheading style.

1. Start Dreamweaver, open the NewCatalyst site that you modified in Tutorial 3, and display the CSS Styles panel. Switch to Local view, if necessary, and then open the catalogue.htm page in Design view in a Document window.

2. Start Word or another word processing program, and then open the Tutorial.03\ Review\Catalogue.doc document located on your Data Disk.

3. Select all the text in the Catalogue.doc document, copy all of the text to the Windows Clipboard, and then exit the word processor.

4. Place the insertion point below the link text in the catalogue page, left-align it if necessary, and then paste the text onto the page. (*Hint*: You might need to toggle the Property inspector mode to see the Align Left button.)

5. Select "Catalyst Catalogue," click the Format list arrow in the Property inspector, and then click Heading 1.

6. Select "CDs," and then select the CatalystSubHeadings style in the CSS Styles list in the Property inspector (the Property inspector must be in CSS mode) to apply the style to the selected text.

7. Select "VINYL," open the CSS Styles panel, click the Apply Styles option button, and then click the CatalystSubHeadings style in the CSS Styles panel to apply the style to the selected text.

Explore   8. Create a third-tier subheading CSS style to apply to the band names and CD titles. Click the New CSS Style button in the CSS Styles panel, click the Make Custom Style (class) Option button, type ".3rdTierSubHeadings" in the Name text box, click the top Define in Option button, select CatalystStyles.css in the Define In list, and then click the OK button.

Explore   9. In the CSS Style Definition dialog box, select Type in the Category list, change the font to Arial, Helvetica, sans-serif, change the size to 16 pixels, and change the color to #FF6600.

Explore   10. Click Background in the Category list, change the background color to #FFCC00, and then click the OK button.

Explore   11. In the Catalyst - Catalogue Document window, select "Dizzied Connections: Spinning Life," and then click 3rdTierSubHeadings in the CSS Styles panel to apply the style. (Make sure the Apply Styles option button is selected in the CSS Styles panel.)

Explore   12. Apply the 3rdTierSubHeadings style to the other band names and CD titles: "Surface Suction: Black Lab"; "Sloth Child: Them Apples"; and "life in minor chords: i believe in ferries."

13. Scroll to the bottom of the page, insert a blank line, click the Characters tab on the Insert bar, and then click the Copyright button to insert a copyright symbol into the page. Skip a space and type "copyright Catalyst, Inc. 2004".

14. Select the copyright line that you just typed, and apply the CatalystFooter style. (If you pick up HTML formatting, select the line of text and click the two Clear commands in the HTML Styles panel—making sure that the Apply checkbox is checked—before applying the CatalystFooter style.)

15. Save the page, preview the page in a browser, and then close the page.

16. Open the label.htm page in a Document window, move the insertion point below the link text, and then click the Align Left button in the Property inspector (in HTML mode), if necessary, to left-align it.

17. Start Word or another word processing program, open the Tutorial.03\Review\Label.doc document located on your Data Disk, select and copy the text, and then exit the word processor.

18. Paste the text into the label.htm page.

19. Apply the Heading 1 style to "CATALYST LABEL" using the Property inspector.

20. Apply the CatalystSubHeadings style from the CSS Styles panel to the following text: "News - HEY, look what they're saying!!!"; "Mission"; "History"; and "Employees."

Explore ▶ 21. Apply the 3rdTierSubHeadings style from the CSS Styles panel to the following employee names: Sara Lynn, Enya Allie, Mark Salza, and Brian Lee.

22. Scroll to the bottom of the page, insert a blank line, click the Characters tab on the Insert bar, and then click the copyright button to insert a copyright symbol into the page. Then skip a space and type "copyright Catalyst, Inc. 2004".

23. Select the copyright line you just inserted, apply the CatalystFooter style (first removing any HTML formatting, if necessary), and then close the Design panel group.

24. Click the Show Code and Design Views button on the Document toolbar and examine the code around the footer in the Code view portion of the window.

25. Select "Brian Lee" in the Design view portion of the page and examine the code around the 3rdTierSubHeading in the Code view portion of the window.

26. Save the label page, preview the page in a browser, and then close the page.

Explore ▶ 27. Upload the pages you modified and the updated style sheet to the remote site. Click the Connects to remote host button on the Site panel toolbar. Switch back to Local view, click the Stylesheets folder, the catalogue page, and the label page in the Local Files list (holding the Control key while you select files enables you to select only these files). Click the Put File(s) button on the Site panel toolbar and click No when asked to upload dependent files.

28. Disconnect from the remote host.

29. Open a browser, and then load the remote NewCatalyst Web site by typing the URL into the Address text box on the browser toolbar, and then pressing the Enter key.

30. Navigate through the NewCatalyst Web site using the menu bar text to link to other pages in the site.

31. Close the browser and exit Dreamweaver.

CASE PROBLEMS

Case 1. Hroch University Anthropology Department Dr. Matt Hart has selected a site design and layout from the submissions that he received. He wants you to replace the design that you created with the final version, explore the new site design, and then add text to the Web site you are creating to present his research about the small rural communities of northern Vietnam. Because his research papers are not complete, you'll add text stating that the papers are in process. Professor Hart has decided he wants minimal text formatting in the site so that his research will be accessible to the widest possible audience. Some of his colleagues live and work in remote areas and have access only to outdated computer systems. Because the site needs to be compatible with old browsers, you will use font tags rather than CSS styles.

1. Start Dreamweaver and open the Hart site that you created in Tutorial 2.

2. Open each page of the site, examine the page, and then close the page.

3. Open the index.htm page. Move the insertion point below the color band at the top of the page by pressing the Shift+Enter keys five times, type "Professor Hart", insert three non-breaking spaces, type "Linguistic Differences", insert three non-breaking spaces, type "Cultural Cross-pollination", insert three non-breaking spaces, type "Rituals and Practices", insert three non-breaking spaces, type "Contact Information", and then insert three, final, non-breaking spaces.

4. Select "Professor Hart" and use the Property inspector to create a hyperlink to the ProfHart.htm page.

5. Use the Property inspector to create hyperlinks between each phrase you typed and its corresponding page: LinguisticDifferences.htm, CulturalCrossPollination.htm, RitualsAndPractices.htm, and Contact.htm.

6. Select all of the links, click Edit on the main menu bar, and then click Copy HTML.

7. Save the home page, preview it in your browser, and then close it.

8. Open the Contact page in a Document window, move the insertion point below the color band at the top of the page, click Edit on the main menu bar, and then click Paste HTML to copy the links onto the page.

9. Save the Contact page, preview the page in a browser, and then close the page.

10. Repeat Steps 8 and 9 to copy the links to each page in the site: CulturalCrossPollination; LinguisticDifferences; ProfHart; and RitualsAndPractices.

11. Open the index.htm page in a Document window.

12. Copy the text in the document Tutorial.03\Cases\Overview.doc located on your Data Disk, and then paste it below the links on the home page.

13. Apply the Heading 1 style to the "Brief History and Overview" heading using the Property inspector in HTML mode.

14. Save and close the page.

15. Open the Contact.htm page, copy the text from the document Tutorial.03\Cases\ HartContact.doc located on your Data Disk, and then paste it below the links on the Contact page.

16. Apply the Heading 1 style to the "Contact Information" heading, using the Property inspector in HTML mode.

17. Save and close the page.

18. Open the ProfHart.htm page, copy the text from the document Tutorial.03\Cases\ ProfHart.doc located on your Data Disk, and then paste it below the links on the ProfHart page.

19. Select all the contact information at the top of the ProfHart page, from the name to the e-mail address, and then click the Bold button and the Align Center button in the Property inspector in HTML mode.

20. Using the Bold button in the Property inspector, format the following text with bold-face: Higher Education, Academic Appointments, Editorial Work, Publications: Books, and Grants and Awards.

21. Save and close the page.

22. Open the CulturalCrossPollination.htm page, move the insertion point below the link text at the top of the page, and then type "Cultural Cross-pollination".

23. Apply the Heading 1 style to the Cultural Cross-pollination heading using the Property inspector.

24. Save and close the page.

25. Open the LinguisticDifferences.htm page, move the insertion point below the link text, and then type "Linguistic Differences".

26. Apply the Heading 1 style to the Linguistic Differences heading using the Property inspector.

27. Save and close the page.

28. Open the RitualsAndPractices.htm page, move the insertion point below the link text, and then type "Rituals and Practices".

29. Apply the Heading 1 style to the Rituals and Practices heading using the Property inspector.

30. Save and close the page.

Explore 31. Open the ProfHart.htm page and change the view to Code and Design views. Select the first link and review the code, then select the bold text and find the bold and align tags.

32. Close the page.

33. Connect to the remote server, select the Graphics folder and all of the pages in the Local Files list, and upload them to the remote folder.

34. Examine the site in a browser. Test all of the links and read the text on all of the pages.

35. Close the browser and exit Dreamweaver.

Case 2. Museum of Western Art C. J. Strittmatter asks you to add text to the Web site you are creating for the Museum of Western Art. He also asked you to create a navigation system on all of the pages. After looking over the pages in the site, you also decide to add a horizontal rule to each of the pages. You'll create HTML styles for the site, and then use these to format the text. Then you'll upload the site to a remote location and preview it.

1. Start Dreamweaver, open the Museum site you created in Tutorial 2, and then open the index.htm page in a Document window.

2. At the top of the page, type "The Museum of Western Art". Use the Property inspector in HTML mode to format the text you typed in the Times New Roman, Times, serif font, size +3, and left-aligned.

3. Make sure the line of text is selected, open the HTML Styles panel, and then click the New Style button.

4. Type "Logo" in the Name text box of the Define HTML Style dialog box, verify that the other attributes match the selected text, and then click the OK button.

5. Save and close the page.

6. Open the Museum.htm page, and then type "The Museum of Western Art" at the top of the page.

7. Apply the Logo style from the HTML Styles panel to the text you just typed.

8. Create a hyperlink from the logo text to the home page.

9. Save and close the page.

10. Repeat Steps 6 through 9 for the remaining pages in the site: Art.htm, Artists.htm, Location.htm.

Explore 11. Insert a horizontal line in a page. Open the home page, move the insertion point to the end of the logo text, and then click the Horizontal Rule button on the Common tab of the Insert bar.

Explore 12. Format the line. Select the line, type 4 in the H (Height) text box in the Property inspector. Type 100 in the W (Width) text box and select % from the list. Uncheck the shading checkbox.

Explore 13. Add a color to the line by adding a color attribute and a value to the code. With the line selected, switch to Code and Design views. In the Code pane, place the insertion point after <hr, press the Spacebar, double-click color in the list box that opens, type "#006666" inside the quotation marks in the code, click anywhere in the Code pane to close the color picker, and then switch to Design view. (The new color will not be visible in Dreamweaver, but it will be visible when you preview the page in a browser.)

14. Save the page, and then use the Copy HTML and Paste HTML commands to copy the horizontal line and paste it into the other pages: Art.htm; Artists.htm; Location.htm; and Museum.htm.

15. On the home page, move the insertion point directly below the horizontal line, and then type the following text with three non-breaking spaces after each word: "Museum"; "Art"; "Artists"; and "Location".

16. Using the Property inspector, change the font of the text you just typed to Times New Roman, Times, serif, the size to None, and then format it as bold and left-aligned.

17. Create a new HTML style named "Menu" that uses the attributes of the selected text.

18. Create hyperlinks between each word you typed and its corresponding page: Museum, Art, Artists, and Location.

19. Save the home page.

20. Copy the hyperlinks you just created using the Copy HTML command.

21. Open the Museum page, move the insertion point below the horizontal line, and then paste the links from the Home page using the Paste HTML command.

22. Save the Museum page, preview the page in a browser to check the links, and then close the page.

23. Repeat steps 21 and 22 to paste the links on the rest of the pages in the site: Art, Artists, and Location.

24. Copy the text from the document Tutorial.03\Cases\Welcome.doc located on your Data Disk, and then paste it below the links on the home page. (*Hint*: If an extra space is created between the horizontal line and the menu text when you move your cursor below the text, then you have a paragraph tag surrounding the text. You must remove both the opening and closing paragraph tags from around the link text in Code view.)

25. Select the WELCOME heading, and then use the Property inspector to change the font to Times New Roman, Times, serif, change the size to +7, set the color to #006666, and change the alignment to right.

26. Create a new HTML style named "Main Headings" based on the Welcome heading.

27. Save and close the page.

28. Copy the text from the Tutorial.03\Cases\Museum.doc document located on your Data Disk. Paste the text on the Museum page below the links on the page.

29. Apply the Main Headings style from the HTML Style panel to THE MUSEUM heading.

30. Save and close the page.

31. Copy the text from the Tutorial.03\Cases\Artists.doc document located on your Data Disk to the Artists page below the link text.

32. Apply the Main Headings style from the HTLM Styles panel to THE ARTISTS heading.

33. Select the "Fredric Remington" heading, and then, in the Property inspector, change the font to Times New Roman, Times, serif, change the size to +2, change the color to #006666, and apply bold formatting.

34. Create a new HTML style named "SubHeadings" based on the selected formatted text.

35. Apply the SubHeadings style from the HTML Styles panel to the "Charles M. Russell" heading.

36. Save and close the page.

37. Copy the text from the Tutorial.03\Cases\Location.doc document located on your Data Disk to the Location page below the link text.

38. Apply the Main Headings style from the HTML Styles panel to THE LOCATION.

39. Apply the SubHeadings style from the HTML Styles panel to the following text: HOURS: and LOCATION:.

40. Save and close the page.

41. Connect to the remote server, and upload the Graphics folder and pages to the remote server. Disconnect from the remote site.

42. View the site in a browser. Visit each page of the site, read the text, and check each link.

43. Close the browser and exit Dreamweaver.

Case 3. NORM With a plan and design in place for the NORM Web site, you're ready to add and format the text for the site. Norm Blinkered, the CEO of NORM, has already written the text for the site. You need to create CSS styles for the site and then include this text on the pages. To do this, you will define CSS styles by redefining an HTML tag, customizing the appearance of hyperlinks, and creating custom styles for headings and subheadings, and then creating an external style sheet. You also will create a navigation system for the pages.

1. Start Dreamweaver, open the NORM site you created in Tutorial 2, open the index.htm page, and move the insertion point to the top of the page.

2. Open the CSS Styles panel, and then create a new CSS style of the Redefine HTML Tag type. Select "p" from the Tag list, select New Style Sheet File in the Define In list, and then click the OK button.

3. In the Save Style Sheet File As dialog box, navigate to the root folder of your NORM Web site, create a new folder named "Stylesheets," open the Stylesheets folder, type "NormStyleSheet" in the File name text box, and then click the Save button.

4. In the CSS Style Definition dialog box, click Type in the Category list, change the font to Arial, Helvetica, sans-serif, change the size to 12 points, change the color to #FFFFFF, and then click the OK button.

5. Create a new CSS style of the Use CSS Selector type, select a:link from the Selector list, and select NormStyleSheet.css in the Define In list.

6. In the CSS Style Definition dialog box, click Type in the Category list, and then change the font to Arial, Helvetica, sans-serif, change the color to #FFFFFF, check the none checkbox in Decoration, and click OK.

7. Create another CSS style of the Use CSS Selector type, select a:visited from the Selector list, and select NormStyleSheet.css in the Define In list.

8. In the CSS Style Definition dialog box, click Type in the Category list, change the font to Arial, Helvetica, sans-serif, change the color to #FFFFFF, and then change the decoration to none.

9. Create another CSS style of the Use CSS Selector type, select a:hover from the Selector list, and select NormStyleSheet.css in the Define In list.

10. In the CSS Style Definition dialog box, click Type in the Category list, change the font to Arial, Helvetica, sans-serif, change the color to #CCCFF6, and then change the decoration to underline.

11. Create a new CSS style of the Make Custom Style (class) type, with the name ".NormHeadings," and defined in the NormStyleSheet.css external style sheet.

12. In the CSS Style Definition dialog box, click Type in the Category list, change the font to Arial, Helvetica, sans-serif, change the size to 40 points, change the case to uppercase, change the color to #FFFFFF, and then change the decoration to underline.

13. Create a new CSS style of the Make Custom Style (class) type named ".NormSubHeadings," and defined in the NormStyleSheet.css external style sheet.

14. In the CSS Style Definition dialog box, click Type in the Category list, then change the font to Arial, Helvetica, sans-serif, change the size to 16 points, change the case to uppercase, change the color to #FFFFFF, and change the decoration to underline.

15. Create a new CSS style of the Make Custom Style (class) type named ".NormBookTitles," and defined in the NormStyleSheet.css external style sheet.

16. In the CSS Style Definition dialog box, click Type in the Category list, change the font to Arial, Helvetica, sans-serif, change the style to italic, and then change the color to #FFCC00.

17. In the home page Document window, type "NORMbooks on the edge", highlight "NORM," and then apply the NormHeadings style from the CSS Styles panel.

Explore 18. Adjust the margins so that the formatted text is above and below the horizontal rule. Click Modify on the main menu bar, click Page Properties to open the Page Properties dialog box, and then type "0" in the Top Margin and Margin Height text boxes.

19. Move the insertion point below the horizontal line, and then type the following words separated by three non-breaking spaces between each word: "company"; "books"; "links"; and "contact". (*Hint*: To move the insertion down one line instead of two lines, press the Shift+Enter keys instead of just the Enter key.)

20. Use the Property inspector to create a hyperlink between each word and its respective page: company, books, links, and contact.

21. Select and copy all the text on the page (using the Copy HTML command), and then save and close the page.

22. Open the company page, and then paste the copied text at the top of the page (using the Paste HTML command).

23. Attach the page to the style sheet by clicking the Attach Style Sheet button in the CSS Styles panel and navigating to the NormStyleSheet style sheet in the Link External Style Sheet dialog box, and then change the Top Margin and the Margin Height to 0.

24. Save and close the page.

25. Repeat Steps 22 through 24 for the books, links, and contact pages.

26. Preview the site in a browser and test the links to make sure that they are working.

27. Open the Tutorial.03\Cases\Home.doc document located on your Data Disk in a word processing program, copy the text, and then exit the word processing program.

28. Open the home page, move the insertion point below the link text, and then paste the text into the page.

29. Apply the NormSubHeadings style to "NORM book list" and "News."

30. Switch the Property inspector to CSS mode, and then use the CSS Styles list to apply the NormBookTitles style to each book title on the page.

31. Save and close the page.

32. Open the books page, move the insertion point directly below the link text, type "Coming Soon", and then apply the NormSubHeadings style to the text you just typed.

33. Save and close the page.

34. Open the Tutorial.03\Cases\Company.doc document located on your Data Disk in a word processing program, copy the text, and the exit the word processing program.

35. Open the company page, move the insertion point below the link text, and then paste the text into the page.

36. Apply the NormSubHeadings style to "Mission" and "Staff."

37. Save and close the page.

38. Open the Tutorial.03\Cases\NORMContact.doc document located on your Data Disk in a word processing program, copy the text, and then exit the word processing program.

39. Open the contact page, move the insertion point below the link text, and then paste the text into the page.

40. Apply the NormSubHeadings style to "Contact."

41. Save and close the page.

42. Open the Tutorial.03\Cases\Links.doc document located on your Data Disk in a word processing program, copy the text, and then exit the word processing program.

43. Open the links page, move the insertion point below the link text, and then paste the text into the page.

44. Apply the NormSubHeadings style to "Links."

Explore 45. Select "Ludlow Press," type "http://www.ludlowpress.com" in the Link text box on the Property inspector to create an absolute link to that Web site, and then delete the URL located beside "Ludlow Press" in the Document window. (*Hint:* Make sure to include "http://" when you type the link because it is an offsite hyperlink.)

Explore 46. Repeat Step 45 for the rest of the links using the URLs listed on the page.

Explore 47. Select Ludlow Press, click the Code and Design Views button in the Document toolbar, and then examine the code for an absolute link.

48. Save and close the page.

49. Connect to the remote server, upload the Graphics folder, the Stylesheets folder, and the pages to the Remote site, and then collapse the Site panel.

50. View the site in a browser. Read each page of the site, check each link, and visit each page to make sure everything was uploaded correctly.

51. Close the browser and exit Dreamweaver.

Case 4. Sushi Ya-Ya Mary O'Brien wants you to start working on the navigation system and the styles for the Sushi Ya-Ya Web. She asks you to create CSS styles, add appropriate text to the site, and then format the text you added. You'll view the code, upload the modified pages to the remote site, and then preview the remote site.

Explore 1. Make a list of the styles you need to create. (*Hint:* You will need to modify the <p> tag to add general text attributes, use the CSS Selector to customize the <a> tag, and create headings and subheadings for the site.)

2. Open the SushiYaYa site you created in Tutorial 2, and then open the home page in a Document window.

3. Change the background color of the home page to #9B0C12 in the Page Properties. (*Hint*: Click Modify on the main menu bar and then click Page Properties.)

4. Open the CSS Styles panel and create your first style. Define the style in a New Style Sheet File, create a Stylesheets folder within the root folder of your site, name the external style sheet "SushiYaYaStyles," and place it in the Stylesheets folder.

5. Create the rest of the styles that you will need for the site.

Explore 6. Create the navigation system for the home page. Remember to create links to all the other pages in your site.

7. Copy the links from the home page to the other pages.

8. Preview the site in a browser, testing the links to be sure they work.

Explore 9. Use the text in the file SushiYa-YaContent.doc in Tutorial.03\Cases to add text throughout the site. Apply the styles you created and create any additional styles needed. Don't forget to save the pages.

10. Upload the site to its remote location, and then test the remote site in a browser.

11. Close the browser and exit Dreamweaver.

QUICK | CHECK ANSWERS

Session 3.1

1. deprecated

2. You may need to update older HTML pages that use these tags. You may need to create pages for older browsers that still use these tags. Some new portable devices, specialized Web access tools, Web appliances, and Web content management systems still rely on HTML 3.2, which uses these tags.

3. type; copy; paste

4. Relative

5. Hyperlinks

6. a relative link

7. Some Text

8. anchor

Session 3.2

1. CSS style

2. Yes.

3. custom style class

4. Yes; it's called an external style sheet.

5. Modifying an HTML tag can make it more useful by giving you more control over the appearance of your Web page because it controls the way elements appear in the end-user's browser rather than allowing the browser to interpret the tag.

6. Some designers prefer to create custom style classes instead of redefining existing HTML tags so they can use a descriptive and meaningful name for each style.

7. a period

Session 3.3

1. .css

2. Yes, but you must export the styles to an external style sheet first.

3. It is a good idea to delete unneeded styles from a style sheet because unneeded materials in a site make the site cluttered.

4. You need to remove the current formatting from text on a Web page before attaching an external style sheet because the older formatting might override the CSS style you apply, or it might combine with the CSS style causing the text to display differently than you had intended.

5. Yes.

6. When you edit a CSS style, any element to which the style is applied is updated automatically to reflect the changes you make.

7. An internal style sheet is also called an embedded style sheet because the styles are embedded in the head of the Web page.

8. No.

In this tutorial you will:

- Add and format a graphic

- Create graphic hyperlinks and an image map

- Create rollovers

- Add and format tables

- Add and format tables in Layout View

- Use invisible graphics as spacers

W O R K I N G
WITH GRAPHICS, ROLLOVERS, AND TABLES

Organizing Content and Layout in the Catalyst Web Site

CASE

Catalyst

Sara Lynn, the president of Catalyst, hired an artist to design a new graphic logo for Catalyst. She wants you to add this new logo to each page of the Catalyst site and to link it to the home page of the site. To match the style of the new logo, she also had the artist create graphics to replace the text links that make up the navigation system on each page. To further update the site, Brian Lee, public relations and marketing director at Catalyst, has asked you to add tables to the tour dates page containing the tour date information for various regions of the country. He also would like you to add a map containing links to the tables. Finally, he wants you to create a table on the catalogue page to hold the graphics and song lists in place.

After meeting with Sara, Brian decided to add a new page to the site to promote new releases. To do this, he asked you to create a table to hold the content of the new page, and then to create a link from the home page to the new promotional page.

To accomplish this, you will first add the new Catalyst logo to all of the pages in the site, and then format it. Then you will add a map of the United States to the tour dates page and make each region of the map a link to a table listing the tour dates for that region. Next you will replace the text links with the new graphics. Then you will add tables to the tour dates page, listing the tour dates for each region in the country. Finally, you will create a new page for the site describing one of the label's bands.

SESSION 4.1

In this session, you will learn about the different types of graphics you can use in a Web site. You'll add the Catalyst logo to each page of the Web site and you'll format the logo by changing its attributes. You'll create a link to the logo graphic, and then create an image map. Finally, you'll insert a rollover object for the Catalyst logo.

Understanding Graphics Compression

Graphics can make a site more interesting. They can also provide the user with valuable information. For example, maps and graphs can summarize information more succinctly and intuitively than a written description. The graphics that you add to your Web site should reinforce the goals of the Web site. For the Catalyst Web site, you will add a graphic logo to each page of the site. The logo will increase the brand recognition of Catalyst, which is a major goal of the site. In addition to the logo, you will add graphics of the CD cover art to the catalogue page of the site. These graphic will help to promote the bands and to sell products, two additional goals of the site. Other graphics will be added as needed to carry the look and feel of the site throughout the pages.

When choosing graphics to add to a page, ask yourself what each graphic will add to the page. Will it add information or reinforce the content of the page? Will it aid the user in navigating through the Web site? Will it help the page to maintain the look of the site? If the graphic does not add anything to the page, it should not be used.

Because graphics files are usually large, the graphics that you add to your Web site are stored in compressed file formats. **Compression** shrinks the file size of the graphic by using different types of encoding to remove redundant or less important information. The smaller the file size of a graphic, the faster it will load in a browser. When considering what file size a graphic should be, you must consider the total file size of all of the graphics on the Web page and the speed of the connection that your target audience will have. If you are only going to include one graphic on a page, the file size of that graphic can be larger. If you are going to include several graphics on a page, the size of each graphic will contribute to the amount of time it takes a user's browser to download the page. In this case, you might want to make the file size of each graphic smaller. In addition, if your target audience is using dial-up service to connect to the Internet, it will take them longer to download graphic-intensive pages, so you might consider keeping the graphics to a minimum or choosing graphics that are small in file size. Finally, you should consider the importance of the graphic when considering file size. A user will be more willing to wait for a page to download if the page is interesting and provides the content that the user is looking for. Figure 4-1 shows the approximate time it takes to download files of various sizes over a standard 56k/sec dial-up connection, over a DSL connection, and over a cable modem connection.

Figure 4-1	APPROXIMATE DOWNLOAD TIMES FOR FILES OF DIFFERENT SIZES				
CONNECTION TYPE (SPEED IN KB/SEC)	**SIZE OF PAGE (IN KILOBYTES)**				
	10kB Very Small Download	50kB Small Download	100kB Medium Download	200kB Large Download	400kB Very Large Download
Dial-up 56kb (~5kB/sec)	2	10	20	40	80
Home DSL 640kbps (~80kB/sec)	less than 1	less than 1	1.25	2.5	5
Cable Modem 1.5Mbps (~190kB/sec)	less than 1	less than 1	less than 1	1	2.1

Current versions of Internet Explorer and Netscape can universally display three file formats for graphics: GIF, JPEG, and PNG. All three of these formats compress graphic files, but each in a different manner. If you want to use graphic images that are in another format, you will need to use a graphics processing program like Photoshop, ImageReady, or Fireworks to convert them to GIF, JPEG, or PNG.

Using GIF

GIF (Graphics Interchange Format) was invented by the CompuServe Company to provide its customers with a means to exchange graphics files online. Unisys, which now owns the patent on the type of compression used in GIFs, requires that software producing GIFs license the GIF patent. However, graphics compressed as GIFs can be used free of charge. Files saved as GIF images have the file extension *.gif*. The GIF format is usually used on images that have large areas of flat, or non-gradient, color. **Non-gradient** refers to color that is one shade and does not vary with subtle darkening or lightening. Many line-drawn graphics and non-photographic images use GIF. GIF supports a palette of up to 256 colors, one of which may be used for single-color transparency. (To be transparent means to be see-through or clear.) GIF transparency is usually used to create a clear background for graphics. For example, if you want an image to appear on your site without its background around it, you can make the background transparent so that you see instead the color of the Web page or the background image behind it. In GIF format, greater compression (and therefore smaller file size) is achieved by further limiting the color palette of the graphic. This means that the fewer colors used in a GIF image, the smaller the file size. It's a balance between how colorful an image you want to use and how fast users can load the image.

The new Catalyst logo that will appear on each page of the Web site is shown in Figure 4-2. Brian has compressed the new logo using GIF because it is comprised of flat colors and a transparent background.

| Figure 4-2 | CATALYST LOGO AS A GIF IMAGE |

Using JPEG

A committee from the **Joint Photographic Experts Group** created the **JPEG** format to digitize photographic images. Files saved as JPEG images have the file extension *.jpg*. The JPEG format is usually used on photographic images and on graphics that have many gradient colors. The JPEG format can support millions of colors but does not support transparency.

JPEG is a **lossy** compression format, which means that it discards (or loses) information to compress an image. Because it was designed for photographic images, JPEG discards the information that is less perceptible to the human eye, such as the fine details in the background of a photograph. However, as an image is compressed further, additional information is discarded and, as the blurry spots increase in size, the image becomes less and less sharp. So, as with a GIF image, you must make a tradeoff between the image quality and the file size (or download time).

The CD covers for use on the bands page will be JPEG images because each CD cover contains photographic images, which will be more effectively compressed using this format. Figure 4-3 shows the *surface suction: black lab* CD cover as a JPEG image.

Figure 4-3	CD COVER AS A JPEG IMAGE

photographic elements and layers of varying color

Using PNG

PNG (Portable Network Graphics), a newer graphic compression format, was created by a group of designers who were frustrated by the limitations of existing compression formats. PNG files use the file extension *.png*. PNG supports up to 48-bit truecolor or 16-bit grayscale. It uses **lossless** compression, so no information is discarded when the file is compressed. It also supports variable transparency. **Variable transparency** is the ability to make the background of the image transparent at different amounts; for example, a background can fade (using gradient shades of color) from a dark color to transparent. Generally, PNG compresses files 5% to 25% better than GIF. For transmission of photographic style images, JPEG is still a better choice because the file size of a photographic style image compressed with JPEG is usually smaller than the file size of a photographic style image compressed with PNG. The biggest drawback of the PNG format is that it is supported only in Netscape Navigator 4.04 or later and Internet Explorer 4 or later, and variable transparency does not always display correctly in Internet Explorer. If you have a wide target audience, PNG may not be the most effective choice.

Figure 4-4 shows a graphic from the Dizzied Connections CD cover saved as a PNG. The graphic has gradient colors fading to transparency, therefore PNG's variable transparency was the perfect choice for compressing this image.

Figure 4-4	PNG IMAGE

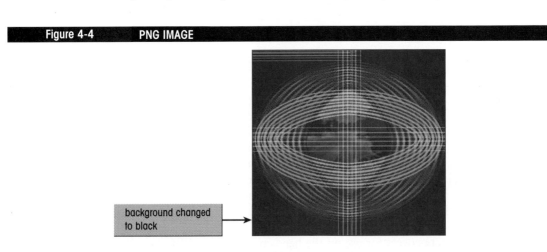

background changed to black

Adding Graphics to Web Pages

Graphics are an integral part of Web pages. When you made your site plan, you decided on the overall look you wanted to achieve. Now that it is time to add the graphics to your site, you need to make sure that each graphic is saved at the proper size for insertion into the pages. Adjusting the size of a graphic after it has been added to a Web page is a bad idea, because the graphic is included at its original size and then resized on the user's machine. This can make your Web pages load much slower. In addition to being sized prior to insertion into the page, each graphic should be compressed to the smallest possible file size you can achieve without losing image quality. Be sure to retain the original uncompressed graphics in addition to the compressed Web versions because you may need to return to the original version to create another variation of the graphic in the future. Once a graphic has been compressed, it cannot return to its original resolution. It is also a good idea to use names that have meaning when you are creating graphics. Logical naming structures will save you time in the future because they will help you avoid confusion. Once you have the final version of all of your graphics, you can add them to the pages in your Web site.

REFERENCE WINDOW   **RW**

Adding Graphics to a Web Page

- Click the Image button on the Common tab on the Insert bar.
- Navigate to the file you want to insert in the Select Image Source dialog box, select the file, and then click the OK button.
- Click the Yes button to copy the file to the local root folder.

or

- Click the Assets tab in the Files panel group.
- Click the Images button on the Assests panel toolbar to display the list of images already stored in the site.
- Click the file in the list of images that you want to insert, and then click the Insert button in the Assets panel, drag the image from the top of the Assets panel to its position on the page, or drag the filename from the list in the Assets panel to its position on the page.

There are two ways to add graphics to a Web site using Dreamweaver: you can use the Insert bar or the Assets panel. The first time you place a graphic in the site you will use the Insert bar to place the graphic in the page. Once a graphic is stored in the root folder, it will appear in the Assets panel and then you can use either method to insert the graphic into your pages.

When you add a graphic to a Web site, you should store it in the Graphics folder within the root folder of the site so that Dreamweaver always knows where to locate the image. You need to include only one copy of each graphic in the Graphics folder, even when you plan to use the same image on several pages.

When you place a graphic in a page, what you are really doing is placing an image (<img>) tag in the page. The image tag tells the page to display the graphic, which you placed in the Graphics folder, at that spot in the Web page. When the same graphic appears multiple times in a site, Dreamweaver will retrieve the graphic from the Graphics folder and display it in the various pages of your site. This is helpful because, if you decide to change the graphics in a site, you can simply replace the old graphic with a new one, and each page that displayed the old graphic will then display the new one.

Using the Insert bar to Add Graphics

The new Catalyst logo is a GIF graphic that will be included in the upper left corner of every page in the site. You will use the Insert bar to add the image. When you insert a graphic, you move the insertion point to the location where you want the image to appear on the page and then use the Image button located in the Common tab of the Insert bar to place the image. If the image is not already stored within the site, you should copy the file to the Graphics folder within the root folder. This ensures that the correct image is always available to Dreamweaver.

Brian asks you to add the redesigned Catalyst logo to the site. You'll start with the home page.

To add a graphic to a page using the Insert bar:

1. Start **Dreamweaver**, open the **NewCatalyst** site that you modified in the Tutorial 3 Review Assignments, and then close the **Untitled Document** in the Document window.

2. Open the **index.htm** page in a Document window in Design view. The home page opens with the insertion point in the upper left corner.

3. Click the **Image** button 🖼 on the **Common** tab of the Insert bar. The Select Image Source dialog box opens.

4. Navigate to the **Tutorial** folder within the **Tutorial.04** folder on your Data Disk, and then click **CatalystLogo.gif**. See Figure 4-5.

Figure 4-5	SELECT IMAGE SOURCE DIALOG BOX

5. Click the **OK** button. A dialog box opens, asking if you would like to save a copy of the graphic in the root folder.

6. Click the **Yes** button. The Copy File As dialog box opens, so you can select the location where you want to save the graphic.

7. Double-click the **Graphics** folder within the root folder of the site, and then click the **Save** button. The Catalyst logo is inserted in the upper left corner of the Catalyst home page. See Figure 4-6.

Figure 4-6 **CATALYST LOGO ON HOME PAGE**

TROUBLE? If the Image Tag Accessibility Attributes dialog box opens, the Accessibility dialog boxes are activated on your machine. Click the Cancel button to close the dialog box. To avoid seeing this and similar dialog boxes as you complete the steps in these tutorials, click Edit on the main menu bar, click Preferences to open the Preferences dialog box, click Accessibility in the Category list, uncheck all of the checkboxes indented in the list under Show Attributes when Inserting, and then click the OK button.

The Catalyst logo is surrounded by a black box with squares in the corners and on the sides. This is because the graphic is selected. The squares are **resize handles**. If you drag a resize handle it will resize the selected object. Remember that this is usually a bad idea. To select an object like a graphic, you can click it. When you click on another area of the page, the graphic is deselected.

8. Click anywhere inside the Document window but outside the logo to deselect it.

9. Save and close the **home** page.

You'll repeat this process to insert the logo on the label page, except that you'll use the GIF image you already saved in the Graphics folder.

To add a graphic from the Graphics folder using the Insert bar:

1. Open the **label.htm** page in a Document window.

2. Click the **Image** button ⬇ in the **Common** tab on the Insert bar. The Select Image Source dialog box opens.

3. Navigate to the **Graphics** folder in the site's local root folder, click **CatalystLogo.gif**, and then click the **OK** button. The Catalyst logo appears in the upper left corner of the label page.

4. Click anywhere inside the Document window but outside the Catalyst logo to deselect it.

5. Save and close the **label** page.

Another way to add graphics to Web pages is to use the Assets panel.

Using the Assets Panel to Insert Graphics

In Dreamweaver, **assets** are the images, colors, URLs, Flash, Shockwave, movies, scripts, templates, and library items that you use throughout your site. The Assets panel is used for managing assets. It helps you keep track of the assets in your site by listing them all in one place. Once a graphic has been stored in the local root folder, you can use the Assets panel to place the graphic in other pages. When you display images in the Assets panel, the graphic image appears in the upper pane and the graphic's filename, type, size, and location appear in the lower pane.

You'll open the Assets panel.

To open the Assets panel:

1. Click the **Assets** tab in the Files panel group.

2. Click the **Images** button 🖼 at the upper left of the Assets panel, if necessary, and then click the **Site** option button at the top of the Assets panel, if necessary. The images in the site are listed in the Assets panel.

3. Click **CatalystLogo.gif** in the Assets panel list. The selected image appears in the top pane of the Assets panel. See Figure 4-7.

Figure 4-7	IMAGES IN ASSETS PANEL

TROUBLE? If you don't see the CatalystLogo.gif file in the Assets panel, click the Refresh button in the Site panel toolbar. If you see additional files in the list, right-click any of the files, and then click Recreate Site List on the context menu.

You'll use the Assets panel to place the Catalyst logo in the remaining pages of the NewCatalyst site.

To insert a graphic using the Assets panel:

1. Click the **Site** tab in the Files panel group, and then open the **bands.htm** page in a Document window. The insertion point is positioned in the upper left corner of the page.

2. Click the **Assets** tab in the Files panel group, click **CatalystLogo.gif** in the Images list, if necessary, and then click the **Insert** button at the bottom of the Assets panel. The logo is inserted on the bands page.

3. Save and close the **bands** page.

4. Open the **catalogue** page in a Document window.

5. Click the **Assets** tab in the File panel group, make sure that **CatalystLogo.gif** is still selected, and then drag the Catalyst logo in the top pane in the Assets panel to the upper left corner of the catalogue page in the Document window.

6. Save and close the **catalogue** page.

7. Using either method, insert the Catalyst logo on the **contact** and **tour dates** pages.

You may want to change some of the formatting attributes of inserted graphics.

Formatting **Graphics**

Some elements of style can be added to the Web site by formatting graphics. When a graphic is selected in the Document window, the Property inspector displays a small picture of the graphic and shows the graphic's attributes. Graphic attributes listed in the Property inspector include:

- **Image.** A descriptive name of the image. The image name is used in some advanced forms of programming to allow you to tell Dreamweaver or the browser what to do with the image. The name does not have to be the same as the filename, but it should enable you to identify the image. The image name must begin with a letter, or an underscore, it can contain letters and numbers, but it cannot contain any spaces or symbols.

- **W (Width)** and **H (Height).** The horizontal and vertical dimensions of the graphic in pixels. You can resize the image by changing the values or dragging a resize handle on the image in the Document window. Although you can resize a graphic in Dreamweaver, if you do, the Web site will load more slowly because Dreamweaver must transmit the original graphic to the end user's machine and then resize the image on the client computer. Also, resizing an image larger than its original size will degrade the image quality. Instead, you should insert images at the size you want to display them.

- **Src (Image Source File).** The file path (which includes the filename) of the graphic. It will either be a relative or an absolute path, depending on what you selected when you insert the graphic. Most often a relative path is used because, if you change your URL or move the location of the root directory of the site, a relative path will still work. You can swap an image by replacing the source file with the path to the new image, clicking the Browse for File button and navigating to the new image, or by dragging the Point to File icon to the new file. You can also double-click the image in the Document window and enter the new path information in the Select Image Source dialog box.

■ **Alt (Alternate).** Text that appears in place of the graphic when the page is viewed with a browser that displays only text or when a browser is set to only download images manually. In some browsers, the Alt text also appears in a tooltip when the pointer is positioned over the graphic. You should give all graphics an Alt message that describes the image. This is extremely helpful for individuals who have visual disabilities and rely on screen readers to verbally communicate the graphic information.

■ **Reset Size.** Returns the selected graphic to its original width and height.

■ **V Space** and **H Space.** The blank space, in pixels, that appears vertically along the top and bottom of the image or horizontally along the left and right sides of the image.

■ **Low Src (Low Resolution Image Source File).** The path (including the filename) to a low-resolution image that displays while the high-resolution image is downloading. This enables clients with slow connections to see something while they wait for the high-resolution image to load. It is not necessary to use a low-resolution image.

■ **Border.** A rectangular group of lines that surrounds a graphic. The width of the lines is measured in pixels. A border of 0 pixels (the default) is equivalent to no visible border. If there is no entry in the Border text box, it will default to the user's browser setting. For most browsers, this is equivalent to 0. If the image is linked, then the border is the link color you specified in the page properties; otherwise, the border is the text color of the paragraph around the image.

■ **Align.** A list of the possibilities for alignment of the graphic with text that is next to it on the page. **Default** uses the browser's default setting for alignment; this is usually baseline. **Baseline** and **Bottom** align the bottom of the graphic to the baseline of the text. (The **baseline** is the imaginary line that the text is sitting on.) **Top** aligns the top of the graphic to the top of the tallest item, whether an image or text, in the same line. **Middle** aligns the middle of the graphic to the baseline of the text. **TextTop** aligns the top of the graphic to the top of the tallest character in the text line. **Absolute Middle** aligns the middle of the graphic to the middle of the line. **Absolute Bottom** aligns the bottom of the graphic to the bottom of the lowest character in the text line, for example, with the bottom of a lowercase *g*. **Left** aligns the left edge of the graphic at the left margin and wraps text around its right side. **Right** aligns the right edge of the graphic at the right margin and wraps text around its left side.

The Property inspector can be expanded to show all the available graphic attributes, or collapsed to show only the most common ones.

You'll format the Catalyst logo by entering alternate text, removing the border, and adding horizontal space along the sides of the image.

To format a graphic:

1. Open the **index.htm** page in a Document window, and then click the **Expander arrow** button ▽ on the Property inspector to show all the attributes, if necessary.

2. Click the **Catalyst** logo. The logo is selected, and resize handles appear around the image.

3. Click in the **Alt** text box in the Property inspector, and then type **Catalyst company logo, link to home page**.

4. Verify that there is no entry in the **Border** text box.

5. Click in the **H Space** text box, type **5** and then press the **Enter** key. See Figure 4-8.

Figure 4-8	PROPERTY INSPECTOR WITH IMAGE ATTRIBUTES SET

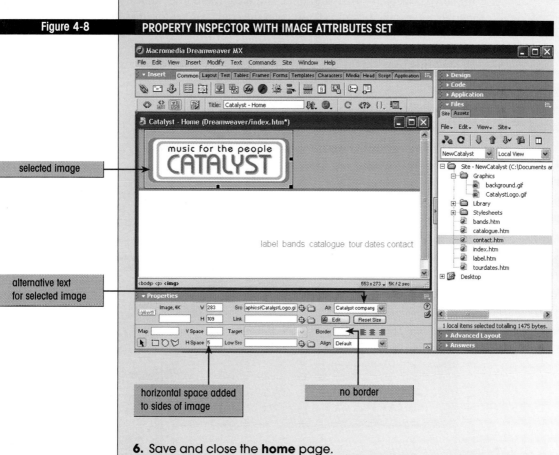

selected image

alternative text
for selected image

horizontal space added
to sides of image

no border

6. Save and close the **home** page.

7. Repeat Steps 1 through 6 for the rest of the pages in the site: **bands.htm**, **catalogue.htm**, **contact.htm**, **label.htm**, and **tourdates.htm**.

Another common use of graphics is as hyperlinks.

Creating Graphic Hyperlinks

As you have seen, graphics are not simply visual enhancements on a Web site; frequently, they are links to other pages and sites. You can create a link for an entire image, or you can divide the image into smaller sections and create a link for each of those sections. Graphic links can be created in the same ways that text links are created. In the Property inspector you can type the path and filename in the Link text box, click the Link Browse for File button and navigate to the location of the link, or drag the Link Point to File icon to the page to which you want to link in the Site panel.

Linking an Image

Creating a graphic hyperlink is similar to creating a text hyperlink. You select the graphic in the Document window, and then use the Browse to File button or the Point to File icon in the Property inspector to browse to the page to which you want to link. Once you have created a link to a page, you can select it as the link for a selected graphic using the Links list box in the Property inspector. When a graphic is linked, the border appears as a rectangle around the graphic (unless the border is 0 pixels) in the color you set for links in the page properties.

You want to create a graphic link to the home page using the Catalyst logo. You'll start by creating the link on the label page, and then you'll repeat the process to create the link on all the other pages in the site except the home page. You do not want to create a link from a page to itself.

To create a graphic hyperlink:

1. Open the **label.htm** page in a Document window.

2. Click the **Catalyst** logo to select it.

3. Click the **Browse for File** button ☐ next to the Link text box in the Property inspector, and then double-click the **index.htm** page in the Select File dialog box. The link information appears in the Property inspector. See Figure 4-9.

Figure 4-9	LINK INFORMATION IN PROPERTY INSPECTOR FOR SELECTED GRAPHIC

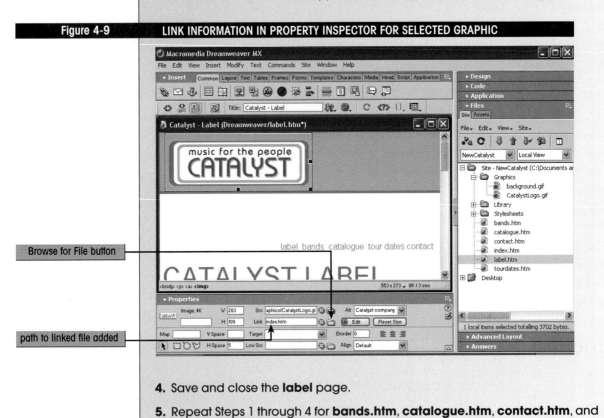

4. Save and close the **label** page.

5. Repeat Steps 1 through 4 for **bands.htm**, **catalogue.htm**, **contact.htm**, and **tourdates.htm**.

In addition to creating a link from an entire image, you can create multiple links from different areas of an image.

Creating an Image Map

An **image map** is a graphic that is divided into invisible regions or hotspots. A **hotspot** is an area of an image that you can click to cause an action to occur, such as loading another Web page. Image maps are useful when you want to link parts of an image to different pieces of information. In a music site, for example, a map could be divided into touring regions and each region would be a hotspot. When the user clicks a particular region, the tour dates for that region would appear on the screen.

REFERENCE WINDOW **RW**

Creating an Image Map

- Select the image.
- Type a map name in the Map text box in the Property inspector.
- Click a hotspot tool in the Property inspector, and then drag over the image to create the hotspot.
- Type alternate text in the Alt text box in the Property inspector for each hotspot.

You can create three types of hotspots: rectangular, oval, and polygonal. When an image is selected, you click the appropriate hotspot tool on the Property inspector, and then drag over the image to create a rectangular or oval hotspot, or click at various points to create a polygonal hotspot. Once hotspots have been created in the image, you create separate links for each hotspot.

You can move or resize a hotspot using the Pointer Hotspot Tool. If the hotspot is a polygon, you can move the individual points as well. When a hotspot is selected, the Property inspector displays the hotspot and pointer tools and displays hotspot attributes, which include:

- **Link.** The Web page or file that opens when the hotspot is clicked. You can type a URL or path and filename into the Link text box, or use the Browse for File button to navigate to the page to which you want to link.
- **Target.** The frame or window in which the linked Web page will open. This option is available only after you specify a link for the hotspot.
- **Alt (Alternative).** The alternate text description for each link.
- **Map.** A descriptive name of the image map. The Map text box is displayed when a hotspot is selected. You do not have to name image maps; however, some advanced coding requires that objects be named so they may be referenced. If you do not name the image map once you create the first hotspot, Dreamweaver will assign the name *Map* to the first image map, *Map2* to the second image map, and so forth. Map names must begin with a letter or underscore, can contain letters and numbers, but no spaces or symbols.

Brian asks you to add a map graphic to the Tour Dates page, and then to use the graphic to create an image map.

To insert a graphic on the Tour Dates page:

1. Open the **tourdates.htm** page in a Document window, and then move the insertion point below the navigation links.

2. Type **TOUR DATES**, apply the **Heading1** style to the text using the Format list in the Property inspector, and then press the **Enter** key twice to move the insertion point down two lines.

3. Click the **Image** button on the **Common** tab of the Insert bar. The Select Image Source dialog box opens.

4. Navigate to the **Tutorial** folder within the **Tutorial.04** folder on your Data Disk, and then double-click **USmap.gif**. A dialog box prompts you to save a copy of the graphic to the root folder.

5. Click the **Yes** button, and then save the graphic in the **Graphics** folder for the site. The map image is inserted into the Tour Dates page.

6. Click the map graphic to select it if necessary, and click the **Align Center** button in the Property inspector. The map is centered on the page.

7. Click in the **Alt** text box, and then type **US map with links to tour dates by region**.

Next, you'll add hotspots to the map, which turns the graphic into an image map. You want to create a hotspot for the West Coast, Central, and East Coast regions on the map. You'll use a polygon hotspot so you can outline the irregular shape of each region.

To create an image map:

1. Click in the text box in the Property inspector to the right of the map image, and then type **USmapIM**.

2. Click the **Polygon Hotspot Tool** button in the Property inspector.

3. Click the upper left corner of the West Coast region. The first point of the hotspot is added to the page. See Figure 4-10.

| Figure 4-10 | FIRST POLYGON HOTSPOT INSERTED |

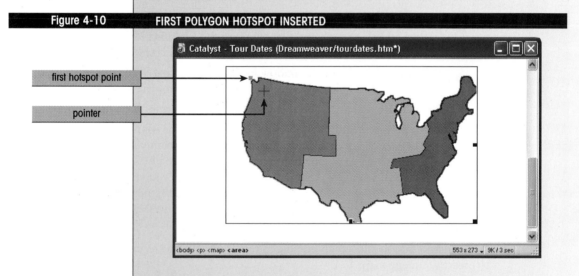

4. Continue to click around the perimeter of the West Coast region to add the hotspot border. See Figure 4-11.

| Figure 4-11 | FINISHED POLYGON HOTSPOT |

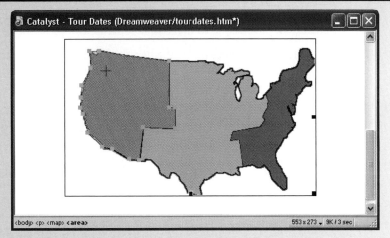

If any parts of the hotspot are not aligned correctly to the region's perimeter, you can drag the appropriate points to realign the hotspot.

5. Click the **Pointer Hotspot Tool** button in the Property inspector.

6. Drag a point on the hotspot to adjust its position, if necessary.

7. Click in the **Alt** text box in the Property inspector, and then type **Link to West Coast tour dates**.

8. Click anywhere outside the hotspot but inside the graphic border to deselect it.

9. Repeat Steps 2 through 8 to create the hotspots for the Central U.S. and East Coast regions of the map. Use the name of each region in the Alt text for the corresponding hotspot. Make sure you click before you click to deselect the hotspot.

Notice that Dreamweaver added a Map name in the Map text box in the Property inspector by appending "Map" to the image name you typed in the Image box to the right of the map thumbnail in the Property inspector.

10. Save and close the page.

In the Review Assignments, you will link the regional hotspots to the text that they reference.

Understanding Rollovers

A **rollover** is an image that changes when the pointer moves across it. In actuality, a rollover enables two seemingly stacked graphics—the original graphic and the rollover graphic—to swap places during a specified browser action, such as a mouseover, and then to swap back during another specified browser action, such as when the pointer is moved off the images. The two graphics must be the same size.

Inserting Rollovers

You can use the Rollover Image button on the Common tab of the Insert bar to insert rollover buttons that change when the user points to them and that link the user to another page when the button is clicked. When you use the Rollover Image button to create rollovers, Dreamweaver does more than just create code to make the images swap. Once you fill in the requested information in the Insert Rollover Image dialog box, Dreamweaver creates all of the code to make four separate things happen:

1. The graphics preload when the Web page is loaded so that they are in place when the browser action (such as a mouseover) occurs.

2. The graphics swap places when the mouse pointer is placed over the graphic.

3. The graphics swap places again when the mouse pointer is moved off from the graphic.

4. If a URL is specified in the When Clicked, Go To URL text box of the Insert Rollover Image dialog box, the user is hyperlinked to the new page when the mouse is clicked.

Technically, a rollover is a JavaScript behavior. JavaScript is a scripting language that works with HTML. A JavaScript behavior is a set of JavaScript instructions that tell the browser to do specified things. In earlier versions of Dreamweaver, you had to create three separate JavaScript behaviors to create a rollover. Now, you simply click the Rollover Image button and enter the image name, the original image source file, the rollover image source file, and a URL, if appropriate; Dreamweaver adds the JavaScripts for you.

The image name is the name that will appear in the Property inspector when one of the rollover graphics is highlighted. The image name does not replace the filename of either graphic you designate. The image name should begin with a letter or an underscore and should not have any spaces or special characters. You should use a descriptive name that includes the word "rollover" so you can easily see that a graphic has rollover behaviors attached to it. Unless the word "rollover" appears in the image name, you cannot tell that a graphic has rollover behaviors attached to it without looking at the code or previewing the page in a browser.

REFERENCE WINDOW | **RW**

Inserting a Rollover

- Click the Rollover Image button on the Common tab on the Insert bar to open the Insert Rollover Image dialog box.
- Type a name for the rollover image in the Image Name text box.
- Click the Original Image Browse button, navigate to the file you want to insert as the original image, and then click the OK button.
- Click the Rollover Image Browse button, navigate to the file you want to insert as the rollover image, and then click the OK button.
- Click the Preload Rollover Image checkbox to check it.
- Type alternate text for the image in the Alternate Text text box.
- Click the When Clicked, Go To URL Browse button, navigate to the file to which you want to link, and then click the OK button.
- Click the OK button in the Insert Rollover Image dialog box.

You'll create a rollover for the Catalyst logo on the bands page. Then, you'll replace the existing logo on each page of the Web site with the new rollover.

To insert a rollover:

1. Open the **bands.htm** page in a Document window, click the **Catalyst** logo to select it, and then press the **Delete** key. The logo image is deleted from the bands page.

2. Click the **Rollover Image** button on the **Common** tab of the Insert bar. The Insert Rollover Image dialog box opens.

3. Type **LogoRollover** in the Image Name text box. Remember, graphic names cannot include any spaces. Whenever you see the name in the Property inspector, you'll be reminded that the image has rollover behaviors.

4. Click the **Original Image Browse** button, navigate to the **Graphics** folder in the local root directory of the NewCatalyst site, and then double-click the **CatalystLogo.gif** file. The path to the graphic appears in the Original Image text box.

5. Click the **Rollover Image Browse** button, navigate to the **Tutorial** folder within the **Tutorial.04** folder on your Data Disk, and then double-click **CatalystLogoRollover.gif**.

6. Click the **Yes** button, and then save a copy of the CatalystLogoRollover.gif graphic in the **Graphics** folder in the local root folder of your NewCatalyst site.

7. Click the **Preload Rollover Image** checkbox to check, if necessary. Both graphics will load with the Web page.

8. Click in the **Alternate Text** text box, and then type **Catalyst company logo, link to home page**.

9. Click the **When Clicked, Go To URL Browse** button, and then double-click the **index.htm** page in the local root folder of the NewCatalyst site. See Figure 4-12.

Figure 4-12   **INSERT ROLLOVER IMAGE DIALOG BOX**

image name

paths to graphics files

check to load rollover image with Web page

enter URL to link to

10. Click the **OK** button in the Insert Rollover Image dialog box. The rollover image is added to the page.

11. Press the **Right Arrow** key to position the insertion point to the right of the logo, and then press the **Delete** key twice to delete the blank lines between the logo and the navigation bar.

12. Click the **rollover** to select it. Note that there is no information in the Property inspector that identifies this graphic as a rollover except the name, just to the right of the image icon in the upper left corner.

Next, you'll test the rollover by viewing the page in a browser, pointing to the logo, and trying the link.

13. Save the page, preview the page in a browser, and then point to the **logo**. The rollover image appears in the browser. See Figure 4-13.

Figure 4-13	CATALYST LOGO ROLLOVER IMAGE

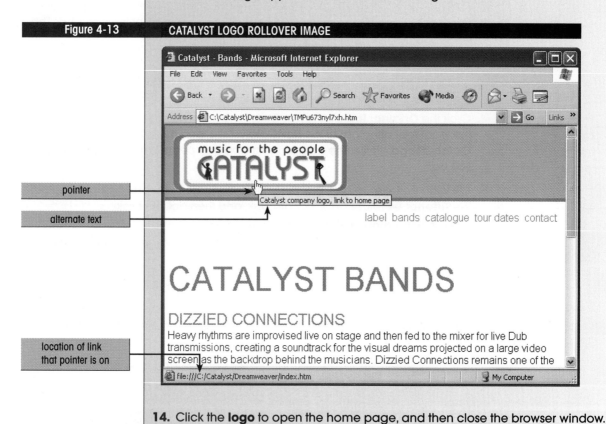

14. Click the **logo** to open the home page, and then close the browser window.

You want the same logo rollover to appear on all the other pages of the NewCatalyst Web site. Rather than inserting the rollover on each page, you can copy it from the bands page, and then paste it on the other pages.

To copy and paste a rollover:

1. Select the **logo** in the bands page.

2. Click **Edit** on the main menu bar, and then click **Copy HTML**.

3. Close the **bands** page.

4. Open the **catalogue.htm** page in a Document window.

5. Select the **logo**, and then press the **Delete** key. The logo is deleted from the page.

6. Click **Edit** on the menu bar, and then click **Paste HTML**. The logo rollover is inserted into the page.

7. With the insertion point blinking to the right of the logo, press the **Delete** key twice to delete the extra lines on the page. Since the new logo looks exactly the same as the graphic you just deleted, you can check to make sure it is the rollover graphic.

8. Click the **logo** to select it, and then verify that the name in the upper left of the Property inspector is "LogoRollover."

9. Save and close the page.

10. Repeat Steps 4 through 9 for the pages **contact.htm**, **index.htm**, **label.htm**, and **tourdates.htm**.

You might want to modify a rollover graphic.

Editing a Rollover

You can edit a rollover by changing the original graphic, changing the rollover graphic, or by editing the code of the rollover. There are several reasons that you might want to edit a rollover. For example, you may need to replace a graphic with an updated design, or you may decide to open the linked page in a new browser window. Dreamweaver does not have a special panel for modifying a rollover. However, you can edit a rollover graphic in three ways:

■ Delete the original graphic and insert a new rollover using the Rollover Image button. This will delete all of the code as well as the graphic and you can create a new rollover from scratch.

■ Replace the original graphic or the rollover graphic with a new one. When you replace a graphic, the attached code remains. You can replace the original graphic by selecting the graphic and then selecting a new source file in the Property inspector. You can replace the rollover graphic by selecting the graphic, opening the Behaviors panel (in the Design panel group), double-clicking onMouseOver in the behavior list, and then selecting a new source file for the rollover graphic.

■ Edit the code for the rollover graphic in Code view if you know JavaScript, or edit the behaviors in the Behaviors panel.

For now, you'll leave the original and rollover images.

Session 4.1 QUICK CHECK

1. What are the three types of file formats that browsers can display?

2. What is the best file format to use for photographs?

3. What can you use the Assets panel for?

4. What is an image map?

5. What is a hotspot?

6. What is a rollover?

SESSION 4.2

In this session, you will work with tables. You will insert a table, and then select, modify, move, resize, and delete the table and table elements. You will create advanced table designs. Finally, you will explore the HTML tags associated with tables, and then redefine the HTML tags associated with tables to modify the external style sheet attached to the page.

Creating Tables

In the early days of the Web, text and images were aligned to the left of the page. Designers soon discovered that they could use tables to provide a vertical and horizontal structure for the content of a Web page. This provided more flexibility in arranging the content and elements on the Web page. Today, tables are used on Web pages to simplify the presentation of data as well as to increase layout options, both of which aid in Web page design.

Tables are grid structures that are divided into rows and columns. **Rows** cross the table horizontally, whereas **columns** cross the table vertically. The container created by the intersection of a row and a column is called a **cell**. The four lines that mark the edges of a cell are called **borders**. Borders can be invisible or visible lines of a width you select. When the borders of the cells of a table are set to 0, the borders still exist but are invisible. The use of tables with invisible borders to place text and images on a Web page presented designers with a whole new world of choices for laying out Web page content.

REFERENCE WINDOW   **RW**

Inserting a Table
- Click the Insert Table button on the Tables tab on the Insert bar.
- Type the number of rows in the Rows text box.
- Type the number of columns in the Columns text box.
- Type a percentage in the Width text box, click the Width list arrow, and then click Percent.
- Type the border width in the Border text box. (Type 0 if you do not want the table structure to appear on the Web page.)
- Click the OK button.

Inserting a Table

You can quickly insert a table into your Web page. Simply move the insertion point to the location on the Web page where you want the table to appear, click the Insert Table button on the Tables tab or on the Common tab of the Insert bar, and then set the parameters for the table. Dreamweaver then inserts the HTML code for the table. The table parameters you can specify are:

- **Rows.** The number of rows that your table will have. You can also add rows to the table later.
- **Columns.** The number of columns that your table will have. You can also add columns to the table later.
- **Width.** The horizontal dimension of the table specified either in pixels or as a percentage of the width of the browser window. Specifying the table width in pixels creates a table that has a somewhat fixed width—the table will still expand to fit the content, if necessary, but it will not change size when the

browser window is resized. Specifying the table width as a percentage creates a table that will adjust in size as the Web page is resized in the browser window. Initially, the table cells all have equal widths; however, you can adjust the height and width of cells, rows, and columns. Be aware that changing the width of a cell changes the width of all the cells in the column, and changing the height of a cell changes the height of all the cells in the row.

- **Border.** The size (in pixels) of the table border. A border of 0 creates an invisible table. By default, the borders of an invisible table are visible within Dreamweaver so you can see the table structure, making the table easier to work with. You must preview the page in a browser to see what the table content will look like without borders.

- **Cell Padding.** The amount of empty space, measured in pixels, maintained between the border of a cell and the cell's content. When no cell padding is specified, most browsers display the table as if the cell padding were set to 1. In most cases, this is fine.

- **Cell Spacing.** The width of the cell walls measured in pixels. Note that if you set the border to 0, then the table still will be invisible no matter what you set the cell spacing to. When no cell spacing is specified, most browsers display the table as if the cell spacing were set to 2. In most cases, this is fine.

You'll create a table to hold the West Coast region tour dates in the Tour Dates page. The table will have 3 columns, 14 rows, and no borders.

To insert a table:

1. If you took a break after the last session, make sure **Dreamweaver** is running and that the **NewCatalyst** Web site is open.

2. Open the **tourdates.htm** page in a Document window, and then move the insertion point below the U.S. map.

3. Click the **Tables** tab on the Insert bar, and then click the **Insert Table** button ▦. The Insert Table dialog box opens. You'll set the table parameters.

4. Type **14** in the Rows text box.

5. Press the **Tab** key, and then type **1** in the Cell Padding text box.

6. Press the **Tab** key, and then type **3** in the Columns text box.

7. Press the **Tab** key, and then type **2** in the Cell Spacing text box.

8. Press the **Tab** key, type **75** in the Width text box, click the **Width** list arrow, and then click **Percent**, if necessary.

9. Press the **Tab** key, and then type **0** in the Border text box.

10. Click the **OK** button. The table appears in the Document window and is selected. Figure 4-14 shows the entire table. You may need to scroll down to see all of it.

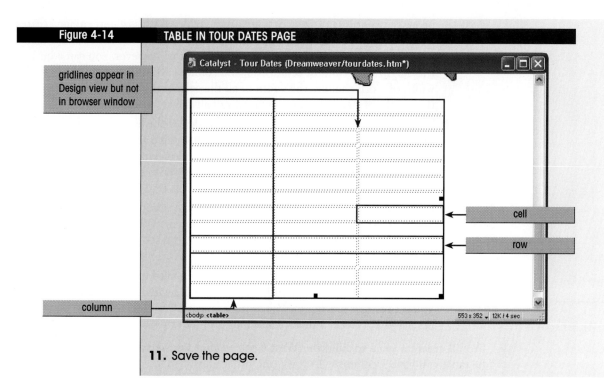

Figure 4-14   TABLE IN TOUR DATES PAGE

gridlines appear in Design view but not in browser window

cell

row

column

11. Save the page.

When you create a table, Dreamweaver inserts a non-breaking space in each cell. Some browsers collapse cells that are empty, thereby destroying your table structure. The non-breaking space is invisible, but it keeps the cells from collapsing. To view a non-breaking space you must be in Code view or Code and Design views.

You will view the non-breaking space in the first cell of the table in the tour dates page.

To view a non-breaking space:

1. Click in the upper left cell of the table on the tour dates page to place the insertion point in the cell.

2. Click the **Show Code and Design Views** button on the Document toolbar. Notice the non-breaking space ( ) in the Code pane. See Figure 4-15.

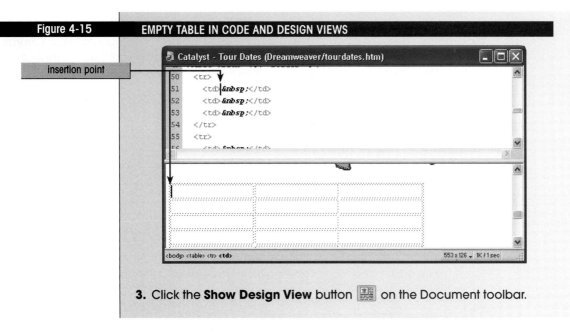

Figure 4-15   EMPTY TABLE IN CODE AND DESIGN VIEWS

insertion point

3. Click the **Show Design View** button ▦ on the Document toolbar.

Next, you will add content to the cells in the table you just created.

Adding Content to Cells

To add text to a cell, all you need to do is click in the cell and type. Pressing the Enter key adds another paragraph within the cell. You can also copy cell data to each cell using the standard Copy and Paste commands. When you type or paste text into a cell, the text wraps within the cell to fit the width you defined. If you check the No Wrap option in the Property inspector, the cell will expand to fit the text in a browser; however the text will still wrap when you view the page in the Dreamweaver environment.

There are several keyboard commands that will help you move through your table. To move to the next adjacent cell, press the Tab key. Pressing the Tab key in the last cell of the table adds a new row to the table. Pressing the Shift+Tab keys moves the insertion point to the previous cell. You also can use the arrow keys to move the insertion point to an adjacent cell.

In addition to text, you can insert graphics into table cells using the Image button on the Common tab of the Insert bar. When a graphic is inserted into a cell, the cell's column width and row height expand as needed to accommodate the graphic.

Brian has supplied the West Coast tour schedule for you to enter into the table on the Tour Dates page.

To add text to a table:

1. With the insertion point in the first cell in the table, type **West Coast Tour Dates**, and then press the **Tab** key. The text appears in the first cell and the insertion point moves to the second column of the first row.

2. Press the **Left Arrow** key and then press the **Down Arrow** key. The insertion point moves to the cell in the first column and the second row.

3. Type the following information into the table, pressing the **Tab** key to move to the next cell (make sure you don't press the Enter key while typing text in a cell; the text will wrap by itself):

Date	Location / Venue	Band
1/4 to 1/6	Seattle, WA / Graceland	Life in Minor Chords, Dizzied Connections

1/11 to 1/13	San Francisco, CA / Bottom of the Hill	Dizzied Connections
1/18 to 1/20	Monterey, CA / The Long Bar	Life in Minor Chords, Dizzied Connections
2/8 to 2/10	Silverlake, CA / Spaceland	Surface Suction
2/15 to 2/17	Arcata, CA / Depot	Dizzied Connections
2/22 to 2/24	San Diego, CA / Casbah	Surface Suction
3/8 to 3/10	Portland, OR / Blackbird	Life in Minor Chords, Dizzied Connections
3/15 to 3/17	Monterey, CA / The Long Bar	Surface Suction
3/22 to 3/24	Los Angeles, CA / Spaceland	Dizzied Connections
4/5 to 4/7	San Francisco, CA / The Dance Hall	Surface Suction
4/12 to 4/14	Seattle, WA / Graceland	Dizzied Connections
4/19 to 4/21	Phoenix, AZ / Modified	Life in Minor Chords, Dizzied Connections

TROUBLE? If you don't have enough rows for all of the entries, press the Tab key in the last cell of the table. If you have a blank row at the end of the table, you pressed the Tab key after the final entry. You'll learn how to delete this extra row shortly.

4. Save the page. Figure 4-16 shows most of the table in Design view. You will need to scroll to see all of the rows.

| Figure 4-16 | TOUR DATES TABLE IN DESIGN VIEW |

All the formatting options available for text on a Web page can also be applied to text in a table. Text formatting attributes are available in the Property inspector when you select a cell, a row, or a column. You can also create CSS styles for table text.

Selecting Tables and Table Elements

You will want to modify your table and its elements to fit the needs of the particular Web page layout or content. To work with a table or table element, you will need to select it. You can select a table cell, a row, a column, or the table itself.

Selecting a Table

When you want to change attributes that affect the entire table, the whole table must be selected. When the entire table is selected, a bold black line surrounds the table and resizing handles appear on the left side, lower right corner, and bottom of the table. The attributes in the Property inspector also change to reflect the entire table.

You'll use two methods to deselect and then select the table in the Tour Dates page.

To select an entire table:

1. Click outside the table to deselect the table.

2. Right-click the **table**, point to **Table** on the context menu, and then click **Select Table**. The table is selected. See Figure 4-17.

| Figure 4-17 | SELECTED TABLE |

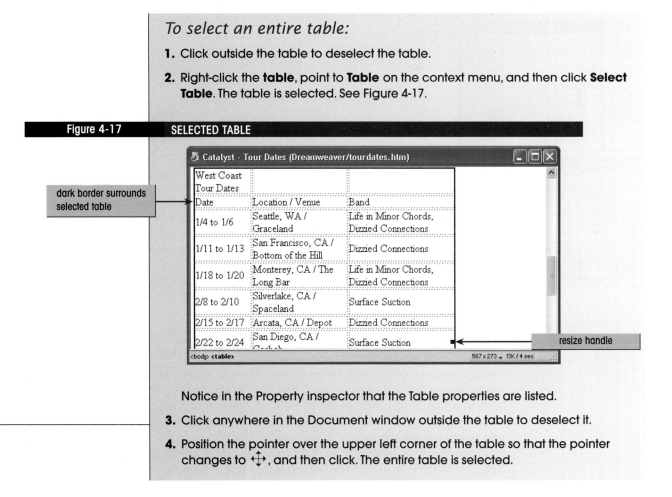

dark border surrounds
selected table

resize handle

Notice in the Property inspector that the Table properties are listed.

3. Click anywhere in the Document window outside the table to deselect it.

4. Position the pointer over the upper left corner of the table so that the pointer changes to ✛, and then click. The entire table is selected.

Selecting a Table Cell

When you want to adjust the attributes of a single cell, you must select that cell. To select the entire cell, you drag across the cell until the cell borders are bold black. If the cell contains any content, the content is selected as well. Clicking in a cell does not select the cell, but it does display the cell properties in the Property inspector. The process is the same to select a group of cells except that you drag across all the cells you want to select; the borders of all the selected cells are bold black. Any content within the selected cells is also selected.

You'll select a single cell and a group of cells in the table on the Tour Dates page.

To select cells:

1. Point to the **cell** at the upper left corner of the table.

2. Drag across the **cell** in the upper left corner of the table. The cell is selected. See Figure 4-18.

   TROUBLE? If you are having trouble selecting the cell instead of the text inside the cell, make sure that you do not release the mouse button until the pointer is outside the cell border. It doesn't matter where in the cell you start dragging, as long as you drag to outside the cell border.

Figure 4-18	SELECTED CELL IN TABLE

selected cell

3. Drag across the three cells in the top row until they have bold black borders. The three cells are selected.

4. Click outside the table to deselect the cells.

Selecting Columns and Rows

You can use the mouse to select one or more columns or rows. To select a column, click above the top border of the column you wish to select. To select a row, click to the left of the row you wish to select. If you want to select multiple columns or rows, you drag across additional columns or rows. The borders of all the cells in the selected column or row are bold. You can also tell that a column or row is selected because the word *Column* or *Row* appears in the Property inspector alongside an icon showing a highlighted column or row in a table. Selecting all the cells in a row or column is the same as selecting the row or column.

You'll select the third column in the table on the Tour Dates page, and then you'll select the second row of cells.

To select a row and a column of cells:

1. Position the pointer above the top border of the third column of the table. The pointer changes to ↓.

2. Click the mouse button. The third column of the table is selected. See Figure 4-19.

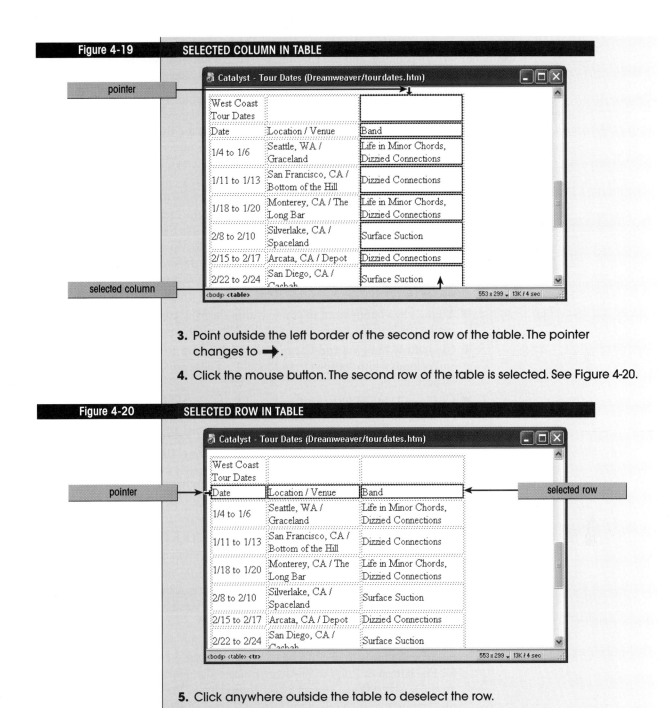

Figure 4-19   **SELECTED COLUMN IN TABLE**

Figure 4-20   **SELECTED ROW IN TABLE**

3. Point outside the left border of the second row of the table. The pointer changes to ➡.

4. Click the mouse button. The second row of the table is selected. See Figure 4-20.

5. Click anywhere outside the table to deselect the row.

Working with the Entire Table

Once a table is selected you can change the attributes of the table, resize the table, move the table, or delete the table.

Modifying Table Attributes

Sometimes it is necessary to change the attributes of a table. You can change the attributes for an existing table in the Property inspector. When the entire table is selected, the

Property inspector includes the attributes from the Insert Table dialog box: rows, columns, width, border, cell padding, and cell spacing, as well as additional formatting attributes. The additional attributes available in the Property inspector include:

- **Table ID.** A unique descriptive name for the table. The table name helps you to distinguish between tables when you have more than one table in a Web page. Also, some programming languages use the name to refer to the table. The Table ID must begin with a letter or underscore, may contain letters and numbers, and may not contain spaces or symbols.

- **H (Height).** The vertical dimension of the table in pixels or a percentage of the height of the browser window. Most of the time it is not necessary to specify a table height. If no value is entered in the Height text box, the cells remain at their default height. Specifying the table height in pixels creates a table that has a somewhat fixed height: the table will still expand to fit the content, but it will not change size when the browser window is resized. Specifying the table height as a percentage creates a table that will adjust in size as the Web page is resized in the browser window.

- **Align.** The alignment of the table within the Web page. Table alignment can be the browser's default alignment, left, right, or center.

- **Clear Row Heights** and **Clear Column Widths.** Removes all row height and column width settings from the table. These are buttons in the Property inspector.

- **Convert Table Widths to Pixels** and **Convert Table Heights to Pixels.** Changes the table width or table height from a percentage to its current width or height in pixels. These are buttons in the Property inspector.

- **Convert Table Widths to Percent** and **Convert Table Heights to Percent.** Changes the current table width or height from pixels to a percentage of the browser window. These are buttons in the Property inspector.

- **Bg Color (Background Color).** The background color for the entire table. You specify a color by typing its hexadecimal value in the Bg Color text box or by selecting the color with the color picker. If a background color is not specified, the Web page background is seen through the table.

- **Brdr Color (Border Color).** The border color for the entire table. You can specify a color in the same manner as for the background color using the Brdr Color text box or color picker. (Note that some versions of Netscape do not display border color correctly.)

- **Bg Image (Background Image).** The background image for the table. You can type the file path and filename in the Bg Image text box, or use the Browse for File button or Point to File icon to select a graphic file to use as the background image. (When you set a background image for the table, Netscape will tile the image in each cell of the table as if you had set the image as the background in each individual cell. Internet Explorer will display the image across all of the cells.)

Because there are differences in the way that browsers handle tables (like the differences in the way browsers display border color and background image), it is very important that you preview Web pages that use tables in all of the different browsers that you intend to support. If you find problems in the way a browser displays the tables you have created, you can look at sites like *www.blooberry.com* as well as support sites from browser manufacturers like *www.microsoft.com* and *home.netscape.com* to look up issues and fixes for specific browsers and browser versions.

You'll name the table in the Tour Dates page *West Coast* and align the table to the center of the page.

To change table attributes:

1. Select the **table** on the tourdates.htm page.

2. Type **West Coast Tour Dates** in the Table ID text box in the Property inspector.

3. Click the **Align** list arrow in the Property inspector, and then click **Center**. The table is centered on the page.

4. Double-click in the **CellPad** text box, type **0**, double-click in the **CellSpace** text box, type **0**, and then press the **Enter** key. The cell padding and cell spacing tighten up. See Figure 4-21.

Figure 4-21	TABLE WITH MODIFIED ATTRIBUTES

cell padding and spacing set to 0

table name

5. Save the page.

Next, you'll change the table's size and location.

Resizing and Moving a Table

Sometimes you know how you want a table to look on a page, but you don't know the exact dimensions to create that look. When a table is selected, you can manually adjust the size (height and width) and position from within the Document window. To resize the table, you drag the lower right corner of the table until the table is the size you want. A dotted border appears as you drag, indicating the new dimensions the table will have when you release the mouse button. When you manually resize a table, Dreamweaver inserts the new width and height values, which you can see in the Property inspector. The values are calculated in the unit of measure (percentage or pixels) that you specified previously for the attribute. If no height value was specified previously, the new value will be in pixels. You can move a table on the page by cutting and pasting the table or by dragging the table to the new location.

You will adjust the size and location of the table on the Tour Dates page.

To resize and move a table:

1. If the rulers are not visible, click **View** on the main menu bar, point to **Rulers**, and then click **Show**.

2. Click **View** on the main menu bar, point to **Rulers**, and then click **Pixels**, if necessary.

3. Click a **resize handle** on the table to make the Document window active and keep the table selected, and then point to the lower right corner of the selected table. The pointer changes to ↖↘.

4. Press and hold the left mouse button, drag down and to the right about 200 pixels. A dotted border shows you the new dimensions of the table. See Figure 4-22.

Figure 4-22	RESIZING A TABLE

TROUBLE? If the exact numbers on your screen are different than those shown (in other words, if the table is in a different position relative to the measurements on the rulers), then your screen size is different than the one shown in the figure. Don't be concerned about this.

5. Release the mouse button. The height and width values change in the Property inspector, reflecting the larger table size. The table doesn't need to be this large, so you'll try a smaller size.

6. Drag the lower right corner of the table up and to the left about 300 pixels to reduce the table size. The new height and width values appear in the Property inspector, reflecting the smaller table size.

   The text is difficult to read in the smaller table, so you'll return to the original table size by resetting the values in the Property inspector.

7. Double-click in the **W** text box in the Property inspector, type **75**, double-click in the **H** text box, and then press the **Delete** key to delete the value in the Height text box. The table returns to its original size.

   Next, you'll move the table to another location.

8. Click **View** on the main menu bar, point to **Rulers**, and then click **Show** to hide the rulers.

9. Position the pointer to the upper left corner of the selected table so that the pointer changes to ✛.

10. Press and hold the left mouse button, and then drag the **table** above the map. The table moves to the new location. See Figure 4-23.

TROUBLE? If there is no blank line between the page heading and the map, release the mouse button when the indicator line is to the left of the map.

| Figure 4-23 | REPOSITIONED TABLE |

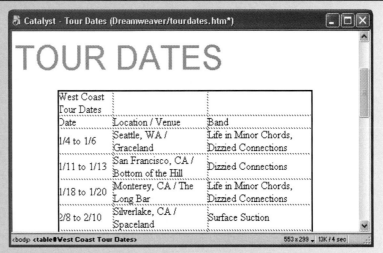

The original position is more appropriate, so you'll move the table back to that location.

11. Drag the **table** to its original position below the map, and then save the page.

TROUBLE? If the window won't scroll when you try to reposition the table, move the pointer near the vertical scroll bar while you are dragging.

Deleting a Table

While creating a Web page, you may need to delete a table completely. To delete a table, simply select the table and then press the Delete key. The table as well as any content contained in the table is deleted from the page.

Working with Table Cells

You can customize tables by modifying individual cells or groups of cells. When a cell or a group of cells is selected, you can change its attributes in the Property inspector, including modifying the formatting attributes of cell content and changing the cell properties.

Modifying Cell Formatting and Layout

Cells have a different set of attributes than tables. Once a cell has been selected, you can change the attributes, and the attributes of any content within the cell, in the Property inspector. Cell attributes include text formatting, because within a table, content can be contained only in cells.

You can format the content of an entire table by selecting all of the cells in the table and then changing the text formatting attributes. Text formatting attributes are not available when you select the table itself, because the HTML code for text formatting is in the tags for the individual cells and rows not in the code for the table itself. This setup allows for formatting variations within cells and makes tables more flexible.

In addition to the familiar text formatting attributes, you can use the following options in the Property inspector to change the cell's layout attributes:

- **Merges selected cells using spans.** Joins all selected cells into one cell. This button is active only if more than one cell is selected.

- **Splits cell into rows or columns.** Divides a single cell into multiple rows or columns. This button is active only when a single cell is selected.

- **Horz (Horizontal).** The horizontal alignment options for the cell's content. Content can be aligned to the browser's default setting, left, right, or center.

- **Vert (Vertical).** The vertical alignment options for the cells content. Content can be aligned to the browser's default setting, top, middle, bottom, or baseline.

- **No Wrap.** Enables or disables word wrapping. Word wrapping enables a cell to expand horizontally and vertically to accommodate added content. If the No Wrap checkbox is checked, then the cell will expand only horizontally to accommodate the added content.

- **Header.** Formats the selected cell or rows as a table header. By default, the content of header cells is bold and centered; however, you can redefine the header cell tag with CSS styles to create a custom look.

- **Bg (Background Image).** The background image for a cell, column, or row. You can type the file path and filename of the background image or browse to select the background image. If no image is specified, the Web page background is seen through the cell. The background image for a cell takes precedence over the background color for the cell. Also, the background image for a cell takes precedence over a background image or color for the table.

- **Bg (Background Color).** The background color for the selected cells. You can specify a color by typing its hexadecimal number in the Bg text box or by selecting the color with the color picker. If no color is specified, the Web page background is seen through the cell. The background color for a cell takes precedence over the background image or color for the table.

- **Brdr (Border Color).** The color of the cell border. You can type a hexadecimal number in the Brdr text box or select a color with the color picker. If the cell borders for the table are set to zero, the border is not seen.

When a single cell is selected, the word *Cell* and an icon of a table with a selected cell appear in the lower left corner of the Property inspector. You can then verify that you have selected the correct element before you begin to adjust the attributes.

You'll merge the cells in the top row of the table, and then make the new cell a header cell.

To adjust cells:

1. Select the three cells in the top row of the table on the tour dates page.

2. Click the **Merges selected cells using spans** button ⊞ in the Property inspector. The three cells are combined into one.

3. Click the **Header** checkbox in the Property inspector to check it. The text in the merged cell is centered and boldface. See Figure 4-24.

Figure 4-24   **CELLS MERGED AND FORMATTED AS HEADER CELLS**

merged cells

check to format selected
cells as header cells

click to merge
selected cells

4. Save the page.

Next, you adjust the height and width of cells.

Adjusting the Row Span and Column Span of Cells

You can adjust the row span and the column span of individual cells of a table. **Row span** is the height of the cell measured in rows. **Column span** is the width of the cell measured in columns. You can change the row and column spans by increments of one. For example, increasing a cell's row span makes the selected cell span the height of two rows of the table. If you increase the row span of a cell twice, the cell becomes three rows high. Decreasing the row span removes one increment. If a cell is only one row high, decreasing the row span does not work. Adjusting column span works the same way. Increasing the column span of a cell makes the selected cell span the width of two columns of the table. If you increase the column span of a cell twice, it becomes three columns wide. Decreasing the column span removes one increment. If a cell is only one column wide, decreasing the column span does not work.

You'll adjust the row span and the column span of cells in the table in the Catalyst - Tour Dates page.

To adjust row span and column span of cells:

1. Right-click the **cell** in the first column and the second row of the table, point to **Table** on the context menu, and then click **Increase Row Span**. The cell's height spans two table rows. (Actually the cell merges with the one below it and the content of both cells is combined).

2. Right-click the **cell** in the first column and the second row of the table, point to **Table** on the context menu, and then click **Increase Column Span**. The cell's width spans two table columns. Because the merged cell was the height of two cells in the adjoining column before you executed the command, the three cells merged and all of the cell content was combined. See Figure 4-25.

Figure 4-25	CELL AFTER INCREASING ROW AND COLUMN SPANS

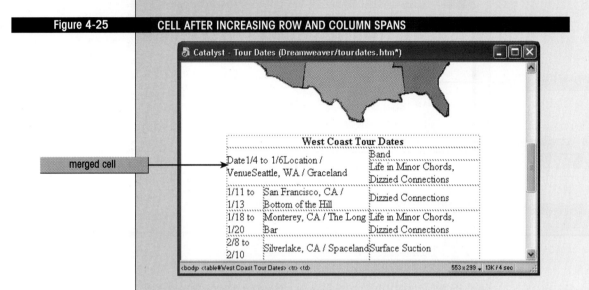

The cell doesn't need to have a different height or width, so you'll decrease the row span and the column span.

3. Right-click the cell in the first column and the second row of the table, point to **Table** on the context menu, and then click **Decrease Row Span**.

4. Right-click the **cell** in the first column and the second row of the table, point to **Table** on the context menu, and then click **Decrease Column Span**. The cell's height and width return their original settings, but all of the text is still in one cell.

5. Right-click the **cell** in the first column and the third row of the table, point to **Table**, and then click **Decrease Column Span**. The cell's height and width return to their original settings.

6. Select **1/4 to 1/6** in the cell in the first column and the second row, press the **Ctrl+X** keys to cut the selected text, click in the first cell in the third row in the table, and then press the **Ctrl+V** keys to paste the cut text.

7. Cut **Location / Venue** from the first cell in the second row, and paste the cut text into the **cell** in the second column and second row of the table.

8. Cut **Seattle, WA / Graceland** from the first cell in the second row, and paste the cut text into the cell in the second column and third row of the table. The text is in the correct cells again.

9. Save the page.

You can also modify entire rows and columns in a table, not just individual cells.

Working with Rows and Columns

Table rows and columns provide the vertical and horizontal structure for the content of the table, as well as for the content of some Web pages. When a row or column is selected, you can change its attributes, and resize, add, or delete the entire row or column. Selecting all the cells in a row or column is the same as selecting the row or column.

Modifying Rows and Columns

The attribute options available for rows and columns are the same as those for cells. When you modify attributes while a row or column is selected, the changes apply to all of the cells in the selected row or column. Before you change attributes, verify that the correct element is selected by looking in the Property inspector.

You want to change the second row of the table to a header row.

To change row attributes:

1. Select the **second row** of the table.

2. Click the **Header** checkbox in the Property inspector to check it. The content of each cell in the row is centered and in boldface.

3. Save the page.

Next you'll resize the columns.

Resizing Columns and Rows

When a table is created, columns are all of equal width and rows are all the default height. You can adjust the width of a selected column by typing a new value in the W (Width) text box or by dragging a column's left or right border to the desired position. When you adjust a column width manually, Dreamweaver calculates the width you selected. You can adjust the height of a selected row by typing a new height value into the H (Height) text box or by dragging the row's top or bottom border to the desired position. When you adjust a row height manually, Dreamweaver calculates the height you selected.

You need to resize the columns in the table to better fit the content.

To resize columns:

1. Position the pointer on the right border of the first column. The pointer changes to ┼╟→.

2. Drag the border so that the content in the first column appears on only one line. See Figure 4-26.

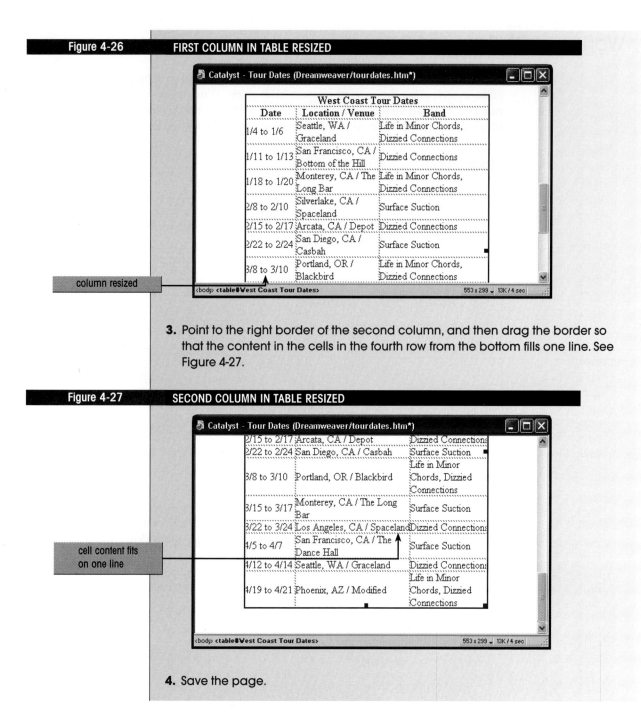

Figure 4-26   FIRST COLUMN IN TABLE RESIZED

column resized

Figure 4-27   SECOND COLUMN IN TABLE RESIZED

cell content fits on one line

3. Point to the right border of the second column, and then drag the border so that the content in the cells in the fourth row from the bottom fills one line. See Figure 4-27.

4. Save the page.

Next you'll delete a row in the table.

Adding and Deleting Columns and Rows

As you work, you might find you need more or fewer columns and rows in a table. To insert a column, you select a cell or a column and use the Insert Column command. A new column of the same width as the selected cell or column is inserted to the left of the selection. To insert a row, you select a cell or a row and use the Insert Row command. The new row is added above the selected cell or row. You can also add a new row at the end of the table by clicking in the last cell of the table and pressing the Tab key. You can add multiple columns or rows by using the Insert Rows or Columns command; when you click this command, a dialog box opens and you set the number of columns or rows you want to insert and where you want to insert them relative to the selection.

If you need to remove extra columns or rows, you can select the column or row and then use the Delete Column or Delete Row command. Be aware that all the content in that column or row is also deleted. Once a column or row is selected, you can also press the Delete key to remove the selected column or row and all of its content.

Brian calls to tell you that the shows in Phoenix on 4/19 to 4/21 have been postponed. He asks you to delete the row with that information from the table.

To delete a row:

1. Select the **last row** of the table.

2. Right-click the selected row, point to **Table** on the context menu, and then click **Delete Row**. The row and all its content are removed from the table.

3. If necessary, delete any extra blank rows from the table.

4. Save the page.

The table still needs additional formatting.

Using Preset Table Designs

Because some commonly used table designs are cumbersome to create, Dreamweaver added the Format Table dialog box. The Format Table dialog box contains a number of preset table designs, as well as other options to further customize the preset designs. Applying the customized designs to tables saves you the time of having to change all of the attributes yourself. The features included in the Format Table dialog box include:

- **Preset table design list.** A list of available preset table designs. When you click a design, the sample table on the right shows the attributes associated with that design. The text in the sample table enables you to preview any text formatting options, but the text will not be included in your table.

- **Row Colors.** The colors and alternating pattern to apply to rows. You can enter the hexadecimal code or use the color picker to choose two colors for the rows in your table. The first color will appear first in the color rotation; the second color will appear second. The Alternate list box enables you to choose the frequency with which the chosen colors are used in the table.

- **Top Row.** Customization options for formatting the cells in the top row of the table. Attributes include align, text style, background color, and text color.

- **Left Col (Left Column).** Customization options for formatting the cells in the left column of the table. Attributes include alignment and text styles.

- **Table.** Customizations that apply to the entire table. You can change the Border size in the Border text box.

- **Apply All Attributes to TD Tags Instead of TR Tags.** If you leave this checkbox unchecked (the default), the attributes are applied to the row tags for the table. If the checkbox is checked, the attributes are applied to cell tags. (Cells are distinguished in HTML with the TD tag; rows are distinguished with the TR tag. Table tags will be discussed in depth in the next section.)

For better readability, Brian wants you to add alternating colors to the table rows. Rather than changing the row colors manually, you'll use the Format Table dialog box.

To use the format table feature:

1. Click anywhere in the table, click **Commands** on the main menu bar, and then click **Format Table**. The Format Table dialog box opens.

2. Click **AltRows:Blue&Yellow** in the preset table designs list.

3. In the Row Colors section, replace the hexadecimal color code in the First text box with **#FF6600**, and then replace the color code in the Second text box with **#FF9900**.

4. Click the **Alternate** list arrow, and then click **Every Other Row**, if necessary.

5. Click the **Align** list arrow in the Left Col section, and then click **Center**.

   You do not need to choose any options in the Top Row section, as you have already applied the Heading 1 style to the top row in the table. If you do not change the Top Row or Left Column attributes in the Format Table dialog box, then they will not change in the table.

6. Double-click in the **Border** text box, and then type **0**.

7. Click the **Apply All Attributes to TD Tags Instead of TR Tags** checkbox to check it. See Figure 4-28.

Figure 4-28	COMPLETED FORMAT TABLE DIALOG BOX

8. Click the **OK** button. The colors are applied to every other row of the table and the content of each cell is centered in the cell. See Figure 4-29.

| Figure 4-29 | TABLE WITH NEW FORMAT APPLIED |

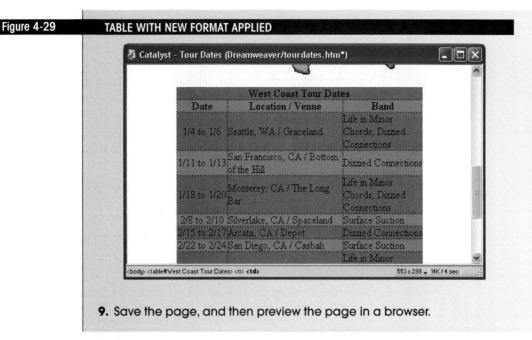

9. Save the page, and then preview the page in a browser.

This look makes the table more attractive and easier to read. Next, you'll explore the HTML tags that define your tables.

Exploring the HTML Code of Tables

Four types of tags are associated with tables: table tags, table row tags, header cell tags, and cell tags. Although Dreamweaver allows you to select columns of cells, there are no HTML tags to define columns. All of the tags associated with tables are **bracketing tags**, which means that they consist of an opening tag and a closing tag that bracket the content to which they are applied. All of the tags can contain a number of parameters for the items they define, as explained in the following list:

- **Table tags.** A set of table tags that surrounds every table. Table tags take the form:

  ```
  <table attribute1="value" attribute2="value">tags
  defining table rows and cells</table>
  ```

  If you apply attributes to the entire table (when the table is selected), the parameters for those attributes appear in the opening table tag.

- **Table Row tags.** A set of row tags surrounds every row. An opening table row tag always appears after the opening table tag, because every table must have at least one row. Table row tags take the form:

  ```
  <tr>all the tags for the cells in the row</tr>
  ```

  If you apply attributes to a row of cells, the parameters for those attributes usually appear in the tags for the cells, not in the tag for the row.

- **Cell Tags.** A set of cell tags surrounds every cell (except those cells you designate as header cells). Cell tags appear between the row tags (they are nested inside the row tags). Every table must have at least one cell. Cell tags take the form:

  ```
  <td attribute1="value" attribute2="value">text in the
  cell</td>
  ```

Every cell in the table has its own set of cell tags (unless it is a header cell), and any attributes applied to the cell are contained in the opening cell tag. Attributes that you apply to columns appear in the cell tags for each cell in the column. If you check the Apply All Attributes to TD Tags Instead of TR Tags checkbox in the Format Table dialog box, then the row attributes you apply will appear in the cell tags as well.

■ **Header Cell Tags.** A set of header cell tags surrounds every cell that you designate as a header cell by checking the Header Cell checkbox in the Property inspector while the cell is selected. Like regular cell tags, header cell tags are nested between the row tags. Header cell tags take the form:

```
<th attribute1="value" attribute2="value">text in the
cell</th>
```

Every header cell in the table has its own set of header cell tags, and any attributes applied to the cell are contained in the opening tag.

A table may seem complex; however, all table code can be broken down into the four types of tags described above.

Figure 4-30 shows the table on the Catalyst - Tour Dates page in Code view.

Figure 4-30   TABLE TAGS IN CODE VIEW

Redefining Table Tags Using CSS

One hallmark of good Web design is to create all the tables in a site with a consistent look. It's also a good idea to keep the fonts and font styles within the table consistent with the font choices you made for the rest of the site. One way to do this is to use a CSS style.

REFERENCE	WINDOW	RW

Redefining Table Tags Using CSS
- Open the CSS Styles panel.
- Click the New CSS Style button.
- Click the Redefine HTML Tag option button.
- Click the Tag list arrow, and then select the table tag you want to modify.
- Click the appropriate option button to define the style in the current page or in a named style sheet.
- Set the appropriate options in the CSS Style Definition dialog box, and then click the OK button.

Brian asks you to format the text in the table so that the font and font styles are consistent with the rest of the NewCatalyst Web site. You will create a CSS style to redefine the HTML tags for header cells and for regular cells.

To redefine header tags and cell tags:

1. Open the **CSS Styles** panel.

2. Create a new style for the table header tag (**th**), selecting the option **Redefine HTML Tag** defined in the style sheet file **CatalystStyle.css**.

3. In the CSS Style Definition for th in CatalystStyles.css dialog box, change the style definition for the **Type** category by setting the font to **Arial, Helvetica, sans-serif**, setting the size to **14 pixels**, setting the weight to **bold**, setting the case to **uppercase**, and setting the color to **#000000**.

4. Change the **Background** category by setting the background color to **#FFCC00**.

5. Click the **OK** button.

   Next, you'll redefine the cell tags.

6. Create a new style for the table cell tag (**td**) selecting the option **Redefine HTML Tag** defined in the style sheet file **CatalystStyle.css**.

7. In the CSS Style Definition for td in CatalystStyles.css dialog box, change the style definition for the **Type** category by setting the font to **Arial, Helvetica, sans-serif**, setting the size to **12 pixels**, and setting the color to **#000000**.

8. Click the **OK** button.

9. Preview the page in a browser. See Figure 4-31.

Figure 4-31	FORMATTED TABLE IN BROWSER WINDOW

10. Drag the lower right corner of the browser window to resize the window first larger and then smaller so that the text in the table rewraps as you resize the window. The table adjusts to fit the browser window.

TROUBLE? If your browser window is maximized, click the Restore button in the browser window title bar, and then try Step 10 again.

11. Close the browser and the **tourdates.htm** page.

In this session, you've created a table, added content, and formatted it in Standard view. In the next session, you'll work with a layout table in Layout view.

Session 4.2 QUICK CHECK

1. Define a table cell.

2. True or False? Table borders can be invisible.

3. Explain the difference between cell padding and cell spacing.

4. Explain what pressing the Tab key does when you are entering data into a table.

5. Describe what happens when you merge two cells.

6. What is the opening HTML tag for a table row?

7. What is the opening HTML tag for a table cell?

In this session, you will learn to work in Layout view. You will draw layout cells and layout tables, and then select, size, move, and modify them. You will add content to the layout table. Finally, you will update the files on the Web and preview the remote Web site.

Planning a Table in Layout View

Tables are frequently used by designers to provide structure for the layout of Web pages. For example, you can use the rough sketches of your Web site as a blueprint to create a table that fills your Web page and that has a cell across the top to hold the company logo, a cell for the navigation system, a cell for the content, and so forth. Creating tables for the layout of a Web page in Standard view can get tricky because it is sometimes necessary to merge and split cells many times to achieve the desired design.

To make it easier to create tables that will be used for Web page layout, Dreamweaver provides a special setting called Layout view, which enables you to draw tables and table cells directly onto a Web page. Drawing individual cells is the most common way of working in Layout view. When you draw a cell on the page, Dreamweaver adds a table that fills the page and additional cells that hold your cell in position. The cells you draw are white with blue outlines; the cells Dreamweaver creates are gray with white outlines. When you add additional cells, Dreamweaver modifies the cells it created to hold all of your cells in place. This method is far more convenient than creating a table in Standard view and then merging and splitting the cells yourself.

In addition to drawing cells, you can also draw tables in Layout view. If you draw a table in an empty page, it is positioned in the upper left corner of the page. Once you have a table, you can draw cells in the table and Dreamweaver will create additional cells to hold yours in place. Additional layout tables created outside the original table will be flush with the lower left corner of the top table. You cannot leave space between layout tables because they provide structure for the page, and leaving spaces between tables makes their position less stable.

If you need to add additional rows and columns that do not align with the structure of the rows and columns you already created, you can draw another table inside an existing table or you can draw a table that surrounds an existing layout table to create a **nested table**. The inside table is the nested table. You cannot draw a nested table inside a cell that you created, only inside a cell that Dreamweaver created to hold your cells in place.

Once you have created tables in Layout view, you can add, resize, and adjust the elements on the page. You cannot create a table in Layout view if the Web page already contains any content. However, you can adjust and resize existing tables even after content has been added to the page. You can switch back and forth between Standard view and Layout view when you are working on your tables. Any table selected in Standard view is considered a regular table and any table selected in Layout view is considered a layout table. This is true regardless of the view in which the table was created.

It is a good idea to sketch the tables for the layout of a Web page before you start to create them. Just like planning the Web site, planning the placement of the cells and tables on the page will help you avoid reworking the page elements, thus saving you time and frustration in the end. Planning the page layout enables you to determine where to place the cells and tables on the page so that your information can be conveyed effectively.

Brian wants you to add a new page to the NewCatalyst site plan. The new page will be titled "What's Hot." There will be a link from the home page of the site that, when clicked, will load the What's Hot page in a new browser window. The What's Hot page will be used to promote new CD releases. It will use tables for structure. It will not have a navigation structure because it is a pop-up promotion instead of another regular page in the site. Figure 4-32 shows a sketch of the layout for the new page.

Figure 4-32   SKETCH OF LAYOUT FOR NEW WHAT'S HOT PAGE

Surface Suction CD cover will go here.

Promotional text will go here.

Song list will go here.

You'll start by creating the What's Hot page, adding a page heading, and attaching the external style sheet to the page.

To create the page and attach the style sheet:

1. If you took a break after the previous session, make sure **Dreamweaver** is running and the **NewCatalyst** Web site is open.

2. Click **File** on the Site panel menu bar, then click **New File** to add a new page named *untitled.htm* to the page list.

3. Type **WhatHot.htm** as the page name, and then press the **Enter** key.

4. Open the **WhatHot.htm** page in a Document window, type **Catalyst - What's Hot** in the Title text box on the Document window toolbar, and then press the **Enter** key.

5. Display the **CSS Styles** panel, if necessary, and then click the **Attach Style Sheet** button . The Link External Style Sheet dialog box opens.

6. Click the **Browse** button, navigate to the **Stylesheets** folder in the root folder of the NewCatalyst site, and then double-click the **CatalystStyle.css** external style sheet located there.

7. Click the **OK** button in the Link External Style Sheet dialog box, and then save the page.

Creating a Table in Layout View

Once you are in Layout view, you can create a table either by drawing a cell and having Dreamweaver create a table around it or by drawing a table and populating it with cells.

REFERENCE WINDOW **RW**

Creating a Table in Layout View
- Click the Layout View button on the Layout tab on the Insert bar.
- Click the Draw Layout Cell button on the Layout tab on the Insert bar, and then drag on the page to draw a table cell.
- Click the Draw Layout Table button on the Layout tab on the Insert bar, and then drag on the page to draw a table.

You'll start by switching to Layout view.

To switch to Layout view:

1. Click the **Layout tab** on the Insert bar. Note that the Standard View button [Standard View] is selected.

2. Click the **Layout View** button [Layout View]. A gray bar at the top of the Document window with the words Layout View written across it indicates that the Document window is now in Layout view.

    TROUBLE? If the Getting Started in Layout View dialog box opens, click the OK button.

3. Click **View** on the main menu bar, point to **Rulers**, and then click **Show**, if necessary, to display the rulers.

Next, you will draw a cell.

Drawing Cells in Layout View

You can use the Draw Layout Cell button on the Layout tab of the Insert bar to create a table or to add cells to an existing table (even if you drew the table in Standard view). A cell cannot exist outside a table. If you draw a cell before you have drawn a table, or if you draw a cell outside a table, Dreamweaver will create a table around the cell to fill the Document window. The number and placement of cells that Dreamweaver creates to fill this table is dependent on the size of the Document window. The cells that you create have a white background, whereas the additional cells that Dreamweaver creates for maintaining the structure are gray. Cells cannot overlap.

While you are drawing a cell, the measurements of the cell, in pixels, are visible on the right side of the status bar. You can use these measurements or the rulers at the top and left of the Document window to help you draw correctly sized cells. You'll draw a cell in Layout view on the Catalyst - What's Hot page. This cell will be the cell in which you will place the CD cover graphic.

To add a cell in Layout view:

1. Click the **Draw Layout Cell** button 🔲 on the **Layout** tab on the Insert bar. The pointer changes to ┼.

2. Click in the upper left corner of the Catalyst - What's Hot page, and then drag down diagonally to draw a square cell approximately 230 pixels by 230 pixels. You can use the rulers to help you measure or you can use the pixel measurements in the status bar at the bottom of the Document window as your guides. The white cell you drew and any gray structure cells that Dreamweaver drew appear in a table that fills the Document window.

   TROUBLE? If the ruler units are not in pixels, click View on the main menu bar, point to Rulers, and then click Pixels.

3. Click the **Collapse arrow** button 🔺 in the lower right of the Property inspector to collapse the Property inspector to two rows, and then drag the bottom border of the Document window to resize the Document window to fill the screen. The size of the gray cells that Dreamweaver drew expand to fill the resized Document window. See Figure 4-33.

Figure 4-33	CELL DRAWN IN LAYOUT VIEW

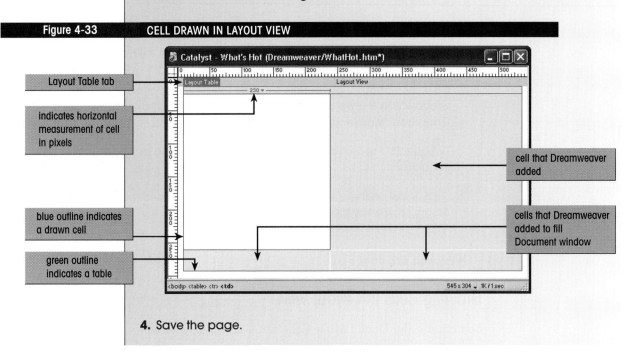

4. Save the page.

Next, you'll add a second table in Layout view.

Drawing a Table in Layout View

You can use the Draw Layout Table button to draw a table in the same way that you drew a cell. Once you have drawn the table, you will have to add cells. You can add more than one table to a page; you can even add a nested table within a table by simply drawing it there. Nested tables are beneficial because each table retains its own attributes. However, some older browsers have difficulty displaying nested tables properly, so consider your target audience before you create a complex table structure for a page layout.

Brian asks you to create an additional table in the Catalyst - What's Hot page to hold the promotional text.

To create a table in Layout view:

1. Click the **Draw Layout Table** button on the **Layout** tab of the Insert bar.

2. Beside the existing cell (and inside the existing table), drag to draw a table that is approximately 230 pixels by 230 pixels. The green outline indicates a table in Layout view.

3. Click the **Draw Layout Cell** button ▥ in the **Layout** tab of the Insert bar, and then draw one cell in the new table. The cell should be the same size as the table. The cell you create has a blue outline. See Figure 4-34.

| **Figure 4-34** | **TABLE AND CELL DRAWN IN LAYOUT VIEW** |

4. Save the page.

Selecting Tables and Cells in Layout View

Once you have created a table, you can work with it in Layout view in much the same way you work with tables in Standard view. Just like Standard view, before you can move, size, and format tables or cells, they must be selected.

Selecting Tables in Layout View

You select tables in Layout view by clicking anywhere in them. You can also click the Layout Table tab at the upper-left corner of the table. To select a table that is completely filled with a cell, you must click the Layout Table tab. After you select a table, the table border changes from a dotted green line to a solid green line, and green resize handles surround the table. Also, an image of a table and the words "Layout Table" appear in the upper-left corner of the Property inspector to indicate that a table in Layout view is selected. You need to select a table to make any other changes to it.

You'll select the tables in the Catalyst - What's Hot page in Layout view.

To select a table in Layout view:

1. Click anywhere in the outer **table**. The resize handles appear and the outer table is selected.

2. Click the **Layout Table** tab at the top of the nested table. The resize handles appear and the nested table is selected, as indicated in the Property inspector. See Figure 4-35.

Figure 4-35	SELECTED TABLE IN LAYOUT VIEW

solid green line and resize handles surround selected table

dotted blue line indicates unselected drawn cell

indicates a table is selected

You can also select cells in Layout view.

Selecting Cells in Layout View

When the pointer is positioned over the border of an unselected cell that you created, the border changes from a dotted blue line to a solid red line. You select a cell in Layout view by clicking the cell's border. When a cell is selected, the perimeter changes to a solid blue line and resize handles appear. Also, an image of a cell and the words "Layout Cell" appear in the Property inspector. Cells in Layout view can be **active**—ready to accept input—but not selected. When a cell in Layout view is active, the border of the cell is a solid blue line and the insertion point blinks inside the cell, but no resize handles appear.

You will select cells on the What's Hot page.

To select a cell in Layout view:

1. Point to the **perimeter** of the left cell. The cell perimeter turns red.

2. Click the red cell **perimeter**. The cell is selected and the perimeter changes to a solid blue line with resize handles visible. See Figure 4-36.

Figure 4-36 | SELECTED CELL IN LAYOUT VIEW

solid blue line and selection handles surround selected cell

dotted green line indicates unselected drawn table

indicates a cell is selected

3. Select the **right** cell, then place the pointer inside the cell and click. The resize handles disappear and the cell is active, but not selected.

Working with Tables in Layout View

Once a table or cell in Layout view is selected, you can change its attributes, resize it, move it, or delete it.

Resizing Tables in Layout View

Once a table has been selected in Layout view, you can drag the table's resize handles to change its size. Nested tables can be moved freely within the outer table. A nested table cannot overlap a cell that you drew in Layout view, but it can overlap the gray cells that Dreamweaver drew to hold the cells that you created in place. Tables in Layout view can also be resized by changing the attributes in the Property inspector while the table is selected.

You'll try resizing the tables in the What's Hot page.

To move and resize a table in Layout view:

1. Click the **Layout Table** tab in the upper left to select the outer table.

2. Drag the right **resize handle** to the right until the width of the table is approximately 815 pixels wide. (Remember to use the rulers to help you.)

TROUBLE? If the rulers are not visible on your screen, click View on the main menu bar, point to Rulers, and then click Show. If the ruler units are not in pixels, point to View on the main menu bar, point to Rulers, and then click Pixels.

3. Drag the bottom resize handle until the table is approximately 500 pixels high.

4. Click the **Layout Table** tab at the top of the nested table, and then drag the table by the tab down to move the nested table below the first layout cell that you drew.

5. Scroll to the bottom of the Document window, click the bottom (green) **border** of the outer table, and then drag the bottom **resize handle** of the outer table up so that the bottom of the outer table is flush with the bottom of the table you just moved.

6. Drag the **Layout Table** tab of the nested table back to its original position, and then drag the bottom resize handle of the nested table down to meet the bottom of the outer table (so that the nested table is approximately 500 pixels high). See Figure 4-37.

Figure 4-37	RESIZED TABLES IN LAYOUT VIEW

7. Save the page.

You can also add formatting to layout tables.

Modifying Table Attributes in Layout View

You can customize tables by changing their attributes. The attributes are visible in the Property inspector when a table is selected in Layout view. You can verify that the table is selected by checking the image and label in the upper-left corner of the Property inspector. The attributes in the Property inspector for tables selected in layout view are similar to those for tables selected in Standard view except for the Autostretch option, Border and Border Color. Table attributes in Layout view include:

■ **Width.** The horizontal dimension of the table. There are two types of widths in Layout view: fixed and autostretch. **Fixed width** is a numeric value, specified in pixels, that does not change when you add content to the cell and applies to the entire table. You can enter a fixed width in the Property inspector. **Autostretch** sets the width of one column to resize automatically with the width of the browser window. Only one column in each table can be set to autostretch. To create a table that autostretches, you select the Autostretch option in the Property inspector and then designate which column you want to autostretch. The default option is fixed width, which you establish when you drag to create the table.

- **Height.** The vertical dimension of the table in pixels. Dreamweaver calculates the height when you draw the table and displays it in the Height box. You can modify this by typing a new value into the Height text box.

- **Background Color.** The background color for the table. You enter the hexadecimal value of the color into the Bg text box or use the color picker to select a color. If a background color is not specified, the Web page background is seen through the table.

- **Cell Padding.** The amount of empty space, measured in pixels, maintained between the border of a cell and the cell's content. When you don't specify cell padding, most browsers display the table as if the cell padding were set to 1.

- **Cell Spacing.** The width of the invisible cell walls, measured in pixels. If the border is set to 0, then the table structure will be invisible despite thick walls. When you don't specify cell spacing, most browsers display the table as if the cell spacing were set to 2.

- **Clear Row Heights** and **Clear Column Width.** Removes the height or width settings for all the cells in a selected table. If there are no cells in the selected table when you clear row heights, the table will collapse completely.

- **Make Widths Consistent.** Resets the widths of the fixed width cells in the selected table to match the cell content when the cell content is wider than the fixed width.

- **Remove All Spacers.** Removes all of the spacer images from the selected layout table. A **spacer image** is a one-pixel transparent image that is inserted into the fixed-width columns in a table created in Layout view that contains an autostretch column to maintain the widths of the fixed width columns.

- **Remove Nesting.** Deletes a selected nested table and adds the cells and their content to the parent table.

Tables that are used for layout are often designated as autostretch because this allows the content of the Web page to adjust to the size of the user's browser window. When you format a table as autostretch, you are asked if you want to create and use a spacer image. The spacer image maintains a minimum width for the fixed width columns in a table with an autostretch column. Without spacer images, the fixed width columns in a table with an autostretch column might disappear in the Design window. The first time you choose autostretch as an option in a Web site, a dialog box opens asking if you want Dreamweaver to create a spacer image file, if you want to use an existing graphic file for your spacer image, or if you don't want to use spacer images in autostretch tables. Usually, you would choose to have Dreamweaver create a spacer image. You can tell Dreamweaver where to store the spacer image it creates. The best choice is in the Graphics folder you created for your site.

When a column in a table is set to autostretch in Layout view, a double set of wavy lines appears at the top of the column. When a column in a table has a fixed width, in Layout view the numeric value of the width appears at the top of the column in the Document window. The sum of the values of the column widths of the table equals the width of the table.

Brian asks that you set the attributes for the outer table in the What's Hot page. You will change the table to an autostretch table so that the contents of the table can scale in the user's browser window. When you select the autostretch option, you will enable Dreamweaver to create a spacer image and you will place it in the Graphics folder in the root folder. You will also change the height of the table to accommodate the graphic and text which you will place in the table.

To set table attributes in Layout view:

1. Scroll to the top of the Document window, if necessary, and then click the **Layout Table** tab of the outer table to select the outer table.

2. Click the **Autostretch** option button in the Property inspector to set the width of the selected table to autostretch. Because you have not yet set autostretch options for this site, the Choose Spacer Image dialog box opens.

   TROUBLE? If the the Choose Spacer Image dialog box does not open skip step 3.

3. Click the **Create a spacer image file** option button, if necessary, click the **OK** button, double-click the **Graphics** folder within the root folder of your NewCatalyst site, and then click the **Save** button. Once the spacer image is set, Dreamweaver will continue to use that spacer image for the layout tables in this site, and you will skip this step.

4. Double-click in the **Height** text box, type **600** and then press the **Enter** key. See Figure 4-38.

Figure 4-38	MODIFIED TABLE ATTRIBUTES SET

outer table selected

height changed
to 600 pixels

Autostretch option selected

5. Save the page.

You can also delete tables in Layout view.

Deleting a Layout Table

You may need to delete a table in Layout view. To delete a table, you need to select the table and press the Delete key, just as you would delete a table in Standard view. If you want to delete a nested table, including the cells and content in the nested table, you select the nested table and press the Delete key. If you want to delete a nested table but add the cells and content from the nested table to the outer table, you first select the nested table and then click the Remove Nesting button in the Property inspector.

You'll delete the nested table from the What's Hot page but you'll add the cells and content to the outer table.

To delete a nested table in Layout view:

1. Select the nested **table** in the What's Hot page.

2. Click the **Remove Nesting** button ▣ in the Property inspector. The nested table structure is deleted from the page, and the cell is added to the outside table.

3. Save the page.

Working with Cells in Layout View

Working with cells in Layout view is similar to working with cells in Standard view. Once a cell is selected, the cell can be moved, sized, formatted, or deleted.

Moving and Resizing Cells in Layout View

When a cell is selected in Layout view, you can move it by clicking the blue border between the resize handles and dragging the cell to the desired location. When the cell is placed in a new location within a table in Layout view, Dreamweaver creates all the additional cells necessary to hold the selected cell in place. To resize a cell, drag a blue resize handle to the desired dimensions, or select the cell and specify the desired dimensions in the Property inspector.

You'll move and resize the cells in the table on the What's Hot page.

To resize and move cells in Layout view:

1. Select the left cell and drag the bottom resize handle until the cell is approximately 425 pixels in height.

2. Select the right cell in the table and drag the bottom resize handle until the cell is approximately 220 pixels in height.

3. Click the left edge of the cell on the right between the blue resize handles and drag the cell below the left cell.

4. Select the cell again, and then drag the resize handle at the bottom of the selected cell down until the cell touches the bottom of the table, if necessary.

5. Select the top left cell and drag the right resize handle to the right until the cell is approximately 425 pixels in width.

6. Click the **Draw Layout Cell** button ▦ on the **Layout** tab of the Insert bar, and then draw a third cell to the right of the upper left cell that fills the gray space on the right side of the table. See Figure 4-39.

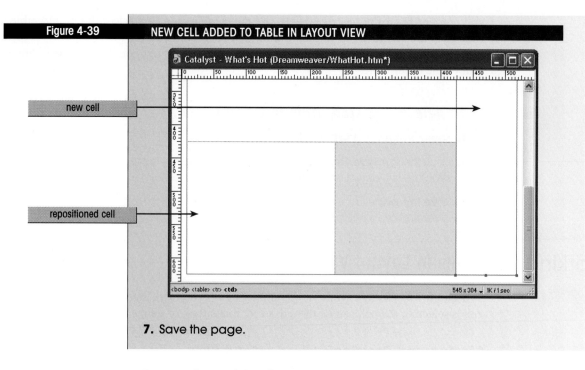

Figure 4-39   **NEW CELL ADDED TO TABLE IN LAYOUT VIEW**

7. Save the page.

You can also modify cell attributes in Layout view.

Modifying Cell Attributes in Layout View

When a cell is selected in Layout view, the formatting attributes for the cell that are associated with the Layout view are visible in the Property inspector. Once a cell has been selected, you can change the attributes of that cell in the Property inspector. Make sure you select the cell to change its attributes. If the cell is only active (ready to accept input), the attributes associated with text appear in the Property inspector instead of the cell attributes. Cell attributes in Layout view include:

- **Width.** The horizontal dimension of the cell. Like a table, in Layout view a cell can be fixed width or autostretch width.

- **Height.** The vertical dimension of the cell in pixels. You can change the value in the Height text box. If you do not change it, the cell remains the height that it was drawn.

- **Bg (Background Color).** The background color for the cell. You can enter the hexadecimal value of a color into the Bg text box or use the Color Picker to select a color. If a background color is not specified, the Web page background is seen through the table.

- **Horz (Horizontal).** The horizontal alignment of the cell's content. Content can be aligned to the browser's default setting, left, right, or center.

- **Vert (Vertical).** The vertical alignment of the content of the cell. Content can be aligned to the browser's default setting, top, middle, bottom, or baseline.

- **No Wrap.** Enables or disables word wrap within the cell.

You can switch back and forth between Standard view and Layout view when you are working with cells. Any cell selected in Standard view is considered a regular cell and any cell selected in Layout view is considered a layout cell. This is true regardless of in which view the cell was created. To modify attributes like border and border color, you must be in Standard view. To modify attributes like autostretch, you must be in Layout view.

You'll set the attributes for the layout cells in the What's Hot page.

To set the attributes of cells in Layout view:

1. Select the cell in the lower left corner of the table.

2. Click the **Fixed** option button, if necessary, double-click in the **Width** text box in the Property inspector, type **400**, and then press the **Enter** key. The cell resizes to 400 pixels wide.

3. Select the **cell** again, if necessary, click the **Horz** list arrow, and then click **Center** to change the horizontal alignment to center.

4. Click the **Vert** list arrow, and then click **Top** to change the vertical alignment to top.

5. Select the **cell** at the upper left corner of the table.

6. Click the **Fixed** option button in the Property inspector, if necessary, double-click in the **Width** text box, type **400**, press the **Tab** key to move to the Height text box, type **400**, and then press the **Enter** key.

7. Change the horizontal alignment to **Left**, and change the vertical alignment to **Bottom**.

8. Select the **cell** at the right of the table, and then drag the left **resize handle** to the left until the cell is flush with the other cells in the table.

   TROUBLE? If the bottom left cell resized to be wider than 400 pixels preventing you from widening the tall cell on the right, select the bottom cell, double-click in the Width text box, type 400, press the Enter key, and then try Step 8 again.

9. Click the **Autostretch** option button in the Property inspector, and then change the horizontal alignment to **Center** and the vertical alignment to **Middle**. See Figure 4-40.

Figure 4-40	MODIFIED CELLS IN LAYOUT VIEW

resized cells

cell set to autostretch

10. Click the **Expander arrow** button ⊡ in the lower right of the Property inspector to expand the Property inspector to four rows, click **Window** on the main menu bar, and then click **Tile Horizontally**. The Document window resizes to fit the work area.

11. Click **View** on the main menu bar, point to **Rulers**, and then click **Show** to turn off the rulers.

12. Save the page.

Now you are ready to add content to the cells you drew in Layout view.

Adding Content to Cells in Layout View

You can add content to cells in either Layout view or Standard view. Adding content to a cell in Layout view is just like adding content to a cell in Standard view. Just click in the cell and start typing. To add graphics to a cell in Layout view, click in the cell and use the Image button on the Insert bar to select the desired graphic.

Brian wants you to place a graphic of a CD cover in the upper left cell and a song list in the lower left cell. You will type the promotional text in the right cell of the table.

To add content to cells in Layout view:

1. Click in the upper left cell of the table. The insertion point blinks at the bottom left of the cell.

2. Click the **Common** tab on the Insert bar, click the **Image** button 🖾, and then insert the Black Lab CD cover **SurfaceSuctionCDcover.jpg** graphic in the **Tutorial.04\Tutorial** folder on your Data Disk.

3. Click the **Yes** button to save a copy to the root folder, and then save the copy to the **Graphics** folder in the root folder of the NewCatalyst site.

4. Open the **catalogue.htm** page in a Document window, select the **Surface Suction: Black Lab CD title** and **song list**, click **Edit** on the main menu bar, click **Copy HTML**, and then close the page.

5. Click in the lower left cell of the table on the What's Hot page, press the **Enter** key, click **Edit** on the main menu bar, and then click **Paste HTML**.

6. Click in the cell on the right side of the table, and then type **Black Lab: The latest release from Surface Suction**.

7. Select the text you just typed, click the **Format** list arrow in the Property inspector, and then click **Heading1**.

8. Press the **Right Arrow** key, press the **Enter** key to skip a line, and then type **Available at record stores in your area**.

9. Select the text you just typed, open the **CSS Styles** panel in the **Design** panel group, if necessary, click the **Apply Styles** option button if necessary, and then click **CatalystSubHeadings**.

10. Save and close the page, and then preview the page in a browser. See Figure 4-41.

Figure 4-41	TABLE ON WHAT'S HOT PAGE IN BROWSER WINDOW

11. Drag the lower right corner of the browser window to resize the window larger and then smaller so that the text on the right rewraps as you resize the window. This is because the column on the right is an adjustable width column, while the column on the left has a fixed width.

TROUBLE? If your browser window is maximized, click the Restore button in the browser window title bar, and then try Step 11 again.

12. Close the browser window.

Finally, you will add a text hyperlink to the home page and target the link to open the What's Hot page in a new window. You can specify where a linked Web page will open by defining a target for the linked page. A **target** is the page or browser window in which a linked Web page will open.

To add a targeted link to the What's Hot page:

1. Open the home page in a Document window.

2. Click the **Layout** tab on the Insert bar, and then click the **Standard View** button Standard View .

3. Place the pointer below the navigation text, and then press the **Enter** key five times.

4. Type **What's Hot at Catalyst**.

5. Select the text you just typed, click **3rdTierSubHeadings** in the CSS Styles panel, and then click the **Align Center** button ☰ in the Property inspector.

> TROUBLE ? If you can't find the Align Center button in the Property inspector, click the Toggle CSS/HTML Mode button.
>
> 6. Click the **Point to File** icon ⊕ beside the Link text box in the Property inspector, and then drag to **WhatHot.htm** in the Site panel to create a link.
>
> 7. Click the **Target** list arrow in the Property inspector, then click **_blank**. Now the linked page will open in a new browser window when the link is clicked.
>
> TROUBLE? If the Target list box is inactive, click anywhere in the Document window to deselect the link text, then select the line again.
>
> 8. Save and close the page.
>
> 9. Preview the home page in a browser, and then click the **What's Hot** link. A new browser window opens displaying the What's Hot page.
>
> 10. Close both browser windows.

Now you will upload the site to the remote server.

Updating the Web Site on the Remote Server

As a final review of the changes you made to the NewCatalyst Web site, you'll update the files on the remote server and review the page over the Internet. You need to upload every page of the site (bands.htm, catalogue.htm, contact.htm, index.htm, label.htm, tourdates.htm, and WhatHot.htm) because you have made changes to every page. When you upload the pages, you will also need to include the dependent files so that the new graphics and new CSS styles are uploaded to the remote server. Then you'll preview the site on the Web.

> ### To upload a site to the remote server:
>
> 1. Click the **Collapse** arrow ▼ in the Design panel group to close the group.
>
> 2. Click the **Connects to remote host** button 🔌 on the Site panel toolbar to connect to the remote host.
>
> 3. Click the **View** list arrow on the Site panel toolbar, and then click **Local View**.
>
> 4. Select **bands.htm, catalogue.htm, contact.htm, index.htm, label.htm, tourdates.htm**, and the **WhatHot.htm** files in the Local view list, and then click the **Put File(s)** button ⬆ on the Site panel toolbar.
>
> 5. Click the **Yes** button when asked if you want to include dependent files, because you have not yet uploaded the new dependent file for the site.
>
> 6. Click the **View** list arrow on the Site panel toolbar, and then click **Remote View**.
>
> 7. Double-click the **Graphics** folder in the Remote file list in the Site panel. Note that copies of the new graphic files (CatalystLogoRollover.gif, spacer.gif, SurfaceSuctionCDcover.jpg, and USmap.gif) were uploaded to the remote site.
>
> 8. Click the **Disconnects from remote host** button 🔌 on the Site panel toolbar, click the **View** list arrow on the Site panel toolbar, and then click **Local View**.
>
> 9. Close the **NewCatalyst** site.

Next, you'll preview the updated site in a browser. The site will include all of the new styles and text that you added to your local version.

To preview the updated site in a browser:

1. Open your browser, type the URL of your remote site in the Address text box on the browser toolbar, and then press the **Enter** key.

2. Open the **home** page, if necessary, and then click the **label** link to make sure that the page was successfully uploaded.

   TROUBLE? If the new CSS styles that you created do not appear in your browser window, click the Refresh button on the browser window toolbar.

3. Move the pointer over the **Catalyst** logo on the label page to see the rollover graphic, and then click the **logo** to return to the home page.

4. Click the **bands** link to make sure that the page was successfully uploaded, move the pointer over the **Catalyst** logo, and then click the **logo** to return to the home page.

5. Click the **catalogue** link to make sure that the page was successfully uploaded, move the pointer over the **Catalyst** logo, and then click the **logo** to return to the home page.

6. Click the **tour dates** link to make sure that the page was successfully uploaded, move the pointer over the **Catalyst** logo, and then click the **logo** to return to the home page.

7. Click the **contact** link to make sure that the page was successfully uploaded, move the pointer over the **Catalyst** logo, and then click the **logo** to return to the home page.

8. Click the **What's Hot at Catalyst** link to make sure that the page was successfully uploaded, examine the What's Hot page, and then close that browser window.

9. Close the browser window.

Session 4.3 QUICK CHECK

1. What is a nested table?

2. Why is it a good idea to plan the page layout when you are using tables?

3. True or False? A cell cannot exist outside a table.

4. What does Dreamweaver do automatically if you draw a cell in Layout view before you draw a table?

5. Can you resize a cell by dragging its resize handles when it is active in Layout view?

6. What is a spacer image?

REVIEW ASSIGNMENTS

You need to create a variety of tables on the other pages of the NewCatalyst Web site to insert content and organize the layout. You'll create tables in Standard view for Central Tour Dates and East Coast Tour Dates in the Tour Dates page. Then, you'll hyperlink the hotspots on the map to the appropriate tables. For the Catalogue page, you'll create a table in Standard view and insert graphics of the CD covers, as well as text of the CD titles and song lists.

1. Open the NewCatalyst Web site that you modified in this tutorial, and then open the tourdates.htm page in a Document window.

2. Click below the West Coast Tour Dates table on the tour dates page, and then create a table with 3 columns and 13 rows, 0 Cell Padding, 0 Cell Spacing, Width 75 percent, and 0 Borders in Standard view.

3. Merge the top row of cells in the new table.

4. Select the top two rows of the new table and make them header cells.

5. Type "Central U.S. Tour Dates" in the top row.

6. Align the table to the Center.

Explore   7. Adjust the widths of the columns so they are the same as the column widths in the West Coast table.

8. Type the information from the table below into the appropriate places in the second table.

Date	Location / Venue	Band
1/4 to 1/6	Cleveland, OH / Grog Shop	Surface Suction
1/11 to 1/13	Chicago, IL / Abbey Pub	Surface Suction
2/8 to 2/10	Minneapolis, MN / 9th Street Entry	Surface Suction
2/15 to 2/17	Iowa City, IA / Gabe's Oasis	Surface Suction
2/22 to 2/24	Lawrence, KS / Bottleneck	Surface Suction
3/15 to 3/17	Denton, TX / Rubber Gloves	Surface Suction
3/22 to 3/24	Austin, TX / Emo's	Surface Suction
4/13 to 4/14	Houston, TX / Sidecar Pub	Surface Suction

9. Click Commands on the main menu bar, and then click Format Table to open the Format Table dialog box. To format the table, click AltRows:Blue&Yellow, type #FF6600 into the First text box, type #FF9900 into the Second text box, select Every Other Row from the Alternate list, select Center in both Align list boxes, type 0 in the Border text box, check the Apply All Attributes to TD Tags Instead of TR Tags checkbox, and then click the OK button.

10. Select the empty cells and delete them.

Explore   11. Create a third table for East Coast Tour Dates using the information from the table below. Format it so that the columns align with the tables above it and the colors are the same.

Date	Location / Venue	Band
1/4 to 1/6	Atlanta, GA / Echo Lounge	Sloth Child
1/11 to 1/13	Carbord, NC / Room Four	Sloth Child
2/8 to 2/10	Baltimore, MD / Ottobar	Sloth Child
2/15 to 2/17	Washington, DC / Black Cat	Sloth Child
2/22 to 2/24	Philadelphia, PA / Unitarian Church	Sloth Child
3/15 to 3/17	Cambridge, MA / Middle East	Sloth Child
3/22 to 3/24	New York, NY / Bowery Ballroom	Sloth Child
4/13 to 4/14	New York, NY / Knitting Factory	Sloth Child

Explore 12. Insert a blank line between the three tables. Click to the left of the Central table, then press the Enter key. Do the same for the East Coast table.

Explore 13. Create a named anchor for the West Coast Tour Dates table. Select the text in the first row of the first table, click the Common tab on the Insert bar, and then click the Named Anchor button. In the Named Anchor dialog box that opens, type "westcoast" in the Anchor Name text box, and then click the OK button. A box with an anchor appears beside the selected text. The anchor cannot be seen outside the Dreamweaver environment.

Explore 14. Create a named anchor for the Central U.S. Tour Dates table. Select the text in the first row of the second table, and then insert an anchor named "central."

Explore 15. Create a named anchor for the East Coast Tour Dates table. Select the text in the first row of the third table, and then insert an anchor named "eastcoast."

Explore 16. Add a link from the West Coast hotspot to the westcoast named anchor. Click the hotspot at the left of the U.S. map, and then type "#westcoast" in the Link text box in the Property inspector.

Explore 17. Add a link from the Central U.S. hotspot to the central named anchor. Click the hotspot in the center of the U.S. map, and then type "#central" in the Link text box in the Property inspector.

Explore 18. Add a link from the East Coast hotspot to the eastcoast named anchor. Click the hotspot at the right of the U.S. map, and then type "#eastcoast" in the Link text box in the Property inspector.

19. Save and close the page, and then test the links to the anchors by previewing the page in a browser, and clicking each hotspot on the map. (*Hint*: If each table does not move to the top of the window when you click the appropriate hotspot in the browser window, you may not have enough blank lines at the end of your Web page. Open the page in a Document window and add extra lines to the end of the page by pressing the Enter key.) Close the browser window when you are finished.

20. Open the catalogue.htm page in a Document window, insert a table below the CDS heading that has 4 rows, 2 columns, 4 cell padding, 0 cell spacing, 75% width, and 0 borders.

21. Select the table, and then select Center from the Align list in the Property inspector.

22. Select "Dizzied Connection: Spinning Life" and the song list below it, cut the selected text, and then paste the text into the first cell in the second row of the table.

23. Select "Surface Suction: Black Lab" and the song list below it, cut the selected text, and then paste the text into the second cell in the second row of the table. (It may be necessary to adjust the column width of the second column by dragging the left border of the column to the left.)

24. Select "Sloth Child: Them Apples" and the song list below it, cut the selected text, and then paste the text into the first cell in the fourth row of the table.

25. Select "life in minor chords: i believe in ferries" and the song list below it, cut the selected text, and then paste the text into the second cell in the fourth row of the table.

26. Click in the first cell in the first row of the table, and then insert the image DizziedConnectionsCDcover300.jpg located on your Data Disk in Tutorial.04\Review. (Save a copy of the graphic in the Graphics folder.)

27. Click in the second cell in the first row of the table, and then insert the image SurfaceSuctionCDcover300.jpg located on your Data Disk in Tutorial.04\Review. (Save a copy of the graphic in the Graphics folder.)

28. Click in the first cell in the third row of the table, and then insert the image SlothChildCDcover300.jpg located on your Data Disk in Tutorial.04\Review. (Save a copy of the graphic in the Graphics folder.)

29. Click in the second cell in the third row of the table, and then insert the image LifeInMinorChordsCDcover300.jpg located on your Data Disk in Tutorial.04\Review. (Save a copy of the graphic in the Graphics folder.)

30. Select each cell with text, and then select Center from the Horz list and Top from the Vert list.

31. Select each row with graphics in it, and then select Center from the Horz list and Bottom from the Vert list.

32. Select the table and make sure the width is 75% by checking the W text box in the Property inspector, and changing it if necessary. (Sometimes the width will change when you add graphics.)

Explore ▷ 33. Preview the page in a browser, check the bottom of page to see if the "VINYL" paragraph appears inside the orange bar, and then close the browser window. If necessary, click below the table and above the orange bar at the bottom of the page, scroll down so you can see all of the orange bar, then press the Delete key as many times as necessary to move the "VINYL" paragraph up so that it is all inside the orange bar when previewed in the browser.

34. Copy the copyright line from the catalogue page to the home, contact, and tour dates page. (*Hint*: If necessary, remove the HTML style and then apply the CatalystFooter style to the pasted text.)

35. Save and close the page, preview the page in a browser, and then close the browser window.

36. Connect to your remote server, upload the site, and then preview the site over the Web.

CASE PROBLEMS

Case 1. Hroch University Anthropology Department As you continue working on Dr. Hart's Web site, you'll add the Hroch University logo to every page of the site and create a hyperlink from the logo to Dr. Hart's home page. Then, you'll create a table to contain the information in each area of research and put placeholder text in the tables while the research is being completed.

1. Open the Hart site that you modified in Tutorial 3, Case 1, open the home page in a Document window, and place the insertion point in the upper-left corner of the page.

2. Using the Image button, insert the HrochLogo.gif located in the Cases folder within the Tutorial.04 folder on your Data Disk. (Save a copy of the graphic in the Graphics folder.)

3. Delete spaces after the graphic as needed so that the links are in their original position.

4. Save and close the page.

5. Add the logo and create a hyperlink from the logo to the home page in the rest of the pages in the site: Contact.htm, CulturalCrossPollination.htm, LinguisticDifferences.htm, ProfHart.htm, and RitualsAndPractices.htm.

6. Open the Linguistic Differences page and place the pointer below the Linguistic Differences heading. Then use the Insert Table button on the Common tab of the Insert bar to insert a table that has 3 rows, 1 column, 0 Cell Padding, 0 Cell Spacing, 100% width, and 0 Borders.

7. Select the table and select Left in the Align list in the Property inspector, select the top cell, and type #910C26 in the second Bg text box (the Background Color text box).

8. Copy the Linguistic Differences heading and paste it into the top cell of the table. (It may be necessary to reapply the Heading 1 tag from the Formatting list in the Property inspector.)

9. Delete the old heading text and any extra spaces, and then click in the second cell and type "Research in process, check back soon." Then press the Enter key twice to add blank lines.

10. Place the pointer in the bottom cell and click the Copyright symbol button on the Characters tab of the Insert bar. Press the Right Arrow key, press the Spacebar, and then type "Copyright Dr. Matthew Hart, Hroch University Anthropology Dept., 2003." Then select the text and select Center in the Horz list in the Property inspector.

11. Copy the table, save and close the page, and then paste it on the Cultural Cross-pollination page in place of the current heading. Replace the text in the top cell with "Cultural Cross-pollination." Save and close the page.

12. Paste the table on the Rituals and Practices page in place of the current heading. Replace the text in the top cell with "Rituals and Practices," and then save and close the page.

13. Preview the site in a browser, then upload the site to the remote server.

14. Open a browser and load the remote site by typing the URL, then check the links and pages to ensure the upload was successful.

15. Close the site.

Case 2. *Museum of Western Art* C. J. asks you to use the new graphics that the art department has provided to create a rollover image out of the new Museum of Western Art logo, then to replace the text logo on each page of the site with the new logo rollover, which will link to the home page of the site. In addition, you will add a table in the home page and move the navigation links into the table. Then, you'll copy the new navigation table to the other pages of the site.

1. Open the Museum site that you modified in Tutorial 3, Case 2, open the home page in a Document window, select the text logo at the top of the page, and then delete the text.

2. Click the Rollover Image button on the Common tab of the Insert menu and, in the Insert Rollover Image dialog box, type MuseumLogoRollover in the Image Name text box. Click the Original Image Browse button and insert the MuseumLogo.gif (located in the Cases folder within the Tutorial.04 folder on your Data Disk) in the Original Image text box. (Remember to include copies of the images in the Graphics folder in your root folder.) Insert the MuseumLogoRollover.gif located in the Cases folder within the Tutorial.04 folder on your Data Disk in the Rollover Image text box, type "Museum of Western Art Logo with link to the home page" into the Alternate Text text box, click the Browse button next to the When Clicked, Go To URL text box, browse to and double-click the index.htm page, and then click the OK button.

3. Preview the page in a browser, place the pointer over the rollover image to see the image change, and then close the brower window.

4. Select the rollover image and then use the Copy HTML command to copy it. Replace the text logo in the Art.htm, Artists.htm, Location.htm, and Museum.htm pages with the new logo rollover image using the Paste HTML command.

5. Save and close all of the pages, then preview the pages in a browser and test the new logo on each page.

6. Close the browser window and open the home page in a Document window.

7. Position the pointer to the right of the navigation text and insert a table with 4 rows, 1 column, 0 Cell Spacing, 0 Cell Padding, 100 pixels in width, and 1 Border.

8. Select the table, if necessary, and select Right from the Align list (the table will move to the right of the Welcome text), type #006666 in the Bg Color text box and #ECB888 in the Brdr Color text box.

9. Using the Copy HTML and Paste HTML commands, copy the Museum text link into the first cell, copy the Art text link into the second cell, copy the Artists text link into the third cell, and then copy the Location text link into the fourth cell. Then delete the original text links from the page and delete any extra lines between the table and the horizontal line.

10. Save the home page and preview it in a browser.

11. Select the table, then, using the Copy HTML and Paste HTML commands, copy and paste the table into the Art.htm, Artists.htm, Location.htm, and Museum.htm pages to the right of the navigation text. Then delete the old navigation text and any extra spaces from each page and save each page.

12. Preview the site in a browser. Upload the site to the remote server.

13. Open a browser and load the remote site by typing the URL. Then check the links and pages to ensure the upload was successful.

14. Close the browser.

Case 3. NORM Mark Chapman asks you to add a new logo graphic to the NORM site and to create a rollover image out of it, linking users back to the home page. Create a two-cell table in the home page, and add the book list to one cell and a new book cover graphic in the other cell of the table.

1. Open the NORM site that you modified in Tutorial 3, Case 3, open the home page in a Document window, select the text logo at the top of the page, and then delete the text.

2. Use the Rollover Image button to insert a new logo with a rollover. Name the image NORMlogoRollover, use the NORMlogo.gif located in the Cases folder within the Tutorial.04 folder on your Data Disk for the original image, use the NORMlogoRollover.gif located in the Cases folder within the Tutorial.04 folder on your Data Disk for the rollover image, type "NORM logo with link to home page" in the Alternate Text text box, and browse to the home page in the When Clicked, Go To URL text box.

3. Save the page and preview the page in a browser.

4. Copy the logo to the books.htm, company.htm, contact.htm, and links.htm pages to replace the text logos on those pages. (*Hint*: Use the Copy HTML and Paste HTML commands.) Save the pages as you go and preview the site when you are finished to ensure that the rollover images are working.

5. Open the home page, place the pointer directly before the NORM BOOK LIST heading, and insert a table with 1 row, 2 columns, 0 Cell Spacing, 0 Cell Padding, 100% width, and 0 borders into the page.

Explore ▶ 6. Select the NORM BOOK LIST heading and the following list of books and authors, drag the selected text into the left cell of the table, then delete the original text and any blank lines from the page.

7. Drag the right border of the first cell to the left until it is directly beside the longest line of content in the cell, then place the pointer in the right cell and type "Featured Book." Select the text and apply the NormSubHeadings CSS Style.

8. Select the left cell and select Top from the Vert list, then select the right cell and select Top from the Vert list.

9. Place the insertion point after the text in the right cell, press the Shift + Enter keys, and insert into the cell the BookCoverPunchSmall.jpg located in the Cases folder within the Tutorial.04 folder on your Data Disk. (Save a copy of the graphic in the Graphics folder.)

10. Save and close the page.

Explore 11. Create a new page in the Site panel. Name the new page FeaturedBook.htm, then open the page in a Document window. Type NORM – Featured Book in the Title text box on the Document toolbar, open the CSS Styles panel, and link the page to the NORMStyleSheet.css. Open the Page Properties dialog box, type #003366 in the Background text box, and then click the OK button. Then click the Layout View button on the Layout tab on the Insert bar.

12. Click the Draw Layout Cell button and, in the upper left corner of the page, draw a cell that is 350 pixels long by 250 pixels wide. Then insert the BookCoverPunch.jpg located in the Cases folder within the Tutorial.04 folder on your Data Disk into the cell and adjust the size of the cell so that the cell is the same size as the graphic.

13. Click the Draw Layout Cell button and draw a second layout cell directly below the first one. The second cell will have the same width as the first cell and should be 85 pixels high. (*Hint*: If you can't draw the second cell to be 85 pixels high, then you need to increase the size of the outer table so that it is at least 435 pixels high.)

14. Draw a third cell to the right of the first cell. The third cell should be the combined height of the first two cells you drew (435 pixels) and 525 pixels wide.

Explore 15. Resize the outer table so that it is no larger than the cells in it. Select the table and click the Autostretch button in the Property inspector. If the Choose Spacer image dialog box appears, select Create a spacer image file, and browse to the Graphics folder in the root folder for the NORM site.

16. Type #003366 in the Bg Color text box.

17. Place the insertion point in the lower left cell, and then type "Punch by Kelly Moore." Then select the text and select the Paragraph tag in the Format list in the Property inspector. Select "Punch" and apply the NormBookTitles CSS style. (*Hint*: The text color will not change to white until you apply the paragraph tag.)

18. Place the insertion pointer in the right cell and type the following: "A wacky, eccentric collection of female voices searching for meaning in a world gone awry. Punch is a hilarious romp." – Melissa Thurman, Voice.

19. Select the text and select Paragraph from the Format list in the Property inspector. Select the cell and select Middle from the Vert list in the Property inspector.

20. Save the page, close the page, and open the home page. Link the book cover graphic to the Featured Book page and target the page to open in a new browser window, then link the text "Featured Book" to the Featured Book page. Target both links to open in another browser window.

21. Select the graphic, and then click the Align Center button in the Property inspector.

22. Save the page and preview the site in a browser window.

23. Upload the site to the remote server, then open a browser and type the URL into the address text box, review the site, and close the browser window.

Case 4. Sushi Ya-Ya Mary O'Brien asks you to add graphics and tables to the Sushi Ya-Ya Web site. You'll add the new Sushi Ya-Ya logo, with a rollover and a hyperlink to the home page, to every page of the site. Then, you'll create a Specials button on the home page. Finally, you'll create a new Specials Web page. You will create tables in Layout view to structure the new page.

1. Open the Sushi Ya-Ya site that you modified in Tutorial 3, Case 4, open the home page in a Document window, select the text logo if there is one, and delete the text.

2. Add the new logo provided by the design team to the top of each page of the site by using the Rollover Image button in the Insert bar to insert the logo into the home page, and then copying the logo and the functionality to the other pages of the site (use the Copy HTML and Paste HTML commands to copy the logo and functionality). Use the SushiYaYaLogo.gif located in the Cases folder within the Tutorial.04 folder on your Data Disk as the original image, and the SushiYaYaLogoRollover.gif located in the Cases folder within the Tutorial.04 folder on your Data Disk as the rollover image. Add alternate text and a link to the home page.

3. Create a new page in the Sushi Ya-Ya site and name it Specials.htm. Open the new page, connect the page to the stylesheet, and set the page properties. Title the page "Sushi Ya-Ya – Specials," and save the page.

4. Design a layout for the Specials page. The special is the Tikka roll. The page will contain a graphic of the roll (use the TikkaRollTuna.gif located in the Cases folder within the Tutorial.04 folder on your Data Disk), the name of the special—Tikka Roll, a description of the special ("The Tikka Roll combines spicy tuna and rice wrapped in a seaweed roll."), and the price, $3.00.

5. Once you have decided on a layout for the page, create a table in Layout view to hold the content, and then place the content into the page.

6. Create a specials link on the home page of the Sushi Ya-Ya site. You can use the graphic you used in the Specials page, as well as text. You might want to create a table to hold the link in place on the page. Target the link to open the Specials page in a new browser window.

7. Save your changes and preview the site in a browser. Then upload the site to your remote server and view the site from its remote location, checking all of the links and the added pages.

8. Close the browser.

Quick | Check answers

Session 4.1

1. GIF, JPEG, and PNG
2. JPEG
3. You can use the Assets panel to manage the assets of your site.
4. An image map is a graphic that is divided into hotspots.
5. A hotspot is an area of an image map that you can click to cause an action to occur.
6. A rollover is an image that changes when the pointer moves across it.

Session 4.2

1. A table cell is the intersection of a row and a column in the table.

2. True.

3. Cell padding is the amount of empty space maintained between the border of a cell and the cell's content. Cell spacing is the width of the cell walls.

4. Pressing the Tab key moves the insertion point to the next cell to the right, or, if the insertion point is in the last cell in a row, to the first cell in the next row. If the insertion point is in the last cell in the table, pressing the Tab key inserts a new row and moves the insertion point to the first cell in the new row.

5. When you merge two cells, the content is merged into one cell and the new cell is the width and the height of the two original cells put together.

6. <tr>

7. <td>

Session 4.3

1. A nested table is a table inside another table.

2. It is a good idea to plan the layout of Web pages when you are using tables because it helps avoid reworking the page elements once you have placed them on the page.

3. True.

4. Dreamweaver inserts the rest of the cells and a table to hold the cell you drew.

5. No. When a cell is active it is ready to accept input. A cell must be selected and the resize handles visible in order to resize it by dragging the resize handles.

6. A spacer image is a one-pixel transparent image that is inserted into the fixed-width columns in a table that contains an autostretch column.

OBJECTIVES

In this tutorial you will:

- Insert a navigation bar using the Dreamweaver Navigation Bar

- Modify a navigation bar

- Create a Web page with frames

- Adjust frame properties and attributes

- Add content to frames

- Create hyperlinks with targets

- Troubleshoot common problems with frames

- Explore the HTML behind frames, framesets, and targets

SHARED

SITE FORMATTING USING THE NAVIGATION BAR AND FRAMES

Creating More Sophisticated Layouts on the Catalyst Web site

CASE

As you add pages to a Web site, you add more and more content that needs to be organized in a way that is easy for the user to navigate and understand, and, at the same time, catches the user's eye. You have organized some of the content using tables and layers. You are now ready to add pages that are organized with frames that you can resize to better fit the content and in which the user can scroll to view the complete contents.

Brian Lee, public relations and marketing director at Catalyst, has reviewed your work on the new Catalyst Web site. He's impressed with your work so far, and he would like you to make a few more changes. He has decided to replace the text navigation system with a navigation bar using a series of rollover elements for the navigation links. Each of the rollover element includes a series of graphics. A different graphic will be used as the link for the four states of each element; up, over, down and over while down. The different graphics will provide the user with additional information, such as which page of the site is currently open. Also, the look of the graphic elements will add to the look and feel of the site.

In addition, Brian would like you to create a Web page for the band Life in Minor Chords. He wants to use this page to promote the band (thus fulfilling another of the site goals). He wants you to add links to the new page from the band's name on the bands page and from the CD cover graphic on the catalogue page. You will use frames when you design the new page.

In this session, you will delete the navigation links and insert a navigation bar into the Catalyst Web site. You will copy the navigation bar to all the pages in the Web site. Then you will modify the navigation bar.

Creating a Navigation Bar Object

There are many ways to add navigation to a Web site. As you learn more advanced Web design techniques, your choices increase. You have used text hyperlinks to enable the user to move between Web pages in the Catalyst Web site. You have defined CSS styles to customize the look of the various states of the hyperlink tags. You have also created a rollover button for the NewCatalyst Web site logo. Now you will replace the customized text links with a navigation bar.

In general practice, any navigation or menu system that is placed in a Web page can be referred to as a navigation bar. In Dreamweaver, however, the **navigation bar** is a specific item, which consists of a series of rollover graphics that change state when specific browser actions occur, such as when the user places the pointer over a graphic. The rollover graphics are held in place on the Web page by a container, such as a table. Each rollover is called an **element** and can have up to four states. The **Up state** refers to the element before the user clicks it. The **Over state** refers to the element when the pointer is positioned over the up graphic. The **Down state** refers to the element after it has been clicked. The **Over While Down state** refers to the element when the pointer is placed over the down graphic. You create a navigation bar by clicking the Navigation Bar button on the Common tab on the Insert bar and filling in the requested information. Dreamweaver will then create all of the components of the navigation bar and insert them for you. When the term *navigation bar* is used in this tutorial, it will be in reference to the specific Dreamweaver navigation bar object.

REFERENCE WINDOW   **RW**

Creating a Navigation Bar
- Click the Navigation Bar button on the Common tab on the Insert bar to open the Insert Navigation Bar dialog box.
- Type a name for the first element in the navigation bar in the Element Name text box.
- Click the Browse button next to each Image text box to navigate to the image you want to display for that element.
- Type alternate text in the Alternate Text text box.
- Click the When Clicked, Go To URL Browse button, and then navigate to the file to which you want to link the element.
- Click the Target list arrow, and then select the target window for the link.
- Click the Preload Images checkbox to check it.
- If this element represents the current page, click the Show "Down Image" Initially checkbox to check it; otherwise, leave it unchecked.
- Click the Insert list arrow, and then select the orientation of the navigation bar.
- Click the Use Tables checkbox to check it.
- Click the Add Item button above the Nav Bar Elements list to add another element to the bar.
- When you have finished adding elements to the navigation bar, click the OK button.

As with any complex process, understanding the components used in the navigation bar will help you understand what it does. The navigation bar uses hyperlinks, rollovers, and tables; therefore, what you have learned about these items will enable you to better understand how the navigation bar works. When you use the navigation bar, several things happen:

- As with a rollover, the graphics in a navigation bar preload when the Web page is loaded, if the preload option is selected, so that they are in place when the browser action occurs.
- A series of navigation bar elements is defined. (Each element is similar to a rollover button with a set of up to four state images.)
- The navigation bar is placed within a table on the Web page if the Use Table box is checked; otherwise, the elements are placed directly in the Web page. It is best to place the navigation bar in a table because it keeps the elements in their proper positions on the page.
- If you set a URL for each element, then the user will jump to the new page when they click an element, just like when they click a text link.

You will open a sample of the bands page of the Catalyst site with a navigation bar inserted in the page so that you can explore the elements of the navigation bar from within a Web page. (You will not be able to jump to the other pages of the site.)

To examine a navigation bar in a Web page:

1. Start your browser.

2. Click **File** on the menu bar, click **Open**, click the **Browse** button, navigate to the **Tutorial.05\Tutorial** folder on the Data Disk, double-click **bands.htm**, and then click the **OK** button. The bands page with a navigation bar is displayed in the browser window. For each of the links, graphics have been created. The bands element is in the Down state because the bands page is currently visible in the browser. The other elements—label, catalogue, tour dates, and contact—are in the Up state. See Figure 5-1.

| Figure 5-1 | NAVIGATION BAR ON WEB PAGE WITH CURRENT PAGE NAME IN DOWN STATE |

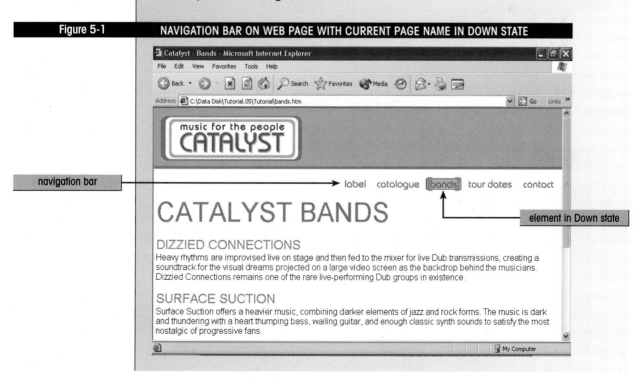

3. Move the pointer over the **bands** element, but do not click. The element changes to the Over While Down state to indicate that the link cannot be clicked because you are currently on that page. See Figure 5-2.

Figure 5-2   POINTING TO ELEMENT INDICATING CURRENT PAGE ON A NAVIGATION BAR

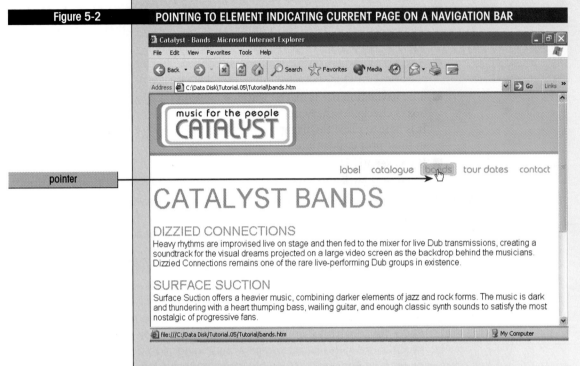

4. Move the pointer over the **label** element. The element changes to the Over state. See Figure 5-3.

Figure 5-3   POINTING TO AN ELEMENT LINKED TO ANOTHER PAGE ON A NAVIGATION BAR

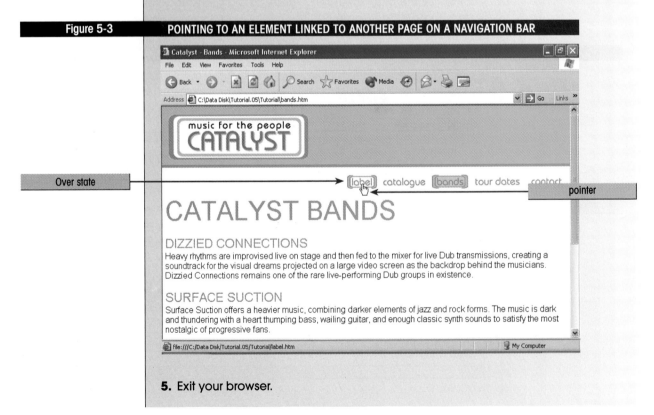

5. Exit your browser.

You will now insert a navigation bar into the pages of the Catalyst site.

Inserting a Navigation Bar

Before you create a navigation bar, you need graphics to use for each state of the elements. The graphics must be saved in one of the Web-safe formats (GIF, JPEG, PNG) to be used in a Web page. You can create graphics in an image processing program, such as Adobe Photoshop, Macromedia Fireworks, or Adobe Illustrator. When you add an image to the navigation bar, you should place a copy of it in the Graphics folder within the root folder of the Web site, just as you have done when adding other graphics to the site. To create a navigation bar, you'll enter the following information:

- **Nav Bar Elements.** A list of elements included in the navigation bar. Once you have created the first element, you can add, delete, or reorder the elements in the list.

- **Element Name.** The name of each element you add to the navigation bar. When you rename an element, its name will change in the Nav Bar Elements list. Element names must start with a letter or an underscore, and they can contain only letters and numbers (no spaces or symbols).

- **Up Image.** The graphic that will be used for the Up state of the element. You can type the path to the image or browse to select the image. You must include a graphic for the Up image for the navigation bar to work. Other states are optional.

- **Over Image.** The graphic that will be used for the optional Over state of the element. You can type the path to the image or browse to select the image.

- **Down Image.** The graphic that will be used for the optional Down state of the element. The **Down state** refers to the element after it has been clicked. You can type the path to the image or browse to select the image.

- **Over While Down Image.** The graphic that appears when the element is in the optional Over While Down state. This optional graphic can be used to give users a visual cue that the button cannot be clicked again while they are in a particular part of the Web site. For example, if the navigation bar includes an Over While Down image that grays out the applicable element, when you are on the bands page of the Catalyst Web site and the pointer is over the bands element of the navigation bar, the image will be gray—indicating that you are currently on that page and that link cannot be clicked. You can type the path to the image or browse to select the image.

- **Alternate Text.** Text that appears in place of the image in browsers that display only text. This is the text that a screen reader will read.

- **When Clicked, Go To URL.** The URL or file path that you want the element to hyperlink, along with the window or frame in which you want the new URL to appear (frames will be explored later in this tutorial). The Main Window option opens the new Web page in the existing browser window.

- **Options.** Options that affect the entire navigation bar, not each individual element. The Preload Images option enables the browser to download all the graphics used in the navigation bar when the page is loaded. If you don't preload images, there might be a delay before the Over image appears when the user moves the mouse over a button. The Show "Down Image" Initially option enables Dreamweaver to display the Down state of an element (rather than the default Up state) when the page is loaded. (The Up state of the element is displayed by default when a page is loaded.) This feature is used to show a user which page of the Web site is displayed. For example, you'll show the Down state of the Label element in the navigation bar on the label page of the Catalyst Web site; when the label page is loaded in the browser, the user knows it is open because the Label button in the navigation bar is in the Down state.

■ **Insert.** The option to insert elements either horizontally to create a horizontal navigation bar or vertically to create a vertical navigation bar. This option applies to the entire navigation bar. Once you have created a horizontal or vertical navigation bar, you cannot change this setting. If you want to switch the orientation of the navigation bar, you must delete the old navigation bar and create a new one.

■ **Use Tables.** The option to use tables to keep the navigation bar elements in place. This option applies to the entire navigation bar. It is a good idea to create navigation bars with tables.

Brian asks you to upgrade the navigation system for the NewCatalyst Web site by deleting the current text links and creating a navigation bar on each page of the site. When you create the new navigation bar on the first page, you will include a graphic for each state of each element. You should include a copy of each graphic in the Graphics folder within the root folder of the Web site. However, when you create the navigation bar on the other pages of the Web site, you should browse to the graphics in the Graphics folder rather than include additional copies of the same graphics for each page. Reusing graphics keeps the Web site lean. Also, if you decide later to change the look of the navigation bar, you have to replace only one set of images instead of a set for each page.

You'll start by creating the navigation bar on the label page. First, you'll open the page and delete the current text links.

To delete text links:

1. Start **Dreamweaver**, and then open the **NewCatalyst** Web site that you modified in the Tutorial 4 Review Assignments.

2. Click the **View** list arrow in the Site panel, and then click **Local View**, if necessary.

3. Open the **label.htm** page in a Document window, and then click the **Show Design View** button, if necessary.

4. Drag to select the **link text** for the current navigation system, and then press the **Delete** key. The text links disappear from the page.

Next, you'll create a graphic-based navigation bar. For each element, you'll include an Up image, an Over image, a Down image, and an Over While Down image. Brian has supplied you with the graphics you should use for each element in the four states. You want the images to preload and you want the element that represents the current page to show the Down image initially. To match the design plan, you'll make the navigation bar horizontal and use tables.

To create a navigation bar:

1. Click the **Navigation Bar** button on the **Common** tab on the Insert bar. The Insert Navigation Bar dialog box opens. See Figure 5-4.

Figure 5-4   INSERT NAVIGATION BAR DIALOG BOX

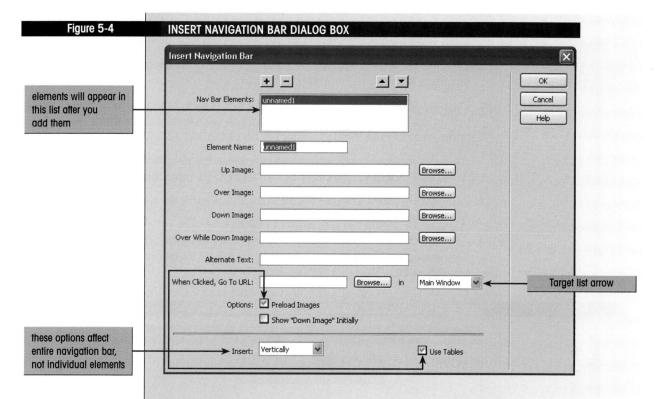

elements will appear in this list after you add them

Target list arrow

these options affect entire navigation bar, not individual elements

2. Type **Label** in the Element Name text box.

3. Click the **Up Image Browse** button to open the Select Image Source dialog box, navigate to the **Tutorial** folder within the **Tutorial.05** folder on your Data Disk, and then double-click **label.gif**. A dialog box opens, prompting you to save a copy of the graphic in the root folder of the Web site.

4. Click the **Yes** button, navigate to the **Graphics** folder in the root folder of your NewCatalyst Web site, and then click the **Save** button. The relative path for the label.gif image appears in the Up Image text box.

   You'll repeat this process to insert the images for the Over, Down, and Over While Down states.

5. Click the **Over Image Browse** button, double-click the **labelOver.gif** located in the **Tutorial** folder within the **Tutorial.05** folder on your Data Disk, click the **Yes** button, navigate to the **Graphics** folder in the root folder of your NewCatalyst Web site, and then click the **Save** button.

6. Click the **Down Image Browse** button, double-click **labelDown.gif** located in the **Tutorial** folder within the **Tutorial.05** folder on your Data Disk, and then save a copy in the **Graphics** folder in the root folder of your NewCatalyst Web site.

7. Click the **Over While Down Image Browse** button, double-click **labelOWD.gif** located in the **Tutorial** folder within the **Tutorial.05** folder on your Data Disk, and then save the graphic in the **Graphics** folder in the root folder of your NewCatalyst Web site.

8. Click in the **Alternate Text** text box, and then type **label**.

9. Click the **When Clicked, Go To URL Browse** button, and then double-click **label.htm** in the root folder of your NewCatalyst Web site.

10. If necessary, click the **Target** list arrow (next to the word "**in**"), and then click **Main Window**.

11. Click the **Preload Images** checkbox to check it, if necessary. Now all of the graphics in the navigation bar will preload.

12. Click the **Show "Down Image" Initially** checkbox to check it. An asterisk appears next to the element name in the Nav Bar Elements list to indicate that the Down image (rather than the Up image) will be displayed initially on the page.

You want to show the Down image initially for the label link to give a visual cue to the user that this is the page of the Catalyst Web site that you are currently on.

13. If necessary, click the **Insert** list arrow, and then click **Horizontally**. The navigation bar will display horizontally.

14. Click the **Use Tables** checkbox to check it, if necessary. The navigation bar will be inserted as a table. You've entered all the information for the first element. See Figure 5-5.

Figure 5-5	INSERT NAVIGATION BAR DIALOG BOX FOR LABEL ELEMENT

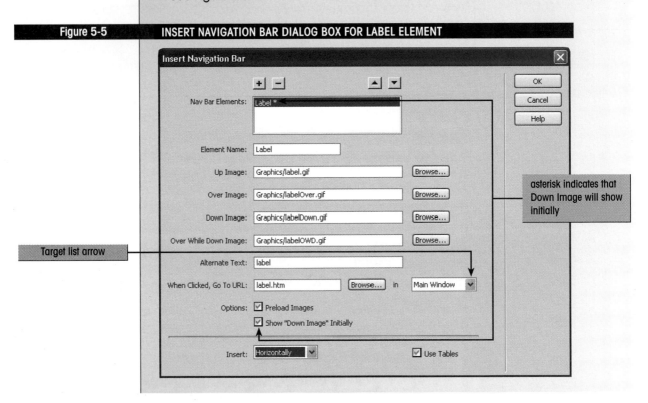

You'll repeat the same process to add the elements for the other pages in the Web site.

To add elements to a navigation bar:

1. Click the **Add Item** button ➕ above the Nav Bar Elements list in the Insert Navigation Bar dialog box. The text boxes and options are cleared so you can add the next element; and the next element name, currently unnamed1, is added to the Nav Bar Elements list.

2. Type **Bands** in the Element Name text box.

3. Browse to the **Tutorial** folder within the **Tutorial.05** folder on your Data Disk to insert the following graphics for each state, saving a copy of each graphic in the **Graphics** folder in the root folder of your NewCatalyst Web site.

Image	Graphic
Up Image	bands.gif
Over Image	bandsOver.gif
Down Image	bandsDown.gif
Over While Down Image	bandsOWD.gif

4. Click in the **Alternate Text** text box, and then type **bands**.

5. Click the **When Clicked, Go To URL Browse** button, and then double-click **bands.htm** in the root folder of your NewCatalyst Web site.

6. If necessary, click the **Target** list arrow, and then click **Main Window**.

7. Verify that the **Show "Down Image" Initially** checkbox is unchecked.

   You do not need to change the Preload Images, Insert, or Use Tables attributes, because these options affect the entire navigation bar, and you already set them when you set the attributes for the first element. You'll follow the same procedure to create the elements for the Catalogue, Tour Dates, and Contact pages.

8. Repeat Steps 1 through 7 for the **catalogue** element, the **tour dates** element, and the **contact** element, using the following files located in the **Tutorial** folder within the **Tutorial.05** folder on your Data Disk for the graphics. For the tour dates element, use "TourDates" (no space) for the Element Name.

Element	Catalogue	Tour Dates	Contact
Up Image	catalogue.gif	tourdates.gif	contact.gif
Over Image	catalogueOver.gif	tourdatesOver.gif	contactOver.gif
Down Image	catalogueDown.gif	tourdatesDown.gif	contactDown.gif
Over While Down Image	catalogueOWD.gif	tourdatesOWD.gif	contactOWD.gif
Alternate Text	catalogue	tour dates	contact
URL	catalogue.htm	tourdates.htm	contact.htm

9. Click the **OK** button. The navigation bar is inserted into the label page in a table, and the table is selected. See Figure 5-6. The label link is in the Down state to indicate that you are on the label page.

Figure 5-6   LABEL PAGE WITH UNFORMATTED NAVIGATION BAR

Down state

selected table containing navigation bar

You want the navigation bar to be aligned along the right edge of the page. You'll make this change, and then test the navigation bar in a browser.

To format and test a navigation bar:

1. Make sure the table that holds the navigation bar is selected, click the **Align** list arrow in the Property inspector, and then click **Right**. The navigation bar moves to the right side of the page and an icon appears at the left of the page. The icon is an anchor point for an aligned element, and it marks the location of the code that is used to align the table. You can select the table by clicking the anchor point. See Figure 5-7.

Figure 5-7   LABEL PAGE WITH FORMATTED NAVIGATION BAR

selected anchor point for the aligned element

TROUBLE? If the anchor point is positioned just above the word "CATALYST," click immediately to the right of the navigation bar, and then press the Enter key.

2. Save and close the **label** page.

Sometimes when you create a navigation bar and you reopen the page, you may see a closing anchor tag highlighted in yellow next to one of the elements. This is a stray tag that sometimes appears and it can be deleted.

3. Open the **label** page. The stray closing anchor tag may appear in the navigation bar. See Figure 5-8.

Figure 5-8	STRAY ANCHOR TAG IN NAVIGATION BAR

stray anchor tag

4. If the closing anchor tag highlighted in yellow appears in the navigation bar, click it to select it, and then press the **Delete** key.

5. Save and close the **label** page, and then preview it in a browser.

6. In the browser window, move the pointer over the **label** link to see how it changes.

7. Move the pointer over the rest of the links to see how they change.

8. Click the **tour dates** link, and watch as the image briefly changes after the link is clicked and before the Catalyst - Tour Dates page opens.

9. Close the browser window.

You need to add a navigation bar to each of the other pages in your NewCatalyst Web site. You do not want to add more copies of the navigation bar graphics to the Web site, because this will increase the size of the site unnecessarily. Instead, you should browse to the Graphics folder located within the root folder of your Web site and use the copies of the graphics that you placed there.

To create a navigation bar on the bands page:

1. Open the **bands.htm** page in a Document window, and then delete the text links.

2. Click the **Navigation Bar** button ▆ in the **Common** tab of the Insert bar.

3. Create the following elements, using the files located in the **Graphics** folder within the root folder of the NewCatalyst Web site for the graphics.

Element	Label	Bands	Catalogue	Tour Dates	Contact
Element Name	Label	Bands	Catalogue	TourDates	Contact
Up Image	label.gif	bands.gif	catalogue.gif	tourdates.gif	contact.gif
Over Image	labelOver.gif	bandsOver.gif	catalogueOver.gif	tourdatesOver.gif	contactOver.gif
Down Image	labelDown.gif	bandsDown.gif	catalogueDown.gif	tourdatesDown.gif	contactDown.gif
Over While Down Image	labelOWD.gif	bandsOWD.gif	catalogueOWD.gif	tourdatesOWD.gif	contactOWD.giv
Alternate Text	label	bands	catalogue	tour dates	contact
URL	label.htm	bands.htm	catalogue.htm	tourdates.htm	contact.htm
Show "Down Image" Initially	unchecked	checked	unchecked	unchecked	unchecked

4. Make sure the Preload Images checkbox is checked, Horizontally is selected in the Insert list, and the Use Tables checkbox is checked.

5. Click the **OK** button. The navigation bar appears in the bands page with the bands link showing the Down state.

6. Right align the **navigation bar**.

7. Save and close the **bands** page.

8. Reopen the **bands** page, delete the stray closing anchor tag from the navigation bar, if necessary, and then save the **bands** page again.

9. Preview and test the **bands** page in a browser, and then close the browser window.

You will copy the navigation bar to the rest of the pages in the site.

Copying a Navigation Bar

You could continue to create the navigation bar for each page manually, but a faster method is to copy an existing navigation bar and then modify the appropriate elements for that page. When you copy the navigation bar to a new page, Dreamweaver will display a series of warnings telling you that the Set Nav Bar Image behavior cannot be copied. This means that Dreamweaver cannot automatically determine which element should be displayed in the Down state and that you must change these elements yourself. You will click OK, then open the Modify Navigation Bar dialog box and manually change the navigation bar to display the element, which represents the current page, in the Down state. Finally, when you copy the navigation bar to a new page, Dreamweaver leaves a stray closing anchor tag (</a>) in the code of the element in the Down state (designated with an asterisk in the Insert Navigation Bar dialog box). You will remove this stray closing tag from the navigation bar on the new page.

To copy the navigation bar to another page:

1. Click the **anchor point** icon to select the entire navigation bar table, click **Edit** on the main menu bar, click **Copy HTML**, and then close the **bands** page.

2. Open the **catalogue** page, select the **link text**, press the **Delete** key, click **Edit** on the main menu bar, and then click **Paste HTML**. A dialog box opens warning you that Dreamweaver cannot copy the "Set Nav Bar Image" behavior.

3. Click the **OK** button in the warning dialog box, and if additional dialog boxes open with the same message, click the **OK** button in each one.

Next, you will modify the navigation bar by changing the bands element so that it shows the Up state initially and changing the catalogue element (the element that represents the current page) so that it shows the Down state initially.

4. Click **Modify** on the main menu bar, and then click **Navigation Bar**. The Modify Navigation Bar dialog box opens.

5. Click **Bands*** in the Nav Bar Elements list, and then click the **Show "Down Image" Initially** checkbox to uncheck it.

6. Click **Catalogue** (the element that represents the current page) in the Nav Bar Elements list, and then click the **Show "Down Image" Initially** checkbox to check it. See Figure 5-9.

Figure 5-9 **MODIFY NAVIGATION BAR DIALOG BOX**

asterisk indicates that Down Image is shown initially

7. Click the **OK** button, and then save and close the page.

8. Open the **catalogue** page again, select the stray closing anchor tag in the navigation bar, if necessary, and then press the **Delete** key.

9. Save and close the **catalogue** page, preview the **catalogue** page in a browser, test the navigation bar, and then close the browser window.

10. Repeat Steps 2 through 9 for the **contact.htm** and **tourdates.htm** pages.

11. Open the **index.htm** page, delete the link text, click **Edit** on the main menu bar, click **Paste HTML**, and then click the **OK** button in any warning dialog boxes that open. You will not designate an element to show the Down Image initially on the index.htm page, because there is no element in the navigation bar that represents the home page.

12. Click **Modify** on the main menu bar, click **Navigation Bar**, click **Bands*** in the Nav Bar Elements list, click the **Show "Down Image" Initially** checkbox to uncheck it, and then click the **OK** button.

13. Save and close the **index.htm** page, reopen the **index.htm** page, delete the stray closing anchor tag, if necessary, and then save and close the **index.htm** page again.

14. Preview the **index.htm** page in a browser, test the navigation bar, and then close the browser window.

Next, you will learn to make additional modifications to the navigation bar.

Modifying **the Navigation Bar**

As a Web site grows and changes, you will undoubtedly need to modify the navigation bar. You might need to add new elements, delete current elements, reorder existing elements, change the graphics associated with the various states of the elements, and update the URLs to which elements are hyperlinked. Remember, you cannot change the horizontal or vertical orientation of a navigation bar once it has been created. To change the orientation of the navigation bar, you must delete the current navigation bar and create a new one.

REFERENCE   WINDOW   **RW**

Modifying a Navigation Bar
- Click Modify on the main menu bar, and then click Navigation Bar to open the Modify Navigation Bar dialog box.
- Click the element you want to modify in the Nav Bar Elements list.
- Change the options you want to modify.
- Click the OK button.

Brian has decided that placing the catalogue element of the navigation bar before the bands element will be more effective in achieving the site goal of promoting CDs. He asks you to modify the navigation bar for the NewCatalyst Web site so that the catalogue element is placed before the bands element.

To modify a navigation bar:

1. Open the **index.htm** page in a Document window.

2. Click **Modify** on the main menu bar, and then click **Navigation Bar**. The Modify Navigation Bar dialog box opens.

3. Click **Catalogue** in the Nav Bar Elements list box to select it.

4. Click the **Up Arrow** button 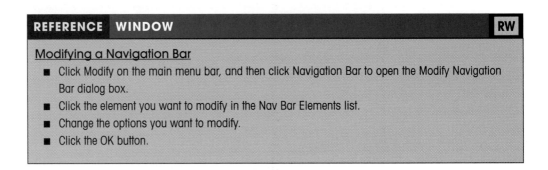 above the Nav Bar Elements list one time so that the element is second in the list. See Figure 5-10.

| Figure 5-10 | CATALOGUE ELEMENT MODIFICATIONS IN MODIFY NAVIGATION BAR DIALOG BOX |

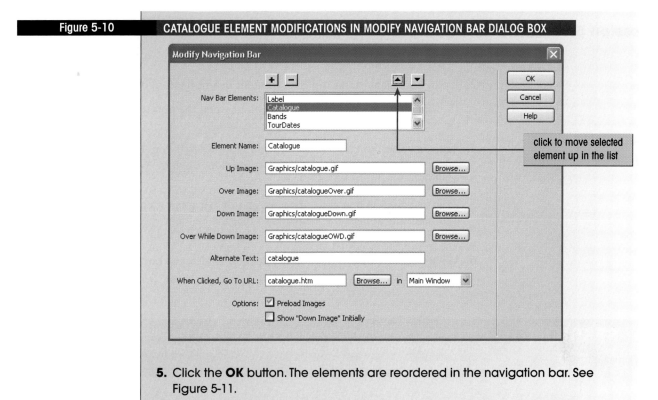

click to move selected element up in the list

5. Click the **OK** button. The elements are reordered in the navigation bar. See Figure 5-11.

| Figure 5-11 | HOME PAGE WITH REORDERED NAVIGATION BAR ELEMENTS |

repositioned element

6. Save and close the **index.htm** page.

7. Repeat Steps 1 through 6 for the **bands.htm**, **catalogue.htm**, **contact.htm**, **label.htm**, and **tourdates.htm** pages.

8. Starting with the **home** page, preview all the pages of the site in a browser.

9. Close the browser.

So far, you have created and modified the navigation on each page of the NewCatalyst Web site. In the next session, you will create frames and framesets.

Session 5.1 QUICK CHECK

1. What is a navigation bar?

2. Up to how many states can each element in a navigation bar have?

3. In which state is a navigation bar element when the pointer is positioned over the element before the graphic has been clicked?

4. True or False? You do not need to add graphics that you use in navigation bar elements to the Graphics folder in the root folder of your Web site because they are used only for the navigation bar elements.

5. True or False? When you copy a navigation bar to a different page, Dreamweaver automatically adjusts the elements so that the element representing the link to the page to which you are pasting is now shown in the Down state.

6. What property of a navigation bar cannot be changed once the navigation bar has been created?

SESSION 5.2

In this session, you will learn about frames and framesets. You will use several different techniques to create frames. You will save the frames page, and then set page properties and attributes for frames and framesets.

Understanding Frames and Framesets

Frames divide one Web page into multiple HTML documents. Each frame contains a single HTML document with its own content and, if necessary, its own scroll bars. For example, you will create a new page in the Catalyst Web site for the band Life In Minor Chords. The new page will have three frames. The top frame will contain an HTML document with the band logo, a frame at the lower-left of the page will contain an HTML document with the menu for the page, and a frame at the lower-right of the page will contain one of the many HTML documents containing content. When a user selects a different menu link, the HTML document containing the requested information will display in the content frame of the page, but the other two frames will remain the same.

A Web page with frames is held together by a frameset. A **frameset** is a separate HTML document that defines the structure and properties of a Web page with frames. The frameset page is not displayed in the browser; its only function is to store the information about how the frames will display on the Web page and to provide the browser with that information when the page is loaded. Every frame must be contained in a frameset. When you create frames in Dreamweaver, code to display NoFrames content is automatically added to the code of the frameset page. **NoFrames** content is content that is shown by browsers that cannot display frames. The NoFrames content is added to provide information for users who cannot view the frames. You will learn more about NoFrames content when you add content to the frames.

The biggest benefit of frames is that they can be used to keep some parts of a Web page static while other parts of the page are updated. For example, frames can keep the portions of Web pages that remain consistent throughout the site (such as logos and navigation bars) separate from the portions of the Web pages that change (such as the content). This is done so that the user does not wait for the logo and the navigation bar to reload every time they click on a new menu item. This makes the user's experience more pleasant because pages load faster.

When used correctly, frames can add a lot to a site; however, there are some problems with using frames. Frames are not supported in browsers earlier than Netscape 2 and

Internet Explorer 3. Also, frames run more slowly in Internet Explorer prior to version 5.5 because older versions open an additional, invisible browser window for each frame in the page. These additional invisible browser windows take processing power and make things slower, eliminating the benefit of using the frames. If you are supporting very old browsers, you should not use frames. Using frames in a page makes it hard for users to bookmark specific content because bookmarks mark the initial state of the frameset. If the user has clicked the menu options and the content of the page has changed, the changes are usually not reflected when the bookmark is loaded. This can irritate users who want to come back to a particular place in your site. Along the same lines, the URL no longer constitutes a complete specification of the information shown in the browser window because the URL marks the initial state of the frameset. You can only create a link to the site as it is initially displayed in the browser. This reduces the usefulness of shortcuts and hyperlinks because you cannot link to specific information, only to the general site. Finally, using frames in a site can make it difficult for search engines to list the site.

Over the years, frames have gotten a bad reputation, primarily because many sites make poor use of them. The two most common mistakes are using too many frames in a page and miscoding frames so that information is loaded into pages incorrectly. Using too many frames in a page fragments the page and makes it hard to read. When frames were first introduced, many designers went crazy, placing so many frames into their pages that users found the sites confusing and hard to follow. When you add frames to a site, ask yourself why you are adding the frames and what they will add to your site. Only add frames when they will contribute to the overall site design. When you create your frameset and frames, it is important to code them correctly. Some common mistakes include targeting a link to open in the wrong frame and miscoding so that multiple instances of the same frame open within one Web page. You will learn the correct way to create frames in this session.

Even if you decide not to use frames in your sites, it is a good idea to develop an understanding of the way they work because as a professional designer you will run into frames from time to time.

Before you start using frames, you will explore a Web page that uses frames from within your browser. The sample Web page is the page that was used during planning stages to develop the Life in Minor Chords frame layout. The borders of the frames have been made visible so that you can see where the frames are located, and one of the sample links is targeted to open in the wrong frame so that you can experience the effects of mistargeting a link (one of the most common mistakes designers make when working with frames). Experiencing the effects of a mistargeted link will help you recognize the mistake if you run into it while you are creating your own frames. The sample Web page contains text placeholders where the finalized artwork, navigation bar, and content will be. Designers often use text placeholders to help with the layout of Web pages while finalized art and content are being created. In the final version of the page, the Life in Minor Chords logo art will be substituted for the text in the top frame, a navigation bar will be created for the left frame, finalized content will be added to content frames, and the frame borders will be invisible.

To explore a Web page that uses frames in a browser:

1. Start your browser.

2. Click **File** on the menu bar, click **Open**, click the **Browse** button, navigate to the **FrameTest/Dreamweaver** folder in the **Tutorial** folder in the **Tutorial.05** folder on the Data Disk, double-click **LIMCFrameSet.htm**, and then click the **OK** button. The sample page with frames loads in the browser window. These are the frames that you will create for the Life in Minor Chords page. The top frame is where the logo will be placed, the left frame will contain the navigation bar, and the right frame will contain the changing page content. See Figure 5-12.

Figure 5-12   SAMPLE WEB PAGE WITH FRAMES

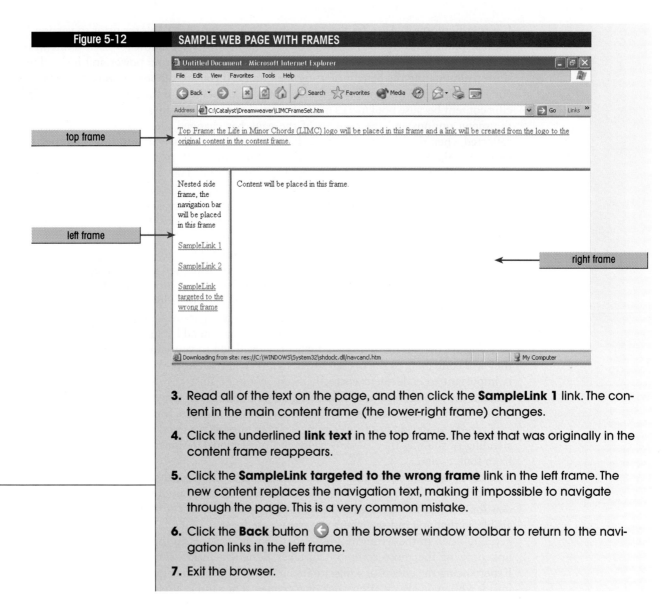

3. Read all of the text on the page, and then click the **SampleLink 1** link. The content in the main content frame (the lower-right frame) changes.

4. Click the underlined **link text** in the top frame. The text that was originally in the content frame reappears.

5. Click the **SampleLink targeted to the wrong frame** link in the left frame. The new content replaces the navigation text, making it impossible to navigate through the page. This is a very common mistake.

6. Click the **Back** button ⊙ on the browser window toolbar to return to the navigation links in the left frame.

7. Exit the browser.

Next, you will explore frames from within Dreamweaver.

Creating a Web Page that Uses Frames

Initially, each Web page can be thought of as one frame. You can then create more frames on any page. There are many ways to add frames to a Web page. You can split the page into frames, you can drag the borders of a page to create frames, you can insert frames, or you can use predefined framesets. No matter which method you use to create frames, you need to set Dreamweaver so that frame borders are visible. To view the frame borders once you have made them visible, the page must be in Design view.

Creating a Web Page That Uses Frames

- Open the page in which you want to create frames.
- Click View on the main menu bar, point to Visual Aids, and then click Frame Borders.
- Click Modify on the main menu bar, point to Frameset, and then click a Split Frame command.

or

- Drag a frame border.

or

- Click the Frames tab on the Insert bar, and then click a Frames button to insert a predefined frameset.

To view frame borders in Dreamweaver:

1. If you took a break after the last session, make sure that **Dreamweaver** is running and the **NewCatalyst** site is open.

2. Open the **home** page in the NewCatalyst site.

3. Click **View** on the main menu bar, point to **Visual Aids**, and then click **Frame Borders**. A gray frame border surrounds the entire page. See Figure 5-13.

| Figure 5-13 | HOME PAGE WITH FRAME BORDER |

frame border

A border surrounds each frame on the page. In this case there is only one frame border because you haven't created any frames yet. To select a frame, you click within that frame in the Document window. The view frame borders option is not a setting that you can save. When you are working with frames, each time you close a page and reopen it, you will need to reset the view frame borders setting.

Next, you'll use the different methods to create frames on the home page.

Creating Frames by Splitting a Web Page

You can create frames in a Web page by splitting the page. When you split a page, the Document window divides into two frames—either vertically (left and right) or horizontally (up and down). The Web page properties and any content move into the specified frame (left, right, top, or bottom). You can continue to split the page by selecting a frame and splitting it until you have achieved the desired number of frames. The four ways to split a page are:

- **Split Frame Left.** Splits the page vertically into two frames, and moves the Web page properties and any content into the left frame.
- **Split Frame Right.** Splits the page vertically into two frames, and moves the Web page properties and any content into the right frame.
- **Split Frame Up.** Splits the page horizontally into two frames, and moves the Web page properties and any content into the top frame.
- **Split Frame Down.** Splits the page horizontally into two frames, and moves the Web page properties and any content into the bottom frame.

If you decide you don't want a frame you just added, you can use the Undo command on the Edit menu to remove the frame.

You'll create frames on the home page so that you can become familiar with the way creating frames affects the content of your Web pages. First, you will create frames by splitting the Web page.

To split a Web page:

1. With the insertion point positioned anywhere in the home page in the Document window, click **Modify** on the main menu bar, point to **Frameset**, and then click **Split Frame Left**. The page splits into two vertical frames with the content in the left frame and nothing in the right frame. The left frame also has its own scroll bar. See Figure 5-14.

| Figure 5-14 | HOME PAGE WITH VERTICAL FRAMES |

2. Click in the left frame to make it active, click **Modify** on the main menu bar, point to **Frameset**, and then click **Split Frame Up**. The left frame splits into two horizontal frames with the content in the upper frame. See Figure 5-15.

Figure 5-15   **HOME PAGE WITH HORIZONTAL FRAMES**

content in top frame

3. Click **Edit** on the main menu bar, and then click **Undo Insert Frame**. The page returns to two vertical frames.

4. Click **Edit** on the main menu bar, and then click **Undo Insert Frame**. The page returns to one frame.

You'll try another method to create frames.

Creating Frames by Dragging Borders

When frame borders are visible, you can create frames in a page by dragging the frame borders at the perimeter of the Web page up, down, left, or right. If a Web page already has frames, you can create additional frames by dragging the borders of the outside frames away from the edges of the page. Dragging the frame borders that do not touch the edge of the Web page will resize the frames. Be careful. The frame (and any content it contains) is deleted if you drag the frame border back to the Web page perimeter.

You'll create frames by dragging the borders of a Web page.

To create frames by dragging borders:

1. Position the pointer over the **left page border** (all the way on the left side of the screen). The pointer changes to ↔.

2. Drag the **border** to the right approximately one-third of the way to the center of the page to create two vertical frames. The Web page content and settings (like the page background) are in the larger right frame. See Figure 5-16.

Figure 5-18 PAGE WITH TOP AND NESTED LEFT FRAMES

- this number will differ on your screen
- Top and Nested Left Frames button
- new left frame border
- content in right frame

Selecting and Saving Frames in the Document Window

Once you have created frames in your Web page, you must save them before you begin working on the page. Each frame contains a separate HTML document, so you will select and save the document in each frame individually. To select the HTML document in a frame, you place the pointer in that frame in the Document window. You select a frame when you want to add content to the HTML document in that frame, or when you want to save the HTML document that is in that frame. Once you have selected the frame, you can save it.

REFERENCE WINDOW RW

Saving a Frame
- Select the frame in the Document window or in the Frames panel.
- Click File on the main menu bar, and then click Save Frame.
- Type a filename in the File name text box.
- Click the Save button.

You will save the top and left frames that you created for the Life in Minor Chords page. You will add a page title and identifying text when you save each frame. (You saved the HTML document in the right frame when you created the page in the Site panel, so you do not need to save it again.)

To save frames:

1. Click in the **top frame** to make that frame active, and then type **LIMC - top frame**.

2. Replace the text in the **Title** text box in the Document toolbar with **Life in Minor Chords top frame**, and then press the **Enter** key.

3. Click **File** on the main menu bar, and then click **Save Frame**. The Save As dialog box opens.

4. Navigate to the local root folder of the NewCatalyst site, double-click the **LifeInMinorChords** folder to open it, select all of the text in the **File name** text box, type **LIMCtopframe.htm**, and then click the **Save** button. The new HTML document appears in the LifeInMinorChords folder in the Site panel and the filename appears in the Document window title bar. See Figure 5-19.

| Figure 5-19 | MODIFIED TOP FRAME |

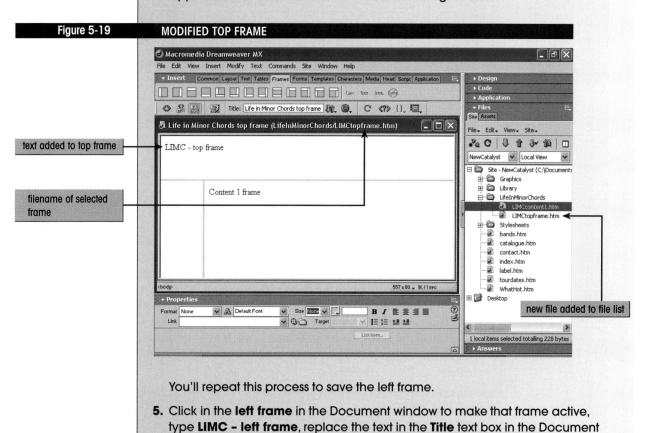

text added to top frame

filename of selected frame

new file added to file list

You'll repeat this process to save the left frame.

5. Click in the **left frame** in the Document window to make that frame active, type **LIMC - left frame**, replace the text in the **Title** text box in the Document toolbar with **Life In Minor Chords - left frame**, and then press the **Enter** key.

6. Click **File** on the menu bar, click **Save Frame**, and then save the frame in the LifeInMinorChords folder with the filename **LIMCleftframe.htm**. See Figure 5-20.

Figure 5-20	MODIFIED LEFT FRAME

left frame filename

content in left frame

Next, you will select and save the frameset.

Selecting and Saving the Frameset in the Document Window

Once you have saved the HTML document in each frame of the page, you must save the frameset. The frameset is a separate page that contains all of the information about how the frames will display in the Web page, and what HTML documents will initially be loaded into each frame. (When you adjust the size of a frame, the attributes of a frame or the attributes of the frameset, that information is stored in the frameset page.) You select the frameset from the Document window by selecting the outer border of the page. (The frame borders must be visible to select the frameset in the Document window.) When the frameset is selected, a dotted line is visible inside the border of one frame or all of the frames in the Document window and the frameset properties are visible in the Property inspector.

REFERENCE WINDOW   RW

Saving a Frameset

- Select the frameset in the Document window or in the Frames panel.
- Click File on the main menu bar, and then click Save Frameset.
- Type a filename in the File name text box, and then click the Save button.

Select the frameset you created for the LIMC page and save it.

To select and save the frameset:

1. Make sure the frame borders are visible, and then click the **border** that surrounds the entire page in the Document window. The frameset is selected.

Figure 5-21 SITE PANEL WITH NEW PAGES

dotted line and name in Property inspector indicate that frameset is selected

2. Replace the text in the **Title** text box with **Catalyst – Life in Minor Chords**.

3. Click **File** on the main menu bar, and click **Save Frameset**. The Save As dialog box opens.

4. Save the frameset in the **LifeInMinorChords** folder with the filename **LIMCframeset.htm**. The filename you give the frameset will appear in the browser window title bar. In this book, we will use the word "frameset" in the filename to avoid confusion, but it is not usually considered good practice in Web site design because it is meaningless to the user.

5. Close the page, preview in a browser the four pages that you created and stored in the LifeInMinorChords folder, and then close the browser window.

Once you have saved the frames and the frameset, you can save any changes you make to the frames or frameset by clicking the Save All command on the File menu. This will resave any frame that has been changed.

If you want to work on or view the Web page that contains the frames, you open the frameset page, because it contains all of the instructions for creating the frames. You can also open each frame individually in a Document window by selecting the desired page in the Site panel.

Next you will explore the frameset and the individual HTML documents that are in each frame.

Adjusting Page Properties for Frames

Once you have saved all the frames and the frameset for a Web page, you can adjust page properties and attributes for each HTML document. Because each frame contains a separate HTML document, you must set page properties and attributes for each frame separately. First, you select the desired document by placing the insertion point in the frame in the Document window or by selecting the document from the Site panel and opening the document in its own Document window. Then, as with other elements, you adjust the page properties in the Page Properties dialog box and you adjust the attributes of any page content by selecting the content and adjusting the attributes in the Property inspector.

REFERENCE   WINDOW   **RW**

Adjusting Page Properties for Frames
- Click in the frame whose properties you want to adjust.
- Click Modify on the main menu bar, and then click Page Properties.
- Change the options you want to modify.
- Click the OK button

You will set the page properties for each of the HTML documents that are displayed in the LIMCframeset page. You will set the background color to light blue (#A1CEF4), the text color to dark gray (#666666), the visited links to light gray (#CCCCCC), the links and active links to white (#FFFFFF), and the margins to 0.

To set page properties:

1. Open the **LIMCtopframe.htm** page in a Document window. The HTML Document that is displayed in the top frame of the LIMCframeset page is open in its own Document window.

2. Click **Modify** on the main menu bar, and then click **Page Properties**. The Page Properties dialog box opens.

3. Type **#A1CEF4** in the Background text box, type **#666666** in the Text text box, type **#CCCCCC** in the Visited Links text box, type **#FFFFFF** in the Links text box, and then type **#FFFFFF** in the Active Links text box.

4. Type **0** in the Left Margin, Margin Width, Top Margin, and Margin Height text boxes.

5. Click the **OK** button, then save the page. See Figure 5-22.

Figure 5-22	FORMATTED TOP FRAME

Next, you will change the page properties of the other pages in the LIMCframeset page from within the frameset page.

6. Close the **LIMCtopframe.htm** page, and then open the **LIMCframeset.htm** page.

7. Click **View** on the main menu bar, point to **Visual Aids**, and then click **Frame Borders**. The frame borders are now visible. The HTML document in the top frame (LIMCtopframe.htm) has the page properties set.

8. Click in the **lower left frame** in the Document window to select it.

9. Click **Modify** on the main menu bar, and then click **Page Properties**. The Page Properties dialog box opens.

10. Type **#A1CEF4** in the Background text box, type **#666666** in the Text text box, type **#CCCCCC** in the Visited Links text box, type **#FFFFFF** in the Links text box, and then type **#FFFFFF** in the Active Links text box.

11. Type **0** in the Left Margin, Margin Width, Top Margin, and Margin Height text boxes.

12. Click the **OK** button, click **File** on the main menu bar, and then click **Save Frame**.

Now set the page properties for the right frame.

13. Repeat Steps 8 through 12 for the **lower right frame**. See Figure 5-23.

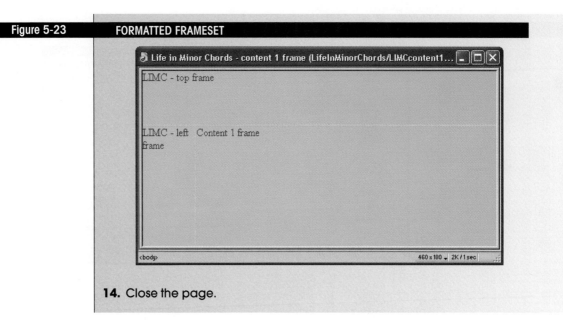

Figure 5-23   FORMATTED FRAMESET

14. Close the page.

Next, you will use the Frames panel to adjust the frame and frameset attributes.

Adjusting **Frame and Frameset Attributes**

You set and adjust attributes for each frameset and frame individually. This enables you to customize the way each frame is displayed in the browser. For example, you can make the borders of one frame visible and make the borders of other frames invisible. To adjust the attributes of a frame or frameset, you must first open the frameset page and then select the frame or frameset you want to modify in the Frames panel. The **Frames panel** enables you to select and adjust the frame and frameset information that is contained in the frameset page. Remember, the frameset contains all of the instructions for creating the frames, and the individual HTML pages contain the content that is displayed in the frames. When you select a frame in the Document window, you are actually selecting the HTML document contained in that frame (because the frameset page is not actually displayed). Selecting the frameset in the Document window is the same as selecting the frameset from the Frameset panel, but it only provides you with access to the main frameset information (not the elements in the frameset page). When you select a frame or frameset from the Frames Panel, you are selecting the information within the frameset page that pertains to the selected item.

You will open the Frames panel and select the frames and framesets in the LIMCframeset.htm page.

To select frames and framesets in the Frames panel:

1. Click **Window** on the main menu bar, point to **Others**, and then click **Frames**. The Frames panel opens in the Advanced Layout panel group.

2. Open the **LIMCframeset.htm** page, click **View** on the main menu bar, point to **Visual Aids**, and then click **Frame Borders**. Frame borders must be redisplayed each time you open a frameset page.

3. Click in the **top frame** in the Frames panel. The top frame is selected in the Document window, and its attributes are visible in the Property inspector. See Figure 5-24.

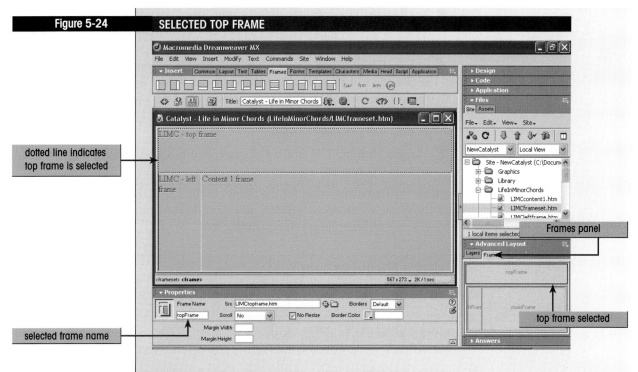

Figure 5-24   **SELECTED TOP FRAME**

dotted line indicates
top frame is selected

Frames panel

top frame selected

selected frame name

4. Click the **left frame** in the Frames panel. The leftFrame element is selected within the frameset, and the leftFrame attributes are visible in the Property inspector.

5. Click the **outermost border** in the Frames panel. The LIMCframeset is selected and the frameset attributes are visible in the Property inspector.

You will now explore frame attributes, then set the attributes for the frames you have created.

Adjusting Frame Attributes

You adjust the attributes of frames by selecting the frame in the Frames panel and changing its attributes in the Property inspector. Frame attributes include:

■ **Frame Name.** A descriptive name you give the frame. The frame name will appear in the Property inspector when the frame is selected, and the name will appear in the Frames panel. The name will also be used for hyperlink targets, so the name must begin with a letter or an underscore and cannot include spaces or special characters. Also, the frameset uses these names as a reference to know where to load the file.

■ **Src (Source).** The filename of the page that will appear in the frame. If you have already saved the frame, the filename you assigned will appear in this text box.

■ **Borders.** The option to turn on the frame's borders so that they can be seen in the browser (Yes), or off so that they are invisible in the browser (No), or to default to the frameset settings (Default). The frame border setting overrides the frameset border setting. However, the border can be turned off only if all adjacent frames borders are also set to No, or if all adjacent frames are set to Default and the frameset is set to No.

■ **Scroll.** The option to display scroll bars when there is not enough room to display the content of a frame within the frame. **Yes** displays the scroll bars. **No** hides the scroll bars. **Auto** displays scroll bars if they are needed. **Default** leaves the decision up to the user's browser setting, which is usually Auto.

■ **No Resize.** The option to prevent users from resizing a frame by dragging its borders. Checking this option does not restrict you from resizing the frame within the Document window.

■ **Border Color.** The color of the frame's border entered as a hexadecimal code or selected with the Color Picker. The frame border color overrides any frameset border color. This attribute does not display correctly in all browsers.

■ **Margin Width.** The amount of space, in pixels, between the frame content and the left and right borders.

■ **Margin Height.** The amount of space, in pixels, between the frame content and the top and bottom borders.

You will set the frame attributes for the frames in the LIMCframeset.htm page. You will customize the frame name of each frame, and then set the borders to 0, scroll bar to no, resize option to no, and margin width and height to 0.

To set the frame attributes:

1. Select the **top frame** in the Frames panel.

2. Select all of the text in the **Frame Name** text box in the Property inspector, type **LIMCtop**, press the **Enter** key, and then verify that **LIMCtopframe.htm** is in the Src text box. The top frame in the Frames panel is now named LIMCtop.

3. Click the **Borders** list arrow, click **No**, click the **Scroll** list arrow, and then click **No**.

4. Click the **No Resize** checkbox to check it, if necessary.

5. Type **0** in the Margin Width and Margin Height text boxes. See Figure 5-25.

Figure 5-25   **TOP FRAME ATTRIBUTES SET**

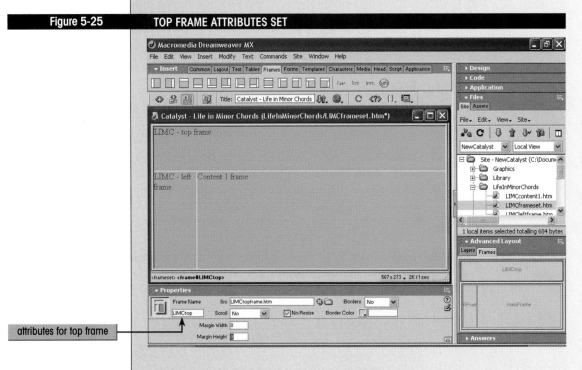

attributes for top frame

6. Click the **left frame** in the Frames panel.

7. Select all the text in the **Frame Name** text box in the Property inspector, type **LIMCleft**, press the **Enter** key, and then verify that **LIMCleftframe.htm** is in the Src text box.

8. Select **No** in the Borders list, select **No** in the Scroll list, and then click the **No Resize** checkbox to check it, if necessary.

9. Type **0** in the Margin Width text box, and then type **0** in the Margin Height text box.

10. Select the **right frame** in the Frames panel.

11. Select all of the text in the **Frame Name** text box in the Property inspector, type **LIMCcontent**, press the **Enter** key, and then verify that **LIMCcontent1.htm** is in the Src text box.

12. Select **No** in the Borders list, select **Auto** in the Scroll list, and then click the **No Resize** checkbox to check it, if necessary.

13. Type **0** in the Margin Width and Margin Height text boxes.

14. Click **File** on the main menu bar, and then click **Save Frameset**.

Next, you will adjust the attributes of the frameset.

Adjusting Frameset Attributes

Frameset attributes are adjusted in the same way that frame attributes are adjusted: by selecting the frameset in the Frames panel and changing its attributes in the Property inspector. When you use nested framesets (like the lower frame of the LIMC page, which is divided into a nested left frame and right frame), Dreamweaver inserts additional framesets within the code of the main frameset page to designate the nested frames. In addition to selecting and setting the attributes of the main frameset for the page, you can select and set attributes for the nested framesets. You select a nested frameset by selecting the raised border that surrounds the nested frameset in the Frames panel. (In this case a raised border surrounds the left and right frame because the lower frame has been split into a nested frameset.)

Frameset attributes include two of the same attributes available for frames: borders and border color. You can also set the border width and the frame size in the frameset attributes. **Border width**, measured in pixels, affects all the borders within the frameset. The frame size is set separately for each frame within the frameset. You can set the **frame size** of frames by clicking the tabs at the top or the left of the RowCol Selection box, typing a value for the selected row or column in the Value text box, and selecting a unit of measure for the selected row or column in the Units list. Frames that are in the selected row or column will resize to the entered values. The unit of measure for rows and columns can be pixels, percent, or relative. **Pixels** sizes the row or column to the specified pixel value. **Percent** sizes the row or column as a percentage of the entire browser window. Frames in the selected rows or columns will expand and shrink as the browser window is resized to maintain the specified percentage of the window area. **Relative** places an asterisk in the code for size. The asterisk means "take up all remaining space in the browser window." If you enter a specific relative value, it will have no effect unless more than one row or column is set to relative. If more than one row or column is set to relative and a value is specified, the value specifies what portion of available space will be designated for each row or column. For example, if two rows are set to relative and have the same numeric value (1, 2, 3, etc.), then each will occupy half of the available space. However, if one column value is 1 and the other column value is 2 (totaling 3 units of measure), then the second column will be twice the width of the first, and together they will occupy all available browser space. If you do not set the width of at least one row to Relative, users with smaller monitors may need to scroll to read all of the content.

You'll set the frameset attributes for the new page.

To set frameset attributes:

1. Click the **outermost border** of the frameset in the Frames panel. The Property inspector shows the frameset attributes.

2. Click the **Borders** list arrow and click **No** if necessary, double-click in the **Border Width** text box, and then type **0**, if necessary.

3. Click the **top box** in the RowCol Selection box, double-click in the **Value** text box, type **130**, and then, if necessary, click the **Units** list arrow, and select **Pixels**.

4. Click the **bottom box** in the RowCol Selection box, if necessary double-click in the **Value** text box and type **1**, and then, if necessary, click the **Units** list arrow, and click **Relative**.

   Next, you will set the attributes for the nested frameset.

5. Click the **border** of the nested frameset in the Frames panel. The nested frameset includes the bottom left and right frames. See Figure 5-26.

Figure 5-26	NESTED FRAMESET SELECTED

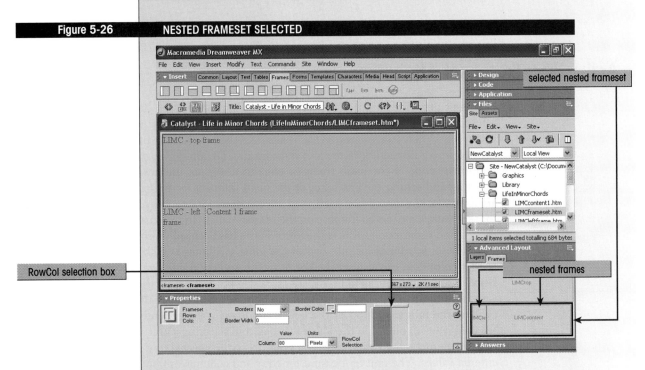

6. In the Property inspector, select **No** in the Borders list, and then type **0** in the Border Width text box.

7. Click the **left column** in the RowCol Selection box, type **100** in the Value text box, and then select **Pixels** from the Units list.

8. Click the **right column** in the RowCol Selection box, type **1** in the Value text box, and then select **Relative** from the Units list.

9. Click **File** on the main menu bar, and then click **Save Frameset**. The changes you made are saved.

10. Close the page.

11. Preview the **LIMCframeset.htm** page in a browser. See Figure 5-27.

| Figure 5-27 | FRAMESET PAGE WITH ALL PROPERTIES SET |

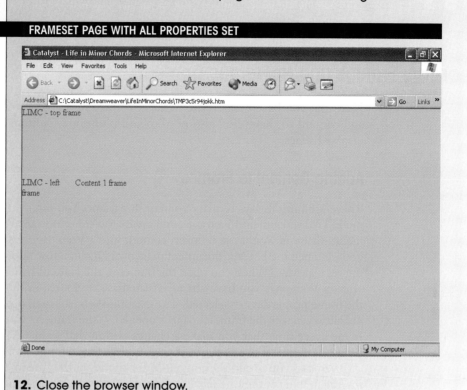

12. Close the browser window.

In this session, you've created a new Web page with frames for the Life In Minor Chords band, set the properties for the HTML documents that are displayed in the frames, set attributes for the frames, and set attributes for the framesets. In the next session, you'll add content to the frames.

Session 5.2 QUICK CHECK

1. What are frames?

2. When a Web page contains frames, what can each frame contain?

3. What is a frameset?

4. Why does Dreamweaver create NoFrames content when you create frames?

5. True or False? The only way to create frames on a page in Dreamweaver is to use one of the preset frames by clicking a button on the Frames tab on the Insert bar.

6. What is a nested frameset?

7. Why do you need to save the frameset?

SESSION 5.3

In this session you will add content to the HTML documents in your frames. You will create hyperlinks and target the links to specific frames. You will review problems that are common in pages that use frames. Finally, you will explore the HTML behind frames and targets.

Inserting Frames and NoFrames Content

Now that you have created the frames for the Life in Minor Chords page, you need to add content to them. You also need to add NoFrames content for browsers that cannot display frames.

Adding Content to Frames

There are several ways to place content in a frame. You can open the frameset page, select the HTML document in a frame, and create the content in the frame using the same techniques that you would use to insert content into a Web page that does not contain frames. You can open the HTML document in its own Document window and create the content in the regular way. (When you open the frameset, the content will be displayed.) You can also select a Web page you have already created as the Source in the Property inspector when the frame properties are selected. The existing Web page will open in the selected frame by default whenever the frameset page is opened. If the frameset is open, you must resave each frame every time that you make a change within that frame. Remember, you can use the Save All command to save all the open frames and the frameset in one step.

Brian asks you to add the content to the frames of the Life in Minor Chords page. You'll insert a graphic of the Life in Minor Chords logo with background artwork taken from their latest CD in the top frame of the new Web page. Then you'll insert and format text in the main frame of the Web page.

To insert a graphic into a frame:

1. If you took a break after the previous session, make sure that **Dreamweaver** is running and the **NewCatalyst** site is open.

2. Open the **LIMCframeset.htm** page, click **View** on the main menu bar, point to **Visual Aids**, and then click **Frame Borders**.

3. Click in the **top frame** in the Document window. This is the frame where you will insert the graphic.

4. Delete the text in the frame, click the **Common** tab on the Insert bar, and then click the **Image** button 🖼. The Select Image Source dialog box opens.

5. Navigate to the **Tutorial** folder within the **Tutorial.05** folder on your Data Disk, and then double-click **LifeBanner.jpg**.

6. Save a copy of the graphic in the **Graphics** folder within the local root folder of the NewCatalyst site. The image is added to the top frame of the page. See Figure 5-28.

| Figure 5-28 | NEW PAGE WITH GRAPHIC |

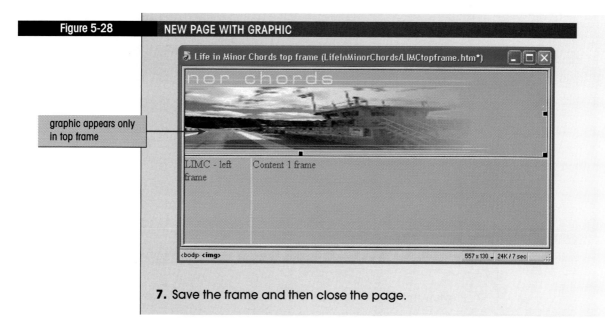

graphic appears only
in top frame

7. Save the frame and then close the page.

Next, you'll open the HTML document that is displayed in the right frame of the frameset page in its own document window and add the text content to the document. Then you will format the text. Brian has supplied the text in a Word document, so you can copy and paste the content rather than retyping it. You also want to format the text you add to the frame.

To paste text into a document:

1. Start **Word** or another word processor, open the **LIMCmainframetext.doc** document located in the **Tutorial** folder within the **Tutorial.05** folder on your Data Disk, copy the entire document, and then close the document and word processing program.

2. Open the **LIMCcontent1.htm** page, select the text in the Document window, and then paste the text you copied. The copied content appears in the Document window.

3. Select the heading text, and then use the Property inspector to set the font to **Arial, Helvetica, sans serif**, the size to **+3**, and the color to **#FFFFFF**.

TROUBLE? If the Font list box is not visible, you are probably in CSS mode. Click the Toggle CSS/HTML Mode button in the Property inspector to switch to HTML mode.

4. Select the rest of the text on the page, and then use the Property inspector to set the font to **Arial, Helvetica, sans serif**.

5. Select the last two paragraphs of the body text (beginning with "'Sure we sold out...'" and ending with "...makes us authentic.'"), and then click the **Text Indent** button in the Property inspector. The text in LIMCcontent1.htm is formatted.

6. Save and close the page, and then open the **LIMCframeset.htm** page. The new content is displayed in the right frame. See Figure 5-29.

Figure 5-29   **NEW PAGE WITH CONTENT**

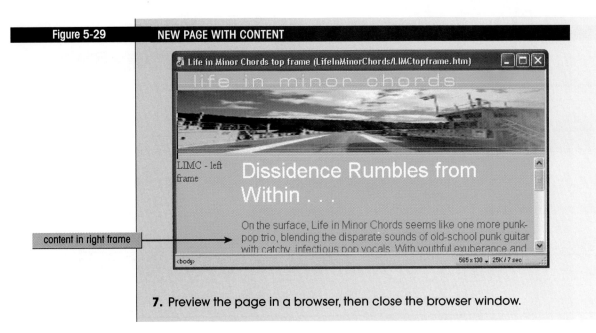

content in right frame

7. Preview the page in a browser, then close the browser window.

Next you will add NoFrames content to the page.

Adding NoFrames Content

The NoFrames code is automatically added to the HTML code for the frameset page when you create frames in Dreamweaver. You can add NoFrames content just as you would add content to any other frame or Web page. The content that you add will be displayed in place of the regular Web page when a user's browser does not support frames. (Frames are not supported in browsers earlier than Netscape 2 and Internet Explorer 3, or in some devices, like PDAs, that support limited Web browsing.) The NoFrames content should be simple text that explains that the page users are attempting to view uses frames and cannot be seen by their browser. The text should also provide a brief explanation of the purpose of the page, links to alternate pages where users can locate information, or contact information so users have an alternate way to get the information they were trying to access by viewing the Web page.

REFERENCE WINDOW   **RW**

Adding NoFrames Content
- Open the frameset in the Document window.
- Click Modify on the main menu bar, point to Frameset, then click Edit NoFrames Content.
- Type the content you want to appear in browsers that cannot display frames.
- Add a link to the home page.
- Click File on the main menu bar, and then click Save All to save the NoFrames content.

You'll add content to the NoFrames code for the LIMC frameset page. The content will be text that provides users with a link to the main Catalyst site so they can get more information about Life in Minor Chords or Catalyst.

To add NoFrames content:

1. With the **LIMCframeset.htm** page still open in the Document window, click **Modify** on the main menu bar, point to **Frameset**, and then click **Edit NoFrames Content**.

2. Type **This Web page uses frames. Click here for more information about the band Life in Minor Chords or about the Catalyst label.**

   You'll link the word "here" to the home page of the Catalyst site.

3. Select the word **here**.

4. Click the **Browse for File** button in the Property inspector, navigate to the local root folder of the NewCatalyst Web site, and then double-click **index.htm**. The path to the home page appears in the Link text box. See Figure 5-30.

Figure 5-30	NOFRAMES CONTENT ADDED

selected link text

link to home page

You will switch back to the frameset page.

5. Click **Modify** on the main menu bar, point to **Frameset**, and then click **Edit NoFrames Content** to toggle back to the frameset page.

6. Click **File** on the main menu bar, click **Save All**, and then close the page. The frameset page is saved with the NoFrames content.

Using Hyperlinks with Frames

When you click a hyperlink in a Web page, the linked page usually replaces the current page in the browser window. In a frames page, where more than one HTML pages compose one Web page, you don't always want the linked page to replace the HTML page in the same frame. For example, consider the common practice of creating a navigation bar in a frame at the left or top of the page. When a user clicks an element in the navigation bar, the linked page opens in the main frame of the Web page (rather than replacing the navigation bar). You can change where a Web page will open by modifying the target for the linked page. In addition to specifying a browser window in which a linked Web page will open, a target can also specify the frame in which the linked page will open. Figure 5-31 lists the target options.

Figure 5-31	TARGET OPTIONS
TARGET OPTION	**DESCRIPTION**
_blank	Opens the link in a new, browser window and leaves the current window open.
_parent	Opens the link in the parent frameset if you are using nested framesets. (Remember, the parent frameset is the frame that holds the nested frameset.)
_self	Opens the new page in the same frame as the link. If there are no frames, self replaces the old page with the new page. This is the default target.
_top	Replaces all the frames and the content of the current Web page with the content of the new page.
named frames	Opens the new page in the frame you select. The names you gave each frame appear at the end of the Target list.

Brian wants you to create targeted hyperlinks for the frames you created for the Life in Minor Chords page. You'll create a navigation bar in the nested left frame and then target the links to the LIMCcontent frame. Brian has another team member creating the content for the additional pages, so you need to create placeholder pages for that content. Also, you'll create a link from the LIMCbanner.gif to the LIMCcontent1frame.htm page and target the link to the LIMCcontent frame. This will provide the illusion that the user is linking to the home page of the LIMC site when the logo is clicked, because the content that displayed when the page was originally loaded will reappear.

You'll start by creating the placeholder pages for the targets. As a shortcut, you'll copy the existing HTML document LIMCcontent1frame.htm, rename the copied page, and then delete the content in the renamed pages.

To create the placeholder pages:

1. Click **LIMCcontent1.htm** in the Site panel, press the **Ctrl+C** keys to copy the page, and then press the **Ctrl+V** keys to paste a copy of the page in the Site panel. (The copy is listed at the bottom of the list of pages in the LifeInMinorChords folder.) You'll rename the copy of the page.

2. Right-click **Copy of LIMCcontent1.htm**, click **Rename** on the context menu, type **LIMChistory.htm**, and then press the **Enter** key. The page is renamed.

3. Open the **LIMChistory.htm** page in a Document window, select the header **Dissidence Rumbles from Within...**, and then type **LIMC History**.

4. Replace the words "content 1 frame" in the Title text box in the Document toolbar with **History**.

5. Select the remaining text on the page, and then press the **Delete** key. See Figure 5-32.

Figure 5-32	LIFE IN MINOR CHORDS HISTORY PAGE

6. Save and close the page.

You'll repeat this process for each placeholder HTML document you need to create.

7. Repeat Steps 1 through 6 for the pages listed below and replace "content 1 frame" in the Title text box with text corresponding to the new header text:

Rename as	New header text
LIMCmembers.htm	**LIMC Members**
LIMCcds.htm	**LIMC CDs**
LIMCtours.htm	**LIMC Tours**
LIMCphotos.htm	**LIMC Photos**

Next, you'll insert the navigation bar in the nested left frame of the LIMCframeset.htm page. Each element in the navigation bar will display graphics. For each element, you'll specify the linked page and the target frame. (You will add alternate text for each element in the Review Assignments.)

To create a navigation bar with targeted links:

1. Open the **LIMCframeset.htm** page in a Document window, click **View** on the main menu bar, point to **Visual Aids**, and then click **Frame Borders** to make the frame border visible.

2. Click in the **bottom left frame** to make it active, select the text in the left frame, and then press the **Delete** key. The left frame is active and empty.

3. Click the **Navigation Bar** button ![navigation bar icon] on the **Common** tab on the Insert bar. The Insert Navigation Bar dialog box opens.

4. Create the first element using the following name and images and saving a copy of each image in the Graphics folder in the site's local root folder. (Note that the Down image is the same as the Over image, so you link the Down image to the same image that you stored in the Graphics folder when you created the Over image.)

Element name	**LIMChistory**
Up Image	**Tutorial.05\Tutorial\LIMChistory.gif**
Over Image	**Tutorial.05\Tutorial\LIMChistoryOVER.gif**
Down Image	**Catalyst\Graphics\LIMChistoryOVER.gif**
When Clicked, Go To URL	**LIMChistory.htm** (in the LifeInMinorChords folder in the local root folder)
Target	**LIMCcontent** (this is the name of the target frame)
Preload Images	checked
Insert	**Vertically**
Use Tables	checked

The Insert Navigation Bar dialog box contains all the information for the LIMChistory element. You did not check the Show Down Image Initially checkbox, because you are using the same navigation bar for every content frame. See Figure 5-33.

Figure 5-33	INSERT NAVIGATION BAR DIALOG BOX FOR LIMCHISTORY ELEMENT

You'll add the next navigation bar element, which is LIMCmembers.

5. Click the **Add Item** button **+** in the Insert Navigation Bar dialog box.

6. Create the second element using the following name and images and saving a copy of each image in the Graphics folder in the site's root folder. Remember you do not need to change the Preload Images, Insert, or Use Tables options for each element.

Element Name	**LIMCmembers**
Up Image	**Tutorial.05\Tutorial\LIMCmembers.gif**
Over Image	**Tutorial.05\Tutorial\LIMCmembersOVER.gif**
Down Image	**Catalyst\Graphics\LIMCmembersOVER.gif**
When Clicked, Go To URL	**LIMCmembers.htm** (in the LifeInMinorChords folder in the local root folder)
Target	**LIMCcontent**

7. Click **+** and then add the third element using the following name and images and saving a copy of each image in the Graphics folder in the site's root folder.

Element Name	**LIMCcds**
Up Image	**Tutorial.05\Tutorial\LIMCcds.gif**
Over Image	**Tutorial.05\Tutorial\LIMCcdsOVER.gif**
Down Image	**Catalyst\Graphics\LIMCcdsOVER.gif**
When Clicked, Go To URL	**LIMCcds.htm** (in the LifeInMinorChords folder in the local root folder)
Target	**LIMCcontent**

8. Click **+** and then add the fourth element using the following name and images and saving a copy of each image in the Graphics folder in the site's root folder.

Element Name	**LIMCtours**
Up Image	**Tutorial.05\Tutorial\LIMCtours.gif**
Over Image	**Tutorial.05\Tutorial\LIMCtoursOVER.gif**
Down Image	**Catalyst\Graphics\LIMCtoursOVER.gif**
When Clicked, Go To URL	**LIMCtours.htm** (in the LifeInMinorChords folder in the local root folder)
Target	**LIMCcontent**

9. Click ⊞ and then add the fifth element using the following name and images and saving a copy of each image in the Graphics folder in the site's root folder.

Element Name	**LIMCphotos**
Up Image	**Tutorial.05\Tutorial\LIMCphotos.gif**
Over Image	**Tutorial.05\Tutorial\LIMCphotosOVER.gif**
Down Image	**Catalyst\Graphics\LIMCphotosOVER.gif**
When Clicked, Go To URL	**LIMCphotos.htm** (in the LifeInMinorChords folder in the local root folder)
Target	**LIMCcontent**

All the elements for the navigation bar are created with the appropriate names, graphics, linked pages, and target frames.

10. Click the **OK** button. The navigation bar appears in the nested left frame. See Figure 5-34.

Figure 5-34   **NAVIGATION BAR IN NESTED LEFT FRAME**

selected navigation bar

11. Click **File** on the main menu bar, click **Save All**, preview it in a browser, and then close the browser window.

Next, you'll use the Property inspector to create the targeted link from the logo in the top frame to the HTML document that was originally displayed in the LIMCcontent frame. Target the link to open in the LIMCcontent frame.

To create a targeted link using the Property inspector:

1. Click the **graphic** in the top frame to select it, click the **Browse for File** button next to the Link text box in the Property inspector, and then double-click the **LIMCcontent1.htm** page in the **LifeInMinorChords** folder in the local root folder of the NewCatalyst site.

2. Click the **Target** list arrow in the Property inspector, and then click **LIMCcontent**. See Figure 5-35.

Figure 5-35	TARGET INFORMATION FOR TOP FRAME

top frame selected

link from top frame will open in content frame

3. Click **File** on the main menu bar, click **Save All**, and then close the page.

4. Preview the **LIMCframeset.htm** page in a browser, click each of the links in the navigation bar in the left frame, and then click the graphic link in the top frame. See Figure 5-36.

Figure 5-36   **COMPLETED LIMC FRAMESET IN A BROWSER**

5. Close the browser window.

Next, you'll add links from the bands page and the catalogue page of the Catalyst site to the LIMCframeset.htm page. Target the links to open in a new browser window so that the LIMCframeset page does not replace the Catalyst page. This enables the user to easily return to the main portion of the Catalyst site.

6. Open the **bands.htm** page in a Document window, select the **Life In Minor Chords** subheading text, click the **Browse for File** button in the Property inspector, and then double-click **LIMCframeset.htm** in the **LifeInMinorChords** folder in the local root folder of the New Catalyst site.

7. Click the **Target** list arrow in the Property inspector, and then click **_blank** to open the link in a new browser window.

8. Save and close the page, preview the **bands.htm** page in a browser, and then click the **LIFE IN MINOR CHORDS** link. The Life in Minor Chords page opens in a new browser window.

9. Close both browser windows.

10. Open the **catalogue.htm** page, select the **Life in Minor Chords CD cover** graphic, and then link the **CD cover** to the **LIMCframeset.htm** page, targeted to open a new browser window.

11. Save and close the page, preview the **catalogue.htm** page in a browser, and then click the **Life in Minor Chords CD cover** graphic. The linked page opens in a new browser window.

12. Close both browser windows.

Reviewing **HTML Associated with Frames and Targets**

When you use frames in a Web page, all the frame tags associated with the Web page are in the frameset page. Additional content pages are simply regular Web pages that are targeted to open in one of the frames. The three following tags are associated with frameset pages (refer to Figure 5-37):

- **Frameset tags.** A set of frameset tags surround the frameset and, if nested frames are used, additional sets of frameset tags surround the nested frames within the parent frameset. The opening frameset tag contains the values for the frameset attributes.

- **Frame tag.** A frame tag is inserted between the opening and closing frameset tags for each frame in the frameset. There is no closing frame tag. It is one of the few HTML tags that is not in a pair. The frame tag contains the values for the frame attributes.

- **Noframes tags.** The noframes tags are inserted after the closing frameset tag. They surround content that is seen by browsers that do not support frames.

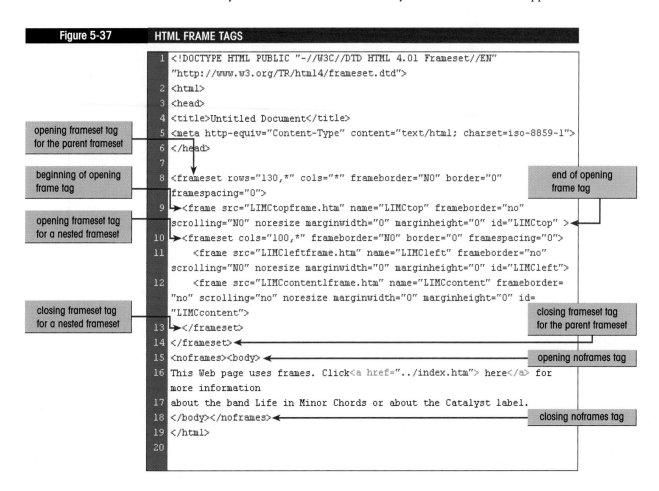

| Figure 5-37 | HTML FRAME TAGS |

```
 1  <!DOCTYPE HTML PUBLIC "-//W3C//DTD HTML 4.01 Frameset//EN"
    "http://www.w3.org/TR/html4/frameset.dtd">
 2  <html>
 3  <head>
 4  <title>Untitled Document</title>
 5  <meta http-equiv="Content-Type" content="text/html; charset=iso-8859-1">
 6  </head>
 7
 8  <frameset rows="130,*" cols="*" frameborder="NO" border="0"
    framespacing="0">
 9    <frame src="LIMCtopframe.htm" name="LIMCtop" frameborder="no"
    scrolling="NO" noresize marginwidth="0" marginheight="0" id="LIMCtop" >
10    <frameset cols="100,*" frameborder="NO" border="0" framespacing="0">
11      <frame src="LIMCleftframe.htm" name="LIMCleft" frameborder="no"
    scrolling="NO" noresize marginwidth="0" marginheight="0" id="LIMCleft">
12      <frame src="LIMCcontent1frame.htm" name="LIMCcontent" frameborder=
    "no" scrolling="no" noresize marginwidth="0" marginheight="0" id=
    "LIMCcontent">
13    </frameset>
14  </frameset>
15  <noframes><body>
16  This Web page uses frames. Click<a href="../index.htm"> here</a> for
    more information
17  about the band Life in Minor Chords or about the Catalyst label.
18  </body></noframes>
19  </html>
20
```

opening frameset tag for the parent frameset

beginning of opening frame tag

opening frameset tag for a nested frameset

closing frameset tag for a nested frameset

end of opening frame tag

closing frameset tag for the parent frameset

opening noframes tag

closing noframes tag

When you set a target for a hyperlink, the target information is added to the HTML code for the hyperlink in the following format:

```
<a href="theURL" target="value">Linked text or graphic</a>
```

where the target value options are the same options listed in the Target list in the Property inspector: _blank, _parent, _self, _top, and named frames.

Next, you will examine the code of the LIMCframeset page and review the frameset, frame, and noframes tags—as well as the hyperlink tags with target information inserted into them.

To examine HTML code in the frameset page:

1. Open the **LIMCframeset.htm** page in a Document window, and then select the frameset in the Frames panel.

2. Click the **Show Code View** button ⟨⟩ on the Document toolbar. The code for the LIMCframeset.htm page appears in the Document window. The parent frameset tags and everything between them are highlighted. See Figure 5-38.

| Figure 5-38 | CODE FOR THE LIMCFRAMESET PAGE |

opening parent frameset tag

closing parent frameset tag

TROUBLE? If your screen does not match the screen shown in Figure 5-38, then click the Show Design View button on the Document toolbar, select the outermost frame in the Frames panel again, and then repeat Step 2.

3. Locate the opening frameset tag and examine the frameset attributes and their values.

4. Locate the closing frameset tag.

5. Find the nested frameset and then locate the first frame in the nested frameset.

6. Examine the frame attributes in the first frame.

7. Click the **Show Design View** button ▦ on the Document toolbar, and then close the page.

8. Click the **Collapse** button ▾ next to the Advanced Layout panel group to collapse the panel group.

Finding Solutions to Common Frame Problems with the Macromedia Dreamweaver Support Center

The Macromedia Dreamweaver Support Center (*http://www.macromedia.com/support/ dreamweaver/*) contains a wealth of information pertaining to frames. It can be a great resource when you need to find solutions for common frames problems. From the Support Center you can also access Macromedia Exchange for Dreamweaver, which contains a number of Dreamweaver add-ons that other developers have written and decided to share. You can download and install these add-on programs to your copy of Dreamweaver free of charge. Two of the most popular frame solutions on Macromedia Exchange for Dreamweaver are:

- **Find Parent Frameset Extension.** One of the problems with pages that use frames is that the individual frames can be loaded independently of the frameset. For example, a search engine might follow the links in your navigation frame and index the individual content pages. Clicking one of these links would then load the content page without its surrounding frameset. Find Parent Frameset is an extension you can download that will insert code into any Web page that uses frames to ensure that your page is always shown in its frameset, even if a user links to the frame directly.

- **Frame Buster.** Some Web sites keep one of their frames open while they display your pages, and some Web pages even surround a page from your Web site with their navigation systems and logo. Frame Buster is an extension you can download that will insert code into your Web pages to prevent them from being loaded within a frameset.

Brian asks you to log on to the Macromedia Dreamweaver Support Center and research possible problems with frames pages.

> ## To do research on Macromedia Dreamweaver Support Center:
>
> **1.** Start your browser, type **www.macromedia.com/support/dreamweaver/** into the Address text box, and then press the **Enter** key. The Macromedia Dreamweaver Support Center page opens. See Figure 5-39.

Figure 5-39

MACROMEDIA DREAMWEAVER SUPPORT CENTER PAGE

2. Click the **Creating and Designing Pages** link to display a list of related links below it, and then click the **Using Frames** link. A list of tutorials, articles, and technical notes appears.

3. Click a link for a document that interests you, and read it. When you're finished, click the **Back** button ⬅ on the browser toolbar twice to return to the Macromedia Dreamweaver Support Center.

4. Click the **Downloads** link, click the **Dreamweaver** link, and then click the **Dreamweaver Exchange** link. The Macromedia Exchange for Dreamweaver page opens.

5. Scroll down to view the Site Help list, click the **What is an extension?** link, and then read about Dreamweaver extensions.

6. Click in the **Search Extensions** text box at the top of the page, type **frame**, and then click the **Go** button. A list of extensions related to frames appears. See Figure 5-40.

Figure 5-40

SEARCH RESULTS FOR FRAME EXTENSIONS

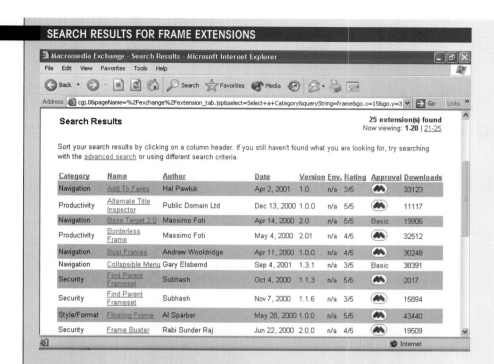

TROUBLE? If your search results differ from the list shown in Figure 5-40, don't worry. Extensions might have been added, removed, or updated since this book was published.

7. Click the **Find Parent Frameset** link, and read about the extension.

8. Click the **Dreamweaver Exchange General Discussion Forum** link near the bottom of the page. The Macromedia Online Forums page opens in a new window.

9. Click in the **Search Category** text box, type **frames**, and then click the **Search!** button. A list of topics related to the keyword "frames" is loaded. See Figure 5-41.

Figure 5-41

SEARCH RESULTS FOR FRAME DISCUSSION TOPICS

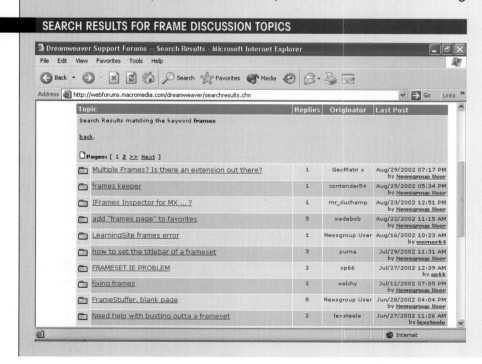

10. Click the link for the top folder to display the discussion related to that topic, and then read the information.

11. Close any open browser windows.

Updating the Web Site on the Remote Server

As a final review of the changes you made to the NewCatalyst Web site, you'll update the files on the remote server and review the pages over the Internet. You need to upload every page of the site because you have made changes on every page. This includes the bands.htm page, the catalogue.htm page, the contact.htm page, the index.htm page, the label.htm page, the tourdates.htm page, and the WhatHot.htm page, as well as all of the pages in the LifeInMinorChords folder: LIMCframeset.htm, LIMCcds.htm, LIMCcontent1frame.htm, LIMChistory.htm, LIMCleftframe.htm, LIMCmembers.htm, LIMCphotos.htm, LIMCtopframe.htm, and LIMCtours.htm. When you upload the pages, you will include dependent files so that the new graphics and new CSS styles are uploaded to the remote server. Then you'll preview the site on the Web.

To upload a site to the remote server:

1. Click the **Connect to remote host** button on the Site panel toolbar.

2. Click the **View** list arrow on the Site panel toolbar, and then click **Local View**.

3. Select the **LifeInMinorChords** folder and the **bands.htm**, **catalogue.htm**, **contact.htm**, **index.htm**, **label.htm**, **tourdates.htm**, and **WhatHot.htm** files in the Local View list, and then click the **Put File(s)** button on the Site panel toolbar.

   TROUBLE? If you can't select only the files you want, click the minus sign (-) next to the LifeInMinorChords folder to collapse the file list in the folder, press and hold the Ctrl key, and then click the folders and files you want to upload.

4. Click the **Yes** button when asked if you want to include dependent files, since you have not selected the new dependent files for the site yet.

5. Click the **Disconnects from remote host** button on the Site panel toolbar, click the **View** list arrow on the Site panel toolbar, and then click **Local View**.

Next, you'll preview the updated site in a browser. The site will include all of the new styles and text that you added to your local version.

To preview the updated site in a browser:

1. Open your browser, type the URL of your remote site in the Address text box on the browser toolbar, and then press the **Enter** key.

2. Open the **Home** page, if necessary, and then explore the remote site.

3. Click the **catalogue** link, click the **Life in Minor Chords CD cover** to open the Life in Minor Chords page in a new browser window, and then close the new browser window that opened.

4. Click the **bands** link on the catalogue page, and then click the **LIFE IN MINOR CHORDS** header to open the Life in Minor Chords page in a new browser window.

5. In the Life in Minor Chords window, click the **history**, **members**, **CDs**, **tour**, and **photos** links to make sure that each link is appropriately targeted and that all of the HTML documents were uploaded.

6. Click the **graphic** at the top of the page in the Life in Minor Chords window to redisplay the original information that appeared on the page when it was opened, and then close the Life in Minor Chords browser window.

7. On the home page, click the **label** link, click the **tour dates** link, click the **contact** link, and then click the **Catalyst** logo to return to the home page.

8. Click the **What's Hot at Catalyst** link.

9. Close both browser windows, and then close the NewCatalyst site.

Session 5.3 QUICK | CHECK

1. Name two ways to insert content into a frame.

2. True or False? You can add NoFrames content to your frameset page.

3. What is typically added as NoFrames content for a frameset?

4. Why is it common practice to place a navigation bar in a frame?

5. True or False? A link cannot be targeted to open in a different frame on the page.

6. What are three HTML tags associated with frameset pages?

REVIEW ASSIGNMENTS

Brian asks you to create a Web page for Dizzied Connections similar to the one you created for Life in Minor Chords. You will create a page with frames and a navigation bar. When the page is complete, you'll link the new page to the band name on the bands Web page. Once all of the changes are complete, you'll upload the NewCatalyst Web site to the Web server.

1. Open Dreamweaver and open the NewCatalyst site. Then, in the Site panel, select New Folder from the File menu and create a new folder named DizziedConnections in the root folder of the NewCatalyst site.

2. Click the new folder in the Site panel and select New File from the File menu to create a new page in the DizziedConnections folder, and name it DCcontent.htm.

3. Open the new page in a Document window.

4. Click inside the DCcontent page in the Document window, then click the Top and Bottom Frames button on the Frames tab of the Insert bar to insert frames into the page.

5. Click inside the top frame, click File on the main menu bar, click Save Frame, in the Save As window, navigate to the DizziedConnections folder in the root folder of the NewCatalyst site and then save the HTML document as DCtopframe.htm.

6. Click inside the bottom frame, click File on the main menu bar, click Save Frame, in the Save As window, navigate to the DizziedConnections folder in the root folder of the NewCatalyst site, and then save the frame as DCbottomframe.htm.

7. Select the frameset, change the title to Catalyst - Dizzied Connections, click File on the main menu bar, click Save Frameset, and then save the frame set in the DizziedConnections folder as DCframeset.htm.

Explore   8. Click in the top frame, change the title to "DC – top frame", and then set the page properties so that the background color is white and all of the margins are set to 0.

9. Click the Image button on the Common tab of the Insert menu bar, and then insert the DCbanner.jpg graphic located in the Review folder in the Tutorial.05 folder of your Data Disk, placing a copy of the graphic in the Graphics folder in the root folder of your NewCatalyst Web site.

Explore   10. Select the graphic and create a hyperlink to the DCcontent.htm page, and then target the link to the main frame by selecting mainFrame from the Target list in the Property inspector.

11. Save all the frames and the frameset.

12. Click in the middle frame, change the title to "DC – content", and then modify the page properties so that the background is white and all of the margins are equal to 0.

13. Open the CSS Styles panel in the Design panel group, and then attach the CatalystStyles.css style sheet located in the Stylesheets folder of your NewCatalyst site.

14. Type "dizzied connections. . ." in the middle frame, select the text you just typed, and then apply the CatalystSubHeadings style from the CSS Styles panel.

15. Save all the frames and the frameset.

16. Select the DCcontent.htm page in the Site panel, copy the page, and then paste a copy of the page in the DizziedConnections folder.

17. Right-click the Copy of DCcontent.htm page in the Site panel, click Rename on the context menu, type "DCcds.htm", and then press the Enter key.

18. Open the DCcds page in a Document window and replace the content in the page with "Dizzied Connections – CDs . . ." in the page. Change the page title to "DC – CDs" and then save and close the page.

19. Repeat Steps 16 through 18 to create DChistory.htm, DCmembers.htm, DCphotos.htm, and DCtours.htm pages. Make sure you type the appropriate heading text on each page (for example, for the DChistory page, type "Dizzied Connections – History…"), and make sure you change the page title for each page.

Explore   20. Click in the bottom frame in the DCframeset.htm page in the Document window, change the title to "DC – bottom frame," and then modify the page properties so that the background image is the graphic file DCbottombanner.jpg in the Review folder in the Tutorial.05 folder on your Data Disk, and all the margins are set to 0.

21. Save all the frames and the frameset.

22. Insert a navigation bar at the top of the bottom frame.

23. Create the first element in the navigation bar using the following name and images. Save a copy of each image in the Graphics folder in the site's local root folder. (Note that the Down image is the same as the Up image, so you link the Down image to the same image that you stored in the Graphics folder when you stored the Up image.)

Element name	DCcds
Up Image	Tutorial.05\Review\DCcdsUp.jpg
Over Image	Tutorial.05\Review\DCcdsOver.jpg
Down Image	Catalyst\Dreamweaver\Graphics\DCcdsUp.jpg
Alternate Text	Dizzied Connections CDs
When Clicked, Go To URL	DCcds.htm (in the DizziedConnections folder in the local root folder)
Target	mainFrame
Preload Images	checked
Insert	Horizontally
Use Tables	checked

24. Click the Add Item button in the Insert Navigation Bar dialog box to add a new element to the navigation bar, using the following name and images. Save a copy of each image in the Graphics folder in the site's root folder.

Element name	DChistory
Up Image	Tutorial.05\Review\DChistoryUp.jpg
Over Image	Tutorial.05\Review\DChistoryOver.jpg
Down Image	Catalyst\Dreamweaver\Graphics\DChistoryUp.jpg
Alternate Text	Dizzied Connections History
When Clicked, Go To URL	DChistory.htm (in the DizziedConnections folder in the local root folder)
Target	mainFrame

25. Add a third element to the navigation bar using the following name and images. Save a copy of each image in the Graphics folder in the site's root folder.

Element name	DCmembers
Up Image	Tutorial.05\Review\DCmembersUp.jpg
Over Image	Tutorial.05\Review\DCmembersOver.jpg
Down Image	Catalyst\Dreamweaver\Graphics\DCmembersUp.jpg
Alternate Text	Dizzied Connections Members
When Clicked, Go To URL	DCmembers.htm (in the DizziedConnections folder in the local root folder)
Target	mainFrame

26. Add a fourth element to the navigation bar using the following name and images. Save a copy of each image in the Graphics folder in the site's root folder.

Element name	DCphotos
Up Image	Tutorial.05\Review\DCphotosUp.jpg
Over Image	Tutorial.05\Review\DCphotosOver.jpg
Down Image	Catalyst\Dreamweaver\Graphics\DCphotosUp.jpg
Alternate Text	Dizzied Connections Photos
When Clicked, Go To URL	DCphotos.htm (in the DizziedConnections folder in the local root folder)
Target	mainFrame

27. Add a fifth element to the navigation bar using the following name and images. Save a copy of each image in the Graphics folder in the site's root folder.

Element name	DCtours
Up Image	Tutorial.05\Review\DCtoursUp.jpg
Over Image	Tutorial.05\Review\DCtoursOver.jpg
Down Image	Catalyst\Dreamweaver\Graphics\DCtoursUp.jpg
Alternate Text	Dizzied Connections Tours
When Clicked, Go To URL	DCtours.htm (in the DizziedConnections folder in the local root folder)
Target	mainFrame

28. Click the OK button, save all the frames and the frameset, close the page, preview the DCframeset page in a browser, and then close the browser window.

Explore 29. Modify the navigation bar in the Life in Minor Chords frameset to include Alternate Text for each element. Open the LIMCleftframe.htm page in a Document window, click Modify on the main menu bar, and then click Navigation Bar. For each element, click the element in the Nav Bar Element list, click in the Alternate Text text box, and then type "Life in Minor Chords – " followed by the name of the element; for example, for the LIMChistory element, type "Life in Minor Chords – History." Click the OK button, and then save and close the page. Preview the page in a browser.

30. Open the catalogue.htm page, select the Dizzied Connections CD cover graphic, and create a link to the DCframeset.htm page, targeting the link to open in a new browser window.

31. Open the bands.htm page, select the Dizzied Connections sub-heading, and create a link to the DCframeset.htm page, targeting the link to open in a new browser window.

32. Save and close both pages, preview them in a browser window, and then test the new links.

33. Close all open browser windows.

34. Connect to your remote server, upload the site, and then preview the site over the Web.

CASE PROBLEMS

Case 1. Hroch University Anthropology Department Professor Hart would like you to create a navigation bar for the site. An artist has already created the graphic elements that you will need. You will create the navigation bar in the home page of the site; then you will copy it to the other pages of the site: the ProfHart.htm page, the LinguisticDifferences.htm page, the CulturalCrossPollination.htm page, the RitualsAndPractices.htm page, and the Contact.htm page. You will then modify the navigation bar in these pages so that the element on the navigation bar that represents the selected page is placed in the Down state when the page is loaded into the browser window.

1. Open the Hart site that you modified in Tutorial 4, Case 1. Open the home page in a Document window, select the text links that you created as a menu bar, and then delete them and place the pointer at the bottom of the red stripes.

2. Click the Navigation Bar button on the Common tab on the Insert bar. The Insert Navigation Bar dialog box opens.

3. Create the first element using the following name and images; save a copy of each image in the Graphics folder in the site's local root folder. (Note that the Down image

is the same as the Over image, so you link the Down image to the same image that you stored in the Graphics folder when you stored the Over image.)

Element name	Hprofessorhart
Up Image	Tutorial.05\Cases\HprofessorhartUp.gif
Over Image	Tutorial.05\Cases\HprofessorhartDown.gif
Down Image	Hart\Dreamweaver\Graphics\HprofessorhartDown.gif
When Clicked, Go To URL	ProfHart.htm
Target	Main Window
Preload Images	checked
Insert	Horizontally
Use Tables	checked

4. Add a second element to the navigation bar using the following name and images; save a copy of each image in the Graphics folder in the site's root folder.

Element name	Hlinguisticdifferences
Up Image	Tutorial.05\Cases\HlinguisticdifferencesUp.gif
Over Image	Tutorial.05\Cases\HlinguisticdifferencesDown.gif
Down Image	Hart\Dreamweaver\Graphics\HlinguisticdifferencesDown.gif
When Clicked, Go To URL	LinguisticDifferences.htm
Target	Main Window

5. Add the third element using the following name and images; save a copy of each image in the Graphics folder in the site's root folder.

Element name	Hculturalcrosspollination
Up Image	Tutorial.05\Cases\HculturalcrosspollinationUp.gif
Over Image	Tutorial.05\Cases\HculturalcrosspollinationDown.gif
Down Image	Hart\Dreamweaver\Graphics\HculturalcrosspollinationDown.gif
When Clicked, Go To URL	CulturalCrossPollination.htm
Target	Main Window

6. Add the fourth element using the following name and images; save a copy of each image in the Graphics folder in the site's root folder.

Element name	Hritualsandpractices
Up Image	Tutorial.05\Cases\HritualsandpracticesUp.gif
Over Image	Tutorial.05\Cases\HritualsandpracticesDown.gif
Down Image	Hart\Dreamweaver\Graphics\HritualsandpracticesDown.gif
When Clicked, Go To URL	RitualsAndPractices.htm
Target	Main Window

7. Add the fifth element using the following name and images; save a copy of each image in the Graphics folder in the site's root folder.

Element name	Hcontactinformation
Up Image	Tutorial.05\Cases\HcontactinformationUp.gif
Over Image	Tutorial.05\Cases\HcontactinformationDown.gif
Down Image	Hart\Dreamweaver\Graphics\HcontactinformationDown.gif
When Clicked, Go To URL	Contact.htm
Target	Main Window

8. Add appropriate Alternate Text to each of the elements.

9. Click the OK button, and then save the page.

10. Preview the page in a browser; then close the browser window.

Explore   11. Select the entire navigation bar, including the table, in the Document window by selecting an element in the navigation bar, and then clicking the <table> tag button in the Document window status bar. The entire table is selected.

12. Copy the navigation bar using the Copy HTML command. Then open the ProfHart.htm page, select the menu text, delete it, and paste the navigation bar into the page using the Paste HTML command. Save and close the page, reopen it, delete the stray anchor tag, if necessary, and then save the page again.

Explore   13. Delete any extra spaces that were added above or below the navigation bar. Then modify the navigation bar to show the Down image of the Hprofessorhart element when the page is loaded. You do this by selecting Navigation Bar from the Modify menu, then selecting the Hprofessorhart element, checking the Show Down Image Initially checkbox and clicking OK. The Down image of the Hprofessorhart element is visible in the Document window.

14. Save and close the page. Repeat Steps 12 and 13 for the LinguisticDifferences.htm page, the CulturalCrossPollination.htm page, the RitualsAndPractices.htm page, and the Contact.htm page using the element that corresponds to the page as the Down image.

15. Preview the Web site in a browser window. Click each link and then close the window.

16. Connect to your remote server, upload the site, and then preview the site over the Web.

Case 2. Museum of Western Art   C. J. asks you to create a page for the artist Fredric Remington. The page will contain small graphics of some of the artist's more famous paintings. When the user clicks a painting, the page will display a larger version of the painting as well as a detailed description. Use frames for the new page and link the page to the artist's name in the artist page.

1. Open the Museum site that you modified in Tutorial 4, Case 2, and create a new folder called Remington in the root folder for the site.

2. Open the Remington folder and create a new page with the filename RemingtonContent.htm.

3. Open the home page and view the page properties for that page. Then add the same page properties to the RemingtonContent.htm page, change the page title to "Museum of Western Art – Remington Content frame," and then save the page. Close both pages.

Explore   4. Create a copy of the RemingtonContent.htm page in the Remington folder, rename the copy RemingtonTop.htm, and open it in a Document window.

5. Add a top frame to the page by clicking the Top Frame button on the Frames tab of the Insert bar.

Explore   6. Make the frame borders visible in the Document window.

7. Select the topFrame in the Frames panel, then, in the Property inspector, link the Src text box to the RemingtonTop.htm page in the Remington folder in your Museum root folder to load that page in the top frame when the page is displayed in a browser.

8. Select the frameset in the Frames panel, change the Title to "Museum of Western Art – Remington," and save the frameset as RemingtonFrameset.htm within the **Explore**   Remington folder.

9. Select the mainframe (the bottom frame) in the Frames panel, then, in the Property inspector, link the Src text box to the RemingtonContent.htm page in the Remington folder in your Museum root folder to load that page in the bottom frame when the page is displayed in the browser.

10. Click in the bottom frame and type "Click any of the Fredric Remington paintings to view a larger version and a detailed description."

11. Click in the top frame and type "The Art of Fredric Remington" and then select the

text and apply the Logo HTML style.

12. Press the Right Arrow key, press the Enter key, and then create a table in the top frame with 4 columns, 1 row, and a cell padding of 5. Then select the table and center align it.

13. Insert the graphic file LoveCallSmall.jpg from the Tutorial.05\Cases folder on your Data Disk into the first cell in the table. Drag the right border of the cell until it is snug against the graphic (there is a cell padding of 5 pixels so the border will remain 5 pixels from the edge of the graphic). Select the graphic and align the graphic to Middle in the Property inspector.

14. Insert the graphic file AmongTheLedHorsesSmall.jpg from the Tutorial.05\Cases folder on your Data Disk into the second cell in the table. Resize the cell horizontally until it is snug against the graphic. Then select the graphic and align the graphic to Middle in the Property inspector.

15. Insert the graphic file LucklessHunterSmall.jpg from the Tutorial.05\Cases folder on your Data Disk into the third cell in the table. Resize the cell horizontally until it is snug against the graphic. Then select the graphic and align the graphic to Middle in the Property inspector.

16. Insert the graphic file RiderlessHorseSmall.jpg from the Tutorial.05\Cases folder on your Data Disk into the fourth cell in the table. Then select the graphic and align the graphic to Middle in the Property inspector. Save all the frames and the frameset.

Explore

17. Resize the frame until you can see all of the table in the top frame. The bottom frame may almost disappear from view if your Document window is small.

18. Copy each of the following pages from the Tutorial.05\Cases folder on your Data Disk and paste them in the Remington folder: AmongTheLedHorses.htm, the TheRiderlessHorse.htm, the TheLoveCall.htm page, and the TheLucklessHunter.htm page. To do this, click the plus sign (+) next to the Desktop icon in the local file list in the Site panel, click the plus sign (+) next to My Computer, then continue clicking plus signs (+) to navigate to the location of your Data Disk. Right-click each of the files you want to copy, click Copy on the context menu, right-click the Remington folder in the Site panel, and then click Paste on the context menu.

19. Open the AmongTheLedHorses.htm page in a Document window, click inside the left column of the table, and insert the AmongTheLedHorsesBig.jpg graphic from the Tutorial.05\Cases folder on your Data Disk in the cell. Make sure you add a copy of the graphic to the Graphics folder in the root folder of the Museum site, then save the page and close the page.

20. Repeat Step 18 for the TheRiderlessHorse.htm page, the TheLoveCall.htm page, and the TheLucklessHunter.htm page using the corresponding big graphic for each page from the Tutorial.05\Cases folder on your Data Disk.

21. Select the small LoveCall.jpg graphic in the first cell of the table in the top frame and link it to the TheLoveCall.htm page. Target the link to open in the bottom frame of the page by selecting mainFrame from the Target list in the Property inspector. Type 1 in the Border text box.

22. Repeat Step 20 for the AmongTheLedHorses, LucklessHunter, and RiderlessHorses graphics. Save all the frames and frameset and then close the page.

23. Open the Artists.htm page, select the Fredric Remington heading text, and link the text to the RemingtonFrameset.htm page. Then target the link to open in a new browser window by selecting _blank from the Target list in the Property inspector and save and close the page. Close the RemingtonFrameset.htm page.

24. Preview the page in a browser, click the Fredric Remington link, and then click the links in the Remington page. When finished, close all of the browser windows.

25. Upload the site to the remote server, and view the Web page over the Internet.

Case 3. NORM The featured book page has generated so much response that Mark would like to improve the page by adding more information. Add frames to the existing Featured books page and expand it to include an author bio, an excerpt from the book, and a navigation bar.

1. Open the NORM site that you modified in Tutorial 4, Case 3, and open the FeaturedBook.htm page. Click the Left Arrow key on your keyboard to move the pointer to the left of the table, then insert frames into the page by clicking the Top and Nested Left Frames button on the Frames tab of the Insert bar.

2. Click in the top frame, change the title to "Featured – top," and then modify the page properties so that the background color is #003366, and all of the margins are equal to 0. Save the frame as FeaturedTop.htm in the root folder of the NORM site.

3. Click in the left frame, change the title to "Featured – left", and then modify the page properties so that the background color is #003366, and all the margins equal 0. Save the frame as "FeaturedLeft.htm" in the root folder of the NORM site.

4. Select the frameset using the Frames panel, and then, in the Property inspector, set the Borders list arrow to Yes, set the Border Width to 1, the border color to #FFFFFF, and the Title to "Featured book – frameset."

Explore

5. Repeat Step 4 for the nested frameset.

6. Select the right frame in the Frames panel, and then, in the Property inspector, select Auto from the Scroll list to enable the frame to display its own scrollbar when the content of the frame extends beyond the borders.

Explore

7. Select the frameset in the Frames panel and save it in the root folder of the NORM site with the filename FeaturedFrameset.htm.

8. Copy the FeaturedAuthorBio.htm and the FeaturedExcerpt.htm pages from the Tutorial.05\Cases folder on your Data Disk and paste the pages in the root folder of the NORM site. To do this, click the plus sign (+) next to the Desktop icon in the local file list in the Site panel, click the plus sign (+) next to My Computer, then continue clicking plus signs (+) to navigate to the location of your Data Disk. Right-click each of the files you want to copy, click Copy on the context menu, right-click the root folder in the Site panel, and then click Paste on the context menu.

9. Insert a vertical navigation bar in the left frame.

10. Create the first element in the navigation bar using the following name and images; save a copy of each image in the Graphics folder in the site's local root folder. (Note that the Down image is the same as the Up image, so you link the Down image to the same image that you stored in the Graphics folder when you stored the Up image.)

Element name	AuthorBio
Up Image	Tutorial.05\Cases\PunchAuthorBioUp.gif
Over Image	Tutorial.05\Cases\PunchAuthorBioOver.gif
Down Image	NORM\Dreamweaver\Graphics\PunchAuthorBioUp.gif
When Clicked, Go To URL	FeaturedAuthorBio.htm
Target	mainFrame
Preload Images	checked
Insert	Vertically
Use Tables	checked

11. Create the second element in the navigation bar using the following name and images; save a copy of each image in the Graphics folder in the site's root folder.

Element name	Excerpt

Up Image	Tutorial.05\Cases\PunchExcerptUp.gif
Over Image	Tutorial.05\Cases\PunchExcerptOver.gif
Down Image	NORM\Dreamweaver\Graphics\PunchExcerptUp.gif
When Clicked, Go To URL	FeaturedExcerpt.htm
Target	mainFrame

12. Create the third element in the navigation bar using the following name and images; save a copy of each image in the Graphics folder in the site's root folder.

Element name	Press
Up Image	Tutorial.05\Cases\PunchPressUp.gif
Over Image	Tutorial.05\Cases\PunchPressOver.gif
Down Image	NORM\Dreamweaver\Graphics\PunchPressUp.gif
When Clicked, Go To URL	FeaturedBook.htm (this is the page that was originally in the frame)
Target	mainFrame

13. Add appropriate Alternate Text for each element.

14. Click the OK button.

15. Adjust the width of the left frame so that the entire image is visible by dragging the right border of the frame.

16. Click in the top frame, and then attach the NormStyleSheet.css located in the Stylesheets folder in the root folder of your NORM site.

17. Create a new CSS style by clicking the New CSS style button in the CSS Styles panel, selecting Make Custom Style (class) from the Type category, typing .FeaturedHeading in the Name text box, and selecting NormStyleSheet.css in the Define In category.

18. In the Type Category, select Arial, Helvetica, sans-serif from the Font list, type 50 in the Size text box and select pixels from the list, type #CCCC33 in the Color text box, and click OK.

19. Type PUNCH by Kelly Moore in the top frame, select the text, and apply the FeaturedHeading style from the CSS Styles panel.

20. Save all the frames and the frameset, close all open pages, preview the FeaturedFrameset page in a browser, test the links, and then close the browser window.

21. Open the NORM home page and select the Featured Book text. Then, in the Property inspector, change the link to the FeaturedFrameset.htm. The link should still be targeted to _blank so that the page opens in a new browser window; if it is not, set the Target to _blank.

22. Select the featured book graphic and change the link to FeaturedFrameset.htm as well.

23. Save and close the page and preview the page in a browser. Click the Featured Book links, then close the browser windows and close the pages.

24. Connect to your remote server, upload the site, and then preview the site over the Web.

Case 4. Sushi Ya-Ya Mary asks you to create a navigation bar for the site, then to create a new page for the Web site. The new page will provide pictures of some common types of sushi. When the pictures are clicked, information about the picture will be displayed. Use frames for this page.

1. Open the SushiYaYa site that you modified in Tutorial 4, Case 4, and open the home page.

2. Select the menu bar text and delete it; place the pointer to the left of the logo, then create a table with 2 columns and 1 row.

3. Drag the SushiYaYa logo into the left column, then adjust the width of the column so that it is snug against the outer border of the graphic.

Explore

4. Click in the right column of the table and insert a horizontal navigation bar with the following elements: company, menu, and contact. Use the images located in the Tutorial.05\Cases folder of your Data Disk with the filenames SushiCompanyUp.gif, SushiCompanyOver.gif, SushiMenuUp.gif, SushiMenuOver.gif, SushiContactUp.gif, and SushiContactOver.gif to create the elements in your navigation bar. Use the Over image as the Down image. Add appropriate alternate text, and link each element to its corresponding page. (If your site does not include pages that correspond to the navigation bar elements, rename existing pages or create new ones now.)

5. Select the navigation bar and right-align it, resize the table wider, if necessary, to accomodate the graphics, delete any spaces that were introduced into the page by the creation of the table, and then save the page.

6. Copy the entire table including the logo and navigation bar to the company.htm page, the menu.htm page, and the contact.htm page. Modify the table in each page so that the navigation bar element that represents the selected page is in the down position when the page is displayed in a browser window. Save and close each page and then close the home page.

Explore

7. Create a new page named SushiDescriptionsFrameset.htm in the root folder of the site; add top and bottom frames to the page so that the page contains three frames; then change the title of each frame and the frameset and save everything with an appropriate name.

8. Set the page properties of the added pages to match the page properties you set for the rest of the site. If you set different page properties for each page, choose one to copy.

9. Attach the top frame to the SushiYaYaStyleSheet.css, type Sushi Descriptions in the top frame, select the text, and apply the pageheadings style.

10. Create a table with 3 columns and 1 row in the middle frame. Set the borders of the table to 1 and the border color to black, then place the SushiCaliforniaRoll.gif graphic in the first column, the SushiTunaHandRoll.gif in the second column, and the SushiSalmon.gif graphic in the third column.

11. Adjust the column widths so that the columns are flush against the sides of the graphics, then center align the table. Select the frameset in the Frames panel, select the middle column in the RowCol Selection box in the Property inspector, type 90 in the Row Value text box, and select pixels for the Row Units.

12. Attach the bottom frame to the SushiYaYaStyleSheet.css, type "Click on the sushi picture to view the name and description," and then press the Enter key. Resize the bottom frame so that it is just tall enough to display one line of text.

13. Save all frames and the frameset.

14. Create three new pages in the root folder of the SushiYaYa site by copying the file containing the bottom frame in the SushiDescriptionsFrameset page. Name the new pages TunaHandRoll.htm, CaliforniaRoll.htm, and Salmon.htm.

15. Start Word or another word processor, open the document file SushiDescriptions.doc in the folder Tutorial.05\Cases on your Data Disk, and then copy the name and description of each type of sushi into its respective page. Click at the end of the description you pasted, and then press the Enter key. Attach each new page to the style sheet, if necessary, format the text using CSS styles, and save and close the page.

16. Click each sushi graphic and create a link to the appropriate description page, and then target the link to the bottom frame.

17. Save all the frames and the frameset.

18. Open the menu.htm page, and then type "Sushi Descriptions" below the horizontal line. (If you do not have a menu page, create one now.)

19. Select the text, apply the subheadings style, and then create a link to the Sushi DescriptionsFrameset.htm page and target the link to open in a new browser window.

20. Save and close the page, preview the page in a browser, testing the new link and the links on the Sushi Descriptions page, and then close the browser windows.

21. Close the Document windows, upload the site to the remote server, view the site over the Web, and then close the browser windows.

QUICK | CHECK ANSWERS

Session 5.1

1. a specific item that consists of a series of rollover graphics that change state when specific browser actions occur, such as when the user places the pointer over a graphic

2. four

3. Over state

4. False

5. False

6. the vertical or horizontal orientation of the navigation bar

Session 5.2

1. A frame divides a Web page into multiple documents.

2. a single HTML document with its own content and scroll bars

3. a separate HTML document that defines the structure and properties of a Web page with frames

4. NoFrames content is added to the frameset so that you can provide information for browsers that cannot view frames.

5. False

6. a frame that is inside another frame

7. because the frameset is a separate page that contains all of the information about how the frames will display in the Web page, and which HTML document initially will be loaded into each frame

Session 5.3

1. You can open the frameset page, select the HTML document in a frame, and create the content in the frame using the same techniques that you would use to insert content into a Web page that is not part of a frameset. You can open the HTML document in its own Document window and create the content in the regular way. You can select a Web page you have already created as the Source in the Property inspector when the frame properties are selected so that page will open in the selected frame whenever the frames page is opened.

2. True

3. Typical content is text that explains that the page users are attempting to view uses frames and cannot be seen by their browser. The text should include a brief

explanation of the purpose of the page, links to alternate pages where users can locate information, or contact information.

4. so that the linked page opens in the main frame of the Web page rather than replacing the navigation bar, and the navigation bar remains on the user's screen

5. False

6. frameset tags, frame tags, and noframes tags

In this tutorial you will:

- Insert a layer into a Web page

- Select, resize, and move a layer

- Add content to a layer

- Adjust layer stacking order

- Adjust the attributes of a layer

- Align layers

- Nest layers

- Add behaviors to a page

- Edit behaviors

USING
LAYERS FOR PAGE LAYOUT AND BEHAVIORS FOR FUNCTIONALITY

Creating Layers in the Catalyst Web Site

CASE

Catalyst

Sara has reviewed the new Catalyst Web site, and she has several suggestions. She likes the general look of the pages, but she would like the site to be more dynamic. She also wants to add more links on the home page to a few more of the label's bands. She and Brian decide to add a small information box about the Dizzied Connections band to the home page. They also decide to create a page for the Sloth Child band and to add a link from the home page to that page. Brian suggests making the Sloth Child page a dynamic page, so that the user can point to or click items on the page to cause the page to change in the user's browser. Sara thinks this is a good idea and gives Brian the go-ahead.

SESSION 6.1

In this session, you will learn about layers. You will insert a layer into a Web page. You will select, move, resize, and add content to a layer. Finally, you will adjust the layer's attributes.

Organizing Content with Layers

A **layer** is a transparent container you place in a Web page to hold different types of content. Like tables and frames, layers can be used to layout a Web page, dividing it into segments that can hold specific text, graphics, and other elements. You can insert more than one layer on a page, and you can draw nested layers. In addition, layers have benefits and potentials beyond the other layout options. Layers can be dragged and positioned anywhere on the screen with great accuracy and reliability, and they stay exactly where you place them relative to the top and left margins of the page regardless of how a user resizes the browser window. This is called **absolute positioning**. While this could be accomplished with some of the earlier layout techniques, it is far less complicated and more accurate when done with a layer. Layers can be stacked one on top of another, so that content overlaps. They can also be animated, made visible or invisible, and the order of stacked (overlapping) layers can be changed.

Layers are part of **dynamic HTML**, which is a combination of HTML enhancements and a scripting language that work together to add animation, interactive elements, and dynamic updating to Web pages. For example, you can use dynamic HTML to hide a layer and then have it become visible in response to something the user does (mouseover, mouse click, and so forth).

A drawback of using layers is that all browsers do not display layers correctly or in the same way. Browsers prior to Internet Explorer 4.0 and Netscape Navigator 4.0 do not correctly display layer properties, such as absolute positioning, so users with older browsers may not see the page you intended. Internet Explorer and Netscape Navigator implement dynamic HTML differently, so some discrepancy in the display of layers exists. Therefore, even users of current browsers may not see the page exactly as you designed.

Brian Lee has asked you to add a new section to the home page of the Catalyst Web site. The new section will contain two text links and a graphic link to the What's Hot page. This new content is designed to promote the new release that appears in the What's Hot page. He wants you to use a layer to contain the new content, because layers can be placed in a page with great accuracy and the new content needs to maintain a consistent position on the page. Figure 6-1 shows how this page will look once you add the new content. Notice that the new layer is positioned at the left of the screen. The layer is selected so that you can see the borders; however, the borders will be invisible when you preview the page in a browser.

Figure 6-1   **HOME PAGE ON CATALYST SITE WITH LAYERS**

new layer

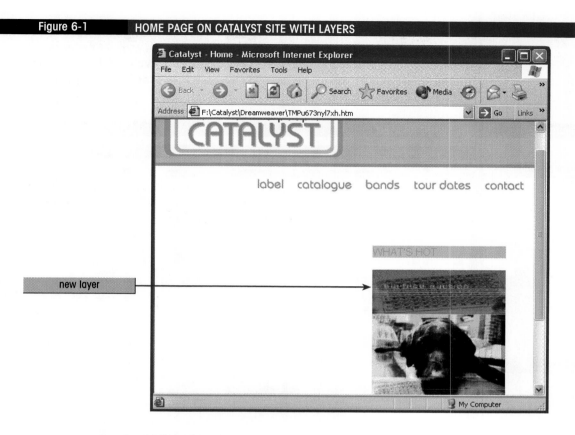

Inserting Layers

To insert a layer on a page, you draw it in Design view. For each layer that you draw on a page, a layer-code marker appears. The **layer-code marker** is a small yellow square that indicates that there is a layer on the page. Sometimes the layer-code marker appears at the top of a page, causing the content of that page to shift in the Document window. This does not affect the placement of the content in a browser window, but it can get in the way when you are trying to work in the Document window. You can drag a layer-code marker to a more convenient location. Repositioning a layer-code marker generally will not affect the position of the layer in the page, and it will have no effect on the way a page will look in a browser. It will, however, affect the order in which layer content is loaded, as well as the order in which the code is interpreted.

You will insert a layer in the home page of the NewCatalyst Web site. The layer will contain a link to the What's Hot page on the site.

To insert a layer:

1. Start **Dreamweaver**, and then open the **NewCatalyst** site you modified in the Tutorial 5 Review Assignments.

2. Open the **index.htm** page of the NewCatalyst Web site.

3. If your rulers are not visible, click **View** on the menu bar, point to **Rulers**, click **Show**, and, if the units on the ruler are not pixels, click **View** on the main menu bar again, point to **Rulers**, and then click **Pixels**.

4. Click the **Draw Layer** button ▣ on the **Common** tab on the Insert bar. The pointer changes to ┼

5. Position the pointer approximately 50 pixels below the navigation bar in the home page, and then drag to draw a layer approximately the width of the navigation bar and 100 pixels high, as shown in Figure 6-2. Don't worry if the layer you drew is not exactly the same as in the figure. You will resize and reposition it in the next section.

Figure 6-2	DRAWING A LAYER

The layer appears as a rectangle below the navigation bar when you release the mouse. The layer-code marker appears at the top of the page, above the Catalyst logo and the logo and the other objects move down. Figure 6-3 shows the Document window enlarged so you can see the layer-code marker.

Figure 6-3	DRAWN LAYER

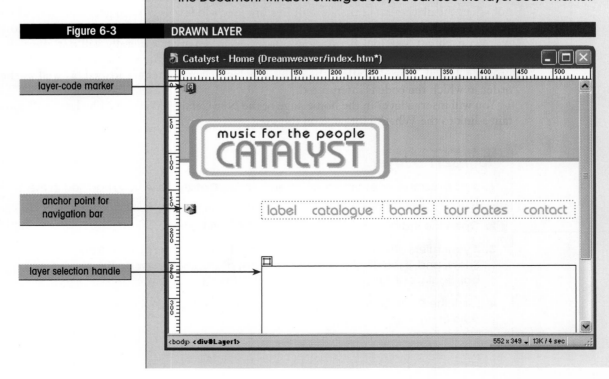

TROUBLE? If the layer you drew snaps to just below the navigation bar, drag it by the square tab at the top of the layer to reposition it.

Even though the layer-code marker seems to have pushed the logo and the navigation bar down a line, the layer-code marker does not appear in the browser window and the other elements will appear in their correct position.

6. Preview the page in a browser, note that the logo appears completely within the orange band at the top, and then close the browser window. Even though the layer-code marker does not affect the placement of the content in the browser window, it can get in the way when you are designing the page, so you will move it out of the way.

7. Drag the **layer-code marker** down and position it to the right of the anchor point for the navigation bar. The logo again appears completely within the orange band.

8. Click in a blank area of the Document window, and then save the page.

Once you have inserted a layer, you can move and resize it.

Selecting, Resizing, and Moving a Layer

As with other container objects like tables, a layer can be selected or made active. You must select a layer before you can reposition or resize it. When a layer is selected, resize handles appear all around the layer, and the layer selection handle appears in the upper-left corner. To select a layer, you click the edge of the layer, click the layer selection handle if the layer is active, or click the layer-code marker. If the page contains multiple layers on top of one another, the selected layer always temporarily becomes the top layer so that you can work with its contents. You can also select more than one layer at a time by pressing and holding the Shift key while you click the layers.

To resize a layer, you drag any of the resize handles until the layer is the desired size. If you know the exact size you want the layer to be, you can also enter the new height and width values in the Property inspector.

At times, you might want to move or reorder layers. Layers are positioned on a page using x, y, and z coordinates, much like graphs. The x and y coordinates correspond to the layer's Left and Top positions, respectively. Left and Top refer to the distance from the left and the top of the page; if the layer is nested inside another layer, Left and Top refer to the distance from the left and the top of the parent layer. When you view a layer in a browser window, the layer remains in the exact same place, even when the browser window is resized. The z coordinate—sometimes called the **z-index number**—determines the layer's stacking order; that is, the order in which the layer is stacked in the user's browser window when more than one layer is used on a page. When layers overlap, the higher numbered layers are at the front of the stack and are seen in front of layers with lower numbers. If a top layer has transparent areas, layers stacked below it are visible wherever this occurs. If a top layer does not contain areas where no content or background color is visible, it covers layers that are stacked below it. You can move a layer by dragging the layer or layer selection handle to the desired location, or by entering new Left, Top, and z-index coordinates in the Property inspector.

You want the layer that you drew to appear below the navigation bar, over to the right. You will reposition the layer.

To select, resize, and move a layer:

1. Click the **layer-code marker**. The layer is selected, and resize handles appear around the layer and the layer selection handle appears. Note the values in the W (width) and H (height) text boxes in the Property inspector. See Figure 6-4.

Figure 6-4	SELECTED LAYER

layer selection handle

selected layer-code marker

resize handles

2. Drag the right resize handle approximately 250 pixels to the left, as shown in Figure 6-5. The size of the layer is adjusted. Note that the W value in the Property inspector change also.

Figure 6-5   **RESIZING A LAYER**

3. Position the pointer over the layer selection handle so that the pointer changes to ⬌.

   You will drag the layer to a new position. Watch the value in the L (Left) text box in the Property inspector change as you drag the layer.

4. Drag the layer by the layer selection handle to the right so that the right edge is aligned with the right edge of the navigation bar above it, as shown in Figure 6-6. The layer is repositioned.

Figure 6-6   **REPOSITIONING A LAYER**

5. Click anywhere in the Document window to deselect the layer, and then save the page.

Now that you've added a layer, you need to add content to it. You will do this next.

Adding Content to a Layer

A layer can contain almost any type of content, including text, graphics, forms, multimedia content, tables, and other layers. Layers cannot contain frames, but you can place a layer within a frame. You add content to a layer using the same methods you use to insert content directly onto a Web page. You can also move existing content from the page to a layer by dragging it. Like layout cells, layers need to be active to accept content. For example, to enter text into a layer, you need to first click inside the layer to make it active.

Brian wants the user to be able to click anywhere in the layer to open the What's Hot page in a new browser window. He asks you to add content to the layer you created in the home page and then create hyperlinks to the What's Hot page.

To add content to a layer:

1. Click in the layer to make it active.

2. Type **WHAT'S HOT**, and then press the **Enter** key. The text is added to the layer. See Figure 6-7.

Figure 6-7	LAYER WITH CONTENT

3. Click the **Image** button on the **Common** tab in the Insert bar, navigate to the **Tutorial** folder within the **Tutorial.06** folder on your Data Disk, and then double-click **SurfaceSuctionCDcover200.jpg**.

4. Click the **Yes** button and then copy the **SurfaceSuctionCDcover200.jpg** graphic into the **Graphics** folder in the local root folder of your NewCatalyst site. The Surface Suction CD cover is added to the layer, and the layer expands to accommodate the content you placed in it.

5. Press the **Right Arrow** key to deselect the graphic, press the **Enter** key to move the insertion point down one line in the layer, and then type **WHAT'S HOT** below the graphic. Notice that the orange bar containing the link text that is already on the page is now partially covered by the layer. See Figure 6-8.

Figure 6-8	LINK TEXT BEHIND LAYER

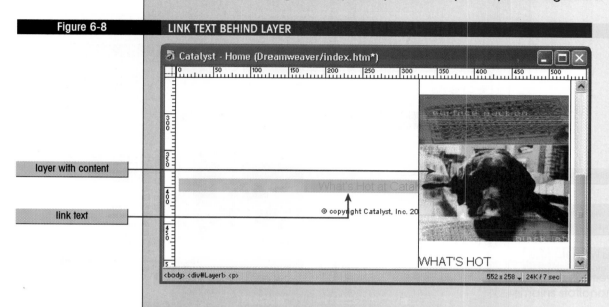

6. Drag to select the **link text** in the orange bar, press the **Delete** key to delete the link text, and then press the **Backspace** key to delete the orange bar if necessary.

7. Press the **Enter** key eight times to move the copyright line below the layer.

Next, you'll format the text you typed in the layer, and then create links from the text and the graphics in the layer to the What's Hot page.

To create links from a layer:

1. Select the **WHAT'S HOT** text at the top of the layer.

2. If the Property inspector is in HTML mode, click the **Toggle CSS/HTML Mode** button in the Property inspector to switch to CSS mode.

3. Click the **CSS Styles** list arrow, and then click **3rdTierSubHeadings**. The selected text is reformatted.

4. Click the **Toggle CSS/HTML Mode** button to switch back to HTML mode.

5. Create a link from the formatted text to the **WhatHot.htm** page, click the **Target** list arrow, and then click **_blank**. When the user clicks the link, the What's Hot page will open in a new browser window.

6. Select the **What's Hot** text at the bottom of the layer, and then repeat Steps 2-5. The text at the bottom of the layer is also linked to the What's Hot page.

5. Close the What's Hot window, and then test the bottom **What's Hot** link by clicking it.

6. Close both browser windows.

With the content placed in the layer, you now need to modify the layer attributes.

Adjusting Layer Attributes

Sometimes it is necessary to change the attributes of a layer. You can change the attributes for an existing layer in the Property inspector. In order to adjust the attributes in the Property inspector, the layer must be selected. When the layer is selected, the Property inspector includes the following attributes:

- **Layer ID.** A unique name for that layer. The layer ID name cannot contain any spaces or symbols, because it will be used in HTML code to refer to the layer. If you don't specify a name, Dreamweaver assigns the name Layer1 to the first layer you draw, Layer2 to the second, and so on.

- **L (Left)** and **T (Top).** The horizontal (L) and vertical (T) positions of a layer measured in pixels from the left margin and the top margin. If a layer is nested within another layer, the values reference the distance from the left and top edge of the parent layer instead of the page margin. As you have already seen, these numbers adjust automatically to reflect the layer's position on the page when you drag the layer.

- **W (Width)** and **H (Height).** The horizontal (W) and vertical (H) dimensions of a layer. You can drag the layer to the desired width and height, or you can type the desired values into the W and H text boxes.

- **Z-index.** A number that indicates the layer's stacking order. Layers with higher numbers are stacked in front of layers with lower numbers.

- **Vis (Visibility).** A list of the layer's visibility options indicating whether the layer is visible when the Web page is loaded. If a layer is hidden when the page is loaded, different actions by the user can make it visible. The **default** option uses the browser's default visibility. The **inherit** option sets the same visibility property as the parent layer of a nested layer. Inherit is the default visibility option for most browsers. The **visible** option displays the layer contents when the page is loaded. The **hidden** option hides the layer contents when the page is loaded.

- **Bg Image (Background Image).** The background image for a layer. You can type the path or browse to select the background image file. If no image is specified, the Web page background is seen through the layer.

- **Bg Color (Background Color).** The background color for the layer. You can type the hexadecimal color code in the Bg Color text box or select a color with the color picker. If no color is specified, the layer is transparent and the Web page background is seen through the layer.

- **Tag.** The HTML tag that is inserted when a layer is created. This tag only affects the way the layer is displayed in older browsers that don't support layers. When you use the **DIV** tag (the default), a paragraph break surrounds the layer, so that the layer appears on its own line or lines as if it were in a new paragraph, separated from the rest of the content above and below it on the page. When you use the **SPAN** tag, the layer appears inline with the rest of the page content; that is, paragraph breaks are not inserted before and after the layer so it is displayed as the next thing in the line of text.

■ **Overflow.** Specifies how a layer will appear in a browser if its content exceeds its specified size. The **visible** option expands the layer to display the overflow content. The **hidden** option maintains the layer's size and prevents the overflow text from being displayed in the browser. The **scroll** option adds scroll bars to the layer in the browser (whether they are needed or not) in Internet Explorer, and behaves as the auto option in Navigator. The **auto** option displays scroll bars for the layer in the browser only if the content overflows. Overflow options are not supported in all browsers.

■ **Clip.** The portion of a layer that will be visible in a browser. If you specify Clip values, only the portion of the layer in the Clip area appears in the browser. Clip does not work correctly in all browsers.

You can use CSS styles to apply layer attributes. If you are going to create many layers with the same attributes, you can create a CSS style with the desired attributes and then apply that style to specific layers.

Because the contents of the layer might overflow the layer boundaries, you need to adjust the Overflow attribute. You also need to name the layer and make sure the Tag attribute is set to DIV. You will do this next.

To adjust the attributes of a layer:

1. Click anywhere inside the layer to make the layer selection handle visible, and then click the **layer selection handle** to select the layer.

2. Double-click in the **LayerID** text box in the Property inspector, and then type **WhatsHot**. (Do not type an apostrophe before the s.)

3. Click the **Tag** list arrow, and then click **DIV**, if necessary.

4. Click the **Overflow** list arrow, and then click **visible**. See Figure 6-12.

Figure 6-12	OVERLAPPED LAYERS

layer name

5. Save and close the page.

So far, you have created a single layer on a page. In the next session, you will create multiple layers, including a nested layer, and you will adjust the stacking order of the layers.

Session 6.1 QUICK CHECK

1. What is a layer?
2. What is dynamic HTML?
3. What is a layer-code marker?
4. Describe three ways to select a layer.
5. What is the z-index number?
6. Describe the Visibility attribute of layers.

SESSION 6.2

In this session, you will adjust the stacking order of layers. You will align layers, create nested layers, learn about the problems Netscape has in displaying layers, and learn to apply Dreamweaver's built-in Netscape Resize Fix to Web pages that contain layers. You will also convert layers to tables and learn about the HTML involved with layers.

Modifying Layers

Designing Web pages using layers gives you more control over the placement of the content on your pages. Once you have added a layer to a page, you will most likely need to modify the layer. You can change the stacking order of layers, you can align layers to each other or to an invisible grid, and you can nest one layer inside another layer.

Adjusting Layer Stacking Order

One benefit of using layers in a Web page is that layers can be stacked or overlapped. Think of each layer as a clear acetate sheet, like those used for overhead projectors. You can stack one layer on top of another and you will be able to see the bottom layer through any transparent portions of the top layer. If the top layer does not have any transparent portions, the bottom layer will be hidden from view. Stacking enables you to create more sophisticated and interesting layout designs. Also, since layers can be animated, stacking enables you to create interesting user interactions. For example, you could stack two layers that contained text, so that the text in the back layer is hidden by the front layer, and then animate the layers so that the stacking order of the layers is switched when the user clicks a button. This would bring the back layer to the front so that you can see the text in it.

Each new layer is assigned a z-index number in the order in which it is created—the first layer you create is 1, the second is 2, and so on. When layers appear on the screen, layers with higher z-index numbers appear in front of the layers with lower z-index numbers. You can change the stacking order of layers by changing the z-index number. For example, a layer with the z-index number of 2 appears behind a layer with a z-index number of 3. If you change the first layer to a z-index number of 4, then it will appear in front of the second layer when the layers are stacked. You change the z-index numbers of layers in the Property inspector.

Another way to change the stacking order of layers is to use the Layers panel. Layers first appear in the Layers panel in the order in which they are created. You change the stacking order by dragging a layer to a new position. When you reposition a layer in the Layers panel, the z-index numbers are automatically updated to correspond to the layers' new stacking order.

Brian wants to add a Dizzied Connections section to the home page. You will add a second layer to the home page, and then you will adjust the stacking order.

To adjust the layer stacking order:

1. If you took a break after the last session, make sure **Dreamweaver** is running and that the **NewCatalyst** Web site is open.

2. Open the **home** page in a Document window, and then draw a new layer approximately 250 pixels wide and 100 pixels high, starting 150 pixels below the navigation bar, and aligning with the left edge of the navigation bar. The new layer should overlap the What's Hot layer that you drew in the last session. See Figure 6-13.

Figure 6-13 **SECOND LAYER ADDED TO PAGE**

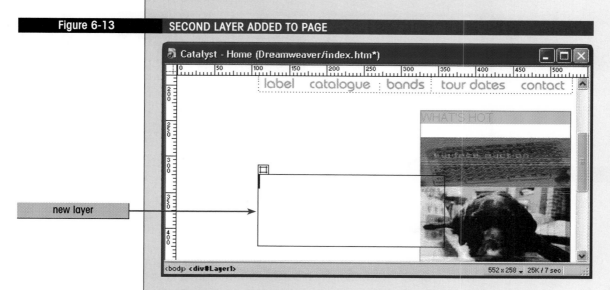

new layer

TROUBLE? If you cannot draw the new layer on top of the WhatsHot layer, the Prevent Overlaps check box in the Layers panel is probably checked. Click Windows on the main menu bar, point to Others, and then click Layers to open the Layers panel. Click the Prevent Overlaps check box in the Layers panel to uncheck it. Click the layer selection handle to select the layer you just drew, press the Delete key, and then repeat Step 2.

TROUBLE? If the layer is not positioned or sized correctly, click the layer selection handle to select it, and then drag it to the new position, or drag a resize handle to resize it.

3. Drag the new **layer-code marker** at the top of the page down next to the first layer-code marker.

4. Click in the new layer to make it active, type **Dizzied Connections**, press the **Enter** key, and then type **Information about the band will be here soon**.

5. Click the **Toggle CSS/HTML Mode** button ![icon], if necessary, to switch to CSS mode, select **Dizzied Connections**, click the **CSS Styles** list arrow, and then click **CatalystSubHeadings**.

You'll look at the stacking order in the Layers panel.

6. Click **Window** on the menu bar, point to **Others**, and then click **Layers**. The Layers panel in the Advanced Layout panel group opens. See Figure 6-14.

Figure 6-14	TEXT ENTERED INTO NEW LAYER

7. Click the edge of the new layer to select it, double-click in the **LayerID** text box in the Property inspector, type **DizziedConnections**, and then press the **Enter** key. Notice that the layer name changes in the Layers panel.

The DizziedConnections layer has a z-index of 2, which means that it is in front of the WhatsHot layer, which has a z-index of 1. This is evident in the Document window.

8. Click **DizziedConnections** in the Layers panel, and then drag it down below the **WhatsHot** layer, releasing the mouse button when the indicator line is below the WhatsHot layer, as shown in Figure 6-15.

Figure 6-15   CHANGING THE STACKING ORDER OF LAYERS IN THE LAYERS PANEL

pointer

indicator line

The What's Hot layer is now stacked in front of the DizziedConnections layer in the Document window, obscuring the text in the DizziedConnections layer.

9. Preview the **index.htm** page in a browser. Some of the text in the DizziedConnections layer is hidden.

10. Close the browser window.

11. Click in the **DizziedConnections** layer in the Document window to make it active, and then click the **layer selection handle** to select the layer. The DizziedConnections layer moves to the front. Back layers temporarily move to the front when they are selected so that you can modify them. Although the DizziedConnections layer now appears in front of the What's Hot layer in the Document window, the z-index in the Property inspector and in the Layers panel is still 1.

12. Click in a blank area outside the **DizziedConnections** layer in the Document window. The layer again appears behind the What's Hot layer.

13. Select the **DizziedConnections** layer, and then drag it approximately 50 pixels to the left so that the text is no longer obscured by the What's Hot layer. See Figure 6-16.

| Figure 6-16 | REPOSITIONED LAYER |

z-index for selected layer

14. Click in a blank area of the Document window, and then save the page.

Once you have more than one layer on a page, you can align the layers. You'll do this next.

Aligning Layers

As you know, you can drag layers around the page to reposition them, using the rulers to guide you. On some pages, you might want to align the elements so that the page looks tidy. You can align layers to the left, right, top, or bottom of another layer. To align layers, you select one layer, press and hold the Shift key, and then click any other layers you want to align. The last layer that you select will remain stationary and the other layers will align to it. The Left Align command aligns the left borders of selected layers to the horizontal position of the left border of the last layer you select. The Right Align command aligns the right borders of selected layers to the horizontal position of the right border of the last layer you select. The Top Align command aligns the top borders of the selected layers to the vertical position of the top border of the last layer you select. Finally, the Bottom Align command aligns the bottom borders of the selected layers to the vertical position of the bottom border of the last layer you select.

Brian asks you to align the layers in the home page. You will align the tops of the two layers.

To align layers using the Align commands:

1. Select the **DizziedConections** layer, press and hold the **Shift** key, click the **WhatsHot** layer, and then release the **Shift** key. The two layers are selected. Note that the Property inspector has changed to indicate that multiple layers are selected. The resize handles on the WhatsHot layer are black, which indicates that this is the layer that will remain stationary and any other selected layers will align with it.

2. Click **Modify** on the menu bar, point to **Align**, and then click **Top**. The selected layers align their tops at the horizontal position of the top of the What's Hot layer. See Figure 6-17.

Figure 6-17	LAYERS ALIGNED AT THE TOP

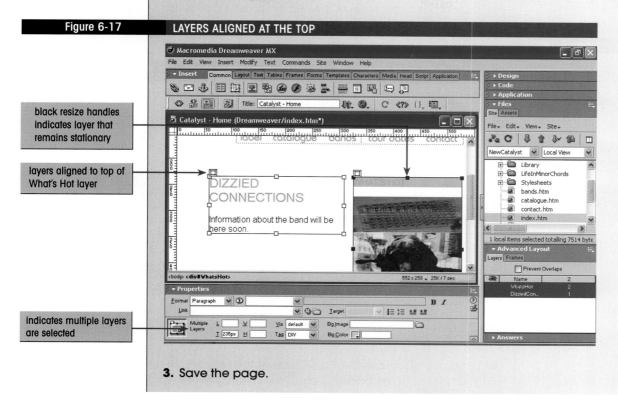

black resize handles indicates layer that remains stationary

layers aligned to top of What's Hot layer

indicates multiple layers are selected

3. Save the page.

Next, you will position the layers on the page using the grid.

Positioning Layers and Other Elements Using the Grid

In addition to the Align commands, you can also use the grid to help you adjust the position of layers and other elements on your Web page. The **grid** is a series of parallel horizontal and vertical lines that overlap to create equal squares in the background of the Document window. The grid provides a guide for positioning or resizing layers or other elements. The default is for the grid to be hidden, but you can display it. If you want to change the size of the grid squares so that you can align elements more precisely, you can adjust the grid's line spacing in the Grid Settings dialog box. You can also use the Grid Settings dialog box to change the appearance of the grid.

You will use the grid to position the elements on the home page.

To align elements using the grid:

1. With both layers still selected, click **View** on the main menu bar, point to **Grid**, and then click **Show Grid**. Grid lines appear in the background of the Document window creating 50 pixel squares.

2. Press the **Arrow** keys to nudge the layers to align the left edge of the DizziedConnections layer with a grid line and the base of the word "Dizzied" with a grid line. The two layers move together because they are both selected. You can also drag the layers with the mouse pointer. See Figure 6-18.

| Figure 6-18 | REPOSITIONING LAYERS USING GRID LINES |

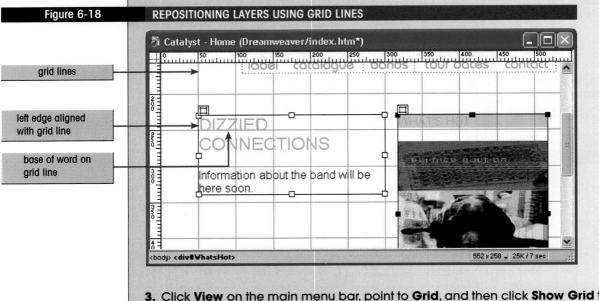

3. Click **View** on the main menu bar, point to **Grid**, and then click **Show Grid** to hide the grid lines.

4. Click in the Document window outside the selected layers to deselect them, and then save the page.

It can be convenient to have two or more layers move together. Next, you will learn how to use nesting to group layers.

Creating Nested Layers

A nested layer is contained within an outer (parent) layer similar to nested tables and nested frames. With layers, nesting does not refer to the physical position of the layers, but to the underlying code for the layers. This means that the nested layer does not have to touch its parent layer on-screen to be nested. Nesting is used to group layers. When layers are nested, if you move the parent layer, the nested layer will move with it. This is because the position of the nested layer is relative to the left and top borders of the parent layer rather than the left and top borders of the page. A nested layer also shares other attributes with its parent layer.

To nest a layer, you draw the parent layer in the Document window, and then you draw the layer you want to nest. You can draw the nested layer anywhere on the page in the Document window. To nest the layers, you use the Layers panel. Press and hold the Ctrl key, and then, in the Layers panel, drag the layer you want to nest over the parent layer. The nested layer is indented under the parent layer in the Layers panel. To un-nest a nested layer, you drag the nested layer to an empty spot in the Layers panel.

Brian asks you to create a new layer that will contain information about the Sloth Child band.

To create a nested layer:

1. Draw a new, 100 pixel square layer below the DizziedConnections layer in the home page. See Figure 6-19.

Figure 6-19	THIRD LAYER ADDED TO PAGE

new layer

2. Click in the new layer, type **Sloth Child**, and then press the **Enter** key.

3. Click the **layer selection handle** on the new layer, double-click in the **LayerID** text box in the Property inspector, type **SlothChild**, and then press the **Enter** key.

4. Press and hold the **Ctrl** key, then, in the Layers panel, drag the **SlothChild** layer over the **DizziedConnections** layer as shown in Figure 6-20, and then release the **Ctrl** key and the mouse button.

Figure 6-20	NESTING THE THIRD LAYER IN THE SECOND LAYER

The SlothChild layer is indented under the DizziedConnections layer in the Layers panel, and the nested layer's layer-code marker moves from the top of the Document window to the top of the DizziedConnections layer. Note that the SlothChild layer shifts down to the bottom of the page in the Document window.

5. Save the page. See Figure 6-21.

| Figure 6-21 | NESTED LAYER ON PAGE |

Netscape Navigator 4 can have difficulty displaying layers properly when the user resizes the browser window. Next, you'll fix this problem on the home page.

Using **the Netscape Resize Fix**

Although Netscape Navigator has been capable of displaying layers since version 4, if someone using Netscape 4 resizes the browser window when viewing a page with layers, the layers tend to move around, scale improperly, or disappear completely. Dreamweaver provides a built-in fix that by default is added automatically to pages that use layers. The **Netscape Resize Fix** is JavaScript code that forces the page to reload every time the browser window is resized, thus eliminating the problems. The Netscape Resize Fix option is available in the Layers category section of the Preferences dialog box. You should turn on the Netscape Resize Fix before adding layers to your pages.

The Netscape Resize Fix should have been added to your pages by default. Brian asks you to examine the Preferences to make sure that it is selected.

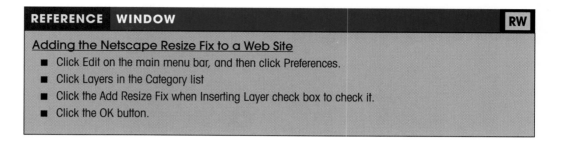

REFERENCE WINDOW   RW

Adding the Netscape Resize Fix to a Web Site
- Click Edit on the main menu bar, and then click Preferences.
- Click Layers in the Category list
- Click the Add Resize Fix when Inserting Layer check box to check it.
- Click the OK button.

To add the Netscape Resize Fix:

1. Click **Edit** on the main menu bar, and then click **Preferences**. The Preferences dialog box opens.

2. Click **Layers** in the Category list.

3. Click the **Add Resize Fix when Inserting Layer** check box to check it, if necessary. See Figure 6-22.

| Figure 6-22 | LAYERS CATEGORY IN THE PREFERENCES DIALOG BOX |

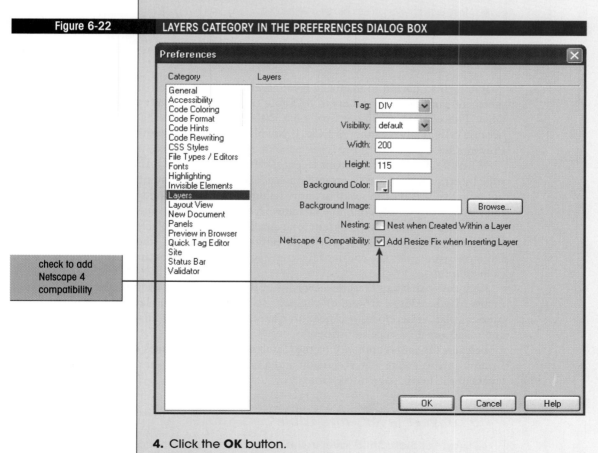

check to add Netscape 4 compatibility

4. Click the **OK** button.

Because older browsers cannot display layers properly, you might decide to create a version of your Web site that uses tables instead of layers. Next, you'll convert the layers on the home page to tables.

Converting Layers to Tables

Layers are great tools for creating Web page layout, but they do have drawbacks. Only version 4 and later of both Netscape Navigator and Internet Explorer support layers effectively, so if your target audience includes users of older browsers, they will not be able to view your pages properly. One solution is to use layers to create the site you want, and then to create another version of the site in which the pages use tables rather than layers. You can then add code to your page that automatically routes anyone using an older browser to the non-layer version of the site.

REFERENCE WINDOW   **RW**

Converting Layers to a Table
- Click Modify on the main menu bar, point to Convert, and then click Layers to Table.
- Click the Most Accurate option button.
- Click the Use Transparent GIFs check box to check it.
- Make sure no other check boxes are checked.
- Click the OK button.

Rather than having to manually create both the layer version and the table version of the same site, you can use the **Layers to Table** command to convert the layers on the page to a table. This command will not work on a Web page with layers that are nested or overlapped, because cells in tables cannot overlap. If you plan to convert layers to tables, you can enable the Prevent Overlap feature in the Layer panel to automatically prevent layers from overlapping.

When a table is created from layers, Dreamweaver maintains the original layout of the page by creating empty cells around the layers to hold that content in place, much like a table in Layout view. This can result in entire columns and rows being empty. In order to maintain the width of any empty columns, Dreamweaver creates a file named transparent.gif, which is (as the name implies) a transparent, one-pixel, GIF file, and places this file in a blank row at the bottom of the table. The row is only one pixel high, the height of the GIF file. Dreamweaver scales the width of the transparent GIF as necessary to maintain the width of each column.

Because of the way Dreamweaver interprets the position of the layers, the various elements may be moved around on the page so that the resulting layout does not reflect your original plan. Therefore, you need to examine the resulting table and overall page layout and make any necessary adjustments.

Because the target audience of the Catalyst Web site includes users with older browsers, Brian wants to create a layer version and a non-layer version of the site. You'll convert the layers in the home page into a table.

To convert layers into tables:

1. Drag the **SlothChild** layer in the Layers panel up to the top of the list to un-nest the layer. The layer-code marker moves from the top of the DizziedConnections layer back up to the top of the page.

2. Drag the **layer-code marker** from the top of the page down to position it next to the other two layer-code markers.

3. Save the page.

4. Click **Modify** on the main menu bar, point to **Convert**, and then click **Layers to Table**. The Convert Layers to Table dialog box opens.

5. Make sure the **Most Accurate** option button is selected, click the **Use Transparent GIFs** checkbox to check it, if necessary, make sure the rest of the check boxes in the dialog box are not checked, and then click the **OK** button.

6. Scroll down the window and compare your screen to Figure 6-23.

Figure 6-23   TABLE CREATED FROM LAYERS

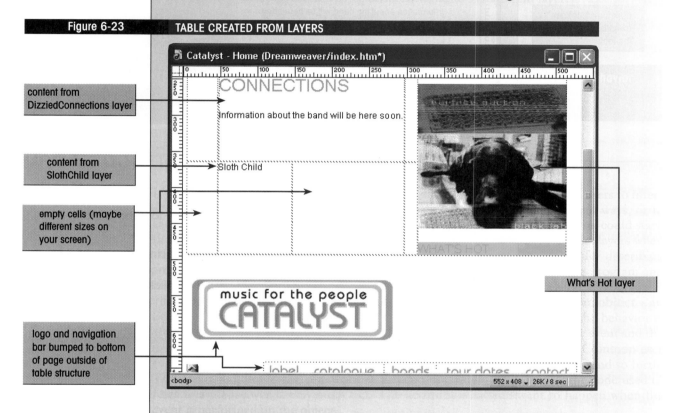

content from DizziedConnections layer

content from SlothChild layer

empty cells (maybe different sizes on your screen)

What's Hot layer

logo and navigation bar bumped to bottom of page outside of table structure

Because you want to keep the home page in its original state with the layers intact, you need to save the page with the table with a new name.

7. Click **File** on the main menu bar, click **Save As**, type **homepagewithtables.htm** in the File name text box, navigate to the root folder of your site, if necessary, and then click the **Save** button. The new page is added to the file list in the Site panel. Notice that the transparent.gif file also appears in the list .

8. Preview the converted Web page in a browser. The logo and the navigation bar need to be moved back to the top of the page.

9. Close the browser window, drag to select all five cells in the top row in the table, then press the **Delete** key.

Using a preset behavior tool is the easiest way to insert behaviors into your pages. Preset behavior tools are buttons that perform common tasks for you and insert the behaviors into your page without your knowledge. They are located throughout Dreamweaver. You have already used many of the preset behavior tools, including the Rollover button and the Navigation Bar button. When you use the Rollover button, Dreamweaver inserts a swap image behavior and a preload behavior as you insert the rollover images. The swap images behavior consists of the action, the images being swapped, triggered by a user event—the user rolling the mouse over the image. The image is the object. The preload behavior consists of the action, the image being downloaded, triggered by a user event—the user loading the Web page into a browser window. The Web page is the object. When you select an object in the Document window and open the Behaviors panel, the behaviors that Dreamweaver inserted for you will appear in the list.

REFERENCE WINDOW   **RW**

Adding the Show-Hide Layers Prewritten Behavior Using the Behaviors Panel

■ Select the layer image or hotspot to which you want to add the behavior.
■ Open the Behaviors panel.
■ Click the Plus (+) button in the Behaviors panel, point to Show Events For, and then click the desired browser choices.
■ Click the Plus (+) button in the Behaviors panel, then click Show-Hide Layers.
■ Click each layer that you want to react to the user event, and then click the Show button to show the layer or click the Hide button to hide the layer.
■ Click the OK button.

You can use the Behaviors panel to create more customized behaviors. When you use the Behaviors panel to create behaviors, you select an object and then you select from lists of prewritten actions and event handlers, which Dreamweaver combines to create the behavior. Dreamweaver will only allow you to choose actions that work with the object you have selected, and it will only allow you to choose event handlers that go with the action you choose. For example, if you select text as your object, you cannot select swap image as your action. Further, you can choose to limit your behavior list choices by browser version or browser brand and version. In general, the more complex behaviors require version 4.0 and later browsers, while simpler behaviors work with 3.0 browsers. If your target audience includes users of browsers older than 3.0, you may need to create an alternate site that does not use behaviors. Some discrepancy exists in the way that different browsers interpret JavaScript, so you need to test pages that use behaviors extensively in all the browsers that you intend to support. In addition, a few users turn off JavaScript in their browsers so that pop-up ads on Web sites will not be able to run. This means that some users with newer browsers will still not be able to access Web sites that use behaviors. Therefore, even if your target audience does not include users of older browsers, you should consider providing links to alternate pages or an alternate site for anyone whose browser has difficulty running JavaScript.

You can add the advanced functionality of behaviors to a Web page yourself by writing your own code (usually JavaScript) in the insert script panel or in the Document window in Code view. When you write the code yourself, the code you create is not actually considered a behavior because it is not added to the reusable prewritten choice lists that Dreamweaver provides in the Behaviors panel. When you write the code yourself, it is considered a custom script. It will appear in the Behaviors panel as a custom script when you select the object to which it is attached.

Adding Behaviors Using the Behaviors Panel

The Behaviors panel is like a sophisticated menu for ordering behaviors. First, you choose an object in the page, then you select a target browser brand and version. The Behaviors panel will display only actions that are compatible with the object and browser you chose. You then choose an action from the list in the Behaviors panel. You can select only the actions that are available for use with the object you selected; actions that are not available for use with the selected object are dimmed. If you don't choose any object, the actions listed are available for the page itself. Once you have selected an action, Dreamweaver provides a list of possible events—with the most common event associated with that action selected as the default. You choose an event from that list. Based on your selections, Dreamweaver creates the behavior and inserts the code.

Sara and Brian like the way the Life in Minor Chords page looks on the site, and they decide that they want you to create a new page for the Sloth Child band. They want you to make this an interactive page, and they want you to use layers and behaviors to show or hide the various layers depending on what the user points to.

You will add a new page for the Sloth Child band, and you will add layers containing graphics to the page. Then you will attach behaviors to the layers to make them hidden or visible, depending on what the user does.

To create a new page:

1. If you took a break after the previous session, make sure that **Dreamweaver** is running and the **NewCatalyst** site is open.

2. Create a new folder named **SlothChild** within the root folder of the NewCatalyst Web site, and then create a new page named **SlothChild.htm** in the Sloth Child folder.

3. Open the **SlothChild.htm** page, change the title to **Catalyst – Sloth Child**, and then modify the page properties as follows:

Property	Attribute
Background color	#000000
Text	
All links	#FFFFFF
Left and Top Margins	0
Margin Width and Height	0

4. Save the page.

You'll add four layers to the new SlothChild.htm page. For each layer, you'll set the properties, insert an image, and then adjust the layer position on the page.

To add layers to a page:

1. Draw a layer in the middle of the Document window, approximately 300 pixels wide and 150 pixels high.

2. Select the layer, and then set the following properties in the Property inspector: type **background** in the LayerID text box, select **DIV** from the Tag list, and select **visible** from the Vis list.

3. Click in the layer, click the **Image** button 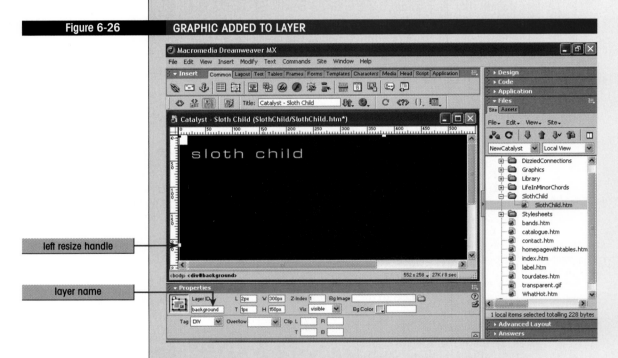 on the **Common** tab of the Insert bar, browse to **Tutorial.06\Tutorial\SlothChildWebPageImage.jpg** on your Data Disk, click the **OK** button, and then save a copy of the image in the **Graphics** folder in the root folder of your Web site. The layer should expand to accommodate the figure, which includes a photo and the words "try an apple" in the lower right and "sloth child" in the upper right.

4. Scroll all the way to the top and left of the Document window, click the **layer selection handle** to select the layer instead of the graphic, then drag the **layer selection handle** to the upper left corner of the page. See Figure 6-26.

TROUBLE? If you have difficulty positioning the layer at the upper left corner of the page, press the Arrow keys to nudge it into position.

Figure 6-26	GRAPHIC ADDED TO LAYER

left resize handle

layer name

Next, you'll draw hotspots on the background graphic.

5. Click in the **layer** to select the graphic. Make sure that the graphic is selected and not the layer by checking to see that "Image" appears in the upper left corner of the Property inspector. See Figure 6-27.

Figure 6-27   SELECTED GRAPHIC IN LAYER

indicates that the graphic is selected

6. Click the **Oval Hotspot Tool** button in the Property inspector, and draw a **hotspot** over the far-right apple, about one-third of the way down in the photo.

7. Draw a second oval **hotspot** over the apple nearest to the center of the apple tree, and then draw a third oval **hotspot** over the apple at the upper-middle of the tree. See Figure 6-28.

Figure 6-28   HOTSPOTS ADDED TO PHOTO

hotspots

TROUBLE? If your hotspots are in the wrong position, click the Pointer Hotspot Tool in the Property inspector, and then drag the hotspots to their new positions.

8. Click the **Rectangular Hotspot Tool** button in the Property inspector, and draw a fourth **hotspot** over the Sloth Child band name in the upper-left corner of the layer.

Now you will modify the attributes of the layers so that they are hidden. You will later attach behaviors to make the layers visible when there is a user event.

To modify the attributes of layers:

1. Click the **Expand arrow** next to the Advanced Layout panel group, to expand the group, if necessary, and then click the **Layers** tab.

2. Draw a second layer on top of the first one, about 25 pixels below the band name, approximately 100 pixels high and the same width as the band name.

3. Select the **layer**, change the name to **SCLayer2**, select **DIV** from the Tag list in the Property inspector, and then select **hidden** from the Vis list.

4. Click in the layer, and then insert the **Tutorial.06\Tutorial\SlothChildLayer2.jpg** graphic on your Data Disk in the layer, saving a copy of the graphic to the **Graphics** folder in the root folder. The layer expands to accommodate the graphic.

   TROUBLE? If you can't see the new layer in the Document window, you clicked outside the layer and the Hidden attribute became effective. Click SCLayer2 in the Layers panel to select the layer and make its borders appear in the Document window.

5. Create a link from the graphic you just added to the **bands.htm** page. See Figure 6-29.

Figure 6-29	LINK ADDED TO LAYER

layer selection handle

link added to image

layer name

6. Click in the outer layer but outside SCLayer2. SCLayer2 disappears because its Visibility is set to Hidden.

7. Draw a third **layer** to the right of the band name and inside the first layer approximately 250 pixels wide and 100 pixels high, select the **layer**, change the name to **SCLayer3**, select **DIV** from the Tag list, select **hidden** from the Vis list, insert the **Tutorial.06\Tutorial\SlothChildLayer3.jpg** graphic on your Data Disk in the layer, and then create a link from this graphic to the **index.htm** page.

8. Reposition the layer, if necessary, so that no part of the image overlaps the band name or the photo of the apples. See Figure 6-30.

Figure 6-30   **THIRD LAYER ADDED TO PAGE**

9. Click in the outer layer but outside the hidden layers, draw a fourth **layer** to the left of the apple tree image approximately 250 pixels wide and 100 pixels high, change the name to **SCLayer4**, select **DIV** from the Tag list, select **hidden** from the Vis list, insert the **Tutorial.06\Tutorial\SlothChildLayer4.jpg** graphic on your Data Disk in the layer, and then create a link from the graphic to the **catalogue.htm** page.

10. Reposition the layer, if necessary, so that the image does not overlap the apple tree image, and so that the bottom of the image (not necessarily the bottom of the layer) aligns with the bottom of the image of the apples. See Figure 6-31.

Figure 6-31   VISUALLY ALIGNED IMAGES

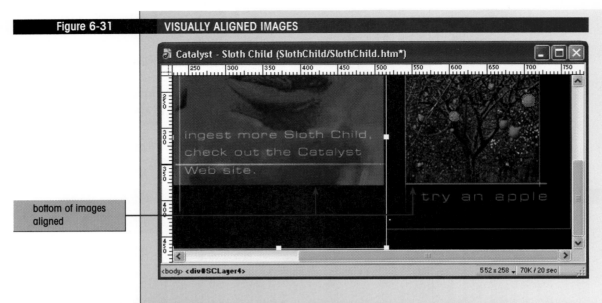

bottom of images aligned

11. Click in a blank area of the Document window. Only the first layer that you drew is visible.

12. Save the page.

Next, you'll add behaviors to the hotspots so that when the user points to the hotspots, the hidden layers will become visible on the page in the browser window.

To add a behavior:

1. Click the **Expand** arrow ▷ next to the **Design** panel group to expand the group, and then click the **Behaviors** tab.

2. In the Document window, click the **hotspot** over the apple on the right to select it. This is the object to which the behavior will be applied.

3. Click the **Plus (+)** button ➕ in the Behaviors panel, point to **Show Events For**, and then click **3.0 and Later Browsers**.

4. Click ➕ in the Behaviors panel, and then click **Show-Hide Layers**. This is the action. The Show Hide Layers dialog box opens. You want the first hidden layer, SCLayer2, to become visible when the user event occurs, and you do not want either of the other two layers to be visible when this happens.

5. Click **layer "SCLayer2"** in the Named Layers list, and then click the **Show** button.

   If either of the other two layers whose Visibility attribute is set to Hidden are visible when the user event occurs, you want them to be hidden .

6. Click **layer "SCLayer3"** in the Named Layers list, click the **Hide** button, click **layer "SCLayer4"** in the Named Layers list, and then click the **Hide** button. You do not need to make a selection for the background layer because it never changes; that is, it is always visible.

7. Click the **OK** button. The dialog box closes and the first behavior is added to the list in the Behaviors panel. Note that the event handler "onMouseOver" is associated with this behavior. See Figure 6-32.

| Figure 6-32 | BEHAVIOR ADDED TO SELECTED HOTSPOT |

You'll repeat the same process to add this behavior to the other apple hotspots.

To add behaviors to the other hotspots:

1. Select the **hotspot** over the apple that is nearest to the center of the apple tree image, click ➕ in the Behaviors panel, and then click **Show-Hide Layers**. The Show Hide Layers dialog box opens.

2. Show **SCLayer3**, hide **SCLayer2** and **SCLayer4**, and then click the **OK** button.

3. Select the third **hotspot** (over the apple near the top of the photo), assign the **Show Hide Layers** behaviors to it, and then hide **SCLayer2** and **SCLayer3** and show **SCLayer4**.

   You decide to have the band and album name appear in the status bar when the mouse pointer is over any part of the background image.

4. Click anywhere in the Document window to select the image in the background layer, click ➕ in the Behaviors panel, point to **Set Text**, and then click **Set Text of Status Bar**. The Set Text of Status Bar dialog box opens.

5. Type **sloth child: try an apple**, and then click the **OK** button.

6. Save the page.

You can also add e-mail links to hotspots. When you click an e-mail link, your e-mail program starts, a blank message window opens, and the e-mail address specified in the e-mail link appears in the To field in the message window.

You need to create an e-mail link from the band name to a general information e-mail address at Catalyst.

To add the e-mail link to a hotspot:

1. Click the **rectangular hotspot** over the band name. The Property inspector changes to show that a hotspot is selected.

2. Double-click in the **Link** text box in the Property inspector, type **mailto:info@ catalystnoise.com**, and then press the **Enter** key.

3. Save the page.

Adding a Custom Script to your Page

When you used the Rollover and the Navigation Bar buttons on the Common tab of the Insert bar, you used the preset behavior tools to insert behaviors; and in the Sloth Child page, you added behaviors to the hotspots using the Behaviors panel. Now you will add a custom script to the Sloth Child page. The script will move the browser window to the front when anything on the screen covers it. You will write the script in the Script dialog box, and then you will add the script to the page.

To create a custom script:

1. Click the **Script tab** on the Insert bar, and then click the **Script button** . The Script dialog box opens. You will write the custom script.

2. Click in the **Content box** in the Script dialog box, type **function toFront(){** and then press the **Enter** key; type **window.focus();** and then press the **Enter** key; type **}** and then click the **OK** button. This script creates the custom action of forcing the Sloth Child browser window to always move to the front. Now you will add the code that references the script to the opening body tag for the page.

3. Click the **Common tab** on the Insert bar, and then click the **Show Code View** button . The Document window switches to Code view and the code inserting the script you just wrote is highlighted.

4. Scroll up a few lines and click inside the closing bracket of the opening body tag.

5. Press the **Spacebar**, and then type **onBlur="toFront()"**. The words "toFront" reference the script you just wrote. The words "onBlur" are the event handler associated with the event of the Sloth Child window being moved behind another window.

6. Click the **Show Design View** button , and then click the **body tag** in the status bar at the bottom of the Document window to select the body tag. The Behaviors panel changes to display your custom script. The object is the page, the event handler is onBlur and the action is toFront(). Notice that your action is listed as a Custom Script.

TROUBLE? If the custom script is not listed in the Behaviors panel, then click in the top left corner of the Document window, press the Up Arrow key, press the Left Arrow key, and then click the body tag in the status bar again.

7. Save the page.

Now you need to test the behaviors you added.

To test behaviors:

1. Preview the Sloth Child page in a browser, and then maximize the browser window.

2. Position the pointer anywhere in the window except on the band name or on one of the apple hotspots. The pointer changes to 🖑 and the status bar shows the band and album name. See Figure 6-33.

Figure 6-33	PREVIEWING GRAPHIC BEHAVIOR IN BROWSER WINDOW

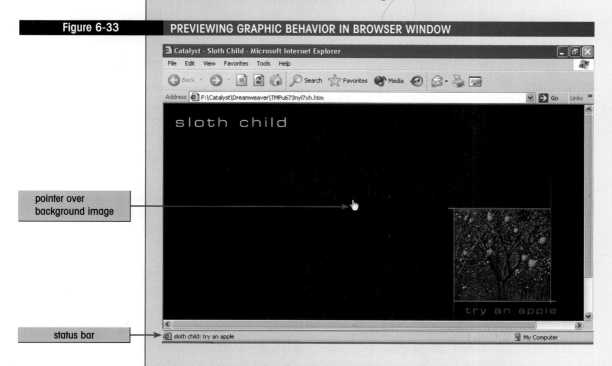

pointer over background image

status bar

3. Position the pointer over the **apple hotspot** on the right of the photo. The image in SCLayer2 appears, and the status bar changes to reflect the file path. See Figure 6-34.

Figure 6-34   **PREVIEWING HIDDEN LAYER IN BROWSER WINDOW**

SCLayer2 image

pointer

4. Point to the **apple hotspot** closest to the middle of the photo. The image in SCLayer2 hides and the image in Layer3 appears.

5. Point to the **apple hotspot** near the top of the photo. The image in Layer4 appears and the image in Layer3 hides.

6. Click the **band name**. Your e-mail program starts and a new message window opens with "info@catalystnoise.com" in the To field. The message window immediately disappears as the Sloth Child window moves to the front. This is the result of the custom script that you inserted.

   TROUBLE? If a new e-mail message window does not open, then your e-mail program may not be configured. Close any dialog boxes and windows that open and continue with Step 8.

7. Click the **New Message** button on the taskbar to move the message window to the front, and then close the message window.

8. Exit your e-mail program, if necessary, and close the browser window.

You can also edit and delete behaviors. You decide to delete the behavior that displays a message in the status bar because you don't want the pointer to look like it is positioned over a link when it isn't. You also want to see if a different event handler would be a better choice for the apple hotspots.

Editing and Deleting Behaviors

Once a behavior has been created, you can change the event handler associated with the behavior or you can delete the behavior. If you want to change the action, you need to delete the old behavior, select the object, and then attach the new behavior. You can do this in the Behaviors panel.

You will edit one of the behaviors associated with an apple hotspot. You also will delete the behavior that displays text in the status bar.

To edit behaviors:

1. Select the apple **hotspot** on the right of the photo. The behavior is listed in the Behaviors panel.

2. Click the **behavior** in the Behaviors panel and then click the **Events** list arrow. The events that are supported by 3.0 and later browsers and the Show-Hide Layers action are listed. See Figure 6-35.

Figure 6-35	MODIFYING THE EVENT ASSOCIATED WITH THE BEHAVIOR

3. Click **onClick**. The behavior's event is changed so that the action will occur when the user clicks this hotspot.

4. Click anywhere in the Document window to select the image in the background layer. The action "Set Text of Status Bar" appears in the Behaviors panel.

5. Click the behavior in the Behaviors panel, and then click the **Minus (-)** button [−] in the Behaviors panel to delete the selected behavior.

6. Save the page, preview the page in a browser, maximize the browser window, and position the pointer anywhere in the window except over a hotspot. The status bar no longer displays "sloth child: try an apple."

7. Click the **apple hotspot** on the right of the photo. The image in Layer2 appears.

   You decide it is better if the user simply points at the apple hotspots.

8. Close the browser window, click the **apple hotspot** on the right of the photo, click the behavior in the Behaviors panel to select it, click the **Events** list arrow, and then click **onMouseOver**. The event is changed back to a mouseover.

9. Save and close the page.

The Sloth Child page is complete. You will add a link to this page in the Review exercises at the end of this tutorial.

Updating the Web Site on the Remote Server

As a final review of the changes you made to the NewCatalyst Web site, you'll update the files on the remote server and review the pages over the Internet. You will upload the pages and files of the site that have changed or been added. This includes the Graphics folder, the SlothChild folder, the homepagewithtables.htm page, the index.htm page, and the transparent.gif file. Then you'll preview the site on the Web.

To upload a site to the remote server:

1. Click the **Connects to remote host** button on the Site panel toolbar.

2. Click the **View** list arrow on the Site panel toolbar, and then click **Local View**.

3. Select the **Graphics** folder, the **SlothChild** folder, the **homepagewithtables.htm** page, the **index.htm** page, and the **transparent.gif** file in the Local View list, and then click the **Put File(s)** button on the Site panel toolbar.

   TROUBLE? If you can't select only the files you want, click the Minus (-) button next to the SlothChild folder to collapse the file list in the folder, press and hold the Ctrl key, and then click the folders and files you want to upload.

4. Click the **Yes** button when asked if you want to include dependent files because you have not selected the new dependent file for the site yet.

5. Click the **Disconnects from remote host** button on the Site panel toolbar, click the **View** list arrow on the Site panel toolbar, and then click **Local View**.

Next, you'll preview the updated site in a browser. The site will include all of the new features and pages you added to your local version.

To preview the updated site in a browser:

1. Open your browser, type the URL of your remote site in the Address text box on the browser toolbar, and then press the **Enter** key.

2. Open the **home** page, if necessary, and then explore the remote site.

3. Click the top **What's Hot** link to open the What's Hot page in a new browser window, and then close the new browser window that opened.

4. Repeat Step 3 for the **graphic** in the What's Hot layer and for the bottom **What's Hot** link.

5. Click in the **Address** text box in the browser window, press the **Right Arrow** key to position the insertion point at the end of the current URL, type **/SlothChild/ SlothChild.htm**, and then press the **Enter** key. The Sloth Child page opens in the same browser window.

6. Point to each of the three **apple hotspots** to test the behaviors.

7. Click the **band name** to open a new e-mail message window, close the message window, and then exit the e-mail program.

> TROUBLE? If a new e-mail message window does not open, then your e-mail program may not be configured. Close any dialog boxes and windows that open and continue with Step 8.
>
> **8.** Close the browser window, and then close the NewCatalyst site.

Sara and Brian are pleased with the new Catalyst Web site. It has a nice look, and useful functionality.

Session 6.3 QUICK CHECK

1. What is a behavior?
2. What is an event?
3. What is an action?
4. Are all behaviors selected and assigned in the Behaviors panel?
5. True or False? You cannot change the action associated with a behavior.

REVIEW ASSIGNMENTS

Brian asks that you complete the NewCatalyst home page. You'll move, resize, and align the layers that you have already created and fill them with content. Then you will create new layers and fill them with content. Finally, you will create links from the content to the other pages of the site.

1. Open your NewCatalyst Web site in Dreamweaver, open the home page in a Document window, and then select the DizziedConnections layer.

2. Move the Dizzied Connections layer so that the left border is approximately 15 pixels from the left page border. (Remember to turn on your page rulers if you need help measuring distance.)

3. Hold down the Shift key and select the Dizzied Connections layer. Both layers should be selected.

4. Click Modify on the main menu bar, point to Align, and then click Top to align the top border of the two layers.

5. Drag the right border of the DizziedConnections layer to the right, leaving approximately 20 pixels between it and the left border of the What's Hot layer.

6. Click after "Dizzied Connections," press the Spacebar, and then type "Heads West."

7. Select the text "Information about the band will be here soon." and then type the following:

   The boys have packed up their toys and are heading to the West Coast to play for a while. Check out the tour dates to see if they'll be stopping by your hometown.

8. Select "Dizzied Connections Heads West," create a link from the selected text to the DCframeset page in the DizziedConnections folder, click the Target list arrow in the Property inspector, and then click _blank.

9. Select the words "tour dates" and create a link to the tourdates.htm page.

Explore   10. If the Dizzied Connections layer is longer than the text inside of it, select the layer, and then drag the bottom resize handle up to resize the layer to a smaller size. If the layer will not resize, click in the blank line at the bottom of the layer, and then press the Backspace key as many times as necessary to move the insertion point so that it is positioned immediately after the end of the last sentence, and then resize the layer.

Explore   11. Use the Align command to align the Sloth Child and Dizzied Connections layers to the left border of the Dizzied Connections layer. (*Hint*: Select the Sloth Child layer first. If the Dizzied Connections layer moves, you selected it first. Click Edit on the main menu bar, click Undo Align, and then try again.)

Explore   12. Select only the Sloth Child layer, and then press the Arrow keys to nudge the layer until the top border of the layer is about 20 pixels from the bottom border of the Dizzied Connections layer.

13. Select the words "Sloth Child," apply the CatalystSubHeadings style, link the selected text to the SlothChild.htm file in the SlothChild folder, and then select _blank from the Target list in the Property inspector so that the link opens in a new window.

14. Select the layer and drag the right resize handle until the words "Sloth Child" fit on one line.

15. Click below the Sloth Child heading, If the CSS Styles list box in the Property inspector still lists CatalystSubHeadings, click the CSS Styles list arrow, and then click No CSS Style.

16. Type the following:

    The new release is shaking things up. Check out the catalogue to see what the buzz is all about.

17. Select the word "catalogue" and link it to the catalogue.htm page.

18. Draw another layer approximately 20 pixels to the right of the Sloth Child layer. Make the layer the same height as the Sloth Child layer, and extend the layer to the right until its right border aligns with the right border of the Dizzied Connections layer above it.

19. Select the layer-code marker and move it to the right of the other layer-code markers.

20. Click in the new layer, type "Life in Minor Chords" in the new layer, press the Enter key, select the text you typed, and then apply the CatalystSubHeadings style.

21. Move the insertion point below the Life in Minor Chords heading, and then type the following:

    If you are an LIMC fan, keep checking their Web site over the next few weeks! The new look is in place and we are adding more every day.

22. Drag the bottom border of the layer up so it just fits to the text.

23. Select the heading text, link it to the LIMCframeset.htm page in the LifeInMinorChords folder, and then target the link to open in a new browser window by clicking _blank in the Target list.

24. Align the top border of the Life in Minor Chords layer to the top border of the Sloth Child layer.

25. Select the Dizzied Connections, Sloth Child, Life in Minor Chords, and What's Hot layers, and then press the Up Arrow key to nudge them up to approximately 20 pixels below the navigation bar.

26. Save and close the page, preview it in a browser window, test the new links, and then close the browser window.

27. Upload the changed pages to your remote server, and then test the pages on the remote server in a browser.

28. Close the browser, and then close the NewCatalyst site.

CASE PROBLEMS

Case 1. Hroch University Anthropology Department Professor Hart is going to be teaching several new courses this semester. He would like you to create a new page for the site with descriptions of these classes.

To do this, you will use layers in the new page. You will also create a layer beside the logo in the home page with a link to the new page.

1. Open the Hart site that you modified in Tutorial 5, Case 1 and, in the Site panel, copy the LinguisticDifferences.htm page and paste a copy of the page in the root folder of the site.

2. Rename the copied page "NewCourses.htm" then open the new page in a Document window.

3. Change the page title to "Hroch University Anthropology Dept. - Prof. Hart - New Courses."

4. Draw a layer approximately 500 pixels wide and 25 pixels high at the bottom of the page; name the layer "Footer."

5. Copy the footer information from the table, paste it into the Footer layer, drag the resize handles so that the layer is the size of the footer, and then position the layer at the bottom of the page approximately 200 pixels below the table.

6. Select the entire Linguistic Differences table and delete it from the page. The table and page content below the Linguistic Differences and navigation bar are removed from the page.

7. Draw a layer approximately 150 pixels square at the left of the window, approximately 20 pixels below the navigation bar and 10 pixels from the edge of the window. Name the layer "CourseList."

8. Insert the HartCourseList.gif graphic from the Tutorial.06\Tutorial\Cases folder on your Data Disk, and then drag the borders of the layer to fit snugly against the borders of the graphic.

9. Draw a third layer approximately 400 pixels wide and the same heights as the Courselist layer about 20 pixels to the right of the CourseList layer, name the layer "OpeningText," and then type the following text into the layer:

> Professor Hart has developed two exciting courses based on the findings of his most recent trip to study the people of Northern Vietnam. To view a course description, select the course that interests you. (These courses are available only to graduate students or by permission of the instructor.)

10. Align the top of the OpeningText layer with the top of the CourseList layer.

Explore ▶ 11. Hide the OpeningText layer from view by clicking below the eye icon beside the layer name in the Layers panel.

Explore ▶ 12. Draw a fourth layer to the right of the CourseList layer, approximately the same size and in the same position as the OpeningText layer. (It is fine to overlap the hidden OpeningText layer.) Name the layer "LinguisticDifferences," and then type the following text in it:

> Anthropological study of cultural patterning in linguistic variations among the people of Northern Vietnam; survey of historical and theoretical development of linguistic evolution in the area; case studies based on Dr. Hart's most recent field work; emphasis on ethnography of speaking and verbal art. Graduate standing or consent of instructor required.

13. Align the LinguisticDifferences layer with the top and left border of the OpeningText layer. (*Hint*: Because the OpeningText layer is invisible, select the layers in the Layers panel. The hidden layer will become visible while it is selected and will return to its hidden state when it is not selected.)

14. Hide the LinguisticDifferences layer.

15. Repeat Steps 12 through 14, but this time name the layer "Rituals," and then type the following text in it:

> How the minority cultures of Northern Vietnam conceptualize the biophysical environment through religious beliefs and ritualistic practices; how images of the environment influence activities and how they are incorporated into tribal life.

16. Drag each of the **layer-code markers** down to just above the navigation bar.

17. Click the **closed eye icon** next to the OpeningText layer in the Layers panel to make the OpeningText layer visible.

18. Select the CourseList graphic, click the Rectangular Hotspot Tool in the Property inspector, draw a hotspot over the top course in the list, and then draw another hotspot over the second course in the list.

19. Click the Expand arrow next to the Design panel group, and then click the Behaviors panel to open it. (You may see a behavior already in the list depending on where the insertion point is in the page.)

20. Select the first hotspot, click the Plus (+) button, and then click Show-Hide Layers.

21. In the Show-Hide Layers dialog box, select each layer in the list, and then click the Show or Hide buttons according to the following list:

Layer Name	Visibility
Layer "Footer"	Show
Layer "CourseList"	Show
Layer "LinguisticDifferences"	Show
Layer "OpeningText"	Hide
Layer "Rituals"	Hide

22. Select the second hotspot, click the Plus (+) button, and then click Show-Hide Layers.

23. In the Show-Hide Layers dialog box, select each layer in the list, and then click the Show or Hide buttons according to the following list:

Layer Name	Visibility
Layer "Footer"	Show
Layer "CourseList"	Show
Layer "LinguisticDifferences"	Hide
Layer "OpeningText"	Hide
Layer "Rituals"	Show

24. Save and close the page, preview the page in a browser, and then test the hotspots by positioning the mouse pointer over each of them in the browser window. Close the browser window.

25. Open the home page, and then draw a layer 100 pixels wide and 75 pixels long in the colored banner at the top of the page positioned approximately above the Contact Information link.

26. Insert the HrochNewCourse.gif graphic file from the Tutorial.06\Cases folder on your Data Disk into the layer (placing a copy of the graphic in the Graphics folder), and then resize the layer so that it fits snugly around the graphic. Drag the layer-code marker down to just above the navigation bar, and then nudge the layer so the graphic is completely within the colored bar.

27. Select the graphic, create a link to the NewCourses.htm page, and target the link to open the page in a new browser window.

28. Save and close the page, preview the page in a browser window, and test the New Courses link. Close the browser windows.

29. Upload the site to the remote server and view the site over the Web.

Case 2. Museum of Western Art C. J. Strittmatter asks you to add the art to the art page of the museum's Web site. Because the museum has so many paintings, C.J. has decided to feature a few paintings at a time from the collection. Use layers to add paintings and descriptions of the paintings to the page, and then use behaviors to show and hide the appropriate layers.

1. Open the Museum site that you modified in Tutorial 5, Case 2, and then open the Art.htm page.

2. Open the home page, use the Copy HTML command to copy "WELCOME" to the left of the menu table, and then close the page.

3. Place the insertion point to the left of the menu table in the Art page, click to the right of the menu table, press the Enter key use the Paste HTML command to paste the text you copied, right-align it select the text you pasted, and then type "ART".

4. Make the rulers and the grid visible in the Document window if they are not already visible.

5. Draw a layer approximately 150 pixels wide and 100 pixels high, drag the layer-code marker to the right of the marker that is already in the page, and then drag the layer approximately 10 pixels from the left border of the page and approximately 20 pixels below the bottom of the menu table (located at the right of the page). (Use the grid to help you position the layer.)

6. Insert the AQuietDayInUtica.jpg graphic from the Tutorial.06\Cases folder on your Data Disk into the layer (placing a copy of the graphic in the graphics folder), drag the borders of the layer so that the layer fits snugly around the graphic, and then name the layer "UticaPic."

Explore   7. Select the graphic, and then add a one-pixel border. Double-click in the Border text box in the Property inspector, and then type "1."

8. Repeat Steps 5 through 7 to add seven more layers. Draw each layer approximately 20 pixels to the right of the previous layer until there are four layers across; then draw the other four layers in a second row approximately 20 pixels below the bottom border of the top row of layers. Use the following list to add graphics to the layers and to name the layers. To add the layers, draw the first layer (to hold the BuffaloRunners.jpg graphic), insert the graphic, name the layer, and then draw the next layer.

Graphic File name	Layer Name
BuffaloRunners.jpg	BuffaloPic
CowpunchingSometimes.jpg	CowPic
IndiansHuntingBuffalo.jpg	IndianPic
AFigureOfTheNight.jpg	FigurePic
TheBucker.jpg	BuckerPic
TheCowPuncher.jpg	PuncherPic
DeerInForest.jpg	DeerPic

9. Select all of the graphics in the top row, click Modify on the main menu bar, point to Align, and then click Top to fine-tune the horizontal alignment of the graphics, and then do the same for the graphics in the second row.

10. Select the two graphics in the first column, use the Align command to align their left borders to fine-tune the alignment of the graphics in the first column, and then do the same for the graphics in the other three columns.

11. Draw a new layer the same width as the UticaPic layer and approximately 50 pixels high below the UticaPic layer, overlapping the FigurePic layer if necessary.

12. Move the layer-code marker for the new layer to the right of the other layer markers on the page.

Explore   13. Name the new layer "UticaID," and then type #CC6600 in the Bg Color text box in the Property inspector.

7. Draw another layer 20 pixels below the JeansPic layer, insert the WasabiPicture.gif graphic from the Tutorial.06\Cases folder on your Data Disk, type 1 in the Border text box, name the layer WasabiPic, and then drag the borders of the layer so that they are snug against the edges of the graphic.

8. Align the top border of the top row of graphics, and then align the top border of the bottom row of graphics.

9. Draw a layer in the center of the page, insert the WasabiOriginal.gif graphic from the Tutorial.06\Cases folder on your Data Disk, name the layer ThermoOriginal, and then drag the borders of the layer so that they are snug against the edges of the graphic.

10. Draw another layer in the center of the page, insert the WasabiCold.gif graphic from the Tutorial.06\Cases folder on your Data Disk, name the layer ThermoCold, drag the borders of the layer so that they are snug against the edges of the graphic, and then hide the layer.

11. Repeat Step 10 for the following graphics:

Graphic	Layer Name
WasabiLukeWarm.gif	ThermoLukeWarm
WasabiToasty.gif	ThermoToasty
WasabiOnFire.gif	ThermoOnFire
WasabiWasabi.gif	ThermoWasabi

12. Select the ThermoOriginal, ThermoCold, ThermoLukeWarm, ThermoToasty, ThermoOnFire, and ThermoWasabi layers in the Layers panel, and then align them Top and Left. The graphics are now stacked and selected.

13. While all of the Thermo graphics are still selected, adjust their position on the page if necessary.

14. Select the ThermoOriginal layer in the Layers panel, click the closed eye icon to open it, click the z-index number, and then type 5, if necessary. The ThermoOriginal layers moves to the number 5 position in the stacking order.

15. Select the graphic in ChiliPic layer, and then add the Show-Hide Layers behavior to it.

16. In the Show-Hide dialog box select:

Layer	Show, Hide, or Nothing
ThermoOnFire	Show
ThermoToasty	Hide
ThermoLukeWarm	Hide
ThermoCold	Hide
ThermoOriginal	Nothing
ThermoWasabi	Hide
ChiliPic	Nothing
HotWingsPic	Nothing
JeansPic	Nothing
WasabiPic	Nothing

Explore ▸

17. In the Behaviors panel select the event, click the arrow, point to Show Events For, click 4.0 and Later Browsers, click the arrow again, and then click (onClick) from the list.

18. Select the graphic in the HotWingsPic layer, and Show-Hide Layers behavior.

19. In the Show-Hide dialog box select:

Layer	Show, Hide, or Nothing
ThermoOnFire	Hide
ThermoToasty	Show
ThermoLukeWarm	Hide
ThermoCold	Hide
ThermoOriginal	Nothing
ThermoWasabi	Hide
ChiliPic	Nothing
HotWingsPic	Nothing
JeansPic	Nothing
WasabiPic	Nothing

20. In the Behaviors panel select the event, click the arrow, and then select (onClick) from the list.

21. Select the graphic in the CharoPic layer, and then add the Show-Hide Layers behavior.

22. In the Show-Hide dialog box select:

Layer	Show, Hide, or Nothing
ThermoOnFire	Hide
ThermoToasty	Hide
ThermoLukeWarm	Hide
ThermoCold	Show
ThermoOriginal	Nothing
ThermoWasabi	Hide
ChiliPic	Nothing
HotWingsPic	Nothing
JeansPic	Nothing
WasabiPic	Nothing

23. In the Behaviors panel select the event, click the arrow, and then select (onClick) from the list.

24. Select the WasabiPic layer, and then add the Show-Hide Layers behavior.

25. In the Show-Hide dialog box select:

Layer	Show, Hide, or Nothing
ThermoOnFire	Hide
ThermoToasty	Hide
ThermoLukeWarm	Hide
ThermoCold	Hide
ThermoOriginal	Nothing
ThermoWasabi	Show
ChiliPic	Nothing
HotWingsPic	Nothing
JeansPic	Nothing
WasabiPic	Nothing

26. In the Behaviors panel select the event, click the arrow, and then select (onClick) from the list.

27. Save the page, preview the page in a browser window, and click each graphic.

28. Close the browser, open the home page, and then create a new layer to the left of the Specials graphic and text.

29. Insert the WasabiPictureSmall.gif from the Tutorial.06\Cases folder of the Data Disk, type 1 in the Border text box, and then click inside the layer next to the graphic and hold the Shift key while pressing the Enter key to move to the next line.

30. Type How Hot Is Wasabi???, apply the subheadings style, adjust the layer so that Wasabi??? appears on a second line, and then select the text and click align center. and enter non-breaking spaces before the graphic so that it is aligned center as well. Name the layer "WasabiHowHot."

31. Move the layer, if necessary, so that it is positioned between the heading text and the Specials text and graphic, Select the Wasabi graphic, create a link to the Wasabi.htm page, and then target the link to open in another window. Then select the text, link it to the Wasabi.htm page, and target the link to open in another window.

32. Save the page, preview the page in a browser, click the Wasabi graphic and text, and then close the browser windows.

33. Upload the site to the remote server, view the site over the Web, and test all of the new links.

QUICK CHECK ANSWERS

Session 6.1

1. a transparent container you place in a Web page to hold different types of content

2. a combination of HTML enhancements and a scripting language that work together to add animation, interactive elements, and dynamic updating to Web pages

3. a small yellow square that indicates that there is a layer on the page

4. click the edge of the layer, click the layer selection handle if the layer is active, or click the layer-code marker

5. It determines the order in which the layer is stacked in the user's browser window when more than one layer is used on a page; higher numbered layers are at the front of the stack and are seen in front of layers with lower numbers.

6. The Visibility attribute indicates whether the layer is visible when the Web page is loaded; if a layer is hidden when the page is loaded, actions taken by the user can make it visible.

Session 6.2

1. True

2. in front of

3. the last layer selected, as indicated by black selection handles

4. a series of parallel horizontal and vertical lines that overlap to create equal squares in the background of the Document window to provide a guide for positioning or resizing layers or other elements

5. No, In fact, it does not need to even be touching its parent layer

6. JavaScript code that forces the page to reload every time the browser window is resized to avoid the layers moving around, scaling improperly, or disappearing completely

Session 6.3

1. code that is added to a Web page that enables users to interact with various elements in the Web page, to alter the Web page in different ways, or to cause tasks to be performed

2. An event is comprised of a user event and an event handler. The user event is what the user does to trigger the action; the event handler is the code used to refer to the event.

3. what happens when an event is performed on an object

4. No, Preset behaviors are available in different areas of the Dreamweaver environment, such as the rollover behavior; you can also write code for new behaviors.

5. False

New Perspectives on

MACROMEDIA
DREAMWEAVER MX

Read This Before You Begin

To the Student

Data Disks

To complete the tutorials, Review Assignments, and Case Problems, you need **five** Data Disks. Your instructor will either provide you with these Data Disks or ask you to make your own.

If you are making your own Data Disks, you will need **five** blank, formatted high-density disks. You will need to copy a set of files and/or folders from a file server, standalone computer, or the Web onto your disks. Your instructor will tell you which computer, drive letter, and folders contain the files you need. You can also download the files by going to **www.course.com** and following the instructions on the screen. You will copy the Tutorial.01, Tutorial.02, Tutorial.03, and Tutorial.04 folders onto one blank formatted high-density disk and label it **Data Disk 1: Tutorials 1–4**; you will copy the Tutorial.05 and Tutorial.06 folders onto a second blank formatted high-density disk and label it **Data Disk 2: Tutorials 5 & 6**; you will copy the Tutorial.07 and Tutorial.08/Tutorial folders onto a third blank formatted high-density disk and label it **Data Disk 3: Tutorial 7 & Tutorial 8 (tutorial partial)**; you will copy the Tutorial.08/Tutorial (continued) folder onto a fourth blank formatted high-density disk and label it **Data Disk 4: Tutorial 8 (tutorial continued)**; you will copy the Tutorial.08 (review and cases) and Tutorial.09 folders onto a fifth blank formatted high-density disk and label it **Data Disk 5: Tutorials 8 (review and cases) & Tutorial 9**. Please note that the Tutorial data files for Tutorial 8 are copied onto two disks and the Review Assignments and Case Problems data files for Tutorial 8 are copied onto a third disk.

Before creating your Data Disks, check with your instructor to find out where you will be storing your Web sites. It is assumed that you are working from the hard drive of your computer; if you are working from a removable disk, then

you'll need to substitute the appropriate drive letter when instructed to navigate to a location.

When you begin each tutorial, Review Assignment, or Case Problem, be sure you are using the correct Data Disk. Refer to the "File Finder" chart at the back of this text for more detailed information on which files are used in which tutorials. See the inside back cover of this book for more information on Data Disk files, or ask your instructor or technical support person for assistance.

Installation Information

We assume a default installation of Dreamweaver MX. The screenshots in this book were taken using a computer running Windows XP Professional and, when showing a browser, Internet Explorer 6. If you are using a different operating system or a different browser, your screen might differ from the figures in these tutorials.

Using Your Own Computer

If you are going to work through this book using your own computer, you need:

- **Computer System** A text editor and a Web browser (preferably Internet Explorer or Netscape Navigator, versions 4.0 or higher) must be installed on your computer. If you are using a nonstandard browser, it must support frames and HTML 4.0 or higher.

- **Data Disks** You will not be able to complete the tutorials or exercises in this book using your own computer until you have your Data Disks.

Visit Our World Wide Web Site

Additional materials designed especially for you are available on the World Wide Web. Go to www.course.com/NewPerspectives.

To the Instructor

The Data Disk files are available on the Instructor's Resource Kit for this title. Follow the instructions in the Help file on the CD-ROM to install the programs to your network or standalone computer. For information on creating Data Disks, see the "To the Student" section above.

You are granted a license to copy the Data Disk files to any computer or computer network used by students who have purchased this book.

CREATING ANIMATION WITH DYNAMIC LAYERS AND BEHAVIORS

Adding Animations to the Catalyst Web Site

CASE

Catalyst

Sara has decided that she wants some animated elements added to the Catalyst Web site. She believes the animated elements will increase interest for the site's target audience. Brian thinks a good place to add the animation that Sara wants is in the tour dates page. He asks you to create an interactive component for the map in the tour dates page. You will animate the route each band will take during its tour. Then you will create a button for each band so that when the user clicks the button, the route for that band will animate.

You'll use layers to add the animated elements to the Web site. Then you will use behaviors with the animated layers to add sophistication and provide advanced functionality to the site.

SESSION 7.1

In this session, you will learn about basic animation. You will explore the Timelines panel. Finally, you will add a layer to the timeline, move layers, and then change the duration of layers.

Understanding Animation

Adding animated elements to a Web site can create interest and interactivity. **Animation** is a series of graphics or images that appear to move over time. For example, think about a flip book with a series of pictures. The picture changes slightly on each page. When you flip the pages of the book quickly, the image appears to move. Creating animation in a Web page uses a similar process. However, you do not have to draw every image for each frame because the computer aids in the process.

You use the Timelines panel to create animations in Web pages. The Timelines panel creates animations by using dynamic HTML code and layers to change layer position, change the source of an image over time, or automatically call behaviors without using Flash, ActiveX, Java, or any other plug-in application. You create animation in the Timelines panel by using the following **timeline actions** to change layer properties over time:

- **Move a layer.** Repositions a layer by changing its X and Y coordinates.
- **Show or hide a layer.** Switches the visibility of a layer between three states: visible, hidden, or default.
- **Resize a layer.** Adjusts the width and height dimensions of a layer.
- **Change the z-index or stacking order.** Changes the order in which layers are stacked on the page by adjusting the z-index number of the layer.

In addition to changing layer properties, you can also change the image source with the timeline. Changing the image source enables you to perform image rollovers within a timeline without using added JavaScript. (Image source is the only image property that a timeline can change directly.)

It is important to plan which elements of your pages will be animated. We have all seen pages that look as though a cartoon has exploded across the page. To avoid overloading the user with unnecessary distractions, you should consider what each animation will add to the page. Include only those animations that support the underlying site goals and provide the user with useful information.

Timelines can be viewed reliably only in 4.0 and later browsers. To begin adding animation to your pages you will need to open the Timelines panel.

To open the Timelines panel:

1. Start **Dreamweaver**, open the **NewCatalyst** Web site that you modified in the Tutorial 6 Review Assignments, and then open the **tourdates.htm** page.

2. Click **Window** on the menu bar, point to **Others**, and then click **Timelines**. The Timelines panel opens below the Property inspector.

3. Close the Property inspector. See Figure 7-1.

Figure 7-1   TIMELINES PANEL IN DREAMWEAVER

Next, you will explore the Timelines panel.

Exploring **the Timelines Panel**

The Timelines panel enables you to create animation. Each element of the timeline controls a different aspect of the animation. If you have used animation software, such as Macromedia Flash or Director, or video editing software such as Premier, the timeline may look somewhat familiar because most time-based software have some similar components. If you have never used a program that enabled you to move objects over time, then the Timelines panel might seem confusing. Don't worry, we will move through it step by step. Figure 7-2 identifies all the components of the Timelines panel.

Figure 7-2   COMPONENTS OF THE TIMELINES PANEL

The Timelines panel consists of a toolbar with buttons that control various aspects of the animation and the timeline area where you create your animation.

The timeline area is divided into frames vertically and into channels horizontally (each frame is in a different column, and each channel is in a different row). In the timeline, frames are not the same as the frames that you used earlier to divide an HTML page so that more than one HTML document is displayed. Timeline **frames** are the units of temporal measurement used in animation. (In film, a frame is one section of the film strip; in traditional animation, a frame is one cell of animation.) As you move to the right on the timeline, the animation progresses in time. **Frame numbers** are visible in the second row of the timeline to help you keep track of what frame you are in.

The **playback head** (the red bar) indicates which frame of the animation is visible in the Document window. You can move forward and backward in the timeline by dragging the playback head. The length of an animation is determined by the number of frames included in the animation and by the speed at which those frames play in the user's browser. The default setting for the **playback rate**, the speed of an animation, in Dreamweaver is 15 frames per second (Fps), which is generally a good average rate. Be aware that there is no way to guarantee the playback rate on a user's machine because browsers always play every frame of the animation, even if they cannot attain the specified playback rate. This means that an animation will run slower on a slow machine and faster on a fast machine, but the fastest it will ever run is the playback rate you specify. To ensure that you achieve the look that you want, it is a good idea to test animations on a variety of computers.

The **Behaviors channel**, the row above the frame numbers, is where you insert any behaviors that will be called from a certain frame in the timeline. The Behaviors channel will be discussed further in Session 7.2.

The numbered rows below the frame numbers are the animation channels. **Animation channels** are the rows in which objects are animated. If you are animating more than one object (a layer or an image) at a time, you use a different animation channel for each object. Unlike other time-based software, the vertical position of a row within the timeline has nothing to do with the z-index number (or stacking order) of the object within the Web page.

The Timelines panel toolbar consists of several buttons:

- **Timelines list.** Moves you to the selected timeline when more than one timeline is added to a Web page.
- **Rewind.** Moves the playback head to the first frame of the timeline.
- **Back.** Rewinds the timeline one frame at a time.
- **Current Frame Number text box.** Displays the number of the current frame of animation.
- **Playback.** Advances the timeline one frame at a time. Holding down the Playback button plays the entire timeline.
- **Autoplay.** Attaches a behavior to the Web page that makes the animation automatically start playing when the Web page is loaded into a user's browser.
- **Loop.** Attaches a behavior to the Web page that makes the animation continue to loop as long as the page is loaded in the user's browser window. **Looping** restarts the animation from the first frame after the last frame is played.

You'll use the Timelines panel to add a layer to the timeline.

Creating a Timeline

The first step in creating an animation is to create a timeline for the layer you want to animate. You create a timeline for a layer by dragging the layer to the Timelines panel. The image or text that you want to animate must be in a layer in the Web page before you can add it to the Timelines panel.

REFERENCE   WINDOW   **RW**

<u>Adding Layers to the Timelines Panel</u>
- Open the Timelines panel.
- Select the layer in the Document window.
- Drag the selected layer to the desired position in the Timelines panel.

Brian wants to create an animated tour path for the Sloth Child band over the U.S. map in the tour dates page. First, you will create a new layer in the tour dates page, drag the U.S. map graphic into the new layer, and then center the layer on the page. Then, you'll create a new layer over the U.S. map and add a graphic to that layer. Placing the new layer and graphic on top of the hot spots on the U.S. map will not inhibit the functionality of the hot spots; they will work through the layer. The map will be the first in a series of graphics you will add to the tour dates page to create an animated path for the Surface Suction tour.

To add a graphic to a layer:

1. Click the **Draw Layer** button 🖼 on the **Common** tab of the Insert bar, and then draw a new layer beside the U.S. map.

2. Select the map graphic, drag it into the layer, and then deselect the layer.

3. Select the layer-code marker at the top of the page, and then drag it to the right of the align anchor point.

   TROUBLE? If the layer-code marker is not visible, you need to display the invisible elements. Click View on the menu bar, point to Visual Aids, and then click Invisible Elements.

4. Select the layer, and then drag the selected layer to about **20 pixels** below the page heading.

5. Align the layer to the center of the West Coast tour dates table.

6. If necessary, position the pointer above the table, and then press the **Enter** key until the table is **50 pixels** below the U.S. map graphic.

7. Open the Layers panel, if necessary, double-click **Layer1** in the Name column, type **USmap**, and then press the **Enter** key to rename the layer. The U.S. map is in a new layer named "USmap," positioned on the tour dates page. See Figure 7-3.

Figure 7-3	TOUR DATES PAGE WITH GRAPHIC ADDED TO USMAP LAYER

repositioned layer-code marker

U.S. map added to layer

repositioned USmap layer

Next, you'll create a new layer over the USmap layer. Then you'll add a graphic to the map that marks the first stop on the tour. Once the graphic is in the layer, you will resize the layer to fit snugly around the graphic and then you will position the layer over the U.S. map.

To create a second layer in the tour dates page:

1. Click the **Draw Layer** button 🗒 on the **Common** tab of the Insert bar, and then draw a layer over the U.S. map in the Document window.

2. Select the layer-code marker, and move it to the left of the right align anchor point.

3. Click inside the layer to make it active, click the **Image** button 🖼 on the **Common** tab of the Insert bar, and insert the **East1.gif** graphic from the **Tutorial.07/Tutorial** folder on your Data Disk, placing a copy of the image in the Graphics folder in the root folder for your site. A graphic with one small black circle appears in the layer.

4. Select the layer, and then resize the layer so that the edges of the layer fit snugly against the edges of the graphic within it.

   TROUBLE? If you cannot locate the edges of the graphic, the graphic image is not selected. Select the graphic to view the edges, and then drag the edges of the layer so that they fit snugly around the graphic image.

5. Reposition the layer so that it is centered over the map. See Figure 7-4.

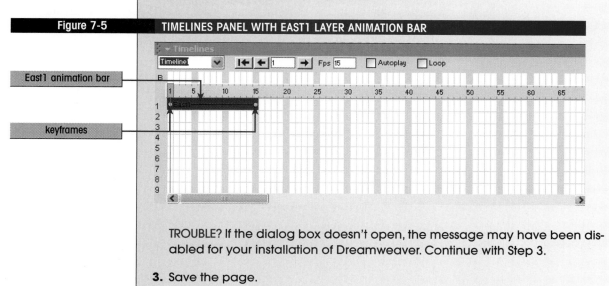

Figure 7-4   TOUR DATES PAGE WITH NEW LAYER SELECTED

borders of new layer positioned around map image

black circle in graphic

6. In the Layers panel, name the new layer **East1**.

Now you'll drag the new layer into the Timelines panel. This creates an animation bar from the layer.

To add a layer to the Timelines panel:

1. Drag the **East1** layer from the tour dates page to frame 1 in animation channel 1 in the Timelines panel. A purple line with a white circle at each end and the word "East1" appear in the first channel of the Timelines panel, indicating that an animation bar has been created. A dialog box opens, explaining the capabilities of the Timelines panel.

   TROUBLE? If the animation bar does not appear, you may be trying to drag the layer from the Layers panel. Drag the layer from the tour dates page to animation channel 1 on the Timelines panel.

2. Click the **OK** button. See Figure 7-5.

Figure 7-5   TIMELINES PANEL WITH EAST1 LAYER ANIMATION BAR

East1 animation bar

keyframes

   TROUBLE? If the dialog box doesn't open, the message may have been disabled for your installation of Dreamweaver. Continue with Step 3.

3. Save the page.

When you drag a layer to the Timelines panel, an animation bar and keyframes are added for the layer. An **animation bar** is the purple line that appears in the channel to which the layer is added. By default the animation bar is 15 frames. The layer name appears at the left of the animation bar and can be used to identify the layer. If you have not named the layer, the default layer name appears at the left of the timeline. The white bullets in the first and last frames of the animation bar are keyframes. A **keyframe** is a frame in a timeline where an event occurs. Every timeline has at least two keyframes—one placed at the first frame and one placed at the last frame of the animation bar.

Next, you will add the other graphics that you will use in the animation to the timeline. For each, you'll create another layer over the U.S. map, insert the graphic into the layer, resize the layer to fit snugly around the graphic within it, align the layer with the East1 layer, name the layer in the Layers panel, and then add the new layer to an animation channel of the timeline. The graphics were designed so that each graphic has the same width and height. When the graphics are stacked and aligned, the points on the tour path will match. To ensure that the points of the tour path align correctly, you need to fit the edges of the layer snugly against the edges of the graphic before aligning the layers. When the stack of aligned layers is positioned correctly over the U.S. map, the tour path will appear over the correct portion of the map. For this reason, it is important that the edges of the East1 layer match with the edges of the U.S. map and that the other layers are then aligned to the top and right of the East1 layer.

To add other graphics to the timeline:

1. Draw a new layer over the U.S. map, and then drag the layer-code marker to the left of the other layer-code markers in the page.

2. Insert the **East2.gif** graphic from the **Tutorial.07/Tutorial** folder on your Data Disk into the new layer, placing a copy of the image in the Graphics folder in the root folder for your site.

3. Resize the layer as needed so that the edges of the new layer fit snugly against the borders of the graphic contained within it. (Remember you must select the graphic to see the edges of the graphic.)

4. In the Layers panel, name the layer **East2**.

   Next, you'll align the East1 and East2 layers.

5. Press and hold the **Shift** key, click the **East2** and **East1** layers in the Layers panel, and then release the **Shift** key. Both layers are selected.

6. Click **Modify** on the menu bar, point to **Align**, and then click **Left**. The left borders of the layers are aligned.

7. Click **Modify** on the menu bar, point to **Align**, and then click **Top**. The top borders of the layers are aligned. See Figure 7-6.

| Figure 7-6 | TOUR DATES PAGE WITH SECOND LAYER |

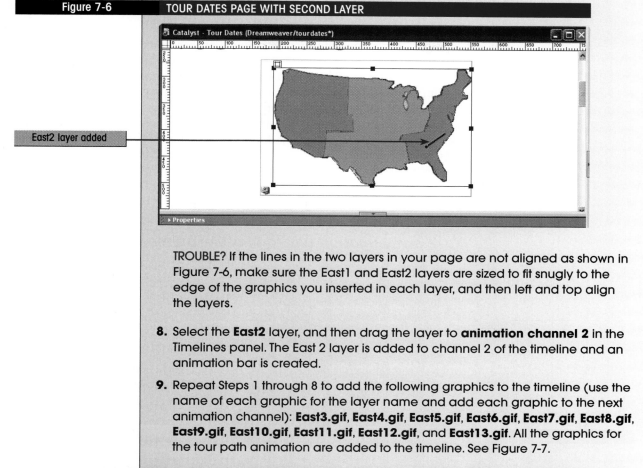

East2 layer added

TROUBLE? If the lines in the two layers in your page are not aligned as shown in Figure 7-6, make sure the East1 and East2 layers are sized to fit snugly to the edge of the graphics you inserted in each layer, and then left and top align the layers.

8. Select the **East2** layer, and then drag the layer to **animation channel 2** in the Timelines panel. The East 2 layer is added to channel 2 of the timeline and an animation bar is created.

9. Repeat Steps 1 through 8 to add the following graphics to the timeline (use the name of each graphic for the layer name and add each graphic to the next animation channel): **East3.gif**, **East4.gif**, **East5.gif**, **East6.gif**, **East7.gif**, **East8.gif**, **East9.gif**, **East10.gif**, **East11.gif**, **East12.gif**, and **East13.gif**. All the graphics for the tour path animation are added to the timeline. See Figure 7-7.

| Figure 7-7 | ALL TOUR PATH ANIMATION GRAPHICS ADDED TO TIMELINE |

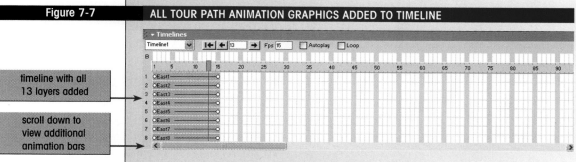

timeline with all 13 layers added

scroll down to view additional animation bars

Next, you will move and resize an animation bar.

Moving and Resizing Animation Bars

You can move an animation bar to another animation channel or to another location within the same animation channel. You can also resize an animation bar to include more or fewer frames.

Moving an Animation Bar

Moving an animation bar to another channel does not affect the layer's stacking order. At times, however, you may need to move an animation bar to another animation channel. Consider the following example: If you place two animation bars in the same animation channel and then decide to add more frames to the first animation bar, you may need to move one animation bar to another animation channel. This way you can add more frames to the first animation bar without changing the frame in which the second animation bar starts. You move an animation bar to another animation channel in the Timelines panel by selecting the animation bar and dragging it to the new channel. To select an animation bar, you click the animation bar anywhere between the keyframes, but not on the keyframes. If you select a keyframe, the animation bar will not move and only the selected keyframe will move either to the left or to the right.

You'll move the East2 animation bar to animation channel 1.

To move an animation bar to another animation channel:

1. Click the **East2** animation bar between its keyframes in the Timelines panel. The East2 animation bar is selected and is a darker purple color.

   TROUBLE? If only a keyframe is a darker purple color, you selected a keyframe and not the animation bar. Click the animation bar, being sure not to click a keyframe.

2. Drag the **East2** animation bar to the right of the East1 animation bar in animation channel 1. Both the East1 and East2 animation bars are in animation channel 1. See Figure 7-8.

Figure 7-8	EAST2 ANIMATION BAR MOVED TO ANIMATION CHANNEL 1

selected East2 layer in animation channel 1

animation channel 2 is empty

3. Select the **East3** animation bar, and then move it to the right of the East2 animation bar in animation channel 1.

4. Select and then move the **East4**, **East5**, **East6**, **East7**, **East8**, **East9**, **East10**, **East11**, **East12**, and **East13** animation bars to the end of animation channel 1. All the animation bars are now in animation channel 1. See Figure 7-9.

Figure 7-9   **TIMELINES PANEL WITH ALL ANIMATION BARS IN ANIMATION CHANNEL 1**

animation bars in channel 1

scroll right to view hidden animation bars

5. Drag the horizontal scroll bar right to view all the animation bars.

In addition to moving an animation bar to another channel, you can reposition an animation bar within the same animation channel. The horizontal position within the channel determines when that animation bar plays within the timeline. Often when creating an animation, you will want each layer to start and end at different times within the animation. One way to do this is to move the opening frame of the animation bar to the frame in which you want the layer to appear. To move an animation bar to a new location within an animation channel, select the animation bar and then drag the animation bar to the frame you want. Remember, frame numbers are located below the Behaviors channel. You can view the frame number of a selected frame or the frame the playback head is over in the Current Frame Number text box on the Timelines panel toolbar.

You'll move the East13 animation bar to the right so that it starts on frame 190 of the timeline.

To move a layer within an animation channel:

1. Select the **East13** animation bar, and then drag it to the right until the first frame of the animation bar is in **frame 190** of the timeline. See Figure 7-10.

Figure 7-10   **EAST13 ANIMATION BAR REPOSITIONED WITHIN CHANNEL 1**

Frame Number text box

frame numbers

East13 animation bar moved to frame 190

2. Select the **East13** animation bar, and then drag it back to **frame 181**. The East13 animation bar is repositioned.

You can also resize an animation bar.

Resizing an Animation Bar

You can resize, or change the length, of an animation bar by selecting the keyframe at either end of the bar and dragging the keyframe to a new position within the animation channel. Lengthening the animation bar increases the duration of the animation by adding more frames, whereas shortening the animation bar decreases the duration of the animation by reducing the number of frames. Longer timelines enable you to create more complex actions as well as more gradual and fluid movements. Although the number of frames over which an animation occurs is one component in the speed of the animation, it is not the only component. Remember that the frame rate of the timeline also affects the speed of the animation. When you change the number of frames within an animation bar, any additional keyframes in the animation bar are spaced proportionately through the timeline so that all of the events in the animation are shortened or lengthened proportionately to preserve the animation.

You'll increase the length of the East13 animation bar to 30 frames.

To increase the duration of an animation bar:

1. Click the ending keyframe of the East13 animation bar to select it.

2. Drag the selected keyframe to **frame 210** in the animation channel. See Figure 7-11.

Figure 7-11	EAST13 ANIMATION BAR RESIZED

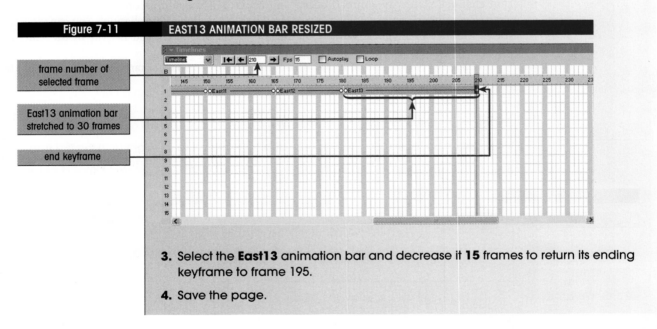

frame number of selected frame

East13 animation bar stretched to 30 frames

end keyframe

3. Select the **East13** animation bar and decrease it **15** frames to return its ending keyframe to frame 195.

4. Save the page.

In this session, you learned about animation and the Timelines panel, and then you added layers to the timeline, moved layers, and changed the duration of layers. In the next session, you will insert keyframes into an animation bar, move layers, adjust the visibility of layers, adjust the size of layers, and then preview the animation in the browser window.

Session 7.1 QUICK | CHECK

1. What is animation?

2. What are the four timeline actions?

3. What are the numbered columns in the Timelines panel called?

4. What is the default frame rate of a timeline?

5. What are the white bullets at the beginning and end of an animation bar?

6. What effect does increasing the duration of an animation bar have on the animation?

SESSION 7.2

In this session, you will insert additional keyframes into animation bars. You will move layers, resize layers, change the visibility of layers, and change the stacking order of layers. Finally, you will preview the animation in a browser.

Adding **Keyframes to an Animation Bar**

Keyframes are where you input instructions for an animation. You can think of keyframes as the control frames of an animation. You need a keyframe in each frame of the timeline where something happens. For example, if you are moving a layer, you need a keyframe each time the movement changes direction, stops, or starts. If you are changing the visibility of a layer, you need a keyframe each time the layer changes visibility.

REFERENCE WINDOW **RW**

Adding Keyframes to an Animation Bar
- Select the animation bar to which you want to add a keyframe.
- Click in the frame to which you want to add the keyframe.
- Right-click the selected frame, and then click Add Keyframe.

You want to create the illusion of movement in the animation path on the tour dates page. You can accomplish this by adjusting the visibility of the animation bars to hidden and then setting them to become visible one at a time. To do this, you must add an additional keyframe to each animation bar. You'll start by adding a keyframe to the second frame of the East1 animation bar, which is the frame in which you want to input instructions.

To add a keyframe to an animation bar:

1. If you took a break after the previous session, make sure **Dreamweaver** is running, the **NewCatalyst** Web site is open, and the **tour dates** page is open.

2. Click **frame 2** of the East1 animation bar in the Timelines panel. The East1 animation bar is selected, the red playback head is positioned over the second frame, and the frame number appears in the Frame Number text box. See Figure 7-12.

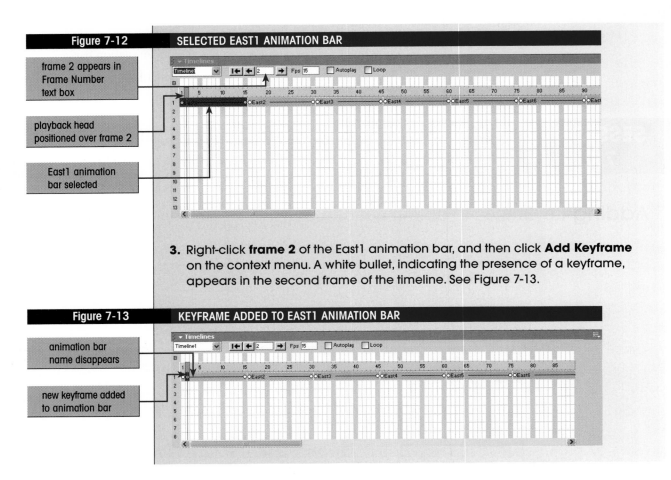

Figure 7-12 | **SELECTED EAST1 ANIMATION BAR**

frame 2 appears in Frame Number text box

playback head positioned over frame 2

East1 animation bar selected

3. Right-click **frame 2** of the East1 animation bar, and then click **Add Keyframe** on the context menu. A white bullet, indicating the presence of a keyframe, appears in the second frame of the timeline. See Figure 7-13.

Figure 7-13 | **KEYFRAME ADDED TO EAST1 ANIMATION BAR**

animation bar name disappears

new keyframe added to animation bar

When you add a keyframe to an animation bar, the layer name disappears. You can tell which layer is being used by selecting the animation bar in the Timelines panel; the layer is then selected in the Layers panel. You can also select an animation bar by selecting the layer in the Layers panel.

Now you will change the visibility of a layer in the Timelines panel.

Adjusting **Layer Visibility in the Timelines Panel**

Changing the visibility of layers is one of the easiest ways to create an animation. The Timelines panel enables you to change the visibility of a layer between visible and hidden over time. For example, you can place a layer with hidden visibility in a page and then change that layer to visible at a designated frame in the timeline, causing the layer to appear on-screen at a specific moment. The change in visibility is not gradual, like a fade; it occurs immediately when the timeline encounters the keyframe with instructions to change the layer's visibility. The three visibility attributes are the same as the normal layer visibility attributes: visible, hidden, and default. The Layers panel includes a column that shows the selected visibility attribute for each layer.

REFERENCE WINDOW   RW

Adjusting Layer Visibility
- Select the desired keyframe.
- In the Layers panel, click the visibility column until the appropriate icon appears.

Now you will animate the layers you added to the timeline by changing the visibility of each layer. First, you will add a keyframe to the second frame of each animation bar. Then, you will set the visibility of the layer to hidden in the first keyframe in each animation bar. Finally, you will set the visibility of the second keyframe to visible. Because the animation bars are positioned one after another in the timeline, this will provide the illusion that the tour path is being drawn over time.

To change visibility of layers in a timeline:

1. Click the first keyframe in the East1 animation bar. The keyframe is selected and the playback head is positioned over the selected keyframe. See Figure 7-14.

Figure 7-14   **SELECTED BEGINNING KEYFRAME IN EAST1 ANIMATION BAR**

playback head over first keyframe

East1 first keyframe selected

2. In the Layers panel, click the visibility column to the left of the layer name until the **closed eye** icon appears. The first keyframe of the East1 layer is set to a hidden visibility. See Figure 7-15.

Figure 7-15	LAYERS PANEL WITH EAST1 LAYER VISIBILITY SET

visibility column

layer visibility
set to hidden

3. Select the second keyframe in the East1 animation bar in the Timelines panel, and then click the **visibility column** in the Layers panel until the **open eye** icon appears. The second keyframe of the East1 layer is set to visible and will remain visible through the remaining frames of the timeline.

You'll repeat this process to add a new keyframe to each of the remaining animation bars and set the visibility for the first and second keyframes of the animation bar. You'll start with the East2 animation bar.

To add keyframes and set visibility for the remaining animation bars:

1. Select the **East2** animation bar, right-click the second frame in the East2 animation bar in the Timelines panel, and then click **Add Keyframe**. A new keyframe is added to the animation bar.

2. Select the first keyframe of the East2 animation bar, and then set the visibility to **hidden** in the Layers panel.

3. Select the second keyframe of the East2 animation bar, and then set the visibility to **visible** in the Layers panel.

4. Repeat Steps 1 through 3 to add a keyframe and set the visibility for each of the following animation bars: **East3**, **East4**, **East5**, **East6**, **East7**, **East8**, **East9**, **East10**, **East11**, **East12**, and **East13**.

5. Save the page.

You have set the visibility of layers in the timeline; now you will preview the animation.

Previewing a Timeline

You can preview an animation in Dreamweaver as you create the animation, and you can preview the animation in a browser. Previewing a timeline in Dreamweaver is helpful because it enables you to see what you are creating while you are working. However, because the animation may run differently in a browser, it is important to also preview the animation in a browser window. In addition, you should test a finished animation on a number of computers after you have posted the animation, so that you can get an accurate view of the playback speed over the Internet and on different computers. Testing the animation helps to ensure that as many viewers as possible see the animation as you intended them to see it.

Previewing a Timeline in Dreamweaver

There are two ways to preview a timeline in Dreamweaver. You can drag the playback head across the timeline in the Timelines panel while viewing the animation in the Document window, or you can click and hold the Playback button in the Timelines panel toolbar while viewing the animation in the Document window. Dragging the playback head enables you to review a piece of an animation quickly. However, when you drag the playback head, you control the playback rate. You need to use the Playback button to preview the playback speed as well as the animation.

You'll use both methods to preview the timeline on which you have been working within Dreamweaver.

> ### To preview a timeline within Dreamweaver:
>
> **1.** Scroll until the U.S. map is visible in the Document window, if necessary.
>
> **2.** Drag the **playback head** across the timeline while viewing the animation in the Document window. The animation plays at the speed you drag.
>
> **3.** Click and hold the **Playback** button ➡ on the Timelines panel toolbar while viewing the animation in the Document window. The animation plays at the frame rate that you input earlier.

You can also preview the animation in a browser.

Previewing a Timeline in a Browser

In order to preview a timeline within a browser window, you must add a behavior to the Web page that instructs the browser to play the timeline. The easiest way to do this is to click the Autoplay checkbox on the Timelines panel toolbar. When you click the Autoplay checkbox, Dreamweaver inserts the Autoplay behavior into the code of the Web page. The Autoplay behavior tells the browser to play the timeline as soon as the page is finished loading. Because the behavior is added to the page and not to the timeline or an object in the timeline, the behavior will not appear in the Behaviors channel in the Timelines panel. You will learn other ways to start a timeline when you add behaviors to timelines.

You'll add the Autoplay behavior to the Web page, and then preview the tour dates page in a browser window.

To preview a timeline in a browser:

1. Click the **Autoplay** checkbox in the Timelines panel. A dialog box opens with an explanation that the Play Timeline action is being added to the Web page.

   TROUBLE? If the dialog box doesn't open, the message has been disabled for your installation of Dreamweaver. Continue with Step 3.

2. Click the **OK** button to confirm that you want to add the action to the tour dates page. The Autoplay checkbox is checked and the behavior is inserted into the code for the tour dates page. See Figure 7-16.

Figure 7-16	PLAY TIMELINE ACTION ADDED TO TOUR DATES PAGE

check to insert Autoplay behavior into code

3. Save the page, and then preview the page in a browser. The timeline runs in the browser window. See Figure 7-17.

Figure 7-17	TIMELINE RUN IN BROWSER WINDOW

tour path animation completed

Next, you will change the stacking order of layers.

Adjusting **Layer Stacking Order in the Timeline**

You adjust the z-index number of layers to change their stacking order. You can change the order in which layers are stacked during a timeline so that the layers appear stacked in different orders. For example, you might have one layer jump in front of another layer. Unlike most other time-based software, the channel in which the animation bar for the layer appears has no effect on the layer's stacking order. Like changes in visibility, the change in stacking order occurs immediately when the timeline encounters a keyframe with instructions to change the z-index number of a layer.

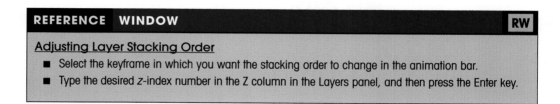

REFERENCE WINDOW   **RW**

Adjusting Layer Stacking Order
- Select the keyframe in which you want the stacking order to change in the animation bar.
- Type the desired z-index number in the Z column in the Layers panel, and then press the Enter key.

Brian has decided to add a new layer to the animation. The new layer will contain a graphic of a tour bus that will eventually move along the tour path that you have already created. You'll add the new layer to the timeline, and then adjust the stacking order of the layers.

To add a new layer to the timeline:

1. Create a new layer approximately **20 × 20 pixels** over the U.S. map, and then drag the layer-code marker to the left of the other layer-code markers.

2. Insert the **BusSmall.gif** graphic from the **Tutorial.07/Tutorial** folder on your Data Disk into the new layer.

3. Drag the borders of the layer so that the layer fits snugly around the graphic, and then move the layer to position the bus over the lowest point on the tour path. See Figure 7-18.

Figure 7-18	BUS GRAPHIC IN TOUR DATES PAGE

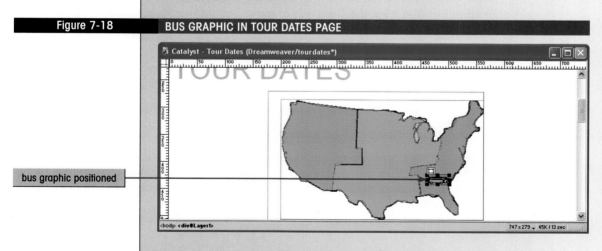

bus graphic positioned

4. In the Layers panel, name the new layer **Bus**.

5. Drag the **Bus** layer to **frame 1** of animation channel 2 of the Timelines panel to add it to the timeline.

6. Preview the page in a browser window. Notice that the bus graphic covers the other layers. See Figure 7-19.

Figure 7-19   **ANIMATION VIEWED IN BROWSER**

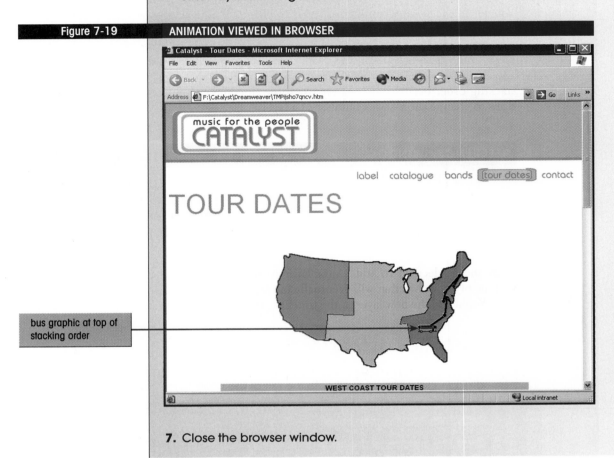

bus graphic at top of stacking order

7. Close the browser window.

Now, you'll change the stacking order of the Bus layer in the ending keyframe of the Bus animation bar. You want the Bus layer to move behind the other layers of the animation in the last keyframe, enabling the user to see the path over the bus.

To adjust the layer stacking order in the Timelines panel:

1. Select the ending keyframe in the Bus animation bar in the Timelines panel, and then select the z-index number of the Bus layer in the Layers panel.

2. Type **2**, and then press the **Enter** key.

3. Preview the page in a browser window. Notice that the Bus layer starts out on top of the animation, and then the path moves over the Bus layer. This is because the stacking order of the Bus layer changes in the keyframe on frame 15 of the animation. See Figure 7-20.

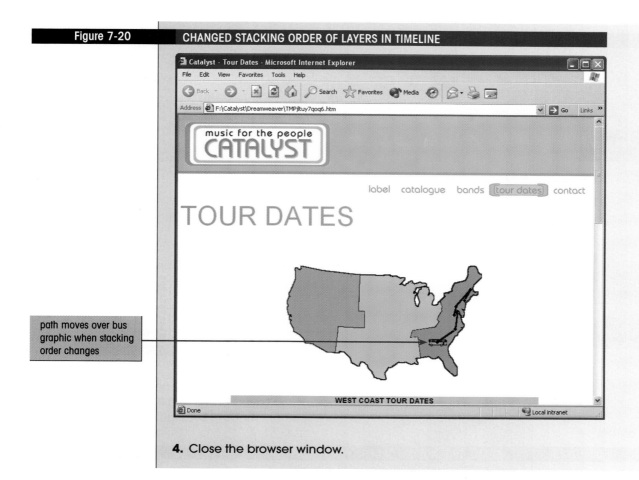

| Figure 7-20 | CHANGED STACKING ORDER OF LAYERS IN TIMELINE |

path moves over bus graphic when stacking order changes

4. Close the browser window.

You can also see the change in layer position from within Dreamweaver after you deselect the layer. The selected layer remains at the top of the stacking order in Dreamweaver so that you can work on it. You'll deselect the Bus layer, and then view the change in stacking order from within Dreamweaver.

To view the change in stacking order:

1. Click the page background beside the map to deselect the Bus layer.

2. Drag the playback head to **frame 1** in the Timelines panel. Notice that the Bus layer has a z-index number of 15 in the Layers panel and that the Bus graphic is the top layer in the animation in the Document window. See Figure 7-21.

Figure 7-21   **FRAME 1 STACKING ORDER**

bus graphic at top of animation

playback head in first frame of timeline

Bus layer has z-index number of 15

3. Drag the playback head to **frame 17** in the Timelines panel. Notice that the Bus layer has a z-index number of 2 in the Layers panel and that the tour path is on top of the Bus graphic in the Document window. See Figure 7-22.

Figure 7-22   **FRAME 17 STACKING ORDER**

animation path moved over bus graphic

timeline on frame 17

Bus layer has z-index number of 2

You'll select the ending keyframe for the Bus animation bar and change the z-index number back to its original z-index number.

4. Select the ending keyframe in the Bus animation bar in the Timelines panel, select the z-index number in the Layers panel, type **15**, and then press the **Enter** key.

5. Save the page.

Next, you'll add animation by moving a layer.

Moving a Layer in the Timelines Panel

Moving a layer is another way to add animation to a page. The timeline enables you to move a layer from one position on the page to another position on the page over a period of time. This technique is frequently used in Web pages to fly headings into the page.

You move a layer by selecting a keyframe and changing the position of the layer. Unlike stacking order and visibility, the layer will not jump to the new position when the playback head crosses the keyframe that contains instructions to change the layer position. Instead, Dreamweaver moves the layer from its initial position to the new position during the intermediary frames, and the layer arrives at its new position as the playback head reaches the new keyframe. Consider the following example: A layer is at the left edge of the screen in the first keyframe of the animation bar. You set a second keyframe in the tenth frame of the animation bar. Then you select the second keyframe and move the layer to the middle of the screen. When you play the timeline, the layer will move one-tenth of the way to its new position in each frame, arriving at the middle of the screen on the tenth frame of the timeline. Adding more frames between keyframes will make the motion slower and smoother.

Brian asks you to move the bus along the tour path for Sloth Child in the tour dates page.

To move a layer in the Timelines panel:

1. Select the ending keyframe of the Bus animation bar and drag it to the right until the Bus animation bar is **195** frames long. The Bus animation bar now ends on the same frame as the East13 animation bar.

2. Click **frame 45** of the Bus animation bar. The Bus animation bar is selected and the playback head is over frame 45.

3. Right-click the selected frame, and then click **Add Keyframe**. A new keyframe is added to the 45th frame of the Bus animation bar.

TROUBLE? If the keyframe is inserted into the wrong frame, drag the keyframe to the 45th frame of the animation bar.

4. Select the new keyframe, and then, in the Document window, drag the **Bus layer** over the second dot on the tour path. See Figure 7-23.

Figure 7-23   **BUS MOVED TO SECOND POINT ON ANIMATION PATH**

Bus layer positioned over second point on tour path

keyframe selected in Bus animation bar

5. Preview the page in a browser to test the first step of the bus animation, and then close the browser window. (Once the bus reaches the second point on the tour path, it will start to move backward. This is because the Bus layer was set to that position in the first and final keyframes when you added the layer to the timeline. The backward movement will stop when you set the final keyframe of the animation bar to its new position in Step 8.)

You will continue to add new keyframes and move the bus along the tour path.

6. Add a new keyframe to **frame 75** of the Bus animation bar, select the **keyframe**, and then, in the Document window, move the **Bus layer** over the third point on the tour path.

7. Add keyframes at **frames 105**, **135**, and **165**, moving the **Bus layer** to the next point on the tour path after you create each new keyframe.

8. Select the ending keyframe for the Bus animation bar in **frame 195** of the timeline, and then move the Bus layer to the final point on the tour path. See Figure 7-24.

Figure 7-24   **ENDING FRAME OF BUS ANIMATION BAR**

Bus layer over final point of tour path

playback head over selected ending keyframe

9. Save the page, and then preview the page in a browser to view the animation.

Next, you'll resize a layer.

Resizing a Layer Over Time

Changing the dimensions of a layer over a period of time is another way to add animation to a page. For example, you can set the background color of a layer to red and then set the layer to a larger size in the ending keyframe of an animation bar. As the timeline progresses, the layer increases in size and the red square appears to grow in size. Adding a background color to the layer enables you to see the layer change dimensions over time. In order to see the layer shrink or grow, the layer's overflow must be set to Hidden in the Property inspector. Resizing a layer does not change the dimensions of images in the layer, but reduces the amount of the images that are visible in the layer as the layer becomes smaller.

Brian wants to try adding a colored square that grows in size behind the U.S. map. To do this, you'll add a new layer to the page, change the background color of the layer, add the layer to the timeline, and then resize the layer.

To resize a layer:

1. Click the **Draw Layer** button 🗒 on the **Common** tab of the Insert bar.

2. Draw a **50 × 50 pixel** layer at the center of the map, and then move the layer-code marker to the right of the other layer-code markers.

3. Select the new layer, and then use the Property inspector to change the background color of the layer to **#FFCC00**.

4. In the Layers panel, name the layer **BackgroundSquare** and change the *z*-index number of the layer to **0**.

5. Select the layer in the Layers panel, and then drag the layer to **frame 1** of **animation channel 3** in the Timelines panel.

6. Drag the ending keyframe of the new animation bar to **frame 100**. The ending keyframe is selected.

7. Drag the resize handles of the layer until the layer is about **20 pixels** larger than the map on every side. Changing the size of the layer in the ending keyframe will cause the layer to grow from its original size in frame 1 to its new size in frame 100 while the timeline is playing.

8. Click an empty space on the page to deselect the layer. See Figure 7-25.

Figure 7-25	TOUR DATES PAGE WITH BACKGROUND SQUARE

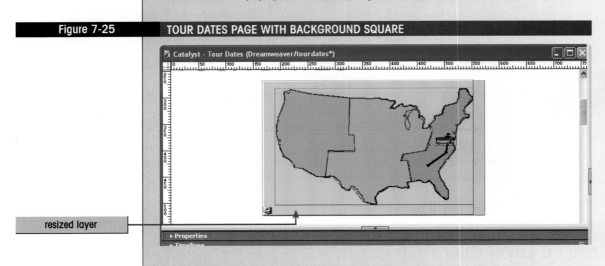

resized layer

9. Save the page, and then preview the page in a browser. The square grows from its original size in frame 1 to its ending size in frame 100, and then remains that size for the duration of the animation. Because the square is behind the other layers, you see the square growing only where another graphic is not covering it.

If you don't need an animation bar, you can delete it.

Deleting an Animation Bar

It is easy to get carried away with animation. Too much can make it difficult for a viewer to focus on the intended message. Remember to ask yourself what each element adds to the page. If you decide that you don't need a specific element, you can easily delete its animation bar.

REFERENCE   WINDOW   RW

Deleting an Animation Bar
- Select the animation bar you want to delete.
- Right-click the selected animation bar, and then click Delete.
or
- Delete the layer from the page.

After previewing the tour dates page with the growing background square, Brian and the rest of the team decide that the growing square makes the page too busy. Brian asks you to delete the background square.

To delete an animation bar from a timeline:

1. Select the **BackgroundSquare** animation bar in the Timelines panel.

2. Right-click the selected animation bar, and then click **Delete**. The BackgroundSquare animation bar is removed from the timeline, but the new layer is still in the page.

3. Select the **BackgroundSquare** layer from the Layers panel, and then press the **Delete** key. The new layer is removed from the page.

4. Save the page.

In this session, you added keyframes to an animation bar. You explored all the timeline actions, including adjusting layer stacking order, moving layers, resizing layers, and changing layer visibility. You previewed a timeline in a browser, and deleted an animation bar from the timeline. In the next session, you will add behaviors to timelines and add multiple timelines to a page.

Session 7.2 QUICK CHECK

1. Where do you input instructions for an animation?

2. What are the four layer actions that you can perform in a timeline?

3. How can you preview a timeline in a browser?

4. How do you change the stacking order of layers in a timeline?

5. True or False? Changing the dimensions of a layer will change the dimensions of an image in that layer.

6. True or False? Once you add an animation to a layer, you cannot delete it.

SESSION 7.3

In this session, you will start your timeline with a button. You will add behaviors to the timeline using the Behaviors channel. Finally, you will add multiple timelines to a Web page.

Starting a Timeline with a Button

Timelines can start when the page is loaded in a browser by using the Autoplay behavior, or they can be started by user interaction. For example, a timeline can start when a user clicks a button. Buttons are a good way to start a timeline because they enable the user to choose when the animation begins and they enable you to tie the animation to a decision. For example, you can pose a question and have the user click a button to indicate his or her answer. The animation that plays is then based on the user's selection.

You start a timeline with a button by adding a behavior to the button that triggers the timeline to begin playing. Using buttons and timelines together enables you to add interesting interactivity to Web pages because the user's choices affect what is displayed in the page. For example, you can create interactive demonstrations, drop-down menus, animated tabs, and so forth.

Brian wants you to add a button (rollover image) to the left of the U.S. map that, when clicked, will start the Sloth Child tour path animation.

First, you will add a rollover image to the page.

To add a rollover image button:

1. If you took a break after the previous session, make sure **Dreamweaver** is running, the **NewCatalyst** Web site is open, and the **tour dates** page is open.

2. Click below the TOUR DATES heading and to the left of the U.S. map in the tour dates page, and then click the **Rollover Image** button 🖼 on the **Common** tab of the Insert bar. The Insert Rollover Image dialog box opens.

3. Type **ScbusRollOver** in the Image Name text box.

4. Click the **Browse** button next to the Original Image text box, and then double-click the **SCbusButtonUp.gif** graphic in the **Tutorial.07/Tutorial** folder on your Data Disk placing a copy of the image in the Graphics folder in the root folder for your site.

5. Click the **Browse** button next to the Rollover Image text box, and then double-click the **SCbusButtonOver.gif** graphic in the **Tutorial.07/Tutorial** folder on your Data Disk placing a copy of the image in the Graphics folder in the root folder for your site.

6. Click the **Preload Rollover Image** checkbox to check it, if necessary.

7. Click the **OK** button. The ScbusRollOver button is added to the page. See Figure 7-26.

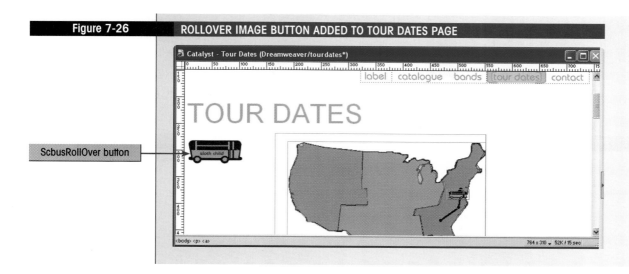

Figure 7-26   **ROLLOVER IMAGE BUTTON ADDED TO TOUR DATES PAGE**

ScbusRollOver button

Next, you will add the Play Timeline behavior to the rollover image, which will enable the user to start the timeline animation.

To add a behavior to a button:

1. Click the **ScbusRollOver** button in the Document window to select it, and then open the Behaviors panel. The Swap Image Restore and the Swap Image behaviors already appear in the Behaviors panel. Remember, these are the behaviors that are added to create the button rollover.

2. Click the **Plus** button ⊞ in the Behaviors panel, point to **Timeline**, and then click **Play Timeline** to add the Play Timeline behavior to the SCbusButtonUp.gif graphic. The Play Timeline dialog box opens. See Figure 7-27.

Figure 7-27   **PLAY TIMELINE DIALOG BOX**

Timeline1 selected

3. Verify that **Timeline1** is selected in the Play Timeline list. You must select the timeline to which the behavior will be added because you can add multiple timelines to a page and you must specify which timeline you want the button to play.

4. Click the **OK** button. The Play Timeline behavior is added to the end of the list in the Behaviors panel.

The Play Timeline behavior usually has the event set to onLoad, which would cause the timeline to play when the ScbusRollOver image is loaded into the browser. Because you want the timeline to start playing when the button is clicked instead of when the button is loaded, you'll change the event to onClick.

To change an event:

1. Make sure the **Play Timeline** behavior is selected in the Behaviors panel.

2. Click the **Events** list arrow, and then click **onClick**. The event changes to (onClick) and the behavior moves to the top of the list in the Behaviors panel. See Figure 7-28.

Figure 7-28	BEHAVIORS PANEL WITH NEW BEHAVIOR

Play Timeline behavior added to SCBusRollOver

TROUBLE? If the onClick event is not in the Events list, your list is set to show events for the wrong set of browsers. Point to Show Events For, and then click 4.0 and Later Browsers. Repeat Step 2.

3. Click the **Autoplay** checkbox on the Timelines panel toolbar to uncheck the checkbox. The Autoplay behavior is removed from the page so that the timeline will not play automatically when the page is loaded.

4. Save the page, and then preview the page in the browser.

5. Click the **Sloth Child tour bus** button to play the animation, and then close the browser window.

You have added a button to trigger the timeline. Now you will add behaviors to the timeline.

Adding **Behaviors to the Behaviors Channel**

You can add many of the behaviors from the Behaviors panel list within a timeline. Placing behaviors in a timeline enables you to make things that are not necessarily triggered by user interaction (such as a mouse click) happen over time within a Web page. You can do something simple such as reset the timeline to frame 1 after the animation has ended so that the timeline can run again. You can also do something a little more complex such as create a timed pop-up window by creating a Click To Begin button that starts a timeline with a behavior in frame 1 that makes a window open and a behavior in frame 200 that makes the window close.

You add behaviors in a timeline by selecting the desired frame in the Behaviors channel and selecting the behavior in the Behaviors panel.

REFERENCE WINDOW   **RW**

Adding Behaviors to the Behaviors Channel
- Select the frame to which you want to add the behavior in the Behaviors channel in the Timelines panel.
- Select the behavior from the behaviors list in the Behaviors panel, and then set any required parameters.

Brian asks you to add four behaviors in three frames of the timeline in the tour dates page to make the animation a little more useful. He wants you to do the following:

- In frame 1, add a Show-Hide Layers behavior, and hide all of the layers in the timeline. This will make the animation invisible in the first frame, which will be helpful when more tour paths and buttons are added to the page.
- In frame 2, add a Show Hide Layers behavior, and show the East1 and Bus layers. This will enable the user to see these layers as the animation begins. The other layers will become visible as the timeline passes the keyframes that change their visibility.
- In frame 215, add a Stop Timeline behavior and a Go To Timeline Frame 1 behavior. This will enable the completed animation to remain visible for 20 frames, and then disappear as the timeline resets to frame 1. Right now, once the button has been pressed and the timeline has run, the layers remain visible.

Adding these behaviors will end the timeline after the animation is complete and reset the timeline, enabling the user to press the button and run the animation again.

To add behaviors to frame 1 of the timeline:

1. Click in **frame 1** of the Behaviors channel in the Timelines panel.

2. Click the **Plus** button ⊞ in the Behaviors panel, and then click **Show-Hide Layers**. The Show-Hide Layers dialog box opens.

3. Click **layer "Bus"** in the Named Layers list, and then click the **Hide** button. The word "(hide)" appears beside the selected layer to indicate that this layer will be hidden in frame 1. See Figure 7-29.

| **Figure 7-29** | **SHOW-HIDE LAYERS DIALOG BOX** |

hide layer behavior
added to Bus layer

4. Repeat Step 3 to hide each of the following layers: **layer "East13", layer "East12", layer "East11", layer "East10", layer "East9", layer "East8", layer"East7", layer "East6", layer "East5", layer "East4", layer "East3",**

When you have multiple timelines in a page, all of the timelines can run at the same time, or you can use behaviors to make one timeline start another timeline and so forth. When using multiple timelines in one page, each timeline should be fairly simple so that the page will be able to run at a reasonable speed. The more movement that occurs at one time in a page, the more processing power it takes to run the animation at the desired frame rate. Too much movement can cause the user's computer to run slowly.

Brian wants you to add a tour path animation for the Surface Suction band to the tour dates page. This timeline will have an animated tour path and an animated tour bus just like the Sloth Child animation. You will create this animation in another timeline. Then, you will add a rollover image button to the page, add a behavior that starts the new timeline with the button, and add behaviors to the new timeline.

To create a second timeline:

1. Right-click a blank frame in the Timelines panel, and then click **Add Timeline** on the context menu. A second timeline is added to the tour dates page.

   You want the second timeline to be named "Timeline2."

2. If necessary, select the default timeline name in the Timelines list box, type **Timeline2**, and then press the **Enter** key. The timeline is renamed. See Figure 7-32.

Figure 7-32	TIMELINE2 IN TOUR DATES PAGE

Timeline2 selected
in Timelines list

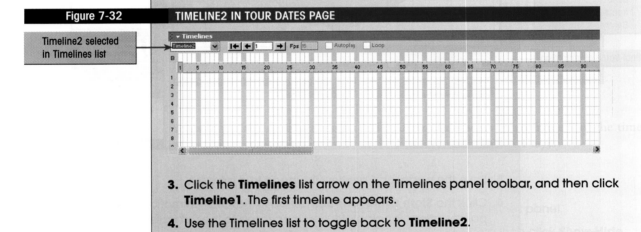

3. Click the **Timelines** list arrow on the Timelines panel toolbar, and then click **Timeline1**. The first timeline appears.

4. Use the Timelines list to toggle back to **Timeline2**.

Next, you will add layers and graphics for the tour path animation for Surface Suction to Timeline2.

To add layers to Timeline2:

1. Click the **Draw Layer** button 🔲 on the **Common** tab of the Insert bar, draw a new layer over the U.S. map, and then drag the **layer-code marker** to the left of the other layer-code markers in the page.

2. Insert the **Central1.gif** graphic from the **Tutorial.07/Tutorial** folder on your Data Disk into the new layer, placing a copy of the image in the Graphics folder in the root folder for your site. A graphic with a small black dot appears in the layers.

3. Resize the layer so that the edges of the new layer are snug against the borders of the Central1.gif graphic that you inserted in the layer.

4. In the Layers panel, name the new layer **Central1**.

5. Press and hold the **Shift** key, click the **Central1** and **East1** layers in the Layers panel, and then release the **Shift** key. The Central1 and East1 layers are selected.

6. Align the layers along their **left** borders, align the layers along their **top** borders, and then deselect the layers.

7. Select the **Central1** layer, drag the **Central1** layer to **animation channel 1** of Timeline2 in the Timelines panel (make sure that Timeline2 is selected in the Timelines list), and then click the **OK** button to close the dialog box, if necessary.

8. Repeat Steps 1 through 7 to create layers and add the following graphics, using the graphic name for the layer name and placing the animation bar for each new layer to the right of the animation bars for previously added layers in the animation channel: **Central2.gif, Central3.gif, Central4.gif, Central5.gif, Central6.gif, Central7.gif, Central8.gif, Central9.gif, Central10.gif, Central11.gif, Central12.gif, Central13.gif, Central14.gif,** and **Central15.gif**. See Figure 7-33.

Figure 7-33	LAYERS ADDED TO TIMELINE2

tour path for
Surface Suction

new layers

Now you'll add the Bus layer to animation channel 2 of Timeline2, and drag the last frame of the Bus animation bar to frame 225. Then you'll create keyframes in the Bus animation bar and animate the bus like you did in the first timeline.

To add the Bus layer to Timeline2 and animate the layer:

1. Select the **Bus** layer in the Layers panel, move the Bus over the first (southernmost) point in the Surface Suction tour path, and then drag the **Bus** layer to **channel 2** in Timeline2.

2. Drag the ending keyframe of the Bus animation bar to **frame 225**.

3. Select the first keyframe in the Bus animation bar in Timeline2, and then change the z-index number of the Bus layer to **32** in the Layers panel.

4. Select the ending keyframe in the Bus animation bar in Timeline2, and then change the *z*-index number of the Bus layer to **32** in the Layers panel. The Bus layer is now the top layer in Timeline2.

5. Select **frame 45** of the Bus animation bar, right-click the selected frame, and then click **Add Keyframe** on the context menu. A new keyframe is added to the animation bar.

6. Select the new keyframe, and then move the bus to the second point on the tour path.

7. Place a keyframe in **frames 75**, **105**, **135**, **165**, and **195** of the Bus animation bar, moving the Bus layer to the next point on the tour path at each keyframe.

8. Select the keyframe in frame 225 of the Bus animation bar, and then move the Bus layer to the final point on the tour path. See Figure 7-34.

Figure 7-34	ANIMATED BUS LAYER IN TIMELINE2

bus at final point on tour path

final frame selected in animation bar

Now that the tour path is animated, you'll add a keyframe to the second frame of each animation bar in channel 1 and then change the visibility of each layer to hide in frame 1 of the animation bar and visible in frame 2 of the animation bar.

To change the visibility in Timeline2:

1. Select **frame 2** in the Central1 animation bar, and then insert a keyframe.

2. Click the **visibility column** of the Central1 layer in the Layers panel until the **open eye** icon 👁 appears. The visibility of frame 2 of the animation bar is set to visible.

3. Select **frame 1** of the Central1 animation bar, and then click the **visibility column** of the Central1 layer in the Layers panel until the **closed eye** icon 👁 appears. The visibility of frame 1 of the animation bar is set to hidden.

4. Repeat Steps 1 through 3 to set the visibility for the following animation bars: **Central2**, **Central3**, **Central4**, **Central5**, **Central6**, **Central7**, **Central8**, **Central9**, **Central10**, **Central11**, **Central12**, **Central13**, **Central14**, and **Central15**. Now all of the animation bars will be hidden until the animation plays the second frame.

You have added the animated Surface Suction tour path to the page. Next, you will add a button to start the new timeline. You'll add a Surface Suction bus rollover image below the Sloth Child rollover image in the Document window. Then you'll add a Play Timeline behavior to the new rollover image.

To add the Play Timeline behavior to a new rollover image:

1. Click to the right of the Sloth Child rollover image in the tour dates page, and then press the **Enter** key to position the pointer below the Sloth Child button.

2. Click the **Rollover Image** button 🖼 on the **Common** tab of the Insert bar. The Insert Rollover Image dialog box opens.

3. Type **SSbusRollOver** in the Image Name text box, click the **Browse** button next to the Original Image text box, and then double-click the **SSbusButtonUp.gif** graphic in the **Tutorial.07/Tutorial** folder on your Data Disk, placing a copy of the image in the Graphics folder in the root folder for your site.

4. Click the **Browse** button next to the Rollover Image text box, and then double-click the **SSbusButtonOver.gif** graphic in the **Tutorial.07/Tutorial** folder on your Data Disk, placing a copy of the image in the Graphics folder in the root folder for your site.

5. Click the **Preload Rollover Image** checkbox to check it, if necessary, and then click the **OK** button. The SSbusRollOver button is added to the page.

Next, you will add the Play Timeline behavior to the SSbusRollOver image so that the button will trigger Timeline2 to start.

6. Click the **SSbusRollOver** graphic in the Document window to select it, and then open the Behaviors panel. The Swap Image Restore and Swap Image behaviors already appear in the Behaviors panel.

7. Click the **Plus** button ⊞ in the Behaviors panel, point to **Timeline**, and then click **Play Timeline** to add the Play Timeline behavior to the SSBusRollOver.

8. Click **Timeline2** in the Play Timeline dialog box, and then click the **OK** button. The Play Timeline behavior is added to the end of the list in the Behaviors panel.

Next, you'll change the event to onClick so that the behavior will be triggered by the event of the mouse click rather than when the SSbusRollOver graphic is loaded.

9. Verify that the **Play Timeline** behavior is selected in the Behaviors panel, click the **Events** list arrow, and then click **onClick**. The event changes to (onClick) and the Play Timeline behavior moves to the top of the list in the Behaviors panel. See Figure 7-35.

| Figure 7-35 | PLAY TIMELINE BEHAVIOR ADDED TO SURFACE SUCTION BUS ROLLOVER IMAGE |

Play Timeline
behavior added

10. Save the page, and preview the page in the browser.

Your next tasks are to add a Show-Hide Layer behavior to the first frame of Timeline2, add a Show-Hide behavior to the second frame, and then add a Stop Timeline behavior and a Go To Frame behavior to the 245th frame of Timeline2. The Show-Hide Layer behavior will hide all the layers in the first frame of the timeline and show the Bus and Central1 layers in the second frame so that the animation will be hidden until the button that triggers it is clicked. The Stop Timeline behavior prevents the timeline from continuing to play and the Go To Frame behavior returns the stopped timeline to the first frame so that it can be played again.

To add behaviors to Timeline2:

1. Click in **frame 1** of the Behaviors channel in the Timelines panel, click the **Plus** button ➕ in the Behaviors panel, and then click **Show-Hide Layers**. The Show-Hide Layers dialog box opens.

2. Select **layer "Bus"** in the Named Layers list, and then click the **Hide** button. The word "(hide)" appears beside the selected layer to indicate that that layer will be hidden in frame 1.

3. Repeat Step 2 to hide each of the following layers: **layer "Central1"**, **layer "Central2"**, **layer "Central3"**, **layer "Central4"**, **layer "Central5"**, **layer "Central6"**, **layer "Central7"**, **layer "Central8"**, **layer "Central9"**, **layer "Central10"**, **layer "Central11"**, **layer "Central12"**, **layer "Central13"**, **layer "Central14"**, and **layer "Central15"**. Do not place anything beside layer "USmap" because that layer should remain visible, and do not place anything beside the "East" layers because they will be reset by the behaviors in the other timeline.

4. Click the **OK** button to close the dialog box and add the behavior to the frame.

   Next, you will add a Show-Hide Layers behavior to frame 2 of the timeline.

5. Click in **frame 2** of the Behaviors channel in the Timelines panel, click ⊞ in the Behaviors panel, and then click **Show-Hide Layers**. The Show-Hide Layers dialog box opens.

6. In the Show-Hide Layers dialog box, show **layer "Bus"** and **layer "Central1"**, and then click the **OK** button. The Show-Hide Layers behavior is added to the second frame of the timeline.

   Next, you'll add the Stop behavior and the Go To Frame behavior to the 245th frame of the timeline.

7. Click in **frame 245** of the timeline in the Behaviors channel, click ⊞ in the Behaviors panel, point to **Timeline**, and then click **Stop Timeline**.

8. In the Stop Timeline dialog box, select **Timeline2** from the list, and then click the **OK** button. The Stop Timeline behavior is added to the frame.

9. Click ⊞ in the Behaviors panel, point to **Timeline**, and then click **Go To Timeline Frame**.

10. Type **1** in the Go to Frame text box if necessary, and then click the **OK** button. The Go to Frame behavior is added to the frame. This will reset the timeline to frame 1 after the animation ends.

Before you finish, you'll save the page and then preview it in the browser. Testing the page ensures that both of the tour bus buttons work. The Sloth Child tour bus button will trigger Timeline1 and the Surface Suction tour bus button will trigger Timeline2.

To preview and test the animation:

1. Save the page, and preview the page in a browser.

2. Click the **Sloth Child tour bus** button. The Timeline1 animation plays.

3. Click the **Surface Suction tour bus** button. The Timeline2 animation plays. See Figure 7-36.

Figure 7-36	TIMELINE1 AND TIMELINE2 IN TOUR DATES PAGE

buttons to start animations

both timelines reset to frame 1 when finished

4. Close the browser window.

Now that the second timeline for the tour dates pages is finished, you will upload the Catalyst site to the remote server.

Updating the Web Site on the Remote Server

As a final review of the changes you made to the tour dates page, you'll update the files for the NewCatalyst site on the remote server and review the page over the Internet. You need to upload the tour dates page and include dependent files so that the new graphics are uploaded to the remote server. Then you'll preview the site on the Web.

To upload a site to the remote server:

1. Click the **Connects to remote host** button on the Site panel toolbar.

2. Click the **View** list arrow on the Site panel toolbar, and then click **Local View**.

3. Click **tourdates.htm** in Local view to select the file, and then click the **Put File(s)** button on the Site panel toolbar.

4. Click the **Yes** button when asked if you want to include dependent files because you have not selected the new dependent files for the site yet.

5. Click the **Disconnects from remote host** button on the Site panel toolbar.

6. Click the **View** list arrow on the Site panel toolbar, and then click **Local View**. The Site panel returns to the local view.

Next, you'll preview the updated site in a browser. The site will include all of the new elements that you added to your local version.

To preview the updated site in a browser:

1. Open a browser, type the URL of your remote site into the Address text box on the browser toolbar, and then press the **Enter** key.

2. Explore the **tour dates** page on the remote site from within the browser.

3. Click the **Sloth Child tour bus** button and view the animation.

4. Click the **Surface Suction tour bus** button and view the animation.

5. Close both browser windows, and then close the page in the NewCatalyst site.

In this tutorial you created animations in the tour dates page that show the tour path for two of the Catalyst bands—Sloth Child and Surface Suction.

Session 7.3 QUICK | CHECK

1. What behavior do you add to a rollover image to start a timeline?

2. Where are behaviors added in the timeline?

3. List one benefit of using behaviors in a timeline.

4. List one benefit of using multiple timelines in a page.

5. How do you toggle between timelines?

6. Why is it a good idea to test pages that contain timelines on a variety of computers?

REVIEW ASSIGNMENTS

Brian asks you to create a timeline for the Dizzied Connections tour path on the tour dates page of the Catalyst site. The band is touring the West Coast. Like the timelines for Sloth Child and Surface Suction, the timeline for Dizzied Connections will have an animated tour bus that follows the tour path. You will add a rollover image for the band, add a Play Timeline behavior to the rollover image, and then add the needed behaviors to the new timeline. Some of the Dizzied Connections tour dates are with the Life in Minor Chords band; however, this will not affect the tour path because Life in Minor Chords will have its own animated tour path added to the page as soon as its tour schedule is finalized.

1. Start Dreamweaver, open the NewCatalyst Web site, and then open the tour dates page.

2. Right-click in a blank frame in the Timelines panel to open the context menu, and then click Add Timeline. A third timeline is added to the tour dates page.

3. Name the new timeline "Timeline3" in the Timelines panel, if necessary.

4. Click the Draw Layers button on the Common tab of the Insert bar, draw a new layer over the U.S. map, and then drag the layer-code marker to the left of the other layer-code markers in the page.

5. Insert the **Dizzied1.gif** graphic from the **Tutorial.07/Review** folder on your Data Disk into the new layer, placing a copy of the image in the Graphics folder in the root folder for your site.

6. Resize the layer so that the edges of the new layer are snug against the borders of the graphic in the layer.

7. Rename the layer "Dizzied1" in the Layers panel.

8. Press and hold the Shift key, select the Dizzied1 and East1 layers in the Layers panel, and then release the Shift key to align the new layer with the existing layers.

9. Use the Modify menu to align the selected layers along their left and top borders. Deselect the layers.

Explore

10. Select the Dizzied1 layer, and then drag the Dizzied1 layer to animation channel 1 in the Timelines panel. (*Hint:* Make sure that Timeline3 is selected in the Timelines list.)

11. Repeat Steps 3 through 10 to create layers and add the following graphics, using the graphic name for the layer name and placing the animation bar for each new layer to the right of the animation bars for previously added layers in the animation channel: Dizzied2.gif, Dizzied3.gif, Dizzied4.gif, Dizzied5.gif, Dizzied6.gif, Dizzied7.gif, Dizzied8.gif, Dizzied9.gif, Dizzied10.gif, Dizzied11.gif, and Dizzied12.gif.

12. Select the Bus layer in the Layers panel, move the Bus layer over the first point in the Dizzied Connections tour path, and then drag the layer to animation channel 2 in Timeline3.

13. Drag the ending keyframe of the Bus animation bar to frame 180.

14. Select the beginning keyframe in the Bus animation bar in Timeline3, and then change the z-index number of the Bus layer to 45 in the Layers panel.

15. Select the ending keyframe in the Bus animation bar in Timeline3, and then change the z-index number of the Bus layer to 45 in the Layers panel. The Bus layer is now the top layer in Timeline3.

16. Select frame 45 of the Bus animation bar, right-click the selected frame, and then click Add Keyframe to add a new keyframe.

17. Select the new keyframe, and then move the Bus layer to the second point on the tour path.

18. Place a keyframe in frames 75, 105, 135, 165, and 180 of the Bus animation bar, moving the Bus layer to the next point on the tour path at each keyframe.

19. Select frame 2 of the Dizzied1 animation bar, insert a keyframe, and then in the Layers panel, set the visibility of the Dizzied1 layer to visible by clicking in the visibility column until the open eye icon appears.

20. Select frame 1 of the Dizzied1 animation bar, and then change the visibility to hidden in the Layers panel by clicking in the visibility column until the closed eye icon is visible.

21. Repeat Steps 19 and 20 for the following animation bars: Dizzied2, Dizzied3, Dizzied4, Dizzied5, Dizzied6, Dizzied7, Dizzied8, Dizzied9, Dizzied10, Dizzied11, and Dizzied12.

22. Click to the right of the Surface Suction rollover image in the tourdates.htm page, press the Enter key to move to the next line, and then click the Rollover Image button on the Common tab of the Insert bar to open the Insert Rollover Image dialog box.

23. Type "DCbusRollOver" in the Image Name text box, click the Browse button next to the Original Image text box, double-click the **DCbusButtonUp.gif** graphic in the **Tutorial.07/Review** folder on your Data Disk, click the Browse button next to the Rollover Image text box, double-click the **DCbusButtonOver.gif** graphic in the

Tutorial.07/Review folder on your Data Disk, check the Preload Rollover Image checkbox if necessary, and then click the OK button. Place copies of the images in the Graphics folder in the root folder for your site. The DCbusRollOver button is added to the page.

24. Click the DCbusRollOver graphic in the Document window to select it, and then open the Behaviors panel. The Swap Image Restore and the Swap Image behaviors already appear in the Behaviors panel.

Explore

25. Click the Plus button in the Behaviors panel, point to Timeline, and then click Play Timeline to add the Play Timeline behavior to the DCBusRollOver, select Timeline3 from the Play Timeline dialog box, and then click the OK button. The behavior is added to the end of the list in the Behaviors panel.

26. While the Play Timeline behavior is selected in the Behaviors panel, click the Events list arrow, and then click onClick. The event changes to (onClick), and the behavior moves to the top of the list in the Behaviors panel.

27. Click in frame 1 of the Behaviors channel in the Timelines panel, click the Plus button in the Behaviors panel, and then click Show-Hide Layers.

28. In the Show-Hide Layers dialog box, select layer "Bus" in the Named Layers list, and then click the Hide button. The layer will be hidden in frame 1.

29. Hide each of the following: layer "Dizzied1", layer "Dizzied2", layer "Dizzied3", layer "Dizzied4", layer "Dizzied5", layer "Dizzied6", layer "Dizzied7", layer "Dizzied8", layer "Dizzied9", layer "Dizzied10", layer "Dizzied11", and layer "Dizzied12". (*Hint:* Do not place anything beside layer "USmap" because that layer should remain visible, and do not place anything beside layer "East" or layer "Central" because they will be reset by the behaviors in the other timelines.)

30. Click the OK button to close the dialog box and add the behavior to the frame.

31. Click in frame 2 of the Behaviors channel in the Timelines panel, click the Plus button in the Behaviors panel, and then click Show-Hide Layers.

32. In the Show-Hide Layers dialog box, select layer "Bus" from the Named Layers list, click the Show button, select layer "Dizzied1", click the Show button, and then click the OK button. The Show-Hide Layers behavior is added to the second frame of the timeline.

33. Click in frame 200 of the timeline in the Behaviors channel, click the Plus button in the Behaviors panel, point to Timeline, and then click Stop Timelines.

34. In the Stop Timeline dialog box, select Timeline3 from the list, and then click the OK button. The Stop Timeline behavior is added to the frame.

35. Click the Plus button in the Behaviors panel, point to Timeline, and then click Go To Timeline Frame.

36. Type "1" in the Go to Frame text box if necessary, and then click the OK button. The Go To Frame behavior is added to the frame, which will reset the timeline to frame 1 after the animation is completed.

37. Save the page, preview the page in a browser, test the animation, and then close the browser window.

38. Upload the page to the remote server, view the page over the Web, and then close the page.

CASE PROBLEMS

Case 1. Hroch University Anthropology Department Professor Hart wants you to animate the New Courses button on the home page of the site to draw attention to the new, featured courses. You will create a timeline with a layer containing the original HrochNewCourse.gif (already in the page) in channel 1. Then you will create a new layer containing the HrochNewCourse2.gif, which is a copy of the graphic with the white circle turned off, and you will move that layer to channel 2 of the timeline. You will add keyframes and change the visibility of the layers so that the white circle appears to be flashing, and then you will add the Autoplay behavior to the page. You will add a Loop behavior to frame 10, and a Stop Timeline behavior to frame 11; then you will add a Go To Timeline frame 11 behavior onMouseOver, and a Go To Timeline frame 1 behavior onMouseOut to the HrochNewCourse.gif and the HrochNewCourse2.gif graphics. This will create a New Courses button with a blinking white border that (1) when moused over, stops blinking but retains the white border, (2) when clicked, opens the New Courses page, and (3) when moused out, begins blinking again.

1. Open the Hart site that you modified in Tutorial 6, Case 1, and then open the home page.

2. Select Layer1 in the Layers panel, and then change the name of the layer to "NCwithRing."

3. Draw a new layer on top of the NCwithRing layer, insert the **HrochNewCourse2.gif** graphic from the **Tutorial.07/Cases** folder on your Data Disk, placing a copy of the image in the Graphics folder in the root folder for your site, and then resize the layer to fit snugly around the graphic.

4. Name the new layer "NCplain."

5. Select the NCplain and NCwithRing layers, and then align the top and left of the layers so that they are stacked. (*Hint:* Use the Shift key to select the layers.)

6. Add the NCwithRing layer to animation channel 1 of the timeline, and then drag the ending keyframe so that the animation bar is 11 frames long.

7. Add the NCplain layer to animation channel 2 of the timeline, and then drag the animation bar to the right so that the first frame is on frame 4 of the timeline and drag the ending keyframe so that the animation bar ends on frame 10 of the timeline.

8. Select the NCplain animation bar, and then add a new keyframe in the second frame of the animation bar.

9. Set the visibility of the first and last keyframes to hidden, and verify that the visibility of the second keyframe is visible.

10. Check the Autoplay checkbox, and then click in the Behaviors channel in frame 10.

Explore   11. In the Behaviors panel, add a Go To Timeline Frame behavior. Type "1" in the Go to Frame text box in the Go To Timeline Frame dialog box, and then click the OK button. This behavior will cause the timeline to loop to the first frame each time the timeline reaches the 10th frame.

12. Click in the Behaviors channel in frame 11, and then, in the Behaviors panel, add a Stop Timeline behavior for Timeline1. If the timeline goes to frame 11, it will stop and remain on frame 11.

Explore   13. Select the HrochNewCourse2.gif graphic in the Document window, and then, in the Behaviors panel, add the Go To Timeline Frame behavior to the graphic.

Explore   14. In the Go To Timeline Frame dialog box, type "11" in the Go To Frame text box, and then click the OK button.

Explore ▸ 15. Click the Events list arrow, and then click onMouseOver. This will cause the timeline to go to frame 11 and stop when the user mouses over the graphic, causing the blinking white circle to stop while the user has the mouse over the graphic. (*Hint:* If you don't see the onMouseOver event, then you may need to change the event settings for 4.0 and later browsers.)

16. Select the HrochNewCourse2.gif graphic in the Document window, and then, in the Behaviors panel, add the Go To Timeline Frame behavior.

17. In the Go To Timeline Frame dialog box, type "1" in the Go To Frame text box, and then click the OK button.

Explore ▸ 18. Click the Events list arrow, and then click onMouseOut. When the user moves the mouse away from the graphic, the timeline will go to frame 1 and play, causing the button to resume blinking. (*Hint:* If you don't see the onMouseOut event, then you may need to change the event settings for 4.0 and later browsers.)

19. Save the page, and preview the page in a browser.

Explore ▸ 20. Mouse over the button you added, and then click the button. Because the HrochNew Courses.gif was already linked, and because it is the graphic that is showing when the mouse is over the graphic, the button opens the new courses page when you click it.

21. Close the browser.

22. Upload the page to the remote server, and then preview the page over the Web.

Case 2. Museum of Western Art C. J. Strittmatter asks you to add a slide show of paintings to the home page of the Museum site. To create the slide show, you will create new layers and add a graphic of a painting to each new layer. You will name the layers, align the layers, and then add each layer to a channel in the timeline. Finally, you will view the new slide show animation in a browser.

1. Open the Museum site that you modified in Tutorial 6, Case 2, and then open the home page.

2. Set the window size to 760 × 420, if necessary. (*Hint:* Click the Window size button on the status bar, and then click 760 × 420 from the list.) Because all the elements in your page are right or left aligned, they should shift to fill the page.

Explore ▸ 3. Draw a layer in the page below the heading, select the body text for the page (not the heading text), drag the selected body text to the layer, and then move the layer-code marker to the right of the logo.

4. Name the layer "Text," move the Text layer so that its top border is positioned at 190 pixels (below the Welcome text) and its left border is positioned at 200 pixels, and then drag its right border even with the right border of the table that holds the navigation bar.

5. Draw a new layer in the empty space at the left of the page, move the layer-code marker to the right of the previous layer-code marker, and then name the new layer "Background."

6. Insert the **SlideShowBG.gif** graphic from the **Tutorial.07/Cases** folder on your Data Disk, placing a copy of the image in the Graphics folder in the root folder for your site, and then drag the borders of the layer to fit snugly around the edges of the graphic.

7. Select the Background layer and reposition it 10 pixels below the horizontal rule and 15 pixels from the left edge of the page.

8. Draw a new layer over the Background layer, name the layer "Painting1," and then insert the **AFigureOfTheNight.jpg** graphic from the Graphics folder in your root folder.

9. Resize the Painting1 layer so that the borders fit snugly against the edges of the graphic, and then move the new layer-code marker to the right of the others.

10. Select the AFigureOfTheNight.jpg graphic, link it to the Art.htm page, and then set the border to 2 in the Property inspector.

11. Repeat Steps 8 through 10 for the following graphics, naming each layer with a later number, such asPainting2, Painting3, and so forth: BuffaloRunners.jpg, TheCowPuncher.jpg, AQuietDayInUtica.jpg, CowpunchingSometimes.jpg, DeerInForest.jpg, IndiansHunting Buffalo.jpg, and TheBucker.jpg.

12. Select all of the Painting layers in the Layers panel, align the left borders, and then use the Left Arrow and Right Arrow keys to move the paintings so that they are centered horizontally inside the Background graphic.

13. Select Painting1, and then center the layer vertically within the Background layer. (*Hint:* Use only the Up Arrow and Down Arrow keys so that you do not change the horizontal alignment of the layer.)

14. Repeat Step 13 for the following layers: Painting2, Painting3, Painting4, Painting5, Painting6, Painting7, and Painting8.

15. Close the Property inspector and open the Timelines panel.

16. Select the Painting8 layer in the Layers panel, and drag it so that the first frame of the animation bar is positioned in the first frame of channel 1.

Explore 17. Select the Painting7 layer and drag it so that the first frame of the animation bar is positioned in frame 14 of animation channel 2. The animation bars overlap by two frames.

18. Select the following Painting layers and drag them to the following positions in the timeline:

LAYER	CHANNEL	BEGINNING FRAME
Painting6	Channel 3	27
Painting5	Channel 4	40
Painting4	Channel 5	53
Painting3	Channel 6	66
Painting2	Channel 7	79
Painting1	Channel 8	92

19. Add keyframes to the second frame of the following animation bars: Painting7, Painting6, Painting5, Painting4, Painting3, Painting2, and Painting1.

Explore 20. Use the Layers panel to set the following visibilities:

ANIMATION BAR	FIRST KEYFRAME	SECOND KEYFRAME	LAST KEYFRAME
Painting8	Visible		Hidden
Painting7	Hidden	Visible	Hidden
Painting6	Hidden	Visible	Hidden
Painting5	Hidden	Visible	Hidden
Painting4	Hidden	Visible	Hidden
Painting3	Hidden	Visible	Hidden

ANIMATION BAR	FIRST KEYFRAME	SECOND KEYFRAME	LAST KEYFRAME
Painting2	Hidden	Visible	Hidden
Painting1	Hidden	Visible	Hidden

Staggering the layer position in the timeline, and then hiding and revealing the layers sequentially, will create an animation that looks like a slide show.

21. Check the Autoplay checkbox and the Loop checkbox.

22. Save the page, and preview the page in a browser window. (*Hint:* If the animation is jerky where it loops, the loop behavior was added to frame 107 in the Behaviors channel. Drag the behavior to frame 106 in the Behaviors channel and preview the page again.)

23. Upload the site to the remote server, and view the site over the Web.

Case 3. NORM Mark Chapman asks you to replace the current link to the Featured Book page with a new animated link. The top text will blink once the page is loaded. When the user mouses over the book cover graphic, a yellow panel will slide out and text will appear. When the text, slide out tab, or book cover are clicked, the user will jump to the FeaturedFrameset.htm page. You will accomplish this by creating two timelines. The TextBlink timeline will make the Featured Book text blink, and the SlideOutTab timeline will control the slide out tab.

1. Open the NORM site that you modified in Tutorial 6, Case 3, and then open the home page.

2. Select 720 × 420 from the Window Size list on the status bar.

Explore

3. Click View on the menu bar, point to Visual Aids, and then click Invisible Elements to uncheck the option. This will prevent the layer-code markers from being visible in the Document window when you add layers to the page. When the layer-code markers shift the content in the Document window and prevent you from viewing the page as it will be seen in a browser, it is sometimes helpful to turn them off.

4. Draw a layer, select the Featured Book text and drag it to the new layer, and then apply the NormSubHeadings CSS Style to the text.

5. Resize the layer so that the text fills one line, name the layer "FeaturedText," and then move the layer so that the top border is at 100 pixels and the right border is at 725 pixels.

6. Select the Featured Book text, and then link the text to the FeaturedFrameset.htm page, if necessary.

7. Draw a new layer, name the layer "BookCover," drag the BookCoverPunchSmall.jpg graphic to the layer, and then move the layer so that it is centered horizontally below the Featured Text text.

8. Select the BookCoverPunchSmall.jpg graphic, and then, in the Property inspector, change the border to 2 and link the book cover to the FeaturedFrameSet.htm page, if necessary.

9. Place the pointer before the NEWS subheading, and then press the Enter key to move down the rest of the text on the page.

10. Create a new layer that is the height of the book cover and 10 pixels in width, name the layer "YellowTab," and then drag the layer to the bottom of the list in the Layers panel so that it becomes #1 in the stacking order.

11. Align the layer to the top and left of the BookCover layer.

12. Change the background color of the YellowTab layer to #CC9933 in the Property inspector.

13. Draw another layer to the left of the BookCover layer, type "Click here to learn more about this amazing new book by Kelly More" in the layer, and then adjust the height and width of the layer so that the layer is the same height as the BookCover and all of the text is visible.

14. Name the layer "TabText," and then drag the layer down in the Layers panel until it is directly above YellowTab.

Explore

15. Open the Timelines panel, and then change the name of the timeline to "FeaturedText."

16. Drag the FeaturedText layer to frame 1 of animation channel 1 in the timeline, and then drag the animation bar to the left so that the bar is 10 frames long.

17. Add a new keyframe at frame 5 of the animation bar, and then set the visibility of the layer to hidden in the new keyframe.

18. Check the Autoplay and Loop checkboxes.

19. Save the page, preview the page in a browser to view the blinking Featured Text animation, and then close the browser.

20. Add a new timeline, name the timeline "SlideOutTab," and then drag the YellowTab layer to frame 1 of animation channel 1 in the timeline.

21. Select the ending frame of the YellowTab animation bar, and then set the width of the layer to 90 pixels in the Property inspector.

22. Use the right arrow to move the YellowTab layer to the right until the left border of the YellowTab is against the right border of the BookCover.

23. Drag the TabText layer to frame 14 of channel 2 in the SlideOutTab timeline, and then drag the ending keyframe of the animation bar to frame 15 of channel 2.

24. Select the keyframe in frame 14 of channel 2, and then change the visibility to hidden.

25. Select the keyframe in frame 15 of animation channel 2, and change the visibility to visible.

26. Select the BookCoverPunchSmall.jpg graphic, and then add the Play Timeline behavior, selecting SlideOutTab from the timeline list in the Play Timeline dialog box, and selecting onMouseOver as the event, if necessary.

27. Save the page, and preview the page in a browser.

28. Upload the site to the remote server, and view the site over the Web.

Case 4. Sushi Ya-Ya Mary O'Brien asks you to delete the old Wasabi graphic on the Sushi Ya-Ya home page and replace it with an animated graphic that links to the Wasabi.htm page. You will create a timeline to animate a tab that moves out when the Wasabi graphic is moused over. Then you will create a second timeline that causes the tab text to blink.

1. Open the SushiYaYa site that you modified in Tutorial 6, Case 4, open the home page, and then change the Window size to 720 × 420.

2. Select and delete the WasabiHowHot layer, including the graphic and the text.

3. Create a new layer to the left of the heading, name the layer "Wasabi," and then insert the **Wasabi2.gif** graphic from the **Tutorial.07/Cases** folder on your Data Disk, placing a copy of the image in the Graphics folder in the root folder for your site.

4. Position the Wasabi layer so that the top border is 10 pixels below the horizontal rule and the left border is 10 pixels from the edge of the page.

5. Create a second layer the width of the Wasabi layer and 10 pixels in height, name the layer "Tab," and then change the background color for the Tab layer to #6666FF.

6. Align the Tab layer so that the bottom and left borders are even with the Wasabi layer's bottom and left borders.

7. Drag the Tab layer to the bottom of the list in the Layers panel to change its stacking order.

Explore   8. Open the Timelines panel, change the timeline name to "Tab," and then drag the Tab layer to the first frame of channel 1.

9. Add a keyframe in frame 8 of the Tab timeline, select the new keyframe, move the Tab layer so that its top border is flush with the bottom border of the Wasabi layer, and then change the Tab layer height to 27 pixels.

10. Select the last keyframe in the Tab animation bar, move the Tab layer so that its top border is flush with the bottom border of the Wasabi layer, change the Tab layer height to 27 pixels, and then drag the right border of the Tab layer until its width is 236 pixels.

11. Draw a new layer over the extended Tab layer, and then name the new layer "TabText."

12. Type "How Hot is Wasabi??" in the new TabText layer, select the text, apply the sub-headings style, and then link the text to the Wasabi.htm page, targeting the link to open in a new window.

13. Drag the TabText layer to center the text over the extended Tab layer.

14. Create a new timeline, name the timeline "TabText," and then drag the TabText layer to the first frame of channel 1.

15. Drag the ending keyframe of the TabText animation bar to frame 10, create a new keyframe in frame 5, change the visibility of the layer to hidden in the first frame and to visible in the fifth frame, and then check the Loop checkbox.

16. Select the Tab timeline from the Timelines list, click in the Behaviors channel in frame 10, insert a Play Timeline behavior from the Behaviors panel, and then select TabText from the Timelines list in the Play Timeline dialog box.

Explore   17. Select the Wasabi2.gif graphic, link the graphic to the Wasabi.htm page and target the link to _blank. Then insert the Play Timeline behavior, and select the Tab timeline from the list in the Play Timeline dialog box.

18. Save the page, and preview the page in a browser.

19. Upload the page to the remote server, and view the site over the Web.

QUICK | CHECK ANSWERS

Session 7.1

1. a series of graphics or images that appear to move over a period of time
2. move, show/hide, resize, and change stacking order (or z-index)
3. frames
4. 15 frames per second
5. keyframes
6. makes the animation run over more frames, which slows the animation and makes the movement more fluid

Session 7.2

1. in the keyframes
2. Show-Hide Layer, Move Layer, Change Stacking Order (or *z*-index number), Resize Layer
3. check the Autoplay checkbox or attach a Play Timeline behavior to a button to play a timeline in a browser
4. Select a keyframe in the timeline, and then type a different *z*-index number in the Z column of the Layers panel.
5. False
6. False

Session 7.3

1. the Start Timeline behavior
2. in the behaviors channel and in keyframes
3. You can make things that are not triggered by user interaction happen over time, such as reset the timeline to frame 1 after the animation ended so the timeline can run again.
4. You can control the animations separately. For example, you can use the Start Timeline behavior attached to a button to play one of the timelines.
5. by selecting a timeline with the Timelines list on the Timelines panel toolbar
6. to get an idea of the average speed at which the timeline will run, because timelines run at different speeds on different computers

ADDING RICH MEDIA TO A WEB SITE

Adding Flash, Shockwave, Sound, and Video Elements to the Catalyst Site

CASE

Catalyst

Sara has gotten great response from the animation that you added to the tour dates page. She has received several complimentary e-mail messages about the animation and heard positive comments from quite a few fans at local shows. Now she wants to incorporate rich media elements into the site.

You will replace the current What's Hot section in the home page with a Flash movie that links to the what's hot page. The Flash movie will draw attention to the new Catalyst products. Some other team members are creating a Shockwave game, which will be added to the bands page. Brian wants you to add a Shockwave promo for the game in the spot that the game will eventually occupy. Also, you'll add some audio samples and some video clips to the catalogue page so that users can get a chance to hear and see the bands.

To add Flash text to Web pages:

1. Open the **bands.htm** page, select the **CATALYST BANDS** heading, and then press the **Delete** key to delete the text from the page.

2. Click the **Flash Text** button on the **Media** tab of the Insert bar to open the Insert Flash Text dialog box.

3. Select **Bauhaus Md BT** from the Font list, type **55** in the Size text box, type **#FF9900** in the Color text box, and then type **CATALYST BANDS** in the Text box.

   TROUBLE? If you do not have the Bauhaus Md BT font, use Arial or choose a font that is similar to the font in the Catalyst logo. It may be necessary to select a different size as well.

4. Click the **Browse** button next to the Save As text box. The Select File dialog box opens.

5. Browse to the **Media** folder in your root folder, type **HeadingBands.swf** in the File name text box, and then click the **Save** button. The Select File dialog box closes and Media/HeadingBands.swf appears in the Save As text box. See Figure 8-8.

Figure 8-8	INSERT FLASH TEXT DIALOG BOX

6. Click the **OK** button. The Flash text appears in the bands page. Notice that the text has some artifacts (it is a bit jagged). See Figure 8-9.

Figure 8-9 BANDS PAGE WITH FLASH TEXT

Flash text in page

7. Save the page, and preview the page in a browser. Notice that the text no longer has any artifacts (it is smooth). See Figure 8-10.

Figure 8-10 FLASH TEXT IN BROWSER

text does not have artifacts

8. Close the browser, and close the page.

9. Repeat Steps 1 through 8 to add Flash text with the page name on the following pages: **catalogue.htm**, **contact.htm**, **label.htm**, and **tourdates.htm**.

Another way to use Flash in a Web page is to add Flash buttons.

Using Flash Buttons

Dreamweaver includes a set of predesigned, customizable Flash buttons that you can use in Web pages to add motion and excitement. You add Flash buttons to a site with the Flash Button button located on the Media tab of the Insert bar. In the Insert Flash Button dialog box, you can select a button style from the Style list. After you select a style, you can view the various states of the button in the Sample box. Move the pointer over a button in the Sample box to view the Over state and click the button in the Sample box to view the Down state. Once you have selected a button style, you can add text to the button, select a font and font size, add a link, select a target, and add a background color for the button. The Sample box will not show changes to text, but the changes will appear in the Document window once you have added the button to the page. You can also download additional Flash button styles from the Macromedia Web site by clicking the Get More Styles button in the Insert Flash Button dialog box.

There are a few downsides to adding Flash buttons to a Web site. Buttons enable the user to navigate through the site; however, users who do not have the Flash Player will not be able to navigate through the pages of the site. Also, Flash buttons are templates, which means that the same buttons will appear on many sites. If you choose to use a Flash button, your site will look more generic and less like an original, professionally designed site.

Brian asks you to review the available Flash button styles and see whether any are suitable for the Catalyst site.

To review Flash button styles:

1. Open the **home page** of the Catalyst site, and then click the **Flash Button** button on the **Media** tab of the Insert bar. The Insert Flash Button dialog box opens with the first button style selected. See Figure 8-11.

Figure 8-11   INSERT FLASH BUTTON DIALOG BOX

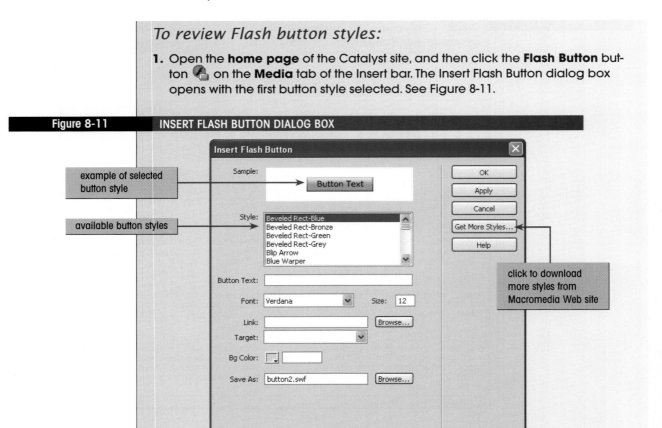

example of selected button style

available button styles

click to download more styles from Macromedia Web site

2. Click the second button style in the Style list, and then view the button in the Sample box.

3. Move the pointer over the button in the Sample box, and then click the button. The button changes states.

4. Review the remaining styles in the list.

5. Click the **Cancel** button to close the dialog box without adding a Flash button.

6. Close the page.

None of the button styles seem appropriate for the Catalyst site. To keep the site unique, you won't add any Flash buttons to the text.

In this session, you learned about the different media you can add to a site. Then, you added a Flash movie and Flash text to the Catalyst site and reviewed the available Flash buttons. In the next session, you'll add a Shockwave movie and sound to the Catalyst site.

Session 8.1 QUICK CHECK

1. What is media?

2. What will a user need to view media in a browser?

3. What is the file extension for Flash movies that you place in Web pages?

4. True or False? The Flash Player in is included with the latest versions of Internet Explorer and Netscape Navigator.

5. True or False? You can create Flash text in Dreamweaver only if you have the Flash program installed on your computer.

6. True or False? You can create customizable Flash buttons in Dreamweaver.

SESSION 8.2

In this session, you will add a Shockwave movie to a Web page. Then, you will add sound to a Web page. You will use a Flash movie to add sound to a page, and you will use a button to play sound. Finally, you will add an MP3 file to a Web page.

Understanding Shockwave

Shockwave is the Macromedia solution for delivering interactive multimedia on the Web. You use Shockwave for more complex interactive media components, such as games, interactive 3D, database driven multimedia, multi-user applications, and educational materials.

Unlike Flash files which are created in the Flash program, Shockwave files are created in Macromedia Director. **Director** is a program that is used to create comprehensive multimedia solutions deployable across multiple mediums, including CD-ROM, DVD, Web, Kiosk, and so forth. Most interactive CDs are produced in Director.

Several file extensions are associated with Director, including:

■ **.dcr (Shockwave).** A compressed file that is viewable in a browser and can be previewed in Dreamweaver. You'll use .dcr files in the Catalyst site for Shockwave movies.

- **.dir.** The source files used by Director when you are creating movies. These authoring files can be opened in Director. Unlike Flash authoring files, .dir files can be called by Director projectors for playback. (**Director projectors** are standalone executable files that do not need any software or plug-ins to run on the client computer.) Files that are going to be viewed on the Web are usually exported from Director as .dcr files.

- **.dxr.** Director files that are locked for distribution. **Locked** files cannot be opened in the authoring environment. Usually, .dxr files are used with Director projectors to deliver material via CD.

- **.cst.** Files that contain additional information used in a .dir or .dxr file.

- **.cxt.** .cst files that are locked for distribution.

Although Flash and Shockwave files are often used in similar ways, there are some marked differences between them. Because Director movies are pre-rendered, Shockwave files are less dependent on the processing speed of the user's machine for playback speed than Flash files, which are rendered on the client machine. For this same reason, the file size of a Flash movie with vector-graphics is usually smaller than the file size of a Director movie with the same content. Shockwave movies tend to process complex coding faster than Flash movies. Shockwave movies can display a wider range of media formats; for example, all Flash video is converted to the Sorenson Spark codec (.flv video files) format, while Shockwave can display video in a wide range of native formats. Finally, the Shockwave Player must be installed on the client machine for Shockwave movies to be displayed. Unlike the Flash Player plug-in, the Shockwave Player is not generally distributed with current browsers and must be downloaded separately by the end user.

Some positive and negative aspects of using Shockwave are listed in Figure 8-12.

Figure 8-12	PROS AND CONS OF USING DIRECTOR
PROS	**CONS**
Shockwave files are less dependent on the processing speed of the client computer for playback speed.	As of September 2002, only 62.6% of users have the Shockwave Player plug-in (or 62.6% browser penetration).
Shockwave movies tend to process complex code faster than Flash movies.	The Shockwave Player is not included with the latest versions of Internet Explorer and Netscape Navigator, and must be downloaded by the end user.
Shockwave movies can display a wide range of media formats.	Shockwave file size may be larger than Flash files because the Shockwave files are pre-rendered.
Shockwave movies will look the same across browsers and across platforms.	
Any fonts can be used within a Shockwave movie because Shockwave is not dependent on the fonts on the client computer.	

You can find additional information and statistics about the pros and cons of using Shockwave on the Macromedia site at *www.macromedia.com/software/player_census/shockwaveplayer*. The Macromedia Web site also provides a Flash and Director comparison (located at *www.macromedia.com/software/director/resources/integration*) and a Shockwave/Flash movie comparison (located at *www.macromedia.com/software/director/resources/integration/flash*).

Brian asks you to research the integration of Shockwave elements into the Catalyst site. You will go to the Macromedia site and review the current Shockwave information and statistics. Then you will review the Shockwave/Flash comparisons.

To research Shockwave:

1. Open a browser window, type **www.macromedia.com/software/
player_census/shockwaveplayer** in the Address text box, and then press the
Enter key. The Macromedia Director Shockwave Player page appears in the
browser window. See Figure 8-13.

Figure 8-13	MACROMEDIA DIRECTOR SHOCKWAVE PLAYER PAGE

2. Click the **Penetration** link to view penetration statistics for the Shockwave
Player. See Figure 8-14.

| Figure 8-14 | SHOCKWAVE PLAYER PENETRATION STATISTICS |

browser penetration statistics

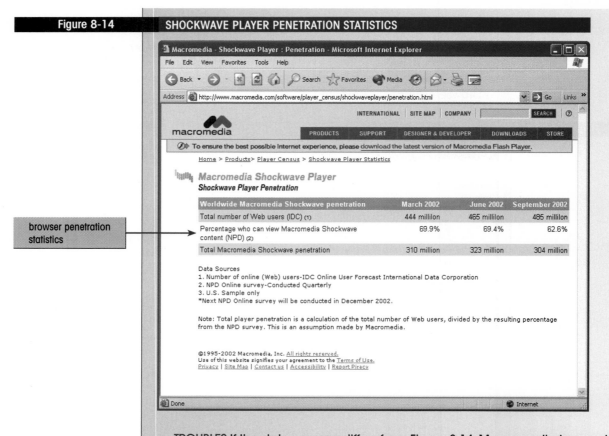

TROUBLE? If the data you see differs from Figure 8-14, Macromedia has updated the data since this book was published. Continue with Step 3.

3. Click the **Back** button ⬅ on the browser toolbar to return to the Shockwave Player page, and then click the **Technology Breakdown** link to view the technology breakdown statistics for the various multimedia plug-ins. See Figure 8-15.

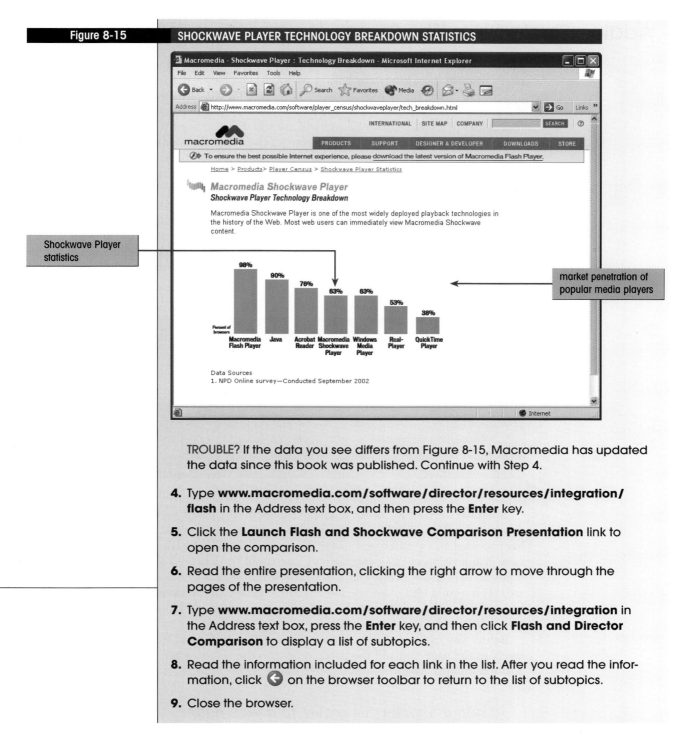

Figure 8-15   SHOCKWAVE PLAYER TECHNOLOGY BREAKDOWN STATISTICS

Shockwave Player statistics

market penetration of popular media players

TROUBLE? If the data you see differs from Figure 8-15, Macromedia has updated the data since this book was published. Continue with Step 4.

4. Type **www.macromedia.com/software/director/resources/integration/ flash** in the Address text box, and then press the **Enter** key.

5. Click the **Launch Flash and Shockwave Comparison Presentation** link to open the comparison.

6. Read the entire presentation, clicking the right arrow to move through the pages of the presentation.

7. Type **www.macromedia.com/software/director/resources/integration** in the Address text box, press the **Enter** key, and then click **Flash and Director Comparison** to display a list of subtopics.

8. Read the information included for each link in the list. After you read the information, click ⬅ on the browser toolbar to return to the list of subtopics.

9. Close the browser.

Now that you have a better understanding of when to use Flash and when to use Director/Shockwave, you will add a Shockwave movie to the Catalyst site.

Adding Shockwave to Web Pages

Adding a Shockwave movie to a Web page is very similar to adding a Flash movie to a Web page. You use the Shockwave button on the Media tab of the Insert menu bar to insert a Shockwave movie into a page. When you insert a movie, Dreamweaver places the code for the movie into the page. When you add a Shockwave movie that is located outside of the root folder to a page, Dreamweaver will ask whether you want to include a copy of the file in the root folder. You should place a copy of the file in the Media folder in the root folder for your site so that all of the materials for your site are located in one place.

Once the Shockwave movie has been added to a page, a small gray rectangle with the Shockwave logo appears in the page. The gray rectangle is 32×32 pixels, regardless of the size at which the Shockwave movie was created. (This occurs because a bug in the Shockwave button prevents the program from seeing the correct dimensions of the movie.) You must enter the correct width and height for the movie in the Property inspector in order to see the movie in a browser or to play the movie from within Dreamweaver. In addition, the Play button in the Property inspector may not play the movie; it may be necessary to preview the page in a browser to view the movie.

REFERENCE WINDOW   RW

Adding a Shockwave Movie to a Web Page

- Open the page, and then click in the layer in which you want to add the Shockwave movie.
- Click the Shockwave button on the Media tab of the Insert bar.
- Navigate to the Shockwave movie file, and then double-click the file.
- Click the Yes button, navigate to the folder in your site where you want to save the file, and then click the Save button.
- Adjust Shockwave movie attributes as needed in the Property inspector.

Brian has decided to add an interactive game to the bands page of the Catalyst site. The new game will be a Shockwave movie. The game is still in production, but the game group has provided an animated promo for the game in the Shockwave format. Although the preview is animation without interactivity and could be delivered as a Flash movie, the team wants to deliver the preview as a Shockwave movie so it can test for problems that might arise. It is a good idea to use the intended final technology when making placeholder objects because it enables you to test the technology in advance. You'll add the Shockwave movie game placeholder to the bands page.

Before you can add the Shockwave movie to the page, you will need to create two new layers in the page and add the page content to the layers. Then you will use the layers to position the text around the Shockwave movie.

To add a Shockwave movie to a Web page:

1. If you took a break after the previous session, make sure **Dreamweaver** is running and the **NewCatalyst** site is open.

2. Open the **bands.htm** page, click the **Draw Layer** button 🗒 on the **Common** tab of the Insert bar, and then draw a layer to the right of the page heading.

3. Drag the layer-code marker to the right of the right align marker, and then name the layer **DizziedConnections**.

4. Select the **DizziedConnections** paragraphs, including the heading and text, and then drag the text to the layer.

5. Draw a second layer over the page heading, drag the layer-code marker to the right of the first layer-code marker, name the layer **RemainingText**, and then drag the remaining text (do not include the page heading, navigation bar, or logo) into the second layer.

6. Turn on the **Rulers** and set them to **pixels** if necessary.

7. Select the **RemainingText** layer and move it down so that the top of the layer is positioned vertically at the 500-pixel mark on the page.

   TROUBLE? If the layer overlaps the footer (the copyright notice), don't worry. You'll fix the footer placement after you work with the DizziedConnections layer.

8. Select the **DizziedConnections** layer, move the layer **15 pixels** below the page heading, and then resize the layer until the layer is the same width as the page heading. See Figure 8-16.

Figure 8-16	BANDS PAGE WITH NEW DIZZIEDCONNECTIONS LAYER

layer-code marker

resized layer positioned below page heading

TROUBLE? If the footer is visible behind the text, you need to reposition it. Click in the page below the page heading, and then press the Enter key until the footer is lower in the page.

TROUBLE? If the text in the layer is displayed in the wrong font, the text is not enclosed by paragraph tags. (Remember that the CSS style for the body text is in the paragraph tags.) Select the text, and then in the Property inspector select Paragraph from the Format list to apply the style.

9. Select the **RemainingText** layer, move the layer **15 pixels** below the DizziedConnections layer, and then align the RemainingText layer to the left border of the DizziedConnections layer.

10. Make sure the Window Size is set to **760 × 420**, select the **RemainingText** layer, and then drag the right border until it is aligned with the end of the last word in the navigation bar. See Figure 8-17.

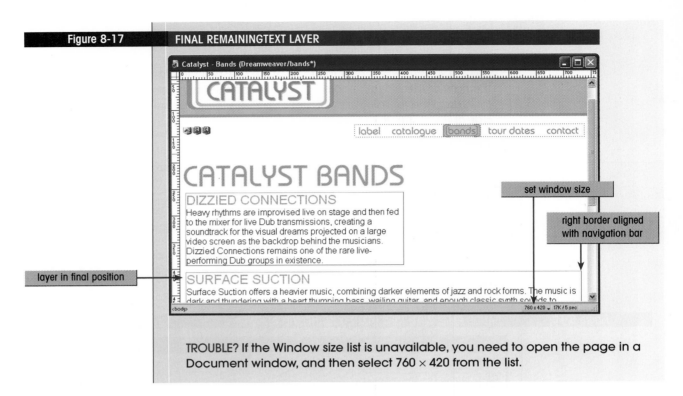

Figure 8-17 **FINAL REMAININGTEXT LAYER**

TROUBLE? If the Window size list is unavailable, you need to open the page in a Document window, and then select 760 × 420 from the list.

Now you will add a new layer beside the page heading, and you will insert the Shockwave movie into the layer.

To insert a Shockwave movie into a new layer:

1. Draw a small layer to the right of the page heading, move the layer-code markers to the right of the other layer-code markers, and then name the new layer **GamePromo**.

2. Move the GamePromo layer so that it is positioned **15 pixels** below the navigation bar and **20 pixels** from the right edge of the page heading.

3. Click in the **GamePromo** layer, and then click the **Shockwave** button ⬛ on the **Media** tab of the Insert bar. The Select File dialog box opens.

4. Double-click the **GamePromo.dcr** file in the **Tutorial.08/Tutorial** folder on your Data Disk, and then place a copy of the file in the **Media** folder. The GamePromo.dcr Shockwave movie is inserted into the layer and a small gray rectangle with the Shockwave logo in the center is visible in the layer. See Figure 8-18.

| Figure 8-18 | SHOCKWAVE MOVIE ADDED TO BANDS PAGE |

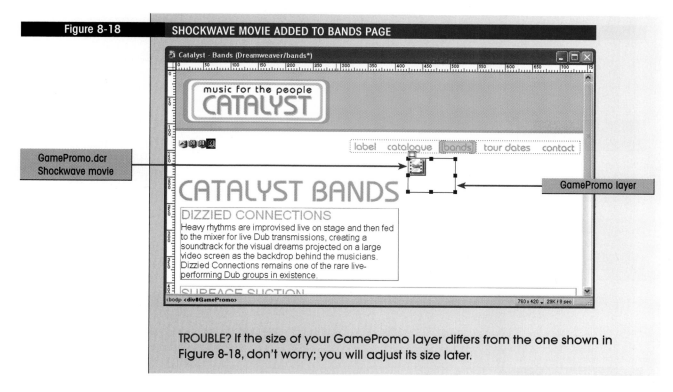

GamePromo.dcr Shockwave movie

GamePromo layer

TROUBLE? If the size of your GamePromo layer differs from the one shown in Figure 8-18, don't worry; you will adjust its size later.

The Shockwave movie is not embedded at the proper size and will not play. You must change the width and height of the movie to its original creation size to view the movie.

Adjusting Shockwave Attributes

Shockwave movies have some of the same attributes as Flash movies. You can adjust the attributes in the Property inspector when the Shockwave movie is selected. Shockwave attributes include: Name, W, H, File, Play, Parameters, V Space, H Space, Align, and Bg. For descriptions of these attributes, refer to the "Adjusting Flash Attributes" section above.

You'll change the width and height of the Shockwave movie so that it will display in the browser.

To adjust Shockwave attributes:

1. Select the Shockwave movie, if necessary.

2. In the Property inspector, type **240** in the W text box, type **240** in the H text box, and then press the **Enter** key. The gray square increases in size.

3. Move the GamePromo layer so that the right border of the layer is aligned with the right border of the RemainingText layer. See Figure 8-19.

| Figure 8-19 | EDITED SHOCKWAVE MOVIE |

resized GamePromo.dcr
Shockwave movie

right border of
GamePromo layer
aligned with right border
of RemainingText layer

CATALYST BANDS

DIZZIED CONNECTIONS
Heavy rhythms are improvised live on stage and then fed
to the mixer for live Dub transmissions, creating a
soundtrack for the visual dreams projected on a large
video screen as the backdrop behind the musicians.
Dizzied Connections remains one of the rare live-
performing Dub groups in existence.

GamePromo layer
overlaps RemainingText
layer but no content is
covered

SURFACE SUCTION
Surface Suction offers a heavier music, combining darker elements of jazz and rock forms. The music is
dark and thundering with a heart thumping bass, wailing guitar, and enough classic synth sounds to
satisfy the most nostalgic of progressive fans.

`<body> <div#GamePromo> <object>`   760 x 420 · 29K / 8 sec

4. Save the page, and preview the page in a browser. See Figure 8-20.

| Figure 8-20 | BANDS PAGE WITH GAMEPROMO SHOCKWAVE MOVIE IN BROWSER |

music for the people
CATALYST

label   catalogue   [bands]   tour dates   contact

CATALYST BANDS

GamePromo movie
playing

COMING

DIZZIED CONNECTIONS
Heavy rhythms are improvised live on stage and then fed
to the mixer for live Dub transmissions, creating a
soundtrack for the visual dreams projected on a large
video screen as the backdrop behind the musicians.
Dizzied Connections remains one of the rare live-
performing Dub groups in existence.

SURFACE SUCTION
Surface Suction offers a heavier music, combining darker elements of jazz and rock forms. The music is
dark and thundering with a heart thumping bass, wailing guitar, and enough classic synth sounds to
satisfy the most nostalgic of progressive fans.

SLOTH CHILD
When Sloth Child plays, there is a dark sway and swirl to the mix of Darren Oren's earnest, wailing vocals

TROUBLE? If a dialog box opens or an icon appears, asking you to install the
latest version of the Shockwave Player, click the Yes button to install the player.
You cannot view the Shockwave movie without the latest version of the player.

TROUBLE? If the movie displays poorly (the words are split between lines and so forth), you are probably viewing the Shockwave movie in the wrong font. You are probably logged in to your computer as a restricted user and do not have access to some system folders that are necessary to view the movie in the correct font. This is one of the potential drawbacks of using media elements in a Web site. Continue with Step 5.

5. Close the browser and close the bands.htm page.

You have inserted Flash and Shockwave movies in the Catalyst site. Next, you'll add sound to select pages.

Understanding Sound

As you create more advanced Web sites, you may want to include sound on some of the pages. Sound can add richness and depth to Web sites when used wisely. Remember, the sound that you add to a site should reinforce the site goals and enhance the user's experience. Some common uses of sound on the Web are music, narration, and sounds paired with user actions, such as sound that plays when the pointer is positioned over a button or other element.

When deciding whether to add sound to a site, you must first consider whether the target audience even has sound playback hardware and capabilities. If they do, then think about issues such as user connection speed and computer speed. You must also determine whether sound is appropriate to the site goals and whether it will truly add value to the site for the end user.

There are two ways that designers add sound to a site. Sound may be embedded directly in a page, or sound may be included as a link. With most sound formats, sound streams to the end user's computer. **Streaming** means that sound can begin to play after only a small portion downloads and will continue to play while the rest of the file is downloading. Streaming is especially helpful to users with slow connections, because they can begin to hear the sound without waiting for large files to download completely.

When sound is embedded directly in a page, the sound files begin to download to the client computer as soon as the page is loaded. Embedded sound files can either start automatically or be set up to start when the user clicks a start button. Either way, the embedded file begins to download as soon as the page loads, allowing relatively quick automatic playback or preloading so that it starts as soon as the user clicks the start button. However, beginning to download many files that a user might not even play wastes the user's time and consumes unnecessary bandwidth.

Many music sites, which often include a lot of sound files, use links to the sound files. When a page is linked to sound files, the file does not download to the client computer until the user clicks the link. The user then decides which sound files are worth downloading, and may have to wait for a partial download of the files before playback begins. However, having to wait after making the choice can become frustrating, especially on slower connections.

Sound files are created or recorded with programs outside of Dreamweaver, such as Sound Forge, Cool Edit Pro, or Pro Tools. You can add sound files to your pages, and in some cases preview them, within Dreamweaver.

Many formats can be used to store and play sound on a computer. Sound files can be fairly large and, like graphics, must be compressed to be delivered over the Web. Remember that compression is the process of eliminating redundant and less important details from a file in order to shrink its size. The different types of compression used for sound are often called **sound formats**. Each sound format uses a different CODEC as the sound is compressed for delivery and decompressed for playback. **CODEC**, short for COmpressor/DECompressor, is the software that converts sound to digital code, shrinks the code to the smallest possible size for faster transmission, and later expands the code for playback on the client machine. There are several different popular CODECs used for sound on the Web, including MP3, RealMedia, QuickTime, and Windows Media. In the past, each format was better for some types of sound and worse for others. Today, all the formats provide high quality sound for nearly any application.

For a client computer to play sound, most sound formats require the end user to download some type of plug-in or player. Plug-ins and players are additional software that knows how to interpret the sound format and convert the code back to sound. When a user installs plug-in or player software, it often includes both browser integration (sound that plays from within the browser) as well as a standalone player with its own interface and controls. Most users have several players installed on their systems, and most players work with a wide range of sound formats. For example, the QuickTime Player will work with QuickTime formats as well as with RealMedia and Windows Media formats.

With care, you can make sure that sound will work for the majority of the target users. However, making sound work the same on all the end users' systems is complex and sometimes impossible. The inability to control a user's experience with sound is one of the challenges to adding sound to a Web page. The difficulties depend on the user's installed players and hardware configuration. For example, a single user might have the RealMedia, QuickTime, and Windows Media players installed on his or her system. When the user visits a site that includes a RealMedia Audio clip, any of the installed players might handle the sound. And, depending on configuration, the sound might just play or a separate player window with sound controls (and ads) might pop up, which is often not desirable. Also, depending on configuration, the sound can either start automatically or require the user to push the Play button on the launched player. For another user who has the same players installed, a different player may respond to the RealMedia Audio clip and that user may have a completely different experience.

One way to alleviate this confusion, and to insure the same sound experience for all site visitors, is to use the Flash format to add sound to your pages. Many professional sites further ease the potential problems by including a choice between two or more sound formats containing the exact same content. This gives the user more control and increases the potential for trouble-free sound playback.

Embedding a Sound-Only Flash Movie

Although Flash is more often thought of as a way to add animation to Web sites, it is also a very consistent and reliable method for adding sound to Web pages. Because the Flash player is widely installed and does not open a separate application when used to play sound, Flash will deliver sound without disrupting the aesthetic of Web pages. When you use Flash to add sound to a page, you are simply adding a Flash movie that does not contain any images. Therefore, you use the same process as you would use to add a regular Flash movie to a page. Because this Flash movie has no visual content and will be used only for sound, it is generally created at a size of 1×1 pixel and with the same background color as the page.

There are two types of sound-only Flash movies: those that prevent automatic play, and those play automatically when the page loads. (When creating a sound-only Flash movie, adding a stop action to the first frame will prevent automatic play, whereas omitting this action will allow automatic play.) Flash movies that play automatically are used to add background sound to pages. For example, a Web page that loads music when the home page loads in the browser might use a sound-only Flash movie that plays automatically. Sound-only Flash movies that do not play automatically are often used to provide sounds that the user can activate with the click of a button. For example, when you include more than one sound-only Flash movie in a page, you can create a Play button for each movie that the user can click to play a particular movie. The Control Shockwave or Flash behavior can be attached to a button to make it control sound-only Flash movies. In addition to creating a Play button, you can use different attributes in the Behavior dialog box when you attach the Control Shockwave or Flash behavior to make other sound control buttons, such as rewind and so forth.

REFERENCE WINDOW   `RW`

Adding a Sound-Only Flash Movie to a Web Page
- Open the page, and then click in the layer in which you want to add the Flash movie.
- Click the Flash button on the Media tab of the Insert bar.
- Navigate to the Flash movie file, and then double-click the file.
- Click the Yes button, navigate to the folder in your site where you want to save the file, and then click the Save button.
- Adjust Flash movie attributes as needed in the Property inspector.

Sara wants to add audio files for some of the songs in the catalogue page of the Catalyst site, and Brian has asked you to make these additions. You will add a sound-only Flash movie to the page that does not play automatically. Then you will add a button to the page and attach a behavior to the button that will cause the sound to play when clicked.

To add sound to a page using Flash:

1. Open the **catalogue.htm** page, place the pointer to the right of the song title "Sunshine" in the Sloth Child song list, and then press the **Enter** key. You'll add the sound-only Flash movie on this new line.

2. Click the **Flash** button 🎵 on the **Media** tab of the Insert bar. The Select File dialog box opens.

3. Double-click the **sunshine.swf** movie in the **Tutorial.08/Tutorial** folder on your Data Disk, and then place a copy of the Flash movie in the **Media** folder. A gray box appears below the Sunshine song title. (Remember that the Flash movie will not be visible in the browser.) See Figure 8-21.

Figure 8-21	CATALOGUE PAGE WITH SOUND-ONLY FLASH MOVIE

4. Select the **sunshine.swf** movie if necessary, type **SunshineFlash** in the unnamed text box in the upper-left corner of the Property inspector, and then press the **Enter** key to rename the Flash movie.

Next, you will add a button to the page. Then you will add a Control Shockwave or Flash behavior to the button, enabling the button to start the sound-only Flash movie that you added to the page.

To start a Flash movie with a button:

1. Place the pointer to the right of the Sunshine song title, and then click the **Image** button 🖼 on the **Common** tab of the Insert bar.

2. Double-click the **FlashSoundButton.gif** in the **Tutorial.08/Tutorial** folder on your Data Disk, and then place a copy of the image in the **Graphics** folder.

3. Select the **FlashSoundButton** image, and then select **Top** from the Align list in the Property inspector.

4. Click the **Plus** button ⊞ in the Behaviors panel, and then click **Control Shockwave or Flash**. The Control Shockwave or Flash dialog box opens. See Figure 8-22.

Figure 8-22	CONTROL SHOCKWAVE OR FLASH DIALOG BOX

5. Click **movie "SunshineFlash"** in the Movie list, if necessary, click the **Play** option button, if necessary, and then click the **OK** button. The behavior is added to the button.

6. In the Behaviors panel, click the **Events** list arrow, and then click **(onClick)**. The image will play when clicked by the user.

7. Save the page, and preview the page in a browser.

8. Click the **Flash sound** image to play the sound-only Flash movie. See Figure 8-23.

Figure 8-23   **CATALOGUE PAGE WITH FLASH IMAGE IN BROWSER**

Flash sound image clicked with sound playing

catalogue page scrolled to bottom

9. Close the browser.

Adjusting Attributes of a Sound-Only Flash Movie

Once you have added a Flash movie to a Web page, you may need to set some of the attributes in the Property inspector. Most of these settings are irrelevant to sound-only Flash movies; they affect only visual aspects of the movie. The only attributes that you set when working with a sound-only Flash movie are the Loop and Autoplay checkboxes. When using a movie that is designed to prevent automatic play, checking the Loop and Autoplay attributes will have no effect, but they will function as usual with a movie that is designed to allow automatic play when the page loads.

You do not need to set any attributes for the SunshineFlash movie you added to the catalogue page.

Embedding Other Sound Formats

Embedding other types of sound files (MP3, RealMedia, and so forth) is a bit more difficult than embedding a sound-only Flash movie, because Dreamweaver does not have a custom control for embedding the other types of files. You can use the generic Plugin button on the Media tab of the Insert bar, but you must type a lot of parameters to make the sound work, or you must download an extension from the Macromedia Exchange. Once you have downloaded an extension, embedding other types of sound files follows the same basic process as embedding a sound-only Flash movie. You will learn more about downloading extensions in the next session when you download the RealMedia extension to embed video in a page.

Session 8.2 QUICK | CHECK

1. In what program are Shockwave movies created?

2. What is the Shockwave file extension?

3. Define streaming.

4. What are two ways to include sound in a page?

5. Name three popular sound formats.

6. What is the one sound format that you should not link directly to?

SESSION 8.3

In this session, you will explore adding video to a site. You will download the RealMedia extension from the Macromedia Exchange. You will embed a video clip in a page. You will download the RealMedia player, if necessary, and you will view the video over the Web.

Understanding Digital Video

Video can add excitement to a Web page and greatly enhance the experience of the site visitor. However, even with compression, video files are relatively large and may be slow to download, especially for users who have dial-up connections. Because video includes moving images and often sound, it requires more focused attention from the site visitor. This can be both good and bad. The positive aspect is that video can really reinforce what you are trying to say. Users tend to pay attention so it is a good way to drive home an important message. The negative aspect is that it is easy to overload the user with too much motion on the page. When the user is barraged with too much motion, or too many messages, the video becomes a distraction and can detract from the effectiveness of the Web site rather than reinforce it. The steeper user requirements (more time to download and more focused attention from the user) associated with video mean that video should be included in a site only when it is truly appropriate for the site goals and the target audience.

When deciding whether to use video in a site, consider that when site visitors must wait for something large to download, their expectations are raised. Or put another way, site visitors will wait for downloads only when they perceive that the content is something worth waiting for.

Video files, like sound files, must be compressed to make them small enough to deliver over the Web. Several major factors affect the file size of a digital video clip, including frame size, playback quality, and sound parameters. Some common video frame sizes used on the Web are 320 × 240 pixels and 240 × 180 pixels—the smaller frame size creates a smaller video file. Playback quality for digital video is often adjusted to match the target connection speed and is usually measured in the amount of data that needs to be downloaded per second. For example, 31 kbps (kilobits per second) might be used with a video clip intended for standard modems, whereas 400 kbps might be used to provide higher quality video to viewers with high-speed connections. Video quality affects the amount of detail and motion in the video image. Higher quality video contains cleaner, more detailed images and smoother movement than lower quality video. Sound parameters in digital video include the choice of stereo or mono and the resolution or clarity of the sound. Stereo and high resolution occupy more file space than mono and lower resolution.

To insure continuous playback of a video clip, it must be **buffered**, which means that the first 5 or 10 seconds of the clip are downloaded before it begins to play. After the clip begins to play, as long as the current download is at or past the current clip playback location, the playback will continue without interruption. A user who has a fast, consistent connection is more likely to be able to download enough of the clip each second to view a continuous playback. If the download does not keep up with the playback (that is, if the next piece of needed file hasn't yet completed downloading), then the video playback will be interrupted. The user may see any of a number of things: the video may stop until the download catches up, the video may become jittery and chunks of it may not play, and sometimes a warning appears telling the user that the download is being interrupted. Any of these things can be very annoying and cause the user to leave the page before he or she has viewed the entire video clip.

Web sites that include digital video use several different solutions to minimize playback interruptions and maximize the viewing experience of the user. These solutions include multiple clip options, multiple formats, and specialized video servers. By offering the same digital video clip in multiple file sizes, a site can satisfy a wide range of visitors. Sites taking this approach often offer each clip in low, medium, and high resolution. They may sometimes instead offer dial-up and broadband sizes, which means that they have used the compression parameters discussed above to offer the same clip in lower quality/smaller frame size for visitors using slower dial-up connections and in higher quality/larger frame size for visitors using faster broadband connections. Some sites also offer different format options, knowing that some users prefer the QuickTime format and player, whereas others might choose RealMedia or Windows Media. In addition, bigger budget Web sites might use a specialized video server to monitor a user's connection and adjust the video quality to compensate for slowdowns, increasing the likelihood that the user can view the video clip without interruption. Another benefit provided by a video server is the ability to allow thousands of users to view the same clip simultaneously, which is impossible when including video on a standard Web server.

Video files are created or recorded with programs outside of Dreamweaver, such as Avid and Premier, but can be added to your pages within Dreamweaver.

Video File Formats

Digital video can have many different formats. Most of the popular sound formats can also be used for video, including RealMedia, QuickTime, and Windows Media. As with audio formats, earlier versions of these video formats were preferred for different uses. Although there are still differences, all three of these formats provide excellent video performance with a wide range of materials. Today, most Web sites that include video offer the user a choice of formats.

On the Web, these formats are identified by their file extensions. Some of the most common extensions are:

- **.mov.** A QuickTime movie that can contain sound, video, and animation tracks. QuickTime is a very popular cross-platform format from Apple used for both Web and CD-ROM video.

- **.rm.** A RealMedia movie, which is another popular format for Web and intranet streaming video. When you add RealMedia to a site, you add an .rm file to your page and Dreamweaver creates an .rpm file for you.

- **.rpm.** A metafile that contains the location of the RealMedia file to be played. When using RealMedia, links should always go to a metafile, which points to the RealMedia file.

- **.smil.** A Synchronized Multimedia Integration Language (SMIL) file used with RealMedia to create time-based multimedia presentations that can include audio, video, graphics, animation, and text.

- **.wmv.** A Windows Media File, which is a format for Web- and CD-based digital video made popular by Microsoft.

- ■ **.avi.** An earlier Microsoft format designation that has largely been replaced by the newer Windows Media format (.wmv).
- ■ **.mpg.** A format created by the Motion Picture Experts Group, and which is generally used for CDs and multimedia pieces rather than for Web distribution.

Most of the popular players will play back both sound and video. The makers of the RealMedia, QuickTime, and Window Media formats each provide a free player that can be downloaded. And, as with sound, the players include both standalone player functionality as well as browser integration, which allows the browser to play video embedded directly in a Web page.

Adding **Video to a Web Page**

There are several steps involved in adding video to a Web page. First, you must download an extension that enables you to insert video into Web pages from the Macromedia Exchange. Next, you use the extension tools to insert video into a Web page. Then you download a player into your browser. Finally, you view the page in a browser.

Dreamweaver does not come with an object designed to embed video the way the Flash object is customized to embed a Flash movie. It does come with a generic Plug-in object that can be used to add a variety of media to your pages. However, because the Plug-in object is fairly generic, you must type quite a bit of code to make any video solution work. Another option is to download an extension from the Macromedia Exchange. Video extensions add tools to Dreamweaver that are designed specifically to embed the video format you have chosen into a Web page. Also, if you do not already have a player installed to view the video in your browser, you will need to download one.

In this session you will use the RealMedia format for video. (You could also choose QuickTime or Windows Media.) No matter which format you use, you will follow the same general process to add video to a Web page:

- ■ Visit the Macromedia Exchange for Dreamweaver site and locate the appropriate extension(s) that will add tools to Dreamweaver that enable you to insert video (in the chosen format) into Web pages.
- ■ Download and install the selected extension.
- ■ Use the extension to add a video clip to a Web page in Dreamweaver.
- ■ Adjust the attributes for the video clip in the Property inspector.
- ■ Save the Web page.
- ■ Visit the format maker's Web site to learn about the format (in this case, the RealMedia site).
- ■ Download the appropriate player from the maker's site and install it in the browser, if necessary.
- ■ Preview the Web page that includes a video clip.

Now that you understand what is involved in adding video to a Web page, you will start the process by downloading the RealMedia extension for Dreamweaver.

Downloading the RealMedia Suite Extension for Dreamweaver

Before you can add video to a Web site using the RealMedia format, you need to download the RealMedia Suite extension for Dreamweaver from the Macromedia Exchange Web site. You must be connected to the Internet to download the extension. If you are not connected to the Internet, see your instructor on how to proceed. You must log in to the site to download the extension. If you have never created a login for the Macromedia Exchange, you must do that before you can begin the download steps.

To download the RealMedia Suite Extension:

1. If you took a break after the previous session, make sure **Dreamweaver** is running and the **NewCatalyst** site is open.

2. Open the **Answers** panel, and then select **Extensions** from the list.

TROUBLE? If Extensions does not appear on the list, then this is the first time you are using the Answers panel. Click the Update button, and then click Extensions from the list.

3. Type **RealMedia** in the Search the Exchange text box, and then click the **arrow** button ➡ to begin your search. A list of all the RealMedia extensions found on the Exchange site appears in the Answers panel. See Figure 8-25.

Figure 8-25   ANSWERS PANEL

list of RealMedia extensions available on Exchange site

TROUBLE? If your list differs from the one shown in Figure 8-25, don't worry; the Exchange is updated frequently and your list shows all of the current RealMedia extensions.

4. Click the **RealMedia Suite** extension. The RealMedia Suite Extension page of the Macromedia Exchange site (*www.macromedia.com/exchange/dreamweaver*) opens in a browser.

5. Click **Windows** to download the Windows version of the extension. The extension starts to download and the File Download dialog box opens.

TROUBLE? If you cannot download the extension, then you are not logged in. Click the Macromedia Dreamweaver Home Page link, log in, and then start again from Step 3. If you do not have a login ID, click the Macromedia ID link, create a login, and then start again from Step 3.

6. Click **Open** to open the extension. The Macromedia Extension Manager dialog box opens and displays the Macromedia Extension Disclaimer.

7. Click the **Accept** button to accept the terms of the disclaimer. The extension installs into the Macromedia Extension Manager, and a dialog box opens indicating that the extension has been installed successfully.

8. Click the **OK** button.

9. Click the **Close** button ☒ in the title bar of the Macromedia Extension Manager window to close it, and then close the browser.

10. Exit and restart Dreamweaver. The downloaded extension becomes active and a RealMedia tab appears on the Insert bar. See Figure 8-26.

| Figure 8-26 | **INSERT BAR WITH REALMEDIA EXTENSION** |

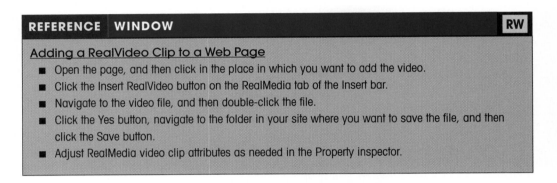

Once you have added RealMedia to Dreamweaver, you can add video clips to Web pages.

Adding a RealMedia Video Clip to a Web Page

Now that the RealMedia tools are installed in Dreamweaver, adding a RealMedia video clip is simple. The Sloth Child band is in the process of shooting a video for its new single, "Sunshine." Sara wants to promote the upcoming video on the Catalyst site.

REFERENCE WINDOW   **RW**

Adding a RealVideo Clip to a Web Page
- Open the page, and then click in the place in which you want to add the video.
- Click the Insert RealVideo button on the RealMedia tab of the Insert bar.
- Navigate to the video file, and then double-click the file.
- Click the Yes button, navigate to the folder in your site where you want to save the file, and then click the Save button.
- Adjust RealMedia video clip attributes as needed in the Property inspector.

You will add a RealMedia video clip with a promo for the upcoming video below the SlothChild layer in the home page.

To add video to a Web page:

1. Open the **home page**, draw a small layer 10 pixels below the SlothChild layer, name the layer **Video**, and then move the layer-code marker to the right of the other layer-code markers on the page.

2. Click in the **Video** layer, and then click the **Insert RealVideo** button on the **RealMedia** tab of the Insert bar. The Select File dialog box opens.

3. Double-click the **sunshineVideo.rm** file in the **Tutorial.08/Tutorial** folder on your Data Disk, and then place a copy of the video clip in the **Media** folder. A black square the size of the video clip with the RealMedia logo appears in the layer. See Figure 8-27.

Figure 8-27	REALMEDIA VIDEO CLIP ADDED TO HOME PAGE

sunshineVideo.rm clip

TROUBLE? If an error message dialog box opens, click the OK button (you may need to do this twice). The error message is most likely because you do not have the latest version of the RealMedia Player installed. (You will install this later.)

4. Make sure the Document window is sized to **760 × 420**, and then select the **WhatsHot** layer.

5. Press the **Right Arrow** key until the right border of the layer is aligned with the last letter of the last word in the navigation bar, and then drag the right border of the DizziedConnections layer to **475 pixels**.

6. Select the **LifeInMinorChords** layer, and then repeat Step 5 to align the layer.

7. Align the left border of the video with the left border of the SlothChild layer.

8. Save the page.

Next, you will adjust the attributes of the video clip.

Adjusting the Attributes of a Video Clip

No matter which video format you use, you can adjust the attributes associated with the video clip in the Property inspector when you select the clip. Some attributes are commonly available within all the formats, whereas others are specific to a particular format.

The attributes that are commonly available in all the formats are:

- **Name.** The name for the inserted object, which can be used for identification and to refer to the object in scripts you write to control the clip.
- **W and H.** The width and the height of the video clip. These dimensions are usually set automatically when you insert the video clip, and should be the actual size of the clip. Setting this value for a size other than that of the clip is not recommended because it may degrade video performance. If you want to change the size of a video clip, the clip should usually be remade at the desired size.

- **Src.** The name of the video clip that you selected when you inserted the RealMedia object. You can select a different video clip to display.
- **Auto-Start.** The option to play the video clip just after the page loads. Users with slower connections may see a short delay before the clip begins to play.

In addition to these common attributes, each format also offers some unique attributes that are not available in the other formats. These attributes are also located in the Property inspector. The unique attributes of the RealMedia format are:

- **Hide Logo.** The option to hide the RealMedia logo. This setting does not have any effect on some systems.
- **Metafile.** The name of a file that was automatically created when you inserted the RealMedia object. This simple text file has an .rpm extension and contains the name and possible location of the .rm file to be played. The metafile controls should remain in their default settings unless you are an advanced user, otherwise the video may not play properly.
- **Allow JavaScript Control.** The option to include JavaScripts that will control the RealMedia object. If you do not include JavaScripts that will control the RealMedia object, then this setting has no effect.

You will name the movie clip that you added to the home page and set the movie to start automatically when the page is downloaded. Then you will view the page. The video clip will not play when you preview the page in the usual way. You must open the page directly to view the video. If you do not have a player, you must install a player before you can view the video.

To adjust the attributes of a RealMedia video clip:

1. Select the **sunshineVideo.rm** video clip.

2. In the Property inspector, type **SunshineVideo** in the unnamed text box, and then click the **Auto-Start** checkbox to insert a check mark.

3. Save the page, and view the page in a browser by clicking the Start button, click **My Computer** on the Start menu, navigating to the root folder of your Catalyst site, and then double-clicking the **index.htm** file. The home page opens in a browser and the video plays if you have a player installed in your browser that plays the RealMedia format. See Figure 8-28.

Figure 8-28

HOME PAGE WITH VIDEO CLIP IN BROWSER

TROUBLE? If the RealMedia logo or an X appears where the video should be, you need to download a player to view the video. Complete the next section, "Downloading the RealOne Player for Internet Explorer," and then repeat Step 3.

The next section provides steps for downloading the RealOne player for Internet Explorer. If you have the player, read but do not complete the steps in the section.

Downloading the RealOne Player for Internet Explorer

To view video added to a Web site, you must install a player in your browser that will enable you to view the video. Installing a player on your computer does not enable other users to view the video on their computers. The player must be installed on the client computer in order for that user to see the video. This is one of the downsides to using video in a Web site as well as one of the reasons to consider the browser penetration of a technology before deciding to use the media in Web pages. The higher browser penetration a media has, the more likely it is that end users will already have the player. Some users who don't have a player will not take the time to download the player, and will simply skip that portion of the site.

Because you are using RealMedia for the video, you will download the RealOne Player and install it in Internet Explorer. If you are using another browser, you will need to download and install the RealOne Player designed for that browser. Remember, most of the new players will play any of the popular video formats, so there is a good chance that other users will not have the exact same viewing experience.

To install the RealOne Player in Internet Explorer:

1. Start Internet Explorer, type **www.real.com** in the Address text box, and then press the **Enter** key. The Real.com page opens.

2. Click the **Free RealOne Player** link, and then click the **Download the Free RealOne Player Only** link. The Download Manager opens.

   TROUBLE? If you don't see the Free RealOne Player link or the Download the Free RealOne Player Only link, then the Web site might have been updated since this tutorial was published. Look for and then click the link to download the RealOne Player.

3. Click the **Yes** button in the Download Manager. The RealOne Player begins to download.

   TROUBLE? If the RealOne Update dialog box opens, you already have the RealOne Player installed on your computer. The RealOne Update dialog box updates the player as needed, and then the RealOne Install Wizard opens. Continue with Step 5.

4. Click the **Yes** button to begin downloading the RealOne Player. When the download is complete, the RealOne Install Wizard appears.

5. Click the **Express Install** option button, if necessary, and then click **Next** to advance to the next page.

6. Click the **Accept** button. The Install Wizard installs the files.

   TROUBLE? If a dialog box opens, informing you that the RealOne Player is already installed, click the OK button to reinstall the player.

7. Click the **Finish** button. The installation is complete, the Install Wizard closes, and the RealOne Player dialog box opens with a welcome page visible.

8. Click the **Next** button to move to the next page. The RealOne Player connects to the Internet and prompts you to enter information into a form.

9. Fill out the form, and then click the button to move to the next page. A confirmation page appears.

10. Click **Confirm** to move to the next page.

11. Click the **Basic Setup** button, and then click **Continue** to move to the next page. The RealOne Player launches.

12. Click the **Start** button, click **My Computer** on the Start menu, navigate to the **index.htm** page in the root folder of your Catalyst site, and then double-click the file. The home page opens in a browser window and the video plays.

13. Close the browser windows.

Updating the WebSite on the Remote Server

As a final test of the media elements you've added to the Catalyst site, you'll view the pages over the Web. You'll upload the pages you changed and the Media folder to the remote server, and then view the site over the Web.

To upload a site to the remote server:

1. Click the **Connects to remote host** button on the Site panel toolbar.

2. Click the **View** list arrow on the Site panel toolbar, and then click **Local View**.

3. Click the **index.htm**, **index.rpm**, **bands.htm**, and **catalogue.htm** files and the **Media** folder in Local view to select them, and then click the **Put File(s)** button on the Site panel toolbar.

4. Click the **Yes** button when asked if you want to include dependent files because you have not selected the new dependent files for the site yet.

   A dialog box opens with the message that the requested file is not found.

5. Click the **OK** button.

6. Click the **Disconnects from remote host** button on the Site panel toolbar.

7. Click the **View** list arrow on the Site panel toolbar, and then click **Local View**. The Site panel returns to the Local view.

Next, you'll preview the updated site in a browser. The site will include all of the new elements that you added to your local version of the site.

To preview the updated site in a browser:

1. Open a browser, type the URL of your remote site into the Address text box on the browser toolbar, and then press the **Enter** key.

2. Explore the **home** page on the remote site from within the browser.

   TROUBLE? If you cannot view the video from your remote server, you need to manually adjust the index.rpm file. Once you make the change, you can no longer view the video locally. See your instructor for the steps to modify the index.rpm file.

3. Click the **bands** link and watch the Shockwave movie.

4. Click the **catalogue** link, and then scroll to the bottom of the catalogue page.

5. Click the **Flash sound** button, and listen to the sound clip.

6. Click the **MP3 sound** button, and listen to the sound clip.

7. Close the browser, and close the **NewCatalyst** site.

In this session, you downloaded an extension from the Macromedia Exchange that enabled you to insert video into Web pages. You used the extension tools to insert video into a page. You downloaded a player into your browser and viewed the video in a browser. Then you uploaded the site to the remote server and viewed the pages over the Web.

Session 8.3 QUICK | CHECK

1. List three things that might affect the file size of a video clip.

2. What is the RealMedia file extension?

3. Why must a video clip be buffered?

4. Name three commonly used video file formats.

5. True or False? Most of the popular sound formats can also be used for video.

6. True or False? Installing a video player on your computer enables all other users to view the video on their computers.

REVIEW ASSIGNMENTS

Brian asks you to add some additional media elements to the Catalyst site. First, he wants you to change the text on the What's Hot page to Flash text so that it can be displayed in the logo font. Next, he wants to you to add a sound-only Flash movie that is set to automatically play to the Sloth Child page. The movie will add sound to the background of the page. Finally, the Life In Minor Chords band is going to be releasing a video of some live performances that were filmed during its most recent tour. The band has created a short promo video to create some buzz. You will embed the video promo in the tour section of the LIMC page.

1. Start Dreamweaver, open the NewCatalyst site, and then open the WhatHot page.

2. Select the text at the right column in the WhatHot page, and then press the Delete key.

3. Click the Flash Text button on the Media tab of the Insert bar to open the Insert Flash Text dialog box, select Bauhaus Md BT (or Arial or a font of your choice that resembles the Catalyst logo font) from the Font list, type "60" in the Size text box, click the Align Center button, type "#FF9900" in the Color text box, and type the following in the Text text box:

BLACK LAB
THE LATEST
RELEASE
FROM
SLOTH CHILD

4. Click the Browse button next to the Save As text box, browse to the Media folder, name the file "WhatsHotText1.swf," and then click the Save button.

5. Click the OK button to close the Insert Flash Text dialog box, and then view the text in the What's Hot page.

6. Place the pointer below the Flash text, type "Available Now in Your Area," and then apply the CatalySubHeadings style to the text.

7. Save and close the page.

Explore 8. Open the Sloth Child page located in the SlothChild folder in your root folder, draw a small layer beside the Sloth Child logo, click inside the layer, and then click the Flash button on the Media tab of the Insert bar.

Explore 9. Double-click the **sunshine_autostart.swf** file in the **Tutorial.08/Review** folder on your Data Disk, and then place a copy of the file in the Media folder in your root folder.

Explore 10. Select the Flash movie, and then check the Autoplay and Loop checkboxes, if necessary.

11. Save the page, and preview the page in a browser. The sound will begin to play when the page is loaded.

12. Open the LIMCtours.htm page located in the LifeInMinorChords folder in your root folder.

13. Draw a layer below the page heading, and then move the layer-code marker to the right of the page heading.

14. Click in the layer, click the Insert RealVideo button on the RealMedia tab of the Insert bar, double-click the **limcVideo.rm** file located in the **Tutorial.08/Review** folder on your Data Disk, and then place a copy of the file in the Media folder in your root folder.

15. Select the layer, and then drag the borders of the layer so that they fit snugly against the borders of the movie.

16. Move the layer so that its top border is 50 pixels below the page heading and its right border is aligned with the end of the page heading text.

17. Select the video clip, and then check the Auto-Start checkbox in the Property inspector.

18. Save the page, and view the page in your browser. (*Hint:* Open the page directly because the video won't work if you preview the page in the usual way.)

19. Upload the site to your remote server, and then view the site over the Web.

CASE PROBLEMS

Case 1. Hroch University Anthropology Department Professor Hart has put together two MP3 audio clips and one video clip that demonstrate some of the linguistic differences he found in northern Vietnam. He asks you to place each example in the linguistic differences page of his site.

1. Open the Hart site that you modified in Tutorial 7, Case 1, and then open the linguistic differences page.

2. Delete the text in the third row of the table, and type "Research in process; in the meantime, click on the video and audio files to preview some interesting findings." in the row.

3. Press the Enter key to create another line in the table row, and then click the Insert RealVideo button on RealMedia tab of the Insert bar.

4. Double-click the **HartHarshSample.rm** file in the **Tutorial.08/Cases** folder on your Data Disk, create a new folder named "Media" in your root folder, and then place a copy of the HartHarshSample.rm file in the Media folder.

5. Check the Auto-Start checkbox in the Property inspector.

6. Insert 14 non-breaking spaces in the page to the right of the video. (*Hint:* Press the Ctrl+Shift+Spacebar keys to insert a non-breaking space.)

7. Type "audio 1," insert another 14 non-breaking spaces in the page, and then type "audio 2."

Explore　8. Select the audio 1 text, click the Browse for File button next to the Link text box in the Property inspector, double-click the **HartHarshwhSample.mp3** file in the **Tutorial.08/Cases** folder on your Data Disk, and then place a copy of the MP3 file in your Media folder.

Explore 9. Select the audio 2 text, click the Browse for File button next to the Link text box in the Property inspector, double-click the **HartModalSample.mp3** file in the **Tutorial.08/Cases** folder on your Data Disk, and then place a copy of the MP3 file in your Media folder.

10. Save the page, and then view the page in a browser. (*Hint:* View the page directly because you cannot view the video when you preview in the usual way.)

11. Upload the site to the remote server, and then view the site over the Web.

Case 2. Museum of Western Art The Museum of Western Art is sponsoring a regional tour of some of their more popular paintings. C. J. Strittmatter asks you to create a new page to promote the tour. The page will eventually include an interactive educational Shockwave movie that provides information about the paintings and promotes the tour. The team that is creating that movie has made a promotional Shockwave movie to be included in the page until the interactive educational movie is complete. You'll add the promotional Shockwave movie to the page. Then you'll add a Flash button to the home page of the site, and link the button to the new page.

1. Open the Museum site you modified in Tutorial 7, Case 2.

2. In the Site panel, copy the Location page, and then paste a copy of the Location page in the root folder for the Museum. A copy of the Location page is visible in the Site list.

3. Rename the Copy of Location page to "Tour.htm," and then open the new Tour page in a Document window.

4. Delete the navigation bar and all of the text below the page heading from the page. The page is empty except for the logo, the horizontal rule, and the heading.

5. Change the page title to "Museum of Western Art – Tour."

6. Change the page heading to "THE TOUR" and then open the **MuseumTour.doc** in the **Tutorial.08/Cases** folder on your Data Disk in a word processing program, copy the text from the document, and paste the text in the new Tour page below the page heading.

7. Place the pointer to the left of the page heading, and then click the Shockwave button on the Media tab of the Insert bar.

8. Double-click the **museumtour.dcr** file in the **Tutorial.08/Cases** folder on your Data Disk, create a new folder named "Media" in your root folder, and then place a copy of the museumtour.dcr file in the Media folder.

9. Select the Shockwave movie, and then, in the Property inspector, type "323" in the W text box, type "240" in the H text box, select Top from the Align list, type "#006666" in the Bg text box, and then press the Enter key.

10. Save the page, and preview the page in a browser.

11. Open the home page of the Museum site, draw a small layer at the right of the logo and above the horizontal rule, and then move the layer-code marker to the right of the other layer-code markers on the page.

12. Click in the new layer, and then click the Flash Button button on the Media tab of the Insert bar. The Insert Flash Button dialog box opens.

Explore 13. Select the Simple Tab style from the Style list, type "Regional Tour" in the Button Text text box, select Times New Roman from the Font list, and then type "15" in the Size text box.

Explore ▶ 14. Click the Browse button next to the Link text box to open the Select File dialog box, browse to the root folder of your Museum site, and then double-click the Tour.htm page.

Explore ▶ 15. Select _blank in the Target list, click the color picker, and then click the eyedropper on the background of the Tour page to select the background color of the page as the background color for the Flash button.

Explore ▶ 16. Click the Browse button next to the Save As text box to open the Select File dialog box, browse to the root folder of your Museum site, type "TourButton.swf" in the File name text box, click the Save button in the Select File dialog box, verify the file path in the Save As text box, and then click the OK button. The Flash button is added to the Tour page.

17. Select the layer and adjust the borders of the layer so that they fit snugly against the edges of the Flash button.

18. Make sure your Document window is set to 760 × 420, and then move the layer so that the button is right aligned to the right edge of the menu table and its bottom edge touches the top of the horizontal rule.

There is a bug that prevents the link in the Flash button from working. You will research the problem on the Macromedia Dreamweaver Support Center Web site, and then you will fix the problem. To enable the link to work, you must select the button, view the code (the button code will be selected), and then delete two parameters from the code.

Explore ▶ 19. Select TechNotes from the list in the Answers panel, and then click Links in Flash objects do not work when previewing in a browser. (If this is not listed, type "Links in Flash objects do not work when previewing in a browser" in the Search Support Site text box, and then click the arrow button. A list of matching terms appears. Click the appropriate link.) The page on the Macromedia Dreamweaver Support Center Web site that explains the bug and provides solutions appears in a browser window if you are connected to the Internet.

20. Read the page, and then close the browser window.

Explore ▶ 21. Select the Flash button in Design view, and then switch to Code and Design view to view the button code. The code is selected.

Explore ▶ 22. Select the <param name="base" value="."> parameter in the Code pane, and then press the Delete key.

Explore ▶ 23. Select the Flash button in the Design pane. All of the code is selected again in the Code pane.

Explore ▶ 24. Select the base= "." attribute in the embed tag, and then press the Delete key.

25. Switch to Design view.

26. Save the page, and preview the page in a browser.

27. Test the button, and then close the browser windows.

28. Upload the site to the remote server, and view the site over the Web.

Case 3. NORM Norm Blinkered wants to increase catalog orders for his publishing company. Mark Chapman has already created a Shockwave movie that contains a catalogue order form. You will create a new page for the site, and then place the Shockwave movie into the new page. Then you will add a Flash button to the top of the home page. The Flash button will link to the new page and will target the page to open in a new browser window.

1. Open the NORM site that you modified in Tutorial 7, Case 3.

2. In the Site panel, add a new page to the site, rename the new page "CatalogueOrder.htm," and then open the new page in a Document window.

3. Open the Page Properties dialog box, type "NORM – Catalogue Order" in the Title text box, type "#003366" in the Background text box, type "0" in the Left Margin, Top Margin, Margin Width, and Margin Height text boxes, and then click the OK button.

4. Place the pointer at the upper-left corner of the page, and then click the Shockwave button on the Media tab of the Insert bar.

5. Double-click the **normform.dcr** file in the **Tutorial.08/Cases** folder on your Data Disk, create a new folder in your root folder named "Media," and then place a copy of the normform.dcr file in the Media folder.

6. Select the Shockwave movie and, in the Property inspector, type "500" in the W text box, type "330" in the H text box, and then press the Enter key.

Explore 7. Press the Play button to preview the Shockwave movie in the Document window.

Explore 8. Click the Stop button in the Property inspector to end the movie.

9. Save and close the page.

10. Open the home page, change the Window size to 760 × 420, and then draw a new layer at the right of the page above the horizontal rule.

11. Click inside the new layer, and then click the Flash Button button on the Media tab of the Insert bar.

Explore 12. Select Translucent Tab from the Style list, type "NORM CATALOGUE" in the Button Text text box, select Verdana from the Font list, type "10" in the Size text box, click the Browse button next to the Link text box and double-click the CatalogueOrder.htm page, select _blank from the Target list, type "#003366" in the Bg Color text box, type "CatalogueOrderButton.swf" in the Save As text box, and then click the OK button.

13. Select the layer, and then move the layer so that the bottom of the button is touching the horizontal rule and the button is centered horizontally over the Featured Book text.

Explore 14. You need to fix the link bug in the Flash button. Select the button in Design view, and then switch to Code and Design view to view the button code. The code is selected.

Explore 15. Select the <param name="base" value="."> parameter in the Code pane, and then press the Delete key.

Explore 16. Select the Flash button in the Design pane. All of the code is selected again in the Code pane.

Explore 17. Select the base= "." attribute in the embed tag, and then press the Delete key.

18. Save the page, and preview the page in a browser.

19. Upload the site to the remote server, and then view the site over the Web.

Case 4. Sushi Ya-Ya Mary O'Brien has decided to add a Sushi-Shell Game to the Specials page. The game will be a Shockwave movie that e-mails the user a coupon for a free piece of the sushi special if the user finds the wasabi hidden under the sushi. Mary also wants you to add a sound clip to the Wasabi page. The sound file is a sound-only Flash movie that will play automatically when the page is loaded.

1. Open the **SushiYaYa** site you modified in Tutorial 7, Case 4.

2. Open the Specials page, and then draw a layer below the table.

3. Click in the layer, click the Shockwave button on the Media tab of the Insert bar.

4. Double-click the **sushigame.dcr** file in the **Tutorial.08/Cases** folder on your Data Disk, create a new folder in your root folder named "Media," and then add a copy of the sushigame.dcr file to the folder.

5. Select the Shockwave movie and, in the Property inspector, type "500" in the W text box, and then type "330" in the H text box.

Explore 6. Press the Play button to preview the movie in the Document window, and try the game.

Explore 7. Click the Stop button.

8. Save and close the page.

9. Open the Wasabi.htm page, place the pointer to the right of the page heading, and then click the Flash button on the Media tab of the Insert bar.

10. Double-click the **wasabisound_autoplay.swf** file in the **Tutorial.08/Cases** folder on your Data Disk, and then place a copy of the wasabisound_autoplay.swf file in the Media folder in your root folder.

Explore 11. Select the Flash movie, check the Autoplay checkbox in the Property inspector if necessary, and then uncheck the Loop check box if necessary.

Explore 12. Click the Play button to preview the sound.

13. Save the page, and preview the page in a browser.

14. Upload the site to the remote server, and then view the site over the Web.

QUICK | CHECK ANSWERS

Session 8.1

1. any special configurable objects that you might add to the pages of your site, which need a player or application that is not part of the browser—such as plug-ins, ActiveX controls, or helper applications—to display within a browser

2. some type of plug-in or player

3. The .swf file is used for the Web.

4. True

5. False

6. True

Session 8.2

1. Director

2. .dcr

3. Sound can begin to play after only a small portion downloads and will continue to play while the rest of the file continues to download.

4. Embed the sound in the page or link to the sound file. When sound is embedded directly in a page, the sound files in the page begin to download to the client computer as soon as the page is loaded. When you link to sound files, the file does not download to the client computer until the link is clicked.

5. RealMedia, MP3, QuickTime, and Windows Media

6. sound-only Flash movies; you should only embed sound-only Flash movies in a page

Session 8.3

1. frame size, playback quality, and sound parameters
2. .rm
3. To insure continuous playback of a video clip, it must be buffered, which means that the first 5 or 10 seconds of the clip are downloaded before it begins to play.
4. RealMedia, QuickTime, and Windows Media
5. True
6. False

In this tutorial you will:

- Explore the head content of a page

- Add keywords to a page

- Add a meta description to a page

- Explore libraries and create a library item

- Add a library item to Web pages

- Create a template

- Create Web pages from a template

- Add a form to a Web page

- Add form objects to a form

BUILDING ADVANCED SITES

Creating Templates and Adding Meta Tags, Library Items, and Forms to the Catalyst Site

CASE

Catalyst

Brian has been reviewing the Catalyst site. Before the site launches, he wants to add keywords and a meta description to each of the pages. Once the site is launched, he will list the pages with search engines. He has also decided that it is a good idea to make some of the commonly used site elements, such as the footer, library items. In addition, he wants to create templates for the site so that new pages added to the site in the future can be easily updated. Finally, he has decided that adding a form to the contact page is a good way to gather some additional information about the users of the Catalyst site.

SESSION 9.1

In this session, you will explore the head content for a page. You will learn how to optimize a page for search engine placement. You will add keywords and a meta description to a page, and then edit them. You will explore libraries and then create a library item and add it to the pages of the site.

Understanding **Head Content**

All Web pages contain head content. Remember that head content refers to anything that is placed within the <head> tags of Web pages. Users usually cannot see elements that are placed in the head of a page when the page is viewed in a browser. Head content typically either adds functionality to a page when viewed in a browser or provides information about the page for search engines. Browsers use head content to work with a page. For example, you placed <link> tags in the head of the pages to link an external style sheet to the page, and you placed <title> tags in the head of each page to display a page title in the title bar of a browser window. Two commonly used tags that add functionality to a page are:

- **Base.** Inserts a base tag into the head, which you use to enter the desired base URL for the page's document relative links.

- **Link.** Inserts a link tag into the head. The link tag is used most often to link an external style sheet to a page.

Link and Base buttons appear on the Head tab of the Insert bar.

Search engines use head content to learn about a page by looking for information in some of the meta tags included in the head of Web pages. A **meta tag** is a tag in the head content that holds information about the page, gives information to the server, or adds functionality to the page. For example, many search engines get the description of the page that is displayed when a user performs a search from the description meta tag in the head of the page. In addition to the page description, you use meta tags to add information such as keywords, author names, a copyright statement, and so forth to the code of a Web page. The exact purpose of a meta tag is defined by its attributes. You can use more than one meta tag in a page. The most important meta tags are:

- **Meta.** Inserts a generic meta tag into the head, and enables you to set attributes, values, and content for the meta tag.

- **Keywords.** Inserts a meta tag with the attribute name="keywords" into the head, which enables you to enter keywords for the page. The keywords meta tag is one of the most frequently used meta tags.

- **Description.** Inserts a meta tag with the attribute name="description" into the head, which enables you to enter a description for the page. The description meta tag is one of the most frequently used meta tags.

- **Refresh.** Inserts a meta tag with the attribute http-equiv="refresh" into the head, which enables you to enter amount of delay, in seconds, before the page is refreshed and choose whether to refresh the current page or open a new URL. Refreshing to a new URL is often used when a site has moved to redirect users who visit the old URL to the new location.

The Head tab of the Insert bar provides buttons for inserting these commonly used meta tags. You'll add keywords and a meta description to the head content of Web pages in the Catalyst site.

Optimizing Pages for Search Engine Placement

Optimizing the pages of a Web site for search engine placement is an important part of designing a Web site, because search engines enable people to find the site. Optimizing a page means doing everything you can to the page to insure that it is ranked highly in target search engines. There are many things you can do to optimize your pages for search engine placement. Be aware that each engine has a different set of formulas that determine page placement. These placement formulas change frequently and are a closely guarded secret to prevent designers from using this information to manipulate page placement. The most basic things you should do to every Web page are to add keywords and a meta description to the head of the pages. Optimizing Web pages does not automatically get them placed in search engines, but it will help a site receive higher listings when it is listed. Having a Web site not listed appropriately with search engines is like having a business located in an unmarked building with no published address. There is no way for people to know about the amazing things inside.

There are hundreds of search engines, but the top 10 to 12 major engines direct 90% of traffic. Some longer-standing top search engines are Google, Yahoo! (which is actually an index), and LookSmart. Unfortunately, the major search engines change frequently. The major engines also feed information to many smaller engines. You should concentrate on getting a site placed in the top 10 to 12 major engines to get the most listings for the site. To list the pages of your site with a search engine you can go to the Web site for each search engine and follow the guidelines to list each page of your site in that engine, or you can pay a service to list your site for you. In addition, some search engines send out **robots**, software that searches the Web and sends information back to the engine, to compile information that is used to list pages in the search engines. However, robots are unpredictable. In order to maintain a favorable listing position (listing within the first page of results), you must list the pages yourself or pay a service to list them for you. Finally, you should re-list the pages of your site with each engine to maintain a favorable position. Some engines allow you to re-list pages monthly, whereas others prefer that you re-list only a few times a year. Guidelines for re-listing can be found with the listing information on the Web site for each major search engine.

In this session, you will begin to optimize your pages for search engine placement by adding keywords and a meta description to each page.

Adding and Editing Keywords

Keywords are one of the elements many search engines use to index Web pages. A **keyword** is a descriptive word or phrase that is placed in the meta tag with the attribute name="keywords". You add one keywords meta tag to the head of each page and then list all of the keywords for the site in that tag. The keywords you choose should be the words you think most people will type into search engines to look for your site or the words you would like people to find your site under. Remember to include the name of the company and products or services in the list. It can also be helpful to include common misspellings of the company or product name. For example, good keywords for the Catalyst site would be Catalyst Records, band names, and album titles.

Keywords can be individual words or short phrases fewer than six words. (Some search engines may penalize you for adding longer phrases by decreasing your ranking order or by dropping the site from the index.) When you use phrases, generally each word is indexed separately and together. For example, if you use the phrase "indie music" for the Catalyst site, the word "indie" and the word "music" will both be indexed as well as the phrase "indie music."

You can use as many keywords as you would like; however, the first 10 words are the most important because many search engines use only the first 10 words in the keyword list to index a site. Additionally, search engines often give higher placement to sites that use the keywords within the content of the pages, so make sure that the content of your Web sites use the keywords many times. For example, because the Catalyst site uses the words "indie" and "music" many times within the text of the pages, the pages of the Catalyst site may be ranked higher in value under these keywords than the pages of a site that uses these keywords but does not use the words in the content of the pages of the site. Another example might be if you use the word "hippopotamus" in the keywords list. The pages of the Catalyst site may receive a lower ranking under that keyword because the word "hippopotamus" never appears in the text of the pages of the Catalyst site. Conversely, using the keywords excessively in the page content of a site may lead to penalties, including decreased ranking of the site or complete removal of the site from the index, because many search engines see this as an attempt at spamming or artificially attempting to inflate your listing position.

Adding Keywords and Examining the Code

Although you can type the keywords meta tag directly in Code view, it is simpler to use a dialog box to add keywords to a page and let Dreamweaver create the code. You add keywords to a page with the Keywords button on the Head tab of the Insert bar. When entering keywords, you should use all lowercase letters because in most search engines lowercase letters represent both upper and lowercase letters while uppercase letters makes an item case specific. You should also separate each word or phrase with a comma. When you add keywords to a page, the following code is inserted into the head of the page:

```
<meta name="keywords" content="keyword1, keyword2, keyword3">
```

Meta tags are unpaired tags. This means that each tag stands alone and not as part of a set of opening and closing tags. Like all tags, the meta tag starts with an opening bracket followed by the name of the tag, meta. The tag name is followed by a series of tag attributes and values. The first attribute in the keywords meta tag is name and the value is the type of meta tag, "keywords". The second attribute is content and its value is the content of the tag, or the list of keywords. The tag ends with a closing bracket.

Brian asks you to insert the list of keywords into the home page of the Catalyst site. Then you'll examine the code in Code view.

To add keywords to a page:

1. Start **Dreamweaver**, open the **NewCatalyst** site that you modified in the Tutorial 8 Review Assignments, and then open the **home page**.

2. Click the **Keywords** button 🖼 on the **Head** tab of the Insert bar. The Keywords dialog box opens so you can type the words you want. Remember to use all lowercase letters and to separate each word or phrase with a comma.

3. Type **catalyst records, indie music, sloth child, dizzied connections, life in minor chords, surface suction, spinning life, black lab, them apples, i believe in ferries, independent scene, denton music, underground sound** in the Keywords text box. See Figure 9-1.

Figure 9-1 | KEYWORDS DIALOG BOX

keywords for Catalyst site

Keywords:
catalyst records, indie music, sloth child, dizzied connections, life in minor chords, surface suction, spinning life, black lab, them apples, i believe in ferries, independent scene, denton music, underground sound

4. Click the **OK** button, and then save the page. The keywords meta tag is added to the head of the page. Its exact location within the head content may vary depending on where the insertion point is located in the page when you click the Keywords button.

5. Switch to **Code view** and scroll, if necessary, to view the keywords meta tag in the Document window. The tag is located somewhere in the head section of the page. See Figure 9-2.

Figure 9-2 | KEYWORDS IN CODE VIEW

keywords meta tag (location may differ on your screen)

closing head tag

Catalyst - Home (Dreamweaver/index*)

```
64  }
65  MM_reloadPage(true);
66
67  function MM_swapImgRestore() { //v3.0
68    var i,x,a=document.MM_sr; for(i=0;a&&i<a.length&&(x=a[i])&&x.oSrc;i++) x.src=x.oSrc;
69  }
70
71  function MM_swapImage() { //v3.0
72    var i,j=0,x,a=MM_swapImage.arguments; document.MM_sr=new Array; for(i=0;i<(a.length-2);i+=3)
73    if ((x=MM_findObj(a[i]))!=null){document.MM_sr[j++]=x; if(!x.oSrc) x.oSrc=x.src; x.src=a[i+2];}
74  }
75  //-->
76  </script>
77  <meta name="keywords" content="catalyst records, indie music, sloth child, dizzied connections, life in
    minor chords, surface suction, spinning life, black lab, them apples, i believe in ferries, independent
    scene, denton music, underground sound, catalist">
78  </head>
79
80  <body bgcolor="#FFFFFF" background="Graphics/background.gif" text="#000000" link="#FFCC00" vlink=
    "#FF6600" alink="#FF9900" leftmargin="5" topmargin="0" marginwidth="5" marginheight="0" onLoad=
    "MM_preloadImages('Graphics/labelDown.gif','Graphics/labelOver.gif','Graphics/labelOWD.gif',
    'Graphics/bandsOver.gif','Graphics/bandsOWD.gif','Graphics/catalogueDown.gif',
    'Graphics/catalogueOver.gif','Graphics/catalogueOWD.gif','Graphics/tourdatesDown.gif',
    'Graphics/tourdatesOver.gif','Graphics/tourdatesOWD.gif','Graphics/contactDown.gif',
```

▼ Properties

Next, you will edit the keywords.

Editing Keywords

Sometimes you'll find that you want to add another keyword to the list, delete a keyword from the list, or correct the spelling of a keyword in the list. You can do any of these by editing the list of keywords that has already been added to a page. To edit the keywords, you open the page in Code view and then either edit the list directly or select the keywords meta tag and edit the list in the Property inspector. You could also open the page in the Document window, switch to Design view, click View on the main menu bar, and then click Head Content. A pane opens so you can select the appropriate symbol for the element you want to edit; you then make the necessary changes in the Property inspector.

Sara's research shows that Catalyst is frequently misspelled as "Catalist." You'll add this misspelling to the list of keywords on the home page.

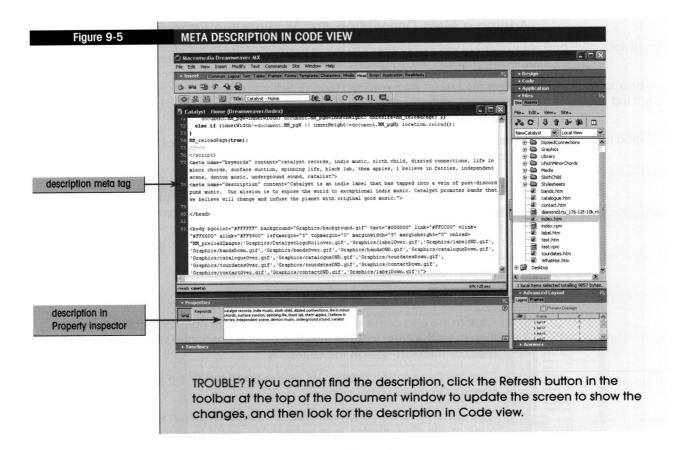

Figure 9-5   META DESCRIPTION IN CODE VIEW

description meta tag

description in Property inspector

TROUBLE? If you cannot find the description, click the Refresh button in the toolbar at the top of the Document window to update the screen to show the changes, and then look for the description in Code view.

Editing a Meta Description

Periodically you may want to update a meta description to reflect changes in the Web site or the company and its products. You can edit a meta description in the same ways that you edit keywords. Click in the description in the Document window in Code view, and then either change the description in the Property inspector or in the Document window.

Keywords and descriptions should be added to all the pages of a Web site. Later you will add them to the remaining pages of the Catalyst site.

Understanding Library Items

Sometimes you need to add an element to many pages in a site. As a site-centric design tool, Dreamweaver has features, such as library items, to help you automate site design and decrease redundant work. A **library item** is a page element (a piece of a Web page) saved as an .lbi file that can be inserted into the other pages of a site. It is useful to create library items for elements that you intend to reuse or update frequently, such as footers or an upcoming events list that will be displayed on more than one page of a site. You can have any number of library items in your site, but making an element a library item is helpful only if you are going to reuse the element a number of times.

A library item can include most elements in the body section of a Web page, including bits of code, text, images, tables, forms, formatting, and so forth. You can even include a navigation bar in a library item, but you cannot use the "show down state initially" feature effectively because every page in which the library item is included would show the Down state for the same button. Library items can only be elements found in the body of a Web page. You cannot create a library item for head content, and you cannot include timelines.

When you include a library item in a Web page, the regular HTML code for the element is inserted into the page along with the a hidden link to the library item. When you edit a library item, Dreamweaver updates each page in which the library item is used and changes the code in each page. For example, you'll create a library item for the footer on the Catalyst Web pages that includes the footer text, formatting, and a link. By making the footer a library item and then inserting the library item into the pages of the site, you can easily change the footer as needed. If, for example, the footer link changes, you simply change the link once in the library item and Dreamweaver changes the link on every page in which the footer library item is used. This can save a great amount of time in a large site.

Library items are stored in the Dreamweaver library for the site. A **library** is a collection of library items that are located in the Library folder in the root folder of the site. Every site created in Dreamweaver that has library items or HTML styles will have a Library folder. You can view the library in the Assets panel when you click the Library button. The Library and library items are Dreamweaver authoring tools (like HTML styles). This means that unlike other items that you have added to your pages, CSS styles for example, libraries and library items do not exist outside Dreamweaver. When you make a change in a library item, Dreamweaver updates each page in which the library item is used and changes the code in each page. When you upload your site to the remote server, you do not even need to upload the Library folder because all the code for each library item is added to the individual pages in which an instance of that item is found.

The downside to using library items is that you cannot change the individual instances of the item without disconnecting the instance from the library item. For example, if you decide that the footer should be bold on one page of the Catalyst site, you cannot change the instance of the library item only in that page. Instead, you must delete the library item from that page and create a unique footer. You could also change the library item, which would change the look of the footer on every page in the site. This all or nothing aspect of library items can be somewhat limiting.

Creating and Using a Library Item

You can create as many library items as you need for a site. To create a library item, you simply create the element in a page, select the element, and then drag the selected element to the library in the Assets panel. It is important to select all the text, the formatting elements, and anything else you want to include in the library item. For example, if you want to include a blank line above and below the footer in the library item, you must select the line break above and below the footer when you create the library item. It is important to pay attention to what you are selecting because everything you select will be included in the library item. It is sometimes useful to switch to Code and Design view so that you can see the tags which are included in the library item as well as viewing the item in the page. Once all the elements are included the library item, you then name the new library item and it will be added to the library. It is a good idea to choose a descriptive name that will help you identify the content of the library item. As with other filenames, use only alphanumeric characters, do not use spaces or special characters, and do not start the name with a number. Every library item is saved as an .lbi file.

Because library items can contain only elements found in the body of a Web page, CSS styles are not included in the library item. Recall that the CSS style sheet code or the link to the CSS style sheet is inserted in the head of the page. When you create a library item from a page that uses CSS styles, a dialog box opens, notifying you that the selection may not look the same when placed in other pages because the CSS style sheet information is not included in the item. The library item will still reference the CSS style sheet and, as long as the pages into which the library item is inserted are attached to the style sheet, the library item will look the same in the new pages.

REFERENCE **WINDOW**   **RW**

Creating a Library Item

- Open an existing page, and then create the page element you want as the library item, if necessary.
- Drag the selected page element to the library in the Assets panel.
- Type a name for the new library item, and then press the Enter key.

or

- Click the New Library Item button in the library in the Assets panel.
- Type a name for the new library item, and then press the Enter key.
- Click the Edit button in the library in the Assets panel.
- Create the page element you want as the new library item, and then save and close the library item.

You will create a library item for the Catalyst site from the Catalyst footer.

To create a library item:

1. Switch to **Design view**, scroll to the bottom of the page, and then select the footer and the blank line above the footer.

2. Open the **Assets** panel in the Files panel group, and then click the **Library** button in the Assets panel. The library is displayed in the Assets panel.

3. Drag the selected footer and blank line to the library. A dialog box opens, warning you that the selection may not look the same when placed in other documents because the style sheet information is not copied with it.

   TROUBLE? If the dialog box does not open, then the message was disabled for your installation of Dreamweaver. Continue with Step 5.

4. Click the **OK** button. An untitled library item is added to the library. See Figure 9-6.

Figure 9-6   LIBRARY DISPLAYED IN ASSETS PANEL

5. Type **CatalystFooter**, and then press the **Enter** key to name the library item. A dialog box opens, asking you whether you want to update the pages that use the library item.

6. Click the **Update** button. The Update Pages dialog box opens, and you can view the update status in the Status section.

   TROUBLE? If a dialog box opens, saying that you cannot copy the SetNavBar Image behavior, click the OK button, and then continue with Step 7. You need to click the OK button in this dialog box every time it opens.

7. Click the **Close** button when the update is complete. The page now contains a link to the library item and must be saved again.

8. Save the page, and then close the home page.

Now you will add the library item to the other pages of the Catalyst site.

Adding a Library Item to Pages and Examining the Code

Once you create a library item, you can add it to any page in the Web site. Simply open the page to which you want to add a library item, and then drag the library item from the library in the Assets panel to the desired location on the page.

The code for the page elements is added to the page along with a hidden link to the library item.

```
<!-- #BeginLibraryItem "/Library/CatalystFooter.lbi"-->
<p align="center"> </p>
<p class="CatalystFooter"> &copy; copyright
 Catalyst, Inc. 2004</a></p>
<!-- #EndLibraryItem -->
```

The library item starts with a comment tag. Comment tags are unpaired tags that are used to add notes to the code that do not appear in the page or affect the way the HTML is rendered. For example, you might use a comment tag to add a note that helps you remember the use or purpose of a section of code. Comment tags are used to denote library items, because they will not cause problems even when the page is edited in another program. The comment tag begins with an opening bracket followed by an exclamation point and two dashes, <!--, and ends with two dashes followed by a closing bracket, -->. Everything that appears between the dashes is considered a comment and will be ignored by the browser. Every library item begins with a comment tag that tells Dreamweaver that a library item has started, #BeginLibraryItem, followed by a path to that library item, "/Library/CatalystFooter.lbi". All code for the page element in the library item follows the comment tag. Each library item ends with a second comment tag that tells Dreamweaver the library item is ending, #EndLibraryItem.

Once the library item has been added to a page you can move it within the page by selecting it and dragging it to the new location. You can add the same library item to a page as many times as you would like, and you can add as many different library items to a page as you would like.

You'll add the CatalystFooter library item to the other pages of the site, and then you will view the code.

To add a library item to a page:

1. Open the **bands** page, and then delete the blank line above the footer and the footer from the bottom of the page.

2. Open the library in the Assets panel.

3. Select the **CatalystFooter** library item, and then drag it to the bottom of the bands page below the RemainingText layer. The CatalystFooter library item is inserted into the bands page.

4. Click in the empty space to the right of the footer to deselect it. The footer is highlighted in pale yellow. See Figure 9-7.

| Figure 9-7 | BANDS PAGE WITH LIBRARY ITEM |

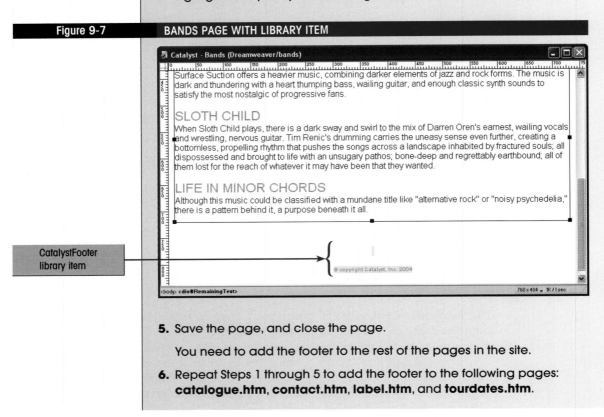

CatalystFooter library item

5. Save the page, and close the page.

   You need to add the footer to the rest of the pages in the site.

6. Repeat Steps 1 through 5 to add the footer to the following pages: **catalogue.htm**, **contact.htm**, **label.htm**, and **tourdates.htm**.

Next, you will open the bands page and view the code for the CatalystFooter library item.

To view the library item code:

1. Open the **bands** page, select the footer, and then switch to **Code and Design view**. The code for the CatalystFooter library item is selected in the Code pane. See Figure 9-8.

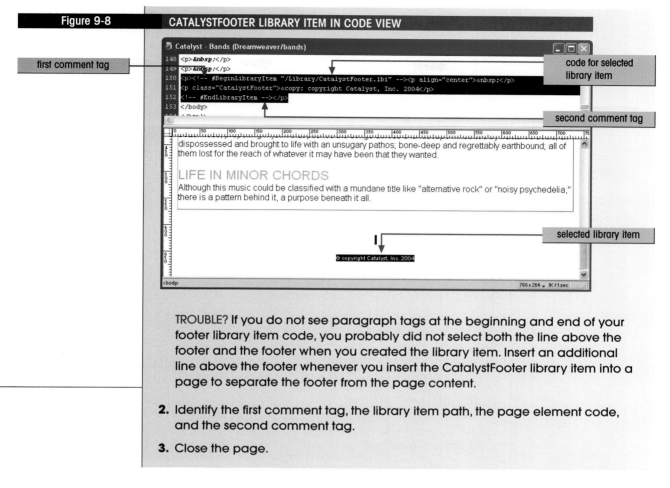

Figure 9-8   CATALYSTFOOTER LIBRARY ITEM IN CODE VIEW

TROUBLE? If you do not see paragraph tags at the beginning and end of your footer library item code, you probably did not select both the line above the footer and the footer when you created the library item. Insert an additional line above the footer whenever you insert the CatalystFooter library item into a page to separate the footer from the page content.

2. Identify the first comment tag, the library item path, the page element code, and the second comment tag.

3. Close the page.

If you discover you need to make a change to a library item, you can edit it.

Editing a Library Item

One of the most useful aspects of a library item is that you can update every instance of the item by editing the library item itself. This is much faster, not to mention possibly more accurate, than having to edit the same element on many pages. To edit a library item, you simply open the library item and make the changes. You open a library item either by double-clicking the library item in the library or by selecting an instance of the library item in a page and clicking the Open button in the Property inspector. Once you have completed the changes, you save the library item in the same way that you would a regular HTML page. Dreamweaver presents a list of all the pages in which that library item has been used and asks if you would like to update the files. When you choose to update the files, Dreamweaver makes the changes to the library item in each page that was listed. After the pages are updated, a log may open, showing the history of the changes made to the pages.

Brian has decided that it would be beneficial to make the CatalystFooter an e-mail link so users can quickly contact the company.

To edit a library item:

1. Open the **bands** page, select the **CatalystFooter** library item, and then click the **Open** button in the Property inspector. A Document window containing the CatalystFooter libarary item opens. See Figure 9-9.

Figure 9-9	DOCUMENT WINDOW WITH CATALYSTFOOTER LIBRARY ITEM

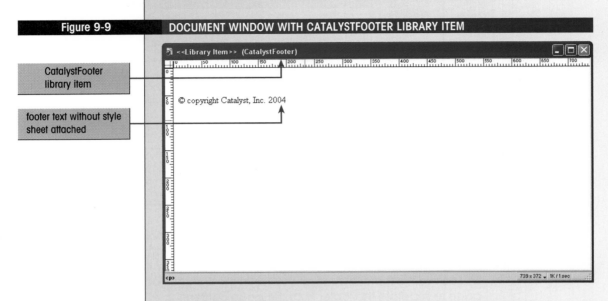

CatalystFooter library item

footer text without style sheet attached

The text does not have the appropriate style because the style sheet is not attached to the actual library item. After you edit the library item and update the pages, the library item will again display the appropriate style. Next, you'll add the e-mail link to the text.

2. Select the footer text, type **mailto:info@catalystnoise.com** in the Link text box in the Property inspector, press the **Enter** key, and then deselect the text. See Figure 9-10.

Figure 9-10	CATALYSTFOOTER LIBRARY ITEM WITH LINKED TEXT

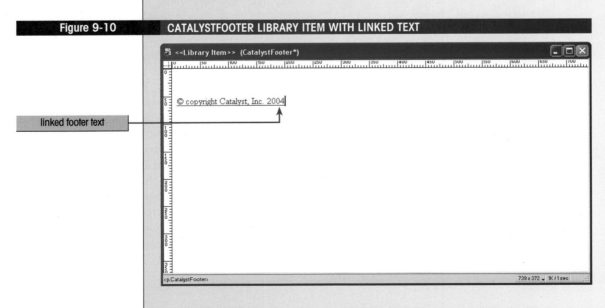

linked footer text

3. Save the Library Item page. The Update Library Items dialog box opens, listing all the pages that contain that library item. See Figure 9-11.

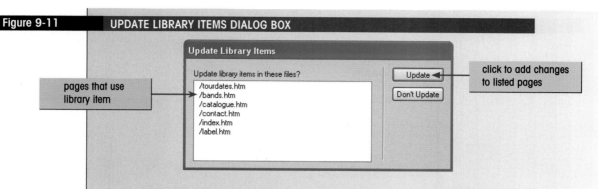

Figure 9-11   UPDATE LIBRARY ITEMS DIALOG BOX

pages that use library item

Update Library Items

Update library items in these files?
/tourdates.htm
/bands.htm
/catalogue.htm
/contact.htm
/index.htm
/label.htm

Update

Don't Update

click to add changes to listed pages

4. Click the **Update** button to update the library item in the listed pages. Dreamweaver updates all the pages that contain the library item and the Update Pages dialog box opens, showing a log of the updates. See Figure 9-12.

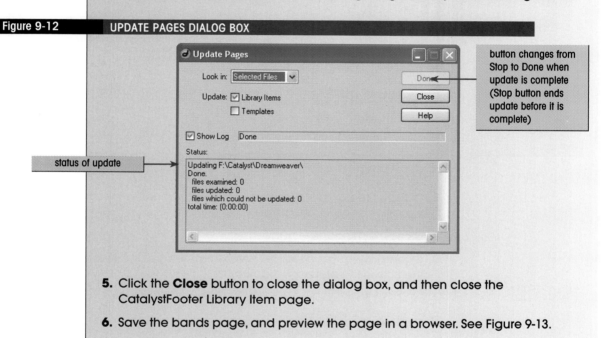

Figure 9-12   UPDATE PAGES DIALOG BOX

Update Pages

Look in: Selected Files

Update: ☑ Library Items
☐ Templates

☑ Show Log   Done

Status:
Updating F:\Catalyst\Dreamweaver\
Done.
  files examined: 0
  files updated: 0
  files which could not be updated: 0
total time: (0:00:00)

Done

Close

Help

status of update

button changes from Stop to Done when update is complete (Stop button ends update before it is complete)

5. Click the **Close** button to close the dialog box, and then close the CatalystFooter Library Item page.

6. Save the bands page, and preview the page in a browser. See Figure 9-13.

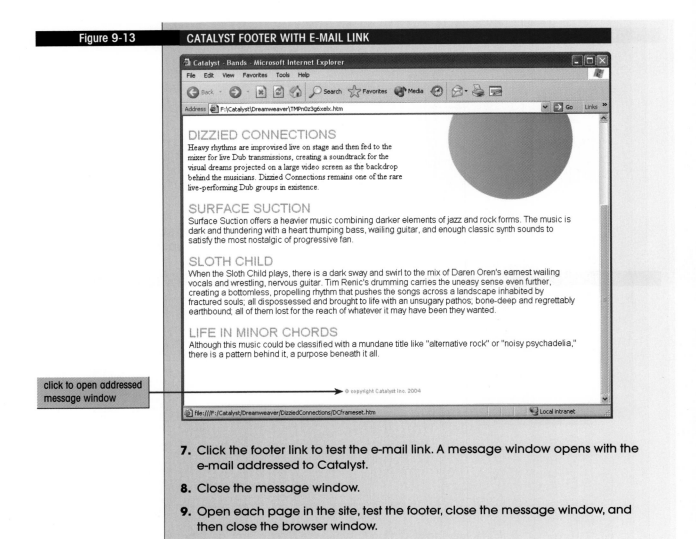

Figure 9-13   CATALYST FOOTER WITH E-MAIL LINK

click to open addressed message window

7. Click the footer link to test the e-mail link. A message window opens with the e-mail addressed to Catalyst.

8. Close the message window.

9. Open each page in the site, test the footer, close the message window, and then close the browser window.

If you don't need a specific library item, you can delete it.

Deleting a Library Item

You can delete a library item from Web pages or from the library. If a library item is no longer appropriate to include on a specific page, you can quickly delete it from the page by selecting the library item on the page and then pressing the Delete key. That instance of the library item is deleted on the page, but it remains available in the library. If a library item is no longer appropriate to include anywhere in a site, you can delete it from the library by selecting the library item in the library and dragging it to the Delete button (trash can icon) in the Assets panel. If you delete a library item from the site while it is being used in the pages of the site, the content of the library item will remain in each page in which it was placed, but the items will no longer be library items. It is a good idea to delete unused library items from the site so that your site remains uncluttered and well organized.

In this session, you added meta tags and library items to the Catalyst Web site. In the next session, you will create templates for the Web site.

Session 9.1 Quick Check

1. What are meta tags?

2. List two frequently used meta tags.

3. Why are keywords important?

4. Where are library items stored?

5. What type of tag begins and ends the code for a library item?

6. What is one of the most useful aspects of a library item?

SESSION 9.2

In this session, you will create a template. You will add regions to the template and then you will create a new page from the template. You will also edit the template and create a nested template.

Understanding Templates

Professional designers often plan and design Web sites based on templates. A **template** is a special page that enables the designer to separate the style of the page from the content by "locking" the page layout. The designer designates what is locked on a page by creating editable regions and noneditable regions. **Editable regions** are areas that can be changed in the pages created from a template. **Noneditable regions** are areas that can be changed in the template but cannot be changed in the pages created from a template. You use a template to create multiple Web pages that share the same layout as well as any content that is placed in the noneditable regions of the template. For example, you can create a template from which to create any new pages added to the Catalyst site. The template should include all of the elements that are used in every page—such as the page properties, Catalyst logo, navigation bar, CSS styles, and footer—in noneditable regions. The template should have editable regions for elements that vary from page to page, such as the page heading and content sections of the pages.

Creating a template for a Web site requires more planning and forethought than creating individual pages for a site. You need to thoroughly plan the layout of the pages prior to creating the site to ensure that you have set up the appropriate editable regions. Recall that editable regions are the only regions that can contain unique page content. For example, you need to include an editable region for the page heading in the template for the Catalyst site because a unique page heading appears in the same location on every page. You also need to include an editable region for page content because each page contains unique content displayed below the page heading. Although it is important to include editable regions for each general area of the page, it is also important not to create too many specific editable regions, which would limit the flexibility of the pages. For example, you do not want to set up separate editable regions for subheadings because subheadings are not used on every page. Adding a separate editable region for a subheading would add a separate subheading region to every page of the site. Instead, you will include subheadings in pages that require them in the editable region that you set up for content. It is tempting to shortcut the planning phase when designing sites with simple pages that are not template-based. When you begin to design large, professional, template-based sites, the pages are more interconnected and the design requires a great deal of forethought.

Templates are an amazing tool because they reduce a lot of the redundant work that goes into creating and maintaining a Web site. You do the work once to set up the layout of a page, including page properties, CSS styles, and a navigation bar, in a template. You or others can use that template to quickly create any number of pages with that same layout. Anyone can then add content to the pages without affecting their layout or design. If you later decide to modify the layout, you need to make the changes only in one place—the template. Any pages created from a template are connected to that template. If you modify a template, all the pages connected to that template are updated to reflect the changes you made. This saves you time and ensures consistency across the pages.

The drawback to using templates is that they can limit your flexibility to vary the content of pages created from the template. For example, to a large extent head content is locked on pages created from templates, so you cannot add many common elements that add code to the head of a page, such as timelines or navigation bars, to the template-based pages. Also, you cannot add content outside the established editable regions.

There is usually only one main template used in a site, but you can use more than one main template if you have distinctly different styles of pages in one site. For example, if Brian decided that each band under the Catalyst label were going to have its own Web page in the Catalyst site, and that the bands pages were going to have a completely different look and feel than the other pages of the site, it would be a good idea to create a separate template for those pages. Using more than two main templates in one site is generally not a good idea because the site can get cumbersome and confusing. In addition, it is easy to forget to make changes that affect the whole site to every template.

Now you will create a main template for the Catalyst site.

Creating a Template

You create a template by opening the page on which you want to base the template, clicking the Make Template button on the Templates tab of the Insert bar, and then naming and saving the template. The page from which you created the template is unaffected and is not attached to the template. The template is saved as a file with the .dwt extension in a Templates folder in the root folder of your site. If the Templates folder does not already exist in the site, Dreamweaver creates one. You can view all the templates for a site in the Assets panel when the Templates button is selected. As with other filenames, use only alphanumeric characters, do not use spaces or special characters, and do not start the name with a number. If you create more than one main template in a site, choose a name that will help you to identify the template.

Templates can be created from a new blank page or an existing page. When you create a template from a blank page, you must add all the elements you want to include in pages made from the template, such as page properties and style sheets, to the template page. In the Catalyst site, for example, you must attach the template to the CSS style sheet and create any new CSS styles you plan to use in the subsequent pages, you must add the Catalyst logo to the top of the template to have the logo appear on the new pages, and you must add the keywords and meta description that will be used in the pages of the site. When you create a template from an existing page, all of these shared elements are already in the page.

Although you can save a template from one site into the Templates folder in another site and use that template to create pages in the other site, it is not a good idea to do so. Copying a template from one site to another causes all the relative links in the template (including links to graphics and other materials used in the template) to become absolute links. To use the template in the new site, you must change the links to relative links and copy the materials used in the template to the new site's root directory. Furthermore, choosing a template from another site when you create a new Web page causes the above problems and it does not move a copy of the template to the new site. Also, if you choose a template from another site and you leave the Update Page When Template Changes checkbox checked (which is its default state), then the links will be in a locked area of the template and you will be unable to change them. Thus, you will not be able to view the template content when you post your new page to the Web. Because of these problems, it is a good idea to create a new template for each site.

Creating a Template

- Open an existing page, and then click the Make Template button on the Templates tab of the Insert bar (*or* open the Assets panel, click the Templates button, and then click the New Template button to create a template from a blank page).
- Type a name for the template, and then save the template.
- If you created a new template from the Assets panel, select the template in the Assets panel, and then click the Edit Template button.
- Add editable regions to the template using the buttons on the Templates tab of the Insert bar.
- Save the template.

You'll create a template for the Catalyst Web site using the existing label page. You'll use the label page because it has the most basic layout of all the existing pages—it doesn't contain any special media elements—therefore it will be the easiest page to modify. Brian is developing a series of new pages with information about indie music and the current underground music scene in the United States. The template will be used to create these new pages of the site. Eventually, the existing pages in the Catalyst site will be converted to the template so that the look of the entire site can be managed and updated more easily.

To create a template from an existing page:

1. If you took a break after the previous session, make sure **Dreamweaver** is running and the **NewCatalyst site** is open.

2. Open the **label** page, and then click the **Make Template** button 📄 on the **Templates** tab of the Insert bar. The Save As Template dialog box opens.

3. If necessary, click the **Site** list arrow, and then click **NewCatalyst**. This selects the site in which you will save the template. See Figure 9-14.

Figure 9-14   SAVE AS TEMPLATE DIALOG BOX

Make Template button

select site to save template in

type template name

label page being saved as template

4. Type **MainTemplate** in the Save As text box, and then click the **Save** button. Dreamweaver creates a copy of the page with the name MainTemplate, a Templates folder is created in the root folder, and the template is saved in that folder. See Figure 9-15.

| Figure 9-15 | NEW MAINTEMPLATE PAGE |

saved template page

Templates folder created in root folder

MainTemplate.dwt saved in Templates folder

You'll delete the page-specific content from the template as you add editable regions to the page.

Adding Regions to a Template

When you create a template, the entire document is locked. In other words, the page is one big noneditable region and only the template itself can be edited. You must add at least one editable region to the template to be able to change page content and other elements in the pages created from the template. Anything outside an editable region can be altered only within the template.

There are several types of regions that you can add to a template:

- **Editable Region.** An area in a template-based page that can be edited. Any area can be defined as an editable region. You can designate either an entire table or a single table cell as editable; however, you cannot designate multiple cells as one editable region. Also, layers and layer content are separate elements. Designating a layer as editable enables you to move the layer. Designating the area inside the layer as editable enables you to change the layer content.

- **Optional Region.** A noneditable region for which you set conditions for displaying the content in that region in template-based pages. You set parameters for displaying the optional region content when you create the template. The regions are displayed in the pages created from the template only if those conditions or parameters are met.

■ **Repeating Region.** A region that can be duplicated within the pages made from the template, enabling the region to expand without altering the page design. For example, you can designate a table row as a repeating region, and then you can repeat the table row in the template-based pages to create expanding lists and so forth. The repeating region is used so frequently with tables that Dreamweaver has a special Repeating Table button in addition to the Repeating Region button on the Templates tab of the Insert bar.

■ **Editable Optional Region.** An optional region that is editable.

You'll create an editable region and a repeating region in the MainTemplate template.

With the exception of the title and a few other page-specific elements, the head content is locked in the pages created from the template. This means that you cannot add navigation bars and many other common elements that place code into the head of the page to template-based pages. Many elements that add code to the head of the page must be added either directly to the template or, sometimes, in a library item that is placed in an editable region.

Regions added to templates are invisible elements. When you show Invisible Elements, a border appears around the regions in both the template and the template-based pages and a tab appears at the top of each region in the Document window. Although the border and tab help you to quickly identify each region, they also interfere slightly with the way the layout appears in the Document window. To view a page as it will appear in browsers, you must hide the Invisible Elements or preview the page in a browser.

You will show the Invisible Elements, if necessary, and then add editable regions to the main template in the Catalyst site. You'll begin by creating an editable region named "PageHeading" at the top of the template page. You want to make the page heading an editable region so that you can change the heading for each new page created from the template.

To add an editable region to a template:

1. If necessary, click **View** on the menu bar, point to **Visual Aids**, and then click **Invisible Elements**. The Invisible Elements are displayed.

2. Select the **Catalyst Label** Flash text. The page heading is selected.

3. Click the **Editable Region** button 📝 on the Templates tab of the Insert bar. The New Editable Region dialog box opens. See Figure 9-16.

| Figure 9-16 | NEW EDITABLE REGION DIALOG BOX |

type name of editable region here

4. Type **PageHeading** in the Name text box, and then click the **OK** button. The new editable region is added to the template, a blue border surrounds the page heading text, and a tab appears over the text. See Figure 9-17.

| Figure 9-17 | EDITABLE REGION ADDED TO MAINTEMPLATE PAGE |

tab with editable region name

editable region

border surrounds editable region

PageHeading

CATALYST LABEL

NEWS - HEY, LOOK WHAT THEY'RE SAYING!!!

"Catalyst perpetuates its legacy of being the best post-punk rock label out there." - BlackDogPrint

"Catalyst has tapped into a vein of post-discord punk that just doesn't quit." - Optioned

"A serious indie rock force to contend with..." - Modern Hits

TROUBLE? If the tab is not visible in the Document window, then Invisible Elements are hidden in the Document window. Click View on the menu bar, point to Visual Aids, and then click Invisible Elements.

You'll change the page heading from the page-specific content to generic placeholder text. You need to create a new Flash text file with the placeholder text, otherwise the Flash text in the label page will change as well because the same Flash text file will be used in both pages.

5. Double-click the **Flash text** to open the Insert Flash Text dialog box

6. Select **Catalyst Label** in the Text text box, and then type **NEW PAGE HEADING**. This is the generic placeholder text.

7. Type **../Media/HeadingTemplate.swf** in the Save As text box, and then click the **OK** button. The placeholder text is saved in the Media folder and appears in the template.

Next, you'll create a repeating region with a table. You will use the Repeating Table button and the table will be added to the repeating region for you. The Repeating Table button also adds an editable area in the table so that you can add content to the table in pages that are created from the template. Remember that repeating regions can be editable or noneditable. If you plan to add content in the repeating region within the pages created from the template, you must add an editable region within the repeating region.

You'll delete the body text from the template page and add a repeating table with an editable region named "Content." You'll use this repeating table to enter the general content for each page that is created from the template.

To create a repeating table:

1. Delete all the text below the page heading and above the footer in the template page.

2. Click the **Repeating Table** button ⊞ on the **Templates** tab of the Insert bar. The Insert Repeating Table dialog box opens. See Figure 9-18.

Figure 9-18   **INSERT REPEATING TABLE DIALOG BOX**

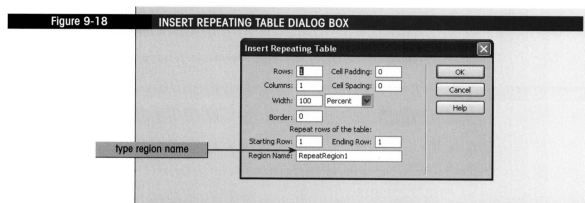

type region name

3. Type **1** in the Rows text box, type **1** in the Columns text box, type **100** in the Width text box, select **Percent** from the list, and then type **0** in the Border text box. This will create a borderless one-cell table the full width of the page.

4. Type **Content** in the Region Name text box, and then click the **OK** button. A repeating table named "Content" with an unnamed editable region is placed in the page below the page heading. See Figure 9-19.

Figure 9-19   **REPEATING TABLE WITH EDITABLE REGION**

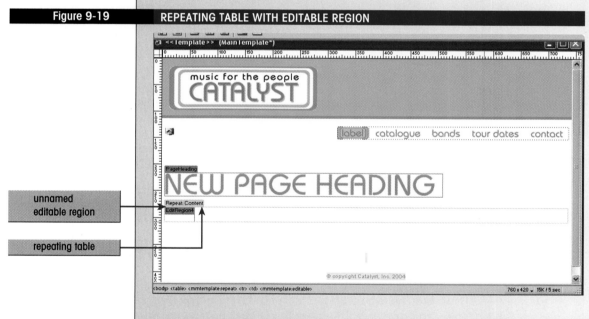

unnamed editable region

repeating table

5. Type **Add content here**. This placeholder text will act as a reminder to enter the appropriate content in the template-based page.

Finally, you will modify the navigation bar so that no images appear in the Down state when the page is loaded. This is necessary because you will not be able to modify the navigation bar in the pages created from the template. If the navigation bar was not altered, all the pages created from the template would display the label button in the Down state initially.)

To modify the navigation bar:

1. Click **Modify** on the menu bar, and then click **Navigation Bar**. The Modify Navigation Bar dialog box opens.

2. If necessary, click the **Nav Bar Elements** list arrow, and then click **Label ***.

3. Click the **Show "Down Image" Initially** checkbox to uncheck it, and then click the **OK** button.

4. Save the template page, and preview the page in a browser. See Figure 9-20.

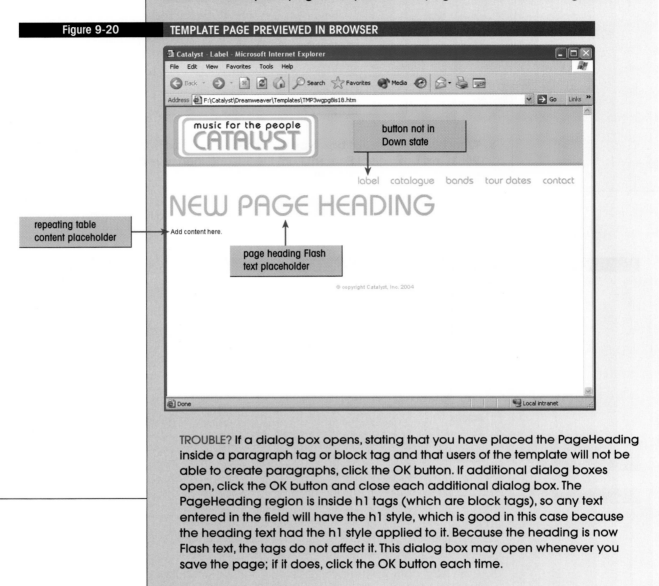

Figure 9-20

TEMPLATE PAGE PREVIEWED IN BROWSER

repeating table content placeholder

page heading Flash text placeholder

button not in Down state

TROUBLE? If a dialog box opens, stating that you have placed the PageHeading inside a paragraph tag or block tag and that users of the template will not be able to create paragraphs, click the OK button. If additional dialog boxes open, click the OK button and close each additional dialog box. The PageHeading region is inside h1 tags (which are block tags), so any text entered in the field will have the h1 style, which is good in this case because the heading text had the h1 style applied to it. Because the heading is now Flash text, the tags do not affect it. This dialog box may open whenever you save the page; if it does, click the OK button each time.

5. Close the browser.

After you create a template, you should test it by creating a page from the template.

Creating a Web Page from a Template

There are two ways to create a Web page from a template. You can create a new page based on the template and then add the appropriate content to the editable regions. Or you can apply the template to an existing page that already contains content.

Creating a New Template-Based Page

Creating a new page from a template is very similar to creating a new page. So far, you have used the File menu in the Site panel to create new pages because pages created from the Site panel are automatically placed in the root folder of the site. However, you should use the main menu bar to create the new page rather than the Site panel menu bar, because the Site panel does not give you the option to create a page from a template. When you select the New command from the File menu on the main menu bar, the New Document dialog box opens. On the Templates tab, you select the current site, and then you select the template you want to use to create the page. Once the page is created, you add content to the editable regions and then save the page as usual.

REFERENCE WINDOW **RW**

Creating a Template-Based Page
- Click File on the main menu bar, and then click New.
- Click the Templates tab in the New Document dialog box.
- Select the current site, and then select the template from which you want to create the page.
- Click the Create button.
- Input the desired information into the editable regions of the page, and then save the page.

Brian wants to see a sample page from the new template before more pages are added to the Catalyst site. You will create a new page from the MainTemplate as a test page, and then add a new page heading and some content to the page.

To create a new Web page from a template:

1. Click **File** on the menu bar, and then click **New**. The New Document dialog box opens.

   TROUBLE? If the New from Template dialog box opens, the Template tab is already selected. Continue with Step 3.

2. Click the **Templates** tab. The Template tab is selected and the dialog box changes to New from Template. See Figure 9-21.

Figure 9-21   NEW FROM TEMPLATE DIALOG BOX

3. Click **Site "NewCatalyst"** in the Templates For list, if necessary, and then click **maintemplate** in the Site "NewCatalyst" list (the list of templates in the site).

4. Verify that the **Update Page when Template Changes** checkbox is checked.

5. Click the **Create** button. The new page opens in a Document window. See Figure 9-22.

Figure 9-22   NEW PAGE CREATED FROM TEMPLATE

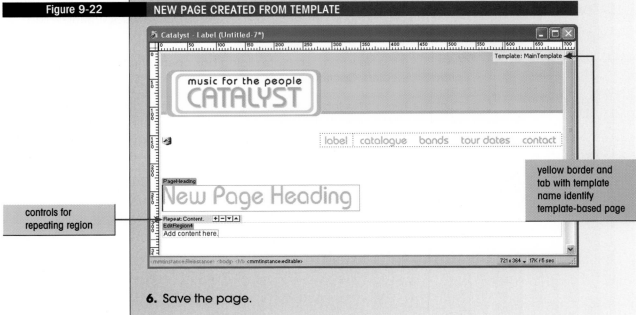

6. Save the page.

As a further test, you'll add content to the editable regions on the new template-based page.

To add content to editable regions:

1. Double-click in the **PageHeading** editable region. The Insert Flash Text dialog box opens.

2. Select the text in the Text text box, and then type **TEST PAGE**.

3. Click the **Browse** button beside the Save As text box, navigate to the **Media** folder, type **HeadingTest** in the File name text box, and then click the **Save** button. A new Flash text file is created for the page heading of the test page.

4. Click the **OK** button. The new heading appears in the PageHeading region.

5. Select the text in the editable region inside the repeating region Content, and then type **Placeholder text for the test page.**

   You'll test the repeating region by adding a second row to the table.

6. Click the **plus** button ➕ in the Repeat: Content tab. A second editable region appears in the page.

7. Select the text in the new editable region, and then type **More text will be placed here.**

8. Select the text in the Title text box in the Document window toolbar, type **Catalyst – Test**, and then press the **Enter** key to change the title of the page. See Figure 9-23.

| Figure 9-23 | TEST PAGE WITH NEW CONTENT |

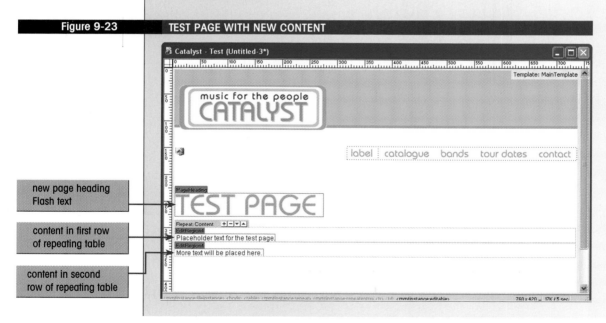

new page heading Flash text

content in first row of repeating table

content in second row of repeating table

When you save the page, you must manually associate it with the appropriate Web site, in this case the NewCatalyst site, because pages created from the main menu bar are not automatically associated with the current Web site.

To save a template-based page:

1. Click File on the menu bar, and then click Save As. The Save As dialog box opens. Because you used the main menu bar to create the file, you must manually associate the page with the Catalyst site.

2. Navigate the Save in location to the root folder of the Catalyst site.

3. Type **test2** in the File name text box, and then click the **Save** button. The template-based page is saved as test2.htm in the root folder of the Catalyst site.

4. Preview the page in a browser. See Figure 9-24.

Figure 9-24   **TEST PAGE PREVIEWED IN BROWSER**

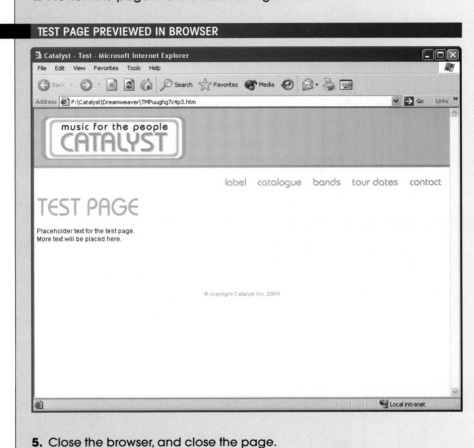

5. Close the browser, and close the page.

If you already have a page with content, you can apply a template to it.

Applying a Template to an Existing Web Page

You can apply a template to an existing Web page by opening the page in a Document window, selecting the template in the Assets panel, and then clicking the Apply button. When you apply a template to an existing page, the page uses the layout of the template page and a dialog box opens so you can designate into which regions the existing content will be placed. This can get a bit confusing at times, especially with complex pages that contain a lot of content. It is usually easier to create a new template-based page and move the content of the old page into the new page.

Editing a Template

One of the most powerful aspects of using templates to create a site is that you can adjust all the template-based pages at once by editing the template. This ability to make a change once saves you time and ensures that all the pages maintain a consistent design. Adjusting the elements inside the editable regions of a template will affect only new pages created from that template. Pages that have already been created are not affected, because updating content in editable regions to reflect the modified template would overwrite any content you have already added to the template-based pages. You can reposition the existing editable regions to change the page layout of the template and any existing template-based pages. You can add new editable regions, which affects the template and any existing template-based pages. You can also delete the various regions from the template. When you delete an editable region from the template, you can choose what happens to the content in that region in the existing pages created from the template. You can either move any content from that region to another editable region or you can delete the content from that region from the page. Any changes made to the noneditable regions in the template affect all pages created from the template—whether new or existing. You can add, edit, or delete content from the noneditable regions.

Brian has noticed that every page of the Catalyst site has a subheading below the page heading. He wants you to add an editable region named "SubHeading" for the subheading to the template.

To edit a template:

1. Place the pointer in the blank area to the right of the PageHeading region in the MainTemplate page, and then press the **Enter** key. A new line is created below the PageHeading region.

2. Click the **Editable Region** button [icon] on the Templates tab of the Insert bar. The New Editable Region dialog box opens.

3. Type **SubHeading** in the Name text box, and then click the **OK** button. The new editable region appears in the site.

   TROUBLE? If the SubHeading text is blocked, you need to hide the invisible elements. Click View on the menu bar, point to Visual Aids, and then click Invisible Elements to hide the tab and view the text.

4. Select the text in the SubHeading region, and then apply the **CatalystSubHeadings** style from the CSS Styles list in the Property inspector. See Figure 9-25.

Figure 9-25   EDITED TEMPLATE PAGE

new editable region
with SubHeading style

5. Save the page. The Update Template Files dialog box opens, asking if you want to update the pages created from the template to reflect the changes in the template. You want this change to appear in the existing template-based pages—in this case, test2.htm.

   TROUBLE? If a dialog box opens, stating that the PageHeading region is in a paragraph or block tag, click the OK button. This dialog box may open whenever you save the page; if it does, click the OK button each time.

6. Click the **Update** button to update the pages, and then click the **Close** button when the update is complete.

7. Open the **test2.htm** page. The subheading is added to this page, which you earlier created from the template.

8. Preview the page in a browser, and then close the page.

Deleting a Template

If a template is no longer relevant for a site, you can delete the entire template. You delete an entire template from a site by selecting the template in the Assets panel and clicking the Delete button (the trash can icon). When you delete a template, the pages that were created from that template still contain template mark-up code. You must also detach the pages from the template. Then they become regular Web pages.

Creating **Nested Templates**

You can create nested templates for a site. **Nested templates** are templates created from the main template so that you can create a more defined structure for some pages of a site. Each nested template inherits all the features of the main template. In other words, each nested template contains the same editable and noneditable regions as the main template and is linked to the main template. You can add additional editable regions to the nested template, but only within the editable regions that exist from the main template. When you make a change to the main template, it affects all the nested templates as well as all the pages created from the main template and the nested templates. When you make a change to a nested template, it affects only the pages created from that nested template.

Nested templates enable you to maintain even greater control over the look of the pages in a site because you further limit the choices people have when they input content into those pages. For example, because many of the pages of the Catalyst Web site have subheadings below the page heading followed by a paragraph of text and another subheading, you could create a nested template with an editable region for a subheading followed by an editable region for text within the editable region that is designated, in the main template, for content.

Nested templates are also very useful when you have more than one major style of page in a Web site. For example, consider a site with both informational pages and product pages. If informational pages have one style and the product pages have the same basic page properties (CSS styles, navigation bar, and so forth) but a somewhat different style, you can create a main template for the site and a nested template for each type of page. Another example is a site with the same basic layout for all pages, but that uses a different background color for each major section of the site. You might create a nested template for each section and change only the background color. You save time and eliminate work because the basic layout for each type of page is already designed and all of your pages are still connected to the same main template.

At some point in the future, Brian plans to add a new page to the site for every CD that Catalyst produces. All the new CD pages will have the same layout. You'll create a nested template based on the main template to accommodate the special layout of these pages. You will add a table with two rows and two columns to the editable region located inside the Content repeating region. Then you will merge the two bottom cells of the table. You will add a placeholder CD cover graphic to the upper-right cell of the new table. Finally, you will adjust the horizontal and vertical attributes for each cell.

To create a nested template:

1. Create a new page from the MainTemplate template, and then click the **Make Nested Template** button 🗎 on the Templates tab of the Insert bar. The Save As Template dialog box opens.

   TROUBLE? If a dialog box opens, stating that the PageHeading region is in a paragraph or block tag, click the OK button. This dialog box may open whenever you save the page; if it does, click the OK button each time.

2. Type **CDPageTemplate** in the Save As text box, and then click the **Save** button to save the template.

3. Delete all the text in the EditRegion, click the **Insert Table** button ▦ on the Common tab of the Insert bar, and then create a table with 2 rows, 2 columns, 100% width, and no border. The new table appears in the nested template.

4. Merge the bottom cells.

5. **Top** align both cells in the top row, and then **Left** align the upper-right cell.

6. Type **Add content here** in the upper-left cell.

7. Insert in the upper-right cell a copy of the **DizziedConnectionCDcover300.jpg** graphic located in the **Graphics** folder in your root folder.

8. Type **Add additional content here** in the bottom cell. See Figure 9-26.

Figure 9-26   NESTED TEMPLATE PAGE

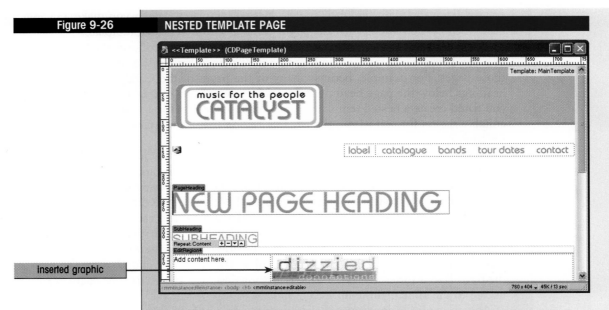

inserted graphic

9. Save the page, and then click the **Yes** button in the dialog box that opens to update all the documents in your local site that use the template. The Update Pages dialog box opens.

10. Click the **Close** button once the pages are done updating, and then close the page. The nested template appears in the Templates folder in the Site panel.

TROUBLE? If you don't see the CDPageTemplate.dwt in the Templates folder, you may need to refresh the Site panel. Click the Refresh button on the Site panel toolbar to display the new template in the Templates folder.

TROUBLE? If a dialog box opens, stating that the PageHeading region is in a paragraph or block tag, click the OK button. This dialog box may open whenever you save the page; if it does, click the OK button each time.

You create pages from a nested template in the same way that you create pages from the main template. The changes you make to the main template flow through to nested templates.

Brian has decided that including the SubHeading editable region in the main template for the Catalyst site is a bad idea and he has asked that you delete it.

To delete a region in a template:

1. Open the **MainTemplate.dwt** page, select the **SubHeading** editable region, and then press the **Delete** key. The region is removed from the template.

2. Save the template. The Update Template Files dialog box opens.

TROUBLE? If a dialog box opens, stating that the PageHeading region is in a paragraph or block tag, click the OK button. This dialog box may open whenever you save the page; if it does, click the OK button each time.

3. Click the **Update** button to update the nested template and the page you created from the template. The Inconsistent Region Names dialog box opens. See Figure 9-27.

| Figure 9-27 | INCONSISTENT REGION NAMES DIALOG BOX |

4. Select **SubHeading**, the region that was deleted from the template, in the Name list, select **Nowhere** from the Move Content to New Region list, and then click the **OK** button. The text that was in the SubHeading region is cleared from the pages.

5. Click the **Close** button in the Update Pages dialog box, and then close the **MainTemplate** page.

6. Open the **CDPageTemplate.dwt** page to verify that the SubHeading region was deleted from the page, and then close the page.

In this session, you created a template, added editable regions to the page, and then created a new page based on the template. You also created a nested template and edited the main template. In the next session, you'll add a form to the site.

Session 9.2 QUICK | CHECK

1. Does creating a template-based site require more or less planning than creating a regular Web site? Explain your answer.

2. What are noneditable regions?

3. How does editing a template affect pages that were created from that template?

4. What is a nested template?

5. True or False? Nested templates inherit all of the characteristics of the main template.

6. What happens when you delete an editable region from a main template?

In this session, you will create a form and add form attributes. Then you'll add form objects. Finally, you'll validate the form data.

Understanding Forms

Forms have become an important element in Web design because they provide a way to interact with users. A **form** is a means of collecting information from users. You can use forms to gather information about the user, create a user log in, gather user feedback, and so forth. Forms encourage user interaction because they enable the user to enter and send information over the Web without leaving the Web site. The user inputs information into the Web page by typing requested data into designated fields or clicking checkboxes, option buttons, lists, and so forth to make selections. Once the form is filled out, the user submits the information, which sends the information somewhere, usually to the server, for processing. Forms do not process information. Once the form information is processed, the server (or information-processing destination) sends requested information back to the user, such as search information, or performs tasks based on the collected information, such as creating a user log in.

Several steps must occur for a form to work:

- The designer creates a form in a Web page.
- The designer installs a script or application in the designated information-processing destination, which is usually a server, to process the form information. (Most forms cannot work without server-side scripts or applications that process the information.)
- The user fills out the form and clicks the Submit button.
- The information is sent to the information-processing destination, such as a server, and a server-side script or application processes the information.
- The server or information-processing destination sends requested information back to the user or performs an action based on the form's information.

You will create a form in the contact page of the Catalyst site to enable users to communicate with Catalyst and to gather information about the users of the Catalyst site.

Creating a Form

You can create a form in any Web page. Before you create a form, you should plan what information you want to collect, how the form should be designed to best collect that information, and in which page to create the form. For example, Sara wants to collect information from users to determine which bands the user is listening to, what types of music the user likes, as well as address and e-mail information for the user. The form will be in the contact page of the site.

Creating a Form
- Add the script that will process the form data to the server or information-processing destination.
- Open the page in which you want a form, position the pointer at the location you want to insert the form, and then click the Form button on the Forms tab of the Insert bar.
- Set the form attributes, including Form Name, Action, Method, Enctype, and Target.
- Add form objects and explanations for each form object to the form, and then set the attributes for each form object, including a name.
- Add a Submit button to the form.
- Add the Verification behavior to the form.
- Test the form in a browser.

The general process for creating a form is to add a form to a Web page, set form attributes, add form objects, and then validate form data.

Adding a Form to a Web Page

The first step in creating a form is to add the form to a page. Basically, adding a form to a Web page places a container in the page for the form content that you will add. You should try to add the form at the page location where you want the form to appear, but you can reposition the form later if you change your mind. When you add a form to a Web page, Dreamweaver inserts <form> </form> tags in the code for the page and a red dotted line appears in the Document window in Design view. The red line designates the form area in Dreamweaver and is invisible in the browser window.

You'll add a form to the bottom of the contact page of the Catalyst site.

To add a form to a Web page:

1. If you took a break after the previous session, make sure **Dreamweaver** is running, and the **NewCatalyst site** is open.

2. Open the **contact** page, and then switch to **Design view**, if necessary.

3. Place the pointer on the blank line below the Directions content, and then press the **Enter** key. You'll insert the form on this new line.

4. Click the **Form** button on the **Forms** tab of the Insert bar. A red dotted line appears in the contact page below the content. See Figure 9-28.

| Figure 9-28 | FORM ADDED TO CONTACT PAGE |

red dotted line
designates form area

Catalyst - Contact (Dreamweaver/contact*)

Catalyst Records
14113 Denton Dr.
Denton, TX 76001
(970) 555-2323
info@catalystnoise.com

DIRECTIONS
Take 35E north from Dallas or Fort Worth to University Dr. Turn right on University Dr. Go straight until you reach Denton Dr. Make a right on Denton Dr. We are located at the end of the street.

© copyright Catalyst Inc. 2004

<body> <form>   763 x 392 ⊣ 16K / 5 sec

5. Save the page.

Next you'll set the form attributes.

Setting Form Attributes

Once you have added a form to a page, you can adjust the form attributes in the Property inspector when the form is selected. You select the form by clicking the red dotted line that designates the form area. It is necessary to set all of the form attributes except the Target attribute, which is optional. Form attributes include:

- **Form Name.** A unique name for the form. The form name enables the form to be referenced or controlled with a scripting language. If you do not name the form, Dreamweaver will generate a unique name for it. The form name can include alphanumeric characters but cannot begin with a number or include spaces or special characters.

- **Action.** The path to the location of the script you will use to process the form data. You must install the script or create the page in the desired location prior to setting the Action. You can also type "mailto:" followed by an e-mail address in the Action text box to send the form information to a specified e-mail address (the mailto: link will work only if the user is on a computer configured to send e-mail), or you can type the name of a JavaScript function in the Action text box if you are using a JavaScript to process the form.

- **Method.** The way form data will be sent to the location specified in the Action text box. **POST** embeds form data in an HTTP request. When you use the POST method, the form data is not visible. POST is the preferred method for most forms. **GET** appends the form data to the end of the path specified in the Action text box. When you use the GET method, form data is limited to 8,192 characters of information and is visible because it is added to the end of the URL. GET is frequently used for search engine requests. **Default** uses the browser default of the user's browser to send form data. The script or application you use to process form data may affect the method that you will need to use to send the form data. It is a good idea to contact the server administrator or your ISP if you are using server-side scripts or applications to process form data.

- **Target.** The target destination for any response from the form. For example, if the script attached to the form sends back a response to the user, such as "Thank you for filling out the form. We have received your information.", that response will appear in the target destination. Target list options are the usual _blank, _parent, _self, and _top.

- **Enctype (Encoding Type).** The Multipurpose Internet Mail Extensions encoding type (MIME type) for the form data. The **MIME type** is a file identification based on the MIME encoding system, which is the standard for identifying content on the Internet. Most forms use the application/x-www-form-urlencoded MIME type. The multipart/form-data MIME type is used for uploading files, such as when you use a file-upload field in a form.

You'll set each of these attributes for the form on the contact page in the Catalyst site. You'll use "ContactForm" as the form name. The action will eventually point to a script placed on the server to process the form data. The programming team is writing the script but is waiting for information from the ISP. In the meantime, they have created a Web page with a script that will enable you to test the form by displaying the data the form will send to the server when the Submit button is clicked. For now, you will place a copy of the test script Web page in the root folder of the Catalyst site and set the action to CatalystFormTest.htm. GET is the method for data delivery. The Enctype is application/x-www-form-urlencoded. The target is _blank.

To set the attributes for a form:

1. Copy **CatalystFormTest.htm** from the **Tutorial.09/Tutorial** folder on your Data Disk to the root folder of your Catalyst site.

2. Click the red dotted line to select the form. You'll set the form attributes in the Property inspector.

3. Type **ContactForm** in the Form Name text box.

4. Type **CatalystFormTest.htm** in the Action text box.

5. Click the **Method** list arrow, and then click **GET**.

6. Click the **Enctype** list arrow, and then click **application/x-www-form-urlencoded**.

7. Click the **Target** list arrow, and then click **_blank**. See Figure 9-29.

| Figure 9-29 | PROPERTY INSPECTOR WITH FORM ATTRIBUTES |

8. Save the page.

Next, you will add form objects to the form.

Adding **Form Objects**

You must add form objects to a form to make it useful. **Form objects** are generally the mechanisms that enable users to input data into a form. Each form object has a specific function:

- **Text Fields and Text Areas.** A text box into which a user can type input in a form. Text fields are usually used for short answer input. Text areas are usually used for long answer input. Text fields are displayed as a single-line box, whereas text areas are displayed as a multiple-line box. Both can accept either single or multiple lines of input. The input can be displayed as typed or as a series of dots or asterisks to protect private information. For example, a password is usually displayed as a series of asterisks when typed into a browser window.

- **Hidden Fields.** Fields used to include information in a form that will be sent along with the form data to the server or designated processing location and which the user cannot see. For example, if a site has more than one form, you can use a hidden field to send the name of the form with the collected form data.

- **Checkbox.** A predefined toggle selection object in a form. Each checkbox can be toggled "on (checked)" or "off (unchecked)". A checkbox is toggled on or off independently, enabling the user to check as many items in a series of checkboxes as is appropriate. For example, you might use a series of checkboxes to have a user select all the types of music he or she listens to.

- **Radio Button and Radio Group.** A group of selection objects that work together in a form. The user can select only one radio button from a radio button group. Unlike a checkbox, which can be toggled on and off independently, a selected radio button can be deselected only when the user selects another radio button within the radio button group. The Radio Button object adds a single radio button at a time, whereas the Radio Group object inserts an entire radio button group.

- **List/Menu.** A list of preset input choices in a form. List presents a list of possible input choices in a designated area, providing a scroll bar, if necessary, that enables users to navigate through the list. The user can select multiple items in a list. Menu presents the user with a list of choices in a drop-down menu. The user can select only one item from a menu.

- **Jump Menu.** A special menu that contains a list of active links to other pages, graphics, or any type of file that can be opened in a browser. When a user selects an item from the jump menu, the new page or document opens.

- **Image Field.** A graphic used as a Submit or Reset button in a form. You can also use graphics as buttons that perform other tasks by adding behaviors.

- **File Field.** A file upload field in the form that enables the user to upload a file from the client computer to the server. The file field contains a Browse button and a text box. The user can select the file using the Browse button or by typing the file path into the text box. You must use the POST method to send files from the browser to the server, and your Web server must be set up to handle this type of file upload.

- **Button.** A button in the form that performs the behavior you specify. The button can be designated as a Submit button or a Reset button or can have no designation at all. The **Submit button** sends the form data to the location you designated for processing. The **Reset button** clears any content from the form so that the user can start over. You can also add behaviors to the button, enabling it to perform other functions.

You'll use text fields, checkboxes, radio buttons, a list, a Submit button, and a Reset button form objects in the contact page form.

You set the attributes for a form object in the Property inspector when that object is selected in the form. Each type of object has its own unique set of attributes. However, every object has a name attribute. It is important to name every form object because the scripting language uses this name to identify the form object. If you do not name an object, Dreamweaver will name it for you. It is a good idea to name form objects yourself because the name of the field will be paired with the date from that field when it is sent to the processing destination. When you view the data collected from forms, you use the name of the field to identify the information beside it. If the name does not identify the field, you may have trouble understanding the information you collect. For example, you'll name the text field where users input their last name "LastName" so that when you view the data you see LastName beside the data captured in the last name field. Without this descriptive name, you might have trouble distinguishing the user's first name from the user's last name.

Creating the Form Structure

You want to add form objects to a form in logical groupings. For example, all similar or related information should be placed together so users can enter that data, such as all their personal information, at the same time. You should also include a label with brief instructions or a description of the information being requested for each object so users know what to do.

The requested information should be organized clearly within the form. You can use line breaks, paragraph breaks, tables, and so forth within forms to lay out the form objects. However, a table is usually the simplest way to keep your forms fairly clean. For example, you could insert a two-column table in a form that includes a separate row for each form object. Then you can right-justify the form labels in the left column and left-justify the corresponding form objects in the right column. This will create a form that is well organized and easy to follow. It will also create a form that is fairly stable across browsers. Different versions of browsers sometimes display form objects in slightly different ways. Putting form objects in a table helps to keep them in the same place on a page regardless of how a user's browser displays the form. However, the form layout may still vary slightly in different browsers.

You'll use a two-column table without a border to organize the form in the contact page.

To add a table to the form:

1. Click in the form, and then click the **Insert Table** button ▦ on the Common tab of the Insert bar. The Insert Table dialog box opens.

2. Type **9** in the Rows text box, type **2** in the Columns text box, type **100** in the Width text box, select **Percent**, type **0** in the Border text box, type **10** in the Cell Padding text box, and then click the **OK** button.

3. **Right** align and **Top** align the left column.

4. **Left** align and **Top** align the right column.

5. Merge the cells of the top row.

   You'll add the form heading to this merged row.

6. Type **Catalyst – Contact Form** in the top row, **Center** the form heading text, and then apply the **CatalystSubHeadings** CSS style. See Figure 9-30.

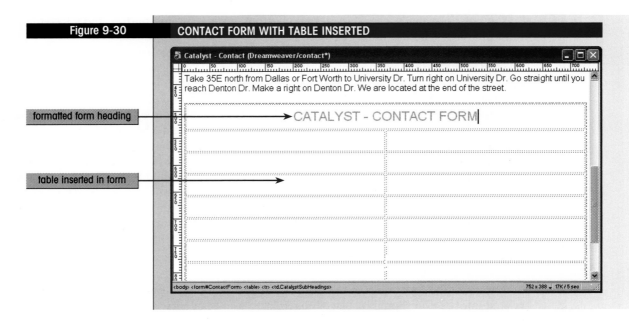

Figure 9-30

CONTACT FORM WITH TABLE INSERTED

formatted form heading

table inserted in form

With the table structure in place, you can begin adding form objects to the form. You will start by inserting a text field into the form.

Inserting a Text Field into a Form

Text fields are used to gather information that a user types. Most commonly, text fields are used for collecting name, address, and e-mail address information. You can set a number of attributes to control how each text field appears and functions in the form. In addition to Name, text field attributes include:

- **Char Width (Character Width).** The maximum number of characters that can be displayed in the text field. When the character width value is smaller than the maximum characters value, the text field will not display all the input.
- **Max Chars (Maximum Characters)/Num Lines (Number of Lines).** The maximum number of characters that the user can input into a single-line text field or the height of a multiple-line text field. You can use Max Chars to limit a user's response. For example, you can limit the number of characters in a text field used to input ZIP code information to five characters.
- **Type.** The designated appearance of the text field. Single line creates a text box that is one line in height. Multi line creates a text field that is more than one line in height and has scroll bars. Password displays the data in the text field as dots or asterisks to protect the data.
- **Init Val (Initial Value).** Text displayed in the text field until the user types new input in the field.

You'll add single-line text fields for collecting the user's first name, last name, and e-mail address. Then you'll add a multi-line text field for collecting user comments.

To add text fields to a form:

1. Click in the upper-left cell of the table below the form heading, type **First Name:** to enter the label for the first text field, and then press the **Tab** key to move to the next cell.

2. Click the **Text Field** button ▯ on the **Forms** tab of the Insert bar. A text field is inserted in the cell. You'll set its attributes in the Property inspector.

3. Type **FirstName** in the unnamed text box, type **50** in the Char Width text box, type **100** in the Max Chars text box, and then click the **Single line** option button, if necessary. See Figure 9-31.

Figure 9-31   **TEXT FIELD ADDED TO FORM**

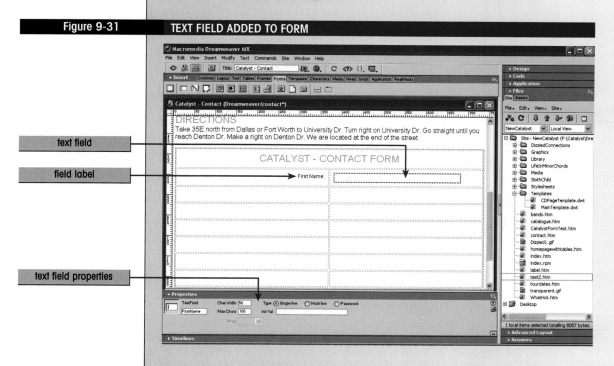

text field

field label

text field properties

Next, you'll add the LastName label and text field to the third row of the table.

4. Click in the left column of the third row of the table, type **Last Name:** to enter the label, and then press the **Tab** key to move to the next cell.

5. Click ▯ to insert another text field, type **LastName** in the Name text box, type **50** in the Char Width text box, type **100** in the Max Chars text box, and then click the **Single line** option button, if necessary.

You'll add the EmailAddress label and text field to the fourth row of the table.

6. Click in the left column of the fourth row, type **E-mail Address:** to enter the label, and then press the **Tab** key to move to the next cell.

7. Click ▯ to insert another text field, type **EmailAddress** in the Name text box, type **50** in the Char Width text box, type **100** in the Max Chars text box, and then click the **Single line** option button, if necessary.

8. Click in the left column of the fifth row, type **Comments:** to enter the label, and then press the **Tab** key to move to the next cell.

9. Click the **Textarea** button ▭ on the **Forms** tab of the Insert bar. A text area is added to the cell.

10. Type **Comments** in the Name text box, type **44** in the Char Width text box, type **10** in the Num Lines text box, and then click the **Multi line** option button, if necessary. See Figure 9-32.

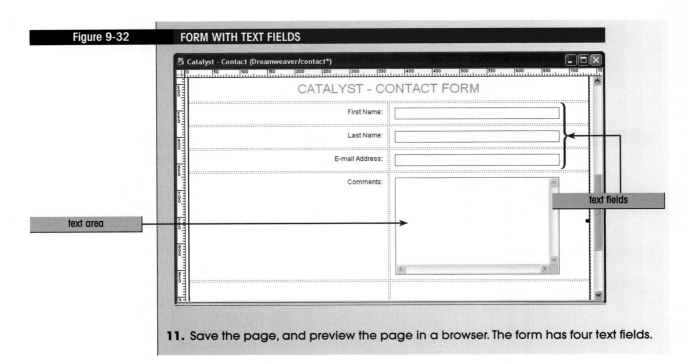

Figure 9-32   **FORM WITH TEXT FIELDS**

CATALYST - CONTACT FORM

First Name:

Last Name:

E-mail Address:

Comments:

text area

text fields

11. Save the page, and preview the page in a browser. The form has four text fields.

Next, you will add a series of checkboxes to the form.

Inserting Checkboxes into a Form

Checkboxes have only two attributes in addition to Name. Because some forms use many checkboxes, it is often convenient to use a code, instead of a name, in the script to process them. The other attributes are Checked Value and Initial State. **Checked Value** is where you can assign a value or a numeric code for a checkbox. The Checked Value is sent to the processing location along with the name when the checkbox is checked. Nothing is sent to the processing location if the checkbox is unchecked. **Initial State** sets whether the checkbox is checked or unchecked initially.

Sara wants to find out what styles of music users enjoy. You will insert a series of checkboxes into the form to enable users to select the types of music they find enjoyable. You will not include a checked value for these checkboxes.

To add checkboxes to a form:

1. Click in the left column of the sixth row, type **Check all of the musical styles that interest you.**, and then press the **Tab** key to move to the next cell.

2. Click the **Checkbox** button ☑ on the **Forms** tab of the Insert bar to insert a checkbox in the cell.

3. In the Property inspector, type **Punk** in the name text box, and then click the **Unchecked** option button, if necessary.

4. Click to the right of the checkbox, type **Punk**, and then press the **Shift+Enter** keys to move to the next line in the cell.

5. Repeat Steps 2 through 4 to create the following checkboxes: **Alternative**, **Trance**, and **Jazz**. See Figure 9-33.

| Figure 9-33 | **FORM WITH CHECKBOXES** |

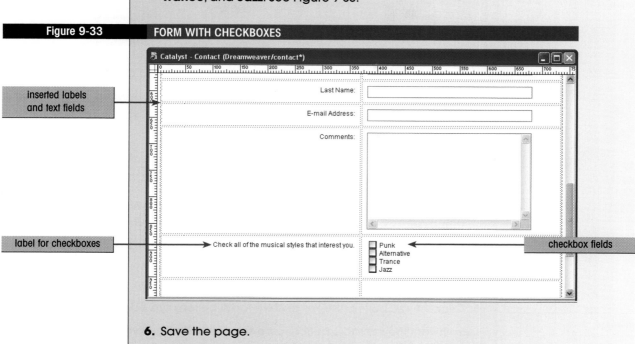

inserted labels and text fields

label for checkboxes

checkbox fields

6. Save the page.

Next, you'll add radio buttons to the form.

Adding Radio Buttons to a Form

Radio buttons are a group of selection objects that work together in a form. The user can select only one radio button from a radio button group. You can insert a group of radio buttons into your form using the Radio Group button. When you click the Radio Group button, a dialog box opens so you can name the radio group, label each radio button with the text you want to appear beside it in the form, and enter a value for the Checked Value of each button. Unlike checkboxes, the label information for a selected radio button does not appear when the information is sent to the processing location. You must enter a unique value for each radio button to distinguish which radio button was selected. When you click the OK button, the radio group is added to the form. When you select a radio button in a form, the name of the radio group to which the button belongs appears in the name text box, its value appears in the checked value, and you can choose checked or unchecked as the initial state for the button.

Brian has decided to start a newsletter and he wants to give users the option to join the newsletter mailing list. You add a radio group with two radio buttons to the form.

To add a group of radio buttons to a form:

1. Click in the left column of the seventh row, type **Would you like to receive a monthly newsletter with updates about the Catalyst bands?**, and then press the **Tab** key to move to the next cell.

2. Click the **Radio Group** button on the **Forms** tab of the Insert bar. The Radio Group dialog box opens. See Figure 9-34.

Figure 9-34   RADIO GROUP DIALOG BOX

click to add radio buttons to group

two radio buttons already in group

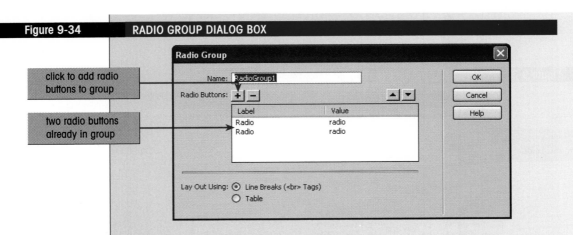

3. Type **Newsletter** in the Name text box, click **Radio** in the first row of the Label column, type **Yes**, click **radio** in the first row of the Value column, and then type **Yes**.

4. Click **Radio** in the second row of the Label column, type **No**, click **radio** in the second row of the Value column, and then type **No**.

5. In the Lay Out Using section, click the **Line Breaks** option, if necessary.

6. Click the **OK** button. The Yes and No radio buttons are added to the form.

   You want the Yes radio button to be selected initially, so you'll change its initial state.

7. Select the **Yes** radio button in the Document window, and then click the **Checked** option button in the Initial State section in the Property inspector.

8. Save the page. See Figure 9-35.

Figure 9-35   FORM WITH RADIO GROUP

checked initial state

Adding a List to a Form

Lists are another way to enable users to choose several items from a group. There are a few attribute choices associated with lists. Height enables you to set how many rows are visible in the list box. You can add as many items to the list as you want. If the list includes more items than are visible in the list box, scroll bars enable the users to view all of the selections. The Selections checkbox enables you to set whether users can select only one item in the list (unchecked) or more than one item in the list (checked). The List Values button opens the dialog box in which you type the items that will appear in a list or edit existing items in a list. You can also associate a value with each item, which can be used by a script to identify the list item. The Initially Selected list enables you to select one or more items from the list to appear selected in the list. This option is often used to create a default selection, such as selecting Dallas from a list of cities because Catalyst is based in Dallas and it is assumed that more users will be from that area. If you prefer the list to appear as a menu, select the Menu button from the Type section.

Sara wants to know which bands users listen to. You will add to the form a list field that includes all the Catalyst bands. The Catalyst bands list will be three rows high, each band will be a list item, and the user will be able to select multiple bands from the list.

To add a list to a form:

1. Click in the left column of the eighth row, type **Select all of the bands that you enjoy from the list.**, and then press the **Tab** key to move to the next cell.

2. Click the **List/Menu** button 📑 on the Forms tab of the Insert bar to insert a list in the cell. A small list box appears in the form. See Figure 9-36.

Figure 9-36	FORM WITH LIST/MENU BOX

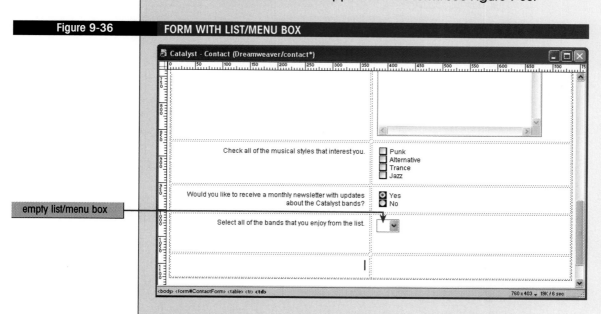

empty list/menu box

3. In the Property inspector, type **BandsList** in the Name text box, click the **List** option button in the Type section, type **3** in the Height text box, check the **Selections** checkbox, if necessary, and then click the **List Values** button. The List Values dialog box opens. See Figure 9-37.

Figure 9-37	LIST VALUES DIALOG BOX

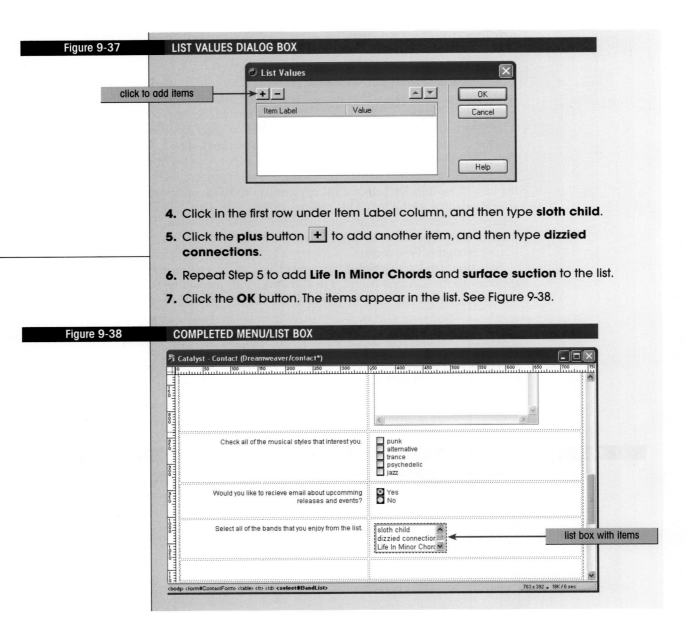

4. Click in the first row under Item Label column, and then type **sloth child**.

5. Click the **plus** button ⊞ to add another item, and then type **dizzied connections**.

6. Repeat Step 5 to add **Life In Minor Chords** and **surface suction** to the list.

7. Click the **OK** button. The items appear in the list. See Figure 9-38.

Figure 9-38	COMPLETED MENU/LIST BOX

Finally, you will add a Reset button and a Submit button to the form.

Adding Buttons to a Form

You must add a Submit button to a form to enable users to send the form data to the location where it will be processed. It is a good idea to add a Reset button as well so that users can clear any data they input into the form with one click and start over if necessary. When you click the Button button on the Forms tab of the Insert bar, it defaults to the Submit form action, which creates a Submit button. You can also choose the Reset form action to create a Reset button, or you can choose None and then add other behaviors to the button. In addition to an action, you should type a name and a label for the button. The label will appear as text on the button, and the name is used to reference the button in the code.

You'll add a Submit button and a Reset button to the form on the contact page.

To add a Submit button and a Reset button to a form:

1. Click in the left column of the last row, and then click the **Button** button 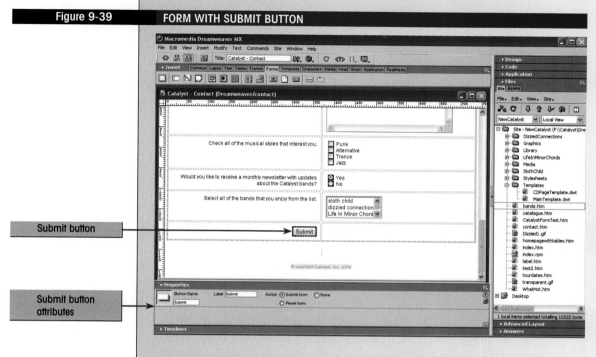 on the Forms tab of the Insert bar. A Submit button appears in the form. See Figure 9-39.

Figure 9-39 | **FORM WITH SUBMIT BUTTON**

Submit button

Submit button attributes

TROUBLE? If your button does not say Submit, don't worry. You need to adjust the button attributes; you'll do this in the following steps.

2. If necessary, in the Property inspector, click the **Submit form** option button in the Action button group, type **Submit** in the Button Name text box, and then type **Submit** in the Label text box.

3. In the Document window, click in the blank space to the right of the Submit button, and then click [ ] to insert another button.

4. In the Property inspector, click the **Reset form** option button in the Action button group, type **Reset** in the Button Name text box, and then type **Reset** in the Label text box, if necessary. The Reset button is added to the form. See Figure 9-40.

Figure 9-40   **FORM WITH TWO BUTTONS**

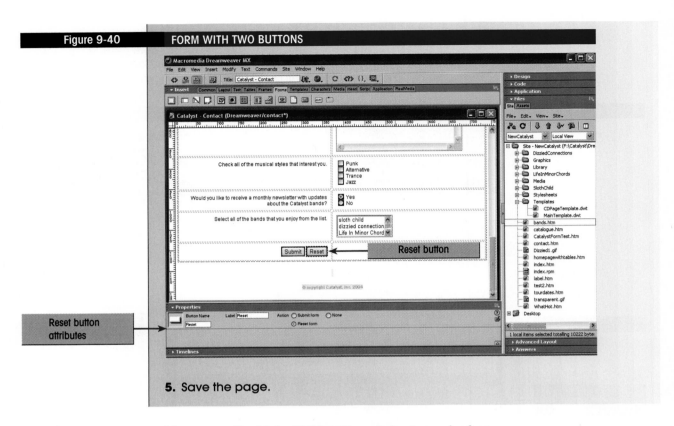

5. Save the page.

Next, you will add the Validate Form behavior to the form.

Validating Form Data

The **Validate Form** behavior enables you to create requirements/limits that check the form data before the form is submitted. When you click Validate Form in the Behavior list, a dialog box opens so you can select each form object and then set limits/requirements. When the user clicks the Submit button, the data is checked to make sure the data meets the limits/requirements that were set for each object in the Validate Form behavior. If information is missing or is not within the set limits, a dialog box opens asking the user to change incorrect information or add missing information and then click the Submit button again.

The Validate Form dialog box displays all of the form objects in the Named Fields list box. You select a field from the list and then set the requirements/limits for that field. You first set whether the selected field is required or optional by checking or unchecking the Required checkbox in the Value section. The user must enter information into a required field in order to submit the form. If the field is optional, the form will be submitted even if the user does not enter information in that field. You can also set a variety of limits for the data the user enters into the selected field in the Accept section of the dialog box. Accept limits include:

- **Anything.** Allows the user to enter anything into the selected field.
- **Number.** Allows the user to enter only numeric values into the selected field. This limit is often used in fields that are used to input phone numbers, or ZIP codes.

■ **Email Address.** Allows the user to enter only information that follows the format of an e-mail address (for example, something@something.atoplevel-domain). This limit does not ensure that the user has inserted a valid e-mail address, only that the submitted address is in the correct format.

■ **Number from.** Enables you to set a range of acceptable numeric values for the field. The first text box is the lowest acceptable numeric value for the field, and the second text box is the highest acceptable numeric value for the field. For example, you might use this limit when you ask a question such as "How old is your teenager?" The lowest value would be 13 and the highest value would be 19. If a user inputs a number below 13 or above 19, the Validate Form behavior would inform the user that the data was outside the acceptable range and then ask the user to input an acceptable value and resubmit the form.

You'll add the Validate Form behavior to the form on the contact page. You'll make the FirstName, LastName, and EmailAddress fields required fields and set the Email Address limit for the EmailAddress field to ensure that all submitted addresses are in the correct format.

To add the Validate Form behavior to a form:

1. Select the form, click the **plus** button ⊞ in the Behaviors panel, and then click **Validate Form**. The Validate Form dialog box opens. See Figure 9-41.

| Figure 9-41 | VALIDATE FORM DIALOG BOX |

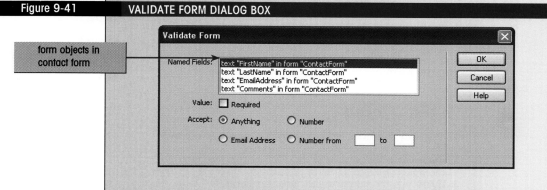

form objects in contact form

2. Select **text "FirstName" in form "ContactForm"** in the Named Fields list, and then check the **Required** checkbox to make the field a required field. The text "(R)" appears after the field name to indicate that the field is required.

3. Select **text "LastName" in form "ContactForm"** in the Named Fields list, and then check the **Required** checkbox to make the field a required field.

4. Select **text "EmailAddress" in form "ContactForm"** in the Named Fields list, and then check the **Required** checkbox.

5. Click the **Email Address** option button in the Accept radio button group to set a limit requiring the data to follow the standard e-mail format.

6. Click the **OK** button.

7. Look at the Behavior list in the Behaviors panel to verify that the Validate Form behavior has been added to the list.

8. Click the **Events** list arrow in the Behaviors panel, and then click OnSubmit, if necessary. This will cause the behavior to run when the Submit button is clicked.

9. Save the page.

Finally, you will test the form.

Testing a Form

You should test your form to ensure that it displays properly in a browser and to ensure that the functionality of the form is working. You should view the form locally to verify that the form objects are laid out properly, and then you should upload the site and test the functionality of the form over the Web. It is sometimes possible to test the functionality of a form locally, but often, when the form processing script resides on a Web server, the script will not work properly until the site is posted to the remote server. When you test a form, you should input data in each field to verify that it is functioning and then submit the form to verify that the processing script is working properly and that any requested information is returned to the end user. If the form returns an error, you should check the form attributes to make sure that the Action, Method, and Enctype are correct. If you are still having problems, you must check the script to make sure that it is in the correct location and that it has been configured correctly. In this case, the script is located in a Web page and is set up to test the form. When you click the Submit button, the script will display the information that would be sent to the server if the script were located there.

You will test the form in the contact page. Because the script is in a Web page, you can test the form locally. The process for testing the form is the same as it would be if you were testing the form over the Web.

To test a form:

1. Preview the contact page in a browser window.

2. Type your first name in the First name text box.

3. Type your last name in the Last name text box.

4. Type **potato** in the E-mail Address text box.

5. Type **testing** in the Comments text area.

6. Check the **Punk** check box. The Yes radio button is already selected, because its initial state was set to checked.

7. Select **sloth child** from the bands list. See Figure 9-42.

Figure 9-42   **CONTACTED PAGE WITH COMPLETED FORM**

Page scrolled down to reveal form

The bottom of the form is not visible in the browser window

8. Click the **Submit** button. A dialog box opens, explaining that the E-mail Address text box must contain an e-mail address. This means that the Validate Form behavior determined that "potato" is not in the correct format for an e-mail address. See Figure 9-43.

Figure 9-43   **FORM ERROR DIALOG BOX**

Validate Form behavior identified incorrect format for e-mail address

9. Click the **OK** button, type your e-mail address in the E-mail Address text box, and then click the **Submit** button. The test script opens another browser window with the form data that would be submitted to the server. See Figure 9-44.

Figure 9-44   FORM DATA THAT WOULD BE SENT TO SERVER

form object names

only the checked checkbox was submitted

data from the form object

F:\Catalyst\Dreamweaver\CatalystFormTest.htm - Microsoft Internet Explorer

Address ☑ dress=info@catalyst.com&Comments=testing&Punk=checkbox&Newsletter=radio&BandsList=sloth+child&Submit=Submit

Form Data Submitted:

- **FirstName:** Guy
- **LastName:** Smiley
- **EmailAddress:** info@catalystnoise.com
- **Comments:** testing
- **Punk:** checkbox
- **Newsletter:** radio
- **BandsList:** sloth child
- **Submit:** Submit

TROUBLE? If you do not have an e-mail address, type "info@catalystnoise.com" in the E-mail Address text box.

TROUBLE? If you notice different symbols in the submitted form data (for example "@" may appear as "%40" and spaces may appear as "%20"), it is due to the URL encoding. This is not an error; continue with Step 10.

10. Close the browser window with the form data, click the **Reset** button in the form to clear the information from the form, and then close the browser window with the form.

The form in the contact page is complete.

Updating the Web Site on the Remote Server

As your last task, you'll upload the site to the remote server and view the site over the Web. This way you can see all the changes you made to the Catalyst site in this tutorial, including the library item footer and the form.

To upload a site to the remote server:

1. Click the **Connects to remote host** button on the Site panel toolbar.

2. Click the **View** list arrow on the Site panel toolbar, and then click **Local View**.

3. Select the **index.htm, bands.htm, catalogue.htm, CatalystFormTest.htm, contact.htm, label.htm, tourdates.htm,** and **WhatHot.htm** files in Local view, and then click the **Put File(s)** button on the Site panel toolbar.

4. Click the **Yes** button when asked if you want to include dependent files because you have not selected the new dependent files for the site yet.

5. Click the **Disconnects from remote host** button 🖧 on the Site panel toolbar.

6. Click the **View** list arrow on the Site panel toolbar, and then click **Local View**. The Site panel returns to the local view.

Next, you'll preview the updated site in a browser. The site will include all the new footer and form that you added to your local version.

To preview the updated site in a browser:

1. Open a browser, type the URL of your remote site into the Address text box on the browser toolbar, and then press the **Enter** key.

2. Explore the **home** page on the remote site within the browser.

3. Click to the **bands** link and test the footer link.

4. Close the message window that opens.

5. Click the **contact** link, and then enter information in the form to test it.

6. Submit the form.

7. Close the browser window, and then close any open pages in the NewCatalyst site.

In this tutorial, you added keywords and a meta description to the head content, created and used library items in pages, created and used templates, and added a form to the Catalyst site.

Session 9.3 QUICK CHECK

1. What is a form?

2. True or False? Forms process data.

3. What is a form object?

4. List three types of form objects.

5. Which behavior do you add to the form that enables you to create requirements/limits that check the form data before the form is submitted?

6. What is the final step in creating a form?

Brian asks you to add the list of keywords and the meta description to every page of the Catalyst site. You'll also add the keywords and description to the template so that future pages will have this head content. Then, you'll create a form in the tour section of the Life In Minor Chords page to enable users to be placed on a list to receive notice when the new tour video is released. You'll use the ContactFormTest.htm file already in the Catalyst site as the form action so that you can test the form.

1. Open the bands page of your Catalyst site, and then click the Keywords button on the Head tab of the Insert bar. The Keywords dialog box opens.

2. Type "catalyst records, indie music, sloth child, dizzied connections, life in minor chords, surface suction, spinning life, black lab, them apples, i believe in ferries, independent scene, denton music, underground sound, catalist" into the Keywords text box. (*Hint:* Use all lowercase letters and separate each word or phrase with a comma.)

Explore ▷ 3. Select the entire list of keywords in the Keywords text box, copy the list, and then click the OK button to add the keywords to the page.

4. Save the page and close the page.

Explore ▷ 5. Open the catalogue page, click the Keywords button on the Head tab of the Insert bar, paste the list of keywords into the Keywords text box, and then click the OK button to add the list to the page.

6. Save the page and close the page.

Explore ▷ 7. Repeat Steps 5 and 6 to paste the list of keywords into the following pages and the template: contact.htm, label.htm, tourdates.htm, WhatHot.htm, and MainTemplate.dwt. (*Hint:* When you add the keywords to the template, be sure to update the pages made from the template.)

8. Open the bands page, and then click the Description button on the Head tab of the Insert bar. The Description dialog box opens.

9. Type "Catalyst is an indie label that has tapped into a vein of post-discord punk music. Our mission is to expose the world to exceptional indie music. Catalyst promotes bands that we believe will change and infuse the planet with original good music." into the Description text box.

Explore ▷ 10. Select the text in the Description text box, copy it, and then click the OK button.

11. Save the page and close the page.

Explore ▷ 12. Open the catalogue page, click the Description button on the Head tab of the Insert bar, and then paste the description in the Description dialog box.

13. Save the page and close the page.

Explore ▷ 14. Repeat Steps 12 and 13 to add the meta description to the following pages and the template: contact.htm, label.htm, tourdates.htm, WhatHot.htm, and MainTemplate.dwt. (*Hint:* When you add the description to the template, be sure to update the pages made from the template.)

15. Open the LIMCtours.htm page located in the LifeInMinor Chords folder, and then press the Enter key until the pointer is positioned below the movie on the page.

16. Click the Form button on the Forms tab of the Insert bar. The form area is added to the page. Next you'll set the form attributes.

17. Type "LIMCvideoForm" in the Name text box, click the Browse button beside the Action text box, and then double-click the CatalystFormTest.htm page in your root folder.

Explore 18. Select GET from the Method list, select application/x-www-form-urlencoded from the Enctype list, and then select _blank from the Target list.

19. Click in the form area, click the Table button on the Common tab of the Insert bar, type "5" in the Row text box, type "2" in the Column text box, type "100" in the Width text box, select Percent from the Width list, type "10" in the Cell Padding text box, and then click the OK button. The table is inserted into the page.

20. Align the left column of the table to the Right and Top.

21. Align the right column of the table to the Left and Top.

22. Click in the upper-left cell, type "First Name:", press the Tab key to move to the next cell, click the Text Field button on the Forms tab of the Insert bar to add a text field into the form, and then type "FirstName" in the Name text box.

23. Click in the left cell of the second row, type "Last Name:", press the Tab key, click the Text Field button on the Forms tab of the Insert bar, and then type "LastName" in the Name text box.

24. Click in the left cell of the third row, type "Email Address:", press the Tab key, click the Text Field button on the Forms tab of the Insert bar, and then type "Email" in the Name text box.

25. Click in the left cell of the fourth row, type "Notify me when the new video is released.", press the Tab key, and then click the Radio Group button on the Forms tab of the Insert bar. The Radio Group dialog box opens.

26. Type "NotifyVideoRelease" in the Name text box, click the first row in the Label column and type "Yes," click the first row in the Value column and type "Yes," click the second row in the Label column and type "No," click the second row in the Value column and type "No," and then click the OK button. The radio buttons are inserted into the page.

27. Select the Yes radio button in the form, and then click the Checked option button in the Property inspector. The Yes radio button is selected initially.

28. Press the Tab key twice to move to the lower-right cell, click the Button button on the Forms tab of the Insert bar to insert a Submit button, and then click the Button button again to insert a second button.

29. Select the second button, click the Reset form option button, type "Reset" in the Name text box, type "Reset" in the Label text box, and then press the Enter key.

30. Select the Validate Form behavior from the Behaviors list in the Behaviors panel. The Validate Form dialog box opens.

31. Select the text "FirstName" in the form "LIMCvideoForm" from the Named Fields list, and check the Required checkbox.

32. Select the text "LastName" in the form "LIMCvideoForm" and check the Required checkbox.

33. Select the text "Email" in the form "LIMCvideoForm", check the Required checkbox, click the Email Address radio button from the Accept button group, and then click the OK button.

34. Save the page, preview the page in a browser, and then test the form.

35. Upload the site to the remote server, view the site over the Web, and then test the form.

CASE PROBLEMS

Case 1. Hroch University Anthropology Department Professor Hart wants you to add keywords to the pages of the site. He also wants you to create a library item for the footer and then add the library item to every page of the site.

1. Open the Hart site you modified in Tutorial 8, Case 1, and then open the home page.

2. Click the Keywords button on the Head tab of the Insert bar, and then type "hroch university, social anthropology, northern vietnam, linguistic differences, cultural cross-pollination, rituals, matthew hart, anthropological research, hroch" in the Keywords text box.

Explore 3. Select the words in the Keywords text box, copy them, and then click the OK button.

4. Save the page and close the page.

Explore 5. Open the Linguistic Differences page, click the Keywords button on the Head tab of the Insert bar, paste the list of keywords into the Keywords text box, and then click the OK button.

6. Save the page and close the page.

Explore 7. Repeat Steps 5 and 6 to add the keywords to the following pages: Contact.htm, CulturalCrossPollination.htm, NewCourses.htm, ProfHart.htm, and RitualsAndPractices.htm.

8. Open the home page, click the Description button on the Head tab of the Insert bar, and then type "Research and study of the language and rituals of peoples of Northern Vietnam by Dr. Matthew Hart of Hroch University." in the Description text box.

Explore 9. Select the text in the Description text box, copy it, and then click the OK button.

10. Save the page and close the page.

Explore 11. Open the Linguistic Differences page, click the Description button on the Head tab of the Insert bar, paste the description into the Description text box, and then click the OK button.

12. Save the page and close the page.

Explore 13. Repeat Steps 11 and 12 to add the description to the following pages: Contact.htm, CulturalCrossPollination.htm, NewCourses.htm, ProfHart.htm, and RitualsAndPractices.htm.

14. Open the Linguistic Differences page, scroll to the bottom of the page, and then select the footer. You'll create a library item for the footer.

15. Click the Library button on the Assets panel, drag the footer to the panel, and then name the library item "footer."

Explore 16. Double-click the footer library item to open it, select the text, and then click the Align Center button in the Property inspector.

17. Save and close the footer library item, and then save and close the Linguistic Differences page.

18. Open the Contact page, and then drag the footer library item from the Assets panel to the bottom of the page.

19. Save the page and close the page.

20. Repeat Steps 18 and 19 to add the footer library item to the following pages: CulturalCrossPollination.htm, index.htm, NewCourses.htm, ProfHart.htm, and RitualsAndPractices.htm. (*Hint:* If a page already has a footer, delete the existing footer before adding the footer library item to the page.)

21. Preview each page of the site in the browser.

22. Upload the site to the remote server, and view the site over the Web.

Case 2. *Museum of Western Art* C. J. Strittmatter has decided to make the Museum site a template-based site, which will make it faster to update the site. C.J. asks you to create a template for the site based on the Museum page that includes a footer library item, which you need to create. There is no need to add the footer library item to the existing pages of the site because you will move the existing pages over to the template once it is approved.

1. Open the Museum site that you modified in Tutorial 8, Case 2, and then open the Museum page.

2. Click the Make Template button on the Templates tab of the Insert bar. The Save As Template dialog box opens.

3. Type "MainTemplate" in the Save As text box, and then click the Save button.

4. Select the page heading in the MainTemplate page, click the Editable Region button, and then name the region "PageHeading."

5. Select the page heading text, and then type "PAGE HEADING" as placeholder text.

6. Delete all the text below the page heading and navigation bar.

7. Click the Repeating Table button on the Templates tab of the Insert bar, type "1" in the Row text box, type "1" in the Column text box, type "100" in the Width text box, select Percent in the list, and then name the region "Content."

Explore ▶ 8. Click in the line below the repeating region, click the Copyright symbol on the Characters tab of the Insert bar to insert the symbol, and then type "copyright Museum of Western Art, 2004."

Explore ▶ 9. Select the copyright text, and then click the Align Center button in the Property inspector.

10. Click the Library button on the Assets panel, drag the text to the panel, and then name the new library item "footer."

11. Save the template and close the page.

12. Create a new page from the template.

13. Type "TEST PAGE" in the PageHeading editable region, type "Test content" in the editable region within the Content repeating region, type "Museum of Western Art – Template Test" in the Title text box, press the Enter key, and then save the page as TemplateTest.htm.

14. Preview the page in a browser.

15. Upload the site to the remote server, and view the site over the Web.

Case 3. *NORM* Mark Chapman asks you to create a template for the NORM site, and then apply the template to the contact page of the site. Once this page is approved, the rest of the template will be applied to the other existing pages of the site.

1. Open the NORM site that you modified in Tutorial 8, Case 3, and then open the contact page.

2. Click the Make Template button on the Templates tab of the Insert bar. The Save As Template dialog box opens.

3. Type "MainTemplate" in the Save As text box, and then click the Save button.

4. Select the page heading text, click the Editable Region button, and then name the region "PageHeading."

5. Select the text in the PageHeading region, and then type "Page Heading" to insert placeholder text.

6. Delete the text below the PageHeading region, click the Editable Region button, and then name the Editable Region "PageContent." The new region appears in the page.

7. Click to the right of the new editable region, and then press the Enter key to move to the next line.

Explore ➤ 8. Click the Copyright symbol on the Characters tab of the Insert bar, insert a space, and then type "copyright NORM, Inc. 2004.", select the text, and then click the Align Center button.

9. Save the page and close the page. Next you will apply the template to the contact page.

10. Open the contact page, and then delete the navigation bar, the logo, and the footer because those elements already exist in the template. The remaining text moves up.

Explore ➤ 11. Click the Templates button on the Assets panel, select MainTemplate, and then click the Apply button at the bottom of the Assets panel. The Inconsistent Region Names dialog box opens.

Explore ➤ 12. Select the Document body region from the Editable Regions list, and then select PageHeading from the Move Content to New Region list.

Explore ➤ 13. Select the Document head region from the Editable Regions list, and then select head from the Move Content to New Region list.

Explore ➤ 14. Click the OK button. The contact page is connected to the template and the page content is moved to the PageHeading region.

Explore ➤ 15. Select the text below the page heading, drag it to the PageContent region, and then, if necessary, remove any extra spaces from the PageHeading region. Delete the placeholder text from the PageContent region, if necessary.

16. Save the page, and preview the page in a browser.

17. Upload the site to the remote server, and view the page over the Web.

Case 4. Sushi Ya-Ya Mary O'Brien asks you to create an online order form for the menu page of the site. You'll add the form to the menu page. Because the server-side script is still being finalized, you'll add the SushiYaYaFormText.htm page to the site so you can test the form.

1. Open the SushiYaYa site that you modified in Tutorial 8, Case 4.

2. Copy the **SushiYaYaFormText.htm** page from the **Tutorial.09/Cases** folder on the Data Disk to the root folder of your SushiYaYa site.

3. Open the menu page, delete the "Coming Soon!" text, and then click the Form button on the Forms tab of the Insert bar. The form is inserted in the page.

4. In the Property inspector, type "Menu" in the Name text box, click the Browse for File button beside the Action text box, double-click the SushiYaYaFormTest.htm page in the root folder, select _blank from the Target list, select GET from the Method list, and then select application/x-www-form-urlencoded from the Enctype list.

5. Click inside the form area, type "menu," and then apply the SubHeadings style.

Explore ▶ 6. Copy the **SushiMenu.htm** page in the **Tutorial.09/Cases** folder on your Data Disk to the root folder of the SushiYaYa site, click the Refresh button on the Site panel toolbar, and then open the page in a Document window.

Explore ▶ 7. Copy the table into the form below the Menu text. The menu table appears in the form.

8. Apply the subheadings CSS style to all of the bold text in the table, if necessary.

9. Click inside the cell in the first column of the second row, and then click the Text Field button on the Forms tab of the Insert bar. A text field appears in the cell.

10. In the Property inspector, type "KappaRoll" in the Name text box, type "6" in the Char Width text box, and then type "2" in the Max Chars text box.

11. Click in the cell in the first column of the next row, add a text field to the cell, type the sushi name as the field name, set the character width to 6, and then set the maximum characters to 2. (*Hint:* Do not include spaces in the field name.)

12. Repeat Step 11 to add text fields for the remaining sushi.

13. Click in the lower-right cell, and then click the Button button on the Forms tab of the Insert bar to add a button.

14. Type "Submit" in the Name and Label text boxes, if necessary, and then select Submit form from the Action radio group.

15. Click the Button button to add a second button, select Reset form from the Action radio group, and then type "Reset" in the Name text box.

16. Select the Validate Form behavior from the Behavior list in the Behaviors panel. The Validate Form dialog box opens.

Explore ▶ 17. Select the first item in the Named Fields list (text "KappaRoll" in form "Menu"), select Number from the Accept radio group, and then type "1" and "10" in the text boxes.

Explore ▶ 18. Select the next item in the Named Fields list, and then set a number limit from 1 to 10.

Explore ▶ 19. Repeat Step 18 to add the validation to all the text fields, and then click the OK button.

20. Save the page, preview the page in a browser, and then test the form.

21. Upload the site to the remote server, view the site over the Web, and then test the form.

Quick | Check Answers

Session 9.1

1. Tags are used in the head of a page to record information about the page or to give information to the server. The exact purpose of the meta tag is defined by its attributes.

2. Keywords meta tag and description meta tag

3. Keywords are one of the elements many search engines use to index Web pages; the keywords you choose should be the words you feel most people will type into search engines to look for the site or the words you want people to find your site under.

4. In the library, which you can access from the Assets panel or in the Library folder in the root folder for the site

5. A comment tag is placed at the beginning and end of every library item.

6. You can update every instance of the item by editing the library item itself.

Session 9.2

1. More—when you begin to design large, professional, template-driven sites, the pages are more interconnected and the design requires a great deal more fore-thought than designing a regular Web site.

2. Areas that can be changed in the template but cannot be changed in the template-based pages

3. When you edit a template, the changes are also made in all the pages that were created from that template.

4. A template that is created from the main template, which enables you to create a more defined structure for some pages of the site

5. True

6. The region is also deleted from the nested template, and you can select whether to move the content to another editable region on pages created from the template or nested template.

Session 9.3

1. A means of collecting information from users. A user can input information into the Web page by typing into designated fields or clicking various elements to make selections. Once the form is filled out, the information is submitted to a server (or other information-processing location) for processing.

2. False

3. The mechanism that enables users to input data into a form

4. Any three of the following: text fields (text areas), hidden fields, checkboxes, radio buttons (radio button groups), menus/lists, jump menus, file fields, image fields, and buttons

5. Validate Form behavior

6. Test the form.

EXTRA CASE

Coffee Lounge

The Coffee Lounge is an all-night coffee bar located on Exposition Parkway, across from Fair Park, at the heart of the Dallas punk music scene. The lounge features live, alternative, and punk music on the weekends; an improvisational psychedelic jazz jam on Thursday nights; poetry slams on Wednesday nights; experimental film screenings on Tuesday nights; and a book club that discusses various titles in the cyberpunk genre on Monday nights. In addition, the lounge encourages public art by allowing patrons and local artists to use the various pens, markers, and paints scattered through the club to add their mark to the walls and tables.

Coffee Lounge owner, Tommy Caddell, has decided that the lounge could benefit from a Web site. Tommy wants to use the site to inform patrons of upcoming and ongoing events, and as a marketing tool to promote featured events, the monthly special—a different coffee blend is featured each month, and sales. In addition, Tommy wants to include a page that features a different Dallas-based nonprofit organization each month. The page should give a blurb about the organization, including contact information and, if possible, a link to the organization's Web site.

You'll create the site for Tommy.

1. Create a list of site goals; review the list for order of importance and wording.
2. Define a target audience, and create a user profile for the site. (*Hint:* Do research as needed about the target audience.)
3. Conduct market research to gather information about at least four competing Web sites or other Web sites that cater to the target audience, and then write a paragraph summarizing your findings.
4. Develop two end user scenarios for the Web site.
5. Create an information category outline for the site.
6. Create a flow chart for the site.

7. Develop a site concept and a metaphor for the site. Write a paragraph explaining your choices.

8. Choose a color palette, fonts, and a graphic style for the site. Write a paragraph explaining your choices.

9. Create rough sketches of two layouts for the site. Write a paragraph explaining which layout you prefer and why.

10. Check the layout of the design you prefer for logic, and verify that your design reinforces the site goals and supports the site metaphor.

11. Create a Local Site Definition and a Remote Site Definition.

12. Create a main template for the site.

13. Add editable regions to the template and insert placeholder text as appropriate.

14. Add a background and colors to the template as appropriate based on your site plan.

15. Add an appropriate list of keywords to the head content of the template.

16. Add an appropriate description of the site to the head content of the template.

17. Create at least three CSS styles to format the text in the site; refer to your site plan for the appropriate colors, fonts, and so forth.

18. Insert a navigation bar into the template, and create appropriate elements. You will not create links in the navigation bar at this time because the pages have not yet been created; you will modify the template and add the links later. (*Hint:* If you do not have access to a graphics program, you can create a series of text links for site navigation instead of inserting a navigation bar.)

19. Create at least two library items for elements that you intend to reuse or update frequently, such as footers or an upcoming events list that will be displayed on more than one page.

20. Use the template to create a Web page.

21. Rename the Web page with a descriptive filename. (*Hint:* Remember to use index.htm as the filename for the home page.)

22. Set an appropriate page title for the Web page you created.

23. Open the Web page, type an appropriate page heading and text content, and then apply appropriate CSS styles if necessary to format the content.

24. Add at least one image to the Web page. (*Hint:* If you don't have an image file to insert, you can use any of the image files on the Data Disk.)

25. Save the page, and preview it in a browser.

26. Repeat Steps 20 through 25 to create a home page and at least three first-level pages for the site based on your site plan.

27. Once you have created all the pages for the site, open the template and modify the navigation bar, selecting each element and adding the link to the appropriate page.

28. Save the template, and update the pages.

29. Create an image map on at least one Web page.

30. Copy the CoffeeLoungeFormTest.htm file from the ExtraCase folder on your Data Disk to the root folder of your site. This will enable you to test the form.

31. Add a rollover button to at least one Web page.

32. Create a form on one Web page to collect appropriate data from visitors. Use a table to organize the form objects. Add at least four different types of form objects to the form.

33. Preview the form in a browser, and test the form.

34. Create a new page not based on the template in which to create animation, rename the page with a descriptive filename, and then type an appropriate page heading.

35. Add animation to the non-template-based page. Create a timeline, add layers to the timeline, move and resize animation bars, add keyframes, adjust layer visibility, and add appropriate behaviors as needed. For example, you might create an animation to advertise the coffee special. (*Hint:* You can add text to layers and move the layers, change visibility, and so forth.)

36. Preview the timeline in Dreamweaver and a browser.

37. Create a link to the new page from at least one of the existing pages of the site, and target the new page to open in a new browser window.

38. Insert a Flash movie, Flash text, Shockwave movie, video, or a sound into at least one page in the site. (*Hint:* If you don't have one of these types of files to insert, you can use any of the files on the Data Disk from Tutorial 8 as placeholders.)

39. Preview the site in a browser.

40. Upload the site to a remote server, and view the site over the Web.

41. Test each page of the form, including the form and the animation.

GLOSSARY

A

absolute font size

based on the standard default base size of 3; sizes 1 and 2 are smaller than 3, and sizes 4 through 7 are larger than 3

absolute link

a path to a document or Web page that includes the domain and protocol and that specifies the complete URL of the page to which you are linking

absolute positioning

when an object stays exactly where it is placed on a Web page regardless of how a user resizes the browser window

accessibility

the quality and ease of use of a Web site by people who use assistive devices or people with disabilities

action

in a behavior, what happens when an event is performed on an object

active link

a text hyperlink in the process of being clicked

additive color system

(*also* **RGB system**) a color system in which new colors are created by adding varying amounts of light; it uses red, green, and blue as its primary colors, and all other colors are created by combining these primary colors

alternative text

also called **Alt text**, text that appears in place of a graphic when the page is viewed with a browser that displays only text or when a browser is set to only download images manually; in some browsers, also appears in a Tooltip when the pointer is positioned over the graphic

anchor point for aligned element

icon that marks location in code used to align an element on a Web page

anchor tag

the HTML tag that defines a hyperlink

animation

a series of graphics or images that appear to move or change over time

animation bar

the purple line that appears in the channel to which the layer is added; by default the animation bar is 15 frames and layer name appears at the left of the animation bar

animation channels

the numbered rows below the frame numbers row in which objects are animated

assets

images, colors, URLs, Flash, Shockwave, movies, scripts, templates, and library items used throughout a site

assistive devices

apparatus that provides a person with disabilities with alternate means to experience electronic and information technologies

B

base font

the default font used wherever a different font is not specifically selected; is overwritten by CSS

base font size

the size of the base font on a Web page; the default base font size is 3; is overwritten by CSS

baseline

an imaginary line on which the text in a line is sitting

behavior

code added to a Web page that enables users to interact with various elements in the Web page, to alter the Web page in different ways, or to cause tasks to be performed

Behaviors channel

the row above the frame numbers, where you insert any behaviors that will be called from a certain frame in the timeline

borders

four lines that mark the edges of a cell

bracketing tags

a pair of tags that surround an element and consist of an opening tag and a closing tag

browser

see **Web browser**

buffer

means that the first 5 or 10 seconds of a video clip is downloaded before it begins to play to insure continuous playback of the clip; after the clip begins to play, as long as the current download is at or past the current clip playback location, the playback will continue without interruption

C

cache

a temporary local storage space in a computer

Cascading Style Sheet (CSS)

a collection of styles inserted in the head of a Web page or attached as an external document

cell

the container created by the intersection of a row and a column in a table

cell padding

the amount of empty space, measured in pixels, maintained between the border of a cell and the cell's content

cell spacing

the width of the cell walls measured in pixels

client

see **Web client**

CODEC (COmpressor/DECompressor)

the software that converts sound to digital code, shrinks the code to the smallest possible size for faster transmission, and later expands the code for playback on the client machine; there are several different popular CODECs used for sound on the Web, including MP3, RealMedia, QuickTime, and Windows Media

columns

vertical dividers across a table

column span

the width of a cell measured in columns

comment tag

the HTML tag used to insert notes in the HTML which will not display in the browser; can also be used to hide new features from older browsers that do not support them

compression

shrinks the file size of a graphic by using different types of encoding to remove redundant or less important information

comps

comprehensive drawings created from a sketch

content

information presented on a Web page

context-sensitive Help

Help topics related to the feature you are using; you access context-sensitive Help by clicking the Help button in any dialog box or toolbar about which you have a question, or by right-clicking any panel tab and then clicking Help

CSS

see **Cascading Style Sheet**

CSS mode

in the Properties inspector, enables you to apply CSS formatting to selected text on the Web page in the Document window

CSS Selector

a style you create to redefine formatting for a particular combinations of tags; most commonly used to customize the appearance of text links

CSS style

a rule that defines the appearance of an element in a Web page by redefining an existing HTML tag or by creating a custom style

custom scripting

your own code (usually JavaScript) included in the HTML or in an external script file

custom style class

(*also* **custom style**) a style you create from scratch and apply to selected text

 D

dependent files

files used in a Web page

deprecated tags

older HTML tags that are in the process of becoming obsolete

Director projectors

standalone executable files that do not need any software or plug-ins to run on the client computer

document relative link

a path from the current page to the linked document or Web page

Document Size/Estimated Download Time

in the status bar of the Document window, the size of the current page in kilobytes (K) and the approximate amount of time in seconds it would take to download the page

Document toolbar

includes buttons for the most commonly used commands related to the Document window

Document window

the main work area in which you create and edit a Web page

domain name

a unique name for a Web site chosen by the site owner combined with a top-level domain

Down state

the way a graphic, link, or button appears after it has been clicked

Dreamweaver

a Web site creation and management tool

dynamic HTML

a combination of HTML enhancements and a scripting language that work together to add animation, interactive elements, and dynamic updating to Web pages

 E

editable regions

areas that can be changed in the pages created from a template

embedded style sheet

see **internal style sheet**

encryption

the process of coding data so that only the sender and/or receiver can read it, preventing others from being able to understand it

end-user scenarios

imagined situations in which the target audience might access a Web site; used to envision actual conditions that an end user will be in while experiencing the Web site

event

a user event plus an event handler

event handler

code used to refer to an event

external style sheet

a separate file that contains CSS styles connected with a Web site

 F

file extension

used by Windows to determine the file type; the file extension for HTML Web pages can be either .htm or .html

File Transfer Protocol (FTP)

common Internet protocol used to copy files from one computer to another over the Internet

filename

the name under which a Web page is saved

firewall

a hardware or software device that restricts access between the computer network and the Internet, thereby protecting the computer behind the firewall

flow chart

a diagram of geometric shapes connected by lines that shows steps in sequence; in Web design, a flow chart provides a visual representation of the hierarchical structure of the pages within the site

font

a set of letters, numbers, and symbols in a unified typeface

font color

the color that is applied to a font

font size

the size of a font

font style

the stylistic attributes that are applied to the font, including bold, italic, and underline

font tag

designates which font and font attributes to use for a given text display

form

a means of collecting information from users over the Web; you can use forms to gather information about the user, create a user log in, gather user feedback, and so forth

form objects

generally the mechanisms that enable users to input data into a form; form objects include text boxes and text areas, hidden fields, checkbox, radio button and radio group, list/menu, jump menu, image field, file field, and button

frame numbers

visible in the second row of the timeline to help you keep track of what frame you are in

frames

divide a Web page into multiple HTML documents

frames (timeline)

the units of temporal measurement used in animation

Frames panel

in the Advanced Layout panel group, enables you to select and adjust the frame and frameset information that is contained in the frameset page

frameset

a separate HTML document that defines the structure and properties of a Web page with frames; it stores information about how the frames will display on the Web page and which HTML documents will initially be loaded into the frame, and provides the browser with that information when the page is loaded

FTP

see **File Transfer Protocol**

FTP host

the FTP site to which you upload the public version of your Web site

 G

generic font families

the three categories of typefaces—serif, sans-serif, and mono—in Dreamweaver

GIF (Graphics Interchange Format)

a graphic file compression format usually used on images that have large areas of non-gradient color; supports a palette of up to 256 colors, one of which may be used for single-color transparency

graphic

a visual representation, such as a drawing, painting, or photograph

graphic style

the look of the graphic elements of the site

Graphics Interchange Format

see **GIF**

grid

a series of parallel horizontal and vertical lines that overlap to create equal squares in the background of the Document window; provides a guide for positioning or resizing layers or other elements

head

the portion of the HTML code between the head tags on a Web page

hexadecimal

a number system that uses the digits 0-9 to represent the decimal values 0-9, and the letters A-F to represent the decimal values 10 to 15

home page

the main page of a Web site

host

see **FTP host**

hotspot

an area of an image that you can click to cause an action to occur, such as loading another Web page

HTML

see **Hypertext Markup Language**

HTML mode

in the Properties inspector, enables you to apply HTML formatting to selected text on the Web page in the Document window

HTML style

in Dreamweaver, a group of text attributes that you save with a name and reuse within the same Web site

HTTP

see **Hypertext Transfer Protocol**

HTTPS

see **Hypertext Transfer Protocol Secure**

hyperlinks

(*also* **links**) nodes that provide the ability to cross-reference information within a document or a Web page and enable the user to move from one document or Web page to another

Hypertext Markup Language (HTML)

the most common language used to provide instructions for how to format Web pages for display of the Web

Hypertext Transfer Protocol (HTTP)

the protocol that controls the transfer of Web pages over the Internet

Hypertext Transfer Protocol Secure (HTTPS)

a protocol that encrypts data transferred between your browser and the server to keep the information secure

image map

a graphic that is divided into hotspots

information architecture

the process of determining what you need a site to do, and then creating a framework that will allow you to accomplish those goals by providing a blueprint for Web page arrangement, Web site navigation, and page content organization

Insert bar

contains tabs that contain buttons for working with the category of objects reflected by the tab name

integrated file browser

enables you to browse files that are outside of your site; located below the local root folder file list in the Site panel

internal style sheet

(*also* **embedded style sheet**) the CSS styles connected with a Web page embedded in the head of the Web page and applied throughout the page

Internet

a huge, global network made up of millions of smaller computer networks that are all connected together

Internet service provider (ISP)

a company that has direct access to the Internet and sells access to other smaller entities

ISP

see **Internet service provider**

JPEG

a lossy compression format for graphic files usually used on photographic images and on graphics that have many gradient colors; supports millions of colors but does not support transparency

keyframe

a frame in a timeline where an event occurs; every timeline has at least two keyframes—one placed at the first frame and one placed at the last frame of the animation bar

keyword

a descriptive word or phrase that is placed in the meta tag with the attribute name="keywords"; you add one keywords meta tag to the head of each page and then list all the keywords for the site in that tag; the keywords you choose should be the words you think most people will type into search engines to look for your site or the words you would like people to find your site under

layer

a transparent container placed in a Web page to layout the page and to hold text, graphics, and other elements

layer-code marker

a small yellow shield-shaped marker that indicates that there is a layer on the page

layer selection handle

a small square that appears at the upper left of a layer when the layer is active or selected; you can click it to select the layer or drag it to reposition the layer

layout

the position of elements, including the navigation system, text, logo, and artwork, on the screen

library

a collection of library items that are located in the Library folder in the root folder of the site

library item

a page element (a piece of a Web page) saved as a .lbi file that can be inserted into the other pages of a site to help you automate site design and decrease redundant work; it is useful to create library items for elements that you intend to reuse or update frequently, such as footers or an upcoming events list that will be displayed on more than one page of a site

links

see **hyperlinks**

local root folder

(*also* **root folder**) the location where you store all the files used by the local version of the Web site

Local Site Definition

the information stored on the computer that you are using that tells Dreamweaver where the local root folder is located

locked files

files that cannot be opened in the authoring environment

logo

stylized text or, more usually, a graphic used by a company for the purposes of brand identification

lossless compression

file compression in which no information is discarded when the file is compressed

lossy compression

file compression in information is discarded to compress the file

machine name

a series of characters, often *www*, that the server administrator assigns to a Web site

Macromedia Director

a program that is used to create comprehensive multimedia solutions deployable across multiple mediums, including CD-ROM, DVD, Web, Kiosk, and so forth; Shockwave files are created in Director

Macromedia Flash

one of the first widely used animation programs that used vector-based graphics; because vector-based graphics can scale and compress to a very small file size without losing quality, Flash has become one of the premier solutions for creating and delivering interactive animations for display on the Web

main menu bar

a categorized series of menus that provide access to all the tools and features available in Dreamweaver

market research

the investigation and study of data about a target audience's preferences for a product or service; includes evaluating the products or services of competitors

MDI

see **multiple document interface**

media

refers to any special configurable object you add to a Web page that needs a player or an application that is not part of the browser, such as plug-ins, ActiveX controls, or helper applications, to display within a browser; some of the most useful media used in Web pages are Flash, Shockwave, sound, and video

meta description

a short summary of a Web page that is placed in the meta tag with the attribute name="description"; the description should contain a concise summary of the site's content and goals

meta tag

a tag in the head content that holds information about the Web page, gives information to the server, or adds functionality to the Web page

metaphor

a comparison in which one object, concept, or idea is represented as another

monospaced font

a serif font in which each letter takes exactly the same width in the line

MP3

a very commonly used sound format because MP3 files can contain very high quality sound with a surprisingly small file size; this is perfect for sending sound over the Web, especially when the end user has a slow connection

multiple document interface (MDI)

enables all of the document windows and panels to be integrated in one, large application window

navigation bar

a specific item in Dreamweaver that consists of a series of rollover graphics that change state when specific browser actions occur, such as when the user places the pointer over a graphic

navigation system

the interface that visitors use to move through a Web site; often appears on every page in the site

nest

to place one set of tags around another set of tags so that both sets apply to the text, table, layer, or frame that they surround

nested templates

templates created from the main template so that you can create a more defined structure for some pages of a site; each nested template inherits all the features of the main template (in other words, each nested template contains the same editable and noneditable regions as the main template and is linked to the main template)

Netscape Resize Fix

JavaScript that forces the page to reload every time the browser window is resized, thus eliminating the problems of layers moving around, scaling improperly, or disappearing completely

network

a series of computers that are connected together to share information and resources

NoFrames content

content that is shown by browsers that cannot display frames in a frameset

non-breaking spaces

special, invisible characters used to create more than one space between text and other elements

noneditable regions

areas that can be changed in the template but cannot be changed in the pages created from the template

non-gradient

color that is flat (one shade) and does not vary with subtle darkening or lightening

nonlinear

information that branches out from the home page in many directions much like railroad tracks branch out from a train station

Over state

the way a graphic, link, or button appears when the pointer is positioned over it

Over While Down state

the way a graphic, link, or button appears when the pointer is placed over it while it is in the Down state

page-centric design

an approach to Web site design that concentrates on designing and creating the Web pages individually and then linking them together, rather than concentrating on the Web site as a whole

page element

either an object or text on a Web page

page properties

attributes applied to an entire page

page title

the name given to a Web page; appears in the title bar of the browser

panel

a set of related commands, controls, and information about different aspects of working with Dreamweaver

panel groups

a collection of related panels

parent

the outer text, table, layer, or frame that holds the nested text, table, layer, or frame

pixel

the smallest adjustable unit on a display screen represented as a tiny dot of light

playback head

(the red bar) indicates which frame of the animation is visible in the Document window; you can move forward and backward in the timeline by dragging the playback head

playback rate

the speed of an animation in frames per second

PNG (Portable Network Graphic)

a lossless compression format for graphic files that supports up to 48-bit truecolor or 16-bit grayscale with lossless compression; supports variable transparency

Portable Network Graphic

see **PNG**

Property inspector

a toolbar with buttons for examining or editing the attributes of any element that is currently selected on the page displayed in the Document window

proportional font

a font in which the width of each letter on the line is proportional to the width of the letter itself

protocol

a set of technical specifications that define a format for sharing information

redefined HTML tag

an existing HTML tag you modify

relative font sizes

font sizes that add or subtract from the base font size

relative link

a link that is relative to the document or the site's root folder; *see* **document relative link** and **site root relative link**

row span

the height of the cell measured in rows

Remote Site Definition

the information stored on the computer that you are using that tells Dreamweaver where the remote server is located and how to connect to it

Reset button

a button in a Web form that clears any content from the form so that the user can start over

resize handles

small squares that appear around a selected object and that you can drag to resize the object

robots

software that searches the Web and send information back to a search engine where it is compiled and used to list pages in the search engine

rollover

two graphics that swap places during a specified browser action, and then swap back during another specified browser action

root folder

see **local root folder**

rows

horizontal dividers across a table

RGB system

see **additive color system**

sans-serif typefaces

typefaces in which there are no serifs

search engine

a Web site whose primary function is to gather and report what information is available on the Web based on specified keywords or phrases

serif typefaces

typefaces in which a delicate horizontal line finishes off the main strokes of each character

server

a computer that stores and distributes information to the other computers in the network

Shockwave

the Macromedia solution for delivering interactive multimedia on the Web; you use Shockwave for more complex interactive media components, such as games, interactive 3D, database driven multimedia, multi-user applications, and educational materials

Simple Mail Transfer Protocol (SMTP)

an agreed-upon protocol used by some e-mail software

site-centric design

an approach to Web site design that focuses on planning the Web site structure and design before creating any pages

site concept

a general underlying theme that unifies the various elements of a site and contributes to the site's look and feel

site definition

the information that tells Dreamweaver where to find the local and remote files for the Web site, along with other parameters that affect how the site is set up within Dreamweaver

site map

a visual representation of how the pages in a Web site are interrelated

site metaphor

a visual extension of the site concept, thereby reinforcing the site message and the site goals

Site panel

in the Files panel group, enables you to manage local and remote site files

site root relative link

a path from the site root folder to the linked document or Web page

SMTP

see **Simple Mail Transfer Protocol**

sound formats

the different types of compression used for sound; each sound format uses a different CODEC as the sound is compressed for delivery and decompressed for playback

status bar

a banner of details about the window's contents that appears at the bottom of a window

streaming

means that sound, video, or animation can begin to play on the user's computer after only a small portion downloads and will continue to play while the rest of the file is downloading; especially helpful to users with slow connections, because they can begin to hear the sound or view the media without waiting for large files to download completely

Submit button

a button in a Web form that sends the form data to the location you designated for processing.

subtractive color system

a color system in which new colors are created by removing varying amounts of light; it uses cyan, magenta, and yellow as its primary colors, and all other colors are created by combining these primary colors

tables

grid structures that are divided into rows and columns

Tag selector

in the status bar of the Document window, displays all the HTML tags surrounding the current selection in the Document window

target

for a link, specifies where the link opens, in the current browser window or in a new browser window or in a named frame

target audience

the group of users that you would *most* like to visit a Web site

template

a special page that enables the designer to separate the style of the page from the content by "locking" the page layout

text link

text that is formatted to link to another document, Web page, or a position in the current page when it is clicked

timeline actions

layer properties you set to change over time to create animation in the Timelines panel

title bar

displays the page title and the filename of the Web page in the Document window; displays the page title in the browser window

top-level domain

the highest category in the Internet naming system that identifies a Web site's type of entity or country of origin

Uniform Resource Locator

see **URL**

Up state

the way a graphic, link, or button appears before the user interacts with it

URL (Uniform Resource Locator)

the unique address of a Web page that Web browsers use to locate it

user event

what the user does to trigger the action in a behavior

user profile

the information that you gather from a list of questions to help you determine the characteristics of the target audience

Validate Form behavior

a behavior that enables you to create requirements/limits that check the form data before the form is submitted to the information-processing destination

variable transparency

the ability to make the background of the image transparent at different amounts; for example, fading from a dark color to transparent

visited link

a text hyperlink that has been clicked

Web

see **World Wide Web**

Web browser

(*also* **client**) the software installed on a client computer that allows users to view Web pages

Web client

(*also* **browser**) the computer an individual uses to access information via the Internet that is stored on Web servers throughout the world

Web pages

the electronic documents of information on the Web

Web Safe Color Palette

a palette of 216 colors that was created so that Web designers would have a reliable color pallet to work with

Web server

a specialized server that stores and distributes information to computers that are connected to the Internet

Web site

a group of related and interconnected Web pages

Window Size menu

displays the Document window's current dimensions in pixels in the status bar of the Document window

World Wide Web (WWW or Web)

a subset of the Internet with its own protocol

WWW

see **World Wide Web**

WYSIWYG

acronym for "What You See Is What You Get"; it means that the document or Web page is displayed in the program window as it will appear to the end user and the code is hidden from sight

z-index number

determines the layer's stacking order in the user's browser window; a layer with a higher number appears at the front of the stack and is seen in front of a layer with a lower number

formatting, 3.06–13
HTML tags for, 3.13–25
links, 2.19–20, 3.13–18, 5.06
positioning, 3.34
spell-checking, 3.05–06
word wrap option, 3.21, 4.32

Text attribute, 8.11

Text Field button, 9.41

Text tab, 1.32

TextTop attribute, 4.10

This Document Only option, 3.35, 3.38

timeline(s). *See also*
Timelines panel
adding behaviors to, 7.34, 7.40–42
adding layers to, 7.21–25
creating, 7.07–11, 7.35–42
deleting animation bars from, 7.30
previewing, 7.19–20
stacking order settings, 7.22–23
starting, with buttons, 7.30–32
visibility settings, 7.16–18, 7.38

timeline frame(s)
described, 7.06
numbers, 7.05, 7.06

Timelines list, 7.05–06

Timelines panel
adding layers to, 7.07, 7.09
components of, 7.05–06
creating multiple timelines with, 7.35–42
described, 7.05–06
moving layers in, 7.25–27
opening, 7.04
timeline actions and, 7.04
visibility settings, 7.16–18

Times New Roman font, 2.18

title bar, described, 1.26

<title> tag, 2.35

titles, for Web pages, 2.31, 2.35

Toggle CSS/HTML Mode button, 3.47, 6.09

Top attribute, 4.10

top-level domains, 1.07

tourdates.htm, 2.37, 2.30, 4.13, 4.21, 4.29, 4.42, 5.13, 7.04–43, 8.13, 9.11

<TR> tag, 4.37–38, 4.40

Tracing Image option, 2.32

transparency
GIF format and, 4.03
JPEG format and, 4.03
PNG format and, 4.04
variable, 4.04

Tutorial folder, 4.06, 4.14

Type attribute, 9.40

Type option, 3.33, 3.35

U

<ul> tag, 3.20

underscore (_), 4.16

Undo Delete Frame command, 5.21, 5.22

Uniform Resource Locators. *See*
URLs (Uniform Resource Locators)

unordered (bulleted) lists, 3.07

Up Arrow button, 5.15

Up state, 5.02–5.09

Update button, 9.11, 9.15

Update Library Items dialog box, 9.14–15

Update Page When Template Changes checkbox, 9.18, 9.26

Update Pages dialog box, 9.11, 9.33

Update Template File dialog box, 9.30

updating
described, 2.40
older HTML pages, 3.02
to remote locations, 2.40–44, 3.57–58, 4.58–59

URLs (Uniform Resource Locators). *See also* **links**
forms and, 9.36
frames and, 5.17
for graphics, 4.09, 4.16
navigation bars and, 5.03, 5.05, 5.14
parts of, 1.07
servers and, 1.07

Use CSS Selector option, 3.41

Use Firewall option, 2.27

Use Passive FTP option, 2.26, 2.28

Use Tables option, 5.06, 5.08

Use Transparent GIFs option, 6.25

user profiles, 2.04–06

Using Dreamweaver command, 1.33, 1.34

V

V Space attribute, 8.09, 8.23

Validate Form behavior, 9.48–50

Validate Form dialog box, 9.48–50

validation, of form data, 9.48–52

Vert (Vertical) attribute, 4.32, 4.54

video. *See also* **movies**
adding, 8.34–40
attributes, 8.37–39
buffered playback, 8.32–33
compression, 8.32
file formats, 8.33–34
file size, 8.32–33
previewing, 8.41
understanding, 8.32–34
uploading, 8.40–41

View menu
Code View Options command, 3.21
Grid command, 6.19
Rulers command, 4.29, 6.03
Text Size command, 3.12
Visual Aids command, 5.19

views, displaying Web pages in different, 1.26–27

visited links
color of, 2.19–20, 2.33, 5.29
described, 2.19–20

W

W (width) attribute, 8.08, 8.23, 8.37

W3C (World Wide Web Consortium)
accessibility technology information resources, 2.14
HTML standards, 3.02

WAI (Web Accessibility Initiative), 2.15

Wasabi2.gif, 7.50–51

wasabisound_autoplay.swf, 8.47

TASK	PAGE #	RECOMMENDED METHOD
Align text to center	DRM 3.14	Select text, click ☰
Align text to left	DRM 3.27	Select text, click ☰
Align text to right	DRM 3.14	Select text, click ☰
Alternate text for graphics or links, add	DRM 4.10	Select link or graphic, click in Alt text box in Property inspector, type alternate text
Animation bar, delete	DRM 7.27	See Reference Window: Deleting an Animation Bar
Animation bar, move to another animation channel	DRM 7.10	Select animation bar, drag to new channel
Animation bar, move within animation channel	DRM 7.11	Select animation bar, drag to right or left as needed
Animation bar, resize	DRM 7.12	Select a keyframe, drag selected keyframe to right or left until animation bar is desired size
Animation bar, select	DRM 7.10	Click animation bar between its keyframes in Timelines panel
Behaviors, add to Behaviors channel	DRM 7.31	See Reference Window: Adding Behaviors to Behaviors Channel
Behaviors, add using Behaviors panel	DRM 6.28	See Reference Window: Adding the Show-Hide Layers Prewritten Behavior Using the Behaviors Panel
Behavior event, edit in Behaviors panel	DRM 6.39	Open Design panel group, click Behaviors panel, click behavior in Behaviors panel, click Events list arrow, click new event
Browser window, close	DRM 1.12	See Reference Window: Closing the Browser Window
Cell, add in Layout view	DRM 4.46	Click ▦ on Layout tab in Insert bar, drag to draw cell in Document window
Cell, format as header	DRM 4.32	Select cells, check Header checkbox in Property inspector
Cell, merge	DRM 4.32	Select cells, click ▦ in the Property inspector
Cell, select in Layout view	DRM 4.48	Click perimeter of cell
Cell, select in Standard view	DRM 4.26	Drag across table cell
Cell, split	DRM 4.32	Select cell, click ⫿ in Property inspector, click Rows or Columns option button, set number of rows or columns in which to split the cell, click OK
Code view, change to	DRM 1.25	Click ◇ on Document toolbar
Code and Design views, change to	DRM 1.25	Click ▤ on Document toolbar
Column, delete	DRM 4.36	Select column, right-click selected column, point to Table, click Delete Column
Column, insert	DRM 4.36	Select column to right of column you want to insert, right-click selected column, point to Table, click Insert Column

TASK	PAGE #	RECOMMENDED METHOD
Column, resize	DRM 4.35	Drag column border
Column, select	DRM 4.26	Click above top border of column
Column span, adjust	DRM 4.33	Right-click in column, point to Table, click Increase Column Span or Decrease Column Span
Custom style class, apply	DRM 3.39	Select text, click style name in CSS Styles panel
Custom style class, create	DRM 3.38	See Reference Window: Creating Custom Style Classes
Custom style class, delete from within document	DRM 3.45	Click Edit Styles option button in CSS Style panel, click style name, click 🗑 in the CSS Styles panel
Custom style class, edit	DRM 3.52	Click Edit Styles option button in CSS Style panel, double-click style name, make desired changes, click OK
Default Dreamweaver MX workspace, select	DRM 1.14	See Reference Window: Selecting the Default Dreamweaver MX Workspace
Design view, change to	DRM 1.24	Click 📰 on Document toolbar
Document window, change size of	DRM 1.27	Click the Window Size menu in Document window status bar, click the size you want
Document window, open a file in	DRM 1.23	Double-click the filename in the Site panel
Dreamweaver, start	DRM 1.15	Click Start, point to Programs, point to Macromedia, click Macromedia Dreamweaver MX
Dreamweaver, exit	DRM 1.36	See Reference Window: Exiting Dreamweaver
Editable region, delete from template	DRM 9.32	Open template page, select editable region, press Delete key, save template, click Update button, resolve inconsistent region names, click OK, click Close
E-mail link behavior, add	DRM 6.36	Click hotspot to which you want to add e-mail link, double-click in Link text box in Property inspector, type "mailto:", type e-mail address, press Enter
Extension, download	DRM 8.35	Open Answers panel, select Extensions, type RealMedia (or media type), click ➡, click extension, click Windows to download Windows version, click Open, click Accept, Click OK, click Close, exit and restart Dreamweaver
External style sheet, attach to a Web page	DRM 3.46	See Reference Window: Attaching an External Style Sheet to a Web Page
External style sheet, create	DRM 3.43	See Reference Window: Exporting Styles to an External Style Sheet
External style sheet, define a new style in	DRM 3.49	See Reference Window: Defining a Style in an External Style Sheet
File, delete from Site panel list	DRM 2.40	Click filename in Site panel, click File on Site panel menu bar, click Delete, click OK

TASK	PAGE #	RECOMMENDED METHOD
Flash attributes, adjust	DRM 8.08	Select Flash movie, change attributes in Property inspector
Flash button, use	DRM 8.14	Click 🔍 on Media tab of Insert bar, click button style in Style list, review button states in Sample box, click OK
Flash movies, add to Web page	DRM 8.06	See Reference Window: Adding a Flash Movie to a Web Page
Flash text, add to Web page	DRM 8.11	See Reference Window: Adding Flash Text to a Web Page
Folder, create new in site	DRM 5.23	Click File on Site panel menu bar, click New Folder, type new folder name, press Enter
Font, change	DRM 3.08	Select text, click Font list arrow in Property inspector, click desired font group
Form, create	DRM 9.35	See Reference Window: Creating a Form
Form object, add to form	DRM 9.35	Click in form, click appropriate button on Forms tab of Insert bar, type name and set attributes in Property inspector
Frame, adjust Page Properties	DRM 5.28	See Reference Window: Adjusting Page Properties for Frames
Frame borders, displaying	DRM 5.19	Click View on main menu bar, point to Visual Aids, click Frame Borders
Frame and Frameset, saving changes	DRM 5.19	See Reference Window: Creating a Web Page That Uses Frames
Frame, create a Web page that uses	DRM 5.44	Click File on main menu bar, click Save All
Frame, save	DRM 5.24	See Reference Window: Saving a Frame
Frameset, save	DRM 5.26	See Reference Window: Saving a Frameset
Graphics, add to a Web page	DRM 4.05	See Reference Window: Adding Graphics to a Web Page
Grid, display or hide	DRM 6.19	Click View on main menu bar, point to Grid, click Show Grid
Help, get in Dreamweaver	DRM 1.32	See Reference Window: Getting Help in Dreamweaver
HTML style, apply	DRM 3.30	See Reference Window: Applying an HTML Style
HTML style, create	DRM 3.26	See Reference Window: Creating a New HTML Style
HTML style, delete	DRM 3.31	See Reference Window: Deleting HTML Styles
HTML tag, modify	DRM 3.34	See Reference Window: Modifying an Existing HTML Tag
HTML tags in Web pages, examine	DRM 3.19	See Reference Window: Examining HTML Tags
Hyperlink, copy	DRM 3.18	Select link, click Edit on the main menu bar, click Copy HTML

TASK	PAGE #	RECOMMENDED METHOD
Hyperlink, create	DRM 3.15	Select text or graphic, click 📁 in the Property inspector, navigate to file to which you want to link, click OK; or drag from ⊙ to filename in Site panel to which you want to link; click Target list arrow in Property inspector, click target window destination
Hyperlink, customize appearance of	DRM 3.40	See Reference Window: Customizing the Appearance of Hyperlinks
Hyperlink, delete	DRM 5.06	Select link, press Delete
Hyperlink, open in new browser window	DRM 5.46	Select link, click Target list arrow in Property inspector, click _blank
Hyperlink, paste	DRM 3.18	Select link, click Edit on the main menu bar, click Paste HTML
Hyperlink, use	DRM 1.09	Click the link in the browser window
Image map, create	DRM 4.13	See Reference Window: Creating an Image Map
Keyframe, add to animation bar	DRM 7.13	See Reference Window: Adding Keyframes to an Animation Bar
Keywords, add to Web page	DRM 9.04	Click 🔲 on Head tab of Insert bar, type keywords in Keywords text box, click OK
Keywords, edit	DRM 9.06	Click in keywords list in Document window in Code view, make changes to keywords as needed in Property inspector or Document window
Layer, adjust stacking order in timeline	DRM 7.19	See Reference Window: Adjusting Layer Stacking Order
Layer, adjust visibility	DRM 7.15	See Reference Window: Adjusting Layer Visibility
Layer, insert	DRM 6.03	Click 🔲 on Common tab on Insert bar, drag in Document window to draw layer
Layer, move	DRM 6.07	Select layer, drag to new position
Layer, move in Timelines panel	DRM 7.23	Select a keyframe and change layer position, repeat for each keyframe where you want layer to move, adding keyframes as needed
Layer, resize	DRM 6.06	Select layer, drag resize handle
Layer, resize over time	DRM 7.25	Select a keyframe, drag layer resize handles to resize layer, deselect the layer
Layer, select	DRM 6.06	Click layer-code marker

TASK	PAGE #	RECOMMENDED METHOD
Layer stacking order, changing	DRM 6.15	Open Advanced panel group, click Layers panel, drag layer to new position in Layers panel
Layers, add to Timelines panel	DRM 7.05	See Reference Window: Adding Layers to the Timelines Panel
Layers, align	DRM 6.18	Select first layer, press and hold Shift, click layer to which you want to align, click Modify on main menu bar, point to Align, click alignment choice
Layers, convert to a table	DRM 6.24	See Reference Window: Converting Layers to a Table
Layout view, switch to	DRM 4.45	Click `Layout View` on Layout tab in Insert bar
Library item, add to a Web page	DRM 9.12	Drag library item from library in Assets panel to desired location on page
Library item, create	DRM 9.10	See Reference Window: Creating a Library Item
Library item, delete from library	DRM 9.16	Select library item in library, drag selected library item to Delete button (trash can icon) in Assets panel
Library item, delete from page	DRM 9.16	Select library item on page, press Delete key
Library item, edit	DRM 9.14	Open library item, make changes as needed, then save the library item, update the library item in all files
Library item, open	DRM 9.14	Double-click library item in library in Assets panel
Local Site Definition, create	DRM 1.17	See Reference Window: Create a Local Site Definition
Local Web page in a browser, open	DRM 1.07	See Reference Window: Opening a Local Web Page in a Browser
Meta description, add to Web page	DRM 9.07	Click on Head tab of Insert bar, type description in Description text box, click OK
Meta description, edit	DRM 9.08	Click in description in Document window in Code view, make changes to description as needed in Property inspector or Document window
Navigation bar, copy	DRM 5.12	Click navigation bar anchor point, click Edit on main menu bar, click Copy HTML
Navigation bar, create	DRM 5.02	See Reference Window: Creating a Navigation Bar
Navigation bar, modify	DRM 5.14	See Reference Window: Modifying a Navigation Bar
Navigation bar, paste	DRM 5.12	Click navigation bar anchor point, click Edit on main menu bar, click Paste HTML
Nested layer, create	DRM 6.21	Select layer in Layers panel, press and hold Ctrl, drag selected layer on top of layer in which you want to nest it
Nested table, remove	DRM 4.53	Select nested table, click in the Property inspector

TASK	PAGE #	RECOMMENDED METHOD
Nested templates, create	DRM 9.31	Create new page from main template, click 📄 on Templates tab of Insert bar, type template name, click Save button, enter template content as needed, save and close page
Netscape Resize Fix, adding to a Web site	DRM 6.23	See Reference Window: Adding the Netscape Resize Fix to a Web Site
NoFrames content, adding	DRM 5.38	See Reference Window: Adding NoFrames content
Non-breaking space, insert	DRM 3.13	Click ⬇ on the Characters tab on the Insert bar
Page Properties, copy	DRM 2.36	Click 📑 on Document toolbar, select the code from the opening to the closing body tags (inclusive), press Ctrl+C
Page Properties, set	DRM 2.32	Click Modify on main menu bar, click Page Properties, set desired properties, click OK
Password, delete from Remote Info	DRM 2.42	Click Site on Site panel menu bar, click Edit Sites, click Web site name in list, click Edit, click Remote Info, uncheck Save checkbox, click OK, click Done
Preview list, add a browser to	DRM 2.37	Click File on the Site panel menu bar, point to Preview in Browser, click Edit Browser List, click Preview in Browser, select browser in list; or click ➕ , type the name of the browser, click Browser, navigate to the browser you want to add, click Open, check Primary Browser or Secondary Browser checkbox, click OK; click OK
Preview page in browser	DRM 2.39	Click filename in Site panel, click File on Site panel menu bar, point to Preview in Browser, click browser name
RealVideo, add to Web page	DRM 8.36	See Reference Window: Adding a RealVideo Clip to a Web Page
Remote host, connect	DRM 2.41	Click 🔌 on the Site panel toolbar
Remote host, disconnect	DRM 2.42	Click 🔌 on the Site panel toolbar
Remote Site Definition, create	DRM 2.26	See Reference Window: Creating a Remote Site Definition for FTP Access
Remote Web page in a browser, open	DRM 1.05	See Reference Window: Opening a Remote Web Page in a Browser
Rollover, copy	DRM 4.18	Select rollover, click Edit on main menu bar, click Copy HTML
Rollover, insert	DRM 4.16	See Reference Window: Inserting a Rollover
Rollover, paste	DRM 4.18	Click Edit on main menu bar, click Paste HTML
Rollover, replace	DRM 4.19	Delete original graphic, click 🖼
Rollover, replace original graphic	DRM 4.19	Select graphic, click the Src Browser for File button, navigate to new source file, or click the Src Point to File icon in the Property inspector, drag to new source file in the Site panel
Rollover, replace rollover graphic	DRM 4.19	Select graphic, open Design panel group, click Behaviors panel, double-click onMouseOver, click Browse, navigate to new rollover file, click OK, click OK

TASK	PAGE #	RECOMMENDED METHOD
Row, delete	DRM 4.37	Select row, right-click selected row, point to Table, click Delete Row
Row, insert	DRM 4.36	Select row below row you want to insert, right-click selected row, point to Table, click Insert Row
Row, select	DRM 4.27	Click to the left of left border of row
Row span adjust	DRM 4.33	Right-click in row, point to Table, click Increase Row Span or Decrease Row Span
Shockwave, add to Web page	DRM 8.20	See Reference Window: Adding a Shockwave Movie to a Web Page
Shockwave attributes, adjust	DRM 8.23	Select Shockwave movie, change attributes in Property inspector
Size, change text	DRM 3.08	Select text, click Size list arrow in Property inspector, click desired relative size
Sound file, link to Web page	DRM 8.30	Select graphic, click Browse for File icon next to Link text box in Property inspector, double-click sound file
Sound only Flash movie attributes, adjust	DRM 8.29	Select sound only Flash movie, change attributes in Property inspector
Sound only Flash movie, embed	DRM 8.27	See Reference Window: Adding a Sound Only Flash Movie to a Web Page
Spelling, check page	DRM 3.05	Click Text on main menu bar, click Check Spelling
Standard view, switch to	DRM 4.57	Click Standard View on Layout tab in Insert bar
Style, define in external style sheet	DRM 3.49	See Reference Window: Defining a Style in an External Style Sheet
Style, edit	DRM 3.52	See Reference Window: Editing a style
Styles, export to external style sheet	DRM 3.43	See Reference Window: Exporting Styles to an External Style Sheet
Table, convert to layers	DRM 6.26	Select Table, click Modify on main menu bar, point to Convert, click Table to Layers.
Table, create in Layout view	DRM 4.47	See Reference Window: Creating a Table in Layout View
Table, format	DRM 4.38	Click in table, click Commands on main menu bar, click Format Table, make selections, click OK
Table, insert in Standard view	DRM 4.20	See Reference Window: Inserting a Table
Table, resize in Layout view	DRM 4.49	Select table, drag a resize handle
Table, resize in Standard view	DRM 4.30	Select table, drag a resize handle; or double-click in W and H text boxes in Property inspector, type new values
Table, select in Layout view	DRM 4.48	Click Layout Table tab

TASK	PAGE #	RECOMMENDED METHOD
Table, select in Standard view	DRM 4.25	Right-click table, point to Table, click Select Table, or click upper left corner of table
Table tags, redefine using CSS	DRM 4.41	See Reference Window: Redefining Table Tags Using CSS
Template, apply to existing Web page	DRM 9.28	Open Web page in Document window, select template in Assets panel, click Apply button, designation in which regions the existing content will be placed
Template, create	DRM 9.19	See Reference Window: Creating a Template
Template, delete	DRM 9.30	Select template in Assets panel, drag it to Delete button (trash can icon)
Text, copy from text file and paste in Web page	DRM 5.37	Open text file, select text, press Ctrl+C, open Web page file in Dreamweaver, press Ctrl+V or click Edit on main menu bar, click Paste
Text, format using Property inspector	DRM 3.08	See Reference Window: Formatting Text Using the Property inspector
Text size, change in the browser	DRM 3.11	Click View on browser window menu bar, point to Text Size, click desired size
Timeline, preview in browser	DRM 7.17	Check the Autoplay checkbox in Timelines panel, click OK to confirm Play Timeline action added to Web page, preview in browser
Timeline, preview in Document window	DRM 7.17	Click and hold Playback button in Timelines panel toolbar while viewing animation in Document window
Timeline, start with button	DRM 7.28	Select button in Document window, click ➕ in Behaviors panel, point to Timeline, click Play Timeline, verify that timeline is selected in Play Timeline list, click OK button, select Play Timeline Behavior in Behaviors panel, click Events list arrow, click onClick, uncheck Autoplay checkbox on Timelines panel toolbar if necessary
Timelines, create multiple	DRM 7.33	Right-click blank frame in Timelines panel, click Add Timeline, rename timeline
Timelines panel, open	DRM 7.02	Click Window, point to Others, click Timelines
Timelines, toggle between	DRM 7.34	Click Timelines list arrow on Timelines panel toolbar, click timeline name
Video clip attributes, adjust	DRM 8.37	Select video clip, change attributes in Property inspector
View file list and site map in the Site panel	DRM 1.20	See Reference Window: Viewing the File List and Site Map in the Site Panel
View previously viewed pages in a browser	DRM 1.11	Click ◀ or ▶ on browser window toolbar
View site from remote location	DRM 2.42	Start browser, type URL of remote site in Address or Location text box, press Enter

TASK REFERENCE

TASK	PAGE #	RECOMMENDED METHOD
Web page, create from template	DRM 9.25	See Reference Window: Creating a Template-Based Page
Web page, create new one in site	DRM 2.29	Click File on the Site panel menu bar, click New File, type a new filename, press Enter
Web page, duplicate	DRM 5.40	Click page in Site panel, press Ctrl+C, press Ctrl+V
Web page, open in a Document window	DRM 1.23	Double-click filename in Site panel
Web page, rename	DRM 5.40	Right-click page in Site panel, click Rename, type new name, press Enter
Web page, save	DRM 2.30	Click File on the main menu bar, click Save
Web site, upload to remote server	DRM 3.57	See Reference Window: Uploading a Site to the Remote Server

Note: *The data files supplied with this book and listed in the chart below are starting files for Tutorials 1 and 2. In Tutorial 3, you will begin your work using the files you created in Tutorial 2. The Review Assignments for Tutorial 3 use the file you created in the tutorial, and then subsequent tutorials and Review Assignments build on the previous one. For example, after finishing Tutorial 3, you begin the Tutorial 3 Review Assignments with your ending files from Tutorial 3; and then after finishing the Tutorial 3 Review Assignments, you begin Tutorial 4 with your ending files from the Tutorial 3 Review Assignments. You must complete each tutorial and Review Assignment in order and finish them completely before continuing to the next tutorial, or your data files will not be correct for the next tutorial. The Case Problems also build on their starting data files in the same manner. Please read the "Read This Before You Begin" page on page DRM 1.02 for important information about how to store your data files.*

Macromedia Dreamweaver MX

Tutorial	Location in Tutorial	Name and Location of Data File or Web Site	Files or Web Sites the Student Creates from Scratch
Tutorial 1	Session 1.1	\Tutorial.01\Tutorial\Catalyst	
	Session 1.2	\Tutorial.01\Tutorial\Catalyst	
	Review Assignments		
	Case Problem 1		
	Case Problem 2	\Tutorial.01\Cases\Museum\Dreamweaver	
	Case Problem 3		
	Case Problem 4		
Tutorial 2	Session 2.1		
	Session 2.2	\Tutorial.02\Tutorial\Catalyst	
	Session 2.3		\Catalyst\Dreamweaver\index.htm \Catalyst\Dreamweaver\bands.htm \Catalyst\Dreamweaver\catalogue.htm \Catalyst\Dreamweaver\contact.htm \Catalyst\Dreamweaver\label.htm \Catalyst\Dreamweaver\tourdates.htm
	Review Assignments		\CatalystBlues\Dreamweaver\index.htm *(Additional filenames will differ depending on the site plan you wrote.)*
	Case Problem 1	\Tutorial.02\Tutorial\HartBackground.gif \Tutorial.02\Tutorial\HartMemo.doc	\Hart\Dreamweaver\index.htm \Hart\Dreamweaver\Contact.htm \Hart\Dreamweaver\CulturalCrossPollination.htm \Hart\Dreamweaver\LinguisticDifferences.htm \Hart\Dreamweaver\ProfHart.htm \Hart\Dreamweaver\RitualsAndPractices.htm
	Case Problem 2		\Museum\Dreamweaver\index.htm \Museum\Dreamweaver\Art.htm \Museum\Dreamweaver\Artists.htm \Museum\Dreamweaver\Location.htm \Museum\Dreamweaver\Museum.htm
	Case Problem 3	\Tutorial.02\Cases\NORMBackground.gif	\NORM\Dreamweaver\index.htm \NORM\Dreamweaver\books.htm \NORM\Dreamweaver\company.htm \NORM\Dreamweaver\contact.htm \NORM\Dreamweaver\links.htm
	Case Problem 4		\SushiYaYa\Dreamweaver\index.htm \SushiYaYa\Dreamweaver\company.htm \SushiYaYa\Dreamweaver\contact.htm \SushiYaYa\Dreamweaver\menu.htm *(Additional filenames will differ depending on the site plan you wrote.)*
Tutorial 3	Session 3.1	\Tutorial.03\Tutorial\Bands.doc \Tutorial.03\Tutorial\Contact.doc	
	Session 3.2		
	Session 3.3		
	Review Assignments	\Tutorial.03\Review\Catalogue.doc \Tutorial.03\Review\Label.doc	

Macromedia Dreamweaver MX

Tutorial	Location in Tutorial	Name and Location of Data File or Web Site	Files or Web Sites the Student Creates from Scratch
	Case Problem 1	\Tutorial.03\Tutorial\Overview.doc \Tutorial.03\Tutorial\HartContact.doc \Tutorial.03\Tutorial\ProfHart.doc	
	Case Problem 2	\Tutorial.03\Tutorial\Welcome.doc \Tutorial.03\Tutorial\Museum.doc \Tutorial.03\Tutorial\Artists.doc \Tutorial.03\Tutorial\Location.doc	
	Case Problem 3	\Tutorial.03\Tutorial\Home.doc \Tutorial.03\Tutorial\Company.doc \Tutorial.03\Tutorial\NORMContact.doc \Tutorial.03\Tutorial\Links.doc	
	Case Problem 4	\Tutorial.03\Tutorial\SushiYa-YaContent.doc	
Tutorial 4	Session 4.1	\Tutorial.04\Tutorial\CatalystLogo.gif \Tutorial.04\Tutorial\USMap.gif \Tutorial.04\Tutorial\CatalystLogoRollover.gif	\Catalyst\Dreamweaver\WhatHot.htm
	Session 4.2		
	Session 4.3	\Tutorial.04\Tutorial\SurfaceSuctionCDcover.jpg	
	Review Assignments	\Tutorial.04\Review\ DizziedConnectionCDcover300.jpg \Tutorial.04\Review\ SurfaceSuctionCDcover300.jpg \Tutorial.04\Review\SlothChildCDcover300.jpg \Tutorial.04\Review\LifeInMinorChords CDcover300.jpg	
	Case Problem 1	\Tutorial.04\Cases\HrochLogo.gif	
	Case Problem 2	\Tutorial.04\Cases\MuseumLogo.gif \Tutorial.04\Cases\MuseumLogoRollover.gif	
	Case Problem 3	\Tutorial.04\Cases\NORMlogo.gif \Tutorial.04\Cases\NORMlogoRollover.gif \Tutorial.04\Cases\BookCoverPunch.jpg \Tutorial.04\Cases\BookCoverPunchSmall.jpg	\NORM\Dreamweaver\FeaturedBook.htm
	Case Problem 4	\Tutorial.04\Cases\SushiYaYaLogo.gif \Tutorial.04\Cases\SushiYaYaLogoRollover.gif \Tutorial.04\Cases\TikkRollTuna.gif	\SushiYaYa\Dreamweaver\Specials.htm
Tutorial 5	Session 5.1	\Tutorial.05\Tutorial\bands.htm \Tutorial.05\Tutorial\label.gif \Tutorial.05\Tutorial\labelOver.gif \Tutorial.05\Tutorial\labelDown.gif \Tutorial.05\Tutorial\labelOWD.gif \Tutorial.05\Tutorial\bands.gif \Tutorial.05\Tutorial\bandsOver.gif \Tutorial.05\Tutorial\bandsDown.gif \Tutorial.05\Tutorial\bandsOWD.gif \Tutorial.05\Tutorial\catalogue.gif \Tutorial.05\Tutorial\catalogueOver.gif \Tutorial.05\Tutorial\catalogueDown.gif \Tutorial.05\Tutorial\catalogueDown.gif \Tutorial.05\Tutorial\tourdates.gif \Tutorial.05\Tutorial\tourdatesOver.gif \Tutorial.05\Tutorial\tourdatesDown.gif \Tutorial.05\Tutorial\tourdatesOWD.gif \Tutorial.05\Tutorial\contact.gif \Tutorial.05\Tutorial\contactOver.gif \Tutorial.05\Tutorial\contactDown.gif \Tutorial.05\Tutorial\contactOWD.gif	

Macromedia Dreamweaver MX

Tutorial	Location in Tutorial	Name and Location of Data File or Web Site	Files or Web Sites the Student Creates from Scratch
	Session 5.2	\Tutorial.05\Tutorial\FrameTest\Dreamweaver\ LIMCFrameSet.htm	\Catalyst\Dreamweaver\LifeInMinorChords\ LIMCcontent1frame.htm \Catalyst\Dreamweaver\LifeInMinorChords\ LIMCtopframe.htm \Catalyst\Dreamweaver\LifeInMinorChords\ LIMCleftframe.htm \Catalyst\Dreamweaver\LifeInMinorChords\ LIMCframeset.htm
	Session 5.3	\Tutorial.05\Tutorial\LifeBanner.jpg \Tutorial.05\Tutorial\LIMCmainframetext.doc \Tutorial.05\Tutorial\LIMChistory.gif \Tutorial.05\Tutorial\LIMChistoryOVER.gif \Tutorial.05\Tutorial\LIMCmembers.gif \Tutorial.05\Tutorial\LIMCmembersOVER.gif \Tutorial.05\Tutorial\LIMCcds.gif \Tutorial.05\Tutorial\LIMCcdsOVER.gif \Tutorial.05\Tutorial\LIMCtours.gif \Tutorial.05\Tutorial\LIMCtoursOVER.gif \Tutorial.05\Tutorial\LIMCphotos.gif \Tutorial.05\Tutorial\LIMCphotosOVER.gif	\Catalyst\Dreamweaver\LifeInMinorChords\ LIMChistory.htm \Catalyst\Dreamweaver\LifeInMinorChords\ LIMCmembers.htm \Catalyst\Dreamweaver\LifeInMinorChords\ LIMCCDs.htm \Catalyst\Dreamweaver\LifeInMinorChords\ LIMCtours.htm \Catalyst\Dreamweaver\LifeInMinorChords\ LIMCphotos.htm
	Review Assignments	\Tutorial.05\Review\DCbanner.jpg \Tutorial.05\Review\DCbottombanner.jpg \Tutorial.05\Review\DCcdsUp.jpg \Tutorial.05\Review\DCcdsOver.jpg \Tutorial.05\Review\DChistoryUp.jpg \Tutorial.05\Review\DChistoryOver.jpg \Tutorial.05\Review\DCmembersUp.jpg \Tutorial.05\Review\DCmembersOver.jpg \Tutorial.05\Review\DCphotosUp.jpg \Tutorial.05\Review\DCphotosOver.jpg \Tutorial.05\Review\DCtoursUp.jpg \Tutorial.05\Review\DCtoursOver.jpg \Tutorial.05\Review\DCbanner.jpg	\Catalyst\Dreamweaver\DizziedConnections\ DCcontent.htm \Catalyst\Dreamweaver\DizziedConnections\ DCtopframe.htm \Catalyst\Dreamweaver\DizziedConnections\ DCbottomframe.htm \Catalyst\Dreamweaver\DizziedConnections\ DCframeset.htm \Catalyst\Dreamweaver\DizziedConnections\ DCcds.htm \Catalyst\Dreamweaver\DizziedConnections\ DChistory.htm \Catalyst\Dreamweaver\DizziedConnections\ DCmembers.htm \Catalyst\Dreamweaver\DizziedConnections\ DCphotos.htm \Catalyst\Dreamweaver\DizziedConnections\ DCtours.htm
	Case Problem 1	\Tutorial.05\Cases\HprofessorhartUp.gif \Tutorial.05\Cases\HprofessorhartDown.gif \Tutorial.05\Cases\HlinguisticdifferencesUp.gif \Tutorial.05\Cases\ HlinguisticdifferencesDown.gif \Tutorial.05\Cases\HculturalcrosspollinationUp.gif \Tutorial.05\Cases\ HculturalcrosspollinationDown.gif \Tutorial.05\Cases\HritualsandpracticesUp.gif \Tutorial.05\Cases\HritualsandpracticesDown.gif \Tutorial.05\Cases\HcontactinformationUp.gif \Tutorial.05\Cases\HcontactinformationDown.gif	
	Case Problem 2	\Tutorial.05\Cases\LoveCallSmall.jpg \Tutorial.05\Cases\AmongTheLedHorsesSmall.jpg \Tutorial.05\Cases\LucklessHunterSmall.jpg \Tutorial.05\Cases\RiderlessHorseSmall.jpg \Tutorial.05\Cases\AmongTheLedHorses.htm \Tutorial.05\Cases\TheRiderlessHorse.htm \Tutorial.05\Cases\TheLoveCall.htm \Tutorial.05\Cases\TheLucklessHunter.htm	\Museum\Dreamweaver\Remington\ RemingtonContent.htm \Museum\Dreamweaver\Remington\ RemingtonTop.htm \Museum\Dreamweaver\Remington\ RemingtonFrameset.htm

Macromedia Dreamweaver MX

Tutorial	Location in Tutorial	Name and Location of Data File or Web Site	Files or Web Sites the Student Creates from Scratch
		\Tutorial.05\Cases\AmongTheLedHorsesBig.jpg \Tutorial.05\Cases\RiderlessHorseBig.jpg \Tutorial.05\Cases\LoveCallBig.jpg \Tutorial.05\Cases\LucklessHunterBig.jpg	
	Case Problem 3	\Tutorial.05\Cases\FeaturedAuthorBio.htm \Tutorial.05\Cases\FeaturedExcerpt.htm \Tutorial.05\Cases\PunchAuthorBioUp.gif \Tutorial.05\Cases\PunchAuthorBioOver.gif \Tutorial.05\Cases\PunchExcerptUp.gif \Tutorial.05\Cases\PunchExcerptOver.gif \Tutorial.05\Cases\PunchPressUp.gif \Tutorial.05\Cases\PunchPressOver.gif	\NORM\Dreamweaver\FeaturedTop.htm \NORM\Dreamweaver\FeaturedLeft.htm \NORM\Dreamweaver\FeaturedFrameset.htm
	Case Problem 4	\Tutorial.05\Cases\SushiCompanyUp.gif \Tutorial.05\Cases\SushiCompanyOver.gif \Tutorial.05\Cases\SushiMenuUp.gif \Tutorial.05\Cases\SushiMenuOver.gif \Tutorial.05\Cases\SushiContactUp.gif \Tutorial.05\Cases\SushiContactOver.gif \Tutorial.05\Cases\SushiCaliforniaRoll.gif \Tutorial.05\Cases\SushiTunaHandRoll.gif \Tutorial.05\Cases\SushiSalmon.gif	\SushiYaYa\Dreamweaver\ SushiDescriptionsFrameset.htm \SushiYaYa\Dreamweaver\ SushiDescriptionsBottomFrame.htm \SushiYaYa\Dreamweaver\ SushiDescriptionsTopFrame.htm \SushiYaYa\Dreamweaver\sushi.htm \SushiYaYa\Dreamweaver\TunaHandRoll.htm \SushiYaYa\Dreamweaver\CaliforniaRoll.htm \SushiYaYa\Dreamweaver\Salmon.htm
Tutorial 6	Session 6.1	\Tutorial.06\Tutorial\ SurfaceSuctionCDcover200.jpg	
	Session 6.2		
	Session 6.3	\Tutorial.06\Tutorial\ SlothChildWebPageImage.jpg \Tutorial.06\Tutorial\SlothChildLayer2.jpg \Tutorial.06\Tutorial\SlothChildLayer3.jpg \Tutorial.06\Tutorial\SlothChildLayer4.jpg	
	Review Assignments		
	Case Problem 1	\Tutorial.06\Cases\HartCourseList.gif \Tutorial.06\Cases\HrochNewCourseButton.gif	\Hart\Dreamweaver\NewCourses.htm
	Case Problem 2	\Tutorial.06\Cases\AQuietDayInUtica.jpg \Tutorial.06\Cases\BuffaloRunners.jpg \Tutorial.06\Cases\CowpunchingSometimes.jpg \Tutorial.06\Cases\IndiansHuntingBuffalo.jpg \Tutorial.06\Cases\AFigureOfTheNight.jpg \Tutorial.06\Cases\TheBucker.jpg \Tutorial.06\Cases\TheCowPuncher.jpg \Tutorial.06\Cases\DeerInForest.jpg	
	Case Problem 3	\Tutorial.06\Cases\BookCoverBasketSm.gif \Tutorial.06\Cases\BookCoverProstitutionSm.gif \Tutorial.06\Cases\BookCoverQueenSm.gif \Tutorial.06\Cases\BookCoverStopGapSm.gif	
	Case Problem 4	\Tutorial.06\Cases\SushiYaYaMenu.htm \Tutorial.06\Cases\WasabiCharo.gif \Tutorial.06\Cases\WasabiChili.gif \Tutorial.06\Cases\WasabiCold.gif \Tutorial.06\Cases\WasabiHotWings.jpg \Tutorial.06\Cases\WasabiLukeWarm.gif \Tutorial.06\Cases\WasabiOnFire.gif \Tutorial.06\Cases\WasabiOriginal.gif \Tutorial.06\Cases\WasabiPicture.gif \Tutorial.06\Cases\WasabiPictureSmall.gif \Tutorial.06\Cases\WasabiToasty.gif \Tutorial.06\Cases\WasabiWasabi.gif	\SushiYaYa\Dreamweaver\Wasabi.htm

Macromedia Dreamweaver MX

Tutorial	Location in Tutorial	Name and Location of Data File or Web Site	Files or Web Sites the Student Creates from Scratch
Tutorial 7	Session 7.1	\Tutorial.07\Tutorial\East1.gif \Tutorial.07\Tutorial\East2.gif \Tutorial.07\Tutorial\East3.gif \Tutorial.07\Tutorial\East4.gif \Tutorial.07\Tutorial\East5.gif \Tutorial.07\Tutorial\East6.gif \Tutorial.07\Tutorial\East7.gif \Tutorial.07\Tutorial\East8.gif \Tutorial.07\Tutorial\East9.gif \Tutorial.07\Tutorial\East10.gif \Tutorial.07\Tutorial\East11.gif \Tutorial.07\Tutorial\East12.gif \Tutorial.07\Tutorial\East13.gif	
	Session 7.2	\Tutorial.07\Tutorial\BusSmall.gif	
	Session 7.3	\Tutorial.07\Tutorial\SCbusButtonUp.gif \Tutorial.07\Tutorial\SCbusButtonOver.gif \Tutorial.07\Tutorial\Central1.gif \Tutorial.07\Tutorial\Central2.gif \Tutorial.07\Tutorial\Central3.gif \Tutorial.07\Tutorial\Central4.gif \Tutorial.07\Tutorial\Central5.gif \Tutorial.07\Tutorial\Central6.gif \Tutorial.07\Tutorial\Central7.gif \Tutorial.07\Tutorial\Central8.gif \Tutorial.07\Tutorial\Central9.gif \Tutorial.07\Tutorial\Central10.gif \Tutorial.07\Tutorial\Central11.gif \Tutorial.07\Tutorial\Central12.gif \Tutorial.07\Tutorial\Central13.gif \Tutorial.07\Tutorial\Central14.gif \Tutorial.07\Tutorial\Central15.gif \Tutorial.07\Tutorial\SSbusButtonUp.gif \Tutorial.07\Tutorial\SSbusButtonOver.gif	
	Review Assignments	\Tutorial.07\Review\Dizzied1.gif \Tutorial.07\Review\Dizzied2.gif \Tutorial.07\Review\Dizzied3.gif \Tutorial.07\Review\Dizzied4.gif \Tutorial.07\Review\Dizzied5.gif \Tutorial.07\Review\Dizzied6.gif \Tutorial.07\Review\Dizzied7.gif \Tutorial.07\Review\Dizzied8.gif \Tutorial.07\Review\Dizzied9.gif \Tutorial.07\Review\Dizzied10.gif \Tutorial.07\Review\Dizzied11.gif \Tutorial.07\Review\Dizzied12.gif \Tutorial.07\Review\DCbusButtonUp.gif \Tutorial.07\Review\DCbusButtonOver.gif	
	Case Problem 1	\Tutorial.07\Cases\HrochNewCourse2.gif	
	Case Problem 2	\Tutorial.07\Cases\SlideShowBG.gif	
	Case Problem 3		
	Case Problem 4	\Tutorial.07\Cases\Wasabi2.gif	
Tutorial 8	Session 8.1	\Tutorial.08\Tutorial\WhatsHot.swf	\Catalyst\Dreamweaver\Media \Catalyst\Dreamweaver\Media\HeadingBands.swf
	Session 8.2	\Tutorial.08\Tutorial\GamePromo.dcr \Tutorial.08\Tutorial\sunshine.swf \Tutorial.08\Tutorial\FlashSoundButton.gif \Tutorial.08\Tutorial\MP3SoundButton.gif \Tutorial.08\Tutorial\sunshine.mp3	\Catalyst\Dreamweaver\Media\GamePromo.dcr \Catalyst\Dreamweaver\Media\sunshine.swf \Catalyst\Dreamweaver\Media\sunshine.mp3

Macromedia Dreamweaver MX

Tutorial	Location in Tutorial	Name and Location of Data File or Web Site	Files or Web Sites the Student Creates from Scratch
	Session 8.3	\Tutorial.08\Tutorial\sunshineVideo.rm	\Catalyst\Dreamweaver\Media\sunshineVideo.rm
	Review Assignments	\Tutorial.08\Tutorial\WhatsHot.swf \Tutorial.08\Tutorial\limcVideo.rm	\Catalyst\Dreamweaver\Media\WhatsHotText1.swf \Catalyst\Dreamweaver\Media\limcVideo.rm
	Case Problem 1	\Tutorial.08\Cases\HartHarshSample.rm \Tutorial.08\Cases\HartHarshwhSample.mp3 \Tutorial.08\Cases\HartModalSample.mp3	\Hart\Dreamweaver\Media \Hart\Dreamweaver\Media\HartHarshSample.rm \Hart\Dreamweaver\Media\ HartHarshwhSample.mp3 \Hart\Dreamweaver\Media\HartModalSample.mp3
	Case Problem 2	\Tutorial.08\Cases\MuseumTour.doc \Tutorial.08\Cases\museumtour.dcr	\Museum\Dreamweaver\Tour.htm \Museum\Dreamweaver\Media \Museum\Dreamweaver\Media\museumtour.dcr \Museum/Dreamweaver\TourButton.swf
	Case Problem 3	\Tutorial.08\Cases\normform.dcr	\NORM\Dreamweaver\CatalogueOrder.htm \NORM\Dreamweaver\Media \NORM\Dreamweaver\Media\normform.dcr NORM\Dreamweaver\CatalogueOrderButton.swf
	Case Problem 4	\Tutorial.08\Cases\sushigame.dcr \Tutorial.08\Cases\wasabisound_autoplay.swf	\SushiYaYa\Dreamweaver\Media \SushiYaYa\Dreamweaver\Media\sushigame.dcr \SushiYaYa\Dreamweaver\Media\ wasabisound_autoplay.swf
Tutorial 9	Session 9.1		\Catalyst\Dreamweaver\Library\CatalystFooter.lbi
	Session 9.2		\Catalyst\Dreamweaver\Templates\ MainTemplate.dwt \Catalyst\Dreamweaver\Media\HeadingTest.swf \Catalyst\Dreamweaver\test2.htm \Catalyst\Dreamweaver\Templates\ CDPageTemplate.dwt
	Session 9.3	\Tutorial.09\Tutorial\CatalystFormTest.htm	\Catalyst\Dreamweaver\CatalystFormTest.htm
	Review Assignments		
	Case Problem 1		\Hart\Dreamweaver\Library\footer.lbi
	Case Problem 2		\Museum\Dreamweaver\Templates\ MainTemplate.dwt \Museum\Dreamweaver\Library\footer.lbi \Museum\Dreamweaver\TemplateTest.htm
	Case Problem 3		\NORM\Dreamweaver\Templates\ MainTemplate.dwt
	Case Problem 4	\Tutorial.09\Cases\SushiYaYaFormTest.htm \Tutorial.09\Cases\SushiMenu.htm	\SushiYaYa\Dreamweaver\SushiYaYaFormTest.htm \SushiYaYa\Dreamweaver\SushiMenu.htm